Curriculum Development

Theory and Practice

Hilda Taba   SAN FRANCISCO STATE COLLEGE

Under the general editorship of
WILLARD B. SPALDING, *Chairman,*
Division of Education, Portland State College

HARCOURT, BRACE & WORLD, INC.
New York, Chicago, San Francisco, Atlanta

ISBN: 0–15–516740–5
Library of Congress Catalog Card Number: 62-20567
Printed in the United States of America

COPYRIGHTS AND ACKNOWLEDGMENTS

The author wishes to thank the following for their permission to reprint the material listed below:

ABRAHAMS MAGAZINE SERVICE, INC.—for adapted material from G. L. Anderson's "Theories of Behavior and Some Curriculum Issues," from *Journal of Educational Psychology,* Vol. 39 (March, 1948).

AMERICAN COUNCIL ON EDUCATION—for adapted material from *With Perspective on Human Relations, A Study of Peer Group Dynamics in an Eighth Grade* by Hilda Taba (1955); and for passages from *With Focus on Human Relations* by Hilda Taba and Deborah Elkins (1950).

AMERICAN INSTITUTE OF BIOLOGICAL SCIENCES—for outline from *BSCS Newsletter No. 6,* Annual Report (December, 1960).

APPLETON-CENTURY-CROFTS, INC.—for material from *Theories of Learning,* Second Edition, by Ernest R. Hilgard. (Copyright, © 1956, Appleton-Century-Crofts, Inc.)

ASSOCIATION FOR SUPERVISION AND CURRICULUM DEVELOPMENT—for adapted material from "A Case Study" by Hilda Taba and Elizabeth Noel, from *Action Research,* Association for Supervisors and Curriculum Directors (1957).

BASIC BOOKS, INC. and DAEDALUS—for excerpts from "The Ends and Content of Education" by Sidney Hook, from *Education in the Age of Science,* edited by Brand Blanchard, copyright 1959 by the American Academy of Arts and Sciences, Basic Books, Inc., Publishers. Reprinted by permission from *Daedalus,* the Journal of the American Academy of Arts and Sciences (Winter, 1959), pp. 7-8, 9, 10.

CONTRA COSTA COUNTY SCHOOLS—for material from *Social Studies, Grades 1-6* (1959).

HARCOURT, BRACE & WORLD, INC.—for excerpts from *Fundamentals of Curriculum Development* by B. Othanel Smith, William O. Stanley, and J. Harlan Shores (1957).

HARPER & ROW, PUBLISHERS—for selections from *The Future as History* by Robert L. Heilbroner (1959).

KAPPA DELTA PI—for excerpts from *Experience and Education* by John Dewey. Macmillan (1938). Quoted by permission of Kappa Delta Pi, an honor society in education.

LOS ANGELES COUNTY SCHOOLS—for list of topics from pages 86-87 of *Educating the Children of Los Angeles County. A Course of Study in the Elementary School* (1955).

THE MACMILLAN COMPANY—for selections from *Aims of Education* by Alfred North Whitehead (1929).

NATIONAL SOCIETY FOR THE STUDY OF EDUCATION—for excerpts from "Designing Programs to Meet the Common Needs of Youth" by Harold Alberty, in *Adapting the Secondary School Program to the Needs of Youth.* Fifty-second Yearbook, Pt. I., University of Chicago Press (1953).

CHARLES SCRIBNER'S SONS—for excerpts from *Curriculum-Making in the Social Studies,* A Social Process Appoach by Leon C. Marshall and Rachel Marshall Goetz. Report of the Commission on Social Studies, Part XIII of the American Historical Association's Investigation of the Social Studies in the Schools. Published by Charles Scribner's Sons (1936).

BUREAU OF PUBLICATIONS, TEACHERS COLLEGE, COLUMBIA UNIVER-
SITY—for selection from *Developing a Curriculum for Modern Living* by F. B.
Stratemeyer, *et al.* (1947).

THE UNIVERSITY OF CHICAGO PRESS—for adaptation of "Evaluation in High
Schools and Junior Colleges" by Hilda Taba, in *Reading in Relation to Experience
and Language,* edited by W. S. Gray. Supplementary Educational Monograph, No.
58, University of Chicago Press (December, 1944). Copyright 1944 by the University of Chicago; and for adaptation of "Basic Issues and Cooperative Techniques in
Evaluation with Special Reference to Reading" by Hilda Taba, in *Cooperative Effort
in Schools to Improve Reading,* edited by W. S. Gray. Supplementary Educational
Monograph, No. 56, University of Chicago Press (September, 1942). Copyright
1942 by the University of Chicago.

W. LLOYD WARNER—for adapted version of Table 7 in *Social Class in America* by
W. Lloyd Warner, *et al.* Harper & Row (1960).

YALE UNIVERSITY PRESS—for summary and excerpts from the Yale University
Press edition of *The Lonely Crowd: A Study of a Changing American Character* by
David Riesman (1950).

Preface

Those who work in curriculum development need to look closely at the path they have been following in order to see more clearly where it is leading, to be sure that they are not going toward unwanted destinations, and to chart the possibilities for future ends. Certain ideas and ways of thinking may not have received the recognition due them, and others may have been played up beyond their legitimate worth and role. It is especially important that the theoretical aspects of curriculum development be re-examined because of the strong tendency to assume that the theoretical foundations of our current curriculum are sound and that the difficulties occur chiefly in translating theory into practice.

Since World War II two developments have lent urgency to such a re-examination. First, there has been a wave of sharp criticisms of the schools and their programs from the lay public as well as from scholars in the various disciplines. These criticisms have a simple logic that may very well be seductive to teachers and citizens alike. Yet the assumptions that underlie both the criticisms and the proposals for revision merit sharper examination than they have received so far, because these assumptions stem from generalizations that tend to overlook the complexities of the educational process.

The sources available to educational thinking have also expanded tremendously. This expansion has made available concepts that can be used to strengthen the conceptual framework of educational thinking. If this new knowledge is to be used profitably, educational writers and planners need to free themselves of the predilections to special ways of thinking that limit the possibility of accommodating concepts from other fields. They also need to recognize that knowledge from other fields does not yield direct answers to educational problems. Productive thinking in education can come about only when this knowledge is used within the framework of an educational thinking free of limitations from doctrinaire positions and ambiguities.

It is interesting to note that many of the new ideas about education, curriculum, and teaching bear a great similarity to the educational thought of the 1930's even though these new ideas come from sources that have not been too closely linked either with educational literature or practice. If a bridge can be found between the presumbly new ideas and former ideas that have not always been kept in clear focus, and if knowledge from other fields is used to elucidate educational thinking, it may be possible to take a step toward an intellectual revival in educational thinking and to correct the unfortunate chasm between those who today are called "educationists" and scholars in other fields. It is possible that a new ground can be laid for educational scholarship.

This book attempts to do some of the things mentioned above: to examine the theory of curriculum development, to reach into fields other than education for strengthening thinking about curriculum, and to link what has transpired with current ideas and problems. The book has been in the making for over twenty years. Its main focus is on a scheme of thinking rather than on the specific ideas suggested at any one point. The idea that there must be a system of thinking about curriculum planning occurred to Dr. R. W. Tyler after a rather confusing meeting on curriculum planning in the 1930's in which conflicting proposals for curriculum designs were being debated. Following this meeting, Dr. Tyler and the writer began to elaborate a scheme for a sequence of questions to be asked and an order of steps to be taken in planning curriculum. The writer tried these out in the next workshop held by the Eight Year Study. Over a period of years, working as a curriculum consultant in several school systems and teaching courses in curriculum development, the author has continued testing and refining the scheme and building a theoretical rationale for it. A real chance at a large-scale application of the idea came in connection with the project on Intergroup Education, which the writer directed. At that time (1945), there were no traditions and few precedents for curriculum in human relations. Furthermore, the essential focus of teaching in this field required a theoretical framework from which to work because the idea could not be contained in any one single subject or in any one particular type of experience.

Since that time, curriculum consultantship in Yolo and Contra Costa Counties, especially in the latter, have provided the author with an opportunity for prolonged and systematic work on curriculum development.

Although the particular answers that the scheme of thinking provided earlier no longer hold, the scheme itself seems to be appropriate to the issues of today. It seems to help in bringing some order into the chaotic positions now held in regard to curriculum, and even to suggest a new vitality for many emphases that were alive in the 1930's, but have been submerged since. One of these emphases is the analysis of the thought processes produced by the evaluation staff of the Eight Year Study.

A book that has been so long in maturing has had more helpers than can be personally acknowledged. Hundreds of teachers in a great variety of programs and places have developed units and invented teaching–learning activities that have added to the store of possibilities for implementation and testing. Special gratitude is due to B. O. Wilson, former superintendent, and Evelyn Jegi, former curriculum director, of Contra Costa County Schools, who supported seven years of continuous curriculum development in social studies for the elementary schools. Mary Durkin, Alice Duval, and Alice McMasters, the curriculum coordinators of the county, helped much with the practical implementation of the theoretical ideas. This program provided an opportunity for studying the problems involved in building a sequential curriculum. Many specific illustrations are borrowed from the materials assembled by the former staff members of the Intergroup Education Project—Elizabeth Brady, Margaret Heaton, Marie Hughes, Helen Jennings, and John Robinson. Appreciation is due also to the many publishers who gave permission to quote from their publications. Lavone Hanna and John DeCecco of San Francisco State College and George Spindler of Stanford University read and criticized several chapters. Helen Storen of Queens College read and criticized the entire manuscript; Deborah Elkins of Queens College helped to check the Bibliography. The author is especially indebted to the careful reading and criticism of two versions of the manuscript by the consulting editor, Dr. Willard B. Spalding.

Last, but not least, is the careful labor performed by Audrey Harris and Mary Wilhelm, who were responsible for typing the many drafts of the manuscript and bearing with the vagaries of a situation created by an attempt to write a book within a schedule of a demanding full-time job.

HILDA TABA
San Francisco, 1962

Foreword

Present criticisms of public education are characterized, as are those of the past, by critics' attempts to base curriculum development upon theories about society, culture, learning, and subject matter. Dr. Hilda Taba's examination of these four bases of educational programs yields a structured synthesis, the lack of which has led to increasing dissatisfaction with schools. The hiatus in wide-scale curriculum development, which has persisted since the late 1930's, will end as educators become familiar with *Curriculum Development: Theory and Practice.*

But, as Dr. Taba points out, curriculum development is sterile if it does not encompass change in classroom practices. Her discussion of theory and practice in the design and use of new programs provides both needed fundamental concepts and specific illustrations of their use in schools, with realistic appraisal of teachers' perceptions of themselves, of their ability to participate in educational planning, and of the many other demands upon them.

Educational programs should stand or fall, persist or be modified, because of the quality of their effects upon students. Evaluation of education, as Dr. Taba sees it, includes both the process of determining what changes in the behavior of students result from an educational program, and that of determining whether these changes actually achieve the objectives specified. Here, as in other parts of the book, theory is clarified by practical examples.

Curriculum Development: Theory and Practice will provide intellectual challenges and professional stimulation to college teachers and educational leaders.

WILLARD B. SPALDING

Contents

1. AN APPROACH TO DESIGNING THE CURRICULUM   1

Crisis in Public Education   1
Confusion in Curriculum Planning   3
Needed: A Theory of Curriculum Development   6
An Approach to Designing the Curriculum   9

PART ONE

The Foundations for Curriculum Development

2. CURRENT CONCEPTIONS OF THE FUNCTION OF THE SCHOOL   16

Education as Preserver and Transmitter of the Cultural Heritage   18
Education as an Instrument for Transforming Culture   22
Education for Individual Development   28
Implications of These Concepts for Curriculum   30

3. THE ANALYSIS OF SOCIETY   31

The Sources for Analysis of Society   31
The Impact of Science and Technology   34
The Implications for the Role of Education   40

4. THE ANALYSIS OF CULTURE   47

The Concept of Culture   48
Personality and Culture   50
The Genesis of Personality   52
The Concept of Cultural Change   53
American Character and Values   57

5. EDUCATIONAL IMPLICATIONS OF THE ANALYSIS OF CULTURE   65

The School as a Countervailing Socializing Agent   65
Education for Values and Feelings   68
Autonomy, Individuality, and Creativity   70
The Dangers of Ethnocentricity   73
The Need for Translators   74

6. LEARNING THEORIES AS A FOUNDATION FOR THE CURRICULUM   76

The Relevance of Ideas About Learning to the Curriculum   76
The Main Theories of Learning   79
The Influence of Learning Theories on the Curriculum   83
The Science of Learning and Educational Strategy   85

7. THE CONCEPT OF DEVELOPMENT   88

The Interrelationship Among Areas of Development   89
The Concept of Readiness and of Pacing   92
The Concept of Developmental Tasks   96
*Implications for Curriculum Making of the Concept
    of Developmental Tasks   97*

8. INTELLIGENCE AND MENTAL DEVELOPMENT   100

The Concept of Intelligence   100
Variables Affecting the Functioning Intelligence   103
The Limitations of Intelligence Tests   105
The Development of Intelligence   107
Curriculum Implications of the Concept of Intelligence   112

9. THE TRANSFER OF LEARNING   121

Three Main Concepts of Transfer   121
Maximizing Transfer   125

10. SOCIAL AND CULTURAL LEARNING   130

The Chief Tenets of Social Learning   130
The Process of Social Learning   131
The Agents of Social Learning   134
Variations in Social Learning   135
The Effect of Acculturation on Learning   145

11. THE EXTENSION OF LEARNING   148

Human Potentiality for Learning   148
Learning as Experiencing and Discovering   151
The Confusion About Direct and Indirect Learning   157
The Effect of Social Setting on Learning   160
Group Relations in the Classroom   162
The Effect of Social Climate on Learning   164
Grouping as a Factor in Facilitating Learning   167

12. THE NATURE OF KNOWLEDGE   172

Content and Process   172
The Levels of Content and Their Functions   174
Unique Contributions of School Subjects to Learning   181
New Concept of Fundamentals   184
The Scope of Content   186
The Sequence of Learning   188
Integration of Knowledge   189

PART TWO
The Process of Curriculum Planning

13. THE OBJECTIVES OF EDUCATION   194

The Functions of Educational Objectives   196
Principles to Guide the Formulation of Objectives   199
Classification of Objectives   206

14. THE TYPES OF BEHAVIORAL OBJECTIVES   211

Knowledge: Facts, Ideas, Concepts   211
Reflective Thinking   215
Values and Attitudes   220
Sensitivities and Feelings   223
Skills   225
Translating General Objectives into Specific Ones   228

15. DIAGNOSIS IN CURRICULUM DEVELOPMENT   231

Diagnosis of Achievement   232
Diagnosis of Students as Learners   234
Diagnosis of Curriculum Problems   237

16. INFORMAL DIAGNOSTIC DEVICES   244

An Open-Ended Classroom Interview   244
Open-Ended Questions and Themes   246
Unfinished Stories and Incidents   247
Records of Discussion   248
Records of Reading and Writing   249
Observation and Recording of Performance   249
Special Assignments and Exercises   250
Sociometric Test   252
Devices for Diagnosing the Out-of-School Environment   254
A Program for Diagnosis   261

17. SELECTION OF CURRICULUM EXPERIENCES   263

The Problems of Rational Selection   263
Problems in Establishing Criteria   265
Validity and Significance of Content   267
Consistency with Social Realities   272
Balance of Breadth and Depth   276
Provision for Wide Range of Objectives   278
Learnability and Adaptability to Experiences of Students   282
Appropriateness to the Needs and Interests of the Students   284

18. ORGANIZATION OF CURRICULUM CONTENT
AND LEARNING   290

The Problems of Organizing   290
Establishing Sequence   292
Providing for Cumulative Learning   296
Providing for Integration   298
Typical Attempts to Unify the Curriculum   300
Combining the Logical and Psychological Requirements   301
Determining the Focus   304
Providing Variety in Modes of Learning   307

19. EVALUATION OF THE OUTCOMES OF CURRICULA   310

A Narrow and a Broad Definition of Evaluation   311
The Function of Evaluation   313
Criteria for a Program of Evaluation   316
A Comprehensive Evaluation Program   324
Techniques for Securing Evidence   329
Interpretation of Evaluation Data   331
Translation of Evaluation Data into the Curriculum   336
Evaluation as a Cooperative Enterprise   328

20. DEVELOPMENT OF A TEACHING–LEARNING UNIT   **343**

The Role of a Model for a Teaching–Learning Unit   343
The Methodology for Planning a Unit   345

PART THREE

The Design of the Curriculum

21. CURRENT PATTERNS OF CURRICULUM ORGANIZATION   **382**

Some Problems of Organization   382
The Subject Organization   384
The Broad Fields Curriculum   393
Curriculum Based on Social Processes and Life Functions   396
The Activity or Experience Curriculum   400
The Core Curriculum   407

22. A CONCEPTUAL FRAMEWORK
FOR CURRICULUM DESIGN   **413**

Deficiencies in the Rationale of Current Curriculum Designs   414
The Functions of a Conceptual Framework for Curriculum Design   420
The Elements of the Curriculum   422
Relationships Among the Elements   424
The Problems and Principles of Organization   426
A Methodology of Curriculum Development   439

PART FOUR

The Strategy of Curriculum Change

23. STRATEGY FOR CHANGING A CURRICULUM   **446**

Curriculum Change in Historic Perspective   446
Current Methods of Curriculum Change   448
The Concept of Strategy for Curriculum Change   454
A Sequence of Curriculum Development   456
Integration of Production and Teacher Training   460
Patterns of Work   465
Levels of Involvement   469

24. WORKING WITH GROUPS   471

Composing Work Teams   472
Climate for Productive Work   475
Differentiation of Tasks for Groups and Individuals   477
Leadership Roles   478
A Case Study of Developing Leadership Roles   482
Conclusion   491

Bibliography   494
Index   515

An Approach to Designing the Curriculum

One need not be a prophet to recognize that the forces in education today have the makings either of a great resurgence in curriculum development or of a grand retrogression, depending on the kind of thinking that has most weight in their shaping. The development of a coherent theory of curriculum making will be one of the items that determine in which direction the scales will tilt.

CRISIS IN PUBLIC EDUCATION

Public education today is facing a crisis which may be deeper and more fundamental than any preceding one. In many ways the present situation is similar to that in the 1890's when "skyrocketing enrollments in the cities" and the mundane problems of students, classrooms, and dollars had become overwhelming, and the rote efficiency of the same drill in the same readers made a depressing contrast to the high-minded philosophies professed by the schools (*Cremin, 1961, pp. 20-21*). Since World War II, the public schools have grown too rapidly to develop unassailable programs. They have been too plagued with growing enrollments, mass attendance, and a shortage of teachers, buildings, and finances to do an adequate job of curriculum development. The practical problems of running a runaway school system have left little room for theoretical pondering about the design for the curriculum or about a theoretical basis for the new mass education. Under the circumstances, one is inclined to agree with Henry Steele Commager that it is a wonder that the schools have done as much as they have for as many.

Today, as in the 1890's, the ferment in education is caused by the transforming effects of technology and science on society, with criticism focusing on the failure of the schools to solve the problems created by that transformation. Today, as then, there is a deep faith in the power of education, a sense of "inextricable relationship between education and national progress" (*Cremin, 1961, p. 8*) and a deep disappointment in schools as instruments of this progress. Today, perhaps more than in the 1890's, education supplies the arena for debating the fundamental predicaments of society. There are differences, however. The "revolt" in the 1890's called for extension of the functions of education.

> A cacophony of voices was demanding educational reforms of every sort and variety. Businessmen and labor unions were insisting that the school assume the classical functions of apprenticeship. Settlement workers and municipal reformers were vigorously urging instruction in hygiene, domestic science, manual arts, and child care. Patriots of every stripe were calling for Americanization programs. And agrarian publicists were pressing for a new sort of training for country life that would give youngsters a sense of the joys and possibilities of farming. . . .

The main thrust in the 1890's was toward a concept of a school as a *legatee* institution, which takes over where society fails in *its* education and which must transform its purposes and methods with each transformation of society (*Cremin, 1961, pp. 116-17*). Today schools are accused of having overexpanded their function and of a "subversive" attempt to take over the duties of parents, the church, and other social agencies.

The criticisms of the 1890's flailed against formalism, hard discipline, narrowness of education, and a conservatism which insisted that if McGuffey had been good enough for mother and dad, he would certainly be good enough for youngsters. The reformers of today are more conservative. The schools are criticized for their softness, anti-intellectualism, progressivism, egalitarianism, lack of emphasis on fundamentals and academic skills, and a misplaced emphasis on life adjustment and emotional development. There are calls for a return to the three R's and for reducing rather than expanding the function of schools. The crisis of the 1890's stimulated reform by creating a profession of education capable of managing the schools according to scientific principles. Today the public is being called upon to undo the damage "educationists" have wrought on schools and to return the shaping of curricula to the scholars and the lay public.

The sources of current criticisms of education are multiple and not as yet clearly understood. The voices also speak with different degrees of authority and varied orientation. Some, no doubt, represent a coalition of citizens opposed to school taxes, radicalism, and progressivism in education. A deepening concern over the expansion of Communism at home and abroad plays a role, as the instant reaction to the technical feat of Sputnik demonstrated.

Many "reformers" are at work whose vision of the task of public education and of the curriculum is all too often narrowed either by a prescientific conception of what learning is like, or by a rejection of the egalitarian nature of public education, or both. But, as Cremin points out, there are many people who simply do not favor the same lines of progress as the educators. A large public is ready for an educational reform away from the goals that they think schools are pursuing.*

* For a fuller description of the current attacks on schools and of the publications bearing on them, see Cremin, 1961, ch. 9.

The strongest pressure for re-examination of the curriculum comes from the drastic changes in technology and culture, ranging from automation to atomic power, the voracious demands of the expanding industry on intelligent man-power, and, in the words of the Rockefeller Report, "the constant pressure of an ever more complex society against the total creative capacity of its people" (*Rockefeller Brothers Fund, Inc., 1958, p. 10*).

CONFUSION IN CURRICULUM PLANNING

Against this backdrop, one is struck by a seeming lack of rigorous, systematic thinking about curriculum planning. One cannot help but note in the literature about curriculum development the eclectic quality of the treatment of such basic matters as curriculum design. Various "approaches" to curriculum development are treated descriptively, with statements of pro's and con's for each which seem to set these patterns into a sharper contrast than they merit. There is little discussion of the methodology of designing curricula and less clarity about the elements that may constitute a design. Child-centered, society-centered, and subject-centered curricula are vying with each other as the exclusive approaches to the entire curriculum. An emphasis on a single basis, such as the content, the needs of society, or the needs of the learner, have produced an unnecessary *versus* thinking with its unfortunate juxtaposition of considerations that should be combined into one comprehensive curriculum theory: interest *vs.* subject matter; life-centeredness *vs.* subject-centeredness; method *vs.* content; emotional development *vs.* intellectual growth; basic skills *vs.* the growth of the whole child, and so on.

Thirty years ago, under the stimulus of the various commissions of the Progressive Education Association, including the Eight Year Study, foundations were laid for a comprehensive theory of curriculum planning. The studies of these commissions indicated the necessity for studying children as growing individuals, and laid a foundation for the examination of the needs, the developmental sequences, and the other complexities surrounding learning in school. They emphasized the necessity for analyzing the nature of society and of its demands on individuals as a basis for curriculum development. But above all, these studies, especially those dealing with emotional life and adolescent development, lifted curriculum development out of the narrow realm of an exclusive concern for skills and content mastery. Most of the "newer" schemes of curriculum organization, such as the broad-fields, core, and experience curricula, were designed in this period of experimental ferment, although they grew out of earlier thinking and studies.

During this period also, and largely as a result of the evaluation studies, there emerged the concept of behavioral objectives of education, a concept which encompassed goals that went beyond acquiring knowledge and academic skills and differentiated the learning processes appropriate to each objective. These studies also provided the first glimmer of differentiation between the kinds of learning goals that constituted general education and those that represented the mastery of specialized factual knowledge (*Adventures in American Education Series, 1942-43; Commission on Secondary School Curriculum, 1938-40*).

The curriculum orientation that emerged from these efforts was more vital and inspired than was the curriculum that preceded it. The latter had been founded in the narrow scientism of the times and envisioned education as an enormous conditioning system for atomized academic knowledge and fractioned skills. In a sense, the progressive education movement in its heyday was a countercyclical movement. To use a phrase of Riesman's, "it was an attack on Colonel Blimps in education, cruelty and uniformity of curriculum and pacing." This movement had its visionary fringe which reached for the possible but did not judge well the attainable, and which could be classified as either sentimental or radical (*Cremin, 1961, ch. 6*). Yet the work of the commissions of the Association reached for a more encompassing science of education. Inspired by the spirited philosophical thought of the times, these studies provided the bricks for a new scientific approach to education in general and curriculum building in particular. Education at that moment was ready for a rationally planned diversity, a scientifically calculated way of meeting and dealing with heterogeneity of individual talents and social backgrounds. It was ready to develop ways and means of measuring intangible learnings, such as the power to think and to create, and by doing this, to rescue these important educational outcomes from the status of concomitants to the main business of mastering facts and academic skills. The experimentation and research of the day contained the essential elements of a renaissance in a theory of curriculum building.

Unfortunately, these beginnings and the possibilities were not exploited in the decades that followed the war. The postwar explosion of school population and a growing conservatism evidently discouraged any further effort, and many of the new educational practices which had developed from these experiments and research began to be regarded as unnecessary or even dangerous. No essentially new designs of curriculum have been developed since. The postwar curriculum development has been confined largely to the refinement, reiteration, and implementation of earlier ideas. Writing about curricula has been confined to choosing sides, criticizing and approving this or that pattern, but proposing very little new. While new research is available to support many of the "articles of faith" of the earlier days, the literature on curriculum-making traffics in concepts and controversies inherited from earlier writers who relied largely on intuitive perceptions, empirical observations, and philosophical speculations. Pronouncements of policy and philosophy are filled with pietistic iteration of beliefs in child needs, in interest as motive power, in education of the total child, in creativity. The literature even voices some antagonism (at least verbal) to "mere content," an attitude carried over from the earlier revolt against sterile subject matter. Phrases such as "democratic education," "emotional and social needs," the "whole child," elicit defenses the more fervid as their meaning becomes less concrete. They are akin to the popular acceptance of certain truths in culture, which are expressed in words with uncertain meanings and which, according to Carl Becker, "having from constant repetition lost their metaphorical significance are unconsciously mistaken for objective realities." Around these magic words assumptions grow up which are regarded as so much "of course" as hardly to require proof. They are passed readily from hand to hand like smooth, worn coins (*Becker, 1932, p. 47*). Cremin calls this phenomenon the "conventional wisdom" (*1961, pp. 328-38*).

In this sense, one might say that in the period following World War II curriculum development has suffered from arrested progressivism. The result is a kind of vacuum. Into this vacuum have stepped proposals for reforms, many of which are animated by the prescientific conception of the discipline of mind and betray ignorance of principles of learning or a lack of familiarity with the nature of school population and social realities. Thus, at a time when developments in teaching technology promise an ever greater yield in learning, many proposals for school reform are contracting rather than expanding the scope of curricular emphasis.

Meanwhile, new developments in behavioral sciences have produced a multitude of new concepts and facts. Some of these new concepts throw doubt on many of the assumptions implicit in the current curriculum patterns. Others lend support and specification to ideas which had been no more than hunches or philosophical beliefs. Still others present entirely new possibilities. New ideas and theories about intelligence, perception, thinking, creativity, and learning are filling the pages of psychological journals, spelling out a new potentiality for human intelligence, and also, consequently, for assessment of ability. Anthropological writing has both elucidated and redeveloped the concepts of culture, socialization, and social learning which are helpful in viewing the school as a culture and as a part of the larger culture. The emerging science of group dynamics contains material which suggests new ways for creating an effective dynamic of learning in groups and for planning the conditions for learning. These developments have more than an immediate significance; they suggest also a new way of thinking about curriculum. The changes in social and cultural realities are being recorded and analyzed by the behavioral sciences. Progress in interdisciplinary matching of ideas, theories, and techniques promises to remove the usual blocks to the use of theoretical knowledge by technicians, including educators.

The very roots of the concerns and problems of education go deep into a variety of behavioral and social sciences—those analyzing our culture and society and its demands, those dealing with the nature of man and the processes by which he learns and develops. The content and techniques of educational processes, including the curriculum, should be constantly redirected by what these sciences discover. Yet, the separation of the scholar from the technician is perhaps more prevalent in education than in other applied fields. Education suffers from a double block in gaining access to current developments in its foundational sciences: the general separation of theoretical concerns from the problems of social technicians, and the traditional gulf between education and other social sciences, which the current attacks may even have extended. In the perspective of social scientists, education is an undesirable orphan. Hence, studies of education as an institution are not exactly abundant or qualitatively significant. (*Brim* describes the "lagging" interest of sociologists in the study of education as an institution up to 1950 in his *Sociology and the Field of Education, 1958, pp. 7-11.*)

Furthermore, in the climate of the current cultural attitude toward the school, many analyses of schools tend to be casual, secondhand, and somewhat hostile in defining the school situation (e.g., *Riesman, 1950, pp. 31-55*). There has been little or no thorough assessment by social scientists of the troubles of public schools, which are patently numerous and serious. Few persons fulfill the function of what could be called "frontier thinkers"—that is, persons with an earnest enough concern about and sufficient understanding of education and a sufficient footing in the social sciences to act as translators: to bring relevant facts and concepts to bear on consideration of educational problems, to interpret school education as a social process, and to lift the sights for educational programs. Only recently have there been efforts which might lead to consolidation of findings in social sciences and to an exploration of their educational implications (*Spence, 1959, pp. 84-95; Allinsmith and Goethals, 1956; and Spindler, 1955*).

NEEDED: A THEORY OF CURRICULUM DEVELOPMENT

To make proper use of these emerging resources, a theory of curriculum development is needed. Such a theory should not only define the problems with which curriculum development must deal, but also elaborate the system of concepts which must be used to assess the relevance of these data to education.

Curriculum development is a complex undertaking that involves many kinds of decisions. Decisions need to be made about the general aims which schools are to pursue and about the more specific objectives of instruction. The major areas or subjects of the curriculum must be selected, as well as the specific content to be covered in each. Choices must be made about the type of learning experiences with which to implement both the content understandings and other objectives. Decisions are needed regarding how to evaluate what students are learning and the effectiveness of the curriculum in attaining the desired ends. And, finally, a choice needs to be made regarding what the over-all pattern of the curriculum is to be.

These decisions are made on several different levels. Some decisions about what content to include in the curriculum are made by state legislatures, such as requirements to teach the constitution or the inclusion of driver training in California schools. Still others emanate from state departments of education, such as the requirement to teach American history a requisite number of times, or suggestions regarding the framework of topics to be covered in social studies. Still others are made by the school districts. Finally, many decisions which shape the functioning curriculum are made by local schools and by teachers, either in groups or individually.

If the curriculum development is to be adequate, all these decisions need to be made competently, on a recognized and valid basis, and with some degree of consistency. The very complexity and multitude of decisions and the fact that they are arrived at by different segments in the educational organization make it all the more important that there be an adequate theory of curriculum development. Yet, a clear-cut methodology of thinking and planning seems to be lacking in curriculum making today. Recent writers on curriculum making point out almost unanimously that confusion is the main characteristic of curriculum theory. The bases used in selecting curriculum experiences are manifold: some subjects or learning experiences are included because of tradition, others because of legislative pressure, and still others, rather vaguely, because of needs of children or adolescents. There is little clarity about organization. Highly specialized courses and units stand side by side with courses or subjects drawn from many disciplines. The sequence of subjects and courses follows no clear-cut principles, and some are placed where they are mainly for convenience. New additions are made without any thorough consideration of overlapping with what is being taught elsewhere.

This confusion has many sources, not the least of which is a lack of clarity and outright conflicts in the basic sciences from which education draws its data and guiding principles. Chief among the conflicts are those in the philosophical and psychological theories regarding the nature of the individual, the nature of learning, the goals of our culture, and the role of the individual in that culture. As will be pointed out in chapter 6, there is as yet no coherent theory of learning, and even what is known about learning has not been clearly brought together and applied by curriculum makers. There are disagreements about the function of the school in our society. Only scattered hints are available about the basic character of the American culture; there are differences about its chief values, and hence, also, about the kind of individual needed in this culture.

When these conflicting ideas are applied to curriculum making, they cease to be mere theoretical details: they acquire pragmatic importance. When, for example, the stimulus-response theory of learning is applied in some teaching and the field theory in others without differentiating the particular aspects to which they are relevant, confusion is apt to reign. When some subjects are selected or retained because they are regarded as a good discipline of the mind, others because of their life utility, and still others because they meet the psychological needs of students, the curriculum tends to become a hodge-podge.

Another source of confusion lies in the pluralism of values, presumably a chief characteristic of our culture. This pluralism is apt to impose conflicting goals on teaching and learning. Policies regarding grouping of students are a good example. Segregation of the gifted is favored by some in order to give talent proper opportunities to develop into an intellectual elite. Such a policy is opposed by others because it contradicts the democratic principle of equality, threatens to introduce a class system into school, and creates a snobbish elite which they feel has no place in a democratic society. Such conflicts prevent consideration of the possibility of individualizing curricula and teaching sufficiently to make it unnecessary to isolate the capable from the incapable.

A review of the history of curriculum making reveals other sources of difficulty. Some commentators have pointed out that the whole history of curriculum revision has been piecemeal—a mere shifting of pieces from one place to another, taking out one piece and replacing it with another without a reappraisal of the whole pattern. The curriculum has become "the amorphous product of generations of tinkering"—a patchwork. This piecemeal approach is continuing today, when additions and revisions in certain areas are made without reconsidering the entire pattern, and when acceleration in one part of the school system is recommended without corresponding changes in the next.

To the above problems could be added difficulties stemming from converting a single criterion or partial basis for curriculum development into a total one. In turn, the logic of content, children's interests, social needs, and practical utility have been claimed as the sole basis for selection and organization of a curriculum and of content. While such monolithic theories never quite succeeded, and in practice modifications and exceptions abounded, the arguments about these contrasting proposals and counterproposals have consumed a great deal of intellectual energy, created a great deal of unnecessary confusion, and probably impeded progress toward a comprehensive and adequate theory of curriculum development. The danger, which Rugg pointed out in 1926, still persists: that without an effort to stand aside and gather perspective, the curriculum makers will commit themselves uncritically to plans and movements and will take up current modes only to discard them as unthinkingly as they adopted them. Much of the machinery of American education has indeed developed in the past fifty years by just this method (*National Society for the Study of Education, 1926, p. x*).

Some sterility in curriculum development may also stem from the lack of a methodology designed to foster experimentation and to facilitate the translation of theoretical ideas into practice. The usual method of curriculum revision is to start by revising the "framework" before experimenting with the more specific parts of a functioning curriculum: the teaching units on specific grade levels. Yet, only on this functioning level can new possibilities be created and tested. The deductive nonexperimental approach tends to end in a curriculum which either is unattainable in practice or, when put into practice, becomes much like the preceding one.

Perhaps before new ideas can emerge about the design of scope and sequence sufficient experimentation with smaller units of curriculum is needed to settle the many problems connected with curriculum building. There is reasonable ground for believing that if the sequence in the curriculum development were reversed—that if, first, teachers were invited to experiment with specific aspects of curriculum and then, on the basis of these experiments, a framework were to be developed—curriculum development would acquire a new dynamic.

AN APPROACH TO DESIGNING THE CURRICULUM

What is considered the domain of curriculum thinking depends, of course, on how one defines curriculum. In this respect, too, there are variations. Some definitions seem too all-encompassing and vague to help precision in thinking. When curriculum is defined as "the total effort of the school to bring about desired outcomes in school and out-of-school situations" (*Saylor and Alexander, 1954, p. 3*) or "a sequence of potential experiences set up in school for the purpose of disciplining children and youth in group ways of thinking and acting" (*B. O. Smith, Stanley, and Shores, 1957, p. 3*), the very breadth may make the definition nonfunctional. On the other hand, excluding from the definition of curriculum everything except the statement of objectives and content outlines and relegating anything that has to do with learning and learning experiences to "method" might be too confining to be adequate for a modern curriculum.

The definition that underlies the development of this volume is somewhere in between these two extremes. A sharp distinction between method and curriculum seems unfruitful, but some distinctions need to be drawn between the aspects of learning processes and activities that are of concern in curriculum development and those that can be allocated to the realm of specific methods of teaching. Only certain objectives can be implemented by the nature of curriculum content, its selection and organization. Others can be implemented only by the nature and organization of learning experiences. Thinking, for example, is one of the latter objectives. It would appear, then, that the criteria for and the decisions about learning experiences necessary to implement major objectives belong in the realm of curriculum design.

With this explanation in mind, we can consider the elements of curricula about which decisions need to be made, and the methodology and the order of making these decisions.

All curricula, no matter what their particular design, are composed of certain elements. A curriculum usually contains a statement of aims and of specific objectives; it indicates some selection and organization of content; it either implies or manifests certain patterns of learning and teaching, whether because the objectives demand them or because the content organization requires them. Finally, it includes a program of evaluation of the outcomes. Curricula differ according to the emphasis given to each of these elements, according to the manner in which these elements are related to each other, and according to the basis on which the decisions regarding each are made. For example, vast differences depend on whether the chief aim of curriculum is considered to be intellectual development or the making of a democratic citizen. The selection of content and of learning experiences differs according to whether or not the program includes among its objectives the development of thinking. Decisions about the nature and sequence of both content and learning experiences vary according to the theories of learning that are applied. And the problems of relationships between various types of content are determined by ideas regarding the basic functions of knowledge in the development of an individual.

Further, if curriculum development is to be a rational and a scientific rather than a rule-of-thumb procedure, the decisions about these elements need to be made on the basis of some valid criteria. These criteria may come from various sources—from tradition, from social pressures, from established habits. The differences between a curriculum decision-making which follows a scientific method and develops a rational design and one which does not is that in the former the criteria for decisions are derived from a study of the factors constituting a reasonable basis for the curriculum. In our society at least, these factors are the learner, the learning process, the cultural demands, and the content of the disciplines. Therefore, scientific curriculum development needs to draw upon analyses of society and culture, studies of the learner and the learning process, and analyses of the nature of knowledge in order to determine the purposes of the school and the nature of its curriculum.

To evolve a theory of curriculum development and a method of thinking about it, one needs to ask what the demands and requirements of culture and society are, both for the present and for the future. Curriculum is, after all, a way of preparing young people to participate as productive members of our culture. Not all cultures require the same kinds of knowledge. Nor does the same culture need the same kinds of capacities and skills, intellectual or otherwise, at all times. Reading would be of no importance in a nonliterate culture. A technological culture requires a greater development in scientific knowledge and skills than does a nontechnical culture. The requirement for world understanding has become a reality in our culture only recently. An analysis of culture and society thus provides some guide for determining the main objectives of education, for the selection of content, and for deciding what to stress in learning activities.

Information about the learning process and the nature of learners offers another set of criteria for curriculum development. A curriculum is a plan for learning; therefore, what is known about the learning process and the development of the individual has bearing on the shaping of a curriculum. Such knowledge should determine which objectives are achievable under which conditions, and what variations and flexibilities in content and its organization are needed to provide for optimum effectiveness of learning. Knowledge about the nature of the learning process also sets criteria for and limits on the shape of the curriculum. If learning is an organic whole, then the curriculum should not be piecemeal. On the other hand, if learning is developmental, then the curriculum should also embody a developmental sequence.

The third source of criteria for making curriculum decisions is the nature of knowledge and the specific characteristics and unique contributions of the disciplines from which the content of curriculum is derived. There are differences in the structure of the various disciplines. It is conceivable, therefore, that each discipline contributes something different to mental, social, and emotional development and that each subject or content area needs to be organized and used in a different way. Furthermore, especially today in the era of exploding knowledge, a constant restudy is needed of the basic disciplines from which the content of school subjects is derived to make sure that the concepts around which the school subjects are organized are consistent with developments in those disciplines.

Facts and ideas from these sources do not automatically yield a platform for a curriculum. Certain considerations and choices of values and philosophies will make some developments seem of greater worth than others. For example, a democratic philosophy of life and of education will prize individual development more highly than would a scheme of education which follows another philosophy. Attitudes toward permanence and change determine the extent to which independent thinking is prized over mastery of heritage and conformity to tradition. Hence, knowledge derived from the sources described above must be sifted through certain value criteria, be these derived from the philosophy of what a good life is, from democratic principles and ideals, or from some other sources.

In this book, a discussion of the sources from which the ideas and criteria for curriculum decisions are derived comprises Part I, dealing with conceptions of the function of the school in our society, ideas and information about society, concepts of learning and learners, the nature of knowledge, and the implications of each for curriculum.

If one conceives of curriculum development as a task requiring orderly thinking, one needs to examine both the order in which decisions are made and the way in which they are made to make sure that all relevant considerations are brought to bear on these decisions. This book is based on an assumption that there is such an order and that pursuing it will result in a more thoughtfully planned and a more dynamically conceived curriculum. This order might be as follows:

Step 1: Diagnosis of needs
Step 2: Formulation of objectives
Step 3: Selection of content
Step 4: Organization of content
Step 5: Selection of learning experiences
Step 6: Organization of learning experiences
Step 7: Determination of what to evaluate and
of the ways and means of doing it.*

Curricula are designed so that students may learn. Because the backgrounds of students vary, it is important to diagnose the gaps, deficiencies, and variations in these backgrounds. Diagnosis, then, is an important first step in determining what the curriculum should be for a given population. Although the explorations described in Part I suggest the general aims that the school might pursue, an intelligent delineation of concrete and tangible curricular objectives can proceed only after some information is obtained regarding the level on which objectives can be reached by a particular group of students and the emphasis that may be required in the light of their experience.

Formulation of clear and comprehensive objectives provides an essential platform for the curriculum. In large part the objectives determine what content is important and how it should be organized. For example, if the goal of studying world history is to produce intelligent judgment about the current world scene, certain parts of history are bound to be more important than others. If the goal is to create a common perception of the past, then other aspects of world history and other ways of learning it become important. If reflective thinking is an important goal, a thorough study of fewer topics and greater opportunities to relate ideas would be more important than a complete coverage of facts.

But selection and organization of the content of a curriculum also involve criteria other than objectives, such as its validity and significance, the making of proper distinctions between the various levels of content, and decisions about the level of development at which to introduce it. It involves, furthermore, consideration of continuities and sequences in learning and of variations in the capacity to learn.

The task of selecting and organizing learning experiences involves more than applying certain principles of learning. In the scheme of thinking em-

* These steps are comparable to a sequence proposed in a syllabus by Tyler (1950). A similar sequence is described by Taba (1945).

ployed in this book, it involves ideas about such matters as strategies of concept attainment and sequences in formation of attitudes and sensitivities. To the extent that learning activities are used to implement some objectives, the planning of learning experiences becomes a part of a major strategy of curriculum building instead of being relegated to incidental decisions made by the teacher at the moment of teaching. Problems such as how to translate the content to be learned into appropriate learning experiences and how to project learning experiences that accommodate variations in ability to learn, in motivation, and in mental systems must be faced here.

Finally, plans need to be made for evaluation. How should the quality of learning be evaluated to assure that the ends of education are being achieved? How does one make sure that there is consistency between the aims and objectives and what is actually achieved by students? Does the curriculum organization provide experiences which offer optimum opportunities for all varieties of learners to attain independent goals?

The above problems are discussed in Part II, which includes chapters on diagnosis, objectives, criteria for selecting and organizing content, the selection and organization of learning experiences, and evaluation. Because it is assumed that the development of units of teaching is a significant task which deserves as much attention and care as any other aspect of curriculum development, one chapter deals with a methodology of organizing a unit in order to show how these multiple decisions relate to and influence each other and to demonstrate that all the major decisions, excepting those of over-all design, are involved at this level of curriculum making.

Part III deals with the conceptual framework for curriculum development. The demands and needs of the culture, the growth and development of children, the principles of learning, the fundamental ideas in the various areas of content, and the unique modes of thought represented in them need to flow into one coherent stream. The fact that this stream must yield a development of ideas, forms of thought, feelings, habits, and skills only makes the task of integrating the complex of learning processes we call the curriculum more difficult. This task requires a conceptual framework which spells out the crucial elements of curriculum and their relationship to each other. The central problems of a curriculum design are to determine the scope of expected learning, to establish a continuity of learning and proper sequence of content, and to unify ideas from diverse areas.

Finally, there are problems of developing a strategy for curriculum change. Perhaps one way of solving the problems inherent in either designing or changing the curriculum is to ask proper questions in a proper sequence, so that working at curriculum change becomes a systematic enterprise to be broken down into smaller enterprises, which are considered one at a time. Curriculum development thus can be undertaken as a series of steps, each of which adds to and revises the decisions made at the preceding step. In other words, it seems necessary for curriculum development not only to follow a rational scheme for planning its various elements, but also to have a methodology for developing these elements and for relating them to each other. This methodology includes the ways of deciding who plays the various roles in curriculum making, who makes decisions and suggestions about the ways in which these roles may supplement each other, and how these decisions may be coordinated and rendered consistent. These problems of mobilizing for the task of curriculum development and installation are discussed in Part IV.

PART ONE

The Foundations for Curriculum Development

Current Conceptions
of the Function
CHAPTER TWO   # of the School

Society's concept of the function of the public school determines to a great extent what kind of curriculum schools will have. Yet, in a complex culture with a pluralistic value system, it is difficult to establish a single central function for any agency. In a democratic society these formulations are further complicated by the fact that different layers of society participate in the process of determining what education in general and public schools specifically should be and do. It is, therefore, more difficult to determine the central function of schools in a democracy than in a totalitarian society where a small power group decides both what society should be and what role schools shall play in it.

Our society today has by no means agreed about what the central function of the school should be. One could even say that "the great debate about schools and their function" is in effect a debate about many of the issues our society faces: the balance between freedom and control and between change and tradition, whether the elite should be of power or of intellect, who should participate in shaping the public policy, and many others. It is generally agreed that the main outlines of the "crisis in education" are shaped and complicated by the convergence of two phenomena: the transformative effects of science and technology on society and the emergence of Communist totalitarianism as an expanding imperialist power. In the light of this setting the examination of the functions of the public school is highly pertinent, but extremely difficult, because the issues tend to be confused and the viewpoints somewhat less than objective.

Whatever the specific viewpoints regarding the functions of the public schools, there seems to be little disagreement about the importance of the role of education. American society has always expected a great deal of education and, in Walter Lippmann's phrase, has expressed great faith in it as the "life-giving principle of national power." Historically the American people have assumed that education has the power to reduce poverty and distress, to prevent child delinquency and crime, and to promote the well-being of the individual, the intelligent use of suffrage, and the welfare and stability of the state. Indeed, even today education, if not the public school, is considered an antidote against evils in the minds of men and an ally in achieving all good causes. The very attacks on the schools express the faith of the American public that the schools matter because of their influence not only on individuals, but on society as well. Some critics, for example, seem to reason that the strength of our current enemies is the *result* of *their* education and, correspondingly, that the weakness in our position is the *fault* of *our* education.

These high expectations and the naïve faith in the power of education are at once a curse and a blessing. No doubt they have given American education a certain vigor by insisting that it respond to social ideologies and needs. They have also made it more subject to passing hysterias and changing moods of the public than may have been good for a healthy development. Anyone tracing the various "trends" in curriculum development in the United States will note a zigzag movement in which one "trend" swallows and annihilates the preceding one with an almost unbelievable discontinuity in theoretical thought. When education is overly sensitive to public opinion, changes are bound to be made thoughtlessly. Continuity in capitalizing on past achievements is jeopardized in the heat of hastily formulated reforms and changes. It is no wonder, then, that in periods of crisis the question of the central function of schools in society becomes a subject of heated controversy, with the nature of the relationships of education to society at the very core of that controversy. It is no wonder also that there are many variations in the conceptions of what the essential function of the public school is.

There is relatively little disagreement also about the idea that schools function on behalf of the culture in which they exist. The school is created by a society for the purpose of reproducing in the learner the knowledge, attitudes, values, and techniques that have cultural relevancy or currency.* There is generally also no quarrel with the idea that of the many educative agencies of society, the school is the one which specializes in inducting youth into the culture and is thus responsible for the continuity of that culture.

However, opinion is divided about the precise nature of this function. The differences range from conceptions which assume a strong cultural determination of everything schools do and should do to postulations about ideals of individual development which are quite independent of cultural norms. This division of opinion extends also to views on the extent to which the program of the school is or should be subject to the values and norms of the culture, and in what measure the materials it uses and the ideologies that control its shaping should be drawn from the life of the culture. While in all concepts it is accepted that schools must transmit culture, there are sharp differences about what should be transmitted and the manner in which it is to be done. Some conceptions emphasize education as an agent of change, while others stress its preserving functions.

* Goodson describes this phenomenon as education-culture isomorphism and refers to education as a culturally "capsulated" social institution (1960, pp. 11-12).

Sometimes, especially in theoretical discussions, these divisions of views appear as rather stark and even unrealistic alternatives. Speaking of the function of general education, Conant states one such alternative neatly:

> Roughly speaking, the basic argument about general education turns on the degree to which the literary and philosophical traditions of the western world, as interpreted by scholars and connoisseurs before World War I, should be the basis of the education of *all* American youth. The watershed between two fundamentally opposed positions can be located by raising the question: For what purpose do we have a system of public education? If the answer is to develop effective citizens of a free democratic country, then we seem to be facing in one direction. If the answer is to develop the student's rational powers and immerse him in the stream of our cultural heritage, then we appear to be facing in the opposite direction. By and large, the first position represents the modern approach to education; the latter the more conventional view. Those who look down one valley regard conventional "book learning" as only one element in the landscape; those who look down the other believe that developing the "life of the mind" is the primary aim of civilization and this can be accomplished only by steeping youth in our literary and philosophical heritage [*1948, pp. 74-75*].

All the same, the overlappings in these conceptions are too great to make possible a refined classification of concepts of the function of education. This chapter, therefore, summarizes views on the functions of education under only three large headings: education as preservation and transmission of cultural heritage, education as an instrument for transforming culture, and education as the means for individual development. Within each concept there are variations, some significant enough to cause sharp conflicts regarding the nature of a desirable curriculum. In the emphasis on individual development, for example, there are differences as to whether education should stress intellectual development exclusively or should also stress social and emotional development, and as to how much the socialization of the individual is also within the purview of the public school. The conceptions of the social role of education divide according to whether the major emphasis is on serving social needs and social change or on a planned reconstruction of society. (*See, for example, Brubacher, 1950, pp. 186-200.*)

EDUCATION AS PRESERVER AND TRANSMITTER OF THE CULTURAL HERITAGE

One group of theorists stresses the preserving function of education: the preserving of the cultural heritage, especially that of the Western culture. This group argues that since all cultural traditions have roots, cultural continuity is possible only if education preserves this heritage by passing on the truths worked out in the past to the new generation, thus developing a common cultural background and loyalties. The specific ideas regarding what this heritage consists of are not always clear. In the main the transmission of the accumulated wisdom of the race and of basic truths and values is emphasized.

The Harvard Report on General Education is one example of an emphasis on the importance of preserving tradition and maintaining roots from the past. This report argues that education can develop a unifying purpose and idea only as it develops this sense of heritage, which in turn requires a common ground in training and outlook. This heritage is basic to education because it uses the past to clarify or even to determine what is important in the present. The report points out that it is the function of education to pass on the *inherited* (italics mine) view of man and society, and that its main task is to perpetuate such ideas as the dignity of man and common beliefs in what is good. "Classical antiquity handed on a working system of truths which relied on both reason and experience and was designed to provide a norm for civilized life." It is the business of education to instill a commitment to these truths.

This assertion of the necessity for imparting the common heritage is, however, modified by a certain recognition of the role of new experience and change. The report attempts to reconcile the necessity for common belief with the equally obvious necessity for new and independent insight by pointing out that a certain tough-mindedness in reaching conclusions by scientific methods of thought, a curiosity, and a readiness for change are also necessary; that education cannot be wholly devoted to the commitment to tradition or to the view that means are valuable apart from ideals; that it upholds at the same time the tradition and the experiment, the ideal and the means, and, like our culture itself, change within the commitment. While the report makes a bow to experiment and change, it seems to say that the basic ideals of what constitutes a good man in our society come from tradition. In other words, since the modern society is only an extension of the traditional one, changes will come from applying the ancient truths to the modern scene. Because the common heritage is a way of building unity in culture, and since the classical tradition has handed down a norm for civilized life, the task of education is to "shape the student" to "receive" this ideal (*Report of the Harvard Committee, 1945, pp. 44-51*).

This preserving or conserving function of education is still more strongly accentuated by a group of theorists philosophically classified as rational humanists and classicists. (See, for example, *Hutchins, 1936, and Adler and Mayer, 1958.*) Their conception of the function of education is intimately bound up with and derived from their conception of human nature, which has as its major premise that the essence of human nature is its rational character. Rationality is a common characteristic of all men, apart and independent of the culture in which they exist. The world can be understood by the exercise of this faculty of rationality. Therefore, the chief function of education is to develop this rationality, and the understanding of the eternal truths revealed by these rational faculties. "Education, if it is rightly understood, is the cultivation of the intellect. Only this is what belongs to man as man, and his individuality is only his caprice, self-will, and unique propensities" (*Hutchins, 1936, pp. 66-71*).

Being preoccupied with the essence of things, this viewpoint also insists that learning should be concerned with *essentials,* that is, the first principles articulated in the great books and the classical tradition. Since rationality is essential, the subjects of greatest rational content should also have priority in the curriculum. These subjects are the liberal arts and, among the liberal arts, the humanities (*Brubacher, 1950, pp. 316-19*).

This viewpoint does not deny that societies differ, that education must train citizens for its own society, or that problems of societies vary. However, it insists that these differences are ephemeral and idiosyncratic and that these problems must be understood and interpreted in the light of the universal eternal truths embodied in the classical literature of great books. Such truths are our main cultural heritage, which education must transmit. They constitute the liberalizing education. Further, liberalizing education is the same everywhere, because "truth" is the same everywhere. Thus is set the case not only for the preserving function of education, but also for the requirements for "essentials" and for the uniformity of curriculum.

A rejection of technical subjects and of vocational education of any sort as a narrowing influence is the logical consequence of this viewpoint. That type of "education" is considered to be not education, but training. It is an uncalled-for "encroachment" on the essential task of liberal education (*Griswold, 1959*).

While this view of the function of education was originally put forth in reference to college education, recently the same orientation has been applied to criticism of and proposals for the public-school curriculum by a group organized around the concept of basic education. (*See, for example, Koerner, 1959.*) This group insists also that the transmission of cultural heritage is the chief function of public schools. This heritage is defined by stress on three points, each of which has consequences on what may be proposed for the curriculum.

First, a strong case is made for intellectual development as the distinctive function of public schools. As defined by Bestor this intellectual development must stress the understanding of principles and the ability to handle and to apply complex ideas, to make use of a wide range of accurate knowledge, and to command the means of effective communication. No one would quarrel with this definition. But there is reason to quarrel with another assumption Bestor makes—namely, that because education has been extended to classes and groups which have hitherto been deprived of it, any "weakness" in intellectual training creates a void into which steps anti-intellectualism. In order to prevent this from happening, the case for this intellectual purpose of the school must be made so clear that the anti-intellectual masses cannot distort it (*Bestor, 1955, pp. 7-9; 1959, pp. 76-78*).

Second, this type of intellectual training is possible only by centering the educational effort on basic skills and disciplines: reading, writing, and arithmetic on the lower level, and logic, history, philosophy, mathematics, science, art, and philosophy on the higher levels. These lead the hierarchy of subjects, or the "basics" of education. The assumption that there is a hierarchy of subjects according to "their power to enhance intellectual development" and that the traditional liberal arts subjects are at the top of that hierarchy runs through most of the writings of the basic educators (*Bestor, 1955, pp. 7-21*).

This belief that certain subjects are superior to others as means for intellectual training is made perfectly clear by Clifton Fadiman (*1959, pp. 6-10*), who argues that since the cultural tradition includes many more things than can be handled in schools "without running into chaos," men in the past have imposed on cultural tradition a form and a hierarchy which is constituted into the disciplines of liberal arts, as encompassed in a New York City public school he attended. It is interesting to compare this simple view of basic subjects with the analysis of the complexities in deciding what knowledge is worth most described by those who have examined the recent explosion of knowledge and of its specialization. (See chapter 3 for some of these ideas.)

The third characteristic of "basic education" is a complete rejection of certain current functions of the schools, among them education for democratic citizenship, for moral values, and for ability to deal with social problems, and the concern for the "whole child" or any form of "life adjustment," including education for vocations. These functions put basic educators in an especially aggressive and combative mood. According to Bestor, modern education suffers from an enormous extension of functions which schools have no business in assuming: In this extension there is peril to basic education and to the development of intelligence. This extension also unnecessarily pre-empts the functions of other agencies. Thus, job training is the problem of industry. Training in cultural traits, mores, and the ethical systems belongs to the family and the church. Neither should the school be concerned about "social conditioning," partly because it works against tremendous odds and therefore is ineffectual, partly because the socialization of the individual is the very means of squelching the creativity and independence of the intellect. A thoughtless transfer of functions from one agency to another only creates problems; this transfer should be resisted, even though pressures exist for it (*Bestor, 1959, pp. 80-87*).

In other words, basic education is a case against any goals for schools beyond those for intellectual development, for a return to the pure form of disciplines as defined by classical tradition, and for limiting general education to those who show a certain level of intellectual promise.

There are, of course, many criticisms of and questions about this definition of the function of the public school. One criticism pertains to the validity of the assumption that, since men are rational and truth is everywhere the same, education everywhere must be uniformly addressed to these truths and to the exclusive task of developing the rational powers. The recent explosion of knowledge seems to have disestablished many truths that were considered perennial. Rational powers seems to be interlocked with cultural conditions and personal factors in a way that forces reinterpretation of ancient truths. "Ancient truths" are not always applicable to the realities and the needs of modern society except in a sense so general as to be unachievable short of a lifetime of study. Further, modern social analysis seems to indicate a greater break with tradition than any of the basic educators are willing to admit, and therefore the transmission of outdated wisdom might even be dangerous. It seems more likely that society today needs to create its own image of the true, the beautiful, and the just.

It is questionable also whether intellectual development can take place effectively in such a grand isolation from the cultural milieu as the advocates of this viewpoint seem to assume. This assumption contradicts the tenor of many studies which point to the relationship between the development of an individual and his cultural milieu. (See chapters 4, 8, and 9.) Further, while while there is a general agreement about the central importance of intellectual development, the weight of recent knowledge about learning points to the fact that intellectuality cannot be neatly separated from other aspects of personality development without the danger of cultivating an academic intellectuality instead of a functioning intelligence.

Finally, the argument for the purified liberal arts disciplines as a sole way to wisdom is strongly contradicted by the very developments in these disciplines. Often so-called practical application of what is known becomes the very mainspring of theory, or "pure" thought.

EDUCATION AS AN INSTRUMENT
FOR TRANSFORMING CULTURE

An opposing view is held by many educators and social analysts who maintain, in effect, that education can and does play a creative role in modifying and even reshaping the culture in which it functions, that education and public policy are intimately related, and that progress in one is limited without progress in the other. They maintain that education must deal with the needs of current culture and even help to shape the future.

The idea that education has a constructive role to play in shaping the society has deep roots in American tradition. It is implicitly expressed in the general public faith in the power of education to deal with problems of culture. It is also articulated in much of educational writing over a long period of time. Horace Mann underscored the integral relationship between popular education and social problems, such as freedom and the republican government. This theme resounds through his twelve reports: "A nation cannot long remain ignorant and free. No political structure, however artfully devised, can inherently guarantee the rights and liberties of citizens, for freedom can be secure only as knowledge is widely distributed among the populace" (*Cremin, 1957, p. 7*). Facing the social reality of the times, the public discord of a nation not yet unified, and "Fearing the destructive possibilities of religious, political and class discord," he sought a common value system which might undergird American republicanism and within which a healthy diversity might thrive. His quest was for *public philosophy,* a sense of community which might be shared by Americans of every variety and persuasion. His effort was to use education to fashion a new American character out of a maze of conflicting cultural traditions. And his tool was the *Common School.* The common school for him was the instrument for his limitless faith in the perfectibility of human life and institutions (*Cremin, 1957, p. 8*). In this sense, then, Horace Mann regarded education as an arm of public policy and an instrument for dealing with the problems facing the nation at that time.

A flowering of the idea that education is a social process, the primary and most effective instrument of social reconstruction, came with the work and writings of Dewey and his followers. The main thesis of this group was that the school is not merely a residual institution to maintain things as they are: education has a creative function to play in the shaping of individuals and through them in the shaping of the culture. Dewey consistently saw the function of the school in both psychological and social terms. As early as 1897 he wrote:

> I believe that: all education proceeds by the participation of the individuals in the social consciousness of the race. This process . . . is continually shaping the individual's powers, saturating his consciousness, forming his habits, training his ideas, and arousing his feelings and emotions. . . . The most formal and technical education in the world cannot safely depart from this general process. . . . This educational process has two sides—one psychological, and one sociological and . . . neither can be subordinated to the other, or neglected, without evil consequences . . . knowledge of social conditions of the present state of civilization is necessary in order to properly interpret the child's powers . . . and that the school is primarily a social institution [*Dewey, 1929, pp. 3-6*].

In subsequent development one fork of this dual orientation of Dewey on the function of education matured into an elaboration of the social responsibilities of the school, while the other centered more emphatically on individual development.

Dewey's concept of democracy was that of an intentionally progressive society, committed to change, organized as intelligently and as scientifically as possible. The role of education in such a society is to inculcate the habits that would make it possible for individuals to control their surroundings rather than merely to submit to them. A progressive society would "endeavor to shape the experience of the young so that instead of reproducing current habits, better habits shall be formed, and thus the future adult society be an improvement on their own. . . . We are doubtless far from realizing the potential efficacy of education as a constructive agency of improving society, from realizing that it represents not only a development of children and youth but also of the future society of which they will be the constituents" (*Dewey, 1928, p. 92*).

This viewpoint dictated priorities for curriculum. Dewey was concerned that essentials be placed first and refinements second, but he defined as essentials the things which are most fundamental socially, which have to do with experience shared by the widest groups. He was also deeply critical of the dualism between culture and vocation and concerned with the effects on democracy of a scheme of education in which there is a narrow utilitarian education for one class of people and a broad liberal education for another (*1928, p. 225*). In addition to insisting on the cultivation of the "method of intelligence" and of scientific inquiry as the first tasks of the curriculum, he also stressed the necessity of introducing vocational subjects not merely to build utilitarian skills but as "points of departure" for increasingly intellectualized ventures into the life and meaning of industrial society. (For a fuller summary see *Cremin, 1961, pp. 117-26.*)

The subsequent elaborations of the social function of the school took on several different shadings, which ranged from emphasis on changing society by changing individuals to stress on planned reconstruction of the social system.

Some of the elaborations stress primarily the responsibility of the school to meet current social needs. The deeper interpretation of this responsibility involves shaping the school program according to a long-term perspective on the realities of the changing society, and an adequate study of a whole range of social needs. A shallower interpretation makes demands on the school on behalf of immediate difficulties and problems. The current insistence on redoubled study of mathematics and physical science, growing in part out of the "somewhat adolescent feeling of national humiliation" at Soviet advances in missile technology and in part out of temporary anxieties regarding manpower needs in these fields, illustrates the shallow perspective.

Others see the social function of education as one of promoting a critical orientation toward the current scene. This interpretation has led to an emphasis on problem solving in the social sciences and to the introduction of problem courses. An emphasis on an understanding of the social forces that generate cultural lag and dislocation is part of this orientation. (See *Brubacher, 1950, pp. 186-201,* for an analysis of the relationship of school to social progress.) Some educators interpret the social function of education chiefly as an instrument for social change, either through gradual reform by reshaping the outlook of the oncoming generation or through planned effort at reconstruction.

But whatever the variations in concepts of the social functions of education, certain fundamental ideas tend to run through all. One is the understanding that education must, and usually does, work in the cultural setting of a given society, at a given time, in a given place, shaping the individual in some measure to participate in that society. All decisions about education, including those about curriculum, are made within the context of a society. The values and forces of that society determine not only what manner of man exists but also to some extent what manner of man is needed. The decision-makers themselves are immersed in the culture and therefore subject to the culturally conditioned conceptions of how education is to serve that society. As Childs puts it (*1935, p. 2*), the schools are doubly social in nature. They are the arm instituted by society for the education of the young. But the very materials which constitute the program of the school are also drawn from the life of that society.

This concept means that not only is intellectual training to be directed to understanding the forces of the culture and to mastering the intellectual tools necessary for that understanding, but also that there is a fundamental responsibility for training in the culture's essential values and loyalties. In this view, then, social cohesion depends not so much on transmission of the common knowledge as the sharing of common values and concerns.

A second important element in these concepts is the profound appreciation of the fact of change in modern culture and of the meaning of social change. If the society and the culture are changing, then it is the task of schools to play a constructive role in that change. Education must adjust its aims and program to changing conditions, and, if possible, foreshadow them, especially under the conditions of rapid change introduced by modern technology. Without a continual reorientation to changing conditions, education becomes unreal and in a sense useless because it does not prepare youth for life's problems and responsibilities. To meet changing conditions means, of course, that both the aims of education and the programs devised to implement these aims, including the orientation brought to bear on materials used, must be changed also. It is of central importance to use critical intelligence (not intellectuality as described in the preceding section) and scientific attitudes in understanding and solving human and social problems. These qualities of mind can be cultivated to the extent that the "subject matter" of education is significant to the ongoing experience and concerns of the culture, and that experience is used as the key for giving meaning to knowledge and for translating subject matter into behavior and action (*Dewey, 1937, pp. 235-38; Kilpatrick, 1935, 1926*).

The third important element of this concept is the idea that education is a moral undertaking. It begins and ends with value decisions. Educational decisions, whether regarding aims or curricular selections, always involve value judgments. For this reason education always will involve an element of prescription. Although scientific inquiry will determine what is, it will not prescribe what should be. Education is a moral enterprise also in that it selects which parts of the culture, what wisdom, which values, what ideals to transmit. No school in any society can be completely neutral; the difference lies in whether the basis for selection is made clear and whether the selection is made with some degree of rational method and scientific inquiry (*Childs, 1935, pp. 1-9; 1959, p. 91*).

The concept of education as a reconstruction of society goes further than any of the above. The proponents of this view speak of education as management and control of social change and as social engineering, and of educators as statesmen. The idea that education should not only foster changes in society but should change the very social order was first expressed by Counts (*1932*). It was later reiterated in *The Educational Frontier,* the thesis of which was that the task of education is "to prepare individuals to take part intelligently in the management of conditions under which they live, to bring them to an understanding of the forces which are moving, to equip them with the intellectual tools by which they can themselves enter into the direction of these forces" (*Kilpatrick, 1933, p. 71*). To implement such an education it would be necessary to launch a massive adult program that would build political and educational support for a radically different school curriculum, to develop a public which is education conscious and wise in the realities of industrial civilization, to reorient professional education, and to alert teachers to the pressing social issues of the day (*Cremin, 1961, p. 230*).

More recently a group of educators who call themselves the "reconstructionists" have argued in a similar vein and with the same sense of urgency about the social mission of education. In analyzing the orientation needed for developing a curriculum theory, B. Othanel Smith concludes by observing: "It is clear that the time for building a comprehensive social perspective is here. We are now living in a time when we can no longer depend upon custom and unconscious control to regulate our social existence. There is no longer any substitute for human management of the vast social machine. As a people we have much knowledge of and techniques for social engineering. The question is: can we learn to use it rapidly enough to control the social machine before it either enslaves us or destroys us?" (*B. O. Smith, March 1950, p. 16*).

The main theses of the reconstructionist position are somewhat as follows: the transformation of society by technological and scientific revolution is so radical as to require a new moral and intellectual consensus capable of molding and directing this transformation. It is the task of educators to analyze the social trends, to discern the problems society is facing, to speculate on the consequences of the current social dynamics, and to project the values and the goals which need to be sought to maintain a democratic way of life. Because social changes today are rapid and radical, and because there are blind consequences to the technological revolution which seem to endanger the democratic way of life, tradition is a poor guide. A continuous critical reexamination of the meaning of the democratic way of life under the altered social conditions is needed. Critical examination and reconstruction of the cultural heritage—or social ideas, beliefs, and institutions—in the light of current problems and conditions, rather than inculcation of traditional ideas, must constitute the core of the educational program of today. In addition, educators must be statesmen, and in cooperation with other agencies must study and discuss the implication of the new "intellectual and moral order" for the "institutional structure of society" (*B. O. Smith, Stanley, and Shores, 1957, pp. 574-82*).

In this scheme a rather exalted role is allotted to education and the schools. Educators must take close account of social forces, of the social institutions, and of their educative effects. They must translate this knowledge of culture and society into "educational policy," that is, a curriculum which will aid students in understanding these forces and in developing the techniques and attitudes necessary for participation in democratic reconstruction. The total educative impact of the school must encompass and coordinate changes in beliefs, personality structures, and social arrangements. Educators must carry the rest of the community to an agreement with their proposals (*B. O. Smith, Stanley, and Shores, 1957, pp. 580-82*). Curriculum planning needs to focus on building "social goals" and a "common social orientation." Individual goals and diverse group goals must be integrated into a system of social ends. Curriculum development in this sense becomes a way of making public policy (*B. O. Smith, March 1950, p. 10*).

The capacity of education in general and of public schools in particular to assume a leading role in changing the society and particularly the social structure has been seriously questioned. To sociologists concerned with the relationship of school and society it seems altogether unrealistic for schools to be animated by goals which differ radically from those of the culture in which they work. They point out that usually the aims of education are conservative—that is, they are consonant with the conceptions of the ideal adult which society wishes to produce—and educational institutions can pursue only those aims that society considers desirable. Historically, the aims of education have shifted, but these shifts have followed, not preceded, the changes in society's ideals of a desirable adult. It is therefore somewhat utopian to think of education as a means for a radical reconstruction of society, such as a new social order (*Brim, 1958, pp. 16-17*).

Other critics suggest, in addition, that it is easy to exaggerate both the actual and the potential ability of any formal institution, including the schools, to contribute to consensus in society, whether the means to achieve this consensus be the formation of basic personality or inculcation of a common set of values. This is especially so in industrial societies with their mass patterns of educational service, in which instruction looms larger than education, and in school settings in which it is impossible except under extreme conditions either to isolate or to exclude from its personnel those groups who do not share the dominant goals of the institution (*Floud and Halsey, 1959, pp. 293-94*). It is possible, of course, that the sociologists and other critics may because of their own limited insight into the dynamics of the educational process underestimate what schools can do. The conditions under which creative educational aims can be conceived and implemented might well form the subject of further serious study and research.

EDUCATION FOR INDIVIDUAL DEVELOPMENT

The other fork from Dewey's philosophy led to an emphasis on individual development as a chief function of education. A large part of the progressive education movement emphasized the creative role of education in society by stressing the development of a creative individual. This point of view was implemented by centering educational effort on the development of all the powers of the individual, and especially on his creative imagination, freedom, independence, right to self-discovery, and physical and emotional powers—in other words, on the "whole child." In the extreme this view led to a conception of the "child-centered school," with its concern for creative self-expression, individuality, activity, freedom from imposition "from without," and growth from within. The counterpart of this conception was experimentation with curriculum built up solely to meet the needs and interests of children. The chief tenet of the child-centered concept of education was to preserve the "whole" child and especially what is creative and spontaneous in him. The idea was to move the child into the center of educational activity and to allow him freedom to develop as a unique personality. (*Rugg and Shumaker, 1928,* is perhaps the classical expression of this view.)

A more moderate conception of individual development included concern with the needs of the individual and with his fullest opportunity for self-realization in an intellectual as well as emotional sense, while recognizing that this development needs to combine social and intellectual discipline and freedom in a reasonable balance. The programs generated by this moderate view had a tremendous vitality for several decades and set in motion numerous studies of individual needs and of patterns of development as well as many experiments in educational practice, such as the Eight Year Study (*Adventures in American Education Series, 1942-43*).

This interpretation of individual development probably has influenced the school programs and practices to a far greater extent than have the concepts of the social function of education. Data on developmental sequences have greatly influenced the grade placement of subjects. The emphasis on the important role of emotional development has led to introduction of guidance practices as well as to a more discerning shaping of the conditions for learning, such as the "permissive" climate and regard for motivation. The intellectual understanding of emotional development has been implemented by introducing the study of personal development into the curriculum. And the concept of individual differences has been expanded to include emotional and social maturity in addition to ability and achievement.

A somewhat exclusive emphasis on education as chiefly an instrument of individual development holds sway even today and is discernible even in the work of the groups which start their thinking from an analysis of the impact of social problems and needs on education. The 1950 White House Conference, for example, started with an analysis of factual data regarding changes in family structure, in population trends, and in technology, and of the social problems created by these changes. Their final report to the President, however, concludes with a statement of goals almost entirely in terms of individual development: "The order given by the American People to the schools is grand in its simplicity: in addition to intellectual achievement, to foster morality, happiness, and any useful ability. The talent of each child is to be sought out and developed to the fullest. Each weakness is to be studied and so far as possible, corrected" (*Committee for the White House Conference, 1956, p. 9*).

Today, however, the conception of individual development is likely to include a concern with the social origins of individual powers, with the differences in backgrounds and capacities that these social origins or the social milieu are likely to impose, and with the problems of equalizing opportunity for development for all youth by using the school as a socializing agent. One theme of this conception is that education, among other things, is a gateway to mobility, an arm of equalization society uses in democratizing its inevitably hierarchical structure of economic, social, and intellectual opportunity. One function of the school, therefore, is to fill the gaps and correct the deficiencies in socialization which occur because of the limitations imposed on opportunities by the social structure. It is the task of the school to select and nurture ability that may be stultified by the limitations imposed by social background.

According to this concept the school must not only introduce the students to the skills and powers necessary for survival or for self-realization in our culture; it must also act as an integrating force in shaping beliefs and attitudes to make them coherent with the requirements of the democratic way of life. It needs to act as an integrator of the pluralistic and contradictory values and expectations engendered in a stratified society. In this sense the school functions at once as a conserving force on behalf of human democracy and as an innovating force by helping individuals rediscover democracy in an environment which is in large measure undemocratic.

IMPLICATIONS OF THESE
CONCEPTS FOR CURRICULUM

The arguments about the relative importance of the social orientation and child-centered orientation were acrimonious enough to split the progressive education movement into two camps, one emphasizing the psychological slant of individual development and the other the slant of social reconstruction. This division helped perpetuate the many *versus* arguments that have plagued education ever since, such as "individual *versus* social needs," and "the child-centered *versus* the community-centered school." The rather unrealistic elaborations of these extremes and the black and white contradictions they engendered have provided grist for the mill of current criticisms of progressive education.

Time will show these arguments to have been largely semantic. For example, one of the most literate and vehement champions of the child-centered school, Harold Rugg, has also written voluminously on the analysis of American society and stressed continually the need for studying the society in order to set the goals for education. The fact that the so-called child-centered school was always in a measure also a society-centered school seems to have escaped the later critics of the progressive movement.

But, semantics aside, these variations in the conceptions of the function of education are not idle or theoretical arguments. They have definite concrete implications for the shape of educational programs, especially the curriculum. They determine the definitions of needs to be served. They illuminate the controversies over such curriculum practices as studying contemporary problems rather than ancient and world history. They provide the theoretical basis for deciding whether the classics or modern literature should dominate the reading diet in high schools. They are also relevant to the whole problem of guidance and its role in the curriculum, and to the questions of individualization of the curriculum content and methods of teaching. If one believes that the chief function of education is to transmit the "perennial truths," one cannot help but strive toward a uniform curriculum and teaching. Efforts to develop thinking take a different shape depending on whether the major function of education is seen as fostering creative thinking and problem solving or as following the "rational" forms of thinking established in our classical tradition. And such differences in these concepts naturally determine what are considered the "essentials" and what the dispensable "frills" in education.

The Analysis
of Society

The discussion of the role of education in society is as old as Aristotle, and this discussion is renewed in every period of social crisis. Whether we view the role as that of transmitting culture, socializing the individual, or reconstructing society, we need to study and to analyze the structure of society in order to determine what the goals and the emphasis of the complex we call education should be. This is especially necessary in a rapidly changing technological society where education "plays a role in relation to all aspects of social structure, demographic, economic, political, and social, as well as ideological and spiritual" (*Floud and Halsey, 1959, p. 290*).

It is not an easy task to establish what demands society makes on education and what contribution education can or should make to culture, especially in a complex society in which vast and rapid changes are occurring. Yet it is precisely in such a society that a continuous examination of the goals and demands of society and of the forces operating in it is necessary in order to keep education reality-oriented: to determine what knowledge is most worthwhile, which skills must be mastered, which values are relevant. These questions are all the more relevant if one conceives of education as a creative agent of social change in reconstructing society or as serving social or individual needs.

THE SOURCES FOR ANALYSIS OF SOCIETY

The difficulty in analyzing society and culture to provide a guide for education does not lie in the impotence of behavioral sciences nor in lack of facts. There seems to be an optimism about the capacity of social and behavioral sciences to understand, predict, and control cultural change. In speaking about the science of man in relation to world crisis, Linton, for example, points out that periods of stress are no new thing in human history. All civilizations have experienced them, and each generation has felt that its experience was the worst. "The only unique thing about the present period is the large number of people who believe that such periods are not inevitable and that they can be avoided by intelligent planning for the future. This attitude seems to be something new in human history."

Because he feels that the current stress is a symptom of a "deeper disorder," Linton thinks it is especially important to know what the disorder is and how to cure it. He does not agree with those who maintain that the future of the society and culture is determined by the interaction of innumerable factors, many of which the scientists cannot ascertain, still less control. He feels there is a "human order" and that these seemingly chance-determined events conform to some sort of pattern. "Although no two events are ever the same, the same patterns of organization and the processes of growth in change repeat themselves again and again" (*Linton, 1945b, pp. 201-03*).

Greater aid to education is available also because a tremendous advance has been made in the sciences which constitute the social foundations of education. Advances in biology, anthropology, sociology, and social psychology have given us a new understanding of man and how he grows and learns. There is more data about culture, as well as more penetrating concepts with which to analyze it, to understand its core values and the direction of changes in it. Hundreds of studies have been made of changes in social institutions: of the direction and significance of population movements, of technological developments, of social stratification, of differentiations in value systems and in the behavioral roles, of effects of urbanization, of family structure, and of the nature of the economic machinery and its consequences on human affairs.

Studies are available also on the trends in the total culture. Such problems as the dichotomy between the ideal of individual dignity and autonomy and the individual's rather anonymous mechanical role in the economic life of our day have been widely studied. Studies abound also on such topics as the conflicts and stresses in family life, difficulties of youth in attaining economic and personal independence, the conflicts between the democratic ideal of life and an amorality created by practices used to attain success, and the stresses and strains of a competitive society. There are also analyses of the conflicts in value systems generated by rapid and uneven shifts in different aspects of the culture: its technology, its institutions, its habits and attitudes.

These studies point to a changed meaning in some of the perennials of the democratic philosophy of the American culture. There are reinterpretations of such basic democratic tenets as equality of opportunity, the sanctity of the individual human being, and his freedom and rights in the light of changes in social arrangements and cultural patterns. Some studies point to the passing of the personal, individualistic concept of freedom. The human and economic concepts of democratic equality have been added to the political one. New applications of the fundamental tenets of democratic living have also been made in examining the conduct of the postwar world and policies regarding interracial relations within the United States as well as abroad. There are analyses of readjustments in economic facilities, and of the new relationships between economic institutions, private individuals, and the government. These new interpretations of democratic values and of the problems involved in applying and maintaining them are of great importance in clarifying what to work toward in education for democratic citizenship as well as in determining how to interpret the social implications of what is taught.*

However, an educator looking for direction in the literature of behavioral sciences finds no easy road to discovering the bearing of this knowledge on education and the conduct of schools. First, social scientists have paid relatively little attention either to studying schools as an institution or to applying their findings to the process of education. Although they recognize the fact that in an industrial society education can and does have a strategic place in determining the economic, political, social, and cultural character of the society, and that the school as a social institution is subject to the social forces which mold and create its aims and policies, there is as yet no orderly and coherent analysis of the "institution of education" or of the impact of social forces on education (*Floud and Halsey, 1959, pp. 289-90, and Brim, 1958*). Even attempts by social scientists to apply their knowledge of society to education are scarce. One is surprised to see, for example, that treatises with such titles as *Some Uses of Anthropology, Theoretical and Applied,* which explore everything from medicine to Indian affairs, omit discussion of education (*Anthropological Society of Washington, 1956*).

There is as yet no "science of man," and as yet no adequate description of a culture of modern society. For example, scarcely a single aspect of modern American culture is described as adequately as is the comparable aspect in scores of primitive societies (*Murdock, 1954, p. 21*). Educators searching for leads must find their way through a morass of concepts and ideas in a wide range of social disciplines, each embedded in a specialized thought system and a specialized language. The many faces of society appear selectively, depending on the thought forms and the concepts used in making the analysis. Each discipline of the behavioral sciences, such as sociology, anthropology, and social psychology, has its own distinct framework of concepts. Each, therefore, not only pays attention to a different set of phenomena in society; each also sees the same phenomena in a different light, and consequently yields a different picture of what society is all about, what its crucial problems are, and what factors significantly influence its functioning. None sees society entire. Neal Gross, for example, points out that anthropological concepts are useful mainly in giving perspective on the socializing functions of the school, while sociology is more adequate in describing the school as a social institution. The basic sociological contribution is to add to the intellectual tools a set of sociological insights and concepts that will allow an educator to take into account in his decision making the organizational, cultural, and interpersonal factors at work in his environment (*1959*).

* *See such sociological writing as Mannheim, 1944, 1952, 1956; Durkheim, 1956.*

What is more, the various disciplines are by no means in consensus or even consistent, nor are their conclusions authoritative. Educators need to see the whole face, but the special disciplines are capable of revealing only a partial face, each according to its special tools and techniques. Integration of such dispersed knowledge is no easy task. It is not a simple matter to translate the ideas from behavioral sciences into social perspective on educational goals and practices. It requires a combined effort by students of education and of the social sciences.

Because behavioral sciences have paid relatively little attention to the study of education as a social force and schools as a social institution, the establishment of a social perspective for educational decisions has been largely a one-way track. A far greater *rapprochement* is needed between educational theory and practice, on the one side, and the complex of disciplines which encompass culture-theory. Meanwhile, educators need to search carefully the literature of social and behavioral sciences to discover the ideas and facts which may yield suggestions as to the ways in which education may play, not a rearguard action, but a constructive role in preparing younger generations to participate in the rapidly changing technologically oriented culture, in acting as a buffer between the pressures of social forces and the preservation of human and democratic values.

In order to develop an adequate educational program, a sustained study of the culture in which education functions and a sustained effort to mobilize the resources of the social sciences and to translate whatever is learned about society or culture into educational policy are needed. We must enlist the best thinking of our generation in determining what our society is and needs, and which of those needs education can serve. Efforts to develop such studies are illustrated by attempts at interdisciplinary comparisons of concepts and methodologies and the growth of institutes of human relations and behavioral sciences. Recently suggestions have even been put forth that education be studied as a social force and the school as a social institution. (See, for example, the special issue of the *Harvard Educational Review* [1959] for a description of sociological studies of the problems of education.)

In this chapter and the next we shall deal primarily with concepts, ideas, and suggestions emanating from an analysis of the impact of technology on our society, and from analyses of the culture and of the process of socialization in our culture.

THE IMPACT OF SCIENCE AND TECHNOLOGY

Analyzing the impact of technology and the changes it has produced or is producing in society has been a favorite way, and up until recently practically the only way, of gaining social perspective in education. Underlying this approach to formulating a perspective has been the assumption that technology is the focus and the core of the American culture, the chief initiator and agency of social and cultural change.

Early diagnoses of the social changes introduced by science and technology were rather optimistic. We were dazzled by the new inventions, new machines, new processes, and new benefits to the standards of living and of health. Technological advance spelled automatic progress and improvement of society, and consequently the task of education was to impress these achievements on the minds of the young. Those who fastened their eyes upon the material advance saw glorious days not so far ahead—saw, for example, an era of abundance in which the average family "enjoys a standard of living comparable to that of the upper middle class today" (*Heilbroner, Jan. 1960, p. 28*).

Heilbroner describes this attitude toward science and technology as harbingers of progress as a peculiarly American philosophy of optimism, a "historic attitude toward the future . . . an attitude based on the tacit premise that the future is benevolent, malleable and will accommodate the striving which we bring to it" . . . and "that the historic environment, as it comes into being, will prove to be benign and congenial—or at least neutral to our private efforts" (*1960, p. 17*).

Gradually it has become evident, however, that technological "progress" cannot always be equated with social progress and that the changes wrought by it are not always in man's control or in accord with his desires. As a recent conference of scientists pointed out, the twentieth century removed a complacency generated by the concept of automatic progress. There is no such order in the universe. Each step in human advance seems to introduce new problems and perils along with the benefits. While technical advance emancipates men in many ways which would enable them to live more wisely, more fully, and more freely, it does not automatically ennoble life. It only removes certain disabilities.

On the score of man's hope, the conference recognized that man, unlike other animals, is a creature who both influences his culture and is influenced by it. But progress seems to be especially difficult to define in the value areas because achievement in these is not cumulative in the way that knowledge is. Each generation must face afresh the demand that it affirm values in its own terms. It is also difficult to specify progress with regard to man's life as a whole or to find a yardstick with which to measure it (*H. Smith, 1955, pp. 14, 46, 47*).

The most recent readings of the map of social changes introduced by technology have something like the following to say: Technology has changed and is changing not only the face of the earth and the institutions of our society, but man himself. Technology, with the institutions it has created, impresses itself on the minds and hearts of all those who are using it. Our minds are controlled by technology and by the thought forms and values created by it. While changing the mode of making a livelihood, science and technology also alter the contour of the economy and transform the system of social relations. They have created the possibility of a new union of men by creating facilities for communication and developing interdependence. They have endowed man with fabulous power. But this power can be used either to enhance or destroy the civilization, depending on the responsibility and understanding of those who use it (*Counts, 1952, parts 3 and 4*).

Expansion of technology has also brought vast changes in what modern man is required to do. Chase enumerates a variety of these tasks that seem important to education. The extension of transportation and communication now requires man to take into account a physical environment which "includes the whole earth, and perhaps outer space." The social institutions to be understood "embrace all the major institutions for all the peoples." The demand for literacy and technical skill has advanced with the elimination of low-skill jobs. The task of intercommunication among the diverse cultures vastly extends the demands put on cultural sensitivity. An interlinked world in which "decisions made by any social group today have widespread and important consequences for all persons in a society" requires that "the free choices of individuals will somehow add up on the side of wisdom and general welfare." To sustain a wide latitude of free individual choice in the world of magnified power and shrunken space and time is an extremely urgent, yet a very difficult task (*Chase, 1956, pp. 7-17*).

Thoughtful analysts are contemplating with some apprehension the changes brought about by technology and its social and economic consequences. The effect of ever-accelerating change and the apparent impossibility of controlling it on behalf of human welfare seem to be of chief concern. Heilbroner describes the impact of the sudden and unpredictable changes as follows:

> History, as it comes into our daily lives, is charged with surprise and shock. When we think back over the past few years, what strikes us is the suddenness of its blows, the unannounced descent of its thunderbolts. Wars, revolutions, uprisings have burst upon us with terrible rapidity. Advances in science and technology have rewritten the very terms and conditions of the human contract with no more warning than the morning's headlines. Encompassing social and economic changes have not only unalterably rearranged our lives, but seem to have done so behind our backs, while we were not looking. . . . We feel ourselves beleaguered by happenings which seem not only malign and intransigent, but unpredictable. We are at a loss to know how to anticipate the events the future may bring or how to account for those events once they have happened. The future itself is a direction in which we look no longer with confidence but with vague forebodings and a sense of unpreparedness. . . . If the future seems to us a kind of limbo, a repository of endless surprises, it is because we no longer see it as the expected culmination of the past, as the growing edge of the present [*1960, pp. 13-15*].

The above quotation illustrates what is now generally understood, that the current technological changes and their impact on society are not just an extension of the industrial revolution but that essentially they spell an end of one era in Western society and a beginning of another. We live in an era of profound social and cultural transition. Since these changes are constantly accelerating, the future becomes increasingly unpredictable. Whereas formerly important changes were counted in terms of centuries and generations, now they are counted in terms of five or ten years. The forces of this historic change are "so vast," their time span "so compressed," and the required adjustments "so convulsive" that it is "as if a huge seismic slippage were occurring in the deepest substratum of history" (*Heilbroner, 1960, p. 57*). This makes "prediction of conditions to which the rising generation must adapt far more hazardous than it formerly was" (*Chase, 1956, p. 16*).

But the imprint on our times is not so much by "the mechanisms of science and technolology" as by the "unadvertised, and often the inadvertent social consequences of those mechanisms. Science appeals to us as the means whereby we gain control over our environment. What we fail to notice is that it also forges a new social environment with formidable powers of control over us" (*Heilbroner, 1960, p. 71*). Among these powers are the ugly by-products of industrial and technological revolution: the huge cities and their festering slums, the impersonality of factories and offices, the threat of nuclear war, and the threat of a moral and psychological disintegration, once power and intelligence have freed themselves of the norms of life.

Many sources attest to the disorganizing effects of technology on man and his values and institutions. B. O. Smith, using Mannheim's analysis of the state of our culture as a basis, maintains that modern technology and the organization of economic life generated by it have produced a dangerous confusion of values and beliefs. The rules by which man in Western civilization has lived no longer hold. This confusion and uncertainty generated by the dissolution of old beliefs and values has reached the point where the individual fails to find meaning for his existence for lack of a "common frame of acceptance." In the industrial age of today "the cohesive and the directive forces of the society have been breached and . . . we now live in an unregulated, and reintegrating period." While America is blessed with industrial power in the form of natural and human resources and technical skill, the individual, instead of becoming more secure and more important, is becoming increasingly more fearful and less significant in his social role and in his own eyes. He is losing his sense of purpose in a "world of men highly organized as a means in a vast industrial and political system." The concepts which gave order and meaning to society and to the efforts of individuals no longer hold. The "frame of conventions which has formed the character of men for the past two or three hundred years is already disappearing. . . . Religious sanctions have all but dissolved . . . the structure of classical economic thought is creaking at its joints . . . the principles of political democracy inherited from a pre-industrial society are in need of serious reconstruction."

Specialization and atomization of work and knowledge have reached a point where an existence of a "whole" man and a "whole" culture is in question, and with it cooperation, common basis for judgment regarding common welfare, and a meaningful relationship between man and his environment. There are no common goals or common perceptions of what is of value. This endangers democracy on two fronts: individual autonomy and the democratic way of life. (*B. O. Smith, March 1950, pp. 3-5.* See also *Mannheim, 1944, pp. 73-94.*)

But omnipresent also are the increasing complexities of social organization created by the presence of machines, before which we experience a sense of impotence and alienation. The industrial process itself is a potent controlling influence, as attested to by a large and eloquent literature which describes the psychological pressure of this environment on men. The ever more refined operations "require of their operators ever lower contributions of creative and spontaneous work" (*Heilbroner, 1960, pp. 72-73*), and the psychological pressures of this environment are such as to "put man's freedom of mind into jeopardy" (*Langer, 1951, p. 238*). In this new environment of machines the areas of life that involve dependence on the organized effort of other human beings are increasing, while those in which man acts independently are decreasing. Although man-made, this new environment is "as demanding, incomprehensible, and even arbitrary as the environment of nature" which we have learned to control (*Heilbroner, 1960, p. 73*). Whereas man made his peace with nature largely as an individual, he makes his peace with technology through social organization. Heilbroner maintains that the advance of technology introduces "an ever higher order of *social control,* which is partly visible in the hierarchies of the huge productive firms and partly in the corresponding hierarchies of public institutions which coordinate, restrain, and buffer their operations. Meanwhile, as their invisible companion, there proceeds as well the psychological socialization of the individual—his steadily enforced conception of himself as a part of a huge and impersonal social machine" (*1960, p. 74*).

Fromm describes this psychological counterpart as a sense of alienation, a concept which denotes a person "who has lost himself as a center of his experience. . . . He does not experience himself as the active bearer of his own powers and richness, but as an impoverished 'thing' dependent on powers outside of himself unto whom he has projected his living substance. Alienation . . . in the modern society is almost total: it pervades the relationship of man to his work, to the things he consumes, to the state, to his fellow man, and to himself. . . . He has constructed a complicated social machine to administer the technical machine he has built. Yet this whole creation of his stands over and above him. He does not feel himself as a creator and center, but as a servant of a Golem which his hands have created. The more powerful and gigantic the forces are which he unleashes, the more powerless he feels himself as a human being." (*Fromm, 1955, pp. 124, 125.* See also *Heilbronner, 1960, pp. 157-61.*)

Man perceives things not in their human consequence, but in terms of their market value: a five-dollar watch, a million-dollar flood catastrophe. This quantification and abstraction produces a loss of human dimension. The act of buying and consuming has become a compulsive irrational act, because it is an end in itself and has little relation to the use of, or pleasure in, the thing bought and consumed. Alienation extends even to man's feeling about himself and to his relations to other men. The self is nothing but the many roles that he plays in relation to others, which have the function of eliciting approval and avoiding the anxiety produced by disapproval. Alone an individual is reduced to nothingness. He uses other men for manipulation only, and even reduces his own person to a market personality: to a means for something else rather than as an end in itself. There is consequently a reduced sense of reality and a reduced sense of responsibility (*Fromm, 1955, pp. 141-48*).

Even today, after decades of analysis, the social and psychological consequences of technology are appraised only in a blurred fashion. Some educators express their concerns about these consequences by raising questions which assume that alternative choices regarding the control of future are available— such questions as: After we have conquered the problem of producing goods, can we conquer the problems produced by this technological revolution? After having created a glorious science, can we learn to use it to reshape our political or social institutions, to protect man himself and a democratic way of life? Can the civilization achieve a durable peace, fashion a stable economy, and bring opportunity, security, and well-being to all? Is it possible to meet the threat to democracy implicit in technology, preserve political liberty, and extend the benefits of democracy to all?

Some analysts of the technological society are quite pessimistic about the possibility of conscious control of the consequences of technology and of the future as shaped by these consequences. Heilbroner, for example, sees at least for the present in the socializing influence of science and technology "one of the forces which are closing in on the American future, shaping for it an historic environment whose attributes may not be of our conscious making" (*1960, p. 75*). In speaking of the dilemmas introduced by economic abundance, he points out that while it is impossible to predict what values and standards will characterize the society of abundance, one *can* predict "a serious decline in our accustomed mechanism of social control." Economic abundance will break down the control exerted by the economic need to work at unpleasant tasks and will make new social controls necessary to get the work of the society done. Technology thus enters as a regulatory force into our social system. There will be a loss of personal mastery over life and a weakening of the capacity of a solitary man to cope with life, whether as job-seeker facing displacement, as a homeowner unable to make elementary repairs without outside assistance, or "as an individual mind treated as part of mass audience" (*Heilbroner, Jan. 1960, pp. 29-31*).

THE IMPLICATIONS FOR
THE ROLE OF EDUCATION

How one views the role of education in a technological society of the near future depends on how deeply one has contemplated the nature of the pending changes. What, for example, are the qualities and powers that individuals must develop even to survive as human beings in such a world, let alone to control the forces let loose? What are the tasks of schools? What manner of curriculum would best serve the society of today?

Some educators take a simple view of the needs arising from a technological society and combine this view with the traditional concept of education. As a consequence, they believe that a technological society simply requires technically prepared people, and that, therefore, the task of schools is to increase and to improve the training in mathematics and in science for everyone and to see that talent is directed into special study of these areas.

Others see deeper implications because of their deeper reading of the map of social changes caused by technology, but bring to their concept of the role of education an optimistic view of the potentiality of both technology and education. Counts, for example, who is animated by a fairly optimistic outlook regarding both the marvels of technology and the potentialities of education, insists that education can help determine whether we enter a golden age or a dark age. He believes that education can be harnessed to reshape men, and through men the society: We need to build individual excellence, which embraces not only intellect, but the whole person. We need to vitalize the principles of equality, of political liberty, of esthetic talent, of a tolerable world order. This requires not only good, but great education; one which confronts the realities of our age, expresses the best in our heritage, and takes full advantage of our prospects. Such an education not only serves the current civilization, but expresses a concept of civilization which it is up to educators to formulate. Today we have only good education, not great, because we have failed to probe deeply into the realities of our age and because of our persistent failure to study the nature of education as a social and a moral undertaking (*Counts, 1952, chs. 19-21, 29*).

Others, impressed with the baffling problems created by the accelerated social changes and consequently by the nature of the new tasks these changes thrust upon education, are not so sure what the role of education should be in a society in which future is increasingly unpredictable. Chase, for example, lists the new conditions which set new tasks for education as follows:

1. A tremendous enlargement of the environment to be understood and the culture to be transmitted.
2. An ever increasing demand for increasingly skilled and literate workers.
3. The necessity for the establishment of intercultural communication

among the diverse cultures of the East and the West as a basis for building a world community.

4. The difficulties involved in sustaining wide latitudes of free individual choice in a world of magnified power and shrunken space and time.

5. A constantly accelerating rate of change which makes forecasting hazardous and outspeeds the efforts of education to draw abreast of needs.

While Chase is sure that these new conditions require a thorough re-examination of the content and of the sequence of learning experiences, he is not sure that education can bring about a new golden age. As a matter of fact he feels that under the conditions of rapid change the only thing that schools can hope to do is to

> aim for an education which will enable man to abstract from culture the understandings and skills through which to maintain his equilibrium in a field of rapidly shifting forces. This necessity erases the controversy between the liberal and specialized education. The old argument among those who would have it beamed at the development of a "liberated" mind is now largely obsolete. The most immediate and pressing demands of our age, when analyzed, will turn out to be not those for narrow vocational skills, or for easy "social adjustment" but for a depth of understanding which will make it possible to apply the accumulated wisdom of the race to new conditions as they arise [1956, pp. 16-17].

This point of view, however, leaves one with questions about the nature of this thorough revision. For example, if social changes are so accelerated that prediction even ten years ahead is hazardous, what can education "adapt" from the wisdom of the race for the six-year-olds of today so that they can participate effectively in the society twenty years from now? What is involved in providing for understanding a much enlarged environment ever better and ever more deeply? Does it mean a more extended study of geography of the world or a battle to eliminate ethnocentricity, which blocks intercultural understanding? What can be done about the problem of preserving freedom of individual choice in the world of mass economy and mass communication, and of powerful "socialization" by the products and processes of technology, which puts "man's freedom of mind into jeopardy"? And what does all this mean for selection and organization of the curriculum?

It is obvious that mere extension and manipulation of the current curriculum is not an answer to such questions. It is obvious, also, that before the detailed contours of the needed curriculum can emerge certain larger criteria and perspectives need to be in focus.

Several such focuses suggest themselves as new mandates for education and for curriculum development. One of these is the need for creating an integral orientation toward the whole society and the whole man. Scientific and technological reasoning tends to be so compartmentalized that specialists can talk only to each other. In contrast, productive insight on social problems requires an integration of facts and insights from many areas. A society which lives by specialization requires an education which can create a balanced over-all orientation and a perspective toward the whole culture and whole man. Education must provide perspectives broad enough to sustain cooperative action to make possible common ground for judgment, to develop an integrated world view in order to re-establish a unity and a meaningful relationship between man and his society, and to counteract the atomization and specialization so characteristic of a technological culture.

This integrated world view cannot come about when education consists of "disordered" knowledge in which one aspect bears no relationship to another and of training composed of a bewildering array of credits, courses and requirements. Knowledge and learning need to be so selected and organized that they will provide a young adult with a sense of unity, of meaningful relationship between himself and his world.

The recognition of a paramount need for education to furnish a perspective toward the whole society suggests, further, the need for strengthening general rather than special education. Perhaps even the whole assumption of the liberalizing function of special disciplines needs to be reconsidered. A problem of crucial importance is the compartmentalized and linear mode of thinking created by specialized training which allocates different ideas to different spheres of activity. Since important social and human matters cannot be perceived adequately by this specialized mode of thinking, education needs to counteract the impact of these specialized perspectives. It needs to cultivate forms of thinking that are more appropriate for dealing with problems that are interdependent and that always include the human variables. Education needs to help individuals to find the bearings which the culture has helped him lose.

Another task seems to be to create minds which can cope with the problems of living in a rapidly changing world. This requires a re-examination of ways of using past wisdom and of the assumption that it is necessary to steep minds in a background of cultural heritage without which it is impossible to think about the foreground. Contemplation of the consequences of technological change raises questions about the extent to which such a background is useful in creating insights for understanding the world today. For instance, to what extent will such steeping in the past heritage blind and condition the understanding of the new by binding the mind to concepts and thought forms that no longer apply? This is obsolescence in a new form—the obsolescence of concepts and of thought forms imbedded in organized knowledge which shape the mind to render it incompetent to deal with the rapidly shifting problems and dilemmas of a rapidly changing culture. As we shall see later, the problem of discovering and encouraging creativity in thinking is also involved. Heilbroner suggests that the American mind deals inadequately with the forces of technological change because it lacks a "fresh sense of what to expect of change" and an "intellectual grasp," because it has set controls only in economic calculation, and having adopted an optimistic philosophy regarding the outcomes of change, has overlooked inertia and the resistance to change. He observes, furthermore, that the "average education is barely adequate to allow the population to cope with the complexities of technological change, and insufficient to allow all but few to understand them" (*1960, pp. 57, 193, 198*).

Perhaps significant in connection with Heilbroner's analysis is the tendency that Brameld calls "reductionism," a pattern of thinking which tries to "explain" social phenomena by reducing them to the sources from which they emerged (*1957, pp. 37-38*). In curriculum this reductionism takes the shape of substituting a historical account of problems or of institutions for an analysis of their nature or implications. The treatment of many problems or institutions, such as problems of family life or the economics of capitalism, often turns into an account of the history of these institutions or the genesis of these problems. While the historic accounts may throw some light on the topic, they are far from sufficient to give students an understanding of the role of these problems or institutions today, let alone to help them gain an insight into their future consequences.

In view of what has just been said about the acceleration of changes, one wonders to what extent a history of a phenomenon gives perspective to its future consequences. If progress creates as many problems as it solves, and if the problems it creates may be more crushing than the ones we are trying to solve, then it is time to train ourselves to foresee the "blows of the future." Exclusive training in the lessons of history may only blind us to these possibilities.

There is need for thinking in terms of multiple causation and multiple consequences, for an ability to deal with the ambiguities and uncertainties of the future in place of certitudes regarding past phenomena. As we shall see later, this involves a greater emphasis on methods of inquiry and discovery. Above all, what is needed is some identification of the forces that are preparing the environment of the future.

Providing for a value orientation is another task of education in a society which emphasizes things, technology, and processes, in which values are apt to be confused and conflicting, and in which alienation is endemic. As was pointed out earlier, in societies with rapid social change there is a cultural lag between the technological change and change in the value systems. While the role of the public school in value education is questioned severely these days, there are also demands for a value-oriented education. No matter how much the legion of critics of education disagree among themselves, one thing they do agree upon is that our society and our schools and colleges, by and large, are neither consistent nor clear about the values they teach. There is still more disagreement about the causes for poor teaching of values and, therefore, about what the cure should be. Some find the cause in the fact that cleavages and tensions are epidemic in the moral, religious, political, and other institutions of our times. Others find it in the fact that the overwhelming shadow of the physical sciences—the attention to *non-man*—has impeded the development of the science of man and of scientific methods appropriate to such a science. This orientation toward physical science and scientific method prevents us from dealing with values and other "compelling forces of concrete realities in the world of man" (*M. B. Smith, 1954, pp. 45-46*). The thought forms appropriate to dealing with the "compelling concreteness" of cultural realities or with beliefs and values have been neglected. This fact had been pointed out long before the advent of the behavioral sciences. Kenneth Burke, for example, observes that "in this staggering disproportion between man and non-man there is no place for purely human boasts for grandeur or for forgetting that men build their cultures by huddling together, nervous, loquacious, at the edge of an abyss" (*1935*).

That science and the scientific method have permitted the cultivation of a sense of "social irresponsibility" is even conceded by scientists themselves. A conference on science and human responsibility pointed out that the science of the three centuries preceding the twentieth tended to dull man's sense of responsibility. "On the one hand, its deterministic assumptions made man wonder whether he could do anything about his lot; on the other, its material gains gave rise to the idea of progress which made man wonder if he needed to do anything beyond the automatic to insure his well-being" (*H. Smith, 1955, p. 14*). The original report of the conference points out that the "obsession" of Western civilization with techniques "has reduced it to its present degree of spiritual ineptitude and schizophrenia," and has made the Western man not so very different from the Marxist man, in that both stress material achievement as a supreme goal (*Casserley, 1956, p. 345*).

Still others contend that because education fails to apply reflective thought to values, and because it spends most effort on developing modes of thought unsuitable for dealing with conflicts in values and goals, the very objects of loyalty which create cohesion and common goals are relegated to "personal prejudice and hidden motives." Reflective thought tends to be spent on means and is withdrawn from goals. As a result, the human mind is captivated by habits and methods of thinking which tend to ignore the problems most threatening and crucial to mankind. There is a tendency for these issues to be resolved by prescientific and irrational methods rather than by empirical treatment.

Some writers insist that it is anti-intellectualism rather than emphasis on science and scientific method that has created the gap between thought and values and fostered the union of knowledge with the nonrational elements of human nature. Meyer, for example, pleads that more, not less, of science and scientific thinking be put into the service of "new morality." Cultural fruitfulness cannot be achieved as long as impulse and reason remain at war with each other (*1957, pp. 22-45*). The fact that there is a cleavage of impulse and reason in our society is fairly widely recognized, as is the failure to include in our vocational and scientific training an appreciation of the influence of science and technology on human relations, human motivations, human character, and esthetic and moral values. "If many of our scientists forget why they do things and place the whole emphasis on how to do things, if they think too much about means and too little about ends, it is because their early education in our schools and colleges failed to clarify the connection of their scientific knowledge with the larger purposes of life" (*Meyer, 1957, pp. 49-50*).

It is possible, of course, that education is overly concerned with factual neutrality and "tends to store its values in the educational attic," as Brameld suggests. Consequently, it leaves intact the values and the character structure which youth absorbs in the culture. The basic values on which democracy rests are either taken for granted or at best treated with a sentimental deference, instead of being treated critically and considered seriously as an important basis to the whole theory and practice of education in a democratic culture (*Brameld, 1957, p. 13*).

If education is to be a countervailing power in a technological culture, it needs to cultivate a conscious commitment to democratic values and a sense of personal and collective goals that lends new meaning to individual effort and achievement. Education must help people think collectively about social ends, since we no longer can count on collective goals emerging from an "accidental coincidence of individual goals." There is also a need for occasions to scrutinize the time-honored patterns of conduct and of the rules men live by. The younger generation needs to realize that not only has the game changed, but also that the rules have changed (*B. O. Smith, March 1950, pp. 11-12*).

This task is difficult, as many writers point out. An attempt to reorganize one's orientation from the past has an impious aspect (*Burke, 1935, p. 106*). Or, as Heilbroner puts it, the very suggestion that the areas dealing with the destructive consequences of technology carry an absolutely overriding piority and take precedence over any and all more "profitable" activities smacks of a suspicious radicalism. "We are simply not concerned, beyond a mild lip-service, with mounting an all-out effort to raise the level of national health or civic virtue, or mass living conditions or average education or upbringing" (*1960, p. 199*). These areas, therefore, tend to be closed to rational consideration in our society as well as in our schools. To bring value education into focus, it is not enough to say that the curriculum needs to have more "social-moral" content, be less neutral and descriptively factual. It needs material and learning experiences which influence students' character, touch the very core of their personality structure, and arouse their deepest feelings. Only as an individual is taught in situations that stir feelings and loyalties can moral commitments be used to develop character.

A new intellectual discipline is needed also. Methods of thought are needed which can incorporate consideration of feelings and values and which are appropriate to the kinds of problems with which people of our age are called upon to deal. It is necessary to master procedures which can challenge feelings and prejudices without managing and manipulating human beings toward ends outside their own goals. New methods and techniques are needed for dealing with social and individual conflicts, methods also calculated to release creative energy for new social inventions to deal with new social problems.

New skills are needed also for collective thinking about private and collective values. This in turn involves some concern about how groups operate and how they can deliberate about matters which cut into deep-seated personality structures. As people depend more and more upon one another in situations that challenge their personality structure, they must employ new procedures and techniques of working together. It is, therefore, important to emphasize methods of group deliberation and group work, in order to give training in the necessary skills and to instill the kind of self-discipline that thinking and working in groups requires. It is important that all individuals develop a sensitivity which permits them to explore sympathetically and realistically the frame of mind, feelings, and values out of which persons with a different orientation think and act. Only as men learn to escape their own narrow personal and ethnocentric perspectives and begin to create and to use new techniques designed either to modify or to immobilize these prejudices in themselves and others can they begin to deal with interpersonal and social conflict with a minimum of force and manipulation.

The development of these techniques, however, requires a new insight into the dynamics of the individual's relations to others and to his culture and a new conception of dynamics by which the individual can transcend his ego-centered goals and embrace the collective aims of groups and of the entire society. This conception is slowly developing in psychological and anthropological investigations. It is paralleled by experimentation with the ways of developing a more cosmopolitan sensitivity, and with techniques that can produce consensus out of disagreement and common purposes out of conflict of values.

The Analysis
of Culture

Scientific understanding of culture and of the personality in culture should be part of the professional equipment of all those who deal with curriculum development. There is an obvious need for a *rapprochement* between the disciplines studying the culture and those studying education, for the real issues that plague schools today are not exclusively rooted in education itself—they spring from the dynamics of the human and social environment. An understanding of what that environment is, what it contains, by what dynamics it operates, and what problems and possibilities it holds should shed light on what education can and must do if it is to play its legitimate role. The conduct of education cannot be founded exclusively in psychological knowledge. Added light is needed from cultural anthropology, social psychology, and cultural sociology, if for no other reason than for evidence that even such psychological characteristics as intelligence and personality may be culturally conditioned, or that teaching always occurs in communities with a heterogeneous culture. It must be recognized also that schools themselves are in a sense cultures, and that these cultures educate individuals, possibly in ways which are not part of the conscious goals and design (*Gillin, 1957, pp. 62-63 and ch. 8 below*).

The behavioral sciences that deal with culture and personality in culture can make a unique contribution to education. As Kluckhohn suggests, the interests of education and anthropology converge because both deal with humanly created techniques of living, with the norms and values attached to these techniques, and with their transmission to the younger generation. Both also deal with the key values of culture: anthropology from the standpoint of selectivity in values in the evolution of cultures, and education from the standpoint of selectivity of goals and direction, whether the emphasis be on the enrichment of mind or the formation of character (C. *Kluckhohn, 1957, p. xii*).

For these reasons anthropological concepts have a special relevance to education, and what anthropologists say about culture—its characteristics and problems—is of unique importance to the development of criteria for curriculum making.

Social psychology can contribute to a clarification of the socializing function of the school and of the role of group processes in creating the climate for learning. Sociological studies of the school as a social institution should bring into clearer focus the relative effects of the formal curriculum and of the school culture, provide a scientific analysis of the ways in which educational aims emerge, throw light on how the various decision-making roles get established, and trace the sources of the cultural learning experiences in school. (See, for example, *Brim, 1958, pp. 15-71; and Floud and Halsey, 1959, pp. 290-92.*)

It is possible to use concepts from the behavioral sciences in several ways. One is to adopt them as curriculum content. Spindler suggests, for example, that anthropology as an area of study would make a forceful contribution to general education and he proposes, therefore, that it take its place in the social science curriculum among such subjects as economics, sociology, and history (*1955, p. 6; 1958, p. 116*).

No doubt certain anthropological, sociological, and socio-psychological ideas would constitute an important addition to the content of what is taught. Among these are the concept of culture, including culturally induced values and cultural change, and ideas about race, personality in culture, and cultural dynamics. But perhaps the greater contribution of these disciplines to education comes from the fresh perspective that they may add to understanding educational processes and problems: defining the goals of education; understanding the impact of the culture on the school; and perceiving the role of the school culture, including the impact of what teachers are doing on the learning of values and standards, the effect of role relationships within the school culture, and the relative roles of social learning, socialization, and knowledge in the formation of the character and the world view of students (*Spindler, 1958, pp. 142-43; and 1955, p. 6*).

The summaries of anthropological and socio-psychological concepts, theories, and findings that follow in this section are presented with an idea that these concepts and findings may prove to be an important corrective to current thinking about education.

THE CONCEPT OF CULTURE

One basic anthropological concept which has influenced thinking in psychology and in education is that of culture. This concept denotes first a complex, in which the component parts form a pattern or a design. The whole of this complex embraces a very wide range of human phenomena, material achievements, and norms, beliefs, and feelings—such as loyalty to certain standards, manners and morals, and methods of self-control and self-expectations. It denotes also certain shared regularities of behavior and expectations. Finally, it is something man acquires by living in a society: he learns culture in his relationships to other persons, by inter-action and imitation. Hence, culturally standardized behavior is transmitted socially rather than biologically (*M. B. Smith, 1954, pp. 39-41*).

Anthropologists also speak of "a" culture on different levels of generality. Only in very primitive societies can one speak of *a* culture, that is, of a fairly common set of expectations, regularities of behavior, and a common pattern of values and loyalties. In a complex culture, and especially in the American culture, these common denominators are few in comparison with the varia-tions of subcultures. In such a complex society there can be no single all-encompassing culture pattern. There are many subcultures—regional, religious, class, ethnic, rural, urban. Therefore, the content of both the values and feel-ings which are incorporated in the personality vary because the immediate and the most potent socializing agents follow a different style of life, pursue different ideals and values, and employ different methods in socializing processes. Numerous studies have documented the differences in value pat-terns, motivation, and expectations of different social classes in America, and in the methods employed in socializing the children (see chapter 10). Some students of American culture—W. L. Warner and Allison Davis among them—feel that American personality and character are marked by few com-mon traits.

Most communities in the United States are heterogeneous in the sense that they are composed of several more or less functionally integrated col-lections of subcultures, each with its own system of values, and hence, presumably, its own modal character. There are differences in how authority is viewed, in the role of overt expression of aggressiveness, in models for success, in how such virtues as responsibility, punctuality, and cleanliness are regarded, and even in the views regarding the value of school achievement and education (*Hollingshead, 1949; Davis, 1952; Warner, Havighurst, and Loeb, 1944; Warner and others, 1949*).

These differences in cultural values and expectations may represent only different degrees of emphasis, or they may amount to outright conflicts in demands, expectations, and valuations. As far as individuals are concerned, such conflicts produce strains of acculturation, of which social mobility is one special case. If the cleavages or discontinuities among the demands are too great, as they may be between the slum culture of American cities and the middle-class-oriented public school, these differences, at best, impede social-ization into the total culture and learning in school, and at worst may lead to neurotic behavior, such as aggression, hostility, and delinquency, and to disintegration (*Allinsmith and Goethals, 1956, pp. 433-38*).

The anthropological concept of culture and the orientation implicit in it has directed attention to the systematic and dynamic influence of the human environment on man. It has also pointed to a new meaning of this environ-ment, and in that sense to a new definition of reality, namely, that human beings, after the period of infancy, are related to the "real" world only through the mediating processes of cultural selection and interpretation. This selection and interpretation is made possible by highly developed symbolic processes, which are "at once the badge of humanity and the core of the cultural heritage." In other words, reality for the individual is defined by the premises of the culture in which he participates (*M. B. Smith, 1954, p. 52*).

PERSONALITY AND CULTURE

Anthropology and social psychology are also concerned with human nature and personality: how they are shaped in the culture and how they function in it. Since the concept of human nature is basic to all sciences that study either man or the management of man, the practices and theories of education, like those of anthropology and psychology, are conditioned by the kind of assumptions that are made about human nature. Whatever is thought and learned about human nature will have deep repercussions on the instructional program in our schools. The anthropological concepts of personality and of its relationship to culture are an interesting contrast to the ideas about human nature that underlie individualistic psychological theories about personality development and learning. The anthropologists recognize that personality consists of both unique and socially standardized elements.

Every man is in certain respects (a) like all other men, (b) like some other men, (c) like no other men.

He is like all other men in the general biological endowments, in that he must adjust to a condition of interdependence with other members of their society, and in that they all experience both gratifications and deprivations.

He is like some other men in that he belongs to the same socio-cultural unit, pursues the same occupations, is intellectual or athlete, or belongs to a certain kind of a race.

He is in many respects like no other men in his modes of perceiving, feeling, needing, and behaving as a result of countless and successive interactions between the maturing constitution and the culture (*C. Kluckhohn and Murray, 1955, pp. 53-57*).

Anthropologists tend to emphasize the social sources of personality, to maintain that the culturally standardized aspects of personality are the dominant part. Some even go as far as to say that, apart from a few reflexes, there is relatively little in an individual's behavioral repertory that is not in some degree standardized by the groups with which he has been affiliated. Social learning is the basic process in this formation of a socially standardized personality. Without this socializing process personality could not emerge. The learned elements of personality, in turn, range from the unique to the universally shared. Unique elements are learned by personal experience in a social group (e.g., a specific individual's personal attitude toward authority).

Shared learned elements are those acquired in some degree by a fair proportion of the members of a social group or a status group within a larger social group (*Honigman, 1954, pp. 29-30*).

While psychological literature is concerned with the individual aspects of personality, anthropologists and social psychologists focus on the common structure, or the modal personality, which the individual shares with other members of his culture—with those behaviors that are socially standardized either within the enduring groups in a culture or within the total culture (*Honigman, 1954, pp. 28-34; Sargent, 1950, p. 15*). In this sense reference can be made to a delinquent personality—the behavior that tends to be common to delinquents—over and above the characteristics of individual delinquents. When this standardization concerns moral values and motivations, reference is made to character structure, which represents the culturally formed conscience. Developing a particular form of character structure is one way in which culture assures conformity to its rules and perpetuation of its values and norms.

In simple cultures and in homogeneous subcultures there is a correspondence between the character, personality, and behavior of individuals and the culture. As Redfield points out, there is a code of values which dominates the culture and controls the behavior of the people. The culture in a sense makes a type of human being. In a homogeneous community the states of mind tend to be alike for all persons in a corresponding age, sex, and the career of one generation repeats that of the preceding. However, larger and more complex societies, characterized by impersonal institutions and atomization of the external world, tend to develop a new, a different, and a more varied character structure (*Redfield, 1955, pp. 5-6*).

Each culture has its basic goals of socialization, or a basic pattern for the formation of personality—in effect, a picture of an ideal adult. These goals emerge from what the culture values as behaviors, characteristics, and capacities. For example, if we can trust the descriptions of American culture, it values getting along with others, independence, material success, achievement, and work orientation. The shared characteristics of individuals in American culture or the modal personality of Americans, therefore, is characterized by motivation to get ahead and to achieve. An individual, to succeed, must "sell himself," and excel. The opposite traits are cultivated in Samoa, for example, where the culture values self-minimization and nonpresumptive behavior (*C. Kluckhohn, 1949, ch. 9; Gorer, 1948; Mead, 1942*).

Culturally standarized personality in a sense also represents a culturally standardized sensitivity. Socially learned characteristics of response determine to a considerable extent what cues individuals heed, what meaning they give to them, and which consequences matter. These culturally favored behavior patterns are flavored with feelings and evaluations. An individual feels the rightness of some acts and the wrongness of others. These valuations reflect the individual's view of the relationship of such acts to norms, whether or not he perceives these norms consciously, and determine the way the motivating core of the personality interprets situations which he encounters. They express a relationship between an individual's world view and his idea of self.

These emotional valuations acquired in the process of learning a personality create at once stability and unity within a culture and a problem of ethnocentricity in intercultural relations. Socialization into one culture inevitably creates barriers to understanding the values of another culture. Because individuals are conditioned to the behavior, values, and norms of a given society, their capacity to understand and to appreciate that which is different from their own culture is limited. In addition to the difficulty of seeing the "other," there is the culturally conditioned incapacity to see members of other cultures in terms of that culture's values and standards. A person of one culture responds to a foreign culture in terms of the values and norms of his own culture—that is to say, ethnocentrically. Procrastination becomes laziness in the eyes of a person reared in a work-worshiping culture. A gadget-admiring American regards as inferior anyone who chooses to spend his money on a vacation instead of a refrigerator (*Taba, 1953, pp. 65-67*). Such projection of the particular values of one's own culture as universal is characteristic of all except those persons who are sophisticated in cross-cultural contact or in cultural analysis.

This ethnocentricity or culture-boundedness may affect even the psychological and educational concepts. M. Brewster Smith points out that even such hardy psychological concepts as perception and adjustment, which so far have been treated by both the psychologists and educators as universal, may be too culture bound to serve in a world in which space and time have shrunk and horizons have extended. According to his views, the weight of cultural anthropology seems to be on the side of phenomenological psychology, which postulates a psychological environment, and not on the side of objectivists, who assume that objective stimuli exist independently of the variations in the perceiver (*1954, pp. 49-52*).

THE GENESIS OF PERSONALITY

While anthropologists generally emphasize the fact that personality and character are learned largely through socializing processes, they differ regarding the nature and timing of this genesis. The patterning of childhood experiences is most frequently propounded as the chief source of these processes.* Kardiner, who initiated the studies of the commonality in personality, proposes that similar experiences, especially those of early childhood, produce similar personality configurations. Each culture generates also certain types of mental systems by identification with the models

---

* In this respect the anthropological ideas reflect a strong influence of the psychoanalytic approach to formation of personality.

of thinking around one and a world orientation that is built by projecting these mental systems into the world (*1945*). The psychoanalytically oriented writers maintain that early training in the family has a determining and a lasting impact on shaping personality and character, and subsequent experiences at best only reinforce the view of the world and of the self formed in these early years (*Honigman, 1954, ch. 10*).

These assumptions about the impact of childhood experiences on personality formation are held strongly enough to be offered as the "postulates of the concept of basic personality." Linton, in introducing Kardiner's volume on *The Psychological Frontiers of Society,* offers the following among many others:

> 1. That the individual's early experiences exert a lasting effect upon his personality. . . .
> 2. That similar experiences will tend to produce similar personality configurations in the individuals who are subjected to them.
> 3. That the techniques which the members of any society employ in the care and rearing of children are culturally patterned and will tend to be similar, although never identical, for various families within the society.
> 4. That the culturally patterned techniques for the care of and rearing of children differ from one society to another [*1945a, pp. vii-viii*].

Others writers postulate a continuous conditioning of personality through response to cultural and social forces. They point out that the early stabilization of personality is more characteristic of simple, unchanging, highly integrated societies than of modern ones. This viewpoint contends that although certain basic motivational tendencies and role requirements are internalized fairly early in the life of a human being, the definitions of the social role of an individual, including his sense of responsibility toward that role, are formed much later, partly through experiences in school and partly by participation in the peer society. Parsons, for example, maintains that the school (1) emancipates the child from the primary emotional attachment to the family, (2) universalizes the socialization pattern, (3) helps the child to internalize a level of social values and norms a step higher than those he can learn in the family, and (4) helps to select, allocate, and train its human resources relative to the adult role system (*1959, pp. 309 ff.*). The influences of the school are discussed in greater detail in the section on character development of this chapter and in chapters 5 and 11.

THE CONCEPT OF CULTURAL CHANGE

Another concept of importance to education is that of cultural change. If education is conceived to be a change agent, ideas about the dynamics of cultural change and its effects on personality and the role of the individual in the culture are of great importance. Although studies of cultural change are largely limited to the analysis of primitive cultures, the concepts emerging from these studies, such as that of acculturation, are suggestive for understanding change in contemporary culture also.

Because cultures are organic, a shift in any one part introduces changes in other parts. The primitive, homogeneous cultures are largely conservative: change comes slowly and the core of the culture is preserved intact. Individuals in such a culture can foresee the future. Theoretically the child in a primitive society can prefigure his future as long as he lives. An adult can consolidate his previous experience in fulfilling current needs and roles. Children can foresee their future in observable adults, and their life experience recapitulates the experience of the preceding generation.

In contrast, the Western cultures, and especially the technologically advanced cultures, are characterized not only by rapid change but also by deliberate change. Because the technological advance is absorbed into the environment and transmitted through artifacts and facilities in a compelling manner, there is usually a cultural lag between the rate of changes in the technological aspects of the culture and that in values, customs, behavior expectations, and social institutions. This unevenness and inconsistency in cultural change introduces cleavages and conflicts, which characterize the Western industrial societies.

The technological change produced in America in the recent decades is so profound that Linton classifies it as one of the three great mutations in the whole of man's history. Yet the required adjustments to these technological changes in other aspects of life are more difficult to make; this is especially true of changes in values, social customs, and social institutions, in which a greater conservatism prevails. We call those who make technical changes inventors, but those who make changes in nonmaterial culture are likely to be called rebels, revolutionaries, and reformers, words which do not carry a positive flavor in the American mind. Neither is our culture predisposed toward planning social change, whereas planned technological change is commonplace.

This discrepancy in rates of change in different aspects of culture and the nonacceptance of a need for certain changes lead to contradictions, tensions, and disorganization of character and personality, matters which are discussed in the latter part of this chapter. Here it is sufficient to point out that anthropologists assume that each culture has certain danger zones which cause conflicts and disturbances in individuals and that it is possible to identify the areas in which anxieties and personal conflicts are likely to arise. It is possible that the American culture today has many such danger zones which need to be identified and understood by all who work in education. We need to understand the ways in which culture may engender unrealizable goals, what discontinuities exist in the socializing processes, and what the psychological consequences are of mobility, striving, and of contradictory demands and expectations.

A rapidly and unevenly changing culture also creates difficulties in the transmission of culture. As Margaret Mead points out, American children are growing up in a most rapidly changing culture, in which changes within one generation are greater than changes in other cultures over a period of centuries. Hence the younger generation grows up without models; the experiences of parents or even of older sisters and brothers are of little use as a guide.

> We as people, parents, teachers, citizens, are rearing unknown children for an unknown world. We can not guess their needs by remembering our own, we can not find the answers to their questions by looking into our own hearts. Only by steadily projecting our vision forward, while we keep our observation finely attuned to the needs and fears and hopes of these new children, can we hope to provide the conditions of growth for the next generation who might deal with problems too vast for us, reared in the punier age, even to think about properly [*1951, p. 17*].

The above paragraph states the difficulty inherent in planning learning for children in American society. Because the social changes are drastic, and the circumstances not foreseeable, the adult images of necessary behavior, of important criteria, of the needed adjustments, are not sufficient to predict or to mold a good personality or a good character. This is also probably the reason for the emphasis on adaptation, and the current concern with creativity, discovery, and experimentation, both in our society and in education. In discussing national character, Gorer observes that only as an individual learns to take account of new circumstances and modify his behavior accordingly can he remain a healthy as well as a productive person while the environment changes. In a changing culture there must be a balance between the methods which are addressed to creating a disposition to live up to the cultural demands (conformity) and the emphasis on the idiosyncratic, on experimentation and invention (*Gorer, 1955, pp. 246-59*).

A still more complex problem is created by a shift in the role of the usual culture agents. Mead points out, for example, that as data accumulate on the more heterogeneous and more rapidly changing cultures, especially the other-oriented American culture, it is quite evident that agents other than the family have assumed and need to assume a stronger role in the shaping of the nuclear personality and character (*1955, pp. 651-62*). For one thing, rapidity of change, urbanization, and industrialization have weakened the capacity of the family to transmit culture. Value conflicts in the culture make parents uncertain of their role. Social and geographic mobility loosens the family influence still further because the child no longer grows up in surroundings in which neighbors reinforce what the family expects. In urban centers, in addition, the shared activities of the family are reduced. As the influence of the family recedes, the influence of peer groups and mass media increases.

In such a society "the child will never be, as an adult, a member of the same culture of which his father stood as a representative." It is a recognized feature of our society that children soon after starting school begin to substitute the standards of other children for the standards set by their parents. This tendency becomes steadily aggravated until at adolescence it often results in a crisis in parent-child relations (*Mead, 1955, p. 658*). The abundant literature on the adolescent peer group makes clear the potent influence of age groups and their standards. Because these groups are involved in the process of emancipation from the family and from adult standards, their value systems often are in conflict with those of the family and are further colored by certain antisocial, anti-authority tendencies.

Concern is also expressed about the quality of values which emanate from the mass media as another socializing agent. Wertham points out, for example, that "ethical development of children, . . . the development of the superego, of conscience, or, more simply, the sense of decency, takes place not only on the basis of identification with parents but also with successive parent substitutes who are at the same time representatives and symbols of group demands and group responsibilities. In this sphere comic books are pernicious" (*1953, p. 100*). One might add that television with its stereotyped content, commercial advertisement, and stress on violence has added to the danger.

Finally, social change accentuates the problems of acculturation—the process of learning new behaviors and values in a new culture. In the usual meaning of the term it is applied to the process of learning the values and conduct of a dominant culture by members of a nondominant or a weaker culture—the learning of the values of the dominant American culture, for example, by subcultural groups which have only partially acquired the values of the larger society. But acculturation is involved also in social mobility, such as making the adjustments required by a rural migrant into an urban area and by a child in a transition from home to school.

Whichever the case, the process of acculturation is usually attended by stress, which may range from a relatively mild anxiety to a severe disintegration. The degree of stress usually corresponds to the distance of the culture to be learned from the original culture, to the distance of the behaviors and the core values to be learned from the values and behaviors of the original culture. The attitudes of Spanish-Americans to American medical care, for example, illustrates only a mild stress. To a Spanish-American, the American practice of going to a hospital is antithetical to his idea of medical care as well as to his concept of human relations. Illness signifies an occasion for family solidarity. The idea of being cut off from his kinfolk, of submitting to such indignities as being undressed and examined by members of the opposite sex, is humiliating and threatening (*Allinsmith and Goethals, 1956, p. 436*).

A disintegrating effect of acculturation on character might be illustrated by the effect of the anonymity and freedom of the urban environment on the

Latin Americans who migrate from a culture characterized by strong family and religious controls and from a fairly simple society to our complex cities. Disintegration of personality and character structure, such as delinquency, often results because the cultural distance to be spanned by acculturation is too great, and because a double task of acculturation has to be faced: adjusting to the culture of the United States and to an urban way of life (*Elam, 1960*).

AMERICAN CHARACTER AND VALUES

Studies of the American character and values are of pertinence to education, inasmuch as education needs to be conscious of both the culturally held ideal of an adult and the inconsistency of that ideal with the character created by contemporary social forces. Studies of American social character are rather recent, and there are as yet no adequate descriptive categories nor dependable methods of consolidating the data on behavior, motivation, and values which are at the root of character structure. Consequently there are many variations in the definitions of character, in methods of distinguishing it from values, and also in the "profiles" of American character. This section deals with only a few characteristics of character and values which have rather obvious implications for education.

As was pointed out above, character is one aspect of personality; it is the social conscience. By social character are meant those characteristics which are shared by the members of a culture; individual character is defined by characteristics in which individuals who belong to the same culture differ from each other.

It is generally assumed that the social character grows out of the necessities of culture. Thus, for example, Americans who needed to work hard in order to attain an industrial world developed a high valuation of the drive to work, punctuality, and orderliness, and these characteristics have become part of the American social character. This cultural origin of social character is described rather boldly in a much quoted statement by Erich Fromm:

> In order that a society may function well, its members must acquire the kind of character which makes them *want* to act in the way they *have* to act as members of the society or of a special class within it. They have to desire what *objectively* is *necessary* for them to do. *Outer force* is to be replaced by *inner compulsion* and by the particular kind of human energy which is channeled into character traits [*1944, p. 381*].

The inconsistencies and contradictions of values in a culture are also reflected in the inconsistencies of social character. Modern American culture abounds in inconsistencies and internal contradictions of its root values. Many of these inconsistencies stem from a discrepancy between the values and goals inherent in the technological economic order, such as success goals and achievement motivation, and the traditional ideals of human values, democracy, and the Christian ethic. The success goals, such as possession of money, winning a position, selling an idea or a piece of goods, may be so important that the ways in which these are accomplished may be immoral by one set of values and yet acceptable by another set.

These conflicts are reflected also in the American social character. We cherish independence but require conformity in many vital aspects of life. We enunciate the ideals of individuality but at the same time put a premium on living up to comparative norms of age, class, and achievement. We expect individuals to be aggressive, to compete, to excel, and at the same time to practice the ideals of cooperation, teamwork, and helpfulness. We are dedicated to the idea of equality, yet regard other cultures and many subgroups in our own society as permanently inferior. We presume to stand for a peaceful world, yet our economists look "with some apprehension to the time when we stop producing armaments, and the idea that the state should produce houses and other useful and needed things instead of weapons, easily provokes accusations of endangering freedom and individual initiative." (*Fromm, 1955, pp. 110-208. See also Spindler, 1959, pp. 2-20.*)

Even schools are not free of this dichotomy. Mary Shattuck Fisher points to the inconsistencies in values and expectations in the very training of children.

> Any success-driven culture such as ours, which contains within itself the dramatic contradiction of the urge for power and the idea for cooperation and love-your-neighbor-as-yourself, inevitably produces personalities which have the basic conflict incorporated at least to some extent within themselves. Any society which says to its growing children, on the one hand, "You will be secure, if you are successful. Get to the top. Dominate before you are dominated. Use people before you get used," and on the other hand, "Be pleasant and polite or people won't like you. Learn to get along with people or they will hurt you. Selfishness is wrong. Love your neighbor as yourself," produces confused individuals who will find it hard to become consistently free and responsible and truly democratic. . . . Many of us accept the conflict as inevitable, discount its importance, and only question its costliness. . . . Those of us who have the greatest difficulty in reconciling or solving the conflict, or who resolve it at too great a cost to our personalities, become what Karen Horney calls in her book, *The Neurotic Personality of Our Time*, the stepchildren of our culture [1953]. (*Fischer, 1953, pp. 21-22.*)

If some important part of the culture, such as the business world, stresses too exclusively technical expediency rather than end values and human consequences, character in the culture tends to be conditioned to normlessness even though other parts of the culture stress the Christian ethic or the ideals of democracy. This normlessness is further abetted by a sense of alienation, which was discussed earlier as one consequence of the expanding technology and the consequent dehumanization of work and life.

Other-Orientation

Perhaps the most interesting, though by no means the most flattering, profile of the changing American character is drawn by Riesman, who explores American character and personality from the vantage point of the effect of a changing culture on character formation (*1950*). He distinguishes three types of socialization, or character molding. According to him, different types of societies or cultures enforce conformity and mold social character in definably different ways.

A relatively unchanging preindustrial society develops a typical character whose conformity is ensured by its tendency to follow *tradition:* its people are *tradition-directed* and the society in which they live depends on tradition-direction for conformity.

In the tradition-directed society the culture controls behavior minutely, and conformity is prescribed by rigid etiquette. The culture, in addition to its economic tasks, provides ritual, routine, and religion to occupy and to orient everyone. Little energy is directed toward finding new solutions for age-old problems, because people are "acculturated" to these problems. In this society the activity of the individual member is determined by characterologically grounded obedience to tradition. While the individual is prized, he can exercise only a minimal amount of enterprise and creativity. Such deviation as exists is fitted into institutionalized roles which make a socially acceptable contribution. Individual life goals exist in a very limited sense, and only to a limited extent is there any concept of progress. These societies "adjust" the individual in the sense that the character of most people appears to be in tune with the social institutions and there are few misfits. Most primitive societies would fall into this category (*Riesman, 1950, pp. 11-13*).

In the post-industrial-revolution society of the nineteenth century, conformity of social character was ensured by a tendency to acquire early in life an internalized set of goals. Such people were *inner-directed* and the society in which they lived was a society which depended on inner-direction for its stability.

Inner-direction is the dominant mode of ensuring conformity in a society characterized by expansion and exploration, colonization and imperialism, by increased personal mobility, by rapid accumulation of capital and an almost constant expansion in production of goods. Tradition is splintered by increased division of labor and social stratification. Too many novel situations are presented, which cannot be encompassed in advance by a code. In an inner-directed society the problem of multiplicity of personal choices is solved by a behavioral obedience to a code and by channeling choices through a rigid though highly individualized character. The direction and nature of this character are implanted early in life by elders and directed toward general goals such as industriousness, courage, and being a gentleman. These directions remain relatively unaltered throughout the individual's life.

This mechanism acts like a psychological gyroscope. Once it is set by the parents and other socializing agents, it keeps the inner-directed person "on the course." The inner-directed person becomes capable of maintaining a delicate balance between the demands put upon him by his life goals and the buffetings of his external environment. He can receive and utilize certain signals from outside, provided that they can be reconciled with the limited maneuverability that his gyroscope permits him (*Riesman, 1950, pp. 14-17*).

Finally, our own Western urban society develops in its typical members a social character whose conformity is ensured by their tendency to be sensitized to the expectations and preferences of others. These people are *other-directed*, and the society in which they live is one dependent on other-direction.

The other-directed character is emerging in the recent upper-middle class of our large cities in which the hard enduringness of inner-directed character is less needed and in which increasingly other people rather than material things create problems. The other-directed person is the product of modern mass economy and mass communication. He is shallower, freer with his money, friendlier, more uncertain of himself and his values, more demanding of approval than are contemporary Europeans, for example (*Riesman, 1950, pp. 19-25*). (See also *Fromm, 1947, pp. 67-82; 1955, ch. 5.*)

"What is common to all other-directed people is that their contemporaries are the source of direction for the individual—either those known to him or those with whom he is indirectly acquainted through friends and through the mass media." This source is internalized and becomes the source of guidance and direction. *"It is only the process of striving itself, and the process of paying close attention to the signals from others that remain unaltered through their life. The goals themselves shift as the associations shift. The conformity comes not from being drilled in behavior itself, but from an exceptional sensitivity to the actions and wishes of others."* Individuals in such a society are more capable of and interested in maintaining responsive contacts with others both at work and at play. While the inner-directed person with a good reputation conformed in his dress, curtains, etc., to the "best" people in his milieu, the other-directed person has his eye very much on the Joneses, aims to keep up with them not so much in external detail as in what experiences to seek and how to interpret them. While the tradition-directed person takes his signals from others, they come in a cultural monotone. The tradition-directed person is parochial. The other-directed person is cosmopolitan: the sources are many and the changes are rapid. While the inner-directed person can go it alone, neither the tradition-directed nor the other-directed person can (*Riesman, 1950, pp. 25-31; Fromm, 1955, ch. 5. Italics added*).

Although other-directedness may be the rule, many inner-directed and tradition-directed types remain in American culture. These types may very well be subjected to characterological struggle, because of pressure from contradictory directions. The reaction to this pressure may take the form of either a resentful or a compliant resistance. Migrants from tradition-directed cultures or subcultures may "make, in one lifetime, the jump from a society in which tradition-direction was the dominant mode of insuring conformity to one in which other-direction is the dominant mode. . . . Or they may be tempted by the new goals . . . and may even seek these goals without reference to the culturally prescribed means for obtaining them." They may be discouraged that the signals do not seem to be meant for them, as is the case with minority groups in professional life. Or they may rebel, as did the zoot-suiters, in a pathetic effort to combine smooth urban ways with a resentful refusal to be completely overwhelmed by the inner-directed norms that are still the official culture of the city public schools (*Riesman, 1950, pp. 31-35*).

Other-directedness and alienation are augmented by many other social developments. As communication increases, relations with the outer world and with one's self are mediated by the flow of mass communication. Permissive modes of child behavior and of socialization increase as the older patterns of discipline are relaxed and the original socializing agents are replaced by others. Business organization exerts its power by demanding and enforcing certain qualities of "other-directedness" in its executives and employees (*Whyte, 1956; Packard, 1959*).

This thesis of Riesman is perhaps more attractive than valid. It contains, however, many eye-opening suggestions regarding the consequences of our technological urban society on character development. Too much writing and thinking has been done on the same theme to deny that the character formation of urban Americans is adversely affected by modern urban life and its complexities.

Yet, other-directedness need not necessarily be only of negative value. As Morris points out, values lie not in the source from which they are received, but in the nature of what is transmitted.

> What makes other-direction so distasteful is its narrowness, its limited perspective, its short-range expediency and shallowness. . . . But we must also remember that other-direction has its long-range dimensions as well. We can receive signals from sources other than our immediate peer group. We can receive them from the other social classes, from individuals in other occupations, in other religions, in other races. . . . And these distant signals . . . may come from across the street in our own community or from the other side of the world. . . . Every culture has its own message to transmit, its own value scheme to offer as hypothesis for value-seeking man. If anthropology has told us anything it has told us this. . . . We can hardly build a better social order until we have clearly in mind what it is we want to make of our American society, and it would seem that a full-scale, other-directed attempt to come into a working understanding of the values and ideals . . . of other people would be the most effective starter [*1956, pp. 239-40*].

One might add also that other-directedness is limiting to the extent that it represents a reading of signals without judgment and selection. No matter how broad the source of signals, or how cosmopolitan the nature of what they communicate, an individual who changes his color according to the constellation of the signal-makers around him is still an individual adrift and without a center of values or integrity. For this reason the relevant question to ask about these characteristics is not just where the signals come from, but the extent to which their reading is consistent with fundamental human values and the democratic ideology.

Autonomy and Conformity

Most anthropologists agree that a degree of conformity to the social norms is essential in any kind of social order if that order is to continue. In complex societies group life, if adequately developed, is also founded in a certain complementary diversity of roles. Individuals must acquire certain role behaviors which are necessary for reciprocal functions and for maintaining the social structure of interrelated statuses. Group interaction is also required to provide continuity of tradition and to transmit skills, values, and techniques. Without these each generation would have to discover anew everything learned and invented by the human race. All this represents conformity, restriction of the freedom of the individual, and the suppression of his individuality, autonomy, spontaneity, and creativity (*Honigman, 1954, pp. 220-25*).

In this dichotomy between creativity, inventiveness, and autonomy of the individual and the necessity for adjustment and conformity lie many problems raised by several recent writers with reference to the American culture and its impact on character and values. In some cultures there is the danger of overconformity—that the process of socialization will fill up, crush, or bury individuality altogether. This is the danger which Fromm and many others insist is present in the American culture, despite its tenets of individuality and freedom. He maintains that an individual's feeling of self-adequacy in American culture is so completely dependent on the estimates of his peers that he becomes but a pale shadow of his current social group. The current American culture builds a kind of character structure in which automatic adjustment to the peer demands (the crowd mind, the market personality) is the mainspring. American culture develops a person who listens too assiduously to varying signals from without, whose main aim is to be and remain popular, accepted, well thought of, who cannot operate standing alone, and who cannot tolerate deviation from group standards in himself or in others.

This conformity is all the more dangerous because in the modern democracy an individual is faced not with an overt authority figure, but with a diffuse and anonymous authority, the subtle and constricting expectations of interpersonal relations, of public opinion and the market, without knowing who asks him to conform. It is hard to rebel against this invisible authority, especially because of the other-directed orientation toward the world and people (*Fromm, 1955, p. 152*).

Conformity is reinforced by requirements for teamwork and for group organization, or by the "company rules" and therefore by requirements for subordinating individuality to group demands and norms, which are part of mass organization. And as we saw in the preceding chapter, the more splendid the technology, the more massive the mass organization required to support and maintain it.

The dehumanizing effects of a technological society, its inroads on individuality, privacy, and autonomy of personality, and the danger of overadjustment, are widely recognized. Much literature, both popular and scientific, attests to these dangers and pleads for "sovereignty" of the individual personality and the right for rigorous independent thought, the spontaneous and the private. Our age has been called the orphan age, severed from its historic past by the transforming impact of a dynamic technology.

Common norms are easily imposed in any mass culture in which units of material possessions, such as houses and cars, are standardized and can be easily compared. The mass culture of America, with its mass media and its vendors, makes individuality and autonomy of taste, conduct, ideas, values, and feeling hard to come by and still harder to maintain. It is difficult for an individual to deviate from the cultural norms in any very important ways and especially difficult for him to assert his individuality when the value of the idiosyncratic is not recognized by those around him.

Riesman describes three modes of reaction to the standardizing influences of modern society: the adjusted, the anomic or thoughtless, and the autonomous. The adjusted is a person who is a sociopsychological fit. He conforms to the demands of his culture. The anomic cannot conform. He sabotages the society or himself, and probably both. He feels uncomfortable with the role society assigns to him. He rebels or becomes catatonic. The autonomous is a person who can choose whether to conform or not. He can conform to the behavioral norms of the society. He can choose his goals and modulate his pace. He is capable of freedom and can decide whether he can or cares to take the risks of deviation. He can cooperate with authority, but also can reserve his private judgment. He does not seek to have approval of himself as a person, but, objectively, of his work or ideas or both (*Riesman, 1950, pp. 287-95; Merton, 1957, ch. 4*).

The question, then, is how to reduce overadjustment, conformity, and *anomie,* and how to support individuality, creativity, and autonomy in the mass age. How, for example, can the aspects of conformity which are the prerequisites of technological culture be brought into balance with the freedom of the individual? How can man attain, much less increase, his modicum of political freedom in the face of the complexities of social machinery? How can the more personal freedoms, which come closer to his creativity and spontaneity, be preserved when he lives among vast impersonal forces beyond his control and indifferent to his worth? For, as Malinovsky has pointed out, "Freedom lies in choice of purpose, its translation into effective action and the full enjoyment of the results" (*1944, p. 137*). Is it possible to develop individuals who are free to contemplate change, who do not respond in adjustive mood to varieties of life experiences and cultural and social contacts and who feel free to choose whether to adjust or not, who are capable of transcending their culture at any time and in any respect?

These questions need to be pondered, not only in order to understand and reduce the sources of conformity but also in order to learn how to strengthen individual autonomy and creativity. Simply honoring idiosyncrasy is insufficient. Nor is it enough to practice deviate rebellion such as is staged by the existentialists and their more commonplace followers, the beatniks—a social revolt against the conformity demands of the society and against the image of the "public" man in technological society.

Neither can one simply assume that group work and teamwork of any sort are merely sentimental togetherness, a seedbed of conformity and a deathbed of individuality, and that autonomous and creative thinking and action will emerge once these techniques are eliminated. The problem goes deeper than that. Clearly a new model of a creative and autonomous individual is needed, one more appropriate for our age—one who stands, not alone, but as an autonomous and creative unit in a group enterprise. Clearly, also, models are needed for interaction of groups which leave life space for and permit constructive use of individuality and deviation.

Educational Implications
of the Analysis
# of Culture

The concepts and data emerging from culture analysis suggest many important implications for understanding the educative process and its conduct. These implications have relevance for a reconsideration of the functions of the school and of the relationship between the school as a social institution and its curriculum. They also sharpen insights regarding certain special tasks schools must face if they are to act as a countervailing force to the dehumanizing effects of the technological revolution.

THE SCHOOL AS A COUNTERVAILING SOCIALIZING AGENT

Analysts of culture do not share the blind faith expressed by some writers on education that under current conditions the traditional agencies of socialization are capable of fulfilling the task of socialization, partly because they see more clearly the changes wrought in these agencies by the changes in society and partly because they also see more clearly the wide ramifications of the task. The facts from culture analysis indicate clearly that as the influence of the primary socializing agents recedes and weakens, the schools of necessity must assume many socializing functions, ranging from the teaching of simple social skills to developing an orientation toward the self and the world. Schools have ceased to be simply transmitters of knowledge and trainers in academic skills. They are also, to use C. Kluckhohn's phrase, "custodians of moral values," of democratic ideals, and of certain aspects of personality development. Kluckhohn points out that our formal educational program has assumed, implicitly or explicitly, some of the functions that used to be those of the family or of the church, and that we hedge in teachers with all sorts of restrictions of their personal behavior precisely because we view them as models of the predominantly middle-class code of our society (*1951, p. 162*).

It is possible, in addition, to think of the school as a culture with a way of life in which learning processes are similar to those in life outside, in which internalization of values and feelings can take place, because the environment provides fairly potent models for identification in the form of significant persons as well as of forceful experiences—in other words, as a socializing agent of some consequence which shapes the values and standards of individuals and adds a measure to their life orientation. This idea of the school affecting a person in more ways than providing academic learning is not new, of course. The school has always been responsible for implanting moral standards and such characterological values as responsibility and respect for individuals. The school has also been held responsible for inculcating such core values of American democracy as the worth of the individual, self-determination, universal opportunity, and freedom for self-actualization and self-expression.

However, these two forces, the impact of school life and of the curriculum, have seldom been seen as complementary. It is not beyond reason to suggest that schools can face a double task: to plan a way of life in school designed to foster certain values and character structure, and to see to it that the school curriculum adds to the shaping of this character structure by providing opportunities to explore important values and to examine social institutions and forces in the light of their consistency with these values.

The school culture can serve as a planned addendum and a corrective to the socializing processes of the home and other character-training institutions—as a powerful source for learning values, self-concepts, and life orientation. This additional emphasis could come through a systematic attention to the climate of peer culture. Probably much of this learning goes on even in our unplanned climate of the peer society, but possibly a great deal of it is negative because this unplanned socialization takes place under the shadow of a conflict between the hidden peer culture and the official school culture. With a planned reduction of this cleavage and with application of the techniques of social change to the shaping of the school climate, peer culture could be made into a powerful ally to the inculcation of positive values, of constructive concerns and self-expectations, and of productive social orientation.

If we consider further the possibility of reproducing in school some features of social learning, such as providing experiences that touch feelings, reinforce motivation through interaction with significant persons, and that mobilize interests and goals, it is possible that changes in personality and character can be brought about in the schools. In such a program lies the possibility of education in school acting as a countervailing force to the impact of culture outside the school. Under such conditions the school could strengthen individuality, breaking the chain of conformity pressures of the other-oriented society; it could clarify conflicts arising out of a discrepancy in demands made on individuals, provide orientation where confusion usually prevails, and help students to move toward a more adequate self-definition and a greater self-esteem as unique personalities. Even the possibility of reorientating the modal character may not be as far out of the reach of the educative process as is usually assumed. This too has happened to individuals in school under an inspiration of rare teachers or the confluence of accidental circumstances. What the ideas about culture and personality add is the possibility that systematic effort can add a mite toward the shaping of the modal personality and character.

It is not suggested that schools become institutions of therapy, but only that educational processes can be used for these ends, provided that educators grasp the meaning of social dynamics, can view the school as a culture, and can employ what has been learned about ways of inducing cultural change in shaping this culture. Educators need also to consider ways in which to integrate learning from the socializing process with learning that occurs as a result of its curriculum without confusing the two.

A cultural perspective on education and its institutions makes it possible also to think of education in school as a change agent. Cultural change need not be wholly the accidental product of blind social and cultural forces. Nor does it seem necessary that there be as great a disparity as now exists between the cultural realities of life and what the customs and expectations permit. Myths need not persist after social realities change. Nor is it inevitable that individuals hold on to interpretations of cultural realities which are no longer valid.

Education could probably devise a means for shortening the cultural lag between social realities and cultural attitudes, between beliefs and expectations, by preparing youth for living in a changing society. If the ways of interpreting the culture perpetuate themselves in the ideology and character of the people longer than the conditions that gave rise to those ways, and if people in a culture maintain a character structure more constricted than the pertinent social realities require, then the leverage for change lies in a conscious and consistent re-examination of the ideas with which we interpret the culture, and the reshaping of values and feelings attached to these ideas. Character changes not so much according to altered realities as according to the altered interpretation of conditions. In other words, this means that in a rapidly changing society one task of curriculum makers and teachers alike is to keep interpretations of society attuned to the "becoming" social realities. It means, further, that the curriculum needs to include processes of interpreting, questioning, and contemplating change. This, of course means that all educational workers, no matter what their area of teaching, need to be familiar with the structure and dynamics of our society. All should constantly keep their goals abreast of changing knowledge about society and about the role of individuals in that society.

Regarding the nature and direction of the role of education as a countervailing agent, the psychological and anthropological sources are meager, probably because the concept of education these writers hold is rather limited. To them formal schooling is still largely the passing on of information and skills and training in intellectual discipline. In a lecture to teacher educators, Linton points out that the task of the modern educator is not only to perpetuate our culture, but also to direct its future development: that the task of teachers is to prepare people for change. Education for readiness for cultural change needs to help the student to cope with change, to think about change, and to think for himself. In a rapidly changing culture people have to cope with a good many situations that are strange to our current way of life. It is the educator's task to train the individual to recognize new situations when they arise and to meet them intelligently.

> In addition to training people to think, and to be willing to think, he [the educator] must provide them with reference points from which to think. Without a definite system of values to act as a thrust block, the keenest and most willing intelligence will dissipate its efforts. It may be able to solve a new problem in immediate personal terms, but it cannot develop a solution worthy to become a culture pattern. Such patterns must serve not only the immediate needs of a multitude of individuals, but also the needs of society as a whole. If they are to perform this large function, they must rest upon some coherent idea of what constitutes the greatest good for the greatest number [*Linton, 1941, pp. 9-10*].

Yet Linton's concept of the changes which schools can make is quite limited. He recommends that teachers confine their efforts on behalf of future developments of culture to "a series of minor but intelligently directed changes in the existing culture patterns (such as techniques for personal relations, diet, and hygiene) and to the inculcation of values whose general acceptance would make for a better society" (*1953, pp. 15-16*).

EDUCATION FOR VALUES AND FEELINGS

Teaching values and feelings has often been regarded as beyond the powers of the school, partly because the idea still prevails that values and feelings somehow belong to the innate aspects of personality that are impervious to change by educational methods, and partly because the techniques of both curriculum development and teaching have been too crude to provide an adequate methodology for this purpose. But anthropological literature hammers home the fact that values and feelings are learned, are malleable and changeable, though not necessarily by direct teaching. Some anthropologists also recognize the crucial role of value orientation. Linton, for example, suggests that the shape of the future depends more on the selection of values we pursue than on the further development of technology. Consequently, if educators can control value patterns of individuals, they can control the future of society. If they can control the feelings toward war, uninhibited accumulation of wealth, social justice, and so on, they can deflect culture change. There is even a possibility that education might contribute to the enhancement of the "inner resources" seemingly so lacking in today's culture (*Linton, 1941, pp. 16-17*).

But the importance of value education can be justified on grounds other than control of the future by educators. The analysis of culture and of the socialization of character and personality points up the pervasive nature of value orientation, and describes the ways in which values are learned. Values are implicit in the very functioning of the culture, from the use of technical devices to the requirements of jobs and civic participation. They are implicit also in institutional dynamics and the forms into which education is cast, from grouping to counseling. This means also that education for values is all-pervasive and largely unconscious. The task of education is to make this process conscious, rationally defensible, and, as far as the role of the curriculum is concerned, more effective.

In view of what has been said about the inconsistencies and pluralities of value orientations in our culture, a special task of education regarding values might also be that of integration and conceptualization. This conceptualization may very well become the basis for the new ethics based on scientific knowledge of man and of society which was referred to earlier as a current need. In a culture such as ours, with many contradictions and ambiquities, individuals need systematic aid in clarifying the contradictions and in making conscious the many emotional habits which the culture implants on an irrational and unconscious level. In this respect it is worthwhile contemplating the ways in which education might help develop self-realization in a culture that fosters alienation, might support efforts toward autonomy of the individual in a culture that engenders other-orientation, and might help develop creative patterns of thought and habits of mind and action rather than the conformity that seems to prevail in the technological mass culture. Especially do the young people of our time need to develop a sense of personal identity, of a personal role in culture, and a personal commitment.

The orientation of students of culture to the learning of cultural values suggests several important points for education. First, in value education the real task is to develop criteria other than adjustment in helping individuals to come to terms with their culture and to acquire an experimental attitude toward it. To accomplish this, educators need to discover what can be done with the raw human material with which it works, how it can be done most effectively, and what sort of training will best fit its charges for life (*Linton, 1941, p. 7*). The implication of this in turn is that educators, as well as social scientists, must be in a position to predict the consequences of their attempts to interfere with the course of human behavior. They need to understand the functioning of the human being in the processes of culture, and the ways in which teaching and learning operate in a culture. Kluckhohn points out that education based on anthropology may help extend "the areas which reason can understand and perhaps to some extent control by the search for discoverable regularities" and thus "help a little to halt the flight to the irrational, the terrified retreat to the older orthodoxies which we have seen on a mass scale in this century" (*C. Kluckhohn, 1957, pp. xii, xiii*). They need, also, to institute processes of learning that are appropriate to acquiring values and feelings. If the analysis of learning of values through socializing processes in culture has anything to teach us, it is that values are not learned in the same manner one learns chemical formulas and historic data. They are learned not by "learning about," but by going through experiences which touch the feelings and thereby affect the very core of personality. It follows, then, that adjustments in the content of learning cannot be counted on to alter patterns of behavior that are motivated by characterological needs. Capacity to behave democratically does not develop from learning facts about the beneficial effects of democracy. Conditions need to be provided which approximate the conditions under which values and feelings were acquired in the first place: in social interaction, under conditions that evoke feeling and entail reality of purposes and drives, in a context that permits identification, and so on. In other words, changes in the content of curriculum need to be accompanied by alterations in the conditions under which learning occurs. These include the character of discipline, the quality of interpersonal relations, the degree of attention to individual needs, and the nature of motivational devices used.

AUTONOMY, INDIVIDUALITY, AND CREATIVITY

Developing autonomy, creativity, and individuality in a culture which tends to foster conformity, alienation, and other-orientation is another problem brought into focus by the analysis of culture. It is at this point that the technological forces in society crosscut the American ideals of democracy. Whereas the former breed uniformity in social and economic arrangements and thus also push toward conformity of mind and manner, the latter is predicated on individuality, difference, uniqueness. Whereas the former alienates an individual from himself as a person and converts him into a cog in a machine, the latter stresses self-actualization and a clear relationship of means to goals. It is perhaps here also that the "countervailing" influence of the schools is most needed and perhaps most practically achievable.

There seem to be two main sources of creativity and autonomy, and therefore two avenues for approaching their development. One has to do with methods of independent thinking, and the other with the development of an adequate self-concept and self-expectations. Work on both needs to converge to produce results. In both respects the school may fail to do what is needed and may even add to the dispositions toward conformity.

School programs are predicated on uniformity of content and of the mental systems required to master that content, and, therefore, enforce conformity in thinking in a great many ways. As one examines current curricula and classroom practices, one cannot help but be impressed with the fact that they foster mental systems which promote docility and contribute little to the development of independent thinking and judgment.

Usually this conformity and lack of autonomous thinking in classrooms is blamed on the teacher: teachers are authoritarian, cannot tolerate ambiguity, demand docility from their pupils, or lack sufficient skills for implementing creative thinking and for fostering an autonomous spirit of inquiry (*Henry, 1955, pp. 33-41*). A recent study of the nature of the "teaching acts" points out that the present cultural conception of the teacher as a purveyor of information actually places limits on the intellectual activity of children. It points out, for example, that the controlling functions, which include selection of what problems to attend to, what to learn about them, how to go about the learning, and which answers to reach, constitute over 40 per cent of all teacher acts. In reverse, conditions favorable to inquiry and a creative approach to problems and tasks are correspondingly minimized (*Hughes et al., 1959, pp. 95-96, 181*).

The same examples demonstrate, however, that conformity pressures are not limited to teacher behavior. They are implicit also in the ways in which the curriculum is put together and in the type of instruction this pattern dictates. Assuming that "the culture makes the person," it is even possible that the kind of curriculum we have in public school creates the type of teacher and teaching techniques we bemoan. Some studies indicate that the graduates of teacher training institutions "bend" themselves in the direction of expectations and attitudes which prevail in the schools they serve.

One aspect of autonomy is the capacity for conceptual mastery of one's environment. To develop this capacity an individual must learn to see things in a perceptual orientation that is his own, to find the principles that govern the relationships between what he sees and knows, to use the principles he has learned to explain and to predict, and to structure problems in his own way. In other words, productive and autonomous thinking is one important aspect of personal autonomy.

It will require both a different curriculum and a different way of learning from those we have now to achieve productive and autonomous thinking. In the first place, attention needs to be focused on the essential principles and ideas which give structure to thinking. Second, learning experiences need to include more opportunities for inquiry, discovery, and experimentation. Current practices, anchored as they are in transmitting rather than creating knowledge, may be too much concerned with "getting the right answer." One need only look at discussions in which the questions asked are so closed-ended that the main intellectual effort of students goes into guessing what the teacher expects as the right answer or into remembering what the book says on the point, rather than into developing a rational method for arriving at answers or solutions and multiple ways for analyzing and interpreting facts.

One need only think of the examinations in which *the* correct answer is required on matters which ought to be treated comparatively and in which alternative answers for alternative conditions should be developed. Independent and productive thought is thus inhibited not by design but by omission: by a failure to provide an organization of ideas and a method of approaching them. (This matter is discussed further in chapter 8.)

The other aspect of the development of autonomy and of individuality to which cultural analysis draws attention is the genesis of an adequate self-concept and reasonable self-expectations. This analysis opens a way to considerations of the impact of school culture and of curriculum on the formation of self-image. It raises questions about the current use in education of the psychological concept of adaptation and its relationship to the "other-oriented" ideal of self and of achievement. C. Kluckhohn, for example, points out that American psychiatry and education have probably overemphasized the concept of adaptation and adjustment in comparison to the concept of internal integration and harmony (*1951, p. 160*). Curriculum patterns, expectations, and standards often fail to account, still less to provide, for idiosyncrasies in thought or conduct; and the wholesale enforcement of rigid criteria of conduct limits the possibility of deviation from the common, and often too narrow, norm, thereby affecting negatively the self-image of many students.

This problem has special significance for methods employed in "acculturating" the cultural deviates, such as individuals from minority groups or from the lower socioeconomic groups. Educators have been slow to recognize that a considerable portion of students meet the problem of acculturation when entering school. The greater the distance between the home culture and the school expectations, the more severe these problems of acculturation. Such problems block learning because they represent an extra burden on energy and a discontinuity in experience. They are also a source of personality conflict and disturbance.

The data from analysis of culture throw a new light on the kind of individualization of learning and differentiation in curriculum and instruction that is needed to protect uniqueness and to provide equality of opportunity to learn. The ideas and facts regarding modal personality suggest that it is both unrealistic and inefficient to deal with these problems as if they were purely problems of individual differences. Ways need to be found for differentiating instruction and curriculum materials according to characteristics and differences shared by categories of pupils from different social and learning backgrounds to make the problem of "reaching" all students more manageable and the goals more achievable. Individualization of curriculum and instruction along these lines would not only make for more effective education, including education for values and character building, but would also serve to prevent many individual problems.

Familiarity with the data on and the concept of modal personalities in the various subcultures would help curriculum makers to know more about the people with whom they are dealing, not only as unique personalities with certain drives, abilities, and individual tendencies, but also as products of their cultural backgrounds. In a heterogeneous culture such as ours this would mean taking into account the distinctions in modal personalities as formed by class and caste culture, an idea that is still repugnant to the beliefs and attitudes of many educators (*Linton, 1941, p. 11*).

Questions arise also regarding the amount of ego suppression that occurs in school, because of a necessity of managing large groups, or because of lack of diagnosis, such as mistaking deviation for meanness. The observation that personality, creativeness, and spontaneity are "flattened out" from primary school upwards is common. Efforts at acculturation may be poorly paced, so that in the process of learning the conduct that is appropriate to school, children also learn to deny their unique ego and their individuality, and hence suffer an ego-hurt. The fact that, in the necessity to stress control and order in mass schools, the administration usually tends to favor fairly authoritarian teaching style and therefore engenders authoritarian teacher personality makes matters all the worse. For it is this type of person, who, according to psychologists, has low tolerance for idiosyncrasy in personality or conduct, for ambiguity, or for what Guilford calls "divergent thinking."

THE DANGERS
OF ETHNOCENTRICITY

The analysis of culture points out forcefully the dangers of ethnocentricity imbedded in the natural socialization processes of any culture. Since a culture has no mechanism within itself to overcome this ethnocentricity, the development of crosscultural sensitivity, whether with regard to other national cultures or in relation to subcultures within a nation, is therefore one of the tasks of the school if it desires to prepare people to live in a vastly expanded world with interdependent heterogeneous cultures. The school, in other words, needs to counteract the inevitable parochialism of socialization patterns in the intimate, and therefore confined, primary group, which, like a cultural shell, encloses a particular family within its own racial background, religious beliefs and sanctions, code of morals, and standards of right and wrong. Furthermore, extension of a cosmopolitan sensitivity requires not only an emotional acquaintance with cultural differences but also objectivity about one's own culture.

The first task in achieving this objective is perhaps to examine the curriculum from the standpoint of its effectiveness in developing cosmopolitan sensitivity. Although living in a world of vastly expanded horizons requires a vastly extended sensitivity and capacity to understand, there is little in the usual curriculum of our public schools that is addressed directly to developing a cosmopolitan sensitivity, to seeing the "culturally other" in its own right. To be sure, there are factual surveys of the geography and the economy of other lands; these have been introduced under the mistaken assumption that knowing the rivers and resources of a country produces an objective insight into the compelling forces in its culture. Such information alone, no matter how pertinent, does not produce insight into the dynamics of the people and into the core values by which they live. The experiments in intergroup education, which wrestled with the problem of ethnocentricity, demonstrated that the development of a cosmopolitan cultural sensitivity required not only new curriculum patterns and materials but also new inventions in the methods of teaching and learning, new ways of combining information and insight, and new ways of enhancing the capacity to put oneself into the shoes of the "other." The development of cosmopolitan cultural sensitivity required conditions similar to those required for teaching feelings and values—using experiences which evoke feelings, such as reactions to literature and life incidents, and enhancing contact and interaction of individuals from different cultural backgrounds (*Taba, 1955b, ch. 5; Taba, Brady, and Robinson, 1952, ch. 4*).

According to studies of school life, only a part of the school's population is involved in the official school life and in the school culture that it promotes. The excluded portion is usually the one that most needs such participation in order to learn the common culture. Further, the composition of activity groups usually reflects the same lack of cosmopolitanism that characterizes the students' academic life and community life. Individuals from the same social class or the same neighborhood social groups are, by and large, thrown together in the same activity groups. These activities, therefore, do not provide the cross-group association they are supposed to provide but show a certain pattern of ingrowingness and parochialism. Finally, they reflect a prestige system similar to the social-class system in the community. The selectivity is governed by factors of social background, and as a consequence seldom do minority group members belong to the so-called prestige clubs and societies. In many cases, they are even assigned to separate clubs and provided different activity patterns (*Gordon, 1955; Taba, 1955b, ch. 1*).

THE NEED FOR TRANSLATORS

To assure a productive use of ideas and concepts from behavioral sciences, it is no longer possible to depend on the usual means of slow seepage of knowledge from one discipline into another. The changes in society today are too rapid to allow time for the leisurely sifting of ideas from the behavioral sciences into educational literature and from there into practice. The usual rate of absorbing new research and new concepts is too slow to permit education to assume a positive role in society, especially the role of assisting social change. It is difficult for educational practice even to keep pace with the change in social and cultural forces. The lag between the realities of life and culture and the ideas upon which the school acts is too great. Witness the optimistic recitations of technological progress and its automatic effects on improvement of life that still fill the junior high school curriculum and the major portions of American history, although social analysis points to contrary effects. Consider also the practice of revising the curriculum by espousing every new development as a new age and introducing it as a topic in the curriculum, instead of reconsidering the usual content of curriculum in the light of new ideas and new developments. Despite a vast literature on cultural conditioning and the differences in that conditioning, devices for diagnosing and grouping children completely overlook the fact of cultural conditioning. Research on peer influence on values and motivation has scarcely touched the motivational devices employed in schools and has not yet penetrated into school life as an additional source for mobilizing the learning of values. In spite of long-standing verbal iteration of the importance of analysis of culture and of social needs, this analysis has never cut deeply into practical curriculum making.

To keep abreast of the fast-moving social events and a rapidly growing knowledge about society and culture, a new role needs to be created among those responsible for setting a pattern for the curriculum. This is the role of a translator of ideas and facts from the behavioral sciences into their educational implications, that is, into questions and suggestions regarding educational practices, the conceptions of the educational tasks, and the ideas about the curriculum and instruction. There should be a constant flow of translated findings from research in the behavioral sciences into a body of ideas and information accessible to those who teach and think about teaching.

Learning Theories as a Foundation for the Curriculum

Sound suggestions for curriculum development can be derived only from a sound psychology of learning. In settling issues of curriculum and method one must take into account all that is known about the nature of man and the nature of the learning process. Historically, there has always been a relationship between education and knowledge of or assumptions about the nature of learning. Melton compares this relationship to the traditional relationship between any pure and applied science, such as between physics and engineering. There is, or at least should be, a mutual dependency between the two, especially "at the frontiers of knowledge of both." Yet, although education needs to use the science of learning, its conduct is not merely a straightforward application of this science any more than engineering is merely a straightforward application of physical sciences (*Melton, 1950, pp. 97-98*).

THE RELEVANCE OF IDEAS ABOUT LEARNING TO THE CURRICULUM

Knowledge about the learner and learning is relevant to making a host of curriculum decisions. A curriculum is essentially a plan for learning. Consisting as it does of goals for learning and ways for attaining these goals, a curriculum plan is a result of decisions regarding three different matters: (1) selection and arrangements of content, (2) the choice of the learning experiences by which this content is to be manipulated and by which the objectives not achievable through content alone can be attained, and (3) plans for the optimum conditions for learning. These decisions cannot be made adequately without knowing a good deal about learners and learning. To know what to teach at any given age level requires a reference to what is known about the development of children. Knowledge about characteristic thought forms at various age levels should determine what is the most propitious time to teach any particular subject, what the sequence of these experiences should be, and how to translate that which is to be taught into learnable experiences. If we know how intelligence functions and how capacities develop, we can tailor curriculum content to the needs and capacities of children. Knowledge about transfer of learning can help in making decisions about the efficiency of learning: how to make whatever can be learned in school most useful for the rest of life and how to apply it to things other than those in which the school experience centers. Knowledge about the total development of the individual can help discover what the total range of objectives can be and how the curriculum can accommodate or develop this range.

The cruciality of ideas about learning and learners to curriculum-making is widely recognized. Most curriculum guides point out the importance of understanding students. Some sketch the developmental stages and processes which will aid this understanding. Many a program is justified on the basis of meeting "the needs of students," even though these needs may be interpreted in many different ways. Various categories of learners are recognized: the exceptional children and the emotionally disturbed ones as well as those with different degrees of academic potential and intellectual capacity. This "psychological" basis of the curriculum is so commonly accepted that some writers even suggest that, in comparison to the emphasis on understanding culture and society, there is an overemphasis on the psychological foundations of education, that there is too much psychologizing, and that both social orientation and the role of content is neglected.

The clarity and precision, however, of the psychological knowledge applied in shaping the curriculum leave much to be desired. Theories of learning seem to have a great capacity for survival. Current curriculum patterns and current methods of teaching reflect traces of all historic learning theories from faculty psychology to the field theory. In effect, the study of the psychological principles underlying curriculum and teaching is somewhat akin to an archeological expedition: one can find the fossilized remains of almost any learning theory that ever existed, no matter how outdated or how discredited it may be. Both the teaching and the curriculum of today reflect composites of many different theories of learning, sometimes unrecognized by those who practice them. Certainly some of our "classical" subjects are often still taught by the principles of mental discipline. The exclusive emphasis on the development of intellectual powers advocated by many today reflects a disregard of the organic wholeness of the learner and of the learning act established by current psychological research. Many practices, such as teaching skills out of context and by rote drill, hark back to the S–R theory of learning. Conditioning is often used as a method of controlling and changing conduct and values. A passive mind is still assumed in too large a part of teaching, and the application of the concept of active learning is shallow and confined to "activities," such as construction, manual work, and artistic experiences. Integration of learning, although talked about for a long time, is still only a word to swear by or to play by, not an operational concept.

Among the many reasons for this confusion is the fact that today there is no coherent theory which encompasses consistently all aspects of learning. There are many theories of learning, but each seems to be derived from a close study of some single type of learning, usually a very simple one. Yet the findings from these specific types of learning are applied to all types of learning (*Hilgard, 1956, p. 9; Sears, 1951, pp. 476-83*).

Learning is complex and there are many different kinds: mastering motor skills, memorizing information, learning feelings, concepts, and intellectual skills, such as generalizing, scientific inquiry, and problem solving. Learning theorists may be deceiving themselves by looking for common laws to explain processes which may have little in common. Such empirical laws of learning as exist are limited to the lowest levels of learning. Little as yet is known precisely about the higher levels of learning, such as thinking, attitudes, and interests (*Spence, 1959, pp. 92-93*).

Theoretical explanations seem to concentrate on certain types of learning or conditions of learning, omitting others. Behaviorist associationist theories, which still dominate the field, overlook ideational learning. Field theories stress the learning of ideas and insights, while the dynamics of learning, such as motivational patterns, are the chief concerns of psychoanalytic theories. Although classroom learning occurs in a social setting, relatively little is available about the social factors in learning. Consequently, although learning is central to the educative process, it is difficult to determine just what it is, under what conditions it occurs, or how to maximize it under school conditions (*Haggard, 1955, p. 150*).

It has been pointed out, further, that current psychological investigations are not really concerned with the nature of learning as it occurs in school. Experimental psychology of learning tends to be more concerned with the precise details of learning in rather short-term situations. The psychology of learning, therefore, has lost contact with the long-term educational effects of learning (*Bruner, 1960, p. 4*).

As a matter of fact, it would not be unjust to say that generally the study of conditions under which learning occurs has been neglected. According to Egon Brunswick, psychology has neglected investigations of the environmental or ecological texture of the phenomena studied, including cognition and learning. "Both historically and systematically psychology has forgotten that it is a science of organism-environment relationships and has become a science of the organism" (*1957, p. 6*).

Although the current experimental studies of learning have contributed much new knowledge, their partial nature has also generated many theoretical disputes. There is theoretical dispute even about such simple matters as what constitutes a reinforcement of learning, whether practice improves learning, and what the effect of controlling learning by reward and punishment is. Different theorists come up with different answers to whether individuals learn essentially habits or cognitive structures. There are different answers to whether learners reach solutions to new problems by trial and error or by insight. Confusion or inconsistency in theories of learning naturally cause confusion in instructional practices.

Meanwhile, the educational psychologists have been absorbed in studies of aptitude and achievement and in the social and motivational aspects of the learning situation. Little attention has been paid to analysis of the more complex learning acts, and especially of their intellectual components, such as the thought processes.

This lack of adequate psychological support for education is recognized by psychologists and educators alike. In a recent symposium on learning it was pointed out that the science of learning and the management of learning should and could be mutually supportive. Yet, while education has a great stake in the acceleration of the sciences concerned with learning, the studies that have to do with the conditions and management of learning are meager. There is even a sign of rift between the science of learning and educational method (*Melton, 1950, pp. 98-99*).

THE MAIN THEORIES OF LEARNING

All theories of learning rest on a concept of man and behavior. Historically there have been essentially two concepts of man. One postulates a mind endowed with certain capacities—such faculties as reasoning, remembering, imagining, which grow with exercise. The second concept postulates that man is an energy system—a system of dynamic forces —attempting to maintain a balance or an equilibrium in response to other energy systems with which he interacts through his sense organs. This energy system encompasses his entire being; it includes his responses to stimuli, his motivation, feelings, and rational processes.

The first concept of man produced a theory of learning often referred to as the theory of mental discipline or faculty psychology. The central idea of this theory is that the mind inherently contains all the attributes, or faculties, and that the task of education is to bring them forth by the exercise of acquiring knowledge. The harder this knowledge is to acquire, the better its acquisition trains the mind. For this reason special merit is found in such "hard" subjects as mathematics and Latin; these subjects are traditionally considered the best trainers of mind, if for no other reason than that they are difficult.

In this theory practice and drill are important not so much to induce proper responses but for their disciplinary value. Motivation does not matter, and individual differences are irrelevant. Transfer is assumed to be automatic and universal, because the training of the mind is general. Training in one field prepares the mind for another. Training in Latin makes a better lawyer as well as a better banker. The best content is that which has stood the test of time.

This idea of learning, now displaced as a psychological theory, would be only a historical curiosity except for the fact that it is by no means yet discarded in practice. Much of teaching and curriculum selection in high school suggests this criterion at work. Many current critics of educational practices seem to make similar assumptions when they advocate toughness and hardness of study per se.

The second concept of man has produced at least two theories of behavior and learning. One is the so-called associationist or behaviorist theory, which assumes that man is a collection of responses to specific stimuli (*National Society for the Study of Education, 1942, chs. 1-4*). Each specific reaction is an exact response to a specific stimulus, and each of these can be accounted for (*Hull, 1943*). This theory has been called elementaristic because behavior is essentially assumed to consist of discrete events (*Asch, 1952, pp. 91-104*). The basic problem of this theory, therefore, is to show how the discrete events of experience get joined together. Associationism—that is, a connection between contiguous events—was the earliest explanation. The later behavioristic theories postulated either classical conditioning or other more complicated mechanisms, such as the idea of operative conditioning developed by Mowrer and Skinner (*Mowrer, 1960; Skinner, 1953, ch. 5; Hilgard, 1956, ch. 4; Holland and Skinner, 1961*).

In these behavioristic theories the higher mental functions have a very small place. Learning takes place largely by trial and error and conditioning. Thought, and individual differences in it, is secondary to the system of establishing responses. Motives can be controlled from without by conditioning, punishments, and rewards. Practice (or drill) is essential, especially when combined with applying the law of effect—that is, with rewards and punishments. Transfer is limited. An individual transfers what he has learned in one situation to another one only if the two are similar in content or procedure. Since the behaviorists, such as Skinner and Mowrer, believe that a science of behavior must be built only on what is observable, this school will not consider such unobservable behaviors as purpose, thought, and insight.

Another set of theories of behavior are referred to variously as the organismic, Gestalt, and field theories. The common feature of these theories is that they assume that cognitive processes—insight, intelligence, and organization—are the fundamental characteristics of human response, present even in the simplest perception of the environment. Human actions are marked by quality of intelligence and the capacity to perceive and to create relationships. This understanding of relationships steers man's actions. His responses are shaped by his purposes, cognition, and anticipation. Man is also an adaptive creature who organizes each subsequent response in the light of his prior experience. In each new perception the object or event is seen differently, because the cognitive structure has been reorganized by each prior perception. Sometimes this reorganization takes place in such a fashion as to create an illusion of intuition or a sudden insight. In this interaction of response and stimulus, a new mode of perception and essentially a new reality is created. Man learns only through his own responses: in part by reacting to selectively organized stimuli (*Gestalten*), and in part by creating new organized wholes. Man is not passive in the face of external stimuli but is an active agent who creates his own "phenomenal" world. Learning is essentially an active process of selecting and organizing.

Not much specific research is available on the nature of this insight and intuitive perception of relationships beyond the experiments of Köhler with apes, the studies by Wertheimer of children's methods of problem solving, and the analysis of classroom learning at the University of Minnesota. (*Köhler, 1927; Wertheimer, 1959; Swenson, Anderson, and Stacey, 1949.* The fullest treatment of the problems of learning from the Gestalt viewpoint are to be found in *Koffka, 1935.*) However, the concepts from these theories have been in educational currency for some time. The new curricula that are being developed in mathematics and physics make much of intuitive perception of relationships or intuitive thinking—the shrewd guess and intelligent conjecture, a way of arriving at an answer without quite knowing how one got it (*Bruner, 1960, ch. 4*).

The field theory, as formulated by Lewin, states that behavior is the function of the present life space. Learning is a change in the cognitive structure, or in the way of perceiving events and giving meaning to them. This theory has also extended the concept of "wholeness" of the learning situation by demonstrating the role played by the cultural and social environment in determining what man responds to and what meaning he gives to what he perceives. The cultural environment of an individual shapes the selectivity of his perception and valuation. The followers of this theory no longer speak of a *learning act,* but of a *learning situation* and the *forces operating* in it: the individual, including his perceptual "selectivity," his purposes and needs, the demands of his culture, and his previous learning (*Lewin, 1954; Hilgard, 1956, ch. 8*). Also of interest in this connection is the so-called phenomenological theory of behavior (*Combs and Snygg, 1959*).

These theories of behavior introduce a vastly complex concept of learning and, hence, of curriculum and instruction—so complex, in fact, that it is difficult to describe it accurately. Specific content is important, but only to the extent that it is a part of a meaningful context, serves a given purpose, or is shaped by constellation of mental processes. Isolated facts, unrelated to meaning, purpose, or a frame of reference, are considered poor stuff for learning. The emphasis in learning is on cognitive process rather than on specific product. Thus, in geometry the important learning is the discovery of the organizing principles rather than the specific answer. Learning specific facts is important to the extent that they feed the formation of ideas. The processes of arriving at ideas and the ways of using them to create new knowledge are more important than the specific facts which "serve" these processes. Those who follow this concept stress integrated learning and relationships rather than the mastering of specific content.

Field theory views learning as essentially a social process. To learn, an organism must interact with others. For this reason, provision for group work and interaction, such as discussion, are an important element of curriculum planning. Individual differences are crucial. Because each individual has a unique sequence of experiences and therefore selects different stimuli to respond to and organizes his responses differently from every other individual, provision for idiosyncratic responses is essential in curriculum planning. Each current experience is colored by and so can build on the preceding ones. This continuity of learning is essential to maturing; therefore, a curriculum is effective to the extent that it incorporates the idea of cumulative learning and plans for accumulative sequences of learning.

Motivation is central in this theory. Learning occurs largely in response to basic motivating needs and goals and is enhanced by interest and motivation as well as by practice, which is not synonymous with repetition. Practice consists of modifying each successive attempt to learn something, not of repeating exactly the same act. Intrinsic motivation—curiosity, sensing the relevance and purpose of what is being learned, a sheer drive to understand, or a quickened awareness—is likely to be a more stable stimulator of learning than extrinsic rewards. Learning engendered by intrinsic motivation is more likely to be retained and used again.

All responses are in effect transferable, in that all situations are new and the responses to them are reorganized applications of the previous ones. While transfer is not unlimited or automatic, as was assumed by the faculty psychology, it is general. The main road to transfer of learning is via grasping the essential principles of a problem, a subject, or a situation, or by evolving an approach to and a method of viewing situations which can be applied to the next situation. This is, as we see later, "a set of learning to learn." One can, therefore, design a curriculum to produce transfer and teach for transfer. If the students understand the principles underlying 2 plus 2 is 4, they can apply this principle to other combinations which they do not always need to learn separately. Conversely, practice without understanding the basic principles is of somewhat dubious educational value. (See chapter 9 on the transfer of learning, and the description of procedures in teaching for transfer in chapters 18 and 19.)

THE INFLUENCE OF
LEARNING THEORIES
ON THE CURRICULUM

As suggested above, these various ideas about learning have influenced the shaping of the curriculum. The curriculum and teaching that lean heavily on the idea of mental discipline tend to be narrow in objectives and unitary in scope, and the sequence of content or the continuity of learning experiences is not considered to be particularly significant. Subjects are studied in their "logical" order, in which "first things come first," regardless of the learners' forms of thinking and characteristic ways of viewing things. Definitions precede illustrations, and scientific classifications precede acquaintance with the objects they represent.

The associationist assumptions about behavior and learning lead to a curriculum dominated by specific content, each part of which is learned anew. Because transfer is limited, "coverage" is important. The assumption of a passive mind necessitates heavy emphasis on detailed presentation, memorization, and recitation. Curriculum is focused on atomistic elements of content to be transmitted, not on central ideas or principles, because presumably these cannot be acquired until a sufficient body of specific knowledge is mastered. The later behavioristic theory added to this an elaborate system of acquiring specific skills, learned bit by bit and step by step through a rigorous mechanical drill or rote learning.

The curriculum organization that parallels this learning theory is fairly simple. One needs to identify the desirable responses and the stimuli that lead to these responses, and then fix the appropriate responses to the appropriate stimuli by repetition and reinforcement or shift the inappropriate ones by conditioning. This idea is implicit in the "teaching machines" introduced by Skinner, which are built to reinforce the appropriate responses by programing each step of learning and rewarding each right response immediately after it occurs (*Skinner, 1954; Holland and Skinner, 1961*).

Because the product or the answer, rather than the process leading to it, is considered important in this learning theory, curriculum development involves making an inventory of all the specific things to be learned and then producing a "program" by which to learn them. The earliest application of this theory of learning in curriculum making can be found in the so-called job-analysis method of curriculum construction (*Charters, 1938*). Bobbitt, for example, listed hundreds of specific objectives, each one presumably to be taught specifically (1924). Minute units such as the Morrisonian units on the comma and writing in a manuscript form are based on similar assumptions. The "programing" for teaching machines and in textbooks is the most recent illustration of a similar approach.

The field theory also leads to a curriculum designed to serve multiple objectives, but this multiplicity represents a wider range of types of learnings seen in more general and organized terms. These objectives include not only the knowledge of subject matter but also the development of cognitive processes, of attitudes, and of orientation to the world. The scope of the curriculum is arrived at by and examination of the learning organism, of the developmental sequence in the maturation of its powers, and of what is "given" in a learning situation—that is, the subject content of learning. The actual sequences of the learning experience are determined by the steps which are necessary to create an increasingly integrated organization of ideas and responses. These steps, while not always specifically predictable, nevertheless follow a fairly recognizable developmental path. The organization of the learning sequences is psychological and that of the content both logical and psychological; an attempt is made to translate the logical structure of content or a problem into the thought forms which are appropriate to the characteristic mental operations of the learner. Moreover, because learning involves the entire or "whole" individual, curriculum planning includes provisions for emotional and social as well as intellectual development.

In field theory, both the organization of content and the ways of teaching stress context, relationships, and organized understanding. Specific facts are used to produce these understandings rather than to serve as ends in themselves. For this reason curriculum units are conceived in large organized wholes. The assumption of an active and a creative mind has led to stress on problem-solving processes and more insistent attempts to use open-ended materials and methods to enhance creativity and discovery. In a sense, the content of learning and the processes of learning constitute one single whole; they are distinguishable but cannot be separated from each other. The act of learning is viewed as a transaction between the content and the learner.*

This brief summary of the three types of theories of learning cannot do justice to the ramifications of ideas about learning both within these theories and outside them. It should be pointed out that the essential differences of opinion today reside not in the traditional schools but around the assumptions of either the mechanistic or the cognitive nature of mental processes. Reference is needed, further, to the concepts about learning which are most often referred to by the social psychologists and which are described in chapter 10 on social and cultural learning. It must be noted, also, that while the Freudian psychodynamics has failed to produce a coherent theory of learning, many concepts from this theory of behavior have found a wide currency in education, especially in explaining motivation, behavior problems, and the role emotions play in learning. Among these are the concepts of the unconscious, anxiety, repression, and projection (*Hilgard, 1956, ch. 9; Martin and Stendler, 1959, ch. 7*).

---

* The above parallel of learning theories and curriculum is an adaptation from *G. L. Anderson (1948)*. For a fuller statement of the theories of learning, see *Hilgard (1956)* and *Bode (1942)*.

THE SCIENCE OF LEARNING
AND EDUCATIONAL STRATEGY

As was pointed out earlier, these theories suggest diverse ideas about learning but have not yet produced a science of learning —a coherent set of explanations, laws, and principles to guide education. The more "scientific" behavioristic observations in experimentally confined situations cannot be used to understand or to guide learning of a more complex nature, such as the development of cognitive processes or the formation of attitudes. On the other hand, field theories of learning present too great a complexity of variable factors, with the result that it is difficult to examine adequately their regularities to translate them into appropriate principles and laws. If the possibility of drawing educational applications were limited only to what the experimental psychologists consider precise laws and explanations, one would have to conclude that there can be little correspondence between the studies of learning and the practice of education. One reason for this is the fact that although there are wide varieties of learning, experimental psychology, which is primarily concerned with developing a theory of learning, deals with only a limited range.

The laboratory studies of learning are concerned with vastly simpler phenomena than those faced by schools. Their subjects are animals, and the experiments are confined to repeated experiences in similar situations. By their own admission, this is only one minute aspect of learning. Spence, for example, classifies types of learning and behavioral situations into six groups: (1) conditioning; (2) selective learning; (3) verbal or serial learning, which includes the rote learning; (4) learning of skills, both perceptual and motor; (5) symbolic learning, including reasoning and thinking; and (6) social learning, which involves the learning of attitudes, interests, and feelings. Precise laws are available for only the first three types. Only some very low-level laws and theories are available on the last three, which presumably constitute the bulk of learning that concerns educators. A theory of a higher order is not available on any (Spence, 1959, pp. 92-93).

According to Spence, there are some empirical laws which could form the basis of education. One of these is the principle of reinforcement, exemplifying the law of effect, which underlies the development of teaching machines. While the psychologists disagree on the meaning or the consequences of the law of effect, it is possible to ignore these differences and proceed to discovering the events that serve as reinforcers. Once these are identified, one can program these reinforcers so that the learning of the given material is kept high. This process is a simple kind of conditioning. It deals only with materials and behaviors that can be learned by conditioning (Spence, 1959, pp. 94-95).

This principle, however, cannot be used to guide the more complex kinds of learning. Nor are the by-products of this particular way of learning clearly understood. The difficulty in developing educational procedures from such a limited set of empirical laws is that in the management of learning process one needs to account for the whole process, to watch for a consistency between the effects of that process and the goals, and to see to it that the procedure for one aspect does not produce by-products which conflict with these goals.

One also searches in vain for a fairly clear statement of what a learning act consists of. Bruner describes the elements of a cognitive act of learning as consisting of three almost simultaneous processes: (1) acquisition of new information, often information that runs counter to or is a replacement of what the person has previously known, but which is at the very least a refinement of previous knowledge; (2) transformation, or the process of manipulating knowledge to make it fit new tasks; (3) evaluation, or checking whether the way we have manipulated information is adequate to the task (*Bruner, 1960, pp. 48-49*). Another description of an act of learning, applicable to problem solving, is contained in the steps of problem solving—identifying the problem, developing hypotheses, securing needed facts to check the hypothesis, developing conclusions, and testing them. (All variants of the problem-solving steps go back to *Dewey* [*1933, pp. 106-18*].)

There seems to be no similar analysis for other types of learning acts, such as acquiring new attitudes and feelings, and a more acceptable and convincing theory of human behavior and learning is a need of the first order. To plan scientifically for the management of learning process in the light of today's goals for education requires the kind of science of learning that does not yet exist, one which encompasses all permanent modifications of behavior, with the exception of modifications brought about by sensory adaptation and fatigue. Such a science should also deal with the interrelationship of learning with motivation and with individual differences in talent.

As Melton points out, educators must know how to manage the learning process. No matter what their ultimate goals are and in what social or political orientation they function, they must learn to inculcate the motivation and attitudes which translate capacities into learning (*1950, p. 96*). It seems, then, that in the managing of learning educational practitioners must rely on general principles, hunches, and conclusions from empirical observations rather than on precise laws and facts.

In spite of the lack of a unified theory and a precise science of learning, many advances have been made in understanding the learning process. These understandings can be consolidated, if not into laws, at least into descriptive principles about learning. While this section has dealt with the differences in learning theories, there are many points on which all theories agree. After reviewing many theories of learning, Hilgard developed fourteen points of agreement:

1. In deciding who should learn what, the capacities of the learner are very important. Brighter people can learn things less bright ones cannot learn; in general, older children can learn more rapidly than younger ones; the decline of ability with age, in the adult years, depends upon what it is that is being learned.

2. A motivated learner acquires what he learns more readily than one who is not motivated. The relevant motives include both general and specific ones, for example, desire to learn, need for achievement (general), desire for a certain reward or to avoid a threatened punishment (specific).

3. Motivation that is too intense (especially pain, fear, anxiety) may be accompanied by distracting emotional states, so that excessive motivation may be less effective than moderate motivation for learning some kinds of tasks, especially those involving difficult discriminations.

4. Learning under the control of reward is usually preferable to learning under the control of punishment. Correspondingly, learning motivated by success is preferable to learning motivated by failure. Even though the theoretical issue is still unresolved, the practical outcome must take into account the social by-products, which tend to be more favorable under reward than under punishment.

5. Learning under intrinsic motivation is preferable to learning under extrinsic motivation.

6. Tolerance for failure is best taught through providing a backlog of success that compensates for experienced failure.

7. Individuals need practice in setting realistic goals for themselves, goals neither so low as to elicit little effort nor so high as to foreordain to failure. Realistic goal-setting leads to more satisfactory improvement than unrealistic goal-setting.

8. The personal history of the individual, for example, his reaction to authority, may hamper or enhance his ability to learn from a given teacher.

9. Active participation by a learner is preferable to passive reception when learning, for example, from a lecture or a motion picture.

10. Meaningful materials and meaningful tasks are learned more readily than nonsense materials and more readily than tasks not understood by the learner.

11. There is no substitute for repetitive practice in the overlearning of skills (for instance, the performance of a concert pianist), or in the memorization of unrelated facts that have to be automatized.

12. Information about the nature of a good performance, knowledge of his own mistakes, and knowledge of successful results, aid learning.

13. Transfer to new tasks will be better if, in learning, the learner can discover relationships for himself, and if he has experience during learning of applying the principles within a variety of tasks.

14. Spaced or distributed recalls are advantageous in fixing material that is to be long retained [*1956, pp. 486-87*].

The Concept
of Development

In addition to ideas about learning, the concept of development and research on developmental trends over the life span have been an influential contribution of psychology to education. This research is most useful to educators when interpreted in relation to classroom learning. The developmental trends over the life span, and especially in youth, the trends in emotional, social, cognitive, and personality development, are all important to planning the content and processes of learning. The concept of development has introduced the idea that there is an orderly and sequential transformation which enhances the ability of the organism to adjust, and that this process involves the whole child reacting to his entire environment. The central questions about development are: how do children grow and develop and under what conditions do they develop in a particular way? Although knowledge about child development does not answer directly the question of how children should be educated, this knowledge, nevertheless, provides a basis for deciding what kind of education and training is desirable.

More and more widely and significantly psychologists are studying behavior in terms of trying to determine how individuals develop the forms of behavior and responses they eventually manifest as adults. Even though the concept of development is fairly recent, the idea of the sequential nature of development—that growth and development are gradual, continuous, and sequential, and that developmental stages occur in a fairly orderly sequence—is probably the most universally accepted in education.

Of the four different lines of development—physical growth, social, emotional, and mental—physical growth has been probably the most adequately traced. The volume of research related to the changes associated with pubescence alone is tremendous. Many of these studies are only descriptive, in the sense that they give an average progress of certain groups of children. One illustration of such descriptive studies is the work done by Gesell and his co-workers, which gives behavior profiles or time-flow maps for advancing age levels. While establishing these typicalities, these studies are also quick to point out that individual differences are almost as normal as they are numerous (*Gesell et al., 1940; Gesell and Ilg, 1943, p. 70*).

The central idea of physical maturation is that there are fairly orderly changes in behavior, which are independent of exercise and training, because they are internally regulated (*Hilgard, 1957, pp. 56-63*). One must remember, however, that while it is convenient to mark off the processes of growth by certain stages, such as age levels, or certain periods, such as early childhood, the middle years, and pre-adolescence and adolescence, these stages are only a convenience for analysis and description. There are actually no such sharp breaks in development.

Evidence also indicates that even physical development is cyclic in nature and manifests itself in periodic accelerations, plateaus, and retardations. *Life* magazine, in describing the work of Gesell and Ilg, used the model of a spiral to describe this phenomenon of the progress upward being followed by a downward gradient before moving into a higher level (*April 14, 1947*). The changes occur in cycles of a fairly long duration rather than within definite years—e.g., the pubertal cycle. The cycles and deviations within them have importance for gauging the expectations of physical attainments. They acquire a greater significance when seen in the light of the fact that the rates and variations in physical development often are accompanied by variations in social, emotional, and intellectual development and, in a sense, determine which social and emotional adjustments can take place or are prevented from taking place. For example, physical changes at puberty usually bring new interests, attitudes, and problems. Rapid physical growth usually is accompanied by a degree of restlessness and uneven temperament. Many maladjustments and emotional problems have their source in deviations from the normal rate of physical development.

The patterns discovered in physical maturation have served as models for the concept of developmental sequence in all other areas. Even though the sequences in social, emotional, and mental growth have been studied less thoroughly, it is assumed that all growth and development (a) follows a sequence, (b) proceeds from less mature to more mature, (c) is cyclical, and (d) is organismic.

THE INTERRELATIONSHIP AMONG AREAS OF DEVELOPMENT

The fact that different dimensions of growth are interrelated is as important as the facts about the sequence of development. Knowledge about these relationships has been less clearly applied to curriculum planning than one would expect, largely because research has been specialized in separate areas of development. The segmentation of research and of ideas has also produced a tendency to find the causal factors for irregularities in development first in one area and then in another. Thus in 1930 the common cause of irregularities in behavior was generally seen in physical development, whereas in 1940 emotional disturbances were more frequently used to explain deviate behavior (*Martin and Stendler, 1953, 1959, pp. 111-12*).

These interrelationships are many, and the pattern shifts during growth. For example, intellectual maturity during the primary school years depends in part on a child's ability to read. This ability in turn depends on the proper functioning of the eye, a function of physical maturity. Many intellectual tasks depend on the ability to concentrate, which in turn is controlled by emotional maturity. Erikson has pointed out that achieving any culturally valued capacity or performance also enhances the individual's self-esteem and ego-identity. Thus a child who can walk or read acquires a different cultural status than one who cannot do these things (*1950, ch. 7*).

Emotional development affects mental growth because emotional factors facilitate or block such mental activities as language and reasoning. When physical changes are unusually delayed or occur unusually early, the individual is likely to find himself socially out of step with his fellows. Being out of step socially affects emotional maturity and in turn intellectual functioning. In any group situation in school, inability to control one's temper is sure to reflect on a student's ability to read in groups and to block his functioning in other settings which require social contact. Late and early maturers behave as they do partly because of other people's expectations of them and their responses to these expectations. In many ways physical development affects emotional reactions because of the meaning the culture gives to particular aspects of physical maturity.

While physical maturity is a kind of a pace setter, one can also note the reverse relationships. Mind influences the body, but the body also influences the mind. Emotional disturbances retard physical development. Children in an institution in which they were cared for by their mothers and received love and emotional support showed different rates of physical development than did the children in another institution where they were under the care of overworked nurses (*Spitz, 1949*). Psychosomatic medicine shows that one's health can be affected by one's emotional state, and vice versa (*Gerard, 1946*).

The observations of these relationships have suggested the concept of organismic age, a "going togetherness" of physical growth and other aspects of development (*Olson and Hughes, 1943*). This concept has been criticized as a spurious extrapolation to later years of a relationship that exists only in the very early years, and an extrapolation of the pattern in acquiring simpler behavior to the more complex cognitive and behavioral development, when the "unique factors of individual experience and cultural environment make important contributions to the direction, patterning, and sequential order of all developmental changes" (*Ausubel, 1959, pp. 248-49*). It is also pointed out that organismic age, that is, the compounding of scores on different kinds of development, obscures important facts. "It is not so helpful, for example, for a teacher to know that Philip has an organismic age of 11.7 years as it is for him to know that the child has a reading age of 10.3 and a mental age of 11.4" (*Martin and Stendler, 1959, pp. 122-23*).

The fact is, of course, that no individual develops evenly. Some youngsters are physically mature but lack a corresponding social and psychological maturity. Others combine a well-developed intellectual capacity with childish feelings and immature social behavior. These unevennesses become a source of additional difficulties when the child is surrounded by cultural expectations which assume an even development. It is common in schools, for example, to expect precocity in intellectual mastery, emotional control, and social conduct because of precocity in physical development. These expectations play havoc with an individual's self-expectations and adjustment. Stoltz and Stoltz illustrated this in the case of Ben, who, because of his high physical development, had a hard time living up both to the goals that he set for himself and to what adults expected of him (*1951, ch. 18*). Cultural expectations of evenness of development are bound to have systematic disruptive effects on children whose social backgrounds produce certain deviations in development, such as inadequate social skills in children from underprivileged homes and deficiencies in language development in children from homes with foreign backgrounds. The sociometric studies conducted by students of the author point out over and over again the circular effect of these deviations. Cultural factors, by causing retardation in social skills and language, promoted isolation and nonparticipation in class, which in turn caused malfunctioning at the learning tasks. As children were helped to establish adequate interpersonal relations and encouraged in self-expression, their achievement in other school tasks improved also. Unless teachers and curriculum makers are sensitized to the consequences of these cultural deviations, they fail to provide the necessary opportunities for proper transitions in "acculturation."

THE CONCEPT OF READINESS AND OF PACING

Generally the idea of sequential development has had a salutary effect on curriculum. It alerted educators to the fact that certain minimum levels of maturity are necessary before certain subjects can be taught with reasonable success and efficiency. It also encouraged curriculum makers and teachers to consider the prevailing limitations in such intellectual factors as the grasp of concepts in arranging and presenting subject matter.

The chief contribution of the idea of development has been the concept of readiness and of pacing—that is, that effective teaching involves timeliness in training and opportunities for activity in a sense of pacing teaching to children's maturity. Hilgard states the chief principles of readiness and pacing, among which are the following:

> 1. *"Skills that build upon developing behavior are most easily learned."* Thus it is difficult to master reading as a mechanical act ahead of a certain level of coordination.
> 2. *"The more mature the organism, the less training is needed to reach a given level of proficiency,"* at least in periods of high growth. Many experiments have shown that older children gain faster with the same amount of directed practice. Children who are taught to read when they are ready to read, read more books than those who are not ready. Those who are "ready" to do arithmetic problems, solve more problems than those who are not.
> 3. *"Training given before the maturational readiness may bring either no improvement, or only temporary improvement."* Premature training often results in loss of skill. Children fall back into the level natural for their development, as experiments with training children to cut with scissors, to recite digits, or to maintain balance have shown.
> 4. *"Premature training, if frustrating, may do more harm than good."* A child exposed too early to an activity may lose his natural enthusiasm for it (*Hilgard, 1957, pp. 60-63*).

Effective learning requires effective pacing as experiences need to be in line with developmental sequence. The learner's effective cooperation is impossible if the learning tasks are beyond his capacity to grasp or call for skills and motivation which his physical or emotional development cannot support. This does not mean that teaching is not necessary (a frequent misinterpretation). The principle of pacing is merely helpful in avoiding wasteful teaching: too early, too much, too great a refinement or speed.

However, these principles of readiness and their educational applications have been subject to several criticisms. One series of questions centers on the extent to which the development of behavior is genetically predetermined, the extent to which behavioral organizations unfold automatically as a function of morphological development, and the extent to which experience and training enter in a determining fashion. As we shall see in chapter 8, this argument is especially keen regarding the development of intelligence. While the assumption of genetic predeterminism is usually implied in explaining the development of unlearned behavior, this assumption also seems to color explanations of the development of learned behavior. Hunt (*1961, p. 35*), for example, insists that this assumption is explicit in the writing of Arnold Gesell. He suggests, further, that experiments with sensory deprivation call into serious question the concept that the basic behavior patterns unfold automatically as somatic and neural structures mature, and that the "concept of a continuous environment-organism interaction would better fit the facts" (*pp. 58, 64*).

Similar criticisms leveled against the concept of readiness assert that it suggests a passive waiting for a "proper level of maturity" instead of an active manipulation of experience to enhance the power of the organism to organize and reorganize his behavior and his capacity to learn. Perhaps the fact that the concept of readiness has been modeled after very early development during the period when behavior is as yet limited by physical coordination has too strongly influenced the entire concept of readiness. It is possible that the effect of manipulating such environmental factors as the amount and nature of stimulation and the opportunity for experience and practice has not been as fully recognized as it should be and that, therefore, certain aspects of training are unnecessarily delayed.

Other critics question a premature specification of developmental sequences as guides to educational action. Ausubel points out that the concepts of developmental sequence are as yet too crude to permit the kind of particularization that is necessary if they are to be used as specific guides for placement of content or for setting expectations regarding levels of learning. Generally speaking, the concept of developmental readiness and the idea that there is an optimal age for every kind of learning are interesting and potentially useful. But there are also dangers in applying these ideas too rigidly. While there is little disagreement about the fact that readiness crucially influences learning and that "attained capacity limits and influences an individual's ability to profit from current experience or practice," this should not be confused with the concept of maturation. Maturation is only one of the two factors that determine an individual's readiness. The other is prior experience. Lack of readiness may reflect inadequate teaching rather than maturational deficiency. Equating readiness only with maturation "muddies the conceptual waters" and makes it possible for educators to use maturation as a convenient scapegoat and an excuse for not subjecting instructional practices to the kind of scrutiny necessary for continued educational progress. He questions especially the "internal ripening" theory of maturation, which leads to the self-selection principle in curriculum development—a principle which assumes that children's interests are an adequate index of their developmental needs and that, therefore, one can develop a curriculum on the basis of children's interests. He is also critical of the widely accepted notion that there is a general "going-togetherness" in growth and achievement, a concept which is used to justify an over-all ability grouping in which a single ability is used as a basis for determining the level on which the student is to work in all areas of the curriculum (*Ausubel, 1959, pp. 247-48*).

The current concept of development and its educational equivalent of readiness also illustrate the overgeneralizations which result from observations in a single culture and which lead to a disregard of the cultural environment in creating readiness. The inevitable stages postulated in the theories of development may be inevitable only in a given cultural pattern, and not in others. The animistic tendencies discovered by Piaget in children's thinking may be due to the language which the child is taught. The "storm and stress" ascribed to adolescence do not seem to occur in all cultures (*Anastasi, 1958, pp. 610-14*). Middle-class children are ready to read earlier than lower-class children because of availability of books and because they are "read to."

Current practices illustrate many of the weaknesses which result from the rigid age patterning of the idea of readiness and from extrapolation of the characteristics of development discovered in one area onto another one.

First, the curriculum gauged to fixed age-level norms of development based on the idea of a fixed sequence may be as guilty of underdevelopment as it may be of overexpectation. The descriptions of growth sequence reinforce the notion of fixed stages by describing the most conspicuous symptoms or characteristics of behavior by age levels—as is true, for example, in Gesell's presentations of the growth cycle. It is easy to submit to the tyranny of fixed age-level norms and forget that there are large individual variations in the time at which certain tasks become feasible as well as in the speed with which individuals can master these tasks. The fact that the mass procedures in diagnosis and in education make it difficult to identify and to accommodate variations in developmental readiness adds to the problem.

A further problem in applying the concept of development lies in the fact that the units of evaluation are in static terms, such as age level, IQ, or grade norms. It is relatively easy to determine a level of academic achievement at a given moment, or a certain degree of emotional maturity at a given moment. It is much more difficult to assess what an individual can do in the light of his previous experience and to fit the information about achievement into a historical or psychological perspective which takes into account his developmental sequence.

Our age-patterned curriculum with its uniform requirements often fails to accommodate persons whose developmental cycles define them as slow maturers and those who are late in starting but who accelerate rapidly after they have started. We often expect the same things of a boy of thirteen who is short and slight and who speaks with a childish soprano as we do of a girl of thirteen who could pass for eighteen (*Lindgren, 1956, pp. 65-66*). The failure to provide a greater allowance for variations in the developmental cycles has increased the phenomenon of retardation. Branding as retarded individuals who are only temporarily so actually causes these individuals to remain retarded. The current emphasis on ability grouping even in the early elementary years means that incorrect but irrevocable curriculum decisions may be made for children whose developmental cycles deviate from the so-called normal.

Questions need to be raised also about setting expectations in terms of cyclical advance rather than in strict age-level terms. For example, should the primary school, rather than the first grade, be the cycle during which all children would be expected to learn to read? What happens to the progress of the so-called late-maturers who have to compete in physical coordination, in attention span, and in reading skills during the first part of their cycle rather than at the time when learning these things is most effective for them? What are the effects of such discrepancies between expectations and developmental maturity on self-expectations, acquisition of habits, social relations, and the future potential for learning? Some experiments in retraining slow readers, conducted by the author, indicate that a large portion of retarded readers are retarded not because of their lack of ability to learn to read, but because in their developmental sequence the crucial initial steps in learning to read came at a time when they were unable to respond to such training (*Yolo County Schools, 1956*).

The interrelatedness between various aspects of development points to still other problems in curriculum and teaching. One is the need for a broader base of diagnosis and assessment in order to determine what curriculum to offer to whom. Exclusive dependence on tests of intelligence or of reading for making decisions about ability grouping, accleration, and retardation may be too narrow a basis for making decisions which have crucial consequences for a student's learning career. If each aspect of the development is contingent on another, a proper prediction of what a student can or cannot do should not be made without examining all significant dimensions of development, including something of his developmental history.

The evidence on interrelationship among the several aspects of growth also suggests that each individual brings to each learning situation a differentiated combination of capacities and abilities, each at a particular level of maturity. This would indicate that readiness to learn is determined by such a constellation rather than by any single individual factor. Diagnosis, then, should attempt to describe these constellations of developmental patterns and the factors affecting them. It is surprising how much the judgments derived from an analysis of these idiosyncratic constellations and of the developmental sequences producing them differ from judgments derived from interpreting separately the linear data on each aspect of growth.

At present, schools tend to disregard both the individual rates of growth and the unique constellations of factors operating in the progress of any individual child. Many a curriculum decision is made on discrete measurements and standards. Children are often grouped by reading ability alone. These allocations in turn influence the child's self-expectations and attitudes toward reading, which begin to act as a brake on reading. The first step is thus taken toward making a permanent "slow learner" out of a child who may only be a slow starter, or who, for the time being, suffers from a handicap in his emotional or social development.

But perhaps the most important implications of the idea of development lie in the suggestion that the child and the adolescent are in the process of becoming. Because of the cumulative nature of behavioral development, it is more important to gauge what the outcome of the current curriculum will be for a student at the age of 25 than at the end of a particular grade. For this reason, a curriculum is needed which aids this process of becoming instead of enforcing static norms of achievement and progress. Since the manner in which an individual classifies and orders his experience changes in each developmental stage, a curriculum which permits variations in learning approaches is more likely to aid more kinds of individuals than a curriculum which is rigid in content, in approach, and in expectations of attainment. Since each individual represents a unique constellation of maturities and of capacities to react, his maturity is more adequately nurtured by a curriculum that permits selectivity in learning activities by offering a broad range of possibilities, especially at the younger age levels. A broader base of experience in the beginning is likely to facilitate higher levels of final organization. By knowing something of the patterns of development, a teacher can make a better prediction of future achievement and plan the current program with more attention to future possibilities.

At present, however, it is possible only to speculate on what the curricular sequence might conceivably be if it took into account precise and detailed, but currently unavailable, research findings on the readiness for different subject matters, for differing levels of difficulty within a subject, and for different ways of teaching the same subject (*Ausubel, 1959, p. 249*).

THE CONCEPT
OF DEVELOPMENTAL TASKS

Still another way of looking at development is to consider the shaping of drives and motivations in the light of the demands of the individual's social milieu. There is a growing realization that an individual faces not only his own needs, but also the demands and tasks imposed on him by the cultural expectations mediated through the interpersonal context around him: his family, school, neighborhood, and community. The concept of developmental tasks represents an effort to chart the developmental sequence in the context of cultural expectations. A developmental task is essentially a task of learning which an individual must accomplish in order to be a successful, productive, and healthy person in our society. Each task arises sharply, or has a crucial period, at certain times in an individual's life, when the successful mastery of that task leads to success with other tasks but failure brings the disapproval of society and failure at the succeeding tasks (*Havighurst, 1953, p. 2*). Erikson, the originator of this idea, stresses in addition the idea of *crisis*—that is, that these tasks are also associated with a conflict of feelings and desires. Although these crises are never solved entirely, because each shift in experience and environment presents them in a new form, yet, if the problem is well handled at the crucial period of its appearance, a basis is laid for a sturdy personality, capable of dealing with subsequent tasks (*Erikson, 1955*).

The educational use of the concept of developmental tasks grew out of an attempt to deal with the cleavages and confusion surrounding the concept of "need" as used in education. This concept was used to direct attention to the role of the learner and of the learning tasks as one criterion for curriculum making. It proved to be a difficult criterion. First, it was difficult to reconcile the psychological concept of "needs" with the educational use of the same term, which included the idea of social or cultural demands and of the gaps between these demands and attainment. There were also as many definitions of psychological needs as there were psychologists (*Prescott, 1938, ch. 4*). As a result cleavages arose among the curriculum theorists as to the relative emphasis on one or the other type of need.

It is assumed that the developmental tasks arise from three interacting sources. First, the maturation of the biological organism sets the conditions or takes the lead in some tasks, such as in making a heterosexual social adjustment in early adolescence. Second, the social and cultural patterns exercise demands on individuals through the socialization processes, such as learning to take responsibility or to treat adults in an acceptable fashion. Finally, tasks such as developing a pattern of preferences and dislikes, and a pattern of personal aspirations, are dictated by the individual personality. These tasks are part of us (*Havighurst, 1953, pp. 4-5*).

Several different descriptions of developmental tasks are available. The one most applicable to curriculum development includes the following categories:

1. Achieving an appropriate dependence-independence pattern.
2. Achieving an appropriate giving-receiving pattern of affection.
3. Relating to changing social groups.
4. Developing a conscience.
5. Learning one's psycho-socio-biological sex role.
6. Accepting and adjusting to a changing body.
7. Managing a changing body and learning new patterns of motor control.
8. Learning to understand and control the physical world.
9. Developing an appropriate symbol system and conceptual abilities.
10. Relating one's self to the cosmos (*Tryon and Lilienthal, 1950, pp. 84-87;* see also, *Havighurst, 1953*).

IMPLICATIONS FOR CURRICULUM MAKING OF THE CONCEPT OF DEVELOPMENTAL TASKS

Several advantages have been pointed out in using the concept of developmental tasks in educational diagnosis and curriculum planning. First, it organizes the knowledge about development, which is usually splintered in several directions. It permits bringing together ideas about physical maturation, socialization, psychological development of drives, motivations, and emotions. While these various dimensions can be distinguished, they are not so separated as to blur the vision of the continuity and wholeness of the self.

Secondly, this concept points clearly to the necessity of understanding and facing the complex relationship between the conditions of learning and the dimensions of development. While it is assumed that there are certain limits to the development of the human body and mind, the possibilities which *do* develop, especially in moral and economic behavior, mental activity, and choice of goals and values, are almost completely the products of social learning rather than of direct teaching. To enhance the learning of these behaviors in school, curriculum planning needs to design, use, and control conditions for learning as well as the content to be learned.

The use of this concept also helps to extend and to clarify the educational objectives and emphasizes the need to discover the teachable moment by guiding the timing and pacing of educational effort so that those things that are related or can be related to the developmental tasks are taught "when conditions are most favorable."

One might point out, further, the influence of success at developmental tasks on academic achievement. If failure at one task creates complications about the next one, it is possible that a great many problems of school achievement are created by a failure or only a partial success at some task of growing up, such as a failure to develop sufficient independence from adults, to adopt a proper level of the giving-receiving pattern, or to disengage from an egocentric view toward the world. This idea has implications for the nature of remedial programs needed as well as for the sequences of the curriculum and expectations of achievement. At which point, for example, can a successful analysis of the society begin? When is the crucial time to attempt to conceptualize the contradictions in moral codes and values? The placement of subjects in a sequence could be determined not only according to the individual's capacity to handle the concepts and skills involved but also according to whether or not the subjects help individuals to develop the resources with which to meet their life tasks—and, vice versa, the context of developmental tasks could be used to facilitate academic learning. One might, for example, consider the possibility of introducing such skills as reading and arithmetic in a context which points up their relationship with a developmental task, especially for groups which may be reluctant to learn these skills. One teacher taught ratios and fractions in her eighth-grade class by inducing them to measure and to compare their own physical growth while systematically arranging assignments for computing percentages and ratios of these comparative measurements. She found that this rather "unteachable" class had no difficulty in mastering the essential concepts and processes in this context (*Warren, 1955*).

The concept of developmental tasks also yields a more sophisticated approach to "needs" than is current. Expressing as it does a combination of an individual need and a social demand, it stresses individual needs without an excessive emphasis on child-centeredness.

One thing to remember is that the nature of developmental tasks varies according to the cultural background. Meeting the developmental tasks represents different problems for the different subcultures in our society. It is one thing to learn to be a man in an Anglo-Saxon white family, and something vastly more difficult for a Negro boy to learn the same thing in a slum in a segregated community. A Negro boy needs not only to be a man but also a Negro man; his developmental task is to learn the do's and don't's of a double culture, that of his own subgroup and, in addition, that of a subgroup in a rather inaccessible dominant culture.

It follows that schools have a special responsibility to help the members of the deviant subculture learn to meet the expectations of the common culture in addition to those of their own. For many socially isolated groups in our society, the school is almost the only place with sufficient face-to-face relations to make it possible for them to learn a common culture. Yet these opportunities are often closed by various segregation devices, such as ability grouping, the consequences of which are not always understood (*Bettelheim, 1958*).

Differentiation can be made among the tasks that are recurrent or continuous and those that are not. For example, learning to get along with age-mates is a recurrent task, although the "crisis" or the sharp edge occurs in adolescence. These recurrent or continuing tasks may also suggest the continuing concerns which could be used to sharpen motivation and to set intellectual tasks related to developing a clearer perspective of the self and its relation to society.

Intelligence
and Mental
CHAPTER EIGHT   Development

Traditionally mental ability is central to the concern of the schools. Children are grouped by measures of intelligence and content is allocated according to ability levels. Measures of mental ability are used to determine who qualifies for continued education. Expectations of performance are set by what is known about levels of mental maturity. All educators believe that the development of intellectual powers is an important goal, and some believe it to be the central objective of all schooling.

THE CONCEPT OF INTELLIGENCE

The above activities are predicated on a certain conception of what intelligence or mental ability is and how it functions. This concept further determines what schools can or should do, such as how subject matter is taught and what is included in the curriculum materials. The concept of intelligence further determines whether the general policy of the schools is to use intelligence functioning at the moment or to develop it.

Yet ideas regarding what intelligence or mental ability is, how it functions, and how it develops are not nearly so clear and precise as one would assume from the assurance with which the results of measures of intelligence are used. Miner points out that although intelligence tests can predict potential success in college or school, they do not tell us what accounts for this successful performance (*Miner, 1957, p. 2*).

For a long time controversies regarding the nature of intelligence have been raging on three issues: (1) whether differences in intelligence are hereditary or caused by environmental factors, (2) whether intelligence is constant or modifiable, and (3) whether it is a unitary characteristic or composed of a series of specific abilities. The scales today are tilting toward the idea that intelligence is a product of an interaction between the environment and heredity and, therefore, not constant but modifiable. This would mean that "within the broad limits set by biological endowment and physical development, the so-called aptitudes are largely a consequence of prior ex-perience" (*McGuire, 1957*). It seems also to be generally conceded that the "variations in environmental demands and life experience lead to under-standable and predictable variations in patterns of perceptual, motor, verbal, and reasoning abilities," and that "new patterns of ability can emerge through control and modification of experiences and the educative process" (*Ferguson, 1956*).

It has been suggested also that the concept of intelligence as a constant and a unitary characteristic, which underlies the very instruments by which in-dividual differences and changes in intelligence are measured today, was developed and persists because of a lack of refined tools by which to analyze the nature of intelligence. A new concept of the structure of intelligence, emerging from recent studies, suggests that the quality called intelligence is not a unitary characteristic but consists of a series of specific functional abilities, some of which have been systematically bypassed by tests available up till now because of the restricted concept of intelligence which underlies such tests.

J. P. Guilford and his associates, pursuing factor-analytic studies, indicate that there are at least 55 known factors of intellect, and even then the total structure of intelligence is not filled in (*1959*). Like Miner, Guilford main-tains that reasoning is highly related to intelligence but that the intelligence tests, especially the group intelligence tests, touch on this ability only slightly. He proposes a three-dimensional model of the structure of intellect, composed

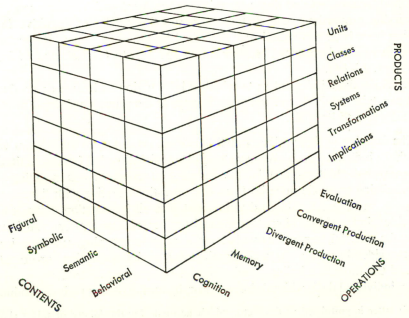

Figure 1 Theoretical Model for the Complete "Structure of Intellect."

of (a) the various operations or abilities, (b) the materials with which these operations deal, and (c) the products or outcomes of these operations, as shown in Figure 1.

Five operations are distinguished by Guilford, described as follows:

1. Cognition, which refers to awareness of objects, qualities, and ideas. This process is complex and includes such variations as the process of knowing about the universe, a flower, the second law of thermodynamics, or a Spenserian sonnet. It is the process involved when one young child looked at oil spilled on a wet pavement and said, "Oh look, Mommy, see a rainbow in a gutter," and the process which led her mother to reply, "That's not a rainbow, that's a dirty oil slick" (*Getzels and Jackson, 1962, p. 13*).

2. Memory and retention: the ability to store information and to retrieve it when needed.

3. Convergent thinking: a mode of thinking which is directed toward finding a "unique" or the "right" answer to problems, the tendency to retain the known, learning what is predetermined, and dealing with the usual and the expected.

4. Divergent thinking, which includes fluency with words, associations, and ideas and the tendency to revise the known, to project new forms of thought instead of depending on habitual forms of thought. These include such matters as changing classes and dimensions of the problem, or adopting different solutions from one problem to another. This type of cognitive functioning is generally oriented toward the novel and the speculative. Getzels points out that both convergent and divergent thinking are employed by all persons, but in varying proportions, and that these contrasting modes of cognitive functioning have been recognized and described by different names. Rogers uses defensiveness and openness, Maslow safety and growth (*Getzels and Jackson, 1962, pp. 13-14*).

5. Evaluation: judgment as to whether information as known or produced meets certain standards and whether the steps in the process or its end product are adequate to its goals.

The function of these primary abilities differs according to the content with which the individual deals. We have long distinguished verbal from quantitative or nonverbal abilities—that is, the building of concepts and meanings by manipulating symbolic material from the operations dealing with figures and quantitative materials. Guilford points out that all information comes to an individual in four kinds of content: figural (or concrete perceptions and facts), symbolic material, semantic or verbal and conceptual meaning, and behavioral, which evidently covers the social intelligence, social perception, or empathy toward the thoughts, feelings, and attitudes of other individuals.*

An individual deals with this information by turning it into various products:

---

* This latter is postulated as the factor which accounts for the failure of talent shown in school and college to turn into success in life (*McClelland et al., 1958, ch. 2*).

forming units and systems of information, establishing relationships, performing transformations, and drawing implications (*J. P. Guilford, 1956, pp. 267-93; 1961, pp. 9-19*).

VARIABLES AFFECTING THE FUNCTIONING INTELLIGENCE

The primary abilities are the outcome of several variables. Miner, for example, points out that the functioning of intelligence is an outcome of three variables: native potential, motivation, and the environmental stimulation (*1957, pp. 4-10*).

Native Potential

Native potential is the basic equivalent of the ability to learn and to reason. While there is a difference of opinion regarding whether the native potential is represented primarily by learning or by ability to reason, in the end these two may represent the same thing. Native ability, when exposed to practice, eventuates in reasoning (*Miner, 1957, pp. 4-5*). This idea is supported by many recent psychological experiments. Harlow, for example, postulates an ability to acquire a "learning set" or a "learning to learn," which is shared by monkeys and human beings. "This 'learning to learn' transforms the organism from a creature that adapts to a changing environment by trial and error to one that adapts by seeking hypothesis and insight" (*Harlow, 1949, pp. 5-6, 61-75; 1950; 1951*). Tomkins suggests, in addition, that human beings can acquire multiple learning sets, which is the manner of initiating the process called reasoning (*1951*).

Motivation

If there is no wish to learn, there is no learning, even though the environment may be rich in stimulation. Learning sets cannot be developed in a motivational vaccum, and a rich learning environment is not an *actual* learning environment for those who will not or cannot take advantage of it. The functioning of intelligence can be hampered by many personal conditions, such as refusal to renounce dependency needs or a passive rather than aggressive orientation toward experience. Intelligence is hampered also by all feelings which have an erosive or a tunnel-vision effect on perception, such as fear and anxiety. Persons subjected to these feelings for prolonged periods of time fail to develop their potential to learn, hence their potential to reason, hence also their cognitive functioning.

But motivation to learn and to integrate what the environment offers is also a function of cultural and class differences in attitudes toward learning and education. In general there is nowhere the same degree of motivation or environmental stimulation in lower- and working-class families as there is in the middle class. Therefore the reduced exposure in these cases is the result both of reduced environmental stimulus potential and of reduced motivation (*Miner, 1957, pp. 6-7*). For example, Davie shows the difference in motivation for further education supplied by middle-class and working-class families (*1953*). A similar difference in aspirations was found by Kahl, who studied social-class influence on the motivation patterns of boys with similar intellectual background and intelligence (*1953*).

The Environmental Stimulus

The environmental stimulus is the third variable in functioning intelligence. Different persons may be subjected to different amounts of stimulation and to different content, depending on the culture in which they live. Some persons receive more stimulation toward verbality, others toward technical reasoning. Primitive people, whose culture lacks technology of any sort, are defective in technical reasoning or intelligence, not necessarily because their native potential does not allow it but because there is no environmental stimulation for its development. Gladwyn, for example, points out that the Trukese, who can navigate by the stars and wind and make extremely subtle and complex adjustments in guiding their boats, are complete failures when its comes to trouble-shooting a car motor (*1960, pp. 23-26*).

If a particular culture is either barren of certain stimulation or undervalues a particular type of learning and thinking, the chances are that the members of this culture will not be able to develop a particular ability. For example, a study by Janke and Havighurst showed that the performance of the ten-year-olds of a city on all their tests showed a consistent tendency for the middle-class children to excel over the lower class. When the same tests were administered to the same group at the age of sixteen, however, one difference disappeared: the higher-class boys no longer excelled the lower-class boys in performance and mechanical assembly tasks. The authors concluded that this shift was caused by a shift of interest and motivation in the higher-class boys away from things mechanical (*Janke and Havighurst, 1945*).

Whether the environmental stimulus is put to use depends both on native potential and on motivation. Individuals may respond selectively, even in an environment that provides multiple stimulation. Some aspects of culture content are of a greater interest value to some individuals than to others. In a sense each individual has a unique *behavioral environment*—a concept advocated by Koffka. This would suggest that the differential abilities are not a function of separate inherited abilities, which "reside in the organism ready to be developed," but that they result from channeling of a unitary native potential into certain types of mental activity or toward certain content areas (*Miner, 1957, pp. 7-8*).

The factor analysis of intelligence test results demonstrates that the most significant variations in intelligence occur according to the factors related to social stratification, such as education, occupation, race, and the subject's own classification of the social class to which he belongs. These variations could be explained by a difference in the degree of actual exposure introduced by these factors.

Assuming that the degree of actual exposure to a content area is a function of the amount of motivation and the degree of environmental stimulation, Miner suggests the following equations to be used for extreme cases:

1. High actual exposure + high native potential = high ability
2. Low actual exposure + high native potential = low ability
3. High actual exposure + low native potential = low ability
4. Low actual exposure + low native potential = low ability (*1957, pp. 9-10*).

This concept suggests that the functioning intelligence is conditioned by the native potential but not completely limited by it. A person of high potential intelligence may have low functioning intelligence because of low exposure or low motivation. A person of low native potential can develop a high intelligence in certain areas, provided his actual exposure is prolonged and his motivation increased. In the latter instance, however, the area of functioning intelligence may have to be rather circumscribed and the development slow.

THE LIMITATIONS OF INTELLIGENCE TESTS

Recently intelligence tests have been criticized from two angles: that they are built on too limited a concept of what intelligence is and that they are culture-bound. J. P. Guilford and his associates have pointed out that the possibility that intelligence is a unitary trait grows increasingly more remote, and that at least the dimensions of creative or divergent thinking and planning have been verified (*1959, pp. 26-27*).

Getzels and Jackson, who explored the meaning of intelligence specifically in relation to creativity, point out that the single metric of the current intelligence tests not only restricts perspective on the more general phenomenon of intelligence but also places on this one concept a greater predictive burden than it was intended to carry (*1962, pp. 6-7*). The conventional IQ type of test requires the subject to know the common association to a stimulus and the accepted solution to a problem. In many of these tests the subject must respond to a stimulus for which only one "unique" answer is correct. He is not asked to innovate, to speculate, to invent, or to come up with an emergent answer. Indeed, if the answer is novel it is likely to be scored wrong. In short, the conventional IQ test tends to emphasize the convergent cognitive processes and exclude the divergent productive or creative processes (*Getzels and Jackson, 1962, pp. 5-8*).

The cognitive style of the type to which the label "giftedness" is most frequently applied seems at once the least explored and the most significant. For all practical purposes the "gifted child" became synonymous with the "child with the high IQ." This limited concept of giftedness blinds us to other forms of excellence and leads to associating creativity exclusively with performance in the arts (*Getzels and Jackson, 1962, p. 7*).

These criticisms have generated an array of studies which are attempting to develop tests of creativity and to analyze the performance of highly creative individuals compared with those with high IQ's. Getzels, for example, found that while the students who were highest in creativity did not have the highest IQ's, their superior academic performance would place them in a pejorative category of "overachievers." This dubious classification implies that an IQ-achievement discrepancy in favor of achievement is a function of "motivational" (as opposed to "cognitive") variables. Getzels suggests that it is perhaps more reasonable to assume that certain types of excellence are not sampled by the "conventional IQ metric" and that the tests may be undiscriminating rather than to attribute the discrepancy to the motivational pathology in the child (*Getzels and Jackson, 1962, pp. 26-27; see also Torrance, 1960; 1961*).

Another set of studies started out with the observation of the cultural origin of the variations in intelligence test scores and analyzed the intelligence tests from the standpoint of their cultural bias. These studies also point out several defects in intelligence testing. First, the current tests are based on too narrow an assumption of what intelligence is; they concentrate too heavily on verbal abstractions. When intelligence is defined as problem-solving ability or reasoning, these tests are not valid measures. Secondly, because it is assumed that intelligence is a native, unchangeable characteristic, little attention is paid to the cultural bias in the existing tests, despite the fact that invariably children from higher-status homes do better on the intelligence tests than do children from low-status homes. Third, these tests are "culture-bound" in the materials they use as well as in operations they require for responses. The common intelligence tests use content which is less familiar to children from lower-status homes, hence are less appropriate for measuring their powers. Their content is usually in verbal abstractions, particularly adapted to the middle-class culture. They systematically underestimate the intelligence of lower-class children from non-Anglo-Saxon homes because they touch neither their motivation nor their experience. Finally, cultural training affects mental development and creates differences in mental systems as well as in motivation for the functioning of mental abilities. The tests concentrate upon the types of mental behavior in which the higher and the middle socioeconomic groups are superior but which are foreign to lower-class students (*Eells, 1953, pp. 288 ff.; Davis, 1952, pp. 46-59*).

Davis describes five factors or phenomena which determine the level of behavior on intelligence tests or in any formal problem-solving situations. These factors are similar to those described by Miner as affecting the functioning intelligence: (1) Heredity, the organic functioning pattern. (2) Cultural influences, or the pupil's experience with the content with which the test deals. (3) Training, which determines the familiarity with the particular situations and symbols used. (4) Cultural motivation; the "drive" at the levels sufficient to impel the pupil to use his full potential to solve the test-problem, and in a manner indicated in the directions. (5) "Speed," which is a combination of hereditary factors, physical condition, stamina, the culturally conditioned habits of work, the student's familiarity with the cultural form and the content of the problem, and his previous experience or training with the specific type of problem.

Out of the five factors affecting performance on tests, four are culture-bound and therefore "unfair" for measuring the native potential of children who deviate from the middle-class culture (*Davis, 1952, pp. 63-65*).

THE DEVELOPMENT OF INTELLIGENCE

Because the assumption of a static intelligence dominated the field until recent times, relatively little work has been done on the development of intelligence and thought. While American educational psychology was preoccupied with debates on the relative importance of nature and nurture in intelligence, the Europeans, notably Jean Piaget and Barbee Inhelder, began to analyze the process of the development of cognition and thought. Their studies pursued the development of intelligence as mental activity, not of intelligence as a hypothetical power (*Piaget, 1957, 1953, 1954, 1950; Piaget and Inhelder, 1947; Piaget, Inhelder, and Szeminska, 1960; Hunt, 1961, chs. 5-9*).

The work of Piaget suggests certain evolutionary sequences from the first sensory-motor reactions to the formation of reflective thought. According to him, the behavior of the human organism starts with the organization of sensory-motor reactions and becomes more intelligent as coordination between the reactions to objects become progressively more interrelated and complex. Thinking becomes possible after language, and with it a new mental organization, develops.

Sensimotor Stage

This development involves roughly three main evolutionary stages. The first stage is the development of sensory-motor intelligence: the coordination of sense impressions and movements. During this stage the child is occupied with establishing relationships between experience and action. During the first step of this stage the child's universe is egocentric. Objects exist only as functional reality—as, for example, something to be sucked or to be swung. But even at this point the intelligent act is based on the sensible organization of the perceptual field.

The second step is formation of habits, of fixed ways of responding. The formation of a habit always involves a means-ends relation: habits are established when behavior is directed toward attaining certain satisfactions. Habit is a passively experienced association, and intelligence, or the beginnings of problem-solving, grows gradually out of it by a cumulative reorganization of habits.

The last step of sensory-motor intelligence is reached when the transition between the simple habit and intelligence is accomplished after vision and apprehension are coordinated. This step brings greater precision and a more generalized behavior. It becomes possible to seek innovation in behavior rather than to suffer change because of need. This sensory-motor or preverbal intelligence, which is perfected after about two years, lies at the bottom of all thought and continues to affect thought through life.

The Stage of Concrete Operations

The second stage is the building of concrete operations—the establishment of reflective grouping of objects. This stage proceeds roughly in three steps. At the preconceptual step symbols are created and *preconceptual symbolic* thought is established. The child begins to represent the world through simple generalizations. This is followed by the development of *intuitive thinking,* during which the perceptual appearance of global and unanalyzable wholes represents the reality. Action images are extended, differentiated, and combined. But distinctions between internal motives and feeling and external realities are yet unclear. The objects and acts are seen as functions of the ego, and events in the material world are attributed to an agent, such as saying the sun moves because God pushes it. Thought is still egocentric and subjective: the child knows his own left hand but not that of his partner who faces him, because he can see only from his point of view.

What is lacking at this point is the concept of *reversibility*. The objects are seen as entities, or *Gestalten,* which vanish when they are taken apart. The child cannot grasp that when the shape of the object is changed, it can be brought back again to its original state, or that a quantity can be composed and decomposed: e.g., if three piles are made from nine marbles, that the three piles of marbles still represent the same quantity.

The third step in the concrete stage, reached when the child is in school, is that of *concrete operations,* the ability to think while manipulating objects and symbols that represent these objects. These operations are the means of getting data about the real world into the mind to be used in solving problems. The child develops an internalized symbolic structure by which he represents the world. This means that he can solve problems in his head in place of using overt trial and error. An abstract and logical grouping of objects is established. The thinking is intuitive, in that the child can see abstract relationships, but only as represented by concrete objects which are immediately present. He cannot deal with the whole range of alternatives that could exist. Objectivity is established and the internal world is separated from the external one. Animism disappears. Reversibility is established also. This period lasts from around two years to eleven years of age.

The Stage of Conceptual Thought

The third stage, that of developing conceptual thought, or *formal operations,* is established somewhere between eleven years of age and adolescence. During this stage reflective intelligence and formal thought, including causal reasoning, are completed. At this point, the child can think with abstract propositions. Instead of being constrained by what is before him, he can deal with hypothetical possibilities. Intuitive grasp of abstract relationships is replaced with conscious concepts. Objective causality is established and now completely replaces intellectual egocentricity and subjectivity. The conceptual system acquires reversibility: abstract wholes can be decomposed into elements and, when the elements are known, reconstituted into wholes. A level of abstraction is attained also: an adolescent can operate with the *form* of an argument while ignoring its empirical content. At this point, the thinking begins to resemble that of a scientist. Instead of grasping abstraction only intuitively and in terms of concrete operations, an adolescent uses formal and conceptually more adequate forms of thought. (*Piaget, 1950, pp. 87-158.* See also *Bruner, 1960, ch. 3, and Hunt, 1961, chs. 5 and 6.*)

Implications of This Concept
of Developing Intelligence

Some very interesting assumptions and implications are involved in this way of explaining the genesis of intelligence and cognitive functioning. Hunt summarizes these as follows:

1. The process of living is a continuous creation of increasingly more complex structures of body, behavior, and thought. The creation of these

structures is the product of an interaction between the organism and the demands of the environment. Simultaneously the organism is accommodating to the external environment by producing an inner organization of physical and mental reactions to cope with the environment, and assimilating the environment by incorporating what he perceives into his inner structures or schemata. The development of intelligence is the essentially one of continuous transformations in the "organization" and the "structure" of intelligence (*Hunt, 1961, pp. 111-16*).

2. In this genesis the forms of organization developed at one stage become incorporated in the subsequent ones. The result is something akin to "a hierarchical organization of symbolic representation and information-processing strategies" (*Hunt, 1961, p. 109*). Whereas sensimotor intelligence is capable only of coordinating successive perceptions of actual objects and overt movements, such reflective thought embraces all kinds of relationships between objects and movements. Whereas sensimotor intelligence is egocentric in the sense of being addressed chiefly to the achievement of immediate goals, reflective thought is addressed to understanding and explaining. Whereas sensimotor thought proceeds in the direction of actual events (is irreversible), reflective thought can proceed in either direction (is reversible) and can even deal with hypothetical possibilities. Whereas sensimotor thought is essentially private and egocentric, formal thought, by using the universal language and a logic of grouping, is communicable and generalized (*Hunt, 1961, pp. 170-71*).

3. At each stage a variety of new competencies becomes available to the individual, so that in the end he possesses a great range of skills. However, these skills are essentially based on a few basic generic operations. These successive mental structures at once simplify the environment and open up an ever widening circle of possibilities for grasping and controlling the world (*Hunt, 1961, p. 231*).

4. These successive organizations and schemata come into existence in a sequence, perhaps even in a fixed one, which is a kind of order of complexity of concepts to be mastered and of cognitive structures and operations to be built and performed (*Hunt, 1961, pp. 255-57*).

5. In these operations means and ends are not separated: motivation is inherent in the very perceiving and acting, and the ends and means become differentiated only gradually. Hence it is unnecessary to assume pre-existing organic needs as stimulators of intellectual activity, and curiosity may be merely a product of interest in novelty, which in turn derives from attempts to perpetuate and to repeat interesting experiences encountered while experimenting with new means to achieve ends.

The whole process is a transaction between the individual and the nature of stimulation available to him. In order that these transactions be useful to him, there must be a match between the individual's mental organization and the nature of stimulation. Otherwise, the environmental stimulation is wasted, or even channeled into unproductive or rigid mental organization and approach (*Hunt, 1961, pp. 267-73*).

Some Questions and Limitations

Numerous studies have been conducted both in this country and abroad to verify or to question Piaget's assumptions and findings. Some of these revolve around the assumption of a more or less rigid age scale in the development of intelligence. Although the results of the studies differ, depending on the aspect of thought processes or the particular concept with which they deal, generally the evidence suggests that it is more correct to speak of a trend than of specific stages in the development of such cognitive operations as the formation of abstract concepts, the ability to differentiate, and the capacity to think objectively, especially in attaining reversibility and conservation of weight and substance. Susan Isaacs, for example, does not agree with the classification of the steps or their age typing. She thinks that between the ages of three and six children's reactions or perceptions of the world are rather mixed. Instead of being completely animistic and egocentric, children see the social world according to the cultural perceptions handed down to them. They view animistically only the things with which they have no experience but reason realistically about objects and phenomena within their experience. It is possible that Piaget observed a certain type of sequence primarily because he was preoccupied with such concepts as time and space. A different time sequence in forming abstract thought might obtain in relation to concepts that refer more directly to the material of the child's direct experience (*Isaacs, 1930, pp. 108 ff.*). Other studies point out that some operations, such as conservation of weight, may not be attained at once for all time, as Piaget suggests, but only with reference to specific situations at first, and then with experience and maturation expanded to others (*Lovell, 1958; Lovell and Ogilvie, 1960*).

Whereas the Geneva school assumes that the thinking of children is essentially dissimilar from that of adults, studies conducted in this country seem to suggest that the thought processes of adults and children are essentially alike, except for the fact that children's thought is more subject to error because of their relative inexperience (*Deutsche, 1937, pp. 7-14*).

Some recent studies also throw doubt on the universal nature of the sequence in the development of intelligence. Cultural variations in the nature of stimulation for which Piaget's observations did not account may introduce modifications both in the pacing of these developmental stages and in their nature. Furthermore, there may also be greater individual differences in the genesis of mental organization than Piaget visualized.

One would also assume that some individual differences will obtain in the ways of seeing objects, grouping their common characteristics, and relating these characteristics, depending on the experiential context in which the individual operates and the personal psychological organization which the individual brings to it. Since the experiential history of an individual is unique and varies according to what is available to him in his environment and according to stimulation regarding the organization of the perception of that environment, one would expect variations also in the ways of reacting to stimuli and in organizing them: in the quality and the nature of conceptualization, in the nature of abstractions formed, and in the quality of reasoning.

One limitation in all these studies is the fact that they have examined the cognitive development of children under "naturalistic" conditions, which did not include training in thinking, or observing the strategies, sequences, or patterns of thinking under given conditions which permit the study of variation. Mogar and Ojeman both have indicated that experience in causal reasoning has a positive effect, from which one may conclude that training may well accelerate the development of certain reasoning processes (*Mogar, 1960; Ojeman et al., 1955*).

Only recently a few attempts are being made to study thinking or functioning intelligence under experimental conditions, in programs that include the development of thinking as an objective, or under conditions that include a systematic and a conscious emphasis on developing reasoning and conceptualization. Bruner and his associates, for example, have examined the strategies of concept formation (*1956*). Suchman is experimenting with training in strategies of inquiry (*July 1961*). If the functioning intelligence is the product of both environmental stimulation and native potential, there is no doubt that providing systematic experience has an influence on the developing cognitive organization, and hence on the ability to see relationships, to reason, to solve problems, and to generalize. Until more is known about how concepts and thought are formed, what patterns of thinking are possible under which conditions, and how particular individuals go about forming concepts and organizing cognitive processes, it is difficult to project educational practices which are effectively focused on developing adequately functioning intelligence and productive thinking, especially on its accumulative development.

CURRICULUM IMPLICATIONS OF THE CONCEPT OF INTELLIGENCE

The above analysis of what intelligence is and how it functions has many interesting implications for curriculum development and for teaching.

The Problem of Heterogeneity

One problem arises in considering the role of the curriculum in the light of the heterogeneity of cultural backgrounds. One would assume that one task of the curriculum is to stimulate and to discover talent wherever it exists. If cultural learning helps to limit and to shape the development of mental capacity, and if a variety of mental systems are developed by this cultural process, and if intelligence tests further fail to detect *existing* talent, then what is the likelihood that the school program as now organized provides an adequate opportunity for all students to develop their native potential? This question has acquired a sharp edge recently from a double angle: the increasing heterogeneity in capacity to achieve in the usual school program brought about by the fact that more students attend school longer, and the stress on the search for and the development of talent.

The increase in the proportion of youth of high-school age who attend high school also increases the proportion of students whose home environment, economic status, personality, or ability level does not render them good academic material for schools as they are now organized. This important change in the student population brings with it a new heterogeneity in mental systems and motivational patterns. The role of these variations has not been studied sufficiently to determine the extent to which the observed lack of achievement is the result of lack of native potential or of a discrepancy between the nature of the intelligence or cognitive organization of the students and the nature of the curriculum and the whole organization of school programs. It is possible that a certain type of talent is continually overlooked and underdeveloped—partly because of a narrow definition of intelligence and of talent and partly because school programs are ill adapted for dealing with deficiencies of home culture in stimulating intelligence. *Time* reports Horace Mann Bond of Atlanta University as saying that the "culturally disadvantaged" families produce only one talented youngster for every 235 from "culturally advantaged" homes. In affluent suburbs, 25% of all youngsters score 125 or above on IQ tests, while in poor neighborhoods only 6% do so. The reason may lie partly in the narrow definition of talent and in the culture-boundedness of the tests themselves, which underestimate the powers of the slum child. Without the advantage of books and conversation, bright slum children also seem to "get dumber" as they grow older. They are labeled as uneducable and treated as such, by being given the worst teachers, the worst equipment, and the least experienced administrators. Little is expected of them, and little is offered. The students, in turn, expect little and get little. With a dwindling sense of worth they accept the verdict of the school and quit (*Time, 1960*).

The schools may be guilty of challenging too narrow a range of mental abilities and cognitive systems and thus not reaching the deviates, be these deviations of cultural or personal origin. By assuming that only certain kinds of mental activities constitute intelligence, the schools then provide only the kind of activities in which this type of intelligence succeeds. Other abilities, including other types of intellectual ability, may not be adequately measured or adequately cultivated.

Those groups in our society who suffer from a systematic underexposure to intellectual stimulation may need more than the current provisions, which consist largely of identifying talent through intelligence tests and achievement scores, programs of ability grouping, acceleration for the gifted, and remedial work in fundamental skills after the pattern of academic failure is already crystallized. Programs such as Higher Horizons, which offer supplementary cultural experience, are better examples of what may be needed. If environmental exposure is a factor in developing functioning ability, more attention needs to be paid to supplementing in school the gaps in exposure at home. But in addition, shool programs also need to correct the underexposure which results from the fact that both the methods and materials used "hook on" inadequately to the outside-of-school learning of a considerable proportion of the students. Thus, for Negroes and lower-class groups the environmental stimulation both inside the school and outside is more restricted, and motivation to learn is least developed. If the school is to preserve and to develop talent, it needs to overcome early the effects of a barren environment prior to school entry and to develop a curriculum which raises the aspiration levels and instills motivation to learn (*Miner, 1957, pp. 148-49*).

The Dilemma of Receptive and Creative Learning

A serious question concerns the possibility of stereotyping of mental functioning and of limiting training to what J. P. Guilford calls convergent thinking to the exclusion of divergent, creative, or productive thinking. If the public-school programs were to take the development of creative thought and intelligence more seriously, they could do so only to the extent that both were more clearly understood (*1956, p. 300*). A limited concept of intelligence no doubt leads to faulty training and to stimulating only a limited segment of the total intelligence. The almost exclusive emphasis on verbal manipulation is one example. Reading is the chief basis for developing all and any mental processes. Early reading, especially, consists largely of learning to recognize symbols and seldom encourages logical thinking. As a matter of fact, the content of primers is entirely illogical, to the point of even being devoid of a sequence of events. Arithmetic centers on learning processes such as multiplying and dividing, often without understanding the rationale for them. A recent survey of problems in mathematical education points out that one difficulty in improving programs in mathematics is that too little is known about how the minds of children can be brought to cope with mathematical concepts; that the repetition of processes without a rationale for these processes is commonplace; and that students of mathematics, especially in high school, "follow the same ruts their grandfathers followed before them" (*Dyer, Kalin, and Lord, 1956, pp. 18, 19, 23, 27*).

Stereotyping of the mental processes is common because both the materials and teaching methods are concerned with *the* right answer or *the* right process rather than with ways of cultivating a variety of methods for getting answers. Because of both a faulty curriculum organization and faulty teaching, the context in which these responses are developed are cognitively disorganized and the expected responses are geared to the lowest level of intellectual activity—guessing and memorizing. Students are thus habituated to unproductive, closed, or convergent types of reasoning instead of open, divergent thinking and creativity.

When curricula, classrooms, and examinations stress only limited methods of looking at problems and limited ways of thinking about them, creative adaptation of learning is reduced, and the functioning of intelligence is blocked. In his study of the patterns of thinking in solving problems, Buswell discovered that high-school and college students alike had difficulties in identifying which facts were relevant or irrelevant to solving certain problems and estimating answers. They had difficulty in discovering generalizations. They were more used to "learning" generalizations than to discovering them. They used formalized procedures in solving problems as if following a recipe (*Buswell and Hersh, 1956, pp. 133-39*). Data such as these raise many questions about curriculum and teaching. What are the ways to creative and productive thinking? What are at least the most common blocks to preserving and enhancing the initial spontaneous creativity of children? Can one "discipline" thought —that is, submit it to the rigors of a scientific method of inquiry—without also at the same time stamping out the very potentiality we are trying to develop?

The answers to these questions are sketchy, but intriguing nevertheless. The conception of the development of the higher mental processes articulated by Piaget suggests some interesting possibilities. First, the idea of an evolution of the cognitive structures and operations of the mind through transactions between the environmental stimulus and the individual's responses suggests a new angle for viewing the learning-teaching process. This concept suggests an active mind, which develops as the material in the environment is shaped to promote active formation of concepts, processing of information, and other mental operations, whereas much of teaching leans too heavily on receptive learning and on prescription of both the end-products of learning and the processes.

Recently some attention has been paid to activating the cognitive processes, and to the consequences of prescriptive teaching. Wertheimer, for example, points out that prescriptive teaching produces nonadaptive learning, because the rationale for understanding is omitted and the judgment of the learner is suppressed. The emphasis on passive mastery of knowledge also produces the least transfer and is the least creative, because such learning conditions the future learning: the learner not only will interpret the future situations as similar to those for which he has been prepared but is also predisposed to reinstate in the current situation the mental acts which he has been taught (*1959, ch. 1*).

It is possible also that a false concept of the relative role of discovery and receptive learning involves a false attitude toward knowledge. Those who overemphasize importance of the mastery of accumulated knowledge are also likely to assume that the best attitude the learner can take toward the knowledge is a receptive or even a reverent one, and that the students need to "acquire a background" before they are able to use their knowledge productively. Those who emphasize the importance of learning by discovery are as likely to insist that nothing of importance can be learned except through self-discovery (*Hendrix, 1961*). While one viewpoint looks to organized knowledge as a chief product of learning, the other looks to formation of cognitive structures and of mental operations, which increase the intellectual power to understand and to control the environment and to process any future information.

As Ausubel points out, these dichotomies may be caused by a defective understanding of the types of cognitive learning that are possible (*1961, pp. 15-16*). Whatever the cause, these extreme positions seem to create an unnecessary dichotomy between learning by assimilation and learning by discovery, and between expository teaching and training in skills of inquiry and productive thinking. What is actually at stake is finding the delicate balance between what to "give" and what to develop in students. To use another mode of expression, it would be necessary to find the match between the existing cognitive organization and new information in order to determine when discovery should be the way of learning and when a presentation of concepts and generalizations is appropriate.

Of course, it would be unthinkable for the student today to develop anew from his current experiences all the generalizations and judgments he needs. It would seem equally unthinkable to get anything functional out of the sheer mastery of organized knowledge without partaking to some extent in the reasoning that has gone into those formulations. To learn science, then, one would have to be a bit of a scientist, to learn history a bit of a historian. The difficulty lies not in using generalizations formulated by others but in using them without any experience that bestows meaning on those generalizations, or on the process of generalizing. If the formulations are presented to the student ready-made, his own perceptions have nothing to do with what is included or omitted from the reservoir of the past. There is no way for him to give meaning to these formulations. He is unaware of the thought forms in terms of which that knowledge is organized. His mind cannot make them his own, use them to form other ideas, and integrate them into a system of generalizations he already has. It is the experience of *inquiring, reflecting, relating,* and *generalizing* that is important, not whether ideas and facts that are used for material come from the past or from the current experience.

The difference between prescriptive, expository teaching and learning and teaching for productive thinking lies chiefly in the delicate balance between what is "given" to the student and what cognitive operations he is asked to perform. It lies also in diagnosing the points at which to "give" and at which to stimulate discovery. Presumably each new "family of basic concepts" needs to be explored anew by the discovery method, but the extension of already mastered concepts can be accomplished by "reception learning." And the question is not that of rediscovering all the discoveries of the past centuries, but that of preparing the reasoning powers of the students in such a way that whatever ready-made generalizations are learned can be incorporated into a system of thought so as to render them meaningful and permit their active use in further thought. To make this possible it is necessary to help students to acquire a perspective on the problem to which a procedure, a generalization, or a fact applies. He needs to understand the essence of the situation (or the "structure" of the subject) and be able to use from his previous experience or from the experience of others that which applies sensibly and significantly. Teaching for creative and productive thinking must help the student in the reasonable restructuring and reorientation which enables him to see problems, events, and ideas in a new perspective (*Wertheimer, 1959, pp. 68-69, 235-36*).

The Problem of Underachievement

But the chief problems which arise from the concept of cognitive development discussed above are the possible under-estimation of potentialities in intelligence and the underachievement of all students resulting from faulty training of cognitive processes. There is the possibility that both the measurement of intelligence and the curriculum conspire to limit the development of the "higher sets for learning to learn" which could release the human potentialities. In other words, the problem of developing talent seems to imply more than simply giving a chance for education to those who have talent or using what intelligence there is. The problem is also to increase the ways and means of raising everyone's level of mental functioning.

There seems to be no doubt that there is a considerable degree of under-achievement of all students. Many students achieve less than their measured capacity warrants. Miner points out that a considerable proportion of the students (54.6 per cent) are intellectually capable of doing work at a higher level. The majority of students are working at a level at least four grades below that at which they could be working (*1957, pp. 108-11*). If this is true, the educational picture is marked by a tremendous wastage.

No doubt motivation accounts partly for this general underachievement: our youth tend to take education for granted and view it to a great extent as a "ticket of passage" either to a job or to social status. But a deeper reason lies in the fact that curricula are not designed for opening up human potentialities, especially for a sequential cultivation of the higher mental powers, including cognitive aspects of creativity. What is needed is the planning of sequential learning experiences which not only proceed from the less difficult to the more difficult materials but also require increasingly more demanding and mature mental activity. In other words, a sequence and scope is needed not only of the content of a curriculum, but also of the mental operations. To do this, some idea of the possible trajectory of mental development is needed, something similar to what Piaget is trying to develop. We need to know more about the cumulative steps that lead to mature thinking and about the steps in the formation and functioning of higher mental processes, such as abstract concepts and generalizations. This knowledge could be a basis for planning the necessary cumulative sequences of learning so that each level of achievement could be used as a stepping stone to reach a still higher power. This knowledge would also aid in translating that which is to be learned into the thought forms of the learners in order to feed and to stimulate their thinking.

Curriculum Strategies for Productive Learning

Finally, there is need for experimenting with curriculum and teaching strategies explicitly addressed to developing increasingly more productive cognitive structures and operations, and for studies of the cognitive functioning developed under these conditions. Since presumably reasoning and thinking can be learned, learning experiences designed to facilitate thought processes could alter the present assessment of age levels at which certain processes of thought can occur and also the speed with which the steps toward mature reflective thought can be taken. The author has noted, for example, that even in a second grade children can master the abstract "if—then" relationships, provided that the content to develop an understanding of these relationships is familiar to them, and that the teaching has stressed inductive formulation of generalizations by the students themselves (*Taba et al., 1950, pp. 21-22*).

If the analysis of complex phenomena into their constituent elements and the synthesis of discrete experiences into generalizations are practiced systematically, and if the examination of causes and consequences is a continuing part of learning any subject, it is possible that the development of thinking and conceptualization can take place more rapidly than is now thought possible. The new curricula in mathematics and science seem to demonstrate that with certain teaching-learning procedures, mathematical and scientific principles previously allocated to high school can be taught in elementary grades. Bruner has suggested that the foundations of any subject can be taught to anybody at any age in some form, because the basic ideas of any science are "as simple as they are powerful." The condition under which this is possible is that we know how to translate the "subject into the thought forms appropriate for the learner but also that these basic ideas be continually deepened by using them in a progressively more complex form" (*Bruner, 1960, pp. 12-13*).

Once these basic ideas are identified, a curriculum could be built which provides for a continual re-examination and the use of these ideas on an increasingly deeper and more formal level. These basic ideas and the mental operations involved in grasping and using them would then constitute the threads of the curriculum, which are revisited in a spiral fashion until a full and mature understanding is achieved. Building such a curriculum would naturally also involve a better understanding of the hierarchies of concept formation and mental operations. A better understanding of the sequences in the development of thought is important also. If there are definite sequences in the development of abstractions of the ability to see relationships, and of causal and logical reasoning, then it would be necessary to apply the principles of pacing, of readiness, and of a sequence to the development of thinking in the same manner they have been applied to reading skills. One would need to choose and place materials of instruction not only for the difficulty of the concepts they involve, but also for the level of challenge they present to reasoning. Curriculum planners would need to analyze the "levels of thought processes" as they now determine the difficulty of materials.

Conscious training in cognitive processes naturally involves a conscious planning of teaching strategies, and planning them not only for a given moment, but for a longer span of development. If the quality of reflective learning on a twelfth-grade level is in part a product of the nature of encounter with one's environment in the first grade, then the experiences in the first grade must in a way forecast and prepare for the mental processes to be employed in the twelfth grade. If the development of intelligence consists of a hierarchical organization and reorganization of concepts and of cognitive structures, then one phase of concept development, such as a clear differentiation of the qualities of objects and events, is a necessary precursor to the next, and a weakness in one will reflect in weaknesses in the next. The development of generalizations is one example. Generalizations are of different levels of complexity and require different levels of abstractions progressively removed from the concrete. There is a progression in abstraction of the common features which are grouped together in one generalization, such as progressing from "this crystal is soluble" to "sodium chloride is soluble." Beyond these are generalizations which represent systems of relationships and of predictions. This, for example, is the case with the proposition "all whales are mammals," a generalization intended to convey the information that if anything is to be considered a whale, it must fulfill the conditions of mammalism. It must be warmblooded, for example. This type of reasoning is not the exclusive prerogative of zoologists. It must be carried on by anyone who studies or develops this proposition. Unless the student goes through the same processes of reasoning as does the scientist, the sentence is only a set of words that are remembered, but not understood (*Cronbach, 1955, pp. 32-33*).

Developing curriculum and teaching strategies of this sort raises several interesting questions. First, what type of experience must students have on a concrete level in order to be able to discover for themselves the general concepts and principles? Must they be able to "perceive" accurately the "things and events" which are the instances of the concepts and generalizations at stake? Must they also experience the processes of search that lead to formation of principles and abstract concepts? If so, how often must this happen (how many encounters are needed), and what are the steps from concrete experiences to the generalization?

Second, how can one plan for cumulative growth of cognitive processes? How can each step in learning produce the greatest mileage? Often there is impatience with spending time on studying any one thing in sufficient detail for fear of "covering" too little. Yet it is possible that such detailed study of an appropriate example of a complex idea is precisely the way to generate a basis for generalizing and for establishing appropriate cause and consequence relationships which pay off in multiple ways by freeing intelligence.

But without sufficient information about developmental sequences, it is quite possible to rush the pacing of intellectual development to a point where it might cause negative consequences on the total personal development. From the standpoint of content mastery it seems like a good idea to teach arithmetic and algebra simultaneously in the primary grades. It seems logical that one would teach simultaneously such matters as two apples and two apples are four apples, two and two are four, and *a* and *b* equal *c*. But the question is whether doing this will crowd the developmental steps and require too rapid pacing of abstractions, for which the individual eventually suffers. At the present moment such questions cannot be answered, and until they are answered through longitudinal studies, it behooves the curriculum makers to exercise care about accelerating the pressure on mental abstractions.

There are also implications for the way of organizing curricula. If the development of concepts, a capacity to handle ideas and principles, is the central business in learning content, then should content itself be organized around central ideas, so that the organization of subject matter aids instead of blocks such thinking and adds to the impact of a method of teaching and learning? (See chapters 18 and 20 for discussion of this way of organizing a curriculum.)

These are matters to which little thought has been given in educational planning or in research, even though they are at the bottom of the inefficiency with which the objective of reflective thinking has been pursued in education. Curriculum planning takes little cognizance of the sequences of conceptualization inherent in the successive parcels of subject matter. The sequence of subject matter often even reverses the sequence—what is offered on a higher grade level may represent a lower order of abstraction and generalization than that which preceded it.

The Transfer of Learning

CHAPTER NINE

The problem of transfer is central to all education. Whatever is taught produces some transfer, but that transfer may be either positive or negative. Being able to apply historic reasoning to new problems, for example, is a form of positive transfer; disliking history as a subject and an area of inquiry is negative transfer. It is hoped that whatever is taught in school is somehow used in the individual's later life—that there is a degree of positive transfer into situations which were not "covered" in school experience and that limited exposure to the materials students learn in school "can be made to count in their thinking for the rest of their lives" (*Bruner, 1960, p. 11*).

Since no program, no matter how thorough, can teach everything, the task of all education is to cause a maximum amount of transfer. The curriculum always must stress those things which promise most transfer, which create a mastery and understanding of matters beyond that which is taught directly. It is presumably possible to teach or to learn American literature in a way that enhances appreciation of all literature, or to study one desert in a way that contributes to an understanding of all deserts.

For these reasons the problem of transfer has been an object of study for a long time. All theories of learning make assumptions about transfer, but there are differences in ideas regarding what it is, how it occurs, and therefore how to develop the capacity to transfer.

THREE MAIN CONCEPTS OF TRANSFER

Chapter 6 described the chief theories of learning and their positions regarding transfer. These theories generated three main ideas of how transfer of learning takes place. All three still affect current curricula and teaching.

One idea is that transfer results automatically from the study of certain

121

subjects, such as mathematics, Latin, and philosophy, that it occurs by training the mind, and that certain subjects discipline the mind better than others.
Locke, for example, advocated mathematics as a discipline of mind, because
it would build in the mind the habit of reasoning closely, and once students
acquired the habit, he estimated, they could apply it to other divisions of
knowledge.

This concept of automatic and unlimited transfer reigned in the United
States until the end of the century. As late as 1892 the "Committee of Ten"
stated that mind developed chiefly in three ways: (1) by cultivating the
powers of discrimination, for which the study of languages was recommended; (2) by strengthening the logical faculty by reasoning from point to
point, which faculty was trained by the study of mathematics; and (3) by
ripening the process of judgment, which was promoted by the study of history
(*National Education Association, 1893, p. 168*).

The idea that the study of certain subjects assures a general and automatic
transfer, is still alive today. It is evident in certain proposals for the study of
liberal arts as the means for developing the intellectual and spiritual powers
of men irrespective of how they are taught (see, for example, *Griswold,
1954*).

Another concept of transfer developed when, following the turn of the
century, these above assumptions regarding transfer were challenged. In the
famous experiment on memorizing, William James demonstrated that practice does not necessarily "strengthen" memory or any other mental function.
A whole series of studies followed, and all showed one result: there is no
general transfer, either from general training of mind or from the study of
specific subjects. Thorndike and Woodworth, for example, showed that improvement in any single mental function rarely brings about equal improvement in any other function, no matter how similar (*Thorndike and Woodworth, 1901, pp. 247-61, 384-95, and 553-64*). These studies demonstrated
that transfer is possible only if there are identical elements in the content
involved or in the process of training—that is, in the method or attitude involved in the training procedure (*Thorndike, 1906, p. 244*).

As late as 1945 Wesman repeated the original study of Thorndike showing that the gains on mental tests could not be attributed to a single subject.
Using standardized achievement tests, he concurred with Thorndike's original
findings (*1945*). Others "proved" that school subjects, as such, had no
disciplinary value. Powers found that those who had not taken chemistry in
high school did about as well in college chemistry as those who had (*1921*).
Others discovered no significant difference in the achievement of those who
had had general science in high school and a group which had not (*Floyd,
1937*). Nor were any relationships found between the number of units or
credits earned in high school in any subject-matter field and scholastic success in college. In the Eight Year Study, for example, it was found that those
who had had one year of mathematics and physics in high school emphasizing

principles and logic did about as well in college physics and engineering as did others of equal aptitude who had several years in these subjects (*Chamberlin, et al., 1942*).

Actually the numerous studies conducted in the 1920's and the 1930's demonstrated little about transfer that was useful. While these experiments and the conclusions from them were rigorously scientific, they were conducted under conditions in which cognitive processes had no place and which therefore prevented any findings on transfer through cognitive means. The majority of investigations proving the absence of general transfer were guided by a mechanistic conception of mind, behavior, and learning. All mental processes were reduced to making responses to specific stimuli and all learning to making connections between various stimuli and responses to them. Hence the experiments in learning and transfer were conducted on the model of blind trial and error, in which no interference of cognitive processes was allowed. The very tests of possibility of transfer were conducted on mental functions too narrow to permit transfer. For example, although James proved that memory could not be improved by practice, he did not prove that memory could not be improved by guiding a person to better methods of memorizing. Similarly, although it was proved that studying Latin did not improve intelligence, it was not proved that studying Latin by analytic processes would not do so (*Symonds, 1959, p. 38*).

These data challenging transfer influenced education tremendously. Their general effect was to shift attention away from producing general understanding to teaching specific knowledge and skills. The more abstract subjects, such as Latin and ancient history, were eliminated because their teaching could not be justified on grounds either of utility or of transfer. Training in specific processes was intensified, with the result that such subjects as spelling and arithmetic became drill subjects, on the assumption that general principles could be understood only as a result of practicing specific processes.

This theory of transfer also lent sanction to the introduction of practical subjects in which knowledge and skills were offered as near to the context in which they were to be used as possible. (Eventually this theory gave rise to the "life adjustment" programs.) All this, no doubt, served to free the American schools from the rigid aridity of the classical curriculum and helped to introduce a more functional education, but there were also drawbacks. The emphasis on narrow specific training deleted from the curriculum the more abstract subject matter. The stress on immediate utility overlooked the possibility of developing the ideas and mental processes which have wider transfer value.

However, certain inconsistencies continued to be observed regarding the way transfer actually worked. It was found, for example, that in certain areas of learning, such as attitudes, transfer was fairly general. In other areas, such as in arithmetical skills, transfer was less than one would expect from the similarity of elements. These inconsistencies led to still another theory of transfer: that transfer occurs not by means of specific identical elements, but through *generalization* either of the content or of the methods employed in learning the content. The classical experiment on demonstrating the role of generalization in transfer was performed by Judd, who had one group of children practice shooting at fish in water, and taught another group the principle of refraction as a means of determining how to shoot the fish but did not give them practice. His conclusion was that theory was not of much value unless it was backed by practice. Combining practice and theory led most effectively to an appropriate solution (*Judd, 1908*).

A similar experiment was conducted by Hendrickson and Schroeder, with similar results, except that theoretical understanding proved to be of aid both in making a transfer and in adjusting to the original situation, and that the effect of the individual discovery of the solution, the sudden insight, was apparent (*1941*).

Other studies demonstrated that the method of instruction can ensure transfer. An early study by Pressey showed that the study of Latin can improve English vocabulary, but only if the students study the similarity of words and the patterns of their derivation (*1944, pp. 514-79*). Others pointed out that when more attention was paid to the principles underlying specific processes (such as principles for deriving a square root) or generalizations combining otherwise unrelated facts (such as that governments imposed by power cannot be changed except by use of power), not only was transfer more assured but learning itself was more stimulating and productive. This was true especially if students were made aware of some applications and guided in making others.

In a sense the recent ideas on transfer have returned to the earlier assumption of the possibility of fairly wide transfer, depending on the level of generalizing that takes place regarding either the content or the method of approach. The more recent experiments with transfer in problem-solving processes have demonstrated the advantage to transfer of all learning that stresses understanding of general principles. This idea of transfer is now supported by the newer theories of learning, which stress the cognitive nature of learning and assume that all learning is a meaningful organization of experience and response.

Consequently, the more recent experiments with transfer give a play to cognitive processes, because it is assumed that learning which involves a meaningful organization of experience and responses can be transposed or transferred with greater facility than learning acquired by rote. Köhler, for example, demonstrated that apes learn by "insight," that is, by grasping a relationship between the objects around them and their goals. Hilgard and others have demonstrated the advantage of learning by understanding if transfer of learning to problem-solving situations is expected (*1953*).

Others have experimented with the role of guiding students in their approach to learning by suggesting guiding principles or a method of procedure. For example, Craig instructed his subjects to find in multiple-choice items the one word in a group of five that did not fit the organizing principle that bound the other four words together. He concluded that the amount of transfer increases as an increased number of clues are provided to aid the discovery of the basic principle (*1953, p. 66*).

Harlow has formalized this idea into the concept of a "learning set," or "learning how to learn." This learning how to learn transforms the organism from a creature that adapts to a changing environment by trial and error to one that adapts by means of hypothesis and insight (*1949, pp. 51-65*). Experiments with problem solving have also indicated that the main difficulty in achieving broad transfer is functional fixedness produced by previous learning experiences. This is a fixation of perception of certain situations or of their features which makes it impossible to make new responses. This functional fixedness, in turn, prevents these experiences from becoming available in problem-solving situations (*Duncker, 1945; Schroeder and Rotter, 1952; Birch and Rabinowitz, 1951*).

These studies provide fairly conclusive evidence that the ability to transfer learning is achieved not by studying a particular subject, or by specific drill and rote learning, but rather by emphasis on cognitive principles applied either to methods of learning or to the understanding of content, and on ways of learning that stress flexibility of approach and that develop an alertness to generalizations and their application to new situations. Positive transfer, therefore, depends on both *how* and *what* an individual learns.

MAXIMIZING TRANSFER

These ideas about transfer suggest several important possibilities for teaching and the curriculum. First, the possibilities of transfer seem almost unlimited. As can be seen from the discussion of how concepts and generalizations are learned, the more abstract the principles and generalizations, the greater the possibility of transfer. But the actuality of transfer depends on whether or not curriculum materials and educational processes are addressed to transfer—on the extent to which both the curriculum and the ways of reacting to its content stimulate the discovery of basic principles, give practice in applying principles, and develop a set for learning, an expectation that whatever is learned will be used in new and different ways.

In this sense educational thought has almost made a circle back to the assumption of general transfer inherent in the formal discipline and the faculty psychology. But there is a difference. Such transfer is not automatic. It takes place only if there is some aid both in abstracting and applying the principle and in developing the method and the "set" for so doing. This involves organizing the curriculum so that the principles of a subject stand out. It involves also "programing" the learning of content in a manner which enables the student to discover generalizations and to incorporate them in his way of thinking, instead of simply "knowing" them verbally. He needs not only to discover these principles inductively but also to differentiate the level of abstraction which the principle represents and to gauge the possible level of its application. And he needs to practice applying these principles.

This analysis of the process of transfer throws a different light on the role of "hard" subjects in lifting the intellectual level of learning. It is unlikely that sheer exposure to hard subjects will develop the kind of productive minds that advocates of those subjects are presumably seeking. Such a development can be expected only to the extent that the content to be learned and the learning processes are designed to lead to fruitful generalizations, thought forms, and methods of applying these in new context.

There is also evidence that principles which the student himself discovers are understood more clearly, retained longer, and used more effectively. For ages there have been educators who found in such a "self-discovery" the key to productive learning. The followers of Dewey stressed strongly the element of discovery, even though they perceived the relationship of this discovery to transfer only vaguely; their emphasis on discovery came about partly because of their rebellion against the rigid domination of subject matter over the development of mind and partly because of their concern for preserving creative and productive thinking.

It is interesting to note, also, that an "unscientific" concept of "learning to learn" was in currency a long time before that and still a longer time before it was confirmed by psychological experiments. Before the turn of the century M. E. Boole, dedicating herself to making accessible to all children "the gateway to the Unseen," and the knowledge and thought of great men, had this to say on discovery and "learning to learn":

> Scientific education is not arrived at, and never can be arrived at, by young people crammed at School and College with ready-made knowledge; and left to find out, after adult life and its duties have come on them, that they are still ignorant of how to learn what they now need to know. . . . Many parents seem to think that all the time is wasted for their children that is not spent in taking in consciously some special idea which some adult already understands. . . . A child comes into science, not only to learn facts and to develop the faculty for doing things, but primarily to establish relations with the laws of nature . . . the laws according to which the world is governed. . . . As preparation for learning electricity, do not be satisfied with once showing the child that sealing-wax rubbed on flannel will attract bits of paper, but let him have a stick of wax, or better, a common vulcanite comb and a piece of flannel, and keep them, and try all the experiments he wants to try. Let him learn by experience that after a time the comb discharges and needs to be rubbed again; that if he touches the table with the charged comb it discharges at once and he has the labor of rubbing it over again. . . . Do not attempt to explain why the comb must be rubbed with wool and the glass rod with silk; but let him find out that so it is [*1904, pp. 29, 47, 58-59*].

Today there are many indications of a new interest in the possibilities of enhancing transfer both by focusing learning on an understanding of what some call "the structure of the subject" and others call simply basic principles, and on something similar to what Harlow has called a "set to learn." In reporting on a curriculum conference, Bruner pointed out that understanding of fundamental principles and ideas "appears to be the main road to adequate 'transfer of training.' To understand something as a specific instance of a more general case—which is what understanding a more fundamental principle or structure means—is to have learned not only a specific thing but also *a model for understanding other things* like it that one may encounter" (*1960, p. 25. Italics added*).

In analyzing the ways of developing productive thinking, Wertheimer points in the same direction. He demonstrates that discovering the fundamental structural elements of the problem, seeing the inner relationships between the different elements of the structure, and organizing the "field" so that sensible thought can be applied to it is at the root of all productive thinking (*1959, pp. 235-36*). Many new curricular developments in science and mathematics, as described in chapter 12 of this book, seem to be based on the principle of "learning by discovery."

There is, of course, a possibility of teaching either too concretely and narrowly or too abstractly for effective transfer as long as we do not know what the appropriate combination of the two might be. Symonds points out that the capacity to understand principles and generalizations, either of the way of learning or of the content, depends on the level of intelligence and mental maturity. The lower the level of abstraction of a generalization or a principle to be applied, the narrower the possibility of transfer, but the greater the number of persons who can apply it. The higher the level of generalizations, the greater the mental maturity required to understand them and to perceive the possibilities of their application. This means that if one teaches concretely, what one teaches is understood by more people, but there will be less transfer. If one teaches toward higher abstractions, fewer persons will understand them, but those who do will have an opportunity for a wide application (*Symonds, 1959, p. 41*).

There are variations, of course, in the extent to which various pupils can transfer learning, no matter how taught. Morrison pointed out thirty years ago that some pupils have an aptitude for forming generalizations and for seeing new relationships. They can transfer what they have learned even under the poorest kind of teaching. Others show no independent power with new material but need to be taught to generalize and to apply their knowledge to new situations. Still others are direct learners. They make poor showing on bookish tasks, but acquire genuine learning and demonstrate transfer when offered opportunities to learn directly, without mediation of words (*Morrison, 1931, p. 57ff.*).

There are possibilities, however, for overcoming both dangers, that of verbalism—a danger in teaching too abstractly—and that of specificity—of too concrete a teaching. Bruner suggests what some good teachers have discovered intuitively—the need to stress the intuitive and heuristic process to grasp ideas instead of using words as middlemen in explaining them (*1960, ch. 4*). Transfer of learning can be aided also by emphasizing what Wertheimer calls "understanding the structure of the problem" (*1959, pp. 35-42*) and Bruner "understanding the structure of the subject matter" (*1960, ch. 2*). Bruner suggests that for a person to be able to recognize the applicability or inapplicability of an idea to a new situation and to broaden his learning thereby, he must have clearly in mind the general structure of the phenomenon with which he is dealing. The more fundamental or basic the idea he has learned, almost by definition, the greater will be its breadth of applicability to new problems. The capacity for transfer requires in addition the development of an attitude toward learning and inquiry, and toward the possibility of solving problems on one's own and preserving some of the "exciting sequences that lead a student to discover for himself." He points out that the Committee on School Mathematics and the Arithmetic Project of the University of Illinois have been devising methods which permit a student to discover for himself the generalizations that lie behind a particular mathematical operation, in contrast to a method in which the generalization is first stated by the teacher and the class is then asked to proceed through the proof (*1960, pp. 20-21;* see also *Hendrix, 1961*).

Experiments are under way with training of elementary children in inquiry methods. Suchman describes a structured pedagogical procedure in developing a logical and systematic approach to scientific inquiry, which consists of a three-step strategy: analysis of episodes to discover the important facts, analysis of relevance to identify the conditions which are "necessary and sufficient" to produce the events of the episode, and eduction of relationships to state the rules that express the relationships among the variables (*1960*).

All this is making more precise and applying to specific subject matter the general principles which were germane to the activity programs in their original theoretical meaning. As Ausubel points out, many features of the activity program are based on the premise that because the elementary-school child perceives the world in concrete terms, he requires considerable first-hand experience with diverse concrete instances of a given set of relationships before he can abstract or apply meaningful concepts. This premise led to attempts to teach information and intellectual skills in real-life functional context rather than through verbal exposition and by artificially contrived drills and exercises (*Ausubel, 1959, p. 253*).

The above also suggests a need for curriculum and teaching processes which take utmost care in translating "knowledge" into the thought forms and experiences characteristic of the learners. To do this, both the meanings on which generalizations are built and the situations to which they are to transfer must be real to students. This means that teachers must create reality experiences at both ends of the process: in clarifying meanings of concepts that are to form the basis for generalizations and principles, and again at the point of application. It is possible that a concerted attention to the processes of transfer will minimize the current discrepancies in comprehending abstract ideas and relationships and will put a wider leap of transfer into the reach of students of all levels of intelligence, including many who are now judged incapable of abstract thought.

All these possible ways of enhancing the processes of transfer seem to indicate that there is no need to return to sheer emphasis on the "hard" subjects and the most abstract content, and no need to turn our back on the so-called practical subjects in order to protect intellectual development. If we rid ourselves of the notion that the higher mental processes are a function of content rather than a function of the cognitive processes that are brought to bear on this content, we might find an educative potency in a great variety of subjects—provided, of course, that the curriculum selection and organization of these subjects reached for the essence rather than ephemera, and provided that learning be focused on understanding and discovering the basic principles rather than following prescriptions.

Social and Cultural Learning

The conventional theories leave many gaps in our knowledge of the nature of learning. For one thing, these theories are largely based on the psychology of the individual and on the conception of learning as exclusively a function of the biological organism. This conception has led to a disregard of social and cultural influences. The behavioristic concept of learning, moreover, is the product of laboratory experiments bearing little resemblance to the classroom learning situation, which is more complex and which, further, occurs in a social setting and is influenced by that setting.

THE CHIEF TENETS OF SOCIAL LEARNING

Although there is as yet no theory of social learning, social psychology, anthropology, and sociology have formulated many ideas about the nature of behavior and learning which are worth examining here, especially because only a few aspects of this knowledge have been applied to classrooms. Some of these ideas were suggested in chapter 4; they can be summarized roughly as follows:

1. Anthropologists and social psychologists define learning more broadly than is usual for the educational and experimental psychologists. Every human being learns the behaviors required by his culture. Learning is defined as the way in which an individual acquires socially standardized behaviors. Among these are not only the approved ways of behaving and believing but also modes of thought and concepts which direct perception and understanding. This behavior, which may be both individual and culturally shared, has sufficient regularities to make it amenable for explanation, understanding, and scientific investigation.

2. Human beings have an unlimited potentiality to respond and to learn. No one has yet discovered the upper limit of these potentialities. The actual

capacity to learn, however, is confined by cultural expectations, by the limitations in behavior patterns which the immediate social environment considers appropriate, and by the self-expectations and motivation patterns which socializing training instills.

3. Human behavior is largely learned. The human organism carries little of unlearned or inherited behavior. Learning is produced by an impact of social environment and by controls exercised in that environment to modify behavior. These controls are exercised in the light of what is considered to be an ideal personality, the image which guides adults in directing the behavior of children.

4. Human beings learn to behave, to think, and to feel in a variety of ways, depending on the culture which surrounds them. Even the specialization of abilities may be conditioned by what the surrounding culture values and encourages.

5. The learning process is primarily social. The innate tendencies of an individual are modified, suppressed, or encouraged according to social demands around him to produce standardized means by which to gratify the primary needs. This is the process of socialization, or the process by which an individual internalizes the demands of his surrounding culture.

6. Socialization is carried on by a variety of culture agents, among which the family is the most potent. But school, the job, and religion continue the process of socialization throughout life. The more inconsistent or discontinuous this impact of the various socializing agents is, the greater the anxiety that accompanies social learning.

7. Most human activity is motivated by covert patterns, called motives, which are secondary drives superimposed on universal basic drives. These secondary drives are culturally patterned. They are also accompanied by strong feelings and, once established, are fairly difficult to change (*Brookover, 1959, pp. 84-87; Gorer, 1949; Honigman, 1954, pp. 172-73*).

THE PROCESS OF SOCIAL LEARNING

The idea of social or cultural learning is central to all anthropological writing and theorizing. While man is regarded as a creator and a recreator of culture, he is also conditioned by his surrounding culture. Generally speaking, man conforms to culture, and even his deviations occur only within certain limitations, unless some agency prepares him for a creative approach to himself and his ways (see *chapter 4, pp. 57, 62-64*). It is, therefore, difficult to understand either behavior or learning except in relation to the particular culture in which it occurs.

In analyzing the process of cultural learning it is important to distinguish the content of learning (e.g., an American boy learns to strive for material success), the form of the learning process (his family insists that he not "let them down"), and the emotional quality associated with learning (he feels a sense of rebellion about having to "make good"). All three elements have an impact on the nature of the final learning. The process of learning and the indirect consequences attending it are as important as what is transmitted directly, or the content of learning. In this process feelings play an important role, and the feelings in turn direct action and conduct.

Individuals learn culture in several ways. First, certain things are taught directly. A child is told what is right and what is wrong. He is also told that certain things cannot be done until he is older.

Other learnings are induced by direct controls. Individuals learn moral standards and how to behave toward other people by being rewarded in some manner for behavior and tendencies acceptable to people around them and being punished for the unacceptable ones.

An individual also learns by imitation and identification. Language is learned by imitation, and so are standards, ideals, and even methods of thinking. Learning by imitation requires the presence of models, and the effect of these models is strongest if they represent significant persons to the learner. These persons are the cultural agents.

Eventually, an individual will have so accepted these controls, values, and behavior patterns that they become part of him. In psychological terminology this is called internalization. (For a further description of this process of socialization, see *Martin and Stendler, 1959, chs. 6-8.*)

Identification and imitation are not always conscious processes. Social adaptation often proceeds by an unconscious absorption. One study of character development describes the socially adaptive type as follows: "[They] acquire a code of conduct by effortless absorption from their social environment. In so doing, a person may learn what is right and what is wrong without necessarily developing a clear-cut rationale of character values, without being deeply contemplative about what is right and what is wrong, and without working through any particular conflicts. These people are successful conformists and have a good character reputation by virtue of adjusting to people around them and adopting an appropriate conduct as a by-product of that adjustment." (*Havighurst and Taba, 1949, p. 143.* See also *Dollard and Miller, 1950, chs. 3 and 4.*)

For an explanation of how learning takes place, or how an individual modifies his behavior, most social psychologists have adopted a definition of learning as essentially a need-fulfilling, goal-seeking, and tension-reducing process. Learned behaviors are responses to *drives,* whether native or acquired. Drive is a forerunner of all learning activity. For a person to learn, he must want to learn. Drives may be initiated either by basic needs, such as needs for food and affection, or by secondary needs, such as seeking status or the approval of significant persons. While the content of basic drives is universal and biologically determined, the method of satisfying them is culturally determined, as is the content of secondary drives.

But in order to learn it is not only necessary to want something; it is also necessary to notice the situations that provide the occasions and the means for the activity with which to respond to the drive. These situations are called cues. Cues or signals have socially determined meaning. Persons from different cultural settings notice different cues in the same situations, or give the same cues a different meaning.

Finally a person makes a response. The responses that are *rewarded* tend to be maintained, and those that are punished tend to be eliminated. Each culture, and even subculture, rewards and punishes different types of responses (*Martin and Stendler, 1959, pp. 257-65*).

The social context adds additional dynamics to this structure of social learning. The signs made by important persons are soon learned by the child and appropriated by him as needs. One learns to get food by the method approved by important persons in one's environment, but soon one learns to seek approval for itself. In this manner secondary drives are generated. While food is a primary need, desire for approval is a secondary need.

Secondary needs are the most fully culturally shaped. These secondary drives elicit the "clues which determine when, where, and how to act." Secondary drives are acquired through experience of the individual and are inculcated through social interaction with other individuals in the learning process.

> Fears and anxieties, desire for prestige, appetites for particular foods are examples of acquired drives. And, since all secondary drives are built up as incentives in order to participate in a society dominated by a particular culture system, the kinds of responses elicited and responded to, as well as the rewards which serve to reduce the various drives, are all colored by this original adaptation [*Irving, 1945, p. 185*].

According to many anthropologists, some of the strongest differences in modal personalities stem from contrasting secondary needs. For example, American education is at least partly a system of social relationships, in which students are pitted to outdo each other. Such education helps an American to feel most adequate in tasks that he can perform better than—or at least as well as—other individuals—in his group. His self-esteem has been conditioned to excelling. Excelling is a secondary drive in his personality.

We thus get a new concept of need. Individuals learn the behaviors which they think they need, which are appropriate in one sense or another. This appropriateness is defined by each person through internalization of the cultural requirements via the "significant others" in his environment. He does so in each significant situation. Self-image, for example, is built in this fashion. This self-image in turn sets important limits to learning and even to intelligence. (See chapter 8 on the concept of functional intelligence as shaped by environmental stimulation which is dependent on culture. See also *Combs, 1952.*)

These are, then, the processes by which the primary instinctual drives are channeled into acceptable forms of expression and satisfaction. By imitation, internalization, control by rewards and punishments, and direct teaching the individual acquires and shapes a whole host of secondary drives which replace the previous drives as motivation of behavior and learning as the child grows up.

THE AGENTS OF SOCIAL LEARNING

The learning in the process of socialization is always a social act: it is being accomplished either in the actual presence of, or symbolically in the presence of, other individuals. The responses are shaped in some milieu of interpersonal relations. Many groups and individuals are in a primary relationship and therefore act as culture agents to shape the process of socialization.

Because the basic socialization of the child occurs in early childhood and in the family, much emphasis has been given to the importance of child-training practices in molding the basic personality and basic modes of learning. This view is accepted by most cultural anthropologists, but especially by those with Freudian orientation. Many cross-cultural studies of socialization, like those by Gorer and Mead, derive their ideas of cultural differences from differences in the patterns of child rearing. Erik Erikson sets a healthy parent in a healthy milieu as a first requirement of healthy personality (*1955, pp. 224-25*).

However, recognition is increasing of the possibility of later changes, and changes through agencies other than the family: the peer group, the work group, the school, the church, friendship groups, and the neighborhood. These groups, too, teach directly as well as control behavior by rewards and punishments, such as acceptance, rejection, or isolation, according to whether or not the individual conforms to certain expected behaviors.

Kluckhohn points out a transition from one influence to another as follows:

The very young child feels only the impact of his subculture (his immediate family), because the family is the psychological agency at this point. Through its socializing procedures the family imposes its style of life on the growing child. This style of life is that which is common to the social group to which the family belongs and to the neighborhood in which the family lives. However, when children enter school their personality is open to the impact of a wider culture. For example, as the child from the middle-class family enters the school he moves out into a wider society, learns about the existence of

Negroes, lower-class children, Southern regional habits—that is, if the school has a heterogeneous population (*C. Kluckhohn, Murray, and Schneider, 1955, p. 244*).

As adolescence is approached, the values and standards of peer groups acquire an increasing importance in controlling behavior and in developing the ethics of interpersonal relations. McGuire points out, for example, that even early adolescents in junior high school develop shared value standards which define what is true and false, what is to be accepted and adopted, what is good or evil. These standards, in addition to those acquired at home, determine the behavior expectations and shape the patterns of interpersonal relations and the self-expectations of individuals (*McGuire, Phillips, and Peck, undated*).

These shifts in social agents also bring discontinuities in social learning. As was pointed out in chapter 4, in societies in which social changes are rapid differences between the ethics and standards of the older generation and those of the children and adolescent peer groups are common. Additional problems are introduced by the variety of emphases in socializing processes in American society because of the heterogeneity of its subcultures. The differences in pressures and expectations exercised by the home and the school will be discussed more fully in another section of this chapter. Because both educators and psychologists have by and large believed personality formation to be largely the product of early childhood family training, the implications of these discontinuities in cultural learning have not yet been explored or understood as widely as they merit.

VARIATIONS IN SOCIAL LEARNING

Although educators have always been aware of the fact that children bring their families and past experiences to school, systematic studies of these patterns, especially of the cultural variations in them, are as yet scarce. The studies of social-class differences are countless, but studies of how these differences affect learning are not as well documented as they need to be to provide a basis for an adequate school program. Generally less is available on differences in social learning produced by ethnic, religious, and regional variations. Such differences as are noted seem to cross the social-class variables and are in general less marked. The discussion in this chapter of differences in social learning according to social class will be limited to those differences that seem most important for educators to understand. (For a fuller discussion of these differences, see *Davis, 1952, pp. 22-37*.)

Gratification of Immediate Needs

One important variation in the social class culture is in differences in methods of gratifying immediate needs, such as satisfying impulses, gaining status, and belonging. While the school culture and the middle-class culture cherish planning for the future, denying immediate desires for future goals, saving, and planning, lower-class children are inclined to a more immediate impulse gratification: they want to use what they have now rather than to save or to plan for future use. This applies to use of money, things, and anything else that involves the denial of current satisfaction for future ends.

Control of Feelings

A difference is observed also in the expression and control of feelings. While the middle-class child learns to suppress or to control his rage urges or to convert them into competitive behavior masked by social skills, the lower-class child learns to express these feelings directly, to fight back. The tendency of lower-class children and youth is to express anger or joy in immediate, often violent, action. Therefore, their behavior impresses the middle-class teachers as undisciplined and violent.

This tendency to express feelings in immediate action has a bearing also on methods of solving conflicts. Lower-class children and youth are given to unrestrained, aggressive conduct, partly because of training in such conduct, partly because they lack opportunities to develop alternate channels for expression and absorption of such feelings. In slum areas, fighting is a necessary skill to survive and to maintain status. Fighting is taught outright by some families for self-defense and is induced by the pressures of the social situation in which slum children grow up: they must take care of themselves, and they are considered sissies if they don't. Fighting for these children has a different meaning than it has for those who have had the opportunity to learn alternate methods of meeting their status needs and dealing with conflicts. Haystack, a little sixth-grade tough from "under the viaduct," a leader of a gang, just could not understand teachers. They were so funny: they were afraid of "a leetle beet of fighting." Haystack had learned one way of achieving status and control. The way of life in school was strange to him, if not a bit silly. And unless Haystack was helped to rechannel his leadership drive without being asked to rescind it, the school's way would remain a stranger to him.

Surveys by the author on "What makes me mad, and what I do about it" showed almost invariably that the occasions causing anger and the reactions of anger occurred equally frequently among the middle-class and the lower-class children. But the latter were more likely to "give back in kind" immediately, while the middle-class children tended to be "nasty-nice" later, teach a "lesson," or just sulk and withdraw (*unpublished material, Intergroup Education Project*).

Schools tend to regard such aggressive and hostile behavior as maladaptive. C. Kluckhohn suggests that this behavior is not maladaptive, and even points out that "The conception that aggression and hostility are neurotic or mal-adaptive . . . is a culture-bound view of our middle-class psychiatrists. In our own society, in lower-class families physical aggression of some types is as normal in the sense of socially approved behavior, as it is in frontier communities the world over" (*1951, p. 159*). And Allison Davis points out that while a middle-class child learns the socially adaptive fear of receiving poor grades, the slum child learns to fear quite different things (*1952, p. 30*).

Cleanliness, Punctuality, and Orderliness

In middle-class homes cleanliness is considered next to godliness. Children are trained early to wash their hands, comb their hair, and keep their clothes tidy. A case in the study of middle-class children in *Who Shall Be Educated* describes such a routine (*Warner, Havighurst, and Loeb, 1944, pp. 2-6*). Similar routines obtain in training for punctuality and orderliness; the middle class is highly time-bound.

Such systematic rituals are not a general rule among lower-class families and certain ethnic groups, partly because facilities and time are lacking and partly because ideas about cleanliness and punctuality are more relaxed. In one school in a Mexican neighborhood, the teachers were bothered by tardiness and tried to establish "disciplinary" methods to eliminate it. Induced to investigate those who were the tardy most frequently, they discovered a variety of reasons. One boy, considered quite irresponsible in school, had the job of picking up coal from droppings from coal trains before coming to school. The family's coal supply depended on him. If the trains were late, so was he. Another student's family owned no clock. Furthermore, different members of his family went to work at different times, all before he was to go to school. There were no rituals punctuating the time in the morning to remind him of the time to go to school. A third one was in the habit of looking at exhibits in the store windows. When these changed, it took him a longer time to inspect them, and no one had taught him to plan his departure from home accordingly. None of these children was subjected to time consciousness, and "time to go to school" had none of the compulsive pressure it has in middle-class families. Training in school was necessary to establish these habits.

Authority, Control, and Punishment

Several studies have pointed out that the distribution of power in the family varies according to ethnic and social-class backgrounds. In some groups authority is concentrated in the father, while in others it is distributed. These differences in power distribution are presumed to affect not only attitudes toward power situations in life, but also value orientation and aspirations. A disciplinary, authoritarian father figure may cause the child to develop hostility toward any authority, handicap communication, and inhibit the child's achievement motive (*Strodtbeck, 1958, pp. 147-49*).

Variations obtain also in the attitudes toward punishment. Some children have learned to respond only to rather violent forms of punishment, such as being beaten with a belt, while others are sensitive to even a gentle reprimand. Some have experienced inconsistent authority, and others have learned to be hostile toward any kind of authority. The first type may interpret such punishments as being sent out of the room or being put in the corner as a rather pleasant pastime, but for others the same measure may represent a traumatic experience. Thus uniform methods of discipline may be neither equally just nor equally effective (*unpublished records, Intergroup Education Project*).

Experiences with authority and control would naturally reflect methods of using freedom. Many lower-class children, especially Negroes and Mexicans, have experienced only the two extremes of control: an absolute freedom in unsupervised play on the streets and the strict limitations imposed in cramped homes or in overdisciplined and crowded schools. Hence they have difficulty with a controlled use of freedom.

In one second grade in a Midwestern school composed of Negro slum children, a teacher decided to teach something about group work and democracy. The school subjected the children to a very strict discipline. They were expected to sit quietly in cramped classrooms, move silently and in rows in the corridors, and generally to behave, or else. Parents used similar "or else" discipline. This teacher used the project of moving some furniture about to create space for resting mats as an occasion for training in committee work, in choosing leaders, and in election procedures. Slowly and painfully this class went through the procedures of setting themselves a task and of planning how to go about it: they were to move a bulletin board, push some chairs about, shift the teacher's desk, etc. For each job a committee was chosen. But when those who were nominated were not elected, they cried. Then it was discovered that the committee chairmen had no skill to tell others what to do. They could only show by doing the job themselves. When finally a patch of floor was cleared, all the children got out of their seats and started dancing up and down. It took two adults fifteen minutes to quiet them down and to get them back into their seats. A bit of free space was more than they could take; the teacher had miscalculated the limit of freedom they could manage (*Taba, et al., 1950, pp. 184-88*).

Motivation, Aspirations, and Achievement

Differences in motivation patterns perhaps cause the most serious problems in school learning. Getting a good grade and making good in school may be a matter of life and death to some students and a matter of small importance to others. While some develop a built-in gyroscope of getting ahead in school, others feel that what they do is to no avail. Some children have learned to respect authority, others are well under way to defying it wherever it appears. Some have already acquired the prerequisite skill for functioning in the school organization; to others the school culture is incomprehensible or even silly.

Several studies have investigated motivation for schooling and for achievement in school. These studies find that among many lower-class families schooling, if accepted at all, is accepted only for practical purposes. Such motives as good grades, excelling in school, achieving in order to make further education possible, are far less potent than they are among middle-class children, who are trained early to respond to such goals and to exercise the controls necessary to achieve them. The differences in what families in different class groups expect of education are illustrated in a study made in New England (*Davie, 1953*). Class I took college education for granted: "How else could one come to really appreciate life?" Class II took a similar attitude, but wondered whether private schools and colleges were an entirely justifiable expense. Class III tended to emphasize the importance of college, if the family could afford it, but expected the child to become self-supporting soon. For Class IV, education beyond high school represented a problem of getting over the hump. Families in Class V and VI wanted "something that will get you a good job" (mechanic or something else involving manual skill). Moreover, the immediate family need determined whether children could remain in the school or not.

Another researcher, who looked into the aspirations of the "common man" boys, discovered that college education was rarely perceived as an objective. Their perception of college and of the kind of jobs college-trained people held were exceedingly vague; they understood that such people were professionals and made a lot of money, but they did not know any such people socially and had no concrete images of what such a life might be.

The aspirations were also subjected to peer-group pressures. If a boy wanted to aim higher than his friends, he had to accept derision or isolation from those who thought it was stupid and sissified to join the "fruits" in the college course who "carried books home at night." Even those who were good students in grammar school somehow lost their ambition after they got to high school (*Kahl, 1953, pp. 193, 200*).

The problem of motivation goes still deeper in a sense that the same stimulus may provoke a different response. A difference of this sort was observed by a fourth-grade teacher in a Negro housing area. She interviewed the students who made errors on intelligence tests in handling synonyms, such as saving and thrift. One such error was identifying "saving" with "mean." The teacher discovered, to her surprise, that the meaning of the term was perfectly clear. The children argued that it was mean to save because then one could not give anybody anything. The motivation for giving the "right" answer was weaker than the association aroused by the word "save" (*un-published term paper, San Francisco State College*). Similar differences, of course, occur also in what motivates response to content and what seems intriguing or worthwhile to study or to discuss.

Self-expectation is an important aspect of motivation. Some children, both at home and in school, go through experiences which make them feel that they are incapable or inadequate in one way or another. Others are constantly encouraged in anything they do: they are given an image of themselves as a person who can achieve. Lower-class children, especially in minority groups, tend to experience this type of encouragement in a smaller measure, both at home and in school. The self-expectations of the minority children particularly are apt to be injured by the very fact of their minority status and by the community reaction to that status. In our communities they themselves, as well as their parents, are apt to be regarded as less than a full measure of a human being. It is much more difficult for them to build a healthy self-respect or a high ideal of success than it is for the ordinary middle-class child. The world is definitely not *their* oyster. Anthropologists observe that Negro youth have unique personality problems which grow out of segregation, formal or informal, and their culturally rejected minority status. They are bothered by cultural ennui, and by lower standards of conduct for lack of appropriate models. They tend to have a sense of unworthiness, which comes partly from accepting white people's evaluation of their skin color and partly from a lack of opportunities to develop an adequate self-image. Surrounded by rejection, stigmatized and rebuffed by the white society, a Negro youth finds it difficult to develop a sense of belonging, except in his own circle. As a result of being a member of a group whose self-respect is constantly put on the defensive, he develops an extraordinary preoccupation with the symbols of social status.

These characteristics were matched almost point by point in a descriptive study of the culture in a Negro high school in a segregated Southern city. These students' personal experiences were extremely limited. They were hemmed into a neighborhood that had little to offer. For entertainment they had nothing to do but to walk the streets or go to the movies once a week. The resources of the city around them were closed to them, and movement within the city was blocked by difficulties of segregated seating in buses, lack of knowledge of where their presence was tolerated, and a constant public rebuff for being a Negro.

These boys and girls had an extremely limited self-image and low self-expectations. Their ideals were confined to being cute, avoiding fighting and cursing, knowing their manners, and knowing their place with reference to adults and the whites. Offense was given and taken easily. They were over-concerned with physical features in their self-appraisals, and underconcerned with other aspects of self-development, such as talent, and skills of various sorts. Graduation was a time of crisis, because it signified that the time had come to look for jobs which they knew were not going to be open to them, or which, if secured, involved taking the kind of rebuff they were not prepared to take (*Taba, 1955a, ch. 2*).

Recent emphasis on development of talent and of manpower have encouraged several explorations of the nature and genesis of the achievement orientation. These studies have noted differences in achievement along the lines of ethnicity and religious backgrounds, though even within these the social-class differences seem to account for the greatest variations.

It has been observed that under fairly similar conditions certain immigrant groups have achieved upward mobility in society more slowly than others. For example, the incidence of mobility is highest among Jews, Greeks, and white Protestants, and lowest among southern Italians, French-Canadians, and Negroes. Some students of the problem explain these differences by the fact of cultural distance: groups with experience in urban environment tend to possess the cultural values and skills which are appropriate to the American environment. But another, more important factor is the nature of the individual's psychological and cultural achievement orientation. Rosen believes this achievement orientation to have three components: (1) achievement motivation, which drives an individual to excel in situations involving standards of excellence; (2) value orientation, which implements the achievement of a motivated behavior; and (3) the level of educational and vocational aspirations (*Rosen, 1959, p. 48*). McClelland and his associates have shown that this motivation is generated by achievement training and independence training, such as getting the child to do things for himself, and do them well, and that this training varies in different subcultures (*1953*). Danziger, in observing cross-cultural variations in achievement motivation, suggests that high achievement motivation is associated with a severity of training, low emotional response from parents and an increasing psychological distance between generations, suppression of immediate emotional response, and enforcement of discipline and demands for independence. Achievement motive is created by a discrepancy between the adaptation level and the stimulation (*1960*).

The general idea seems to be that families with tradition to encourage children to do well and to succeed beyond the level of the family are more likely to encourage achievement motivation than are families who tend to be relaxed about achievement, either because of their own attitudes of resigned fatalism, or because of a more permissive attitude toward child-rearing. While some socio-cultural systems encourage individuals to strive for long-term goals, others encourage them to put short-term advantages to the family above individual aspirations and long-term goals.

Strodtbeck suggests that a value orientation which leads to high achievement includes the following elements:

1. A belief that the world is orderly and amenable to rational mastery: that, therefore, a person can and should make plans which will control his destiny.

2. A willingness to leave home and to make one's own way in life.

3. A preference for individual rather than collective credit for work done (*1958, pp. 150, 186-87*).

Actually these values represent a formula for success in the contemporary American system of individual enterprise, and as such may be less universal than proposed.

Cues and Meanings

Perhaps the most troublesome and also the least studied discrepancies between school demands and social learnings lie in the differences in meanings attached to the commonly used words, symbols, and events that represent the curriculum content. The particular culture of the child determines what these meanings are. The meanings learned in a subculture do not always coincide with the meanings assigned to them in school. When these differences are not diagnosed, the teaching is misdirected and the intended learning does not take place.

A fourth-grade class in an Eastern industrial city was starting to study community helpers, among them the policemen. In trying to diagnose her pupils' understandings, the teacher asked them to talk and to write about their notions of policemen, particularly what they would do if a policeman stopped them on the street. One boy's story of his views and feelings about policemen was as follows:

> To tell the truth, I don't like policemen, because one day I was walking on Broad Street and I saw a police car on Western Avenue. There were no police there. I waited for a while. Soon the police came out of the house. They had a man and a girl with them. The man and the girl were put in the police car, and taken away to the jail. I don't know what they had done, but the reason I don't like cops is because they are so rough when they arrest people. They did not have to push that girl down when they put her in the car.
>
> Yes, I would have run home if a cop had stopped me fighting in the street, because I am afraid of a cop. I did run away once, and I hid in a house. I was playing on the roofs of some houses with some other boys and a ball went through a skylight and broke it. The cops heard us and chased us. I ran home, but some boys must have told him, for he came to the house and rang the doorbell. I wouldn't let him in and nobody else was home. He said that if I didn't let him in he was going to come in the window and get me. I knew I had to open the door then. He said, 'Why did you break that skylight?' I said, 'Huh, what skylight?' Then I said, 'I ain't seen no skylights, I ain't been out; I been right here like my father told me.' He said, 'You are lying, boy, because I saw you run.' I kept right on lying and he left. I was afraid, just shaking, and I felt like busting out crying, but the cop didn't know that. He thought I was tough [*Taba, et al., 1950, p. 11*].

In contrast, children in an upper-class community in California said that the policeman is a nice man; he helps you across the streets, takes you home when you are lost, and watches over your property when you leave for vacation.

A different approach is needed to the study of community helpers in classes representing these different viewpoints regarding policemen. To tell the students who have experienced policemen as tough people who arrest you that policemen are nice leads them to believe that the teacher just does not know the facts of life. They need new experiences with policemen to extend their meaning of and to change their feelings about what policemen are and do.

A reverse limitation was shown by children in an upper-upper-class community. Their experiences had led them to believe that houses, shoes, food, and other necessities came like air and water. They were free gifts to anyone and having them represented no effort on anyone's part. When the teacher, recognizing this gap, read them a story in which a family had to save pennies in order to buy a child a pair of shoes, their first thought was that it was a fairy tale. Things did not happen this way. After they were convinced that it could happen, they were sure that there was something wrong with the father who would not buy his child shoes. The perception of the circumstances of poverty was totally lacking, and so was any sensitivity to the values and feelings of those who did not have all the necessities. Their social learning, confined to the swank side of the economic street, created an orientation that was as remote from reality as was the orientation of the slum children toward a policeman.

There are no doubt classrooms in which the cultural distance is so overwhelming that even a well-intentioned teacher is at a loss regarding what to do. This is the case when habits, motivation patterns, and content meanings all present a vast cultural distance. A first grade in an Eastern industrial city will serve as an illustration. The pupils came from a transient and disorganized lower-class neighborhood, a little island of white people in the midst of the Negro section of a segregated city. The teacher had only private-school experience. When the class was first observed by the writer, the children were seated in a circle of thirty in order to read by turns and to listen to stories. There was no control, nor was reading being done. The teacher was completely baffled, and had begun to doubt her ability to teach.

After the problem of differences in the background was pointed out to her, she began to study her class, observing and recording what they did, thought, and felt. She noted the following characteristics: These children had no training in any kind of group behavior. Their families did not have dinner together, so that the children had no experience in any kind of social routines, such as sitting down for a period and observing certain common rules. They ordinarily took food from the stove whenever they felt hungry. The adults in the family worked, so that the children were largely left to themselves. They played in the alleys, jostling around, and had no training for organized play. Sitting down in a reading circle was an entirely new experience to them, as was the orderly verbal communication which this routine required. None of them had learned to listen to anyone else for any period of time. While quite obedient to the teacher's invitation to sit down, each individual would get up whenever his mood moved him, and go his own way. In cases of difficulty or conflict, children would simply leave and start going home, because this is what their family members did: when they "got mad" they went to a baseball game, or "went to work and stayed all night," as the children's stories about "what makes me mad" indicated.

Paper of any kind was a novelty. They might cherish a piece of toilet paper, and tear a page from a book for a marker in another one. Verbal expression was very meagerly developed, and being addressed publicly was an embarrassment. When in the sharing period the teacher said, "Patsy has a new dress," Patsy's head disappeared under the table, because being spoken about in public was embarrassing. They seemed to talk with their elbows and feet, tripping others when they wanted to say "hello." The teacher said she had difficulty in distinguishing whether they were fighting or merely communicating. Often she would watch a cluster of children jostling, their faces red and teeth clenched. But when she approached them and asked them to stop fighting, they would look at her in surprise and say "We ain't fighting."

There was difficulty with punishments also. The teacher's usual method was to send an offending child into the corner. The first time she did this, the whole class wanted to be put in the corner, because they thought it was an interesting game. The punishments they knew consisted of such things as severe lickings with a belt. It was not until they had learned to value participation in their group that isolation became a punishment.

These children had learned certain skills but had failed to learn others which our schools take for granted and expect. They had learned certain ways of solving conflicts and expressing their anger. They had learned certain concepts of family, home, and conduct, but these had no resemblance to those offered in the primers they were reading.

It seemed obvious that an entirely new curriculum pattern and learning program had to be instituted. Training in new habits was needed before reading could be introduced. The methods of discipline and motivation needed to be changed to produce more effective learning and control of behavior. The reading program had to be initiated around content which had meaning for these children; materials which drew more clearly on their experiences had to be developed. Formal reading was postponed till April. Yet in the remaining two months of school the reading achievement was higher than in previous groups where unsuccessful attempts at reading had continued through the year.

THE EFFECT OF ACCULTURATION ON LEARNING

The differences in social learning discussed above create many problems of acculturation which need to be faced by curriculum makers if opportunities to learn are to approach equality for all. One of these is the effect of acculturation problems on the freedom and ability to learn.

As anthropologists see it, in the process of acculturation a person continues to respond to the same primary drives and possibly even to some of the same secondary drives. But he needs to learn a radically different adaptation: he must learn new symbols, new cues, and new ways of accommodating his drives. This means that in order to understand acculturation processes, one needs to understand what is involved in shifting the patterns of habits, of motivation, of responses, of feelings of self-esteem and of self-expectations. Essentially, the problems of acculturation are problems of culture conflict, and the severity of this conflict varies according to the degree of correspondence between the values and orientation of the original culture and those of the culture to be learned. To the adult already organized around his own culture, the transition is difficult enough. He must select from the new cues what resembles the familiar and add new learnings by trial and error. For the child who is still in the process of learning his social role, the responses inherent in the transition create still greater problems, and, as a consequence, children are more subject to maladjustment (*Elam, 1960, pp. 258-59*).

Acculturation is usually attended by anxiety which, if accentuated, tends to reduce the capacity to learn. Anxiety accompanies even the usual middle-class process of socialization. Davis shows that anxiety about social punishment and drives for social prestige are the normal by-products of socialization in the middle class (*1944, ch. 11; Havighurst and Davis, 1955*). In acculturation the stresses of anxiety could be expected to be even greater. Reactions to acculturation in a subculture at odds with a dominant culture have been shown to range from those producing little stress to those producing severe tensions or even disintegration (*Allinsmith and Goethals, 1956, pp. 435-38*). For the many groups from our subcultures who have only partially acquired the values and the behavior patterns of the dominant culture represented by the schools, school education may represent a strain in acculturation of which social mobility is only one. This strain may be greater to the extent that idiosyncratic solutions of the conflicts encountered are not permitted, and that the school culture itself is rigid, unyielding, and punitive toward deviation.

For a child in a given subculture has not only learned certain values and behaviors but has also invested them with positive feelings. To destroy these and to ask him to acquire a new set of values represents a threat of ego-destruction and of destruction of his sense of belonging to his own culture. By being asked to take on new values, he is in effect asked to reject himself and his parents. If he adjusts to one set of demands, he is bound to be disloyal to the other. This conflict is especially difficult for individuals who tend to be insecure to begin with, and especially so when the program, in form or in content, offers no bridges. It is probably no overstatement to say that for many children from "deviate" cultures much school learning falls under the heading of achieving "meaningless content, conflicting motivation, and incomprehensible goals," and that many nonlearners in our classrooms are persons with severe acculturation problems or else individuals for whom the rewards school offers for loyalty to its values are perhaps not the most attractive (*Loeb, 1953, pp. 170-71*).

When class differences are compounded by differences of race and ethnicity, as with Puerto Ricans in New York City, the consequences are also compounded. Elam points out that these children face not only the problem of learning a new language, but also the problems of cultural identification and conflict, which add to their feeling of inadequacy. These children cannot solve the problems themselves nor can they seek the help of their parents, and some children reason it is better not to try. Thus the acculturation process and problems invade the realm of motivation: one evades the responsibility for functioning because functioning means failure. The result is a syndrome described by many psychologists as consisting of apathy, lack of responsiveness, depressed intellectual functioning, inability to form meaningful relationships, hyperactivity, aggression, and lowered intellectual potential (*Elam, 1960*).

The problems of acculturation are not limited to those of controlling and changing behavior or motivation. The difficulties of learning the content of curriculum and academic skills are also involved. When much of the content that the school offers has meager meaning for the student and is paced as if there were no serious gaps in social learning which block other learning, naturally learning is handicapped.

As the school population becomes more heterogeneous, both because a larger percentage of an age group remain in school longer and because of an extension of mobility, the problems of acculturation become correspondingly more serious and more prevalent, and the curriculum, motivation techniques, and expectations become inappropriate to a larger number of students.

These facts suggest that the school itself is a contributing agent to some of the difficulties in learning. It creates nonlearners by systematically alienating a substantial portion of the growing youth, not all of whom are individuals of inferior ability. They are simply persons in whom our current approach to curriculum and teaching touches no spark, who are immobilized by their acculturation problems, or to whom the school society fails to give adequate social space and a sense of belonging. Being rejected and stigmatized by students and teachers alike, these students live in a hostile environment in which both healthy growth and identification with the majority culture is made psychologically impossible.

Since there is no scientific reason for assuming that the native potential is distributed unevenly in the various groups of population or that talent is more scarce among the lower-class and minority groups, the explanation of differences in achievement and the functioning of learning ability among these groups must be found in the conflict between the content of social learning and the content of the curriculum, and in the discrepancies between the motivational devices that the school uses and the actual motivation.

It would be easy to relegate the causes of nonlearning to home background and to solve the difficulties of heterogeneity by establishing ability groupings and different curriculum tracks as some current proposals suggest, except for two reasons: the democratic commitment to provide the best possible opportunity to learn to all the children of all the people, and the problem of manpower. We need all the talent and all the intelligence that can be developed.

It seems, then, that it is important for educators to consider the conflicts and discontinuities involved in adjustment to school culture. These conflicts are closely allied to the many recurring problems schools face, such as the increasing problems of discipline and the increasing hopelessness in teaching the academic curriculum to a considerable portion of the student body. Modification of curricula and of methods to help close the gap between social learning and the school culture might be the key to opening the avenues to learning for many more students.

The schools today urgently need to overcome their psychological naïvete about the role of social learning and acculturation in academic learning and to begin to shape curricula and teaching, as well as school life and activities, to the end of reaching a greater range of students and thereby opening up a greater range of talent. There are many indications that the problems of schools have increased mainly because they are not prepared to deal with the growth in cultural, social, and intellectual heterogeneity. Some empirical evidence is available to the point that with a greater understanding of the nature of social and cultural learning processes, approaches to curricula and teaching can be devised which will not only raise the quality of achievement of the current nonlearners, but also open ways to a higher standard of learning by all students.

The Extension of Learning

It is the business of education to transform potentialities to learn into actualities. This involves the questions of the limits of human potentialities and the capacity of schools to approach them. There are, however, differences of opinion about the scope of human potentiality and the range of qualitative differentiation of these potentialities. Still greater differences of views exist regarding the extent to which the school does, can, or should reach for the maximum potentiality to learn.

As was shown in chapter 2, some educators believe that the chief function of the school is to develop intellectual powers. These educators insist that the modern school has overextended itself and had better return to its true focus, intellectual education. Others, in criticizing the pursuit of multiple goals, point to the limitations that arise from lack of resources: the schools have neither the financial resources nor the trained personnel to pursue multiple goals; therefore, priorities must be set as to which goals are to receive the most emphasis. A great deal of current writing insists that intellectual development is one such priority and that other types of learning either do not merit attention or are beyond the scope of the school (*Woodring, 1960, pp. 49-50*). Still others point out that the schools should not act as if no other social agencies existed by assuming the responsibility for all aspects of development and training. Kotinsky, for example, asks whether mental health is germane to education in the school, and if it is, what the limits are to what the school can do (*Kotinsky and Coleman, 1955, p. 268*).

HUMAN POTENTIALITY FOR LEARNING

But there are also suggestions that the potentialities to learn far exceed those that are actualized under current conditions. Limits are imposed on the actualization of human potentialities because both the culture and formal education have not yet discovered the means by which to unlock potentialities and because both culture and education exercise a standardizing impact on human mind and heart. Ruth Benedict has suggested that each culture uses only a segment of the raw material for learning, suppressing or neglecting much of it. She suggests this idea of unused potentialities in describing the idea of an *arc of uncountable potentialities* for response:

> The culture pattern of any civilization makes use of a certain segment of the great arc of potential human purposes and motivations, just as any culture makes use of certain selected material techniques or cultural traits. The great arc along which all the possible human behaviors are distributed is far too immense and too full of contradictions for any one culture to utilize even any considerable portion of it [*1946, p. 219*].

Gardner Murphy, carrying this idea still further, speaks of opening up an "ever widening theatre for the development of new potentialities." He disagrees with those who assume that there is *a* human nature and that growth and learning lure into being that which is implicit in that nature, and with those who say that man becomes what the culture dictates through educational and cultural learning. He proposes a third hypothesis, that human potentialities are limitless, provided both education and culture stress within human equipment those satisfactions which are capable of progressive development and support an active effort at self-fulfillment.

> Such an approach would mean not simply the fulfillment of the known biological nature of man, nor the elaboration of the known potentialities of culture, but a constant probing of new *emergent* qualities and forms of experience given by a system of relationships that can today hardly be glimpsed; a leaping into existence of new realms of experience; not an extrapolation of the present, but new in kind.
>
> The realization of human potentialities, I suggest, lies in studying the directions in which human needs may be guided, with equal attention to the learning powers of the individual and the feasible directions of cultural evolution. Such study, I suggest, will give the esthetic satisfactions, the scientific satisfactions, and the interpersonal satisfactions a larger and larger place in the total way of life, and rather than achieving a goal, will define an ever widening theatre for the development of new potentialities [*1953, pp. 4, 5-19*].

In other words, possibilities for a qualitatively new development are open both for the culture and for individuals in it, and learning can be channeled into entirely new directions, if the "transactions between environment and the individual" are addressed to releasing potentialities instead of a disciplined mastery of "all that one's culture has achieved" or of "measures to assure cultural conformity" (*Murphy, 1953, p. 13.* See also *1958, chs. 2, 7, 8, 11*).

The ideas about social learning discussed in the preceding chapters suggest also the value of a wider scope of learning than has been actualized in school. Contrary to current charges that education is attempting too much, it would seem that it is attempting too little. The analysis of social learning suggests that human beings learn not only facts and ideas but also feelings, behavior norms, motivation, and even personality. The concept of intelligence and of mental development indicates the possibility of increasing intellectual potency by increasing stimulation, stressing highly transferable methods of thinking and "a set to learn." Learning is also multiple.

An examination of educational literature reveals a chorus of voices speaking out for extension of the scope of learning in various directions, among which the need for education of the emotions and for creativity stand out. The tenor of a fairly substantial literature on mental health in education is that however much we might attempt to isolate the task of the school as that of intellectual discipline, we cannot escape the fundamental emotional aspects of all learning (*Wall, 1955; Jahoda, 1958, ch. 3*). According to many critics, school programs are altogether too neutral to be effective in developing deep concerns, loyalties, values, and beliefs (see *chapter 3, p. 43*). Others, especially those concerned with aesthetic development and art education, speak of the necessity of an integrated orientation to life which combines the intellectual and emotional in order to realize man's fullest capacities. Since, theoretically, man is "the sum total of psycho-physical, intellectual and emotional" potentialities, what he knows he could also feel, if he would train himself in both spheres. In fact, it is his historic struggle to arrive at an "integrated life in which he would function to the fullest of his capacities through a synthesis of the intellectual and the emotional, through the coordination of penetrative thinking and profound feeling. To reach this goal—to feel what we know and to know what we feel—is one task of our generation" (*Moholy-Nagy, 1947, pp. 10-11*). Moholy-Nagy warns, further, that without a correlated education of perception and emotion, the latter is a private, hit-or-miss affair which results in emotional illiteracy. One way to eradicate this illiteracy is to use art for activating and expressing emotions, for it is the artist who "produces structure, refinement and direction to the inner life of his contemporaries" (*1947, p. 11*).

Still others would like more emphasis on cultivating "the inward life of imagining and feeling," upon the health of which depend "the quality of our living and the quality of our convictions. If any training of the sense of values, any growth of a deep sense of purpose is to be possible, children must not lose their power to experience" (*Niblett, 1955, p. 107*).

Kubie even suggests that education should deal with the unconscious feelings. He proposes, for example, that after emancipation from the "fetish of discipline" and "the fetish of trained mind" education might pay attention to the "trained heart." It should now be the task of education to carry on the emancipation and to widen the concept of the scope of learning to include emotional maturation in the sense of developing self-knowledge in depth and a harmonious coordination and integration of the conscious and unconscious levels of personality. Education today should master the technique by which to prevent, correct, and limit the "fatal and universal dichotomy in human development," the dichotomy between conscious and unconscious psychological processes. By so doing it should help to reduce the distortion of human personality and to release the highest capacities of man. This, to him, seems the more important goal of education. "My bias in the matter . . . is that curriculum changes and curriculum concepts (of today) are of importance in the education of the head, but almost meaningless in the education of the heart" (*Kubie, 1949, pp. 241-46*).

Cultivating *creativity* is another way of extending the scope of learning which recently has received much attention. Traditionally creativity has been associated with the arts, but whether one believes that the aesthetic experience is confined to enjoyment and creation of art products or that existence itself is only possible on an aesthetic level, as Read (*1943*) and Dewey (*1934*) assert. There is general belief that creative response or aesthetic experience is an important aspect of self-actualization, and that without the creative dimension liberal education is an "empty convention." There seems to be an agreement also that creative expression, like language and religion, cultivates human experience and thus is basic to adequate development (*McFee, 1961, p. 176*). Recently creativity has been associated also with the cognitive processes: the importance of a sense of discovery, the possibility of creating something new, solving new problems, or finding new answers to old problems (*H. H. Anderson, 1959*). Chapter 8 of this book described divergent thinking—fluidity of association, flexibility, and innovation—as one factor in intelligence which has been associated with creativity (*see also J. P. Guilford, 1959*). Sir Frederic Bartlett (*1958*) speaks of closed and adventurous thinking.

Little as yet is known about the process of creativity, cognitive or otherwise. According to Dewey, creativity is at the root of intelligence: "a full act of intelligence does not occur, save as some increment, some addition, or some newness accrues." Involved in this concept is that of creative inquiry which, in essence, is a kind of experience that involves "provision of and a control over qualities that are intimately associated with the mastery of both the method of inquiry and the subject matter children had to learn" (*"Dewey and Creative Education," 1959, pp. 21-23*). Hilgard suggests that creative thinking occurs largely in the context of problem solving and involves originality and the ability to reconstruct both the problems and the method of solving them (*1959*). Rogers postulates that for the creative process there must be something to observe, a novel construction and an individual stamp on that construction (*1959*).

LEARNING AS EXPERIENCING AND DISCOVERING

As one considers the possibilities of extending the scope of school learning, it seems fairly clear that the real problem is not so much in the limitation of human potentiality to learn as in the fact that education is governed by concepts which reduce its power or in the inadequate mobilization of available technology and resources for stimulation of learning, including an adequate control of the conditions under which learning occurs.

Most vital learning is experiencing of a sort. To learn to think, one needs to go through certain processes of inquiring, analyzing, and concluding, instead of becoming familiar with the conclusions from someone else's inquiry. To learn a principle means to see how it operates, what it explains, what it predicts or organizes. To learn sensitivity is to experience a feeling of identifying oneself with something, putting oneself into another person's shoes.

One condition for extending the scope of learning is to create situations which make possible such experiencing in the sense of an active transaction.* Experiencing classification rather than remembering ready-made classifications is needed in order to learn that ideas, qualities, and properties can be grouped and that certain things can be inferred from this grouping: deriving a concept of "primitive" from the process of comparing and contrasting relevant aspects of primitive and civilized ways of doing things—such as using tools, securing food, and raising children—developing an appreciation of art, not from being told about good art, but by looking at and comparing good and bad paintings and sculptures.

These processes are usually either completely absent or inadequately developed in educational practice which is dominated by the ideal of the standardized product and a concept of learning which emphasizes the acquisition of information about external things and which "is characterized by getting the 'right answer' by a feedback rather than by creative inquiry" (*Dewey and Creative Education," p. 23*). This concept leads to an emphasis on subject matter and a subject curriculum which is easy to administer and to teach, since knowledge of subject matter alone is required of teachers. Such a curriculum is made to order for administrative efficiency, for mechanical teaching devices, for easy evaluation and mass teaching. Inherent in this emphasis on mastery of subjects are processes which evoke conformity and diminish creativity in inquiry.

As was pointed out in chapter 5, a good deal of stereotyping of responses is inherent in the socialization processes. As a consequence, the culture in which we live has a vital effect on discrimination, conceptualization, and evaluation. Individuals tend to perceive many situations not with a fresh eye but with culturally determined "glasses." As Sir Frederic Bartlett points out, in everyday thinking a great many generalizations are taken over, ready-made, from the society into which a person is born. This makes it difficult to create novel ideas. Even in science experimentation, the established thought forms and generalizations often make new observations difficult because they put

---

* Experience is a weasel word, used in many senses, including some esoteric ones. Learning by experience has become so much a cliché that we have forgotten what it means. For discussion of these meanings see G. L. Anderson and Gates (1950) and Hanson (1961).

blinders on observers, preventing them from noting the phenomena which do not "fit the scheme," so to say (*Bartlett, 1958, pp. 182-84*).

Present research points out, in addition, that the perception of a situation is often patterned according to the conformity demands of a group situation. Group pressures have been found to distort judgment and to create in an individual a tendency to view the situation with the eyes of other persons who are significant to him (*Asch, 1958; Lippitt, 1958*).

Values and standards are especially subject to cultural stereotypes and prejudices, and many areas are closed to rational thought. These areas are influenced, in addition, by ego defenses, wishes, and desires. Consequently, there is a danger of a limited tolerance of reality, and facts are mobilized not according to objective reality but by what an individual believes exists (*Combs and Snygg, 1959, p. 84*).

These psychodynamically and culturally dictated limitations in individualization of perception, thought, and feeling tend to be further reinforced by the standardizing influence of education, which by being concerned with ready-made answers fosters stereotyped thought and response instead of freeing thought and cultivating idiosyncratic responses. The development of independent thinking is a widely acclaimed objective of education, but in many ways the school curriculum and methods of teaching fall short of freeing intelligence and thought and of generating creative patterns for solving problems and organizing ideas. The pressures for stereotyping the perception of problems and for developing closed ideas and meanings are many.

In the first place, the curriculum, especially in the higher grades, represents a fairly fixed body of materials which forces a more uniform perception of facts of life than is perhaps either wise or necessary. To use the terminology of Sir Frederic, our curriculum deals largely with closed systems of thought, that is, problems to which predetermined answers are sought. Further, these required answers are arrived at by stereotyped processes which often disregard the multitude of idiosyncratic meanings and images of children. Textbooks have been criticized for their dull, repetitive, and unproductive models of thinking. Handlin reports: "With few exceptions (the textbook) is dogmatic and dull, an obstacle rather than an aid to learning. . . . There has been no alteration in the basic assumption . . . that learning consists of remembering and that the function of the book is to supply the material to be remembered. . . . Generally, publishers, authors and teachers follow one another in a frustrating circle that strengthens the pattern. The publisher is constrained by the market to turn out books for existing courses; the author writes what will be published; and the teacher shapes his course by the available texts. The result is endless imitation" (*1957, pp. 110-12*).

Further, methods of teaching in many disciplines address themselves to acquiring ready-made answers and learning "about," rather than to encouraging autonomous thought and inquiry. Evidently, a great deal of teaching seems to concentrate on inhibiting productive thinking. The teaching of mathematics is criticized because its processes are taught mechanically and without understanding the underlying principles and because the "explanations" offered by teachers of mathematical processes have "not the remotest connection with mathematics" (*Beberman, 1959, p. 162*).

Classroom techniques not only fail to set problems that permit idiosyncratic approaches to solving them but are, in addition, often either prescriptive or intellectually chaotic. "A right answer" is sought no matter how it is arrived at, else the student is set to guessing what the teacher wants. Records of classroom discussions abound in such docility-inducing devices (*Henry, 1955*). A recent study of teaching acts indicates that over 40 per cent of all teaching acts are controlling rather than freeing (*Hughes, et al., 1959*).

Actually, right answers may even be less important than adequate processes of arriving at them. If the processes are not sensibly related to the answers, the learned skill cannot be used. Burton gives an extreme illustration of a proficiency in giving the right answer without understanding, by describing a child who could add, multiply, subtract, and divide accurately when told to do so. Since she passed "standard" tests, the teachers and parents were satisfied. But she was unable to use these skills. Left to herself, she was likely to subtract numbers meant to be multiplied, or vice versa. Oral diagnosis elicited the following statement:

> I know what to do by looking at the examples. If there are only two numbers, I subtract. If there are lots of numbers, I add. But if there are just two numbers and one is littler than the other, then it is a hard problem. I divide to see if they come out even, but if they don't, I multiply [*Burton, 1952, p. 139*. See also the description of arithmetic processes used by children in *Brownell and Hendrickson, 1950, ch. 4*].

This idea of learning as a product rather than as process and experiencing has had a peculiarly distorting effect on the teaching of feelings and values. The chief educational means for altering values is to teach *about* values and to use content which on the surface seems related to the desired behavior, but which does not touch the psychological dynamics or reach the motivational springs which alone can translate the ideas contained in the content into beliefs, values, and conduct.

Such practices are almost perfect designs for conformity. They encourage dependence, an adherence to stereotyped methods of solving problems, and an attitude of looking for answers chaotically and irrationally. It must be noted, however, that these practices are inadvertent products of other difficulties, such as lack of awareness of what it means to develop independent thinking, a conception of subjects as a collection of information rather than as disciplines, and possibly the fact that creativity and idiosyncrasy threaten teachers whose own capacities to reorganize ideas in new dimensions are not well developed.

In contrast, one could visualize teaching which encourages learning by discovery by reorganizing and transforming evidence in such a way that one is enabled to go beyond the evidence so reassembled to additional new insight (*Bruner, 1961; Taba, 1962*). Such learning is characterized by active experiencing of inquiry: by structuring the very method of attacking problems, by looking for regularities and reasonable patterns, by using previous experience in the search. To develop this approach to learning, students should be helped to experience rational processes rather than be allowed to arrive at the right answer by whatever process they choose. This approach also presupposes an open-ended curriculum, organized for creating questions and hypotheses.

One important condition for productive learning or learning by discovery is the cultivation of intuitive insight and thinking in contrast to depending exclusively on verbal symbols for understanding. An intuitive grasp can be developed from manipulating the processes and things themselves instead of symbols. Even young children can manipulate the different number bases when they would have great difficulty in understanding the verbal explanations. They can see how the rise of a thermometer is related to the degree of warmth.

Bruner describes this intuitive thinking as the "intellectual technique of arriving at plausible but tentative formulations without going through the analytic steps by which such formulations would be found to be valid or invalid conclusions" (*1960, p. 13*). Such intuitive thinking also means avoiding the task "of mastering the 'middle language,' classroom discussions and textbooks that talk about the conclusions produced by intellectual inquiry rather than centering upon the inquiry itself" (*1960, p. 14*). It is his contention also that it may be of "first importance to establish an intuitive understanding of materials before we expose our students to more traditional and formal methods of deduction and proof" (*1960, pp. 58, 59*. See also *Suchman, July 1961*).

In other words, insights can be "caught" before words come to explain them. And in some kinds of learning insights never need to lead to verbalization. Their functioning in thinking and in action would be a sufficient test. This is contrary to an assumption which prevails in both current teaching and educational literature that the most evident characteristic of concepts and generalizations is that they are predominantly verbal, that they are also used through the agency of words (*Brownell and Hendrickson, 1950, p. 93*).

Stressing intuitive knowledge ahead of verbalization does not mean, of course, that there is no place for verbal learning. It only means that a certain type of learning, such as learning feelings or perceiving something truly new, requires experience other than a verbal description as the first step. Words stand for something. They are no entities. Once a basic meaning is established by direct experience, conceptualization can be carried on by verbal abstractions and through a vastly extended vicarious learning. The vast bulk of human knowledge and experience is empirical in its origin. From these experiences mature minds have fashioned mental constructs which are no longer directly related to experience and which cannot be observed in the actuality. What must be recognized is that learners also need to get their primary insights intuitively and empirically and then extend these insights by means of rational processes of abstracting, deducing, comparing, contrasting, inferring, and contemplating. While the vicarious experience supplements and extends direct experience, critical analysis corrects both. This means that both direct and vicarious verbal experience must be subjected to critical analysis to be fruitful. The mistake of the so-called experience curricula was that they failed to emphasize sufficiently conceptualization and critical analysis because it was assumed that experiencing alone produces adequate learning.

In curriculum planning, then, direct experiencing needs to be part of the learning sequence, so calculated that it produces intuitive understandings of ideas, relationships, processes, and feelings without interposing verbalization until maturity of understanding permits such verbalization to be useful. The customary approach to curriculum development is weak in this respect because the proper pacing of direct and verbal learning is left to the discretion of the teacher, while the proposed materials add to the conviction that verbalization is the only way of teaching all manner of things from the way of cleaning teeth to the manner of taking a square root. Verbalization usually precedes instead of following the experience.

A curriculum which alternates intuitive and analytic thinking, experience and verbal learning, also needs to be a spiraling curriculum. The matters treated on an intuitive and experiential level should be revisited on the level of greater abstraction and conceptualization. To plan such a curriculum requires identifying clearly the basic ideas and the central mental processes so they can thread throughout the entire curriculum sequence. Such a planning would avoid the discontinuities of learning because the fundamental ideas taught on the primitive beginning level of understanding would represent a beginning of a truth to which later learning adds, but which it need not revise.

A number of experiments involving revision of curriculum which stress both the modification of content and the approach to mental functioning seem to testify that the problems described above can have a positive answer. New programs in mathematics and physical sciences stress the analysis of the logical principles underlying mathematical processes and the pursuit of new ideas by a method of discovery. (These programs will be described in greater detail in the next chapter.)

Several programs in human relations have attempted to free students of stereotyped reasoning and encourage exploration of causes and consequences. Ojeman and his co-workers, for example, found that the current content of general and special readers and of social-studies and health materials relating to human behavior is largely descriptive. Discussion is focused principally upon what people do, not on understanding the forces underlying their behavior or causes for human behavior. When the program was changed to include materials and methods of teaching that provoked some consideration of causes of human behavior, the moralistic, rigid, and punitive approach exhibited by many upper-elementary-grade children tended to vanish because the children were able to face the problems of human relations with a degree of rational thought which gave them mastery over their own impulsive reactions (*Stiles, 1950; Ojeman, 1953; Ojeman, et al., 1955*).

Similar experiences were common among the teachers who, in connection with the project in intergroup education, attempted to train students in objectivity through handling feelings as facts, in reading for causal explanations of behavior, and in situational analysis of conflict incidents. They emphasized a method of thinking which encouraged students to explore and to express their own reactions, to compare and contrast them with those of others. This was found to give cognitive mastery over life's problems and improve control over one's impulses and feelings. Training by discussions of stories and life incidents, for example, increased markedly the ability to explain human behavior rather than to judge or evaluate it and increased the capacity to generalize while decreasing self-reference and irrelevant remarks (*Taba, 1955b, pp. 100-38*). This emphasis built up a body of concepts useful in rational interpretation of human behavior, such as concepts of motivation, causation, and learning. Understanding the motivation which underlies behavior increased tolerance of differences and respect for the integrity of the feelings and concerns of others. Because the technique was open-ended, a wide range of personality types and intellectual ability was accommodated and affected. Students low in academic performance showed unsuspected intellectual prowess and emotional responsiveness. The method showed promise in developing understanding of fairly complicated concepts and rendering them applicable to new areas of life. This method of encouraging abstracting and generalizing from personalized experience enhanced both emotional responsiveness and abstract thinking. Greater transfer to on-going peer-group life was also observed. Judgmental attitudes were reduced because of an increased sensitivity to the various situational pressures which operated on individuals. There was also transfer to other areas of study: ideas generated in the context of discussing personal problems were applied to the problems of minority groups in social studies (*Taba, 1955b, pp. 137-38*).

THE CONFUSION ABOUT DIRECT AND INDIRECT LEARNING

The confusion about direct and indirect learning, or what in educational terminology is called direct and concomitant learning, is another obstacle to the extension of the scope of learning. If anthropological and social-psychological studies have contributed anything, they have contributed a sharper distinction between what is learned by direct instruction and what is learned from the context surrounding the learning and from the conditions under which learning occurs. As the preceding pages have pointed out, even in the most traditionally academic school no person can learn only one thing at a time. The secondary drives are always in the picture, if only producing indirect learning. These secondary drives, values, and feelings are affected by the conditions and the climate under which learning occurs. Because these conditions are usually unplanned, they often produce negative learning or learning which is inconsistent with what is taught directly. As one considers the so-called indirect, situational, or concomitant learnings, one is struck by the fact that these processes bear a great similarity to the processes of social learning, or to learning by identification, by imitation, and by forming emotional reactions to the conditions of experience. It is probably with this definition of learning in mind that Brookover suggests that "the process and the organic mechanisms necessary for learning culturally required behavior are not different from the process and mechanism necessary to learn the type of behavior required in classroom," and if there is a difference, that difference is not in the process but in the conditions under which learning takes place (*Brookover, 1959, p. 85*).

A limited concept of school learning also limits the idea of what is expected of it. This explains why those anthropologists who accept a wider scope of learning the culture allocate only a limited role to formal education in changing either personality or culture. Linton, for example, suggests that the discoveries of anthropologists can help education to clarify the problems of performing its two main tasks—to perpetuate the culture and to direct its future development. Yet he doubts seriously that education can change the culture in any but minor ways, primarily because, in his judgment, education can alter only minor overt behavior patterns, such as hygiene, food habits, and techniques of interpersonal relations. It is less equipped to do much about changing personality structure or values, because these are not susceptible to direct attack (*Linton, 1941, pp. 10-11*).

If curriculum planning is to be guided by the idea of an optimum learning, it seems evident that one of its tasks is to bring the whole scope of multi-dimensional learning within the realm of controlled planning, instead of treating some of the most influential learnings simply as the unmanageable by-products of such academic tasks as learning to read or to solve algebraic formulas. This task involves at least two principles.

One is the fact that multiple learnings occur in any single learning act, and that their range and quality are governed by the conditions under which the direct or focused learning occurs. It is quite evident that multidimensional learning occurs in school, no matter how narrow the focus of formal learning may be. An act of learning inevitably generates a wide range of reactions and produces a wide array of simultaneous changes. When the planned focus of learning is narrow, or the conditions under which learning occurs and the methods by which it is accomplished are inappropriate, these so-called by-products can be, and often are, negative. Learning history by memorization may develop (a) a dislike of history, (b) an idea that historic facts are un-fathomable, erratic, and incongruous, (c) a habit of approaching intellectual matters by memorizing the verbalizations rather than by analyzing the mean-ings. The conditions surrounding formal learning can also generate low or high self-expectations, feelings of security or insecurity. One can acquire, for example, either conformist or self-directive autonomous attitudes from the type of questions asked in history lessons or on examinations, and high or low self-expectations from being assigned to a particular ability group.

These learnings are also interrelated. Self-expectations affect academic learning and vice versa. Academic success will enhance self-expectation, and failure will erode it. Feelings have an impact on the development of concepts, and conceptualization affects the development of new feelings. Mental skills are not wholly independent of the quality of emotional reactions.

To make sure that this range of multiple learnings is not only positive but also productive, it is important to exercise control both over the focused learn-ing and over the conditions that accompany this learning. It is possible, for example, to set the conditions for learning a new idea so that the idea is mastered and, at the same time, the student acquires an attitude toward a method of inquiry, a new feeling toward himself and toward the meaning of the idea, and a new set of skills. To foster positive multiple learning means also planning for a complete act of learning rather than setting up a curriculum pattern which isolates one kind of learning from another. The usual provisions for curriculum tend to break this completeness of a learning act. Facts are learned apart from problems or questions which they elucidate. They are learned "to think with later." Feelings are separated from meanings when concepts such as democracy, cooperation, and interdependence are dealt with apart from the experience that already has endowed these symbols with cer-tain feelings. Skills are often practiced outside of the context in which they can be used, as when one learns about paragraphing in lessons on grammar but uses paragraphing in classes on composition. Learning to spell columns of words still poses the difficulty of using the right spelling for the right meaning and in an appropriate context.

Curriculum planning for a complete act of learning, including its condi-tions, poses the problem of integrating learning in such a fashion that the learning acts remain whole, that all specific elements of the learning situation are mobilized and set into appropriate relationship.

Another principle is that the multiple learnings represent different types of behavior, each of which requires a distinct and a different type of learning ex-perience. For example, curriculum makers need to realize more clearly than they do now that the learning of feelings and values involves processes that differ from those involved in acquiring knowledge or mastering skills. Learn-ing them, therefore, also requires the use of different types of content and of learning experiences. Adjustments in the content of direct learning alone cannot be counted on to alter values or feelings. For example, study of facts about democracy in texts and propaganda materials do not change attitudes toward democracy or increase the psychological dynamic to operate by democratic processes. Nor does a refutation of stereotypes by facts change the feeling about them or prevent their use, because the motivation for using or not using stereotypes is largely a product of indirect learning. It is probably in this sense that Kilpatrick insists that "they learn what they live." Explicit provisions are needed to reach feelings, whether in a sense of learning new feelings and values, of extending sensitivity to them, of enlarging the capacity to enter into the feelings of others, of developing an understanding of their role, or of understanding and controlling one's own feelings. Materials are needed which stimulate the learner to experience feelings and values. Learning processes are required which encourage personal reactions to these experiences and which are helpful both in extending the capacity to feel and in developing a rational orientation toward them. In addition, the conditions surrounding the classroom need to exemplify democracy.

The school curriculum has abundant resources for the education of emotions and of imaginative thinking. Literature, for example, by offering a distillation of human experience, also offers significance comparable to that of life. Literature uses special ways to *evoke* feelings (*Loban, Ryan, and Squire, 1961, pp. 121, 275*). What is needed, in addition, are open-ended procedures which permit each individual to identify with such material as novels, films, and even episodes of experience. Because education of feelings can take place only to the extent that the individual is involved and builds on his current experience, these materials need to be chosen in the light of diagnostic evidence on problems students have with feelings and values. Fair beginnings have been made to release literature from the exclusive confines of the language arts curriculum and to make it available in all parts of the program that involve human experience. Such procedures as open-ended discussions and sociodrama have also been worked out for training in capacity to project into the feelings of others, for recognizing feelings as facts to be accounted for in understanding human and social situations and in exploring value dilemmas encountered in life. While some of these techniques were initiated as part of special programs in human relations, they have gained acceptance as a part of curricula in language arts, literature, and social studies, especially in the elementary school (*Heaton, 1952; Heaton and Lewis, 1955; Jennings, 1950b; Loban, 1953; Taba and Elkins, 1950, chs. 3 and 6; Taba, 1955b, pp. 100-38; G. and F. Shaftel, 1952*).

THE EFFECT OF SOCIAL SETTING ON LEARNING

Perhaps the greatest source for mobilizing unused potentialities for learning and for controlling the factors which block or retard learning is the efficient use of group relations in the classroom and the school.

The traditional concept of the class is that of a group that collectively forms only a backdrop for what transpires but that has no collectively active role. The usual model of interaction involved in learning in classrooms is also monadic or at most dyadic: learning occurs in the interaction of an individual with the material or at most with the teacher or another student. Social interaction with peers has been traditionally considered to be inimical to learning and therefore discouraged and even forbidden. In this model, recitation or even discussion is nothing more than taking individual turns in answering questions posed by the teacher or by other students. Workbooks, blackboard assignments, television lectures, and teaching machines further reduce even this amount of communication.

It is possible, of course, to project another model of an instructional group in which learning is predicated on the proposition that students learn from each other and from the climate of the group. In such a model interaction would be an important condition for learning, as would be the quality of interpersonal relations and the classroom climate. Such a model would mobilize interaction and grouping on behalf of the direct learning tasks, such as solving mathematical problems. It would also look to the group climate as a source for extending the scope of learning.

The preceding chapters have elaborated on the social sources of much of learning. Chapter 8 pointed out that the very formation of a functioning intelligence is largely a social process. It occurs in interaction with other individuals, and its channeling is affected by the degree of stimulation in that interaction. The preceding sections of this chapter pointed out, in addition, that many so-called intangible or indirect learnings, such as acquiring a democratic outlook or developing a cosmopolitan sensitivity, are generated by the quality of interpersonal relations that surround the learner. It seems, then, that the social setting in which classroom learning occurs represents an array of factors which affect productivity of all learning and constitutes a direct source for certain kinds of desirable learning. Studies of group relations—of the structure of groups and their dynamics, of the processes of learning and achieving productivity and the psychological effect of groups on individuals—have aroused considerable interest among educators. There have been efforts to introduce group processes as teaching techniques. Countless sociometric studies of the structure of classroom groups have been made. Many researchers have studied the relationships between the social status of individuals in groups and their adjustment and achievement (*Gronlund, 1959; Jennings, 1959; Taba et al., 1955*).

Possibly because of the imperfect theoretical synthesis of the science of group dynamics, these borrowings are in the nature of gadgeteering, of using the spectacular techniques. The basic concepts of group dynamics have not yet become as prominent a part of educational process as they might. The avalanche of sociometric testing has resulted in only a few experiments with sociometric grouping, and the consideration of using classroom dynamics plays as yet only a small role among the means used to attain certain educational objectives. Seldom is the social setting considered as a factor in planning for improvement in learning. Many current plans for curriculum improvement not only overlook but reject outright the possibility of a role for the social dynamics in learning. Only recently has there been an effort to translate the knowledge from studies of groups into a systematic view of the dynamics of instructional groups and to suggest a theory of viewing classroom groups as social systems of some consequence to the practice of education (*National Society for the Study of Education, 1960*).

Kurt Lewin first recognized the role of group dynamics in social change and learning. He insisted that groups, including the classroom, have a dynamic of their own and develop a "climate" of their own. The social climate in which children learn affects them as does the air which they breathe: it governs their productivity and determines the content of their secondary learning. Each individual in a group, furthermore, has a different life space. On this life space depend such developments as ego-expectations, role expectations, anxiety and security in performing learning tasks, motivation, and possibly the very level and quality of learning. Lewin's own pioneering study of group climate demonstrated the effect of three different climates on behavior, productiveness, and standards (*Lewin and Lippitt, 1958*). He pointed out further that the real dynamic of education does not reside in programs but in the conditions which constitute the influence of education on the behavior, the personality, and the ideals of the growing child (*Lewin, 1945, pp. 4-5*).

Following this start there has been a veritable avalanche of studies in group relations.* Some of these studies examine the effects of group structure, and of the climate produced by it on productiveness in groups. Others deal with the nature of the dynamics and of learning in small groups. Still others explore the nature of roles performed, including that of leadership (*Cartwright and Zander, 1960; Hare, Borgatta, and Bales, 1955; Jennings, 1950a*).

GROUP RELATIONS
IN THE CLASSROOM

The general ideas about the socio-psychological dynamics of groups might be summarized as follows: Whenever two or more persons come together a system of social interaction begins to emerge. Networks of relationships are built, based on accepting some persons, rejecting others, and overlooking still others. Thus a system of social status emerges: some individuals are important to many, have a strong social status and a sense of belonging, and others are outsiders, either overlooked or rejected. Groups also adopt role expectations for their members. Some are expected to

* A summary of these studies is available in the *Review of Educational Research, (1959).*

lead, to succeed, to play positive roles. Others are expected to follow, to be nonachievers, rebels, or goofers. There are also group "floors" to expectations —norms of behavior which individuals cannot violate and still belong. A system of social relations also generates group motives, expectations, purposes, values, and ideals, a composite which is often referred to as group climate. If the expectations are high, a climate conducive to learning will result. If the group values individual differences, the available social space is extended and idiosyncrasies and deviations are tolerated and permitted a positive role. In reverse, a group which values conformity and uniformity develops a climate intolerant of deviation, be it in conduct or in ability. The availability of roles is narrowed and interaction is hemmed in by exclusiveness or narrowness of scope.

Such characteristics are true of classrooms as well as other small groups. Classrooms, too, have social structures, and the networks of interpersonal relations are part of this structure. Jensen differentiates several dimensions, among which are the following: work relationships, which are closely related to progress toward educational objectives; authority relationships, which determine who makes decisions and the way in which they are made; social acceptance relationships, which determine who has social acceptance and influence in the group (1960, pp. 92-95). The networks of social acceptance and rejection represent an informal social order of the classroom, in contrast to the formal order expressed in the organization of the school. This informal order includes the patterns of human relations, the channels of informal communication, the system of belonging and non-belonging (Dahlke, 1958, parts III and IV).

This system of interpersonal relations is only one of the "cultures" of the school. Getzels and Thelen describe three such systems. One is the system of norms and role expectations, standards and values which the school follows because it is a social institution with certain responsibilities and obligations. This is the institutional culture of the school. In addition to that, the school and the class have a social climate which is generated by unofficial peer culture. This climate also imposes norms, expectations, values, and patterns of conduct. Finally, these groups are composed of individuals with certain personality structures, need motivations, and dispositions. Individuals are subject to demands and pressures from all these norms and expectations. Often the three types of demands are in conflict with each other. The values of the culture outside the school may conflict with the institutional requirements of the school. Conflicts may exist between the goals of the school as an official institution and the expectations of the unofficial peer culture. Both may be at odds with the personality needs and dispositions of individuals (Getzels and Thelen, 1960, pp. 68-82).

THE EFFECT OF SOCIAL CLIMATE ON LEARNING

The social structure and the climate of an instructional group affect learning in many ways. They affect participation and communication; the networks of interpersonal relations are in effect communication lines. In classrooms with open networks of interpersonal relations the lines of communication are open. Classrooms beset with interpersonal cleavage are also characterized by blocked communication. Communication and interaction generate a task orientation which makes it possible for one individual to stimulate another or to extend the ideas offered by another. In a classroom with blocked communication this is impossible. Ideas offered by a rejected person, for example, are not "heard," or are rejected regardless of their merits. Similar blocking of communication occurs when strong stereotypes enter, such as a notion of a teacher "who is after you," or of other students as competitive and threatening. Furthermore, within any group, access to communication lines as well as to gratifying roles are distributed unevenly.

The social climate of instructional groups also affects motivation to learn, sets the levels of aspirations and the norms for behavior, and defines the limits for ego expectations and roles. For example, powerful group forces operate on the unaccepted child, and these forces influence not only his motivational system but also his functioning capacity to learn. Since peer relationships are important, especially to adolescents, they can absorb or release their energy and erode or create motivation to learn. An instructional group, for example, may or may not be achievement-oriented. If it is not, a teacher may have difficulty in stimulating adequate effort. It may be divisive, or congenial and supportive. It may provide need fulfillment to many or be ego erosive, develop common purposes or not, permit a sense of belonging or not. The climate of a classroom also defines the life space that is available to individuals. Some classroom groups have low tolerance of diversity. Students who deviate from the norm, including those of higher or lower than average ability, are cut out from communication lines, from the common stream of ideas, and therefore also from the motivation generated by peer support and expectation. There may be differences in the eligibility of individuals for gratification. Productive roles may be available to many or to only a few (*Jensen, 1960, p. 105*). Differences in mental systems and creative approaches to learning tasks may be encouraged or devalued. In many routinized and standardized classrooms any difference or idiosyncrasy becomes an irritation and a disturbance. Getzels and Jackson's study suggests that truly creative individuals are especially subject to rejection by teachers as well as students (*Getzels and Thelen, 1960*).

A poor climate and cleavage-ridden interpersonal relations also create anxieties which, as several studies demonstrate, narrow perception, which in turn retards the ability to learn (*Beam, 1955, pp. 549-50*). Discipline and task orientation are affected also. In hostile, disrupted classrooms, or class-rooms in which interaction with significant persons is blocked, individuals tend to spend their time and energy in making their presence known, projecting their ego needs, indulging in attention-getting devices, and blocking the task-centered activities. Such a climate immobilizes mental activity, dissipates effort, and diverts attention from the task. In one twelfth-grade classroom, for example, over 50% of the discussion time in a history review lesson was spent in arguing with Joe, or talking down Joe, whose smart remarks provoked the class. The learning efficiency of the class was thus cut in half (*unpublished term project, San Francisco State College*).

Empirical evidence indicates that instructional groups with amenable interpersonal relations, open communication lines, and an ego-supportive climate stimulate self-actualization and achievement motivation, and through supportiveness aid individuals in their struggle for status and self-respect even when home conditions are unfavorable (see *Taba, 1955b, chs. 3 and 4,* for a description of the effect on individuals of a favorable social structure and value system in one classroom).

Such a group is also capable of task-centeredness and of a sense of re-sponsibility. It enhances motivation by adding to the stimulus which indi-viduals can marshal for themselves or which the teacher can communicate. The author has observed many classrooms in which group thinking produces by cross-stimulation chains of ideas which reach a fullness and maturity no single individual could achieve alone or with only the help of the teacher. Oeser reports that learning of difficult subjects, such as mathematics and physics, proceeds more efficiently in small groups in which interaction is permitted and used to set standards of performance and to plan appropriate approaches to the tasks. Small group work enhanced the morale—the liking for the subject, self-imposed discipline, voluntary homework—all of which enabled the class to cover the curriculum of two years in only one (*Oeser, 1960, p. 267*).

Studies are in progress to determine the effect of social climate and of the quality of peer association on achievement. McGuire, for example, is work-ing on the hypothesis that educability is only partly a function of academic ability. One condition among several others which makes it possible for stu-dents to translate their academic potential into achievement is the quality of their peer affiliation. Peer affiliations determine "both the motivational orien-tation and the values which permit the ability to be translated into 'academic potential'" (*McGuire, 1956*).

Several studies have been made which have demonstrated that group-centered learning can be more productive, at least with certain kinds of tasks (*Berkowitz and Levy, 1956; French and Thomas, 1948; Haigh and Schmidt, 1956; McKeachie, 1958*). These studies leave no doubt that the social cli-mate and interpersonal relations in the classroom have a powerful effect on achievement. This effect alone is sufficient to suggest the necessity of planning the patterns of interpersonal relations at least as carefully as the content of what is taught. It suggests also that the major barriers to changing a student's behavior may lie in the nature of the classroom group rather than in the individual student. "To deal effectively with the child may require isolating the group forces that work on him and inducing change in the norms of cliques" (*Gross, 1959, p. 281*).

These studies concern largely the effects of the social structure of instructional groups on academic achievement. Practically no attention has been paid to using a knowledge of the structure of group relations and the climate in classrooms as a basis for extending the scope of learning—for a more effective impact in areas of learning in which at present the school is ineffectual, or which are even considered to be beyond the power of the school.

In the beginning of this chapter it was pointed out that to extend the scope of learning, more conscious planning of experiences was necessary for learning feelings and values and for approximating the conditions for social learning. The social climate of the instructional groups and of the school is precisely such a source of experiences and such a condition. The social climate of the classroom is a way of life which approximates the conditions of social learning in the family and in out-of-school peer relations. Students as part of a school group learn values, feelings, and orientation to life in practically the same manner—by internalization, imitation, and social pressures. There are significant persons among peers in school as well as in the family to provide models, and the social rewards and punishments are as influential. Students adopt goals such as being a good achiever, a rebel, a popular guy, a cooperative and responsible human being, according to how these goals are socially valued. Consequently, depending on the climate, the school or the classroom can contribute to the development of social sensitivity or social perception, either negatively or positively. The classroom group and the school can be a laboratory of human relations in which students can extend their ability to perceive the feelings and viewpoints of others, especially if the classroom is a heterogeneous one. Opportunities can be provided for developing such social skills as using authority democratically, moving from dissension to consensus, subordinating personal wishes to the requirements of the task, and assuming a responsible role and self-imposed discipline. Because peer association is an acknowledged source of values and standards, the interpersonal relations in the classroom can aid in developing a moral code and in giving reality to the ideal of democratic human relations.

To make use of the potentialities of the social setting of the instructional groups, several lines of action are needed. One is a more careful diagnosis of the social structure and the dynamics of the instructional group to identify more accurately the erosive effects of conflict and tension which block the effectiveness of the school, but more importantly, to discover new sources for extending the scope of learning. This extension of learning may include such things as self-definition through clarification of experience and establishment of self-esteem, suggested by Friedenberg as being among the moral responsibilities of the school as an institution responsible for the welfare of youth as social human beings (*1959, chs. 3 and 4*).

It has been pointed out that while the classroom psychodynamic is a real one, under current conditions this dynamic is neither mature nor completely autonomous and hence on its own cannot be expected to be fully educative. To make it an educative force, the conditions producing it need to be planned and used thoughtfully (*Downey, 1960, p. 257*).

The interpersonal structure of the classroom groups, their social climate, dynamics, and morale, need not be an accident. They can be planned, provided the factors which produce them are known. Thelen, for example, points out that it would be important to make a classroom group rather than the gang or a clique an important reference group for the students. Students could then establish standards and release their intelligence, strivings, and motivations in the classroom rather than elsewhere and on behalf of learning rather than for other ends (*1959, pp. 77-78*). Social relationships probably are manageable at least in the same extent that the work relationships are managed now. The authority and leadership patterns can be modified to produce greater involvement. As far as values and standards are concerned, the influence of the peer group is probably even greater than that of the teacher and parents. Currently the tenor of these values tends to be independent of and even in opposition to that which the school emphasizes, but with greater attention to the study and management of the peer-group climate it could probably be brought to a more constructive role. At least the evidence from quite a number of classrooms suggests that this is possible (*Taba and Elkins, 1950, ch. 7; Taba, 1955b; Taba et al., 1950, chs. 5 and 6*).

GROUPING AS A FACTOR IN FACILITATING LEARNING

Grouping is one factor in creating classroom climate which deserves special attention, especially since the problems of grouping have drawn considerable fire recently because of an increased emphasis on ability grouping and on the segregation of both the gifted and the retarded. The chief purpose of these efforts is to make the instructional groups more homogeneous under the assumption that homogeneity in ability is a necessary condition for effective teaching and learning. It seems, however, that the arguments for both heterogeneous and homogeneous grouping as well as research on either rest on a limited analysis of what is involved. First, only the factors of intelligence and academic achievement are considered. This, as was pointed out earlier, is insufficient even from the standpoint of accounting for important abilities.

Second, the chief assumption underlying ability grouping seems to be that academic learning is facilitated when everyone in the group has a nearly equal capacity to grasp the content. This is a necessary condition for successful learning only if the program is uniform in content and pacing and uses closed methods of teaching. Both of these conditions are prevalent enough, but do not have to be so. When teachers can formulate open-ended learning tasks capable of being handled on several levels and can compose small groups by following the lines of relationships and communication among the members, heterogeneity becomes an asset rather than a handicap. Differences and independence in perception and thinking need not be abrogated, except under conditions which require a forced consensus as an end outcome, or under very standardized procedures. These differences can enhance the quality of perception by all members of the group, because they correct errors and steer the social process in accordance with felt requirement.

Third, these methods of grouping assume that homogeneity of ability enhances all varieties of learning. It was shown earlier that there are types of learning—sensitivity to human relations being one—in which a diversity of levels of perception and of the content of social learning add to the end product. Finally, those who favor the practice of homogeneous grouping completely overlook the rather grave social and psychological consequences: the effects on the self-conceptions of individuals, on group climate and, above all, on social stratification in school. An interesting analysis of this aspect is made by Bettelheim (*1958*). In his study of gifted children, Haggard also found adverse effects on group climate and on individuals from the pressure for high achievement that ability grouping tends to create. When pressures for achievement by parents, peers, and teachers converge, some individuals can stand up under it; others become tense, anxious, rebellious, or guilty and perform less productively than they might under a more relaxed regime. All develop hostility toward adults (1957).

This discussion of group relations suggests that grouping of students for instructional purposes is a more serious matter than merely providing for teaching convenience or acceleration of academic learning. It has wider consequences than have been perceived, and it is capable of greater contribution than is visualized. Hence, more thought needs to be given to analyzing both the purposes which grouping can serve and the basis or criteria for managing it.

Although there may be a variety of reasons for grouping, the essential one is to facilitate learning, and learning of the widest possible scope. Grouping could be considered an important part of the strategy to create conditions for aiding not only academic learning but also the type of learning for which direct teaching is ineffective. If, for example, it is important to learn democratic values, adequate self-expectation, sensitivity to how other persons feel and think, and a sense of a responsible role in a common undertaking, and if experiencing is an important ingredient of these types of learning, then grouping individuals together who can serve as stimulants and models to each other would be highly relevant. It is not unreasonable to expect that grouping together with thoughtfully planned interaction around a variety of learning tasks from performing chemistry experiments to reading and reacting to literature could markedly extend the capacity to learn and the scope of possible learning.

In grouping for such purposes complementation which takes account of differences rather than similarities may have to be the chief principle, and developing group cohesion and adequate social space not only to accommodate but also to aid and abet individual differences may have to be the chief characteristics to strive for. For example, a student with low self-expectation may be helped by another who can be supportive; one who needs acceptance needs someone who can pay attention to him and treat him as a human being. Such complementation does more than provide for "social adjustment." It provides a setting for releasing intelligence, for motivation to learn, and for acquiring values and orientation to life. In several experiments such an effort to form small groups by complementation of needs and to provide association and interaction in small work groups within the usual arbitrarily composed class group brought remarkable results in achievement and in group morale and a strong impact on values. The analysis of one instructional group in which this principle of composing small work groups within the class was observed and in which much of the study and work involved interaction suggested that with fair understanding of the group and with a reasonable effort at creating a psychologically favorable climate and psychologically sound sequences for learning, the school can be fairly effective in modifying at least the socially conditioned aspects of personality and in controlling and counteracting some rather potent social learning. It is possible that the school program, by focusing on values, can make itself a powerful force for education in democratic human values. (See *Taba, 1955b, pp. 28-44 and 95-99* for discussion of these factors, individual cases, and the description of group climate.)

The principle of grouping for psychological cohesion and for complementation can be applied to grouping for work also. A working group may be put together to assemble the needed intellectual and social resources by a designed heterogeneity. The best group for this purpose is the smallest one that encompasses the needed resources. Experimentation with small work groups on two criteria—a designed heterogeneity in abilities, skills, and resources and a psychological cohesiveness—has brought reports of greatly heightened learning, partly because grouping by psychological cohesiveness greatly reduces the irrelevant activities and discipline problems and partly because the climate induced increased motivation as well as increased cross-fertilization of ideas (*Taba et al., 1950, pp. 177-83*). The author knows of only one attempt to compose classroom groups within a grade by accounting for sociometric choice patterns and in addition by matching teachers and students (*unpublished report by Eleanor Crouch, Director of Curriculum, Carmel Public Schools, Carmel, California*).

The above analysis suggests several general points about grouping. First, it seems idle to talk about grouping in general. Manageable productive and dynamic learning groups can be put together only in the light of the specific purpose, the specific situations, and the nature of learning processes employed. It makes, for example, a great deal of difference how rigid and uniform the learning situation is, whether it requires participation and interaction or not, and how much self-expression is desired. Further, it is necessary to match the techniques of learning and teaching to the kind of grouping employed. If a teacher uses small groups and then expects to proceed as usual, making the same type of assignments and organizing the learning processes in the same manner, grouping will have little bearing on achievement or anything else. Only when a carefully considered grouping pattern is accompanied by appropriate ways of teaching-learning experiences can one expect an increased productivity of learning.

It seems clear also that multiple rather than single criteria need to be employed for designing groups if productivity and extension of the scope of learning and the creation of adequate social and emotional space are to be the outcomes. Classrooms composed exclusively by expedience and convenience of scheduling can easily contain groups composed of human ingredients which are impossible to manage or which create an unhealthy social environment. The idea of reducing differences by homogenizing groups on a single basis is always an illusion, as homogeneity in any one respect is bound to introduce heterogeneities in many others. Reducing heterogeneity also impoverishes the stimulation for learning by reducing the variety of background and experience. It is an asset only in learning tasks in which uniformity in content and in pace is desirable.

It seems also that groups are more productive when they (a) share purposes, (b) are trained in productive procedures, and (c) are composed to produce a climate which provides a latitude of social space and supportiveness. If the psychological structure of the group supports communication and participation, the difficulties encountered in learning tasks are more easily overcome and the communication of learning from person to person and across the social divisions is facilitated. This has been demonstrated by many empirical experiments. Teachers who have used sociometric analysis to aid them in composing work groups, who have trained their students in the processes of shared thought and action, who have developed in their classrooms some literacy about human relations, have found that their classes operate on a vastly higher level of performance, that they have a greater capacity to perceive abstractions, a better grasp of rational processes, and a higher productivity and efficiency in using time and talent. Evidently the classrooms which capitalize on group settings, group processes, and the psychological potentialities of group interaction develop a level of performance that classrooms predicated on individualistic and isolated performance and on elementaristic notions of learning could not possibly produce. This has a special bearing on classrooms composed of individuals with heterogeneous social learning. In such classrooms, the intelligent use of scientific grouping based on planned heterogeneity can be a new source for creating a learning dynamic which is practically impossible to achieve in classrooms composed and conducted in the traditional fashion.

Finally, any efforts to manage the group climate for whatever purposes must take care to avoid conditions that induce conformity. As Asch points out, shared action that rests upon the voluntary or involuntary suppression of individual experience is a malignant social process which "produces the basis for mass submission to any, even a frightful, Weltanschauung." When the purposes and the ideas of a group rest upon the insight of its individual members, group action and thought can have an entirely different dynamic (*Asch, 1952, p. 492*). It is possible to create groups in which individuals feel that they can afford to be independent and assert their *selves;* in which they feel they can afford to acknowledge their shortcomings without the loss of self-respect and accept criticism without a feeling of being rejected by the group.

The Nature
of Knowledge

The question of what knowledge is of most worth is, as Kazamian points out, a perennial challenge to a sound curriculum development. It was argued by Mills and Spencer some hundred years ago over the problem of introducing sciences into the curriculum of liberal education, which up to that point had contained only the classical subjects. Today this question is again debated, chiefly around the problem of intensifying the role of sciences and mathematics.

Even though the tables are reversed, and the humanistic subjects rather than sciences are now on the defensive, the essential ingredients of the argument are the same: what constitutes disciplined knowledge, what kind of knowledge has the greatest educative impact, and how one develops the higher mental processes (*Kazamian, 1960, p. 308*).

Much of the confusion and debate about such issues as the merit of different kinds of content and what constitutes the fundamentals of the curriculum ensues from the fact that such terms as subject, subject matter, disciplines, and content are used with different meanings and without sufficient analysis of what knowledge in any subject or discipline consists of. This lack of analysis in turn causes misunderstandings about the role of knowledge in learning and in curriculum.

CONTENT AND PROCESS

In the first place, each area of knowledge—a subject or a discipline—has at least two main characteristics: it has its own fund of acquired information and a specialized method of inquiry, or a strategy of acquiring that knowledge. Downey, for example, differentiates physics and history by describing physics as characterized by a theoretical, analytical method of experimentation and by accumulation of concepts and principles; history, by documentary, doubt-removing methods of verification and by an acquired fund of historical information. From this it follows that the study in a subject area should result, first, in the acquisition of skills, attitudes, and "disciplined habits necessary for the discovery of new knowledge in the field" and, second, "in the acquisition of the most useful fund of information possible of mastery within the limits of the time available for the subject" (*Downey, 1960, p. 254*).

Throughout the history of curriculum making, one of these two characteristics of a subject has been emphasized to the detriment of the other, with the result that usually schools have been less than successful in achieving this dual purpose.

The criticisms of education today are addressed to the shortcomings in achieving both purposes, but the recommendations differ depending on the interpretation of what constitutes adequate knowledge, what the function of content is in the school curriculum, and how to attain disciplined thinking. There are several different viewpoints regarding the proper function of subject matter in the school curriculum, just as there were a hundred years ago, even though the meaning of the terms and their scope have changed.

At one extreme is the viewpoint that content per se is important. According to this view each bit of each subject has an inherent worth and skipping as much as an iota of it leaves a gap in the educational edifice and in the background of students. To reduce the study of American colonies to less than thirteen is something akin to a crime against education. The mastery of the names and functions of all the bones in human anatomy is of equal importance in understanding the function of the bone structure of the body, for without the first the other does not exist. One needs only to debate with a history teacher the problem of coverage or attempt to be selective about the content of a civics course to run across evidence of this cherishing of every minute fact as precious knowledge fully worthy of teaching, learning, and remembering.

Others look not to content to discover the worth of the subject but to the mental discipline which its mastery induces. Two contrasting views prevail here. One assumes that subjects have power to discipline the mind. In the old school of mental discipline, it was assumed that the *form* of the subject trained the faculties, and these, once trained or strengthened, could transfer the power so acquired to anything else. The modern concept of mental discipline is more analytical and more likely to be concerned with scientific or critical thinking, the ability to solve problems, and the capacity to understand and to pursue the methods of inquiry. It also accepts the fact that the nature of the content determines what these processes are and how they operate.

But there are differences regarding how these effects on cognitive processes come about. Some writers on the role of subject matter assume either explicitly or implicitly that the "structure" of the subject affects mental discipline no matter how the subject is taught and learned, and, furthermore, that such subjects as mathematics and physics exercise this impact to a greater extent than others. This viewpoint seems to equate knowledge of a "discipline" with disciplined intelligence. This assumption is the primary basis for rejecting the so-called applied subjects and for proposing that the school curriculum concentrate on the "hard" subjects, or academic disciplines. At the other extreme, the source of the educative impact is seen not in the content but in the mental activity that the student or the teacher brings to bear on it. Often this position is interpreted to mean that the various school subjects as such have no unique functions at all, except as bodies of specific knowledge needed for a specific occupational goal or as a treasure of "cultural heritage" to be cherished for its own sake, like a lovely poem or a bright saying. As far as impact on cognitive processes is concerned, any subject can be equally effective or ineffective, depending on what methods of instruction and of learning are employed. For example, if memorizing is the chief method of learning, it makes little difference whether historical dates, mathematical formulas, or the classification of plants are the subject. If problem solving and analysis are the approach, almost any subject can have an impact on critical reasoning.

Both extremes—the valuing of subjects per se and of processes per se—operate as criteria for curriculum development, often as assumptions hidden in the manner of selecting and organizing content and of determining what the fundamentals are. Stated boldly, both these extreme concepts of the function of subjects in curriculum are equally untenable. The idea that the content of a subject has an inherent worth is unacceptable if one assumes that learning results from the interaction between the content and the mental processes of the student. In the light of modern ideas about learning one cannot conceive that a passive mastery of content can produce a disciplined mind, a scientific attitude of inquiry, or any other of the outcomes claimed. A concept such as justice is of educative value only to the extent that the student can do something more with it than to repeat the verbal definition. An unthinking absorption of the accumulated core of the wisdom of the past is by itself of little educative value, especially since the retention of such learning is minimal. Neither can one accept the idea that the content of the subjects studied makes no difference whatever to the development of mental processes. There is a relationship between the cognitive processes and the content. There are differences in the thought systems of the various subjects, and each has something unique to contribute to a balanced intellectual development.*

THE LEVELS OF CONTENT
AND THEIR FUNCTIONS

Some of the confusion in the discussion of the function of subject matter in the curriculum and in the decisions flowing from this discussion can be prevented by a clearer analysis of what knowledge con-

* The discussion of the differences in impact of different content areas is pursued in the latter part of this chapter.

sists of and by clearer distinctions of the levels of content and the differences in functions that these levels may serve.

Specific Facts and Processes

One can view school subjects as consisting of knowledge on four different levels. One level is that of specific facts, descriptive ideas at a low level of abstraction, and specific processes and skills. Descriptions of the branches of government, of the characteristics of the digestive system, dates of events, specific rules of usage, and the computational processes in arithmetic and algebra belong in this category. It may be important to master some facts as facts, although it is not clear just what these may be in any given area. Agreements regarding what these fundamental facts are may also be more difficult to reach in some areas than in others. There are still disagreements as to which classics are worth reading by all students. The author's experience in looking for "landmark" events and facts in United States history revealed a disconcerting disagreement among historians both in the selection of these facts and in the degree of generality and specificity of the listings. A report on the discussions of scientists on what is important to learn in science points out that the only facts worth knowing are those that reconstruct a host of details when needed, such as basic scientific or mathematical formulas. Perhaps another kind are those that lure students onward, such as the discovery that metals bend when heated.

By and large the merits of mastering specific content and specific techniques are considered to be quite limited. This kind of knowledge is described as static, "dead end." Its mastery does not produce new ideas, does not lure the mind onward. Besides telling only part of a story of a discipline, the specific facts also have a pitifully short life even if remembered: they are highly obsolescent (*Bruner, 1960, pp. 24-25*). The "facts" of today easily become the "fiction" of tomorrow. White describes this danger of obsolescence in geography by commenting on the futility of introducing new units about any place that happens to be in the news. "In our earnest concern to prepare young people to live in an increasingly conflicted world, we are in danger of trying to teach them so many facts about the world as it was last year that we shall teach them little of the ways of thinking about the world that is becoming" (*White, 1958, pp. 63-71*).

This difficulty has been recognized by many educational writers and expressed in the use of the derogatory term "mere subject matter" when discussing the role of content in learning. Dewey described such knowledge as "dead baggage" well ahead of the more specific studies in learning and thinking which proved it. But many of Dewey's followers, failing to discriminate among the levels of knowledge, applied this view to all subject matter.

Specific facts, however, constitute the raw material for the development of ideas. Facts are "food for thought," the material from which to derive generalizations and insights and with which to make thinking precise. There-fore a careful choice of the details to study is as important as ever, and they need to be chosen selectively, to be related to and interpreted in the context of the ideas which they serve.

Because facts as such are only raw material from which to shape concepts and ideas, their role in the learning process is a fleeting one. They do not con-stitute the fundamentals in the sense that all students must master precisely the same content details. Nor should their mastery be the chief focus of in-struction or of evaluation.

Basic Ideas

Basic ideas and principles represent another level of knowledge. The ideas about causal relationships between human culture and natural environment are of this sort. So are scientific laws and mathe-matical principles, the ideas stating relationships between nutrition and the metabolism of the human body, or ideas about how such factors as climate, soil, and natural resources produce unique constellations of a geographic environment.

Such ideas and principles constitute what currently is referred to as the "structure" of the subject: ideas which describe facts of generality, facts that, once understood, will explain many specific phenomena. Bruner uses as an illustration the principle of tropism, the idea that among simple organisms such a phenomenon as regulation of locomotion according to a built-in stand-ard is a rule. There is a preferred level of illumination toward which these or-ganisms orient, a preferred level of salinity, of temperature, and so on. The idea itself can be understood by studying some one phenomenon in detail, such as watching an inchworm climb a sheet of paper mounted on a board. When the board is straight, the animal walks straight; when the board is tilted 30°, the animal walks at an angle of 45°; when the board is tilted at 60° the animal walks at an angle of 75°. Evidently the inchworm "prefers" to travel uphill along an incline of 15°. Once understood, many other bio-logical phenomena can be explained in the light of the idea of tropism. To understand "structure," then, means to learn how things are related (*Bruner, 1960, pp. 6-7*).

The idea that subject matter has structure and that understanding this structure should be the central objective in teaching is not entirely new. In the 1920's there were innumerable studies in social sciences searching for generalizations to guide and to unify the "unfortunate particularism" in this field (*Billings, 1929; Meltzer, 1925*). Marshall in his social-processes studies was seeking some unifying synthesizing approach to provide "greater unities of human experience" (*Marshall and Goetz, 1932*). In 1933 Parker, in deal-ing with the problem of distinguishing the descriptive facts of geography and the principles that explain things, admonished teachers that "pupils should be held responsible for independent use of familiar ideas, but also be shown new ways in which geographic ideas would aid them in solving problems" (*1933, pp. 73-177;* see also *Quillen and Hanna* [*1961, ch. 2*] for an analysis of social concepts and generalizations).

Several yearbooks on teaching science have suggested that the teaching of science be organized around broad principles, because most facts serve as means to the end of gaining an understanding of concepts and principles, of inculcating scientific attitudes, and of providing skills in the use of scientific method (*National Society for the Study of Education, 1947, chs. 2 and 3*).

In mathematics such an approach is recent. Only in the last few years have mathematicians begun to examine the structure of their subject and to identify the basic principles which underlie and unify all aspects of mathematics: arithmetic, algebra, and geometry. But the recent programs in mathematics and science have gone further than simply to examine and to enunciate these ideas. They have also begun to produce materials to make sure that the teaching of principles can become an actual fact (*Keedy, 1959, pp. 157-88; Beberman, 1959, pp. 162-88*).

The basic ideas give control over a wider range of subject matter, organize the relationships between facts, and thereby provide the context for insight and understanding. As the concept of tropism illustrates, these ideas and principles represent the kind of knowledge that is dynamic rather than dead-end, that can be applied to understanding a wide range of events, facts, phenomena, and problems and used to explain and to predict them. This type of knowledge frees the mind to explore more complex phenomena with some sense of excitement in discovery. A student can do much more with an understanding of "relations" as a general mathematical idea than by knowing only the specific aspects of mathematical relations, such as a coefficient. The idea that the existence of a physical frontier represented a stimulus to technological development and a safety valve for discontent helps interpret many single phenomena of American history, setting them into a pattern which is productive of reasoning and insight.

Such basic ideas are the fundamentals, in the sense that when carefully chosen, they represent the most necessary understandings about a subject or a field and thus constitute in a sense the core curriculum for everyone— something that every student would learn, even though in a different depth. As we shall see later (chapter 22), they may also be used as centers around which to organize the curriculum.

It must be pointed out, however, that it may be difficult to reach agreement as to what constitutes basic ideas and principles for a given field. The experience of the California State Commission on Social Studies in obtaining a listing of general ideas around which to organize the social-studies curriculum in elementary and secondary schools suggests that agreement may be reached only on a level of such generality as to produce statements which have little meaning for curriculum guidance (*California State Dept. of Education, 1957*).

This does not mean, however, that an identification of these basic ideas and generalizations is not a necessary step in enhancing the contribution of a field to learning.

Concepts

A third level of content is composed of what one might call concepts, such as the concept of democracy, of interdependence, of social change, or of the "set" in mathematics.

Concepts are complex systems of highly abstract ideas which can be built only by successive experiences in a variety of contexts. They cannot be isolated into specific units but must be woven into the whole fabric of the curriculum and examined over and over again in an ascending spiral. For example, a recent report on mathematics curriculum points out that the concept of a "set" can be advantageously used on all levels. It can be used to develop a number concept in elementary arithmetic, such as birds pictured on a page, or pencils in one's hand. The secondary level needs to explore the idea in a more abstract and formal way, such as applying the concept of "null set," which is empty of any elements, and of a universal set, which contains all elements under consideration (*National Council of the Teachers of Mathematics, 1959*). For an illustration of the idea of the "set" see *Rourke, (1958), p. 74.*

In a similar fashion, the concepts of multiple causation, of interdependence, or of democracy can be developed only if they run through a great deal of social science. From dealing in the first grade with interdependence of roles in the family and how its members help each other, one can progress in the twelfth grade to the notion of the economic and political interdependence of nations, a vastly more complex and abstract concept.

These types of concepts are usually in the background, and therefore are often relegated to incidental teaching. In a sound curriculum development they should constitute what some have called the "recurrent themes," the threads which run through the entire curriculum in a cumulative and overarching fashion.

Thought Systems

The academic disciplines also represent thought systems and methods of inquiry. These thought systems are composed of propositions and concepts which direct the flow of inquiry and thought. Each discipline represented by a school subject presumably is organized around some such system of interlocking principles, concepts, and definitions. These systems direct the questions asked, the kind of answers sought, and the methods by which they are sought.

Presumably the most valuable contribution of a field of study lies in generating certain disciplined methods of forming questions, developing logical ways of relating ideas, and following a rational method of inquiry. Because the greatest need in the scientific age is for persons who can use their minds as well as their knowledge and who can apply their knowledge to new problems, systematic thought needs to be given to the ways and means by which the acquisition of knowledge simultaneously becomes also a method of inquiry and a method of thinking. For this reason, the problem of organizing the curriculum and teaching so that learning leads to disciplined thought is a critical issue of education today, especially on the secondary level.

Some educators seem to assume that a prolonged study of each discipline *qua* discipline in its "integral form" is necessary to achieve this end. This position is predicated on the assumption that disciplines, such as chemistry, physics, history, or sociology, have an inherent coherence, and that a sufficient amount of systematic exposure in each is needed in order to acquire a disciplined way of thinking about that subject.

The whole idea of departmentalized school subjects is based on this assumption. One reason that the newcomers in subject organization, such as integrated courses and broad fields curricula, have had a difficult time is that usually the new organization was introduced without revising the old assumptions about the fundamentals or the scope of the subject matter. Thus, while there has been a considerable movement away from fragmented subject matter, the major objective still is to "cover subjects." Only in cases where there has been a sufficient analysis of the "structure" of the subject has there been a concerted effort toward consolidation of subjects. For example, those exploring the possibilities for the new mathematics curriculum are convinced that integration of the separate subjects of arithmetic, algebra, and geometry around some basic concepts, such as the "set," is a way to a new unity of perception of the "structure" and the method of mathematics and the best way of acquiring mathematical thinking (*Rourke, 1958, pp. 74-75*).

However, a curriculum organized around selected basic ideas may offer another possibility of mastering the special methods of thought and inquiry inherent in the various disciplines without spending enormous amounts of time in mastering the entire subject. It is quite possible that a study in depth of a few such basic ideas provides the necessary experience in developing insights into the ways in which a particular discipline asks and answers questions. It is conceivable that with an intensive study of the landmark ideas, combined with an articulated emphasis on intellectual operations as the minimum essentials for general education in the elementary and high school, a much smaller coverage of facts will produce a vastly greater orientation toward the world, a vastly superior intellectual equipment, and vastly improved skill in using ideas to produce other ideas.

Let us assume for a moment that it is possible to identify the really basic ideas in all subjects. Let us assume, further, that it is possible to sample content so that sharp contrasts and comparisons become available as concrete examples for study. Let us assume, finally, that it is possible to develop a way of learning and teaching in which awareness of the method of thinking, such as awareness of the nature of causality and of various levels of universality in generalizations, is developed consciously and systematically in connection with studying any of these ideas. Would prolonged attention to a discipline and a wide coverage then also be necessary to understand which questions science asks about the world and nature, what types of causality operate in each discipline, and what levels of generalization are possible for which kinds of data? It should be possible, for example, to study a few crucial social phenomena, such as wars, by asking all the questions a historian might ask: what are the factors that create wars; how are wars affected by conditions, such as the tools of warfare and the political institutions that surround them; what is the history of causation of wars, and so on. One might, in other words, conceivably learn the essential ways of being a historian without covering all of history, but by studying something of history in sufficient depth to discover the essential ways of thinking, of discovering appropriate causalities, of handling generalizations, and of establishing conclusions.

The way of learning would have relevance also. An analysis of *teaching acts* seems to show that *prescriptive* teaching and controlling acts dominate the classroom procedure (*Hughes et al., 1959, pp. 85, 181*). The assumption seems to prevail, also, that teaching consists largely in presenting something in a verbal form. This assumption seems to underlie even the studies of teaching, the chief aim of which is to point attention to the need for logical thinking. For example, while B. Othaniel Smith suggests that the new way of thinking about didactics may be needed, his classification of teaching acts seems too nonfunctional to permit a dynamic relationship between teaching acts and learning acts (*Feb., 1950*). Both need to be related to each other and to the analysis of the nature and function of content as well as to the analysis of educational objectives and social needs.

To learn a disciplined way of thinking requires more active modes of learning and teaching than are current today. A different didactic is needed, one which keeps an active development of concepts, creative thinking, and the discovery methods in the foreground. These types of learning do not necessarily result from sheer presentation of content. One may learn descriptive facts by remembering what has been presented. But one certainly does not learn a way of deriving fundamental ideas or the way of applying these ideas to new problems by this method. To learn such ways demands some activity besides recall from the learner and techniques other than presenting materials from the teacher.

The reports of new curricula in mathematics and science stress the method of discovery, the ability not only to perceive principles and procedures but also to invent them. Hildebrand, for example, suggests that an understanding of mathematical concepts and some skill with mathematical techniques are insufficient to enable one to apply mathematics in new situations or to create new mathematics. To apply and to invent mathematics one must also develop proficiency in *problem solving* or *reflective thinking*. To apply mathematics, and even more to create new mathematics, one must be not only interested and curious but also able and alert in perceiving interrelationships between apparently different concepts and in identifying generalizations, analogies, special cases, and *idealizations*.

Although discovery might be a special realm for the gifted children, nevertheless "we would like to emphasize with proper modifications in the amount of help given by the teacher, the size of the perceptive leaps expected of the students, and the time allotment given to the various steps of the process, that *all students should repeatedly and continuously be 'led' to discover or 'invent' mathematical concepts and ideas for themselves. . . .* Such discovery techniques help students to develop in their ability to think mathematically as well as in their understanding of the mathematics so developed" (*Hildebrand, 1959, p. 371*).

UNIQUE CONTRIBUTIONS OF SCHOOL SUBJECTS TO LEARNING

Each discipline offers something distinctive to the education of students on each level of knowledge discussed in the preceding section. This is true also of the school subjects. This uniqueness is most obvious on the level of factual information, but distinguishing the similarities and differences in the contribution of school subjects to learning is most crucial on the level of ideas and principles.

Each subject also involves a specific mode of thinking. Subjects differ in the logical demands they make on students, independently of the kind of instructional methods used and the rigor of intellectual activity demanded by these methods. Not all thought processes can be equally well taught in all subjects. Presumably laboratory chemistry requires a precision analysis of the type that would be inappropriate if applied to analyzing literature. Interpretation of a statistical graph involves processes and criteria that differ from those used in interpreting a poem or a painting.

Each science has also its own logical language, its own canons of using facts and symbols, its own way of relating facts and principles to each other, its own way of dealing with causal relations, and so forth. There are differences from subject to subject in how facts and ideas are treated, in how inference and deductions are used, and in the degree of dependability and universality represented in its generalizations. Generalizing in science is a different matter from making judgments about social or historical events. (See chapter 14 for discussion of variations in the nature of generalizations.)

Some subjects demand a greater level of abstraction than others. For example, the idea of a functional relationship is present in all content fields, but only in mathematics can one explore it in a pure abstract form, undistorted by the peculiarities of special content. Nor do the so-called logical processes of thought have exactly the same meaning in all contexts. Assumptions in a political argument are analyzed differently from those in an argument on evolution. A process of moving from propositions to conclusion may be sufficiently different to merit a different emphasis in a geometry problem and in a chemistry experiment. The way in which a hypothesis is tested in physics differs from the manner of testing a hypothesis in history. In some instances this difference may be only in the degree of rigor with which the processes need to be applied.

In this sense, each discipline has its own logic, its way of viewing and organizing the events and phenomena with which it deals. In this sense, then, also, each discipline contributes a different angle to the orientation toward the world. By the same token, each subject also makes a different impact on the mind and offers a different type of mental training. This principle in part defines the concept of a balanced curriculum and of balanced education.

The fact that the disciplines or subjects vary in their impact on the mind of the student means that a sound theory of curriculum development needs to analyze what these variations are. Knowing what these differences are would enable the curriculum makers to see to it that these different types of impact are capitalized upon and brought into balance in organizing the curriculum content and in instruction.

Currently, however, there are several obstacles to making such an analysis of the impact of subjects on the minds of students. Many teachers in high schools and colleges seem to assume that subject matter has its own built-in logic and that the study of specific facts in a subject reveals and implants that logic. Many content-field-oriented persons assume further that certain subjects inherently have a greater power to train the minds than do others. The advocates of solid subjects, therefore, argue that any didactic discourse about the way that curriculum or teaching may assure proper learning of this "logic" is so much hogwash that the professional educators have invented to make jobs for themselves. This position obscures the need for analyzing which subjects do what to the mind.

Legitimate questions can be asked also regarding whether simply exposing students to the process of thinking imbedded in a certain kind of subject matter is sufficient for them to grasp the methods of thinking in that subject's discipline. To be sure, some students "catch on" without being taught. But those are the few especially talented. Regarding mathematics, for example, Stone maintains that "it is not enough to give students an intuitive grasp of mathematical situations by using concrete analogies and illustrations. He needs to be led from this level of understanding to the higher one of abstraction and logical analysis" (*1958, p. 398*).

The failure to identify the basic ideas of the various subjects, combined with the assumption that the specific content shapes the higher mental processes, has led to a habit of a stereotyped "specializing" of the impact of subjects. Mathematics, for example, is held to be the best means to develop logical thinking and abstraction—even, by some, as the only way. Science is supposed to develop causal thinking and the rudiments of experimental method. Whenever the development of creativity is mentioned, thought immediately turns to creative arts. Social studies and literature tend to be associated with the development of attitudes and values. However, it is obvious that the impact of school subjects cannot generally be so "specialized." One could also reverse the argument and maintain that the development of creativity is as important in mathematics as in creative arts, but it will be creativity of a different sort, and in some cases of a different degree. Abstracting should be a process which is cultivated in all areas, but perhaps the particulars of the process may vary, and various "subjects" may contribute to the development of this capacity in a different manner.

Perhaps equally unacceptable is the contention that there are no differences in the logical demands which the subjects of instruction make on students, that any differences that exist are introduced by methods of instruction that circumscribe and determine the nature and the rigor of intellectual or logical processes which the student develops. From this it follows also that any subject is equally capable of developing logical thinking and that all subjects will develop the same type of logical thinking and give the same intellectual training. As we will see shortly, this line of thinking leads to training in logic in isolation from subject content as a way of assuring maturity in critical thinking. This procedure may also be questionable if for no other reason than that learning abstractly the rules of logical thinking may not transfer any more readily into thinking with the content of subjects than knowing the rules of grammar translates into correct writing and speaking.

Perhaps the main problem lies in the lack of clarity about what disciplined thinking is. This confusion makes it easy to identify disciplined thinking with any single aspect of logical thinking or of scientific inquiry. Those who equate disciplined thinking with logic would abstract the canons and the processes of logic and train students in such matters as detecting assumptions, evaluating the validity of conclusions, assessing the available evidence, and identifying fallacies of reasoning (*B. O. Smith, undated; 1957*).

No doubt some attention to logic as such would be helpful. But the canons of logic do not cover all matters of disciplined thinking in all varieties of disciplines, nor do they help necessarily with the processes of concept formation, generalizing, and applying generalizations in a variety of content.

Reflective thinking is also identified with the process of problem solving. As stated in educational literature, the steps in problem solving are essentially the steps of a complete act of thought as described by Dewey's idea of the process of inquiry, a pattern which, according to him, covers adequately all forms of reflective thinking and includes all logical operations.

But to maintain that all aspects of thinking are involved in problem solving or in the process of inquiry is one thing. To assume that following these steps also provides sufficient training in all elements of thinking is something else. For training purposes it is important both to master the various aspects or elements of thinking—such as generalizing, concept formation, analysis of assumptions, application of principle—and to use these processes in an organized sequence in problem solving. (See chapter 13 on objectives for fuller description.) If these elements are not consciously recognized and mastered, problem solving can turn into a ritualistic process of defining any kind of question, collecting any kind of data, hypothesizing any variety of solutions, and so on.

Subsuming all reflective thinking under the category of problem solving has also caused certain elements of thinking to be neglected, especially those which, although involved in problem solving, are not fully attended to *while* solving problems. Among these are such mental processes as concept formation, abstracting, and various methods of induction.

NEW CONCEPT OF FUNDAMENTALS

These distinctions of levels of knowledge and the discussion of the role of methods of inquiry or of thought systems throw a new light on many questions that have plagued education and curriculum development.

One problem in today's curriculum is that of obsolescence of curriculum content. Elsewhere in this book (*pp. 37-38*) it was pointed out that it is difficult to plan education today, because even the fairly near future is only barely over the horizon as far as our image of it is concerned. Oppenheimer points out that today the balance between the old truths and the new have been unhinged, and that, therefore, in addition to the need to improvise, to create new things that grew out of the frontier conditions, there is a new source of change which is even more radical and universal: the unprecedented explosion of knowledge and with it technological explosions unlike any the world has seen. When formerly the shift in fundamental notions could be counted in centuries, now it is counted in decades (*1958*). This explosion of knowledge also creates an increasing rate of obsolescence, especially in knowledge composed of specific facts, but to some degree also in the structure of basic concepts and patterns of thinking. The problem is felt keenly today in science and in mathematics, because the past few decades have brought a rather thorough reshaping of the basic concepts and ideas in these fields. Obsolescence has always been a problem in social studies, because the basic ideas in these disciplines have changed even more rapidly not only from time to time, but also from theory to theory.

This explosion of knowledge and of technology means that a first grader getting his first innings in science will face an entirely new science when he reaches college. A mathematician trained in a high school today is likely to face a new mathematics as a practitioner of engineering. Under these circumstances the knowledge of most worth is least likely to be found among the specific facts and concrete descriptive ideas, for these will change most rapidly and are the least productive of new ideas. An understanding of the general principles which have the broadest range of application and which are the most potent for creating new knowledge is a more promising and creative educational investment. It seems, then, that the common heritage most needed for the future and the background needed to equip the young generation to live in our culture is contained less in the common bodies of factual knowledge than in the way we fit people to think about whatever knowledge they have or about the problems on which this knowledge bears. These, then, should be the fundamentals to which curriculum, teaching, and evaluation should be addressed.

Much of current practice and of current criticism of education is based on a concept of the *fundamentals* the reverse of that stated above. The usual concept of the *fundamentals* is that of the three R's: that is, the specific mastery of computational processes in arithmetic, reading, and the rules of grammar, and such factual knowledge as historic dates and place names in geography. Evidently this concept is based on confusing *precedent* knowledge with *fundamental* knowledge. This assumption seems to be invalidated both by the newer ideas about learning and by studies of achievement. As was pointed out in the preceding chapters, creativity and discovery are considered fundamental in intellectual functioning. Recent research shows, for example, that skill in computation is one of the least significant factors in ability to solve arithmetic problems. Instead, a high ability to solve these problems has been found to be related to computational reasoning, ability to interpret vocabulary, assessment of the operations involved, and the familiarity with the problem's setting (*Corle, 1958; Post, 1958*). A better understanding of mathematics and a greater sensitivity to "reasonable" and "probable" answers was generated when the emphasis on unifying principles was increased in comparison to time spent on computation (*Grubb, 1958*).

A differentiation of the functions of a particular content is inextricably bound with differentiation in learning experiences and also, therefore, in teaching acts. What these differences might be needs to be studied more carefully. At present an observer in classrooms in the elementary or high schools, especially in the latter, is struck by the uniformity of learning processes employed no matter what the content or the particular objective. There is the usual heavy reliance on memorization, the ability to dig in the texts and to answer specified questions on the content of the text or on the teacher's lecture. When discussion is used, it is harnessed less to discovery of new ideas than to sharing of facts or opinions already held by the members of the class.

If subjects have any distinct functions, it seems there should also be distinct ways of learning in order to permit these functions to come into their own. For example, memorization may play a stronger role in learning some things than others; the method of discovery of new ideas may be more important in some areas of learning than in others; the application and use of ideas or their expression in a new integration or a new medium may be more relevant at some points than at others. Not all forms of reflective thinking can be practiced in all subjects with equal emphasis, or in all parts of a subject with the same strength or benefit. An interesting subject of study would be to see which elements of thinking are most appropriately trained in which context. An approach tailored to the development of thinking could conceivably produce much economy in learning and, furthermore, permit more frequent and systematic practice of the variations in learning processes according to the variations in mental systems of students. It is possible that some students grasp the essence of causal relations better in one context than in others. Thus, if the development of disciplined causal thinking were an objective of the same importance as the acquisition of facts, one might conceive of a program in which different types of students pursued different content, but all were engaged in exploring the nature of causal relations or in analyzing the quality and the level of abstractions used.

THE SCOPE OF CONTENT

With a clearer distinction of the levels of knowledge, a new assessment of the problem of scope is possible also. The concept of scope as "coverage" of content has for a long time blocked promising leads in curriculum development, including a proper emphasis on thinking and on other well-recognized objectives of education.

When content is viewed exclusively as an assemblage of information there is no criterion by which to distinguish relevant from irrelevant material. Hence all facts and information seem to have the same significance. For this reason, there always seems to be too much to cover to allow time for developing creative methods of thinking about the content, for developing adequate understanding of relationships between ideas, or for depth study of important ideas. The author has met this difficulty in many a consultant conference, when, after what seemed like an exciting elaboration of the possibilities of developing thinking or some other well-recognized aim, someone would sigh and say, "But we have so much to cover that I don't see how we can fit this in." As the explosion of knowledge continues, the lore and the storehouse of facts will extend to the point of leaving no room in curriculum for anything else except "covering the facts."

Gilbert White illustrates this dilemma growing out of "coverage" in discussing the problem of developing an understanding of the world through the study of geography. He points out that an effort to sharpen the understanding of the world by "covering the world" results in superficiality. For example, the consciousness of the politically emergent Africa has led to units on Africa (as the problem in Palestine led to units on the Middle East, and so on). This is the easy way to extend knowledge of the world, but also distressing, for each such new unit will detract from time for the more fundamental understandings (*1958, pp. 69-70*).

If the content fields are viewed not as treasures of knowledge to be transmitted but as a way of understanding a limited number of basic ideas, the problem of scope acquires a different meaning. One does not ask, for example, what array of particular biological facts could be packed into students, but what basic ideas need to be clearly understood, what questions need to be asked and answered, and how these varieties of ideas, questions, and answers fit into developing an orientation to the world. Instead of asking which particular topics or facts to include or exclude, one examines the basic ideas and principles to determine which are most relevant to gaining a balanced orientation to the nature of the world. Only after the basic ideas are determined does the question emerge as to what specific facts are necessary to accomplish this task most effectively. In this scheme of viewing subject matter it may even be important to study the same specific content from a variety of angles. With the reduction of the scope of factual material, time is released for developing appropriate relationships and for making applications of what is learned. By reducing the load of obscuring detail, attention can be devoted to developing a clear and precise understanding of ideas.

The scope of the study in any field or across several fields, then, needs to be defined along two lines. One is the range of important ideas and concepts to be covered. White illustrates the possibility of using important ideas to define scope by analyzing the role of one basic idea—namely, that there is a regional association of phenomena on the earth's surface: the distributions of the climates, soils, vegetation, minerals, and population occur in distinctive combinations and the change in any one of these elements in the complex will bring about profound changes in others. A thorough study of a few samples of specific combinations of these factors in order to discover or to develop such ideas may eventuate in a better understanding of the world than does a superficial coverage of many details about many places (*1958, p. 70*). And if one teaches for transfer and for application, a concept once mastered for one area, especially if this mastery is achieved by active learning processes (discussed on *pp. 126-28*), becomes applicable to any other area, and students can no longer regard little-known areas as being "as uniform as the color shadings on the map."

In a similar fashion, third graders who learned to analyze "what makes a desert" in studying the environment of nomadic tribes in the Sahara were able to use this knowledge to discover that there was a whole belt of deserts and that the factors which made them as well as conditions of life they created were similar.

Scope is also determined by delineating the kinds of reactions, mental or otherwise, to be cultivated. This concept of scope would include such matters as the methods of interpretation and generalization to be cultivated, the type of logical processes to be mastered, the type and the level of application to be pursued, the kinds of attitudes to be generated, or the sensitivities to be developed—in other words, the behavioral objectives. This double-track concept of scope should lead to a kind of curriculum which would at the same time prepare students for a more profound understanding of whatever they are studying and help them form a "set to learn" in school as well as after they leave school. (See chapters 20 and 22 for further discussion of this method of curriculum development.)

THE SEQUENCE OF LEARNING

Differentiating the levels of knowledge suggests also a new aspect of the sequence of acquiring knowledge. The usual sequence pattern has been to concentrate first on specific facts and to reserve the explorations that lead to fundamental principles and thought systems for the more mature stage of education. This sequence has produced a curriculum with a heavy concentration on factual knowledge in the elementary and secondary schools and with an apparent retardation in the development of ideas about these facts and of higher mental functions. When knowledge is perceived as consisting of the four levels described above, it is clear that thinking and acquiring knowledge need not be separated. The data on the development of thinking indicate that the capacity of general and abstract thinking develops sooner than has been assumed by the usual sequence; hence it is not necessary to amass knowledge with which to think later.

The idea that thinking and learning facts need not be separated by a wide time span is also supported by the learning theory which maintains that cognitive organization is the fundamental characteristic of all intellectual learning, but that the selection and organization of learning experiences needs to aid and abet the conscious formation of general ideas and their relationships.

This new procedure is what is evidently happening in mathematics—the subject considered the most "sequential" of all. The time-honored sequence of arithmetic, algebra, and geometry has been upset by proprosals to teach algebra and arithmetic simultaneously by induction into the nature of the number system. One is further inclined to question the whole idea that a sequence of content topics represents continuity in any real sense, or that the present gradations in difficulty of subject matter are valid. If it is possible in mathematics to reverse the usual order of difficulty, how much greater is the possibility in subjects which are less "logically tight"? Experiments by the author have shown that certain anthropological abstractions are within the compass of third graders, without the traditional sequential study of anthropology, provided that these anthropological ideas are introduced in an understandable context and that curriculum units have provided for the *development* of these ideas, and not simply for "covering" them.

It seems, then, that while sequence and continuity are important in learning, the sequence consists not so much in the succession of details in the various areas of knowledge as in the continuity of learning steps leading toward the formation of ideas and the use of cognitive processes. This suggests a twofold sequence for learning experiences: the sequence of ideas to be dealt with, in the order of their complexity and abstractness, and the sequence of cognitive processes in the order of increasingly demanding intellectual rigor, such as the precision of analysis required or range of application expected. Such a concept of sequence would avoid several traps into which the planning of a sequence in a curriculum tends to fall. One is that of devoting years to unreasoning accumulation of facts and mastery of specific procedures and then trying to superimpose thinking onto this accumulation. Naturally one needs facts in order to think, but one need not assume that a time span must separate the two steps; both processes can go on in the context of the same learning act.

Such a sequence would also prevent the discontinuity in the perception of ideas which is usually present when "simple facts" are taught out of their context. If all learning experiences on all levels are programmed in relation to the basic ideas which they are to illuminate, the danger of young children acquiring ideas that need to be corrected at a more mature stage is minimized. Finally, such a sequence stresses the need for cumulative development in the maturing of the cognitive processes. When only the content sequence is considered, this development is often overlooked. Students bring to subjects appearing at a later step in a sequence mental processes which are at the same level as, or even less demanding than, the mental processes required at an earlier step.

INTEGRATION OF KNOWLEDGE

The differentiation of the levels of knowledge also throws new light on the problems inherent in efforts to integrate curriculum content. Integration of knowledge is an important issue, both from the standpoint of explosion and specialization of knowledge and from the standpoint of the social impact of exploding technology. As the number of specialized fields increases, the pursuit of specialized subjects in school becomes increasingly fruitless or impossible, and more rather than less emphasis is needed on integrating knowledge. General education, in the sense of an integrated mastery of basic fields of knowledge, is needed today more than ever. Both the layman and the specialist of tomorrow need to have a foundation that is general enough to permit him to be intelligent about what goes on in a world decimated by specialized pursuits. As Oppenheimer points out, by the very nature of the knowledge of today, men must limit the number and the kind of new truths with which they have to deal in their professional lives. This makes the intellectual scene that of the specialists, and even the specialists in any one field, for all their surface similarities, are varied in their experience and foreign to each other in the very tongues they speak. This specialization has its dangers. Today the knowledge of the essential nature of nature is no longer a common heritage. Its most fundamental truths are not definable in terms of common experience. There are no common fundamentals of science—only an absence of contradiction between one part and any other part. The fundamental truths are the treasure of many communities of specialists which often become completely cut off from each other in their own rapid growth. When decisions are made, they are made by a collection of experts who have no way of communicating their knowledge to each other. When a consensus is reached, it is limited to statements so vague that they can mean anything to anybody, or to situations so threatening that no theoretical interpretations, no world view need interfere.

The need, therefore, is to "develop habits of mind which permit truths from one field to elucidate facts in another, which develop a dedication and search for order in novelty, variety, and contingencies" (*Oppenheimer, 1958*). For the greatest need today is to develop some common factor which will make communication possible between persons engaged in different specialized phases of human endeavor. This need in a way sets a tasks for general education. Stressing specialized knowledge rather than ideas which integrate knowledge only widens this gap among specialists and between the specialists and the lay public. Such minds as Oppenheimer suggest that what we need cannot be developed by a pursuit of distinct disciplines in their separate "unities." Instead of pushing specialization to an earlier age in school, the greater need is to develop common perceptions by dealing with ideas which cut across fields.

In the light of the direction in which our culture is moving, it seems that our schools would be misguided to let their programs be governed by pressures to become preparatory schools for specialization. Instead, the curriculum needs to move toward broader fields and integration of knowledge. Yet, because of concern for disciplined thinking and basic skills, the idea is gaining that studying specialized disciplines is the only way of achieving discplined thinking. For example, in discussing the nature of text materials needed in modern education, Cronbach wonders whether the "most precious possession of the field" is not lost when students have no opportunity to acquire the "methods of asking questions" that are unique to a field of study, because "the *identity* of a subject is lost to the point that the discipline does not appear in *its integrated* form in student's education" (*1955, p. 51*).

The past attempts at integration of knowledge illustrated by the broad-fields curricula, such as general science, social studies, and language arts, and by the integrated core courses, have been criticized because in these courses the breadth is accompanied by vagueness, lack of precision, and a failure to offer training in disciplined thinking. White, for example, complains that what the students learn from social studies—a combination of geography and history—is familiarity with social problems, but probably not a disciplined way of thinking about them, and that both the historical and geographic modes of thinking seem to have lost their precision (*1958, p. 71*).

Although some of the critics may be biased in favor of maintaining the integrity of their own fields, these criticisms are by no means unfounded. The broad fields and integrated courses have been guilty of vagueness and imprecision, but these characteristics are not inevitable consequences of integration. These courses were often composed by combining existing topics from several fields, or by combining subjects rather than by selecting overarching ideas and then combining facts from several fields in order to study these ideas. This method of organizing by enlarging the topics to be covered prevented focusing on the depth study of any subject or on the application of intellectual rigor in relating facts to principles.

The differentiation of the various levels of knowledge opens up the possibility of a more adequate method for integrating knowledge which does not involve the dangers of vagueness and lack of precision. With a more careful analysis of basic ideas in the various fields, it should be possible to identify ideas that have relevance to several disciplines in the same area, or even across areas. If the substance for developing these ideas were drawn with equal care from diverse fields, integration of knowledge and broadening the subject offerings should be possible without a corresponding loss in depth, precision, and intellectual discipline. The more basic the ideas, the more they tend to point to interrelationships with ideas in other fields, at least in subjects within the same large field. With a proper selection of ideas to pursue, with ample detail from the several disciplines to pursue them in depth, it should be possible both to preserve the distinctive flavor of the ideas as interpreted in the context of the subject, and to achieve breadth and scope in understanding and perceiving relationships. One need not lose, for example, the distinctive method of geographical reasoning merely because geographic ideas are taught in relation to historical facts and reasoning. Rather, the relationship of the two should add to insight and understanding as well as to the scope of application that is possible.

If one assumes that each discipline has a unique contribution to make, it is possible to argue that to "cover" those functions or impacts, contact is needed with material from a variety of subjects around some single focus. It is possible to conceive that the most effective training in a variety of mental operations might be achieved by "integrating" material from many disciplines in the study of a topic or a problem because the student then is exposed to comparative methods of thinking, is faced with the necessity of using different types of logic and different levels of abstraction, and is required to apply knowledge in a diversified manner and by diversified canons.

In doing this, it might be possible to take a new look at the current stereotypes regarding the superior role of academic over applied subjects in intellectual training. The points about the unique contributions of disciplines could be easily construed as an argument for inequality of subjects as educational vehicles. Already there are strong tendencies toward programs composed only of the so-called solids, on the assumption that the knowledge encompassed in these is of most value for all people and for all general education purposes.

Furthermore, if ideas are learned clearly only to the extent that they are applied, one can see an almost necessary role for the applied subjects in the very intellectual training that these subjects now are supposed to shortchange. If there were clear roads to relating the applications to the basic principles, the applied fields might offer special opportunities for completing the "acts of thought" by requiring the use of basic principles and concepts in an entirely new context. The wider the range of application, and the larger the "perceptive leap" from the original context in which the idea was developed to the problem area to which it is applied, presumably the better the idea is learned and the higher its utility in the person's thought system. One would then think that a marriage of the theoretical and applied fields would afford maximum opportunity for acquiring clear, well-understood ideas and for learning how to use them.

PART TWO

The
Process
of
Curriculum
Planning

The Objectives

of Education

An educational program, like any activity, is directed by the expectations of certain outcomes. The chief activity of education is to change individuals in some way: to add to the knowledge they possess, to enable them to perform skills which otherwise they would not perform, to develop certain understandings, insights, and appreciations. The statements of these expected or desired outcomes are usually called either educational aims or educational objectives.

The introductory chapter describes several sources from which ideas for educational aims and objectives are and should be derived. One of these is the analysis of the particular culture and society which the educational program serves: what its problems, needs, and requirements are, and therefore what it demands of individuals living in it. The analysis of society leads to consideration of the competencies and qualities necessary to sustain a culture and to survive in it. Chapters 3 to 5 suggest several broad aims, such as developing an adequate orientation toward the whole society, a mind that can cope with problems of living in a rapidly changing world, an intellectual discipline adequate to grasping complex social phenomena, new skills for collective thinking, and a cosmopolitan sensitivity.

It is equally important to consider what is known about individuals as persons and their needs for self-development and self-fulfillment, for education must be both vital to national life and essential to individual development. Chapters 6 to 11 suggest several aims that are essential to individual development, such as autonomy of thought, appropriate ego-ideal, and the development of a healthy personality. Studies of the learner and of the learning process also yield insights regarding the outcomes of learning, such as the necessity of fostering multiple development toward social, intellectual, and emotional maturity. Information from these studies serves an additional function of helping to determine what is feasible at any one point of development, or the approximate level on which these outcomes are attainable. Thus the studies of developmental sequence should indicate what degree of intellectual, emotional, or social maturity can be attained by students at different age levels with different abilities and varying patterns of social learning.

Finally, it is necessary to study the subjects which compose the school program in order to decide which intellectual skills and understandings are appropriate to each. Chapter 12 elaborates some of the requirements inherent in the nature of knowledge and in the various disciplines which represent that knowledge. This source suggests such aims as the ability to think in a disciplined way, the command of the symbols in which thought is expressed, and the range of understandings that the subjects represent.

Naturally, the purposes derived from each of these sources are not—nor should they be—mutually exclusive. For example, the objectives related to the development of the individual and those concerned with his development as a citizen are complementary, at least in a democratic society. Although the demands of academic disciplines *qua* disciplines sometimes obscure the vision of what their study might contribute either to the social role of the individual or to his self-development, nevertheless the two aims need to supplement each other in setting the sights for the educational program.

The facts and ideas from these sources do not translate themselves automatically into balanced educational objectives. One danger of imbalance lies in the selective use of these sources, as illustrated in chapter 2. Each concept of the function of education described in that chapter put a premium on insights derived from some one source and overlooked or understressed others. Those who are oriented to social and cultural analysis tend to overstress the social functions of education. Those who derive their concept of the function of education largely from the analysis of the requirements of academic subjects are likely to favor intellectual discipline over some other equally important qualities. Today, with the pressure of national needs uppermost in our minds, there is a danger of allowing the objectives which promise to serve these needs to overbalance the program in comparison to the objectives which are related to the fullest development of the individual as a human being.

Thus, the platform of educational aims may be either narrow or comprehensive, balanced or imbalanced, depending on what is referred to as educational philosophy, which is the selection and interpretation of facts and ideas from the above-mentioned sources, but which may actually be only a specialized orientation. If educational philosophy is the synthesizing of all pertinent knowledge and ideas to determine the chief ends and values of education, then this specialized orientation toward the function of education is in effect a failure in philosophic synthesis.

This specialization of orientation also creates conflicts which a philosophical synthesis might be able to reconcile. Today, for example, the lay public as well as educators are divided between those who think that the nature of our technological society demands a greater stress on the development of technical and scientific competencies and those who think that the greatest need is for rationalization of human relations and for a stronger commitment to a democratic way of life. Perhaps a more systematic examination of the ideas from all sources from which educational aims are derived would yield a more comprehensive and balanced statement of aims and eliminate the current conflicts.

THE FUNCTIONS
OF EDUCATIONAL OBJECTIVES

Educational outcomes can be, and have been, stated on several different levels. One level is that of the broad aims of education, such as were described in chapter 2 and in the preceding paragraphs. Statements that education should transmit culture, reconstruct society, or provide for the fullest development of the individual, stake out the broad aims. A similar function is served by statements of such aims as the development of a democratic way of life, of civic responsibility, creativity, economic self-sufficiency, or self-actualization. This latter group of statements refers to life activities of individuals in society, and expresses the dynamic center of educational activity. To the extent that educational objectives are related to the universal wants or needs of men, as created by the activities of life, education becomes more functional and dynamic (*Thompson, 1943*).

The chief function of stating aims on such general levels is to provide an orientation to the main emphasis in educational programs. Aims on this level establish what might be described as a philosophy of education and are only a step toward translating the needs and values of society and of individuals into an educational program. They are an insufficient guide for making the more specific decisions about curriculum development, such as what content or which learning experiences to select or how to organize them.

The general aims can be satisfied only if individuals acquire certain knowledge, skills, techniques, and attitudes. These latter represent a more specific platform of goals. The outcomes on this more specific level are usually referred to as educational objectives and they will be so referred to in this chapter.

Objectives on this level are of two different sorts: those which describe the school-wide outcomes and the more specific ones which describe behaviors to be attained in a particular unit, a subject area, a course, or a grade-level program. Thus, while one may consider the development of critical thinking a school-wide objective, each of the school subjects may contribute to this development in a different way, and hence needs to be guided by a more specific statement of this objective, such as "to understand mathematical proof," or "to perceive relationships between life and literature."

Presumably such large and complex objectives as the development of democratic values or of critical thinking cannot be accomplished by any specific part of the school program. Concepts such as that of interdependence cannot be developed on any one grade level or in a single subject. Neither can these objectives be attained successfully if each division of the curriculum proceeds as though no developments were taking place in another division. If there is no agreement in a high school about the way of treating the process of generalizing in different subjects, it will be difficult for students to achieve a consistent pattern of generalizing and of using generalizations. Nor will differences in the process of generalizing related to the context be sufficiently stressed. Conflicting or unintegrated development of a concept in different contexts is equally inadequate. Therefore, there needs to be an integrated view of common objectives overarching across many parts of the program by which to guide supplemental analyses of the unique contributions of the various subjects (*Pace, 1958, pp. 69-83*).

The chief function of the more specific platform of objectives is to guide the making of curriculum decisions on what to cover, what to emphasize, what content to select, and which learning experiences to stress. This level, in other words, contains the heart of the educational objectives in their usual sense, and clarification of the functions of objectives on this level is essential to arriving at a serviceable guide to curriculum development. Naturally these more specific objectives should be consistent with the general overarching ones and in their totality express the vision of the general aims.

Educational objectives have a variety of functions. Perhaps the most important one is that of guiding decisions about the selection of content and of learning experiences and of providing criteria on what to teach and how to teach it. Because the possibilities of knowledge and of learning are boundless, curriculum makers and teachers always face the problem of selection: what content, which learning activities are the most important, most necessary, and most effective. A platform of desired objectives supplies a criterion for these decisions. No matter what its nature, the statement of desired outcomes sets the scope and the limits for what is to be taught and learned.

A clear statement of objectives helps to select from vast areas of knowledge in the various disciplines that which is realistically necessary for some valid outcome. If the aim of social studies, for example, is to produce intelligent participation in democratic life, then the decision is needed regarding what irreducible substance of knowledge students must acquire in order to participate intelligently in a democratic way of life. If the concept of "intelligent participation in democracy" were further analyzed, a more direct guidance might be forthcoming regarding the content to be taught and the skills and behaviors to be mastered. A similar problem of narrowing through focusing presents itself in developing a content topic, such as that of transportation in the elementary social-studies curriculum. One can deal with the subject of transportation in several different dimensions: what its means are, what is being transported, what changes have occurred, what its effects are, and so on. Which of these is chosen depends on what the objectives of teaching this topic are, what particular concepts, social orientation, attitudes, or understandings are to be the outcomes.

Since education does not consist solely of mastery of content, objectives also serve to clarify the types of powers, mental or otherwise, which need to be developed. The definition of these powers determines how subject matter is selected and how it is handled in the classroom. In teaching literature, it makes a good deal of difference whether the intent is to familiarize students with the content of literary masterpieces, to sensitize them to a greater range of human values, to develop familiarity with the forms of literature, or to develop a personal philosophy of life. What is selected for reading, as well as how it is taught, depends largely on whether one or all of these objectives are stressed. If the emphasis is on creating a personal philosophy of life, literature would be examined to develop insights into the values of other people and for some clarification of a student's own values. In teaching the use of the library resources, different skills will be emphasized depending on whether the objective is solely to develop the ability to locate the needed information, or also on the ability to judge the relevance and value of the information for different purposes.

Whitehead puts this focusing and clarifying function of objectives neatly in criticizing the school reform in England:

> This question of the degeneration of algebra into gibberish, both in word and in fact, affords a pathetic instance of the uselessness of reforming educational schedules *without a clear conception of the attributes* which you wish to evoke in the living minds of the children. A few years ago there was an outcry that school algebra was in need of reform, but there was a general agreement that graphs would put everything right. So all sorts of things were excluded, and graphs were introduced. So far as I can see, with no sort of idea behind them, but just graphs. Now every examination paper has one or two questions on graphs. Personally, I am an enthusiastic adherent of graphs. But I wonder whether as yet we have gained very much. You cannot put life into any schedule of general education unless you succeed in exhibiting its relation to some *essential characteristic of all intelligent or emotional perception.* It is a hard saying, but it is true; and I do not see how to make it any easier. In making these little formal alterations you are beaten by the very nature of things. You are pitted against too skillful an adversary, who will see to it that the pea is always under the other thimble [*1929, p. 12. Italics added*].

A platform of objectives is needed also to provide a common, consistent focus for the multifarious activities we call the curriculum. The program of the school is managed by many people. There are many subjects, classes, and teachers. Some unity in emphasis, some common focus is needed to make these efforts converge on certain common, consistent goals. Furthermore, many types of growth cannot be developed without a consistent emphasis throughout the whole program. Clarification of the main school-wide objectives should define these common areas of concern as well as the contribution of each area of activity to these common purposes. If there is a discrepancy among these various areas of objectives, or in the experiences used to achieve them, the net result will be less than adequate. These problems argue for the establishment of school-wide objectives and for the examination of the consistency of specific objectives in specific areas of experience with the school-wide objectives—in what they represent, in how their achievement is paced, and in what sequence the achievement occurs. Statements of objectives should then indicate the general school-wide emphasis and the unique tasks of specific areas of instruction or of activities.

Finally, the objectives serve as a guide for the evaluation of achievement. Discrepancy between what is taught and what is evaluated is a common fault of school programs. The scope of evaluation of achievement is usually much narrower than the scope of the objectives for the program. Partly this discrepancy is caused by limitations in the available means of measuring a sufficiently broad range of achievement: adequate and easily administered evaluation instruments are available only for measuring the achievement of information and skills. But largely this discrepancy between the expected outcomes and evaluation is caused by the fact that the objectives themselves are not clearly formulated. The often-referred-to intangibility of some objectives is nothing but a smoke screen for lack of clarity. Such objectives describe neither the behavior nor the content clearly enough to make adequate analysis possible. Therefore, evaluation tends to be concentrated on the most obvious but not always the most important outcomes, such as remembering information rather than thinking with it. This deficiency has a circular effect. It is well known that those things that are most clearly evaluated are also most effectively taught. Since the intended changes do not become effective changes unless there are clear-cut provisions for them in the curriculum, the curriculum also is narrowed and weakened in its effect when some important outcomes are unclearly defined. This weakness is quite obvious today. It is difficult to defend the "frills" from current attacks because attainments other than those in "essentials" are not readily demonstrable. It is therefore easy to brand emphases on thinking, social sensitivity, and creativity as unnecessary frills. With a clearer platform of objectives and more adequate evaluation data, both the necessity and the efficacy of many aspects of the school program would be vastly more defensible.

PRINCIPLES TO GUIDE THE FORMULATION OF OBJECTIVES

In order for objectives to serve their functions well, a systematic approach to the formulation and organization of objectives is needed. There must be a rational basis for the conception of the desired outcomes of learning and for the grouping and classification of objectives.

Because the particular content of objectives varies from situation to situation, depending on the approach to education as well as on local needs, a general chapter can only develop certain criteria for the process of formulating objectives. Some of these criteria are dictated by the function of the objectives. Others emerge from a consideration of the difficulties arising out of the sources for and the levels of objectives. These criteria should be useful in avoiding confusion in stating objectives and in developing sharper distinctions among them without imposing an element of inflexibility or prescription by specifying the particular content of the objectives.

A statement of objectives should describe both the kind of behavior expected and the content or the context to which that behavior applies. Too often educational objectives are stated so that only the coverage of the content is explicit, and it is not clear whether this content is to be memorized, thought about, or acted upon to produce a change of attitudes. In other words, the expected behavior is not specified. At the other extreme are generalized statements of behavior, such as developing an ability to think logically or to express oneself clearly, without any indication of the kind of content in which this behavior is to apply.

This twofold specification is important for two main reasons. First, the specification of behavior is necessary in order for the objectives to serve as a platform for both curriculum development and evaluation. The chief cause for a narrow emphasis in curricula and teaching is the fact that, when a description of content is the sole definition of objectives, too narrow a range of behaviors is envisioned as outcomes of learning and only a limited set of outcomes is evaluated. Secondly, although such behavioral outcomes as thinking, interpreting, and appreciation probably are applicable to wide varieties of content, the specific processes vary sufficiently from area to area to make distinctions necessary.

The most useful and clearest statements of objectives are those which specify both the kind of behavior reaction that is expected and the content to which it applies, such as the ability to interpret accurately data on taxation, or the ability to differentiate between facts and opinions. If the behavior denotes knowing or remembering, the statement of objectives should also indicate what is to be known or remembered. If the statement specifies an attitude, then it should also state what the attitude is about.*

Such a twofold specification of objectives expresses a concept of achievement which relates content mastery to the intellectual skills and affective reactions and thus helps point attention to the fact that the process of education consists both of mastery of content and of the development of powers. This concept of achievement should prevent the usual limitation in the evaluation of achievement by which erudition becomes the sole mark of an educated person. It should further aid in extending the concept of scope so as to include both the range of content to be used and the range of behaviors to be cultivated.

This double concept of scope should go a long way toward eliminating the bugaboo of coverage as the sole index of achievement and growth which has

* A two-dimensional chart for analyzing objectives appears in Tyler (1950, p. 33).

so far prevented sufficient attention to thoughtful understanding of what is studied. It may make it possible to see that to enrich learning one need not always add new content, that a more limited coverage accompanied by a more profound understanding, deeper analysis, or a more skilled handling of ideas may add up to more adequate learning. It even suggests the possibility of using the same content to promote different kinds of achievement, such as reading and discussing a novel both to develop an appreciation of good form and to gain insight into the temper or values of the times.

Complex objectives need to be stated analytically and specifically enough so that there is no doubt as to the kind of behavior expected, or what the behavior applies to. Too often statements of educational objectives lack the concreteness and clarity that are needed if they are to serve as a guide for making decisions about the curriculum or about evaluation. They are stated in terms too general or too vague to be translated into educational practice. Such statements as "to develop a method of inquiry," a "mind that can cope with complexities of modern life," "appreciation of the beautiful," "loyalty to truth," or "a knowledge and attitude basic to being a responsible citizen" are too broad, too vague, or both. They may be useful in suggesting a general policy but are useless in deciding which learning experiences are appropriate to a course or how to go about getting evidence on the degree of their attainment. Often such terms as "understanding" or "competence" are used, which include the additional difficulty of being complexes of several different kinds of behavior, such as knowledge, thinking, and skills. Such statements easily become decorations in front of a curriculum guide which have no effect either on the content of the guide or on the teaching that follows it. Such statements are also subject to multiple interpretation. For example, "to understand something" may mean a literal comprehension; it may mean a translation of a communication from one language into another one, or it may mean interpretation in the sense of bringing the various parts of a message, of a work, or of a piece of data into relationship with each other and reorganizing them into a new configuration.*

This principle of clarity and specificity suggests the need to analyze complex behaviors into their particular components, so that the precise behaviors intended are clearly perceptible and so that the qualities expected of them are fully understood. It is necessary, for example, to break down such objectives as "clear thinking" into the ability to make inferences from specific facts, to apply principles, to use logical processes in detecting assumptions, and to generalize, before this objective represents a reasonable platform for selecting curriculum materials, for a teaching emphasis, and for evaluation. Many important educational objectives have been insufficiently analyzed and are therefore neglected in curriculum planning and evaluation because they are

* See Bloom (1954, pp. 74-81) for a discussion of the meaning of comprehension, translation, and interpretation.

considered too "intangible." This is true to some extent of all objectives except those that deal with the mastery of information and skills: the development of thinking, of values, attitudes, cooperation, and creativity. The term "intangible" conveys a suggestion that these objectives are inherently incapable of being fully understood, hence also incapable of serving as a focus for teaching, learning, and evaluation. An adequate behavioral analysis of these objectives should dispel this notion.

A clear specification of expected behavior also reveals the extent to which the same behaviors can be attained in many different subjects. Clear thinking is not the monopoly of science or mathematics, as has been tacitly assumed by many educators. It is involved, although in different terms, in interpreting literature and in producing a painting. Nor is creativity limited to the arts or to writing: it is possible to think creatively in mathematics. This method of specifying objectives makes it possible to find the common elements in many educational experiences and to look for common patterns of growth in the total school program, as well as to discover the specific variations from one field of activity to another.

Conversely, it becomes evident that manifold behaviors are involved in achieving certain generalized objectives which formerly were regarded as unitary. Citizenship, from the standpoint of behavioral analysis, is a multiple objective. It involves knowledge of certain facts and ideas, certain modes of thinking and of relating ideas to each other, certain attitudes and loyalties, as well as skills, interests, or concerns. Achieving health involves understanding the principles of nutrition and of body functions and an ability to apply these principles to the use of exercise, rest, and food. It means pursuing hygienic practices and skills.

Objectives should also be so formulated that there are clear distinctions among learning experiences required to attain different behaviors. Lack of such distinction is probably the greatest obstacle to effective provision for attaining many objectives. Too often little distinction is made among the kinds of behavior required to master knowledge, to learn to think, or to develop attitudes, interests, and skills—even though, according to the psychological analysis of the processes involved, each behavior category requires a different learning experience. Learning experiences necessary to master manual skills are not necessarily suitable for developing thinking. Experiences calculated to create interests may not necessarily help to change attitudes. In teaching international relations, for example, it is important not to confuse the acquiring of information about various nations and their governments with the experiences needed to assure the development of sympathy or tolerance toward these governments or a concern with the problems of these peoples. This lack of distinction is responsible for an insufficient emphasis in some important areas of growth; it is assumed that the attainment of all objectives in these areas is an automatic by-product of some single attainment, such as the mastery of content. The development of attitudes is most frequently relegated to this category of concomitants. But often the various aspects of thinking are treated in a similar way—the ability to think logically, for example, may be assumed to develop as a by-product of absorbing logically organized content.

This analytical approach to formulating objectives should not blind us to the fact that in the reality of a learning act the various types of behavior represented by these objectives occur simultaneously. They can be distinguished from each other in analysis but cannot be separated from each other in actual learning experience. In curriculum planning this perception of differentiated behaviors should guide the planning of learning experiences aimed at multiple objectives, such as creating learning tasks and situations which call at the same time for learning new facts, adding something to the tool chest of thinking skills, and affecting changes in attitudes and feelings.

Objectives are developmental, representing roads to travel rather than terminal points. Objectives need to be conceived in terms of a continuity of growth over a long period of time and through different contexts, each more exacting than the previous one, rather than as terminal points, confined to a subject, a grade level, or even a specific activity. This principle means also that the achievement of educational objectives needs to be planned for continuity and with a full appreciation of the developmental steps within that continuity.

When objectives consist solely of the highly specific outcomes of single units or courses, an impression is created that all objectives have this terminal quality. It is dangerous to view even relatively specific objectives, such as the ability to think and to write in paragraphs, as if they could be learned for once and forever at a certain level. Even such a comparatively specific skill as paragraphing requires different operations as the thought which is being paragraphed increases in complexity. The developmental approach to both visualizing and implementing objectives is still more important in relation to such matters as the formation of abstract concepts, developing methods of inquiry, or acquiring a tolerant attitude toward differences. These objectives require cumulative development over a period of time. For example, in developing sensitivity to differences, one might begin by helping young children to understand and accept a boy or a girl with different dress, mannerisms, or ways of thinking. Later one might add experiences which help to understand differences that come from variations in economic circumstance or in social and cultural background. This capacity to respond with understanding may be gradually extended to all varieties of differences—racial and religious, political and cultural. Eventually it may encompass the "generalized other," the general welfare of mankind, and include not only a vague tolerance but also an objective understanding of the forces that produce differences and their psychological consequences. A cumulative growth includes not only an increasing range in the objects of sensitivity, but also an increment in the depth, sophistication, and subtlety of the response.

To apply the concept of developmental continuity to the formulation of objectives requires a fine analysis of the particular behaviors involved in the objectives and of the content to which the behavior refers. For example, it is difficult to see the need for a developmental accumulative growth in the ability to think reflectively if it is not clear what reflective thinking consists of or what particular matter it may be applied to. The same would be true of aesthetic sensitivity, which may range all the way from appreciating good color in a dress to responding to a cubist painting.

The concept of developmental sequences, or of the unfinished business of objectives, introduces a new dimension to the planning of curriculum and instruction. Curriculum builders have learned to apply the principles of developmental continuity to the planning of content. In academic skills the idea of a developmental sequence of behavior to be expected is also fairly clear and fairly well observed. Nothing similar has been done regarding continuities in developing mental powers, discrimination, or attitudes. If an upgrading in them occurs at all, it does so as an incidental by-product of upgrading in the difficulty of the content. The developmental growth of attitudes especially suffers from expectations of changes in shorter time and with less varied exposure than is feasible. Even in research it is not rare to see attempts to measure changes in such complex attitudes as prejudices as a result of reading a book or seeing a film.

This tendency to convert objectives which require developmental treatment into short-term terminal expectations occurs partly because little is known about the developmental sequences of more complex behaviors such as higher mental processes and attitudes, and partly because of a lack of sophistication in the nature of the ways in which behavior is changed and learned. The image of how facts are learned shapes the notions of how everything else is learned. A careful study of developmental sequences in thinking and in the maturation of feelings and sensitivities is necessary before we can hope for an efficient cumulative plan for these behaviors. Viewing objectives as developmental sequences and learning to formulate them so that their statements on successive levels reveal accumulative additions to basic behaviors would be a first step in this direction.

Objectives should be realistic and should include only what can be translated into curriculum and classroom experience. There is an almost traditional discrepancy between what is professed and what is practiced. It is tempting to overelaborate objectives without regard to whether they can be attained or whether there are realistic conditions for their attainment. Such objectives, in effect, represent a hope and a prayer, without any expectation of implementing them. Units with elaborate objectives decorating their front pages and with no sign of experiences planned to make them an actuality are legion.

As the discussion of human potentialities in the preceding chapter suggested, this lack of realism does not necessarily mean that higher performance is expected than is reasonable. The programs of public schools are more likely to be guilty of underexpectation than of overexpectation. Evidence is already accumulating that elementary students can handle concepts and methods of inquiry heretofore reserved only for high school or college students. It is possible that, with proper provisions, a greater maturity in social attitudes and a finer discrimination in taste can be attained. What the principle of reality suggests, however, is that the objectives set higher expectations than the provisions made for their attainment warrant or than the developmental sequence of experiences permits. Using the attainment of precision as an example, it is possible that even young children can be more precise about what they perceive, how they handle symbolic expression and thought, provided they have had experiences in learning, to do so. At the same time, older students, short of such experiences, may be expected to be no more precise than are young children.

The scope of objectives should be broad enough to encompass all types of outcomes for which the school is responsible. Lack of comprehensiveness is a commonly voiced criticism of educational objectives. The statements of objectives do not always include all the types of educational outcomes which are considered important. They are too narrow to encourage the manifold aspects of development for which education can or should be responsible. Even attempts to compile a great range of stated objectives and to classify them in an orderly fashion have ended in uncertainty about the comprehensiveness of the resulting classification scheme (*Bloom, 1954, pp. 6-13*).

The lack of comprehensiveness in the scope of objectives comes about in several ways. In some cases the platform of objectives for a school is nothing more than a compilation of specific objectives formulated separately by teachers of various subject areas. This compilation reflects the specialization of emphasis: the objectives which look important from the standpoint of mastering specific subjects are strongly represented, while the overarching general abilities, especially the behaviors that are least affected by a specific content and most by a way of learning, are neglected. There is also a tendency to "specialize" these more intangible and general objectives—such as assuming that geometry, and geometry alone, cultivates logical thinking, that abstracting is a process which belongs only to mathematics, or that appreciation of beauty can be developed only in arts and not also by algebraic formulas.

The result of this weakness in the general platform of objectives is that the various school subjects emphasize a more limited set of outcomes than is desirable. Many objectives are left to the tender care of incidental emphasis, which often means no emphasis at all. There is a tendency to give lip service to such objectives as democratic loyalty, integrity, responsibility, tolerance, and openmindedness, whereas the actual content, time, and effort is dedicated to acquiring information and academic skills. Usually this imbalance works in favor of the objectives that are easiest to understand and simplest to teach. Objectives that have to do with modifying attitudes and feelings tend to receive the least attention because they are most difficult to describe concretely and require more unusual techniques of teaching and learning.

CLASSIFICATION OF OBJECTIVES

Formulation is only the first step in arriving at a reasonable platform of educational objectives. The statements of objectives after formulation are apt to be on different levels of generality and are usually too numerous to give a rational perspective either for defining an approach to curriculum planning or for evaluation. A grouping of the specific objectives is needed to permit rational thinking about them and to suggest the types of learning experiences needed to attain them and the types of evaluation techniques necessary to their adequate appraisal.

Many statements of objectives appearing in curriculum guides have been criticized for a lack of organization capable of conveying a consistent approach, a logical conception of their scope, a hierarchy of importance, or a sequence of attainment. After examining a spate of the statements of objectives, Bloom described the field of educational objectives as chaotic, because persuasive skills rather than research findings determined priorities, and because definitions and classifications were confused (*1954, p. 13*). A variety of confusions exist. Some schemes of classification confuse the general aims of education with the objectives for curricula and instruction (e.g., listing the development of literate citizenship on the same level as reading comprehension).* Often the outcomes to be achieved are confused with statements of the means by which to attain these outcomes (e.g., not differentiating between "providing a democratic atmosphere" and learning to behave democratically). Further problems occur because of the apparent difficulty in making a clear-cut differentiation of various behaviors without implying a separation of these behaviors in actual learning. This prevents some people from making any differentiation. An orderly classification is one aspect of orderly thinking about educational objectives: it synthesizes and organizes a variety of specific objectives, provides at once an over-all perspective to curriculum planning and a nonspecific guide to implementing its specific parts in instruction, and supplies a clear basis for evaluation. Such a classification must combine a logical order with a regard for the functional realities of the curriculum and teaching. For example, a statement of objectives needs to be logical in the sense that it is consistent with the major aims of education and related to some dynamic objectives of the culture. It also needs to be practical in the sense that what it contains is capable of being translated into curriculum planning and teaching strategy. (See *Thompson* [*1943, pp. 196-99*] on the type of thinking that needs to go on regarding educational objectives.)

The first problem encountered in developing a logical scheme for grouping objectives is the variety of categories in which objectives can be and are being stated and grouped. It is possible, for example, to group educational objectives in terms of life needs of individuals, the needs of society, the content

* See the discussion of levels of objectives, pp. 197-98.

fields, or behaviors to be achieved. Each method tends to favor some aspect of development and neglect others. The subject classification, for example, tends to favor academic skills in subject areas and to subordinate qualities necessary for the development of the individual as a person. Objectives stated and classified in such terms as democratic citizenship, economic competency, or areas of life needs tend to stress cultural requirements but to be weak in expressing the scope of behaviors to be cultivated. Objectives stated in terms of individual competencies, such as initiative or clear thinking, do not always convey clearly to what activities of life or subject areas these competencies apply. Sometimes these three classifications are combined in such a manner that no clear criterion for the selection of content, for social direction, or for the competencies emerges.

Historically, American education has demonstrated several of these specific emphases in the conception and classification of objectives. Originally the objectives, if stated at all, were solely in terms of subject mastery. The growth of pragmatism and of the science of education engendered a discontent with the academically aloof and static pattern of education. The result was a series of efforts to state the purposes of education in terms of the needs of society. The Cardinal Principles of Secondary Education was one such. This report stated the chief aim of education as follows: "The purpose of democracy is so to organize society that each member may develop his personality primarily through activities designed for the well-being of his fellow members. . . . Consequently, education in a democracy, both within and without the school, should develop in each individual the knowledge, interests, ideals, habits, and powers whereby he will find his place and use that place to shape both himself and society toward even nobler ends." On the basis of these aims the Commission proposed seven cardinal principles as the basic objectives of secondary education, as follows: (1) health, (2) command of fundamental processes, (3) worthy home-membership, (4) vocation, (5) citizenship, (6) worthy use of leisure, (7) ethical character (*Commission for the Reorganization of Secondary Education, 1918, pp. 7, 10-11*).

These principles actually only described the areas of life activity which should be of concern to educators but did not elaborate the behaviors needed to attain these ends. It is no wonder, then, that even though the Commission did not intend to suggest that these areas be introduced as school subjects, this is precisely what happened. The statement of the cardinal principles became an incentive for introducing courses such as civics, health, leisure, and home and family, and also became a model for many subsequent formulations of objectives. Many groups, lay and professional, followed this scheme of stating the scope of objectives.

The Educational Policies Commission made an effort to combine a statement of the chief areas of life needs with a description of the behaviors and qualities necessary to attain each, to combine ideas about social needs with those about individual needs. In *The Purpose of Education in American De-*

mocracy, the objectives are listed under four main categories describing areas of life needs: the objectives of self-realization, of human relationships, of economic efficiency, and of civic responsibility. But each category includes certain behavioral goals, such as the inquiring mind (an aspect of self-realization), respect for humanity (an aspect of human relations), and critical judgment (an aspect of civic responsibility) (*1938*). This was a laudable effort to achieve rationality by relating general social aims to behavioral objectives. Unfortunately, the behavioral objectives were stated in terms too general to provide concrete guidance to curriculum makers or teachers.

The *Imperative Needs of Youth,* which appeared in a later document of the Educational Policies Commission, classifies the desirable outcomes in terms of behaviors that people in our society need to master, while subordinating the areas of life or subject fields to which these behaviors apply. For example:

1. All youth need to develop salable skills and those understandings and attitudes that make the worker an intelligent and productive participant in economic life (economic competency).

2. All youth need to develop respect for other persons, to grow in their insight into ethical values and principles, and to be able to live and work cooperatively with others (democratic values).

3. All youth need to grow in their ability to think rationally, to express their thoughts clearly, and to read and listen with understanding (thinking). (*1952, p. 216.*)

The result is a mixed list of objectives which combines several categories of behavior in one statement and employs no single basis of classification.

The above documents have been discussed widely and their influence has been great. But their influence has been more marked in extending the scope of school programs than in producing a realistic relationship between what the educators proclaimed they stood for and what the curriculum actually attained. Such highly generalized objectives as citizenship and an inquiring mind provoked either a ritualistic iteration as pieces of conventional wisdom or else a tendency to bestow on these statements a varied meaning according to individual beliefs and preferences. As a result, when someone strongly favored citizenship as an objective, no one knew whether he favored military training in high schools, instilling internationalism dogmatically, or teaching facts about the constitution.

To solve this problem of vagueness in formulating and stating educational outcomes, another type of analysis and grouping of objectives was introduced in the 1930's. This approach insisted on stating and classifying objectives in terms of behaviors they represented and on differentiating and grouping these behaviors according to the learning processes they required.

This method of analyzing and classifying objectives was developed in the evaluation program of the Eight Year Study and has remained a standard method since. It was based on the assumption that the business of education is to change people and that consequently the objectives should spell out the desired behavioral changes. It was understood, further, that because the nature of the objectives, and especially the evaluation of these objectives, dictated the nature of the curriculum and of instruction, care must be taken to stress a wide range of behaviors in order to ensure a wide scope of learning. Since it was evident that essentially the same types of behavior applied to a wide range of subject-matter content at different levels of education, these behaviors were fitted into a relatively small number of classes, each of which represented distinctions in types of behavior and the ways in which they are learned, rather than in types of life needs they serve or subject content in connection with which they are learned. This classification differentiates behaviors classifiable as acquisition of knowledge, the intellectual skills representing thinking, the behaviors classifiable as attitudes and feelings, and those referred to as academic skills and study habits.

Using homogeneous types of behavior as a basis for classification, this approach yielded the following grouping of educational outcomes:

1. The development of effective ways of thinking
2. The acquisition of important information, ideas, and principles
3. The development of effective work habits and skills
4. The development of increased sensitivity to social problems and aesthetic experiences
5. The inculcation of social rather than selfish attitudes
6. The development of appreciation of literature, art, and music
7. The development of increasing range of worthwhile and mature interests
8. Increased personal-social adjustment
9. Improved physical health
10. The formulation and clarification of a philosophy of life (*E. Smith and Tyler, 1942, p. 18*).

This classification by types of behavior has been found useful in determining the areas in which evaluation is needed and in suggesting the needed emphasis in curriculum development. But it must be remembered that the concept of scope such a scheme conveys is that of range of behavior and not of life needs or of content, at least not explicitly.

Actually, no single scheme of formulation and classification of objectives covers all the functions that seem important: indication of the focus and scope of the curriculum and teaching; provision of a concrete platform for instruction and evaluation; indication of a clear-cut relationship to the major functions of education in society and a consistent approach to the task of translating general ideas about this function into educational practice. Except in a particular school and with reference to particular students, it would be difficult, for example, to specify both the level of expected behavior and the particular *content* or *context* in which that behavior is to be applied. It would be difficult to specify what "improved understanding and attitudes which facilitate desirable relationships within a family" would mean precisely for eighth graders in Harlem, in Pasadena, and on the North Shore of Chicago. This difficulty is evident in a recent publication which attempts to visualize specifically the meaning of general objectives in terms of specific context. The result is a complicated taxonomy in which the areas of aims, such as self-realization, human relationships, and economic efficiency, have been supplemented with listings of specific behaviors necessary to reach these aims and the content to which they apply (*W. French et al., 1957*).

Another publication uses for primary classification areas of development, such as physical development, social relations, quantitative relationships, communication, and aesthetic development, and follows this classification with statements of behavioral objectives classified as those of knowledge, skills, competencies, attitudes, interests, and action patterns (*Kearney, 1953*). Here, also, the attempt to relate a specific behavior to specific content results in apparent rigidity and a nondevelopmental approach. It is difficult to visualize the curriculum pattern in terms of such concrete prescriptions as that a primary child should "know the meaning of the skull and cross bones on bottles." Nor is one quite satisfied about placing "asking thoughtful questions in discussion" in the upper grades rather than projecting this as a behavior to be sought throughout the school. The difficulty seems to lie in attempting to describe a behavior and a standard of achievement in general terms at the same time, and in attempting to convey comprehensiveness and specificity simultaneously and in the same order of classification.

The difficulties described above raise the question whether the formulation of objectives does not involve a twofold task. One is that of determining the main aims of education; this belongs in the hands of persons qualified to consider the whole field of education and to study carefully the sources from which to derive the aims. The other task is the definition and determination of the more specific curricular objectives, including the determination of the specific context in which to achieve the aims and the specific levels of attainment. This formulation should be in the hands of those who develop the local curriculum guides and specific units—the local curriculum groups and the school staffs. A rational and functional platform of objectives emerges, however, only to the extent that the specific objectives are consistently related to the general aims.

The Types
of Behavioral

CHAPTER FOURTEEN

Objectives

An organized statement of objectives should be more than a mere grouping of individual objectives. It should also convey the fundamental rationale on which the very conception of objectives is based. This rationale should indicate what is important in education and where the subsidiary values lie. Such a statement should be useful in establishing priorities in the grand design of the curriculum, as well as in the smaller decisions such as those about sampling content for a particular unit or whether to spend time on analyzing historic documents. It should yield some criteria for the scope of the educational effort and set some limits for the specificity or depth desired. In this sense an organized statement of objectives expresses the philosophy of education of a particular school system or of a particular school.

The two-dimensional model of stating and classifying objectives by a description of behavior and of the content to which this behavior applies illustrates both the advantage of greater clarity and the difficulty of living up to it. It conveys the idea that the fundamental point in education is to change behavior. It also creates some difficulty in producing a clear-cut classification. Either one or the other could be used as a basis for classification. If the types of behavior are used for a basis, the kinds of content to which the behavior is addressed is bound to be less clearly represented and less systematically sampled. If the content of behavior is used for a basis, the types of behavior involved tend to be obscured, as do the areas of life to which these behaviors are related. Recently, however, classification by types of behavior has been favored because it seems more functional as a basis for curriculum development and for evaluation than classification by content.

KNOWLEDGE: FACTS, IDEAS, CONCEPTS

In the simplest behavioral definition this area of objectives is that of remembering, of recalling facts, ideas, or phenomena in the form in which they were experienced or learned. The broader definition involves the idea of "understanding" or "insight," implying that knowledge which cannot be reorganized and used in new situations, which does not also involve seeing relationships and making judgments, is of little value. There is therefore some obscurity as to where possession of knowledge leaves off and the behavior called thinking starts.

On the surface, the objective of acquiring knowledge should require no discussion. Acquisition of knowledge is the dominant objective today as it has been for centuries. For many educators the change in the amount and the kind of knowledge is the primary or even the sole objective of education. Even the so-called progressives, who revolted against the tyranny of packaged knowledge, wanted more, not less, knowledge.

It is assumed that knowledge of any sort is an index of one's acquaintance with reality. As an individual increases his knowledge he also increases his understanding of the world around him. Knowledge is also regarded as a prerequisite to the development of intellectual powers. Often the maturity and the intelligence of an individual is judged by the amount of knowledge he possesses. In addition, teachers often prize information for its own sake simply because it is more easily taught and learned than any other educational outcome. For these reasons such objectives as "factual information about current events," "knowledge of the physical and chemical properties of common elements and compounds," or "familiarity with important historic events" figure heavily among the statements of objectives. There is some emphasis on knowledge of the ways and means by which to deal with specific facts, such as "knowledge of the standard representational devices used in maps and charts," and knowledge of the various classifications and categories, such as "familiarity with the types of literature," or "the ways of classifying plants and animals."

Because knowledge is vast and of different levels of relevance, one problem in organizing an adequate statement of the objectives of knowledge is to achieve both a proper scope and a proper differentiation of priorities of significance. The levels of knowledge described in chapter 12—differentiating the specific facts, basic ideas, concepts, and thought systems—in effect represent such a sequence of priorities among the objectives of knowledge.

Specific facts have only a temporary utility as means of acquiring ideas. Therefore, their acquisition and retention probably should have the lowest priority. Factual information is too vast, is increasing at too great a rate, is too much subject to obsolescence, and is too difficult to retain even if it were useful. Research has shown that about 80% of disconnected facts are forgotten in two years or so. Thus, to learn isolated facts is inefficient, even if their possession were important. A careful differentiation is needed between those facts which are important per se and those which are used as instruments for attaining some other objectives, and hence need not be regarded as a permanent equipment to be retained and recollected over a long period of time.

Much of the curriculum today operates on an assumption almost the reverse of the above. It stresses largely knowledge of the first level, the accumulation of specific, often isolated facts. Proceeding on the assumption that one has to have facts before one can generalize or think, the educators have also fallen into the trap of assuming that a great deal of knowledge needs to be piled up before thinking can begin. No doubt a defective concept of how intelligence develops and functions has contributed to the prevalence of this assumption (*see chapter 8, pp. 100-05, 107-12*).

Undifferentiated concentration on specific facts has created several phantoms that have tended to reduce the level of productive learning. One is the phantom of "covering the ground." When mastering facts alone is the measure of knowledge, "coverage" can become onerous, absorbing so much time that there is little room to learn anything else. The other phantom is that young people cannot deal adequately with complex concepts, that they lack the intellectual resources for handling abstract thought processes. This phantom has reduced the level at which the higher mental processes are challenged. There is a measure of truth in the assumption that when neither the organization of the curriculum nor the methods of teaching supports an organized development of concepts and abstractions, only a few bright souls catch on. Evidence is accumulating, however, that abstract concepts can be developed much earlier and at a higher level, provided that the curriculum is organized to focus on ideas and that teaching is guided by adequate knowledge of how concepts are learned (*see chapter 8, pp. 118-20*). The explorations of the author in curriculum development have indicated, for example, that third graders can learn concepts such as those of comparative culture and comparative geography, provided the curriculum and teaching are organized to this end. (Contra Costa County Schools, 1959*a*. See also chapter 20 on developing a unit.)

The second level of knowledge, the knowledge of principles and basic ideas, is represented in objectives such as "understanding the principle of gravitation or the biological laws of heredity and reproduction," the basic ideas of the "ways in which cultures differ and are similar to each other," or the generalizations about "the effect of frontier in shaping the way of life in the United States." These basic ideas naturally vary tremendously in their degree of abstractness and complexity. They range from a simple idea, such as that "community services change to meet community needs," which is appropriate for the second-grade study of community workers, to ideas that describe the control of the economy by the government or the nature and the behavior of the atom.

Knowledge on this second level is more useful than that on the first, mainly because it is more general and therefore more widely applicable. This type of knowledge is also productive in a sense that it can create new knowledge. General ideas are transferable: they can be applied to understanding things and events not learned directly. For example, the idea developed in connection with the study of one desert that deserts form a belt around the earth and that they occur only in certain latitudes under certain climatic and topographical conditions, provides a more transferable knowledge than would all the available details about all deserts.

Basic ideas are the fundamentals of content. But even here a choice is indicated, because the number of basic ideas that can be mastered is also limited. A variety of criteria can be used to select the basic ideas: they must have scientific validity; they must be learnable at the age level at which they are offered; they must have utility in our current culture. Historically, each of these criteria has been stressed separately and in turn. Our earlier curriculum committees, largely composed of specialists who had more insight into the requirements of becoming a specialist than into processes of learning or cultural needs, were most concerned with scientific validity of the content and produced a curriculum centered on concepts with a highly academic orientation. An increasing awareness of the difference in the knowledge required for the general education of youth from that required to become a specialist and an emphasis on producing alert and intelligent citizens led to applying the test of utility and learnability to the ideas to be included in the curriculum. This emphasis produced a curriculum strong in "learnability" but weak in scientific validity. It is possible that the current method of cooperative curriculum projects, in which curriculum workers and teachers work with content specialists, might prevent this one-sidedness and produce curricula which have a valid content but are also oriented to produce intelligent laymen, and have content which is learnable and has social importance in the culture of today.

The third level of knowledge—the concepts which relate bodies of generalizations and principles—is represented by objectives such as the understanding of the concepts of evolution, of number, of measurement, or of personality. This type of knowledge is seldom acquired in a brief treatment; it is usually a product of many experiences over a long period of time and in many different contexts. This is especially true of concepts such as justice, which have no concrete sense referents and denote abstract qualities of behavior. These last two categories of knowledge involve more than memorization and recollection; such knowledge must be developed by abstracting from many experiences of differentiating and synthesizing.

The problem of how to master facts, ideas, and concepts has been debated for a long time in education. The earliest model for learning concepts was derived from learning arbitrary facts which had no special logic. As Brownell and Hendrickson show, there is no special logic in calling a certain river "Euphrates." Learning such facts is a matter of arbitrary association (*1950, p. 95*). A different problem altogether is involved in acquiring abstract ideas and concepts, for they must be invested with meaning by the learner if they are understood at all. Learning them involves what Dewey called transactional experience (*1933*), and what more recently has been called the discovery method (*Bruner, 1961; Taba, 1962*). Both these terms imply active learning. They also involve the question of whether learning concepts and ideas is purely verbal or whether there is such a thing as intuitive perception of the relationships which constitute the concept or the principle (*Ausubel, 1961; Hendrix, 1961*). A recent study is postulating further that discovery of concepts and general principles comes through using the inquiry method (*Suchman, July, 1961*).

Precision stands out as one criterion for such knowledge, especially with reference to scientific knowledge. A vague concept of "vacuum" (e.g., as identified with emptiness or suction) makes the concept useless for either prediction or explanation. Perhaps for concepts which have no concrete referents, such as justice or democracy, operational differentiation of their meaning in various contexts takes the place of the kind of precision that these concepts cannot achieve by verbal definition.

REFLECTIVE THINKING

One scarcely needs to emphasize the importance of critical thinking as a desirable ingredient in human beings in a democratic society. No matter what views people hold of the chief function of education, they at least agree that people need to learn to think. In a society in which changes come fast, individuals cannot depend on routinized behavior or tradition in making decisions, whether on practical everyday or professional matters, moral values, or political issues. In such a society there is a natural concern that individuals be capable of intelligent and independent thought.

But this concern does not ensure that the meaning of critical thinking is clearly understood or that there is an adequate analysis of the behaviors that compose it. The status of this objective is similar to that of other "intangible" objectives: the behavior called thinking has many meanings and is called by many names. All intellectual skills and abilities from concept formation to problem solving are likely to be identified with thinking.

The psychologists are even debating about the distinctions between thinking and concept formation. The term "understanding" is often used to encompass processes of investing verbal symbols with meaning and of making inferences. A fairly recent yearbook on measurement of understanding found it difficult to define understanding. It seemed easier to say what it was *not* than to describe what it was (*National Society for the Study of Education, 1946, p. 2*). It is no surprise, then, to find that the development of thinking is an objective to which we pay lip service, but which we do not practice.

Critical thinking involves many different processes, each of which must be distinguished fairly clearly if this objective is to serve as a guide either to curriculum development or evaluation.

Interpretation of Data

One cluster of behaviors is related to the ability to interpret data of various sorts and to generalize from them: to distill meaning from a literary passage, to "read" a cartoon, a statistical table, or a series of mathematical formulas. Essentially the process of interpretation involves singling out important facts or ideas from a context, relating them to each other, and deriving generalizations from them.

Specifically, interpretation may consist of a simple reading of points or of trends, of comparing these points or trends, and of inferring causes or consequences. Evaluating the dependability of data and recognizing their limits is involved also. These processes naturally include the ability to read the meaning of symbols of all sorts and the capacity to analyze or to break down complex sets of data into their components. Logically this process is described as inductive thinking.*

The operations necessary to make legitimate and valid interpretations also differ according to the character of the data, such as whether their content is scientific or literary, quantitative or verbal, highly abstract or concrete. For example, in interpreting quantitative graphic data about the relationship of the changes in the price of cars to the wages paid to automobile workers over a period of years, precision and accuracy are important and the generalizations that can be drawn are limited to what is given in the data. The interpreter must refrain from extrapolating possible causes of these changes, their effects or purposes, unless data on these are included. Different processes and criteria are involved in reading a pamphlet about problems of delinquency, studying the statistics on slum conditions, or reading a play like *Dead End,* even though each deals with the same subject. To learn what these materials have to offer, a student should be able to ferret out the relevant facts and ideas in each and draw appropriate inferences by using appropriate processes. But ferreting pertinent facts from statistics on slum conditions involves a more exacting process than does reading a pamphlet on delinquency. The play offers less precise data on delinquency but more adequate information on the psychological dynamics of becoming or being one. The interpretation of a play, therefore, has more latitude; while "going beyond the data" is a fault in reading a chart, "reading between the lines" is a necessity in interpreting a play (*Taba, 1940*).

Application of Facts and Principles

Applying facts and principles to the solution of new problems and to the prediction and explanation of new phenomena is another aspect of thinking. To predict the consequences of an increased sales

---

* For a fuller description of the processes involved in various aspects of interpretation, see Bloom (1954, pp. 74-81) and E. R. Smith and Tyler (1942, pp. 38-47).

tax on cigarettes, one may apply what is known about the effect of the sales tax on various groups in society and about the general principles of taxation, including the principles of democracy. When a car is skidding toward a ditch on a wet pavement, the principles of friction could be applied to predict what the driver needs to do to bring it out of the skid.

This process involves first a sufficient grasp of the principle. It involves discrimination of the principles that have relevance to the particular problem from those that do not. It involves also a sufficient understanding of the new problem or phenomenon to see the relationship between it and what one knows. And it always involves restructuring and reorganization of knowledge to make it appropriate to new problems and situations.

As in interpreting, the process of applying principles involves using criteria to determine the quality of the process and of the product. The process of application may be limited or productive, may involve precise reasoning or reasoning by analogy, or even misconceptions. The inferences may represent convergent thinking in the sense of being limited to the most obvious and immediate or be divergent in the sense of introducing innovation and subtlety (*E. R. Smith and Tyler, 1942, pp. 77-84; Bloom, 1954, pp. 110-15*).

As in interpreting data, the processes used in application vary depending on the content with which one deals. Generalizations, principles, and facts, for example, vary in the degree of universality which can be assumed. Some generalizations or principles, especially those of the physical sciences, are relatively universal and dependable. For example, the law of gravity is universal and dependable: a stone will fall in the U.S. *and* in Russia. Other generalizations are both less dependable and less universal, such as generalizations regarding causes of revolutions. (At different times and in different places different circumstances lead to revolutions.) Many social-science generalizations lack universality and dependability: some are little more than hypotheses, others involve value judgments and beliefs. These types of generalizations must be applied and used in a different manner from those of physical science, and their application needs to be surrounded with different sets of qualifying conditions.

Most social and human phenomena are also subject to multiple causation. One can assume no one-to-one connections between *a* principle and *a* solution, *a* prediction or *an* explanation. Usually a constellation of qualifying facts and generalizations must be considered, and the conclusions are at best much more tentative than is the case with applying the principles of science.

Value judgments and feelings also enter in interpretations. Thus in explaining why delinquency exists or predicting how it will change if certain measures are employed, it is necessary to consider not only the ways in which human behavior is caused but also what one believes about equality, justice, and other democratic values and how one feels about the worth of all human beings, about deviate behavior, or about adolescents. These feelings may interfere with the clarity of thinking; they may block rational thought processes, and touch off subjectivity, irrationality, bias, and wishful thinking. We know, for example, that correct facts and valid principles about such matters as the role of racial minorities in American society, even if known, are either distorted or not applied because they contradict feelings or emotional dispositions. Some recent research has demonstrated that emotionalized and autistic thinking prevails over rational processes in many "closed" areas, among which are the problems of minority groups and race relations (*Adorno et al., 1950, pp. 145-50*).

Because of these difficulties, learning to apply principles of science or some other "neutral" material is no assurance that the same processes will be used in fields that present various obstacles to clear thinking. Learning to reason logically about abstract and emotionally neutral problems is no guarantee of logical reasoning on more complex issues or on issues which involve feelings and values (*Taba, April 1944, p. 394*).

The fact that the effectiveness of school learning depends on the extent to which students can apply to new situations what they have learned makes the transfer of learning an extremely important objective. And the greater the leap of transfer, the more profitable the learning. Yet, as has been pointed out before, this ability is by and large not well provided for in our curriculum (*chapter 8, p. 115*). Students in high schools and colleges are not especially adept either at analyzing and attacking problems or in using what they know to solve them.

Logical Reasoning

The ability to reason logically and critically and to analyze ideas for the same qualities is another aspect of thinking. Conflicting statements on the same issue may appear in different sources. Many conclusions are based on a mistaken or hidden assumption. Convincing arguments are supported insufficiently or with unacceptable evidence. Advertising and propaganda often try to impress us with the desirability of buying a certain soap to make us beautiful or of supporting a political platform which guarantees the best government by using distorted logic and emotional appeal.

Since all such reasoning is carried on with reference to assumptions, defensible or not, hidden or open, the ability to detect faulty assumptions and to formulate adequate ones is important. The individual in modern society needs to judge assumptions and to weigh evidence discriminatingly if he is not to be at the mercy of salesmanship of all sorts. He needs to judge where facts end and opinions begin and to recognize conclusions based on faulty assumptions or faulty logic. For example, when reading a plea for economy in government or hearing a discussion of the causes of war, students should be able to ask themselves what the author takes for granted, whether he has considered all the important factors, and how relevant his facts and arguments are to his conclusions. In many contexts, such as reading novels, it is especially important to examine intelligently the assumptions being made about human motivation.

It is also necessary to recognize fallacious devices, such as attacking a person to discredit an idea, deliberate shifting of definition, or the use of emotionally charged words. In many cases the use of the principles of logical inference, such as the "if-then" principle, is a necessary part of criticizing arguments. Or one may need to be aware of the crucial words and phrases and their definitions and to recognize that changed definitions may produce changed conclusions.

The ability to judge critically other people's arguments does not automatically improve one's own logic, and awareness of the specious qualities in other people's reasoning does not assure avoidance of the same qualities in one's own reasoning. Sound argumentation involves the capacity to follow a logical chain of reasoning from assumptions or premises to conclusions, and to construct a logical structure of argument, and not, as Salinger points out, "trying to make a very convenient generalization stay still and docile long enough to support a wild, specific premise" (*1950, p. 65*). (For further descriptions of these aspects of thinking, see *Taba [1950]; R. Smith and Tyler [1942, chs. 2 and 3]*).

It is clear that thinking is not a simple thing to be learned in a few easy lessons, in a single subject, or in one unit. Its development requires continued practice in many different contexts. While it is possible that certain subjects provide special opportunities for special forms of thinking, such as pursuing proof in geometry, an effective skill develops only by practicing thinking in a variety of contexts.

Furthermore, thinking is something that can be learned only by doing. Whichever of its elements one considers—deciding what is important to think about, analyzing facts, generalizing, pursuing the steps of logical inference, or comparing and contrasting different sets of facts—all require consistent practice for mastery.

Neither can the ability to think critically be taught all at once, no matter how thorough the emphasis. Serious provisions for thinking require some continuity. A course in logic, which has been proposed as a means for lifting the level of thinking, will not solve the problem. Thinking as a behavior has a developmental sequence, and therefore a developmental plan is needed to learn it effectively. Unfortunately, as was pointed out earlier, too little is yet known about the nature of the developmental sequence in thinking: which skills and processes can be mastered at which age level, which aspects must precede which others, what type of generalizations and what level of abstraction young children can master in contrast to high school students.

There are several ways to strengthen the implementation of this objective. One is the more careful planning of sequences in the development of thought, such as providing for accumulative sequence in the development of abstract ideas, in the rigor used in applying generalizations, or in the development of the facility to follow a logical sequence of thought. A sequential development is possible only if there is a clear enough understanding of both the specific behaviors that compose thinking and of the necessary steps in their development. In such a sequence concrete experiences with pertinent examples must precede the development of perception of abstractions. To become capable of being logical or insightful about the "democratic freedoms" requires a preceding exploration of both democracy and freedom in a concrete context which is sufficient to give meaning to these abstractions.

Second, the organization of curriculum might take greater account of the fact that the basic process of thinking is the common factor among the various subjects. A form of integration in pooling forces for this development is therefore possible, no matter how diverse the content of these subjects. Discriminating thinking, like discriminating taste, is best developed by comparison. If thinking were stressed in the various subjects and the differences in the processes of interpretation and application according to context were made conscious, comparative training in thinking would become a matter of course. Students would experience variations in the rigor and the precision of thinking and would learn discrimination in the use of data, generalizations, and principles according to the degrees of their universality. A comparison of the process of proof in geometry and in an article on politics would add greatly to the understanding of what logical proof is all about.

Third, it is quite evident that the usual separation of curriculum planning from the planning of teaching strategies adds up to insufficient provision for the development of thinking. Effective and consistent training is possible only if the whole gamut of decisions, ranging from the selection and organization of content to the choice of materials and the method of asking questions or of making examinations, are focused continuously on this objective. Too often the organization of content constitutes a veritable "obstacle course" to thinking at all, let alone to thinking critically, so that unusual methods, such as special training in inquiry or courses in logic, must be resorted to in order to encourage thinking. Or again, when the treatment of content is persistently addressed to seeking *the* right answer, or *the* only cause, special occasions must be created for creative and divergent thinking.

VALUES AND ATTITUDES

This is an area of objectives of the greatest concern to those who are oriented to social analysis and the study of cultural needs of today. As was shown in chapters 3 and 4, the mainsprings of culture and of human motivation and action lie in the realm of values and feelings. There seems to be consensus that the technological culture of the twentieth century is increasingly in danger of submerging its social and human values to things and techniques, whether in nuclear weapons, skyscrapers, or urban renewal, and that education could or should be a countervailing force to this danger.

Many who judge the problem of values to be the most compelling find it at the same time the most perplexing one. There are criticisms to the effect that the school curriculum stresses fact finding to the exclusion of the study and the development of values, that this emphasis has produced a dangerous pseudo-neutrality toward moral issues, and that in many areas, such as morality, religion, minority relations, nationalism and patriotism, decisions are governed by blind emotional reactions, prejudices, and taboos (*chapter 3, pp. 35-39; chapter 4, pp. 57-64*).

The statements of objectives in this area do not reflect this urgency. There is perhaps even less clarity in the area of values and attitudes than in the area of thinking, and this lack of clarity extends to all important aspects of formulating objectives: the identification of important values, attitudes, and areas of sensitivity, the differentiation among various types of values and attitudes, and the analysis of specific behaviors which would be part of "valuing" or "having an attitude."

The consequences of this confusion and vagueness of definition were well illustrated in the attempts a few years ago to develop a sharper emphasis on moral and spiritual values. Most symposia and conferences held on the subject and the pamphlets that followed ended in relegating this task either to religious education or to education for democracy, because, defined vaguely, these values seemed to have something to do with either religion or democracy. It seemed impossible to secure a fresh analysis of what was meant by moral and spiritual values and to specify the behavior involved. This lack of clear specification characterizes statements of objectives pertaining to values and attitudes in other areas also. Statements regarding respect for the individual, the democratic way of life, and responsible citizenship abound among curricular objectives, but behavioral analysis of these objectives is hard to come by.

A great deal more analysis is needed to produce more functional objectives in this area. It may be important to distinguish the different kinds of values in order to gain clarity about how values can be acquired. Getzels, for example, distinguishes two different kinds: those representing the democratic creed in American society, which he calls the "sacred values," and those he calls the "secular values," which guide daily conduct in our culture and which shape the American character (*1958, p. 149*). Among the "sacred values" are the traditional democratic tenets, the values which everyone cherishes and presumably wants his children to cherish. These include faith in democracy, the idea that the welfare of the many is more important than the welfare of the few, that those who are affected by consequences of decisions need to be involved in making them, and that the people are the best judges of their needs. They involve also the tenets on freedoms, such as the freedom to hold a wrong opinion, to speak out, to assemble, and to organize.

Another facet of the democratic creed is that the individual is a source of initiative and responsibility and has a right to self-development. The political and economic implications of individualism involve the right to free enterprise, to government by the citizenry, and such privileges as living one's own life in one's own way and choosing one's own religion.

From the principle of individualism flows the principle that all individuals, whatever their personal capacities, must have equal opportunity to develop themselves and equal rights before law and justice. Part and parcel of the democratic creed is the belief in human perfectibility, an optimism about improving people as well as the human condition.

Some of the secular values were described in the section of chapter 4 dealing with character development in American society. Among these are the values referred to as the work success ethic: acceptance of the value of competitive achievement, the ideal of individual success, and respect for the value of work and work responsibility. Still other "secular" values flow from the democratic ideals and the Christian ethic: tolerance, cooperation, regard for the welfare of others, and respect for individuals. From the basic orientation toward the future—another characteristic of the American character— emerge such values and attitudes as the importance of planning for the future, of sacrificing current needs for future ones, of thrift, and of using time economically and wisely.

The conflicts inherent in these values are also reflected in the objectives dealing with values and attitudes. There is, for example, a cleavage between the objectives which stress independence and individuality and those which emphasize the importance of obedience to rules, getting along with others, and adjustment (according to certain interpretations of it). This cleavage of values produces a certain hesitancy in specifying the content of these objectives and also, therefore, a difficulty in analyzing clearly the behavior involved. As a consequence, there is little to guide a teacher or a curriculum maker in deciding exactly what behaviors to seek or how these behaviors could be learned. It is no wonder, then, that the statements of objectives of social values largely cling to generalized clichés about democracy and the worth of the individual personality. Only in the area of personal living can one find more concrete statements of values and attitudes to be achieved, such as willingness to undertake and to carry through a job to a completion (responsibility), and willingness to help others and to work with others for desirable group goals.

These difficulties naturally affect the quality of the curriculum and teaching. The teaching of values is largely of three types: teaching about them, moralizing, and hoping that they will emerge as a by-product of other things in the program. It is no wonder, then, that school programs have less of an effect on the development of values than might be expected, and offer meager experiences for the internalization of important values.

SENSITIVITIES AND FEELINGS

Sensitivity is the term used by those who are concerned with the experiencing of feelings and values instead of descriptive learning about them. Sensitivity can be defined as a capacity to respond to the social and cultural environment and as a personal and unique quality in perception, meaning, and response. Involved in this capacity is the empathic ability, or the capacity to "take the role of the other," and to respond empathically to social and human situations (*Cottrell, 1950, pp. 706-08*).

In some programs concerned with human and intergroup relations the development of a cosmopolitan social sensitivity, the capacity to respond empathically across the barriers of cultural differences, has been regarded as a cornerstone for democratic human relations. The rationale for this emphasis is based upon the analysis of social needs in today's world. As was pointed out in chapter 3, living in today's world demands an understanding and acceptance of a vast scope of cultural and human differences. We are required to meet and to understand ways of life, attitudes, values, and feelings of a diversity of people undreamed of in earlier days. We cannot afford not to learn to "see" other people as they see themselves and to communicate across the personal as well as cultural barriers. The normal socializing process does not prepare individuals for this demand, because in any society the process of socialization tends to be parochial. Chapter 4 pointed out that an individual is socialized in a sense in a cultural shell: in a family with a particular style of life, according to its social status, religious orientation, and cultural or national background. This "cultural location" circumscribes the values and standards which are internalized and become the criteria for conduct and expectation. Eventually these standards and valuations are universalized and applied as criteria in judging all behavior. Socialization also trains the individuals to accent certain behaviors and to reject others as unfitting. The more successful this unconscious socialization is, the greater the danger of prejudice, of rejection of differences in values and behavior and of ethnocentricity in feelings, valuations, and standards. This unconscious socialization seldom prepares an individual for either a sympathetic understanding of differing values and feelings or objectivity in assessing their role in his own conduct or in that of the others.

Attempts to analyze social sensitivity as an objective in education and to measure growth toward it began as early as 1935. Early definition was largely concerned with the cognitive aspects of sensitivity and included such behaviors as "concern about social problems, events and issues," the capacity to evaluate problems and action in terms of values, consequences and purposes, and loyalty to democratic values and principles as a personal point of view (*Taba, 1936; 1942, pp. 160-61*).

The studies in intergroup education extended the definition to include empathy and feelings. Chief among the behaviors of social sensitivity stressed in these programs were the following: "Capacity to identify oneself with the feeling, values, and aspirations of others . . . the ability to project oneself into the lives, problems, and dilemmas of other people and the capacity to understand them in their own terms rather than interpreting them ethnocentrically." Some emphasis also was put on the capacity to communicate across the barriers of differences, the ability to accept differences, and the capacity to use cosmopolitan value criteria in interpreting and assessing human situations (*Taba, Brady, and Robinson, 1952, p. 41*).

Extension of feelings is an important aspect of sensitivity, whether social, moral, or aesthetic. Feelings figure in most human situations. It is difficult to understand people without understanding their feelings. Feelings are also at the bottom of many forms of distorted reasoning: hostile stereotyping, an uncritical use of ethnocentric assumptions, and so on. In conflict situations, persons with no understanding of how feelings function tend to counter feelings with feelings. Only one who is literate in the ways of feelings, who can read and interpret them, can use them as factual material from which to fashion solutions to conflicts.

But besides understanding feelings, there is also the problem of generating feelings and extending the capacity to identify, to empathize, and to make "a really personal contact and entry" (*Niblett, 1955, pp. 36-37*).

Feelings, values and sensitivities are matters that need to be discovered rather than taught. Neither democratic values nor feelings of tolerance can be developed solely by teaching about them. This means that the provisions for these objectives must include opportunities for direct experiencing of some sort and materials which affect feelings. A much more conscious use is needed of the experience of students, of literature, and of other materials which reproduce life in its full emotional meaning and which express and affect feelings and values.

This makes the modification of attitudes and feelings one of the most difficult of educational tasks. Many question whether it is a proper task for education, or one that is attainable by means available to schools (*see chapter 2, pp. 18-21*). However, experiments in many schools have demonstrated the feasibility of extending by educational means the capacity to "feel with," to accept and understand, and to modify the standards and values learned in one's own immediate culture. Using literature systematically for extending the capacity to feel and to respond and to identify values has been among the chief ways.

Because feelings are learned by imitation, the extension of feelings and sensitivities also requires a living laboratory. Therefore, assembling groups with heterogeneities of backgrounds and providing for open interaction among these heterogeneities has been another method. The incongruity of teaching democratic principles and ideals but allowing the classroom climate and the life in school to instill the antithesis has long been recognized.

Finally, it is well to remember that to change sensitivities and feelings requires indirection and a lot of freedom on the part of the individual to do his own examining and changing.*

SKILLS

There are skills to be learned in connection with any area of competency. The objectives pertaining to skills, therefore, range from the basic academic skills, such as reading, writing, and arithmetic, to skills in democratic citizenship and group living. Usually the objectives pertaining to skills are concentrated on the "three R's," which constitute the basis for academic study. In the minds of some persons these constitute the essentials, at least on the elementary level.

The skills necessary for independent and creative intellectual work—the ability to locate and evaluate information from sources other than textbooks and the processes of solving problems and analyzing data—have received some emphasis. These skills are especially important in programs that have made a transition from "following the textbook" to assignments which require the use of multiple sources.†

Emphasis on problem solving suggests a need for additional skills, such as the ability to define problems of investigation, to plan a method of inquiry, to assess discriminatingly the appropriateness and limitations of the sources for particular purposes and the ability to master simple research skills, such as tabulating and classifying information and experimenting with different ways of organizing and interpreting.

An especially neglected area of skills is the complex pertaining to the management of interpersonal relations and the conduct of groups. These are usually referred to as social or group skills. The emphasis on these skills has not always been very broad in scope, nor pertinent. Often training is confined to the routines of polite etiquette and to mastering parliamentary procedure. In some primary schools with acculturation problems the training in the common routines of social communication, such as saying "hello," expressing appreciation or regret, may be pertinent. But it must be recognized that even in such schools many children are not prepared for group living in school. There are children whose homes have not given them much training in the ordinary social disciplines, whose com-

* For examples of programs addressed to this objective see Taba and Elkins, 1950; Taba *et al.*, 1950; Heaton, 1952; Heaton and Lewis, 1955.
† See Taba and Elkins, 1950, pp. 157-64, for the problems encountered and the skills needed in such a transition.

munication skills are at a minimum, and who have only a minimal mastery of such common routines as group listening, controlling the impulses of anger, or following rules of conduct. For these children acquiring a "common culture" in the sense of developing a modicum of common social skills becomes a necessity. For the students from minority groups or from homes on lower economic levels, the problem is even more serious. The deficiency in the needed social skills leads to an almost inevitable failure in social situations and to a defensive "chip-on-the-shoulder" attitude, hostility, or withdrawal.

Because the problems of interpersonal relations, especially those of handling interpersonal conflicts, rebuff, misunderstanding, or criticism, are with us everywhere, the skills in managing interpersonal relations have acquired some importance. There is scarcely a child or adolescent who does not face such conflicts with peers, family, or adults and who would not benefit from some emphasis on the skills needed to deal constructively with interpersonal conflict, or for the development of constructive human relations. The deficiency of these skills showed clearly in responses to a survey on the question, "What makes me mad and what I do about it," conducted by the Intergroup Education Project (unpublished material). The results showed that the range of skills brought to solving conflicts were as meager as they were ineffective. Both children and adolescents resorted with equal frequency to retaliation in one form or another as the major device. Withdrawing from a situation or taking it out on someone else or something else followed in frequency. Few thought of talking it through. A special feature of these replies was the tendency to "blame" someone. Practically no one looked at the situation to discover what factors provoked the conflict, because he did not have even the idea of a situational causation of behavior, much less the skills for conducting such an analysis.

To manage conflict situations it is also necessary to gauge the feelings of the opposite party, to assess objectively the reactions of people to one's own behavior, and to discover the situational rather than the personal causes of difficulty. Many difficulties in interpersonal relations occur because individuals are unaware of the discrepancy between their own motives and their actual conduct. They don't realize how what they do looks from the "outside." Understanding and applying certain simple principles of behavioral causation, such as that anger begets anger, that hurting stimulates further hurting, or that a smile produces a smile, helps to extend perception of what goes on in human interaction and with it the rational control over conduct even for the misbegotten and maladjusted.

Still another needed skill is that of managing authority democratically. In school as well as out of school there are many occasions to exercise authority. The usual practice on such occasions is to resort to authoritarian controls, including using the power to mete out "punishments according to crime." Many a monitor or traffic boy will tend to enforce his authority by authoritarian methods, not so much because he admires these procedures as because he knows no alternatives. This practice not only causes much conflict but also teaches undesirable methods of control; both dangers could be avoided by a development of skills in democratic use of authority.

Training in the ways of using authority democratically would greatly reduce the cleavages on which schools spend such a large amount of time. For example, sociodramatic training in resolution of conflicts provides opportunities for learning the more difficult democratic procedures for control (*Taba et al., 1949, pp. 109-17*).

The growth in sophistication about group relations and group processes have opened up still another area of skills, those related to participation in and the conduct of groups. Group activity is becoming increasingly important in modern life, so much so that many students of society insist that the fundamental relations of men are now with groups rather than with individuals as such. As a consequence the development of vastly improved techniques of group deliberation and of making group decisions is considered one of the major tasks of society today—and, therefore, of the schools today. Furthermore, most of the work of the schools is carried on in groups, and much of it wastefully, at worst, and less productively than it might be, at best. In surveying the status of group skills, the staff of the Intergroup Education Project pointed out that one serious deficiency was a lack of skills in the effective functioning of groups: thinking, planning, making group decisions, participation. While the schools recognized the importance of these skills, scarcely any analysis was available of what the skills entailed, much less any tangible methods for learning them (*Taba, Brady, and Robinson, 1952, pp. 47-52*).

Productivity in group situations requires a variety of skills: doing orderly thinking, planning group goals, focusing on the central task, controlling egocentric drives, managing conflicting ideas, progressing from dissension to consensus. A series of skills are involved also in making group work productive—focusing, clarifying, involving, initiating ideas, harmonizing feelings, and a host of others (*Cunningham et al., 1951; Benne and Sheats, 1951, pp. 98-104; D. Hall, 1957, ch. 12*).

Many a committee or a work group, adult or child, founders because individuals in it are energized by their own personal needs and are insufficiently sensitive to the need for focusing on the group task, do not know how to help the group effort, cannot discover the group goals, or fail to identify with them. Giving social space to a variety of viewpoints and feelings is as much a matter of skill as it is a matter of inclination. Group discussions can be more than either a rambling conversation or a strait jacket in which there is no room for all to participate constructively. It is possible to learn ways of moving from dissension to consensus. In other words, besides good will and democratic intent, many specific skills go into making groups productive and effective. These skills can be learned and, if learned, make group work vastly more effective (*Taba et al., 1950, chs. 5 and 6*).

Learning appropriate leadership roles is another factor in group productivity. The conventional concept of leadership, derived largely from the operation of the official leadership positions, assumes that a few persons are the leaders and the rest the followers. Recent experiments and studies in group procedures have disclosed a wide range of possible leadership roles, all of which can be performed by a large number of group participants. A wide distribution of these roles is both needed and possible.

Training in carrying on a variety of these roles is important both for immediate effectiveness and productiveness and for ultimate maturity in group participation in adult life. Distribution of leadership is further useful for opening up leadership opportunities to those who most need it: students whose home backgrounds have left them short in adequate group skills and, hence, incapable of assuming a part in the school's program or activities. This reversal of emphasis is needed if we are to correct the current practice of throwing into leadership roles persons who already show capacity and who, because of their home environment or cultural advantages, already have developed the qualities and skills necessary for assuming such roles (*Taba, 1955a, p. 115*).

TRANSLATING GENERAL OBJECTIVES INTO SPECIFIC ONES

A platform of general objectives, no matter how well defined, is still an inadequate guide for the specific aspects of curriculum, such as the selection of content and experiences for particular units on a particular grade level. These general objectives need to be translated into more specific ones. The term "translation" is used to emphasize the fact that these more specific objectives should be clearly related to the major objectives and that the greater specification of objectives is for the purpose of adjusting the major objectives to the specific content and to the developmental needs of the particular group.

Too often there seems to be little consistency between the school-wide objectives, usually stated in broad strokes, and the objectives of specific courses in specific subjects, or the specific units. This inconsistency is especially bound to occur when one group in the school system is responsible for the development of the general framework of the curriculum and another for the generation of more specific curriculum plans. Under these circumstances it is easy to forget that the specific aspects of the program are responsible for implementing the general objectives.

To maintain this consistency it is necessary, first, that the general objectives be clear enough so that what follows from them is clearly understood. In addition, those in charge of curriculum development must pay some attention to the process of implementing the general objectives in all its steps: to the formulation of the objectives in subject areas for specific units, and to the examination of consistency among the learning experiences to assure that they indeed are providing opportunities for the attainment of the major objectives.

A handbook to guide the use of the resource units developed under the direction of the central curriculum committee in one school system illustrates this process of helping teachers translate the general objectives into the more specific ones. The general objectives for the social studies were stated as follows:

CHILDREN NEED TO UNDERSTAND (knowledge)

1. That all peoples of the world are in some way dependent upon each other and must get along with each other
2. That our world is constantly changing
3. That events, discoveries, and inventions may improve some ways of living but create problems in others
4. That people have established communities and governments to meet their needs
5. That groups develop traditions, values, and ways of doing things, and new generations learn these from their elders
6. That the physical geography of a place affects the way people live

CHILDREN NEED TO LEARN HOW (skill)

1. To seek information from many sources and to judge its validity
2. To organize facts and form generalizations based on facts
3. To carry on a discussion based on facts and to make generalizations or conclusions
4. To plan, to carry out plans, and to evaluate the work and the planning
5. To accept responsibility as part of living
6. To develop a set of values for judging right and wrong actions

CHILDREN NEED TO BECOME (attitude)

1. Willing to undertake and carry through a job to completion
2. Anxious to help others and to work with others for desirable group goals
3. Appreciative of others like and unlike themselves [*School City of South Bend, 1949, p. 10*].

The booklet then proceeds to illustrate how to translate such general objectives as the concept of interdependence. It points out that if the teacher wishes to develop the concept of interdependence in the second-grade unit on community helpers, she must first define what is important to learn about interdependence and what can be learned in this area by second graders. This analysis may lead to the selection of such understandings as that families depend on the services of other persons for some of their needs.

In contrast, a sixth-grade unit concentrating on the relationship of the city to the world might include the following understandings to implement the concept of interdependence: Communities with specialized industries (like South Bend) depend on many other communities and nations for raw materials and manufactured goods; many communities and countries depend on South Bend for manufactured goods. Similar suggestions are given for the development of skills. The skill of planning together is one of the general skill objectives for the city-wide curriculum. Yet, planning for kindergarten children might involve only such objectives as having the child develop an ability to listen to other children's suggestions and decide what he thinks ought to be done and which job he would like to do. A fifth-grade program might aim to develop the ability to select good leaders, to contribute to group planning, and to help others in the group to contribute by asking them questions (*School City of South Bend, 1949, pp. 17-18*).

From the foregoing it should be evident that the task of translating general objectives into specific ones is not simply that of a more specific elaboration of the general statement. It involves rethinking of the meaning of the general objective in terms of the particular curriculum content or learning experiences, and the selection of a particular emphasis in the light of what is both logical and appropriate to the growth potential of the given age or maturity level. In other words, the specific objectives must be seen as developmental aspects of the general objectives and placed accordingly. Some aspects of any general objective, be it a concept or a form of thinking, may be beyond the possibility of a given maturity level to acquire, and others could be emphasized only if the preceding experiences have built a background for such emphasis. The criterion that objectives be developmental does not mean simply an age-level placement of expectations; it means also a planning of sequences to upgrade these expectations.

Finally, it should be pointed out that the formal statement of the school-wide objectives, no matter how adequate, is only a part of the total platform. It would, therefore, be foolhardy to attempt to incorporate all the necessary qualifications and specifications in such a statement. Such an attempt would only result in a cumbersome complexity which would communicate little to anyone except those who formulated it. Such general statements are vastly more useful when they are relatively simple. These statements, however, need to be supplemented by the more specific descriptions of the grade-level steps toward these objectives, and of the special contribution of the various subject areas. To attempt to serve both functions in one general statement would make the listing too lengthy and chaotic to serve as a general guide. On the other hand, to limit the statement of objectives only to those pertinent to the grade levels and various subjects would make obscure the perspective which a systematic statement of objectives should provide.

Diagnosis
in Curriculum
CHAPTER FIFTEEN # Development

Diagnosis is an essential part of curriculum development and of curriculum revision. To keep the curriculum in tune with the needs of the times and of students, and to help determine which objectives to stress, diagnosis should be a continuous part of ongoing curriculum and teaching. There is a continuous need to accommodate different types of learners, to introduce new materials or a new emphasis. These adjustments should be made not blindly, but according to definite diagnostic checks on what the students know and can understand, what skills they have, or what mental processes they have mastered. Diagnostic evidence is also needed to gear plans and expectations to the upper limits of potentiality.

Diagnosis is essentially a process of determining the facts which need to be taken into account in making curriculum decisions. These decisions may concern small matters, such as determining the level at which to work in a given class. They may concern matters of general consequence, such as whether to teach the arithmetical and algebraic approaches to the number concept simultaneously.

Since curriculum decisions are of different levels of generality and importance (see ch. 1, p. 67, and ch. 22), diagnosis should and does also operate on different levels. At one extreme one can speak of diagnosing the whole state of the educational system, including its resources and facilities, in order to determine where the weaknesses are and where improvements are either necessary or possible. At the other extreme one can speak of diagnosing an individual student or a group of students to determine what causes problems and difficulties in their learning or behavior.

This chapter deals largely with diagnosis as the first step in curriculum development and improvement, whether for building a course in mathematics or social science, developing a particular unit in a given subject, modifying the organization of a unit or a course, or changing the materials used. It is, therefore, concerned with the kind of diagnosis that lies somewhere in between

231

the two extremes suggested above. The type of diagnosis described here is concerned chiefly with determining the educational needs of students, the conditions of learning in the classroom, and the factors that affect optimum achievement of educational objectives.

DIAGNOSIS OF ACHIEVEMENT

One important function of diagnosis is to determine how well students have achieved important educational objectives. The scope of this diagnosis naturally depends on the scope of the objectives. It may include such matters as what concepts and information students have mastered, what patterns of thinking they find easy or difficult, what maturity in attitudes and feelings they possess, which skills they can or cannot use, and what their interests are. (Chapter 14 on objectives discusses the types of achievement that may be considered.)

Diagnostic information can be used in a variety of ways. Most frequently it is used to establish standards. This is especially so with the results of achievement tests, as in the comparison of group scores and national norms on an arithmetic test to decide whether or not a greater emphasis in arithmetic is needed to "bring achievement up to the expected norm." This is perhaps the narrowest interpretation of diagnosis of achievement and of least use in changing the character either of the curriculum or instruction.

Diagnostic data can also be used to locate the causes of weaknesses and strengths in the attainment of students. This purpose is served when diagnostic data are analyzed in sufficient detail to indicate not only the particular areas of strength and weakness but also their possible causes. Bloom illustrates this approach in his analysis of the difficulties students encounter when attempting to solve mathematical problems on tests. He found that unsuccessful students failed at several necessary processes. They had difficulty in understanding the nature of the problem. Some misinterpreted the directions, and therefore tended to approach the problem quite differently from the manner in which it was posed. Others refused even to attempt any solution which appeared abstract and complex. They either decided that they knew the answer or could not get it anyway. Many students who had the necessary information were unable to relate it to the problem. They could attack the problem only if it was similar to one that they had originally encountered in the text or lectures. A frequent difficulty was an aimless drifting through the problem rather than making a methodical approach (*Bloom, 1947, pp. 156-60*). A similar analysis was used by Buswell and Hersh, as described in chapter 8, page 115, in observing that high school and college students could recognize generalizations they knew but could not discover new generalizations on their own (*1956*).

This type of analysis describes not only the end product of achievement but also the processes by which the answers are obtained and the error-causing flaws in processes. It is conceivable that a diagnosis of these difficulties and help with these processes would make the difference between failure and success. Such evidence is helpful in locating the particular points which need attention in order to make curriculum and teaching more effective. When such information is available on a wide range of objectives, it is also possible to determine whether the achievement of students in all educational objectives is balanced or whether it is systematically high in some respects and shows equally systematic weakness in others, such as a high achievement in information about current events, but equally high gullibility in accepting the commentators' interpretations of their meaning.

Diagnosis also provides the information needed to gauge the level of attainment that is possible. Diagnostic information can be used to decide at which points to start in any particular grade, subject, or unit. Thus, in developing a unit for the third-grade study of community relations, it is important to know which concepts the students already have about the community, what level of reading they can handle so as to know which material to select, and the extent to which they can generalize and abstract, so as to decide on what level to provide learning experiences requiring abstraction. Knowing that a certain group has had little experience with problem solving would indicate what preparation is needed if problem solving is to be used. Similarly, if there were weakness in written expression, one would not introduce learning experiences that involve writing until proper preparation had been made. In others words, on this information depend decisions regarding what content is appropriate, the level on which this content needs to be treated, what particular materials are usable, and which learning experiences are likely to be effective.

Without such information the curriculum can either overreach or underreach the students and teach what they already understand or expect what is impossible for them. Many a curriculum innovation fails because its focus was misplaced in one way or another. Much of current curriculum is weak in continuity of learning because no diagnosis is available regarding levels of thinking. Students "progress" from one area of content to another one, but not necessarily from one level of thinking to a more demanding one, or from one level of sensitivity to a more comprehensive or subtle one.

One source of aid from careful diagnosis lies in the fact that diagnostic data help bridge the gap between a knowledge of the general needs of students and of the particular needs of a given group. Although most teachers accept in general the principle of starting where the students are, without adequate diagnosis this principle lacks concrete applicable meaning. One of the chief deterrents to applying the principle that curriculum should serve student needs has been the lack of sufficient or adequate means to determine concretely what these needs are.

An illustration of an error in curriculum emphasis that comes from applying general knowledge about needs without checking the specific needs of a group is supplied by what happened in a combined first- and second-grade class. Generally it is known that children, especially children from deprived backgrounds, need training in perception to develop reading readiness. Acting on this general knowledge, the teacher assiduously pursued a curriculum of perception training: the children visited and observed, and painted and told stories about what they saw. An appraisal of these paintings and stories indicated that these students, though from deprived home backgrounds, had extraordinarily clear perceptions of the environment around them. They could reproduce anything, including action, in greatest detail. At the same time, classroom observation revealed them to be quite defective in oral communication and in an awareness of time sequences and consecutive sequences of events. They could not talk or tell a story. It was quite evident that a different curriculum emphasis was needed—one emphasizing perception and communication of sequential events.

Diagnosis of the status in attaining educational objectives also serves to set up benchmarks for evaluation of progress. Actually, all evaluation of progress is merely a comparison of status at different points of the program, and hence diagnosis of the levels of attainment is the first step in evaluation.

To serve these purposes, diagnosis of levels of attainment should be as comprehensive as are the objectives of the curriculum. If the curriculum objectives encompass a variety of dimensions, such as the development of important concepts and of relevant patterns of thinking, extension of sensitivity and feelings, and a range of academic and social skills, then diagnosis of attainment should have a similar scope. It should provide information on all areas of growth which the school considers important and provide it in sufficient depth to reveal not only gaps and difficulties, but also their causes.

DIAGNOSIS OF STUDENTS
AS LEARNERS

To develop effective curriculum units and plans for learning experiences, it is important to know a great deal more about students as learners besides their status in the attainment of educational objectives and their abilities. In the light of the ideas about learning discussed in chapter 10, it is necessary to know something about students' cultural backgrounds, motivational patterns, and the content of their social learning, such as the particular meanings they bring to school, their particular approach to learning tasks, and the expectations they have of themselves and of others. In learning to read, for example, the choice of content and the approach to learning depend on whether the students are largely slum dwellers or from the middle class. Units on community need to be approached from the standpoint of the experiences with community life students have had. Existing differences in mental systems and in the students' understanding of common concepts and symbols need to be taken into account in choosing an approach to learning tasks, in determining what materials to use, in selecting the specific content with which to develop the basic ideas and the type of incentives used to generate learning. A survey of the problems students have in learning would suggest needed modifications in pacing of learning as well as in the organization of learning experiences.

One would not, for example, select the same array of community helpers for children in a well-to-do suburb and in a slum area to study. Each group is already likely to be acquainted with a certain type of community helper, and needs a different addition for a balanced view. One would need to introduce such aspects of community life as the services of a policeman in a different context to a slum child than to a child in an upper economic neighborhood, because each has had different experiences with policemen, and hence have invested them with different meaning and feeling. (*See chapter 10, pp. 135-44.*)

Curriculum makers and teachers also need to know what differences there are in the mental systems of children, in their approaches to problem solving, and in the functioning of their intelligence. Research points out, for example, that some individuals approach new tasks more readily through verbal symbolizations, and others, who function on a similar level of abstraction, approach them more readily through some visual representation or manipulative operation. They get the idea of "interchange of trade," for example, from figures on export and import rather than from a description in the book, and they understand what tolerance means through a series of analogies to their own experience, rather than directly from a description in a novel.

In other words, it is important to gauge a student's special approach to problem solving, to abstracting, and to meaning-getting. Only through such knowledge is it possible to provide the roads of learning that are appropriately individualized. Curriculum-makers as well as teachers need to know also what variations there are in the amount of concrete illustrations needed to grasp an abstract idea or concept. The diagnosis of these differences determines the range of learning methods that is made available in order to give everyone an equal opportunity to learn. The requirements in today's heterogeneous classrooms are gauged to the lowest common denominators at least partly because too little is known about the variation in mental and motivational systems to provide flexibility for known reasons and for known purposes.

This lack of information has caused the rather common assumption that, except for rate and capacity for learning, the basic ways of learning are essentially similar, and, therefore, individual differences can be accommodated by adjusting either the pacing or the amount and difficulty of content. Not much thought has been given to varying the approach to learning concepts and abstract ideas to accommodate differences in mental systems. This assumption of a uniformity in mental systems is largely responsible for the failure to reach a considerable proportion of the students; their potential has not been awakened because the approach to learning has failed to provide the best stimulation and optimum conditions for them.

Similar problems obtain also as far as motivational patterns are concerned. Recent research has established pretty clearly that motivational patterns vary according to the cultural backgrounds of the students and that the level of achievement depends as much on the use of appropriate incentives as on the level of mental ability. A better diagnosis of interests and concerns would probably suggest a wider range of motivating devices, including modifications in the approach to curriculum content and in the specific details used to learn basic ideas, instead of simply calling on the achievement motive per se, which today represents the major stock in trade among the incentives for learning.

In this diagnosis of individual differences in mental systems, in motivational patterns, and in special needs lies the key to the development of differentiated opportunities for learning, which goes beyond the surface provisions of differentiation in the amount of work required or in the amount of help given by the teacher. Such diagnosis amounts to searching for optimal approaches to learning. It would go a long way toward the kind of flexibility in curriculum which provides variant approaches to the learning of fundamentals. It would also help prevent the learning difficulties caused by curriculum and teaching methods in which there are discontinuities in expectation and poor adaptation to student needs, which involve inappropriate pacing or use inappropriate content. When diagnosis is inadequate, underachievement is discovered too late, after the effects of the factors responsible for underachievement are already fixed and the remedial measures are ineffective. The effectiveness of remedial measures is further impaired when they overlook the motivational deviation and depend on such incentives as requiring harder work, demanding more homework, and insisting on a more intensive intellectual discipline. An early diagnosis of the factors affecting learning and an earlier attempt to deal with the difficulties introduced by these factors could probably prevent a great deal of underachievement in the later stages of schooling (*Bowman, 1960*).

Diagnosis is needed also of the conditions under which learning occurs, because these conditions have the power to enhance or to inhibit learning. Chief among these conditions are the structure of interpersonal relations, the atmosphere or the climate in the classroom, and the group values which control both.

Chapter 11 drew attention to the fact that the nature of interpersonal relations in classrooms is a source of many kinds of learning and that an important factor in school achievement is the individual's social status in the peer group and his sense of belonging in it. A diagnosis of the social setting of the classroom, therefore, would aid in determining not only what patterns of teaching and learning are feasible but also what changes are needed to improve the group structure in classrooms before curriculum and teaching can function effectively.

Diagnostic information about the nature of learners and the factors that affect learning does not provide bench marks for evaluation of growth. It is useful chiefly to discover the problems to be dealt with in order to create optimum learning conditions. However, no clear line can be drawn between the information which is useful for evaluating growth and that which is not, because such usefulness depends on what the curriculum is supposed to accomplish. A study of motivation patterns, for example, could be used chiefly to make wise decisions about what conditions of learning to provide. But if the curriculum and teaching are addressed to changing motivation patterns, diagnosis of these patterns also serves as a bench mark for evaluation of growth. In some schools knowledge about interpersonal relations is used chiefly to help guide the classroom organization and processes. In others, in which the improvement of group relations is an objective, changes in the structure of interpersonal relations fall into the category of objectives sought, and hence their diagnosis is also the first step in evaluating progress.

DIAGNOSIS OF
CURRICULUM PROBLEMS

In most school situations it is extremely difficult to carry on a continuous diagnosis on as broad a scale as described in the preceding section. A comprehensive diagnosis is usually reserved for special cases, such as for classrooms in which curriculum experiments are carried on or for the study of special problems. Hence, some differentiation is needed between the type of data which can and should be secured as a matter of course for the whole student population, and the data which are secured selectively—either for certain groups of students or for certain aspects of learning. For example, the general ability to read may be diagnosed widely through a diagnostic reading test, but special information on ability to read for precision may be important only in certain subject areas. All teachers need to know with what range of ability they deal, but history teachers planning a revision of a history course, or a teacher of third grade developing a unit on community study, need additional information about the concepts and meanings which their students have in these specific areas. Comprehensive case studies which include information about early childhood and require description of personality characteristics are too time-consuming to be made available for all children. Such intensive diagnostic data may be needed, however, in preparation for remedial action for a few students whose behavior suggests personality disturbances.

A special case of diagnosis is presented by a necessity to analyze curriculum problems: the necessity to find the causes of underachievement, the difficulties encountered in teaching world history in high school, or the evident failure of the curriculum to reach a considerable portion of the students. Such problems have many ramifications and when studied without a design involve assembling tremendous amounts of data. Since the causes of such problems may lie almost anywhere, it is obvious that diagnostic data are needed in more than one dimension. Furthermore, since, as we learned in chapter 7, the various behaviors are interrelated, the difficulty in one type of behavior, such as achievement, may be caused by difficulties in other types of behavior, such as motivation.

To study problems of this sort, it is necessary to assemble the diagnostic data by some criteria of priority in order to "narrow down the possibilities" before attempting to collect a vast assortment of data. Establishing hypotheses regarding the more reasonable causes of the difficulty before launching diagnostic studies is a way of accomplishing this. For example, in order to study the problem of retardation in reading, one needs to hypothesize what the possible causes of this retardation may be. If difficulties in reading are caused either by (a) lack of mental ability, (b) difficulties in some skill involved in reading, (c) some unfavorable habit in reading, (d) emotional difficulties, or (d) lack of experiential sophistication, then all these factors need to be examined before it is decided what to do in the reading program. Yet, before studying any of them in detail, the most likely causes need to be established to eliminate fruitless data gathering.

With such a pattern or design, it is possible to limit the study and to secure sufficient information on pertinent aspects to locate the causes of difficulty. A depth study of selected aspects also permits bringing into view the conditions which, although on the surface not connected with the difficulty, nevertheless may have contributed to it. For example, it is difficult for teachers to assume that their methods of teaching may be a source of difficulty in learning to read. Data on the socioeconomic status may seem like a far cry from reading difficulties. Yet as influences on motivation for some student groups, these data may provide the most direct clues to the causes of their reading difficulties.

Diagnosing curriculum problems by the process of determining what to study and of formulating hypotheses, assembling data, and interpreting them is likely to add up to a stimulating and new perspective about the fundamental aspects of the curriculum, learning, or teaching.

For this reason diagnosis conducted in such a manner that it raises theoretical questions and stimulates application of psychological principles to educational procedures can be a powerful method of teacher training. To serve this purpose fully, it is necessary that teachers participate in the entire process: identify the problems to study, analyze the dimensions of the problem, determine the factors that affect it, formulate hypotheses regarding the causes, and invent or select the methods by which to validate or disprove these hypotheses. Pursuing diagnosis becomes a device for teacher education in the measure that teachers have a part in building the conceptual basis for the whole process. The broader the implications of the diagnostic data, the stronger the impact on teacher orientation.

If we assume, as is assumed in this book, that the functioning curriculum is in the hands of teachers and that, whatever the role of curriculum outlines and guides, the final creative touch of translating the general and often vague objectives and plans into an operating curriculum depends on the capacity of the teachers as curriculum makers, then any studies which enhance the capacity of teachers to pursue creative and theoretical thinking about curriculum are worth their price. It is they who can put flesh on the bare bones of curriculum plans and outlines. They also are in charge of that vastly intricate process of making something happen in the minds and hearts of the students by combining into one dynamic flow of experience the multiplicity of facts, ideas, and considerations that comprise the curriculum. For this reason, experience in careful diagnosis is a *sine qua non* for creative work in curriculum development and teaching: for producing the insights with which to modify content or learning experiences, for devising activities and approaches with which to unlock the problems of learning, through which to overcome the rigidities borne of tradition and routine, and so on.

This concept of diagnosis as a means for teacher training is shared by many proponents of action research (*Association for Supervision and Curriculum Development, 1957; Taba and Noel, 1957; Corey, 1953*). Action research is essentially a method of systematically diagnosing the practical problems of curriculum, and its chief purpose is to help those who are doing it "to acquire a more adequate perspective regarding their problems, to deepen their insights as to what is involved in their task and to extend their orientation toward children, toward methods of teaching them and toward what is significant in content of learning" (*Taba and Noel, 1957, p. 2*). This approach to diagnosis approximates research to the extent that the process, in addition to providing solutions to immediate problems, will be centered on carefully analyzed realistic and significant problems, that the data are secured under conditions to assure their validity and dependability, and that the interpretations are thorough enough to break through the conventional assumptions to important principles and concepts.

Too often diagnostic data are either too meager or too poorly interpreted to lead to anything but confirmation of existing assumptions or reinstitution of procedures which have little effect on eliminating the basic causes of difficulty. Such a diagnosis fails to raise new questions, to set new sights, to produce fresh insight, or to enlarge the conceptual framework for development or teaching.

Systematic diagnosis involves several steps. These steps are discussed and illustrated by the case study of the problem of retardation which follows (Summarized from *Taba and Noel, 1957, pp. 12-27 and 39-48*).

Problem Identification

The first step in a diagnostic study of curriculum problems is the identification of problems which concern teachers. Unless the suggestions of problems to be studied come from them, it is difficult to involve teachers in serious study because their identification with the problem is weak. In a workshop on curriculum development, one group of teachers was concerned with the problem of slow learners. They complained that their classes contained large numbers of children who were slow in learning to read and that this slowness retarded them in all their work. The descriptions these teachers gave suggested that they viewed all slow learners as being alike, that slowness to them was a monolithic quality shared by all retarded children in a like manner. For this reason they treated all slow learners alike: they either intensified drill, gave individual help, or emphasized punishments and rewards. The thought that the slowness might have been caused by different factors in different individuals and hence also be correctible in different ways was both strange and unacceptable.

Problem Analysis

The initial identification of the problem only suggests the difficulty. The next task is to analyze this difficulty sufficiently to discover the real dimensions of the problem. Depending on the difficulties involved, the analysis may be simple or complicated, and the processes may be straightforward or roundabout. In this case, the teachers were convinced at first that slow learners were identifiable by certain characteristics. They therefore attempted to assemble a list of characteristics which were common to all slow learners by asking other teachers to supply a list of characteristics which were common to slow learners in their groups. The attempt yielded a long list of characteristics, such as low vitality, short memory, lack of self-confidence, and poor parent-child relationships. There was a wide diversity of opinion about the importance of each item in the list. Furthermore, none of these characteristics applied exclusively to slow learners. There were good achievers with low self-confidence and from poor home conditions. Not all adequate achievers were blessed with a good memory, and so on. It seemed clear also, that starting from such a list could lead only to a use of generalized devices which, while presumably applicable to all slow learners, would not help any of them.

The failure of this procedure suggested the need for another design, that of studying intensively a sample of slow learners to discover the factors which operate in each case and, through the study of these, to discover the pattern in these factors. Seventeen cases, one for each teacher, were selected. By using information which was fairly accessible, preliminary "case studies" were composed, noting recurring difficulties.

All seventeen cases showed retardation in academic achievement, most frequently in reading, but also in spelling and writing. Most were also discipline problems of some sort. Most had an average or only slightly below average I.Q. This suggested immediately that low mentality was not the sole cause of slowness and not even the primary one. It seemed that multiple causes were at work, and that each individual may have been retarded for a unique combination of these causes. While the general difficulties were repeated in many individual cases, they tended to combine into a unique cluster or a syndrome for each individual. If this tendency were verified by a systematic study, it would mean that a different curriculum and teaching procedure were needed to help each syndrome of difficulties.

Formulating Hypotheses and Gathering Data

The preliminary explorations serve as a source for formulating scientific guesses or hypotheses. These hypotheses focus the problem and narrow the job of data gathering to the most promising leads. The hypotheses themselves need to be checked against the easiest available data, to eliminate those which are the least promising. Narrowing the field makes it possible to spend the available energy on securing adequate data and on making thoughtful interpretations.

Using the information contained in their preliminary explorations, the group began to formulate hypotheses by listing the clusters of factors which figured most frequently and which seemed most crucial in causing slowness in reading for a guide to further studies. This list was as follows:

1. Mental ability
2. Physical handicaps, such as difficulties with vision or hearing, lack of vitality, nervousness, frequent absences because of colds or other illnesses
3. Feelings, such as fears, anxieties, hostilities, inferiority, and the context in which these feelings occurred
4. Emotional climate at home: broken homes, relationship of parents with children, nature of controls used, stability of home life and family relationships
5. Relationships with other children, such as the degree of isolation at home and at school, degree of belonging, adequacy of social skills, the nature and frequency of contacts with peers
6. Cultural and social environment: the degree of cultural deprivation, newness to the country or the area, values and patterns of using leisure time at home, patterns of child rearing practiced by parents
7. Behavior at school, consistencies and inconsistencies: outburst of

temper, restlessness, inattentiveness, unwarranted attention seeking, whether these behaviors and slowness showed in all situations, which situations seemed to provoke them, what contrasts existed in behavior manifested in controlled (classroom) situations and free (play) situations (*Washington School District, 1956b, pp. 5-8; and Taba and Noel, 1957, p. 38*).

With such a list of relevant points as a guide, the teachers assembled information systematically about each of the seventeen cases. They used a variety of techniques. Besides anecdotal records of their observations of consistencies and inconsistencies of behavior in the classroom and on the playground, they examined data on intelligence, reading readiness, health, and previous school history. Occasionally a special test of achievement or of mental maturity was administered. In two instances, in which severe mental retardation was suspected, individual tests were given by the psychologist. On two cases health information was secured from the county health officer. A few open-ended questions and themes, such as "Three Wishes," were used to get data on reality orientation. Students also wrote on "What makes me mad and what I do about it" for diagnosis of their attitudes toward conflict and their skill in dealing with it. Sociometric tests were used to determine their social status. Parents were interviewed to gain insight into the emotional and cultural climate in the home and in the neighborhood.

The results showed that lack of mental ability was not a cause except in one case. Only one child suffered from a physical handicap—a deformed arm. Several suffered from anxiety and inferiority feelings. Many more had broken homes, were pressured by parents, and had unstable home life. Several seemed to be isolated, rejected by others, or had unstable relationships with peers, some because of their own idiosyncrasies. Only a few seemed to show disturbed behavior, and usually when facing certain learning tasks, such as spelling.

Experimenting with Action

Immediate action is not the only product of diagnostic studies, important as this is. Such studies are also valuable in producing perspective on the curriculum and suggesting action patterns which go beyond the problem that caused the study. However, action hypotheses need to be tested before they can become curriculum recommendations for general use.

One important discovery which emerged from the above diagnostic procedure was the fact that while these slow learners had many characteristics which were also common to many other students, there was usually some one additional factor which "broke the camel's back." If the "action" was addressed to this factor, results showed fairly soon. This means, of course, that when precise diagnosis of the causes of difficulty is available and changes in curriculum or teaching are addressed to the crucial source of the difficulty, these changes have a greater chance of success.

It was clear also that the causes of the difficulty may lie in areas other than the one in which the difficulty manifests itself. Reading difficulties, by and large, were the result of difficulties elsewhere, such as blocking from too great an anxiety to succeed, lack of concrete experience, problems of cultural adjustment in the family, and so on. This realization led to a different perspective on the treatment of the problem of retardation: an acceptance of differentiation in the treatment, and an application of remedial procedures to the causes of difficulty rather than to the area of apparent difficulty.

In this instance, each teacher tried out the most promising action possibility for her own "case." Those who were blocked because of fear of failure were helped when their learning tasks were broken down into smaller steps to assure success. Others improved when teachers capitalized on their special talents and interests, to give them a needed role in the group and with it needed self-respect. Several needed enriching experiences in school because their home environment was too barren to develop the needed perceptions. Still others needed acceptance from peers, either from another student or from the entire group, to enhance their self-concept. Still others changed when pressures for achievement at home and in school were released.

A variety of changes were reported. All but one student improved in achievement, including the quantity and quality of reading. Improvements were noted also in work habits, in social relations, and in attitudes toward school and the learning tasks. These students started to work harder at their tasks, learned to complete assignments, started to talk to other students about their work, played better with other children, and seemed happier and more self-confident. All began to take greater responsibility for their work.

Perhaps the most significant result was the change in the attitudes and the insights of the teachers. They evolved a concept of the slow learner which differed markedly from the monolithic one they held before the study began. They learned gradually that to get at real causes, one needs to explore fairly comprehensively instead of focusing his efforts on the particular difficulty first noticed. They discovered that the child's school problems are part and parcel of his life problems, and his life problems are a part and a product of his school problems. They learned that difficulties in learning have multiple causes and are produced by a whole syndrome of factors, within which there is usually the "straw that breaks the camel's back." They also discovered that although in the preliminary analysis the "blocks" to learning seemed complex, multiple, and ramifying, the steps to removing these blocks were fairly clear and simple, once the "crucial" factor was identified.

Informal

CHAPTER SIXTEEN Diagnostic Devices

Diagnosis of the scope suggested in the preceding chapter is too extensive to depend on formal instruments or to be carried on all at once, such as at the beginning of a year or of a course. Rather, one needs to think of diagnosis as a continuous process which may center on some formal diagnostic tests but is also aided by many less formal means. These informal means are especially necessary in areas in which few objective devices have so far been developed, as in the areas of thinking, attitudes, feelings, and some skills, or in cases in which diagnosis needs to be fitted into a more or less unique context and therefore needs to be flexible.

That much of this diagnosis is possible without resorting to objective tests has long been recognized. The advice of a yearbook on measurement of understanding strongly recommends extending the base for diagnosis and evaluation by using devices other than tests (*National Society for the Study of Education, 1946, pp. 326-28*).

Ingenious teachers and curriculum consultants have over a period of time compiled many devices which combine flexibility of use with the advantage of providing fairly dependable information. An added advantage is the fact that many of these devices can be incorporated into instructional procedures and thus serve both an instructional and a diagnostic purpose. This chapter is devoted to describing some of these informal diagnostic instruments and procedures.

AN OPEN-ENDED
CLASSROOM INTERVIEW

This procedure consists of asking the class questions designed to elicit the meaning certain things have for them, what they are familiar with, or descriptions of experiences they have had which can be used to interpret their background and their feelings toward or understanding of certain phenomena or concepts. These interviews have proved especially helpful with younger children and have been used to guide the selection of ideas and content for new units or to test the appropriateness of the existing ones to students with deviate backgrounds. One teacher, in developing a unit on cowboys for a kindergarten class, asked the class to describe what cowboys do. To her surprise she got a startling array of notions, evidently gathered from television viewing: cowboys get on rocks and jump on people, kill people, jump on bad men in hideouts and take them into bars, steal money from banks, wear spurs so people won't step on their feet in the bars, and so on. This response suggested that a conventional cowboy unit was not appropriate for this group.

Before developing units on home life for the first grade for a group consisting largely of children of agricultural workers, many of whom had foreign backgrounds, one teacher conducted a series of such interviews on questions which covered the chief dimensions of the unit, such as: what happens at breakfast, who does things in our house, what happens when adults are gone, how are we punished? The information obtained became the introductory content for each part of the unit and the insights into the conceptions of family life gained from these sessions guided the selection of basic ideas and their development for the remainder of the unit.

Similar class interviews can be conducted to discover what understanding students have of concepts on which a unit or a course is predicated. One sixth-grade teacher, who was developing a plan for a study of Latin America which was to stress the economic conditions, government, educational level, communication, transportation, and rights and freedoms, spent some time in discussing what the students had learned about the concepts which underlie these topics in the five years of their school life. The old social-studies books were re-examined and the units they had covered were reviewed. Students were asked to state what they knew regarding these topics as related to the United States.*

This review helped both the teacher and the class to decide on what level to pitch their study of Latin America and which ideas or content to stress in the contemplated units. For example, the study of government in Latin American countries would not have been fruitful if the students' idea of government itself was fuzzy.

Another possibility is to ask students to propose questions describing what they want to know about an area of study which is about to be launched. A fourth-grade teacher who was redeveloping her world geography units for a greater emphasis on understanding of people had children propose questions they wanted answered about each region they were to study. She did this to diagnose their level of understanding and to detect any misconceptions that needed correction. Some interesting misconceptions were revealed in discussing the questions proposed by children. For example, children wanted to know

* From an unpublished curriculum study, Contra Costa County Schools, Pleasant Hill, California.

where the Baffin Islanders got their vitamins and how they kept clean. Evidently these children had learned that one needs to eat spinach and other green vegetables to get vitamins. How then could people who live in snow and ice secure them? Taking baths to them was the only way of keeping clean, and consequently people with no bathtubs could not possibly be clean.

OPEN-ENDED
QUESTIONS AND THEMES

Responses to certain themes are frequently used as a diagnostic device to tap the ideas, concepts, and feelings of a given group. This device is especially useful when students are old enough to write. These open-ended questions are homemade projective tests which provide a stimulus sufficiently unstructured not to cue the students as to what response might be expected. Students can write on these questions and themes, discuss them in class, or play them out in sociodrama. (*See Taba et al., 1955a, ch. 6, for a description of how to administer these questions.*) The themes can be formulated on any pertinent point: the concepts of what students think a community is, their feelings about certain foreign people, what it means to be poor, to suffer hardships, to be civilized or primitive. The main requirement is that the questions tap spontaneous rather than studied responses and thus reveal the functioning conceptions, feelings, and misconceptions. Because feelings are easily suppressed or distorted, thoughtful planning of the questions used to tap feelings and sensitivities is needed to make sure they contain no cues which might limit freedom and spontaneity of expression. Furthermore, projective themes or questions pertaining to feelings are successful only with good rapport.

The range of these questions is limited only by the ingenuity in inventing them. Teachers have experimented with themes to study children's self-concepts ("What I like about myself" and "What I criticize about myself"), attitudes toward their homes ("What I like about my home" and "What I would like to change about my home"), wishes ("My three wishes"), attitudes toward possessions and money ("What I would do with *x* dollars"), and an array of others that have seemed appropriate for diagnosis of attitudes and feelings.*

To diagnose skills in dealing with interpersonal conflicts many teachers have used the theme: "What makes me mad and what I do about it." The analysis of the results, described in chapter 14, usually led to new emphasis on training in skills to deal with conflict, such as a systematic incident analysis or

---

* See Taba and Elkins, 1950, for examples of such writing. A list of themes used in the Intergroup Education Project is in the Appendix of Taba *et al.*, 1955, ch. 6.

an analysis either in discussion or sociodrama of stories presenting human conflict.*

UNFINISHED STORIES
AND INCIDENTS

Discussion of cut-off or unfinished stories and incidents provides still another avenue for diagnosing the quality and the level of feelings, judgment, and sensitivities. The major idea of the technique is the reading of a story sequence or the description of an incident which involves a dilemma, such as a conflict between a parent and a child or a problem of conflicting loyalties or divided feelings. This incident or story sequence is then probed by discussing it, or by playing it out. If a systematic diagnosis is needed, a sequence of questions can be employed in probing, somewhat as follows:

1. What happened in this story or in this incident? This question is asked to get a picture of the level of sensitivity and of perception. Some students may only restate the surface facts, while others may perceive the crux of the situation. Some may discern the motivations and causes and others may not.

2. Why did these things happen? The replies to this question suggest the level of the rationale of which the class is capable: whether they see causes for behavior and what kind of causes.

3. How did those involved feel? This question diagnoses the capacity of the group to put itself into another person's shoes, and reveals any gaps in sensitivity. For example, in situations involving children, adolescents, and parents, students find it hard to identify and empathize with parents; they are much more realistic about the feelings of other children or adolescents.

4. Has anything like that happened to you? This question probes the level of abstraction students reach and therefore the level of transfer that is possible. A low level of abstraction leads to searching for examples that are like some detail in the described situation, such as the fact of being spoken to in a harsh voice. A higher level of abstraction would produce examples on a more subtle level, such as meeting rejection in an entirely different situation, or difficulties encountered in interpreting the same situation in a different way.

5. What would you do to make this situation come out better? The replies to this question reveal the level of application of the perception, feelings, and understandings.†

---

* The method of this analysis is similar to the method of analyzing cut-off stories described below.

† For examples of discussions of stories, see Taba *et al.,* 1955, ch. 6; Taba and Elkins, 1950, chs. 3 and 6; Albany Public Schools, 1953; Heaton, 1952; George and Fannie Shaftel, 1952; Jennings, 1950*b*.

RECORDS OF DISCUSSION

Analysis of the records of discussions constitutes another diagnostic device. The content of discussions can be analyzed for sensitivity to values and feelings, for concepts students master and apply, and for the ability to see relationships and to generalize.

Recently discussion records have been used also to diagnose the ability of students to play constructive roles in discussion, leadership, and participation by subjecting these records to participation analysis in addition to content analysis. This source for diagnosis has become much more readily available since the advent of tape recorders. Records of discussions, however, require a fairly careful analysis and a summary to be fully useful. One example of a fairly voluminous recording of discussions as a means of diagnosis is provided by Taba and Elkins (*1950, chs. 3 and 6*). In this example, the teacher used novels and stories systematically as a prelude to factual studies of problems in human relations in social studies and English classes to enhance sensitivity to these problems, thus determining the needs to be met in the curriculum. Subsequently the data were reanalyzed for more systematic evaluation of the methods of thinking about human relations, by tabulating the frequencies of remarks in fifty discussion records in each of the following categories:

1. *Projections:* the attempts to understand the story, to explain and to evaluate the behavior, and to propose reasonable action for the solution of the dilemmas described.
These were further subdivided into the following types of statements:
(a) *Explanations:* statements which explain behavior by stating cause-and-effect relationships, explaining motivation, or analyzing the circumstances which made the behavior necessary. ("Marion showed she was growing up because . . .")
(b) *Evaluation:* statements which evaluate behavior by applying some general principles. ("This was a very immature thing to do," or "It is not natural for teen-agers to act that way.")
(c) *Action:* statements which suggest courses of action for the characters in the story. ("Father should not have been so harsh," or "Ann would have done better if she talked it over first.")
(d) *Experience:* statements which attempt to explain behavior through illustrations from personal experiences.
(e) *Facts:* statements which merely give factual items from the story without interpretation, reasoning, or evaluation.
2. *Generalizations:* interpretations carried beyond the immediate facts given in the story, which involve distillations of many facts and attempts to express the principles governing the events and behaviors.
Two types of generalizations were further distinguished: generalizations which were merely inferences from the immediate facts of the story, and normative generalizations which expressed moral norms regarding the right type of behavior.
3. *Self-references:* statements expressing references to or applications to personal experiences.

4. *Irrelevancies:* statements without bearing on or connection with the points of the story under discussion (*Taba, 1955b, pp. 110-11*).

This analysis revealed the extent to which students used cause-and-effect relationships to explain behavior or were satisfied with analogical self-references. It sifted out those who dominantly translated the unique material in stories into generalizations about human conduct in general, from those to whom the specific feelings and situations only suggested further specifics.

Analysis of records of discussions permits also an examination of the dynamics of individual and group roles. To what extent is conformity in values either created or enforced? To what extent do strong individuals influence the values of the group? What affects the quality and quantity of contributions? What variations exist in the basic methods of thinking, such as the tendency to blame or judge instead of to explain? To what extent do moral principles come into play? What is the scope of explanations and the degree of objectivity in accounting for causal factors? How consistent is the thinking, and how did the ability to abstract function? (*Taba and Elkins, 1950, pp. 110-38*).

Analysis of informal discussion of books reveals a good deal about the maturity of reactions to reading, the type of content and style the students enjoy, the material that they consider significant, boresome, or trivial. These discussions are also useful in detecting the extent to which students can relate ideas they find in books to their own lives and concerns.

RECORDS OF
READING AND WRITING

When systematically collected and carefully analyzed, records of reading are a good source of information about scope, variety, quantity, quality, and maturity of interests, and for diagnosis of patterns of perception and thinking.

Records of writing can be used in a similar way. Folders containing all of a student's writing can be analyzed for the quality of ideas expressed, for discrimination in the use of sources, for organization of thought, for originality and sensitivity in interpretation. In order to secure comparative information and diagnosis of growth, all writing can be filed and summarized at the end of the year.

OBSERVATION AND
RECORDING OF PERFORMANCE

Records of performance are especially useful for the diagnosis of skills and work habits. If one wants to see what skills a committee chairman has in working with a group, one can watch him in action.

If it is necessary to diagnose the skills of a committee at work, have the group describe how they proceeded and what troubled them. If one needs to know whether students use correct procedures to arrive at correct answers in arithmetic, one must somehow secure a record of what they do in solving problems. To discover how adequate or inadequate the work habits of students are, one can observe them taking notes, browsing in books, or planning dimensions of a topic to study. This can be done on a simple level by occasionally observing students at work, as one sixth-grade teacher did. As he watched his committees, in exploring a new topic, thumb through books as if they expected important information to fly out at them, he discovered the need for teaching the use of the index and the table of contents. Another example comes from a tenth-grade biology class who were sent to the library to examine texts about frogs. The observer noticed that the students proceeded to copy down the very first sentences they found in chapters on frogs, usually definitions using Latin phrases. None stopped to consider the questions he was to answer before selecting what information to copy.

Occasionally, more systematic observations are needed, such as the application of time sampling to the behavior of a student or a group of students to discover what is wrong with their work habits. The record below is from a fourth-grade class whose teacher thought their extreme slowness was caused by over-meticulousness. To test her contention, it was suggested that a time sample of one fairly typical student be taken, recording everything he did during one arithmetic work period. The table on p. 251 shows her results.

This record suggested that the boys and girls in this class were far from meticulous: they had got into the habit of all sorts of unnecessary activities while appearing to a casual observer to be meticulously busy.

Similar performance records can be made of interaction and participation. In one instance, a student who appeared to be participating in all sorts of groupings turned out to be only a fringer—always on the edge of groups, but never in them. In another instance, a classification of remarks during a history review lesson revealed that over half dealt with arguments growing out of interpersonal conflict, and less than half with history. Primary schools have used observation checks to discover the length of attention span, signs of nervousness, and stability and instability of social relations. Playgrounds afford opportunity for observations of free interaction.

SPECIAL ASSIGNMENTS AND EXERCISES

One method of sizing up the level of concepts used, the degree of abstraction students are capable of, the ability to interpret either verbal or quantitative materials, or any other aspect of thinking is, as a prelude to teaching, to introduce assignments which require the performance

Time and Motion Observation—ARITHMETIC

Time	Activity	Time	Activity
11:32	Stacked paper		Watched me
	Picked up pencil		Watched L.
	Wrote name		Laughed at her
	Moved paper closer		Erased
	Continued with heading		Hand up
	Rubbed nose		Made faces at girls
	Read problem—lips moving		Laughed. Watched D.
	Looked at Art's paper		Got help
	Started to work. . . .	11:50	Looked at Lorrie
11:45	Worked and watched		Tapped fingers on desk
	Made funny faces		Wrote
	Giggled. Looked at Lorrie and smiled		Slid down in desk
			Hand to head, listened to D. helping Lorrie
	Borrowed Art's paper		Blew breath out hard
	Erased		Fidgeted with paper
	Stacked paper		Looked at other group
	Read		Held chin
	Slid paper around		Watched Charles
	Worked briefly		Read—hands holding head
	Picked up paper and read		Erased
	Thumb in mouth, watched Miss D.		Watched other group, chin on hand
11:48	Worked and watched		Made faces—yawned—fidgeted
	Made funny face		Held head
	Giggled. Look and smiled at Lorrie		Read, pointing to words
	Paper up—read		Wrote
	Picked eye		Put head on arm on desk
	Studied bulletin board		Held chin
	Paper down—read again		Read
	Fidgeted with paper		Rubbed eye
	Played with pencil and fingers	11:55	Wrote [Taba, 1957, pp. 60-61]

of these processes. Special assignments and exercises can be addressed to specific processes. Students can be asked to interpret specific passages in books to discover how well they can discern relationships between facts and ideas or decipher abstractions. Asking students to interpret charts and graphs as a normal part of teaching will show their ability to get accurate meaning from precise facts. Students can analyze passages that contain assumptions and distorted logic to discover their awareness of fallacies, of logical processes of proofs, and so on. Ability to classify ideas can be diagnosed by asking students to bring some order into disordered series of facts or ideas.

Similar exercises can be used to diagnose the ability to apply known information and generalizations, such as being asked to determine what might grow in a certain undetermined locality with a given altitude, amount of sunlight, water, and type of soil. Even in the second grade it is possible to work on exercises involving principles of logic such as "if—then": "If the baseball comes flying at one, what will a girl do, a boy do, a mother do, a teacher do?" "If a father comes home late for dinner, what will the mother do?" "If a newcomer comes to this class, what will we do?"

SOCIOMETRIC TEST

No diagnosis for the purpose of guiding curriculum making is complete without some idea of the crucial conditions which affect learning and achievement and determine what is possible in a given classroom. Many an efficient curriculum plan has failed because of insufficient awareness of the important conditions that either block learning or enhance it.

The structure of interpersonal relations which prevails in classrooms is one such factor. Its relevance was discussed in Chapter 11, which pointed out that the structure of interpersonal relations affects the atmosphere of the classroom, controls the energy available for learning, determines the range of roles individuals can play and also, therefore, their access to opportunities to learn, determines the communication lines, and influences the frequency of discipline problems. Therefore, the diagnosis of interpersonal relations is important even in schools which do not include the improvement of human relations among their objectives.

The sociometric test is one method of diagnosing the pattern of interpersonal reactions. One such test consists of asking students to choose three persons they would want to sit with, be on a committee with, go to a movie with, or do any of the things that can be done in small groups. The main requirement for a valid test is that the situation be realistic, that the arrangements which are implied in the question will actually be carried out. (In this respect the sociometric test referred to here differs from such devices as "Guess Who," in which individuals assess others in reference to certain traits or behavior and the tests which ask individuals to identify their best friends.)

These choices can be tabulated in a systematic way and studied to discover the nature of the networks: what cleavages exist, which subgroups there are, the degree of isolation, or the degree of focusing on a few individuals. This information can be used to discover the extent to which these cleavages and divisions occur because of some general factors, such as differences in ability, racial background, or sex, as a consequence of certain school practices or styles of teaching, or because of personal qualities. The measures taken to improve the relationship naturally depend on what the diagnosis is: whether it is necessary to help individuals, or to change the values of the group. They include reseating, composing groups by new criteria of psychological cohesiveness, training in group procedures, and changes in curriculum.*

McGuire and Clark have devised a way of recording sociometric choices which is applicable to large groups and which, therefore, could be used for composing classrooms in a manner to create an optimum learning environment and to minimize erosive conflict (*Clark and McGuire, 1952; McGuire and Clark, 1952; Thelen, 1959*). This method has been used in at least one school system with some success in minimizing interpersonal conflict, reducing discipline problems, and enhancing self-directed activity on the part of the students (*Crouch, unpublished report*).

The record of sociometric choices, naturally, describes only the pattern of interrelationships and not the causes for these patterns. To get information on the values which create these patterns and consequently also about the ways in which curriculum might help to change these values, it is useful to ask for reasons for the choices. When categorized, these reasons reveal the values which prevail in the entire group, and thus throw light on the psychological factors of the climate. Some individuals depend on long acquaintance. They find it hard to experiment with new relationships. In other classrooms ability and achievement are the chief criteria of high sociometric status. Students in these classrooms may need help in discovering other important qualities which people possess. Still other classrooms are controlled by popularity. They seek people who are outgoing, friendly, popular, fun to be with. Some classrooms give weight to what might be described as moral character: dependability, loyalty, trustworthiness. Still others judge people by qualities which are important in human relations, such as helpfulness, understanding, and common interests. Few students with no training in human relations differentiate between these personal factors in association and the factor of skill. Most student groups select companions even for work situations by a criterion of personal affinity rather than by a criterion of skill.†

Summaries of the values underlying sociometric choices also provide a basis for judging whether the values of the class are congenial to good class

---

* For further information on administering, recording, and interpreting sociometric tests, see Taba *et al.*, 1955*b*, ch. 5; Gronlund, 1959, ch. 3; Northway and Weld, 1957.
† For descriptions of typical choice patterns and values, see Taba, 1955*b*, chs. 3 and 4; Taba and Elkins, 1950, pp. 190-94; Atkinson, 1949; Northway and Weld, 1957, ch. 10.

relations or create brittleness, division, and social distance. They describe the degree to which the classroom atmosphere either thwarts or enhances the development of a democratic orientation, such as the capacity to accept diversity and individual autonomy and to function in a heterogeneous social group without a personal necessity to reject, to dominate, or to indulge in ego derogation.

From such diagnoses emerge indications of the directions in which the class needs to grow and suggestions for program emphasis, both as to the extension of sensitivity and the skill training needed. Teachers who have explored this line of diagnosis have also derived many insights into the whys and wherefores of the peer society, into the social needs of their classrooms, as well as into the effects of the group atmosphere on academic learning.

Some practical and immediate purposes are served also. For one thing, sociometric data provide a more adequate basis for grouping students for a variety of purposes: for composing classes, committees, discussion groups within the classroom, and teams for projects of various sorts. Many teachers have found that smaller face-to-face groups are an aid in learning and use committees to work for regular classroom tasks as well as special projects. If these groups are composed by considering not only the commonality of interests, skills, and abilities but also the psychological cohesion, conditions are set for more productive work than is otherwise possible. (*See ch. 11, pp. 164-71.*)

Finally, sociometric data are useful in diagnosing the effect of ways of organizing the curriculum, of teaching techniques, and of grouping on the social structures in otherwise comparable groups of children. They can correct wrong assumptions about the ways to organize groups or about the causes of difficulties in existing groups. In one school a few children usurped all leadership roles. Sociometric data helped identify a wider group of leaders, as well as a wider range of leadership roles these leaders could carry. In another school sociometric data helped to uncover the practices in school which fostered intersex cleavages. In still another school ability grouping was found to impose on an already existing ethnic segregation a heightened social exclusiveness, sharp cleavages between subgroups, and a high concentration of choices on a few leaders.

DEVICES FOR DIAGNOSING THE OUT-OF-SCHOOL ENVIRONMENT

Knowledge about the social and emotional climate in which students live and learn outside the school is indispensable to the teacher. When students come from styles of life and backgrounds which are unfamilar to the teachers, such information is needed to make it possible to adjust the curriculum to the important differences in backgrounds.

Schools have recognized that studying the home background of students is an important ingredient of adequate program development. Many schools have some way of establishing contact with the home, such as parent conferences and home visits. These procedures are useful, but they reproduce the same categories of awareness teachers already have. Teachers see the homes in the light of their own middle-class biases. These methods also yield only the objective facts about the home. They fall short of describing the psychological and the social world in which the children live, knowledge of which is useful in creating new awareness and new insights.

To diagnose social-class background, a simplified version of the techniques anthropologists use in their studies of communities is useful. For example, Warner used a variety of criteria by which to describe the social-class status of families: type of housing and of neighborhood, occupation, level of education, source of income, association patterns, and so on (*Warner, Meeker, and Eells, 1960*). It has been found that occupational level seems to be a fairly dependable index of socioeconomic status. To get a rough estimate of social-class status of students, a list of the occupations of parents can be composed either from the entrance cards or by checking with students themselves. These can then be classified by social-class level, type of occupation, using a chart of job classification such as the one employed by Warner. (See Figure 1 below.) For school purposes a three-way classification of social class is sufficient: upper class (Warner classes one and two), middle class (Warner classes three to five) and lower class (Warner classes six and seven). With this information, it is possible to begin to infer what the major features of social learning and the major gaps in the experience, interest, and skills of the students are.

One new high school was beset by many problems. It had recently split from a conservative high school (in an established rural town) with a very traditional program. The new school continued the program of its parent school, including the pattern of activities and clubs. There was a good deal of trouble with participation in activities. Even though the school obviously drew from an unskilled labor group, the staff needed some demonstration that program revision was in order. The tabulation of the occupations of the parents on a blank matrix sheet such as the one given in Figure 1, using only three social-class classifications, revealed at a glance a heavy concentration in the lower socioeconomic class and in semiskilled occupations. These data challenged the staff to explore the value patterns and the social backgrounds typical of this social group. Besides raising many questions about the appropriateness of the activities program and of the motivating devices used by the staff, the data and the discussions they generated also stimulated questions about the appropriateness of the heavy academic emphasis in the curriculum. In other words, the information, inadequate as it may have been from a research standpoint, nevertheless was highly useful for diagnosis, for reorientation of the staff, and for stimulating a reconsideration of the program.

FIGURE 1

REVISED SCALE FOR RATING OCCUPATION*

[Class] Rating Assigned to Occupation	Professionals	Proprietors and Managers	Business Men	Clerks and Kindred Workers, Etc.	Manual Workers	Protective and Service Workers	Farmers
1	Lawyers, doctors, dentists, engineers, judges, high-school superintendents, veterinarians, ministers (graduated from divinity school), chemists, etc., with post-graduate training, architects	Businesses valued at $75,000 and over	Regional and divisional managers of large financial and industrial enterprises	Certified Public Accountants			Gentleman farmers
2	High-school teachers, trained nurses, chiropodists, chiropractors, undertakers, ministers (some training), newspaper editors, librarians (graduate)	Businesses valued at $20,000 to $75,000	Assistant managers & office & department managers of large businesses, assistants to executives, etc.	Accountants, salesmen of real estate, of insurance, postmasters			Large farm owners, farm owners
3	Social workers, grade-school teachers, optometrists, librarians (not graduate), undertakers' assistants, ministers (no training)	Businesses valued at $5,000 to $20,000	All minor officials of business	Auto salesmen, bank clerks, postal clerks, secretaries to executives, supervisors of railroad, telephone, etc., justices of the peace	Contractors		
4		Businesses ...		Stenographers, book- ...	Factory foremen,		Dry cleaners, butch-

					ers, sheriffs, railroad engineers and conductors
	$2,000 to $5,000	keepers, rural mail clerks, railroad ticket agents, sales people in dry goods store, etc.	electricians, plumbers, carpenters	} owners, business	
5	Businesses valued at $500 to $2,000	Dime store clerks, hardware salesmen, beauty operators, telephone operators	Medium-skill workers, carpenters, plumbers, electricians (apprentice), timekeepers, linemen, telephone or telegraph, radio repairmen	Barbers, firemen, butcher's apprentices, practical nurses, policemen, seamstresses, cooks in restaurant, bartenders	Tenant farmers
6	Businesses valued at less than $500		Moulders, semiskilled workers, assistants to carpenters, etc.	Baggage men, night policemen and watchmen, taxi and truck drivers, gas station attendants, waitresses in restaurant	Small tenant farmers
7			Heavy labor, migrant work, odd-job men, miners	Janitors, scrubwomen, newsboys	Migrant farm laborers

* From *Warner, Meeker and Eells* (1960), pp. 140-41.

Other schools have simply asked the students to write about their lives out-side the school. One high school in a slum area of a segregated Negro neigh-borhood was developing a general education program in the ninth grade. The staff was anxious to develop a program which truly served the needs of these students but was undecided about what these needs were and ambivalent about accepting the fact that these students, under their cultural conditions, might have some unique needs. One assumption, rather commonly accepted, was that since so many students lived in broken homes, security was a central need.

Among the many diagnostic devices used to develop some hypotheses about the needs and the focus of the program was that of asking the students to write on the following questions:

1. How many persons are in your home with you?
2. How many of these persons are relatives and how are they related to you?
3. What things do you like about your home?
4. What things would you like to change about your home?
5. What, if anything, are you especially unhappy about or dissatisfied with?
6. What, if anything, are you especially glad about?
7. Have you ever helped support the persons with whom you live? If so, what work did you do?
8. What do you need that you do not have in your neighborhood?
9. What other persons older than yourself (grown-ups) are there with whom you find it easy to get along? Explain in what ways it is easy to get along.
10. What persons older than yourself are there with whom you find it diffi-cult to get along? Explain in what way it is difficult [*Taba, 1955a, pp. 39-40*].

The results confirmed many previous assumptions. Most students lived in large, mixed family units which included relatives and boarders. Fewer than half lived with both parents. Contrary to staff expectations, however, nearly everyone found something to like about his home, and nearly one-third of the students liked everything about their homes. While the physical conditions were rather deplorable, the expectations were also low. Students were glad to have such "advantages" as a radio, telephone, refrigerator or piano, and even such ordinary conveniences as an inside toilet, a new stove, steam heat, a bed of their own, or a living-room chair. Their demands for privacy were limited.

The greatest surprise was the tenor of attitudes toward family relations. While the staff had assumed insecurity and poor family relations, the students were pleased by the emotional atmosphere and by the way the family treated them. Many expressed gratitude for being able to live with their parents and for pleasant family friendships, cooperation, happiness, love, and understand-ing. It was clear also that these students took crowdedness, quarrelsomeness, loud talk, and offensive language for granted as a general condition and were happy when their families were free of it. Instead of the usual adolescent rebellion and discontent with adults, so common in middle-class white families, these adolescents expressed security, trust, and dependence on adults for understanding and supportiveness.

The school faculty was induced to revise many premises on which their general education program was to be developed. They began to visualize needs they had not suspected and found that some on which they had worked were not crucial at all. These data, together with the discovery of extremely limited self-expectations revealed in the themes on "What I like about myself" and "What I would like to change in myself," opened up an entirely new perspective regarding what was needed in the new program (*Taba, 1955a, pp. 39-60*).

The use of diaries is still another method for tapping the out-of-school environment through the child's own view of it. This is an angle that objective surveys of home conditions often miss, yet which from a standpoint of social learning is extremely important. A child's or an adolescent's judgment of his environment may be distorted; nevertheless, *his* social and psychological *reality* is what he lives with and what he reacts to. Hence, devices appropriate to examining the child in *his world* are an important facet in the total diagnostic battery. A diary consists essentially of a record of a few sample days in which children describe in brief time intervals everything they do. With proper directions and rapport, students can be induced to describe what they do and with whom, and perhaps something about the circumstances or a manner in which events occur. However, the diaries usually do not provide explanations of the reasons for these events. The feelings and views of children on such matters are better explored by questions designed to elicit this information.

Diaries can be assigned on any grade level on which students have learned to express themselves in writing. As an instrument of diagnosis, the validity of a diary depends on rapport, for diaries which omit activities that students are afraid to reveal are not useful. Like the instruments described above, diary material needs to be subjected to careful summary if it is to reveal the group characteristics rather than presenting only interesting vignettes of individuals.*

Under conditions of good rapport, diaries provide information useful for many purposes. In the first place, they describe the life space of children and youth in different communities and in different homes. For example, in a Negro school the experiences of students were limited by segregation. Their ideas as to what to do with their leisure time were extremely meager, and the school needed to help them. Families tended to be permissive and free in their expression of both anger and affection, but training for independence was at a minimum.

In other lower-class white neighborhoods, diaries revealed extremely meager contacts with parents. The time at home was usually spent on house chores,

* For a method of administering and interpreting diaries, see Taba *et al., 1955a*, ch. 2.

and mealtimes were occupied with settling conflicts and with discipline. There was scarcely any communication about the experiences different family members had, no time for guidance, and no concern about children's school experiences. This kind of life space and experience content differs from that of the usual middle-class family. Children learn to make decisions for themselves, but they get little support for achievement in school. In middle-class families, school achievement tends to be more important, and the adult controls are much more perceptible, but children also have fewer opportunities to make decisions, because their life is more routinized, patterned, and highly controlled.

Diaries also describe the work load and the roles children play in families. Some subordinate themselves to routines established by elders, others carry nearly adult responsibilities. In some families children are treated as unwelcome roomers, and in others they are a center of attention and accommodation. Some experience only demands and authority pressures, others receive a good deal of support and help.

These experiences set the background for school learning. They make a difference, for example, in the assignments that are possible, the amount of homework one can count on, and so on. Children with limited experiences with peers out of school need opportunities in school to learn even the ordinary social skills. The isolated lone wolf is apt to be a problem case in school because group controls are foreign to him. A student whose home continually explodes in cleavages cannot calmly forget these explosions and do arithmetic full tilt. Analysis of diaries also tells what the teacher can anticipate in managing the classroom and what gaps need to be filled in for school learning to have a proper effect. They also indicate what meanings or skills required for school work are lacking and need to be developed in school. They give clues on how to approach academic learning and what type of content is most likely to bring response and create interest.

Diary material provides a clearer explanation of such problems as inability to get along with other students, difficulties with homework, or apparent lack of success in adjusting to school demands. It suggests the causes of many discipline problems, such as deficiencies in a sense of belonging and poor ways of using time.

The main contribution of diaries, however, is to uncover the gaps in social learning which the school program needs to fill, such as the fact that the home life is barren of any education in values and ideals and that a greater emphasis on these matters in curriculum is needed (*Taba, 1955b, ch. 2; Taba and Elkins, 1950, chs. 1, 3, and 4*).

A PROGRAM FOR DIAGNOSIS

There is no doubt that if curriculum development is to avoid routinized tinkering on the one hand and thoughtless changes on the other, more imaginative diagnosis is needed. If it is to provide insight into factors which affect learning, this diagnosis should also be of a much broader scope than is current today. It is necessary to extend diagnosis to cover the whole range of objectives, especially those that involve the so-called intangible learnings. Information is needed about the problems encountered in learning and about the conditions which may affect learning either favorably or adversely or which promise to enhance it.

Each of these dimensions of diagnosis will add fruitful hypotheses about the objectives which the curriculum needs to serve and about the limitations and conditions which must be taken into account in projecting learning experiences for a particular group of students.

It seems clear also that diagnosis cannot be limited by the availability of objective tests and instruments. Even if these were available in all areas, they still would be too limited to permit the flexibility of exploration that the varied conditions and problems involved in curriculum development require.

There is much to be said in favor of using the kinds of informal procedures described in this chapter. First, these devices can be incorporated into instruction; therefore it is easier for teachers to use them at the time when they need them and to put the findings into action almost immediately. This flexibility makes it possible also to serve unique needs in a unique manner and to explore the growing edge of the broader educational needs. All of this will help to keep the curriculum from becoming too stereotyped and too uniform to respond to new ideas or new needs. The instructional utility of the diagnostic devices will also invalidate the usual excuse for limiting diagnostic activities—that they take time away from instruction.

Another virtue of informal diagnostic data lies in the fact that they provide more telling clues than do the formal data and that they add concreteness and vividness to the events, circumstances, and behaviors studied. They are, therefore, highly suggestive as to what procedures and materials to use and what to emphasize in curriculum and instruction; in fact they are far more helpful than rows and rows of test scores which, while more generalizable and objective, are also less descriptive.

These merits of the more informal diagnostic devices should not blind one to their many shortcomings. They are subjective and, unless great care is taken in processing and interpreting the results, can easily lead to misinterpretation and biased conclusions. Their very concreteness and vividness tend to stimulate crystal gazing and focusing on the striking detail instead of on the common features, unless methods of interpretation are used which limit the conclusions according to the nature of the data and their weaknesses. It is therefore extremely important to develop adequate categorization and objective interpretation of these data. Data from informal devices are also some-what unreliable and spotty, and therefore judgments from them are dependable only if the conclusions from data from several sources are consistent. Even fairly undependable data acquire a greater reliability when they show consistency with other data secured from different sources. Objectivity of interpretation is enhanced also when data are assembled not in helter-skelter fashion but according to a rational set of hypotheses. Without such a design diagnosis will lack focus and any one thing will seem as important as anything else. There are no criteria by which to decide what is most crucial to study, which relationships of facts to examine, or which principles to apply in finding meaning. For example, discussion is analyzed in one way when the chief purpose is to distinguish mature reactions from the immature, and in another way if the point is to discover what level or pattern of sensitivity students have toward the problems of human relationships.

Without such rationale even the most objective and reliable data could be misleading, especially if they pertain to an isolated aspect of behavior, such as the IQ or achievement in arithmetic. Because human beings act as organic units, and behavior or growth in one dimension is affected by, and in turn affects, behavior and growth in other respects, one has to look for rational constellations of factors to discover the real meaning of any particular datum.

Careful interpretation of the diagnostic data is essential also. This seems almost a platitude. Yet, too often, proportionately too much time and energy is spent on data gathering, and much less on getting objective and appropriate meaning from them. This is true of the data assembled school-wide as well as of the more informal information secured by teachers on students in their classes.

It is obvious, of course, that a diagnostic program of a reasonable scope cannot be managed through the isolated efforts of individual teachers. Cooperative work is needed in planning as well as in securing the data. This involves reasonable differentiation between the kind of information to be secured on a fairly wide scale and the kind which is secured for special purposes only, on small groups or for special samples, and requires a rational way of relating the first type of information to the other.

Even the informal devices require proper technical treatment if their results are to be worthwhile. Technical help in planning and analysis is needed to assure objectivity and validity in data and their interpretation. Technical aid is needed also to make sure that the devices are dependable and that the interpretations are more than impressionistic.

Finally, there is the problem of translating the findings into perception of needs to be served by the curriculum. The weight of tradition and of routinized thinking tends to show itself at its heaviest in this process of translating diagnostic findings into educational objectives, and therefore competent help in imaginative thinking about the curriculum is most needed at this point.

Selection
of Curriculum

CHAPTER SEVENTEEN

Experiences

Selecting the content, with accompanying learn-
ing experiences, is one of the two central decisions in curriculum making, and
therefore a rational method of going about it is a matter of great concern.

THE PROBLEMS
OF RATIONAL SELECTION

Selection, of course, has always been a problem
in curriculum development. There has always been more to learn than any
student could learn in twice the time at his disposal. Today the problem of
a rational basis for selecting curriculum content is especially crucial for several reasons. First, because of the ferment in education, proposals for what
to include in the curriculum or to exclude from it emanate from a variety of
sources, based on a variety of considerations, some of which are either insufficient, irrational, or both. Educators themselves seem to be confused
about the criteria by which to decide what the content of curriculum should
be or the ways in which learning should be organized and managed. Second,
the explosion of knowledge has made the classical simplicity of school subjects impossible. As specialized knowledge increases, it is necessary either
to add more subjects or to assign new priorities in the current offerings to
make room for new knowledge and new concepts.

New requirements for what constitutes literacy have also emerged. This is
well illustrated by what is happening in the requirements of geographic knowledge. Areas of the world that formerly were treated as continents known
only by their general physical characteristics now are populated by specific
nations. In addition, effective knowledge of the current world conditions requires more than familiarity with place names. It requires also an understanding of a "bewildering variety of living conditions" and the "sobering
inequality in these conditions" (*White, 1958, pp. 63-71*).

In addition, the extension of the objectives of education has called for new areas of learning which were not part of the classical curriculum, such as subjects dealing with the sociology of the family or with personal development, the development of creative thinking, or an objective understanding of the cultures of the world. The usual method of accommodating new demands, especially on the high-school level, has been to introduce new subjects or to put new units into existing subjects. To make room for these additions, older subjects have been "scaled down" until some, such as world history, may be nothing more than a collection of generalized points, offering little material for thoughtful understanding. This additive method of curriculum revision has eventuated in a curriculum that is both amorphous and disorganized. To prevent this danger, new additions call for sharper reassessment of the offerings throughout the curriculum.

Finally, an improved educational technology presumably permits an expansion of what can be learned in a given period of time. New technical aids for self-teaching, for communicating information, and for learning a variety of skills are shifting the balance of time and of effort needed for acquiring a substantial portion of the current curriculum. These developments call for a reconsideration of what it is possible to offer and a re-evaluation of the scope of objectives for which the school can be responsible.

When more and more diverse content is pressed into the same amount of time, it becomes impossible to preserve unity, depth, or sequence in learning. It is not unfair to say that, under these conditions, the more one "covers" the less one learns. While new content and new emphasis are needed, it is also important to prevent the curriculum from becoming a cafeteria offering, an indigestible mélange of sundries rather than a patterned diet for learning.

Lately there has also been pressure toward a greater efficiency of curriculum because of an overabundance of students and shortages of facilities and teachers. This pressure has generated questions about the need to speed up what has been considered to be too leisurely a pace of educating the young, and proposals for reconsideration of what are the fundamentals in curriculum and what the dispensable frills.

All this naturally has led to the question of priorities in curriculum content. Some critics maintain that the curriculum both in our colleges and high schools does not reflect an order of priorities, and that there are no criteria for establishing such priorities. Years ago Hutchins eloquently criticized the college curriculum for a lack of any such criteria and for an unwillingness to establish any: "The crucial error is that of holding that nothing is any more important than anything else, that there can be no order of goods and no order in the intellectual realm. There is nothing central and nothing peripheral, nothing primary and nothing secondary, nothing basic and nothing superficial. A course of study goes to pieces because there is nothing to hold it together. Triviality, mediocrity, and vocationalism take over because we have no standard by which to judge them" (*1943, p. 26*).

Priorities are also a matter of concern in many recent reports on education, although sometimes it is not clear on what basis these priorities are established. Gardner boldly states that, at least in the elementary curriculum, reading is the most important subject, and mathematics second only to reading (*1960, pp. 86-87*). Since Sputnik, priorities are being established by assigning more time to science, foreign languages, and mathematics on the ground that scientific and mathematical literacy is necessary in technological culture and that competition with Russia requires that we develop more scientists and technicians. According to some other critics, this priority has thrown the curriculum woefully out of balance.

All this demonstrates a need for establishing rational criteria for determining what schools shall teach, which subjects the curriculum should include, and what to cover in each. These criteria are needed for assurance that temporary needs and feelings of urgency will not overwhelm other basic functions of education, that omissions will be considered as carefully as additions, and that in the course of establishing priorities of time spent, the possibilities of increased efficiency in learning and teaching will not be overlooked.

PROBLEMS IN ESTABLISHING CRITERIA

To develop criteria for rational priorities in selecting curriculum experiences it is necessary to clarify some prior points. First, it is important to understand that the curriculum consists of two different things: the content and the learning experiences, or the mental operations that students employ in learning content. Although in the actual learning act the two are in constant interaction—one cannot deal with content without having a learning experience—for the purposes of establishing rational criteria the two need to be distinguished. It is possible, for example, to deal with significant content in a manner that results in inadequate learning, or to apply fruitful learning processes to content that in itself is not worth knowing. One can speak of effective learning only as both content and processes are fruitful and significant.

The failure to make this distinction has caused many a misunderstanding in the discussion of curriculum theories. As we shall see later (chapter 22), many a reasonable criterion for organizing or selecting curricula has been misapplied or misunderstood by critics, because what was intended as a criterion for selecting learning experiences came to be used as a criterion for selecting curriculum content or even for organizing the entire curriculum. For example, the discussion of the role of subjects as means for training in disciplined thought has been obscured because of the assumption that disciplined thought is the direct function of the type of content rather than of the mental operations employed while learning it. It is possible to learn mathematics by rote, and to learn welding by analyzing and applying some basic principles. In other words, depending on the nature of learning experiences, any subject can be reduced to *learning about* or become the means for the learning of the *how* of disciplined thinking. A clearer distinction between the content of the curriculum and the learning experiences or the processes which students employ in dealing with content would be helpful in classifying such problems of selection as determining which criteria apply to which aspect of curriculum.

The discussion of the behavioral objectives shows also that some educational objectives are served by the content, whereas others are best implemented by certain learning experiences. The objectives described as acquisition of knowledge—the concepts, ideas, and facts to be learned—can be implemented by the selection of content. On the other hand, the attainment of objectives such as thinking, skills, and attitudes cannot be implemented by selection and organization of content alone. To attain them students need to undergo certain experiences which give them an opportunity to practice the desired behavior.

If curriculum is a plan for learning, and if objectives determine what learning is important, then it follows that adequate curriculum planning involves selecting and organizing both the content and learning experiences.* This means, of course, that not all decisions pertaining to the kind of experiences students are to have in classroom are purely methodological. Some, such as having balanced opportunities for the development of thinking, attitudes, and skills, are curricular decisions, inasmuch as on these decisions depend the opportunities for achieving a considerable portion of the educational objectives. There has been perhaps a greater separation of the domain called curriculum and the domain called method than is good for adequate curriculum planning and practice, and the line of distinction may be in the wrong place. For this reason, in this chapter, the criteria for selecting curriculum content and learning experiences are not discussed separately, but distinctions will be made regarding what pertains to selection of content and what to selection of learning experience.

It needs further to be kept in mind that because content represents several different levels, as suggested in chapter 12, different levels of choice are also involved in selecting it, and each may be subject to different criteria. One needs to decide which subjects to include in the total program, such as whether to include world history, chemistry, family life, vocational orientation, conservation, driver training, and the like. On another level, decisions need to be made regarding what topics to cover in each area or subject, such as whether world history should include the study of ancient civilizations, medieval period, Asian developments, and modern Europe, or what aspects of community should be studied in the third grade. Further, organizing each subject involves selecting the basic organizing concepts, such as that of social change or of inter-

---

* For an analysis of the role of selecting learning experiences in curriculum planning see R. W. Tyler, 1950, pp. 41-56; Tyler and Herrick, 1950, ch. 6.

dependence; selecting the basic ideas, such as that the United States is a multiculture society; and selecting the specific facts, such as the descriptions of certain plants or the location of certain rivers and cities. Since the concepts and ideas represent the fundamentals, and the specific facts serve as means for elucidating these fundamentals, different considerations apply to the choice of each. For example, coverage is a much more relevant criterion in selecting the fundamental concepts and ideas than it is in selecting the specific facts. The idea of depth has more meaning when applied to understanding of concepts than when identified with absorbing more facts. Flexibility to follow student interests is much more applicable to the sampling of specific content than to the choice of basic ideas.

The formulation and application of criteria for the selection and organization of the curriculum is essentially a device by which to translate considerations derived from the study of the sources for curriculum development into the functioning curriculum. These criteria should, therefore, encompass and integrate the implications from the views regarding the functions of school in society, from the study of the needs and requirements of the society, from the studies of the learners and the learning process, and from the analysis of the nature of knowledge and of the subject matter. Furthermore, these criteria can be applied realistically only to the extent that diagnosis reveals the particulars of a given situation. This means, then, that a different orientation to the task of the school in society, to the needs of the culture, and to learning will also produce different objectives and a different set of criteria for a good curriculum.

Finally, it is evident that whatever the criteria, they need to be applied as a collective set of screens through which to sift the possibilities in order to assure that only experiences that are valid in the light of all pertinent considerations find their way into the curriculum. An exclusive use of any one criterion or of a limited set of criteria involves a danger of an unbalanced curriculum. To produce an effective as well as efficient curriculum it is necessary to retain only that content and those learning experiences which survive the sifting process after the application of all relevant criteria of a good curriculum.*

VALIDITY AND SIGNIFICANCE OF CONTENT

Curriculum content should be valid and significant, but validity and significance imply several different specific considerations. In one sense *curriculum content is valid and significant to the extent that it reflects the contemporary scientific knowledge.*

One consequence of rapidly changing knowledge is the equally rapid obso-

* Some of the following criteria are discussed more fully in Taba, 1945.

lescence of subject matter used in school curricula. Obsolescence itself is of various sorts: obsolescence of facts, obsolescence of the underlying concepts and of theories which organize and interpret the facts, and obsolescence of the approach or the mode of thought used, including the kinds of questions asked and answered. Today the obsolescence of content seems to be an especial problem in science and mathematics. In both fields the fundamental concepts around which their content is organized no longer hold. It is pointed out that it has been the "destiny of the twentieth century to sweep away stone by stone the very foundations on which the nineteenth century built the house of science. Newtonian dynamics was rejected in favor of relativity. The deterministic corpuscular view of matter was abandoned in favor of the statistical wave conception fundamental in quantum theory" (*Stone, 1958, p. 396*). The curriculum in physics is described as antiquarian in perspective, technological in emphasis, overly inclusive in content, and confused in structure, because the physics textbooks present the material from the point of view which dates back half a century (*Calandra, 1959, p. 20; Little, 1959*).

Defining the curriculum as a prescription for what pupils should learn and teachers should teach, the authors of *Problems in Mathematical Education* say that: "To be a useful prescription, the curriculum needs to be in vital contact with at least three areas of reality: the growing body of knowledge in the field itself, the specific mathematical needs of the sciences and professions, and the minimal understanding of mathematics an ordinary person must develop if he is to live comfortably in a technical culture." They find that the current mathematics curriculum does none of these things and that the "mathematics curriculum in general use today looks remarkably like the 1890 model" (*Dyer, Kalin, and Lord, 1956, pp. 18-19*). Another report on mathematics points out that this subject, which "pulsates with the challenge of new ideas," is presented in the classroom in the "matrix of pre-seventeenth century thought" (*National Council of the Teachers of Mathematics, 1959*).

Similar questions are being raised also about social studies, and English, that is, whether their content reflects the most valid and up-to-date concepts. Whether these questions are raised less loudly in these areas because the curriculum has been under a more constant scrutiny or because at the present time less money is being made available for basic studies in these areas is not altogether clear. There is reason to believe, however, that the "new" is currently more acceptable in sciences and mathematics than in social sciences and humanities. Some local curriculum proposals seem to accept progress of knowledge in the sciences and mathematics but exclude new knowledge in such areas as sociology and anthropology in favor of history. In commenting on the proposals for the Portland curriculum study, for example, Gustafson points out that "whereas most of the separate reports, concerned with subject matter, reveal awareness of the progress of knowledge and of the need and existence of innovation in thought and method, the report of history and social studies looks toward the past . . . such as eliminating all sociological material about the family in the high school. Only strong pressure obtained approval for some courses in anthropology and sociology in the undergraduate preparation of prospective social science teachers" (*1960, p. 467*).

Shortcomings are bound to exist in regard to using in the school curriculum ideas and knowledge from newer disciplines, which may offer important needed insights to understanding and interpreting the world today. Anthropologists, for example, point out that anthropology, the one science which specializes in the "whole" culture and the "whole" man, is conspicuously absent both in the content of curriculum and among the concepts with which social phenomena are explained and interpreted. Social studies curricula make meager use of the anthropological concepts which represent generalized knowledge of man and which have much that is valuable to say on culture, history, human nature, values, universals and culture change (*Spindler, 1958, p. 116*).

"It is possible that social studies programs have tended in general to deal more or less exclusively with the formalized *end-products* of human behavior. The results of the personality and culture studies, along with the values and the cultural change researches, may eventually be used to help the social studies teacher to present more of the dynamics" (*Spindler, 1958, p. 138*).

But perhaps the more important question about validity of content is how fundamental the knowledge is. Chapter 12 described the different levels of knowledge and pointed out that the mainstay of current curriculum, specific facts, is the least fundamental, and that the main core of school subjects lies in the basic ideas, concepts, and modes of thought which organize the kaleidoscope of concrete facts and events.

The problem of distinguishing surface details from basic knowledge exists in mathematics when the mechanical intricacies of solving a linear equation overshadow understanding the principle of it. Science experiments in the elementary school may be neither truly scientific nor experimental. The history curriculum may be so studded with historic facts that no basic ideas about historic causation or of the essential nature of such movements as immigration in American history can emerge.

The more fundamental the idea, the greater will be its breadth of application, for the idea is "fundamental" precisely because it has wide as well as powerful applicability. If a student has mastered the idea of the wave theory of light, he could then apply this to the understanding of sound. Since the concepts which have wide applicability must also be built on a wider range of direct experience to develop their meaning, deeper inquiry into selected parts of the subject is more likely to develop these concepts than a survey of the whole subject. To develop an understanding of such concepts it is necessary to move up vertically with each idea instead of laterally from idea to idea (*Easley, 1959, pp. 4-12*).

The practical counterpart of this suggestion is to focus study on a limited number of carefully selected principles which constitute the basic core of a subject, and then to use these ideas as the criteria for *sampling,* rather than *covering,* the more specific content necessary to develop them. These ideas could be considered the essentials or universals of the curriculum.

Often the curriculum is loaded with insignificant detail because there is no way to determine what is important and what is not. Without a reference to basic ideas any one detail is as important as any other. It is easy to indulge in broad coverage of facts under the illusion of providing for depth when actually this practice invites a neglect of insight, prevents thoughtful reactions, and stultifies inquiry.

It is evident, then, that the criterion of validity and significance is especially relevant to the selection of the basic concepts and ideas. Since the more concrete facts, events, and experiences are only the means for elucidating the basic ideas, it is probably more important that they be sufficiently connected with the experience of students to provide an adequate road to comprehension of ideas and principles than that they represent the ultimate in significance. Often fairly simple, commonplace experience content will serve to elucidate important ideas, especially on the elementary level.

In current discussions of the curriculum in physics and mathematics especially, these fundamental ideas, concepts, and laws are sometimes referred to as the "structure of the subject matter" (*Bruner, 1960, pp. 6-8, 17, 32*). Possibly the essence of the content of social studies or literature is less likely to be defined in this way. The use of this term could easily convey an impression of the necessity to focus on individual and separate disciplines, when actually the more fundamental the idea is, the more likely it is to point to relationships between the subjects. The new mathematics curricula which are addressed to the "structure" of mathematics have found it necessary to combine the formerly separated subjects of arithmetic, algebra, and geometry. This seems to be the case with the basic ideas in other fields also. To explore the idea that specialization leads to greater productivity in work as well as to greater ennui in living, one needs to dip into economic as well as sociological and historical facts. In a similar manner, study of "a way of life in a modern community" requires a study of materials ordinarily classified as economics, sociology, and anthropology. The relationship of the concepts of mathematics and physics is more than a desirable ingredient of the curriculum: the two sets of concepts reinforce and support each other. This should remind us that school subjects are but convenient categories of classification, subject to change as knowledge changes or ideas about learning are modified.

It seems, then, that the objective of disciplined thinking about basic ideas does not eliminate the possibility of organizing the curriculum around ideas which cut across many disciplines and are supported by the study of facts combined from many subjects. The chief obstacle to "integrated" curriculum is not the fact that integrated knowledge *per se* jeopardizes disciplined thinking, but the fact that it is more difficult to plan an integrated curriculum adequately and to teach it competently.

Knowledge becomes significant also to the extent that its pursuit conveys the spirit and the method of inquiry. To learn significant history means to learn to ask and to answer the kind of questions a historian would ask and to learn to treat historic evidence, facts, and ideas as a historian would.

This concept of knowledge as a spirit and a method of inquiry is not new. As Easley points out, in connection with analyzing the educational theory that underlies the work of the Physical Science Study Committee, the method of inquiry has been emphasized in curriculum theory by such groups as the Progressive Education Association, and by such philosophers as John Dewey, for a long time (*1959, pp. 6-7*).

In describing the function of science instruction, *General Education in a Free Society* suggested that "science instruction in general education should be characterized mainly by broad integrative elements—the comparison of scientific with other modes of thought, the comparison and contrast of the individual sciences with one another. . . . These are areas in which science can make a lasting contribution to general education" (*Report of the Harvard Committee, 1945, p. 155*).

The idea has not been implemented in practice because of insufficient study of the relationship of scientific inquiry to learning process, and because the method of inquiry is not easy to apply.

Decisions regarding which concepts and ideas are valid, significant, and basic are not easy to make. First, teachers as well as curriculum makers are not always sufficiently at home in the frontiers of knowledge in their subjects. The decisions involved here require high enough competence to put the best minds in the respective disciplines to the task of sifting the ideas and concepts and the methods of inquiry. But the task of developing valid, significant, and fundamental curriculum content goes further than selecting basic ideas. A problem of establishing significance exists also in making such minor decisions as the choice of the particular objects or activities with which to represent the "Indian way of life" in a mural, if this representation is to correspond to the "truth" about the way of life as an anthropologist or historian would see it. This means that the particulars of the content must also represent the structure of the subject matter. To apply this criterion adequately and consistently calls for the re-establishment of the now largely defunct cooperation between teachers and specialists in curriculum and in content fields.

Perhaps the greatest difficulty lies in translating this criterion into consistent classroom practice. For example, while the ideas on the importance of methods of inquiry are not new, they have not been applied even in subjects whose prime objective is scientific method. Much of science teaching, instead of being an induction into inquiry, is quite dogmatic. Laboratory experiments are even prescriptive. All the student has to do is to follow the directions. It is not an easy task to translate the principles, ideas, and methods of inquiry into the thought systems appropriate to the developmental levels of students. The fact that little is known about the developmental sequence in the higher mental function was pointed out in chapter 8. Ausubel seems to feel that at least for the present the task is almost hopeless, because the deficiencies in "particularizing developmental generalizations" are far too great even to begin to tell what the readiness is for different subject matter areas, for various levels of difficulty within each, and under different styles of learning and teaching (*1959, p. 249*). It seems, then, that although theoretically it might be possible to teach "anyone anything at any age, provided one knows how to translate complex ideas into the appropriate modes of thinking," as Bruner claims, in practice, at least for the time being, trial and error must be the guide. Current curriculum practice makes as many errors in the direction of spending time on expounding concepts which are insufficiently understood and therefore can only be memorized, as in filling students' minds with trivial facts unrelated to basic ideas.

CONSISTENCY WITH SOCIAL REALITIES

If the curriculum is to be a useful prescription for learning, its content and the outcomes it pursues need to be in tune with the social and cultural realities of the times. Applied to the selection of content, this criterion further selects from the scientifically valid and fundamental knowledge that which is also significant. Some knowledge has the additional value of providing the most useful orientation toward the world around us. While the study of algae and of the atom could be equally fundamental, the latter is presumably of greater significance, at least as general education for understanding the world around us.

There is a difference between responsiveness to the demands of the immediate situation and achieving a thoughtful reality orientation to the basic needs of the culture. As was pointed out earlier, American education is almost overly responsive to immediate social pressures, which usually work on behalf of the demands of the immediate situation. Increasing the emphasis on science and mathematics in elementary schools because there is presumably a shortage of technically trained personnel and disregarding the fact that this shortage may no longer exist by the time the present elementary-grade youngsters become employable illustrates the danger of taking the cues from the demands of the immediate situation.

Analysis of culture and society has pointed out many areas of problems in our culture and in the world, literacy about which is crucial to living comfortably in society or to preserving its essential features. These areas, presumably, provide at least the cues which the curriculum makers must use in searching for content and learning experiences which, in addition to being valid and fundamental in a scientific sense, are also significant in a social sense. Chapters 3 to 5 described several, many of which have perhaps not been sufficiently considered in the selection of curriculum experiences. Only a few problems can be commented upon here. One of these is that *the curriculum should develop the knowledge and perspective which is commensurate with the kind of world in which we live,* a world that has shrunk unbelievably as far as contact and interdependence is concerned, and yet is composed of an unlimited variety of outlooks, backgrounds, and standards of living. In such a world cultural ethnocentricity is probably among the most dangerous incapacities of men. Yet, it seems quite possible that our curriculum perpetuates a far greater degree of provincialism and ethnocentricity than is either wise or healthy. Its anchorage is not only in the Western culture, but even in a national one, and this anchorage unconsciously and inadvertently engenders incapacity to understand cultures, that of other peoples as well as our own, because of lack of comparative material or of a comparative approach.

While the first criterion applied largely to the way of sorting out the more or less important content in the existing subjects, this second criterion introduces the problem of extending the boundaries of the current subjects into new areas of knowledge. It is doubtful that our present curriculum, with its year of world history and a smattering of world geography, can begin to build the foundation needed to develop a cosmopolitan orientation toward the diversities of the cultures of the world.

Further, there are also limitations in the responses cultivated to whatever content is used. Questions can be raised, for example, about the extent to which the materials about other areas of the world are interpreted by applying ethnocentric valuations and about the extent to which there is a concerted effort to lift the perception of issues, such as those of freedom, of government, of the use of resources, of the human condition, to the world perspective.

The development of a cosmopolitan instead of an ethnocentric orientation depends not exclusively on introducing new material and new subjects. Much can be accomplished even on the elementary level by treating such ordinary topics as the studies of community, of patterns of government, of work, and of resources comparatively: by widening the examples of communities to include samples from a variety of cultures, or by introducing patterns of work or ways of using technology in other parts of the world along with those dominant in the United States.

Orientation to cultural and social realities also involves value education. Chapters 4 and 5 documented the problems involved in developing loyalties to democratic values, especially when the technology tends to mold the social institutions in directions which may be inimical to democratic human values. They also described the dangers and difficulties involved in the conflict of values in our society and in the alienation of the individual from the basic sources on which to build a value orientation. One would assume that curriculum makers should be concerned about introducing materials and experiences which encourage examination of values and of value conflicts.

Presumably literature, the arts, and the social sciences are the most appropriate subjects for examination of values and value conflicts in our culture. These are precisely the areas that are being pushed into the background by demands for increased emphasis on science and mathematics. Not only that, but the approach to these subjects may be described as neutral and bland. Whether this blandness can be ascribed to the influence of the theory of adjustment, as Bruner and many other critics of education suggest, may be questioned. But there is reason to think that there is a good deal of "shutting our eyes to the turmoils of human life" through a systematic omission of opportunities to weigh conflicting values and to deal with issues that tend to be closed to rational thought (*Bruner, 1959, pp. 189-91*). Furthermore, one need not assume, as Ryle points out, that intelligent mental operations are limited to cognitive processes of conceptualization (1960). Extension of capacity to feel and to identify is as important an aspect of value education as is the understanding of the role of values and of value conflicts.

Selecting the values to examine, including the ways to penetrate into their essence, is a more difficult task than that of identifying the fundamental concepts of physics or the basic sociological ideas about urban society. If direct experience with the relevant "instances" is important in developing concepts, it is even more so in extending sensitivity to values and feelings. In this respect the current curriculum is as defective as it is in the development of intellectual powers, and the task of translating these issues into appropriate experiences is even more complicated.

Many critics point to "pablum" treatment of human issues and values: to the nonsensical content of our readers, to the descriptive neutrality of book reviews students are asked to write, to the literary selections which omit the crucial problems in the human condition, to the general avoidance of value issues, and to the failure to re-examine or reinterpret traditional values. As Brameld remarks, these values are either put into an educational attic or treated with sentimental deference. Both these policies prevent re-examination of values in the light of changed conditions and thereby deprive youth of an opportunity to become skilled in examining "the rules men live by" and in changing them rationally. If, as the anthropologists and psychologists tell us, in the human and social realm feelings are facts to be reckoned with, and if by controlling the feelings one can control social change, then vastly greater attention needs to be devoted to the study and cultivation of feelings and values. Literature on the role of arts is especially adamant that education of feelings and of the capacity to express them should be a part of the conscious development of all men.

Change is still another aspect of the contemporary social reality. Chapters 3 and 4 dealt with some consequences of rapid changes on all aspects of social life. Of particular importance is the discrepancy between the rate of change in technology and in social institutions. This poses the problem of the ways in which curriculum can help bridge the gap. *Essentially the problem of cur-*

riculum building is to include sufficient materials and experiences to develop
a conceptual understanding of the phenomenon of change and of the prob-
lems introduced by it and to develop minds that can cope with change and
reasonable techniques for doing it.

One special aspect of this problem is the possibility that curriculum content
is too strongly oriented toward the past to provide a realistic understanding
of the current social scene. We may depend too much on the "lessons of
history" which no longer suffice to give proper perspective toward the forces
of the future, or even to develop a facility to apply them to future contingencies. In social sciences, for example, the "background" receives more attention
than does the "foreground," as far as both material and interpretation are
concerned. Knowledge is regarded as significant to the extent that it has
"stood the test of time" and has been helpful in the centuries of development
of man and his society. Yet, it is possible that social transformation today is
deep enough to render the lessons of history inapplicable. Under these conditions the curriculum should offer only that wisdom which sheds some light
on today and opens vistas for tomorrow. Unless this is done there is a possibility that education will be hopelessly behind the times, and that the gap
between what is taught today and what today's students will need as adults
will gradually increase.

If education is to serve an unpredictable future, it is especially important
to cultivate the type of mental processes which strengthen the capacity to
transfer knowledge to new situations, the creative approaches to problem
solving, and the methods of discovery and inventiveness. Furthermore, since
complexity, anonymous control, and large-scale organization seem to be increasingly the order of the day, with the consequent dangers of conformity
and other-orientation, *autonomous thinking and independent judgment need*
to be cultivated with special care if even the minimum of latitude in the
freedom of individual choice essential to democracy is to be maintained.

Another aspect of social reality that has assumed a greater significance than
it had even a few decades ago is the role that group organization and human
relations in groups play in social life and in decision making. *Understanding*
the culture of the groups—how they function, the ways decisions are made,
how they influence individual behavior—is as significant a part of literacy
about our society as is the understanding of its political and economic func-
tioning. Constructive citizenship depends a great deal on skills in group participation and leadership which enable decision making and group deliberation to become productive, while preserving the democratic quality of its
goals and human relationships.

The criterion of social reality supplements the preceding criterion in that,
within the valid knowledge, we are asked to search in addition for knowledge
that sharpens the social perspective. This criterion supplies the basis for
examining the extent to which the conventional subjects do justice to the
needed social perspective. It is easy to turn back the educational clock and

to settle for the "formal discipline" of the conventional subjects and for the "training of the mind," while considering only the need for intellectual discipline suggested by the first criterion. The criterion of relevance of knowledge to the current emerging social realities raises sharply the question of *restoring and maintaining the balance between intellectual proficiency and intelligent social perspective*. Intellectual excellence without a value orientation and a social perspective can be easily put to serving unhuman ends, as recent history has well demonstrated. As even those most concerned with development of disciplined thinking in science programs maintain, "ultimately, science is a human study which has meaning only in terms of human values. Our attitudes toward science and what we should do with it are more crucial to the future of the earth and the quality of human living than the sciences themselves are" (*Joyce, 1961, p. 216*).

BALANCE OF BREADTH
AND DEPTH

Curriculum should represent an appropriate balance of breadth and depth. Yet depth of understanding and a breadth of coverage are two contradictory principles. One cannot practice both to an extreme. They are especially contradictory when subject matter or content is viewed as an accumulation or collection of specific descriptive facts rather than a disciplined way of seeing the important relationships between facts and the central ideas. The followers of this view see depth as an extension of coverage. This view of "depth" leads to a broad coverage which practically prevents spending time on the mental processes to make the knowledge truly useful. It also leads to the necessity of concentration on a few fields, which prevents sufficient scope for the broadening of perspective or for serving a greater variety of needs.

According to the second view, depth means understanding fully and clearly certain basic principles, ideas, or concepts, as well as their application. To achieve depth of understanding, one needs to explore ideas fully enough and in sufficient detail to comprehend their full meaning, to relate them to other ideas, and to apply them to new problems and situations. To begin with, one could study the concept of light in sufficient depth without necessarily covering all the phenomena of light. Secondly, if one has "understood" the functioning of the wave theory of light, it may not be necessary to do the same regarding sound. The depth understanding of one principle might make it unnecessary to "cover" certain other areas of physics.

This definition of depth suggests that it might be possible to achieve a reasonable balance of breadth and depth by selecting a sufficient range of ideas to study which have the greatest applicability and the greatest power to transfer, and by spending enough time on studying each. Such an approach to depth of understanding permits the student to penetrate into the way of thinking sufficiently to acquire the "discipline" of the subject. Combining the selection of ideas representing a sufficient scope of knowledge and a method of studying which moves up vertically with each idea might eliminate the current conflict between the requirements of scope and depth and restore the balance which now seems to be lacking. An experience in studying comparatively and deeply fewer ideas from a greater range of subjects might even, instead of leading to confusion and imprecision, contribute to a clearer understanding of the similarities and differences in the use of principles, laws, and concepts in various disciplines.

Some writers concerned with a depth in curriculum come close to suggesting a much criticized position of making methods of inquiry instead of content the chief focus of effort. In viewing "what shall we teach" from the standpoint of learning theory, Shoben suggests that in the future most of the world's work will be done by people "who have simply mastered in one degree or another the technique of disciplined thought." He proposes that, at least in elementary curriculum, greater attention be devoted to "such matters as intelligent use of evidence, the processes of inference, and the interrelationships between the fields of knowledge." The specific subject matter could range from baseball to astronomy, provided that the student knows something, can order that something in a logical manner, and can present the evidence in a communicative manner, and provided that he is helped "toward a greater degree of subtlety and comprehensiveness in applying these methods and toward a greater awareness of both what he is doing and the usefulness of doing it." Shoben's position is that the basic intellectual skills can be acquired, at least in the beginning, through any suitable content, and that while the growing command of sequential and orderly thought should retain its primacy, it will gradually assume the form of a concentration on particular content (*1959, pp. 274-76*).

It seems that, so far, the problem of what is meant by depth and of the balance between the needed depth and coverage is being argued on the basis of strong feelings and assumptions rather than in terms of definite knowledge of the role of each. There is, for example, no evidence on how many different encounters with the concrete facts of a subject are needed either to understand a basic idea or to acquire a particular method of thinking. It is possible that a judicious sampling of contrasts and comparisons of content may accomplish the same ends as unsampled but wider coverage of similar facts and points. Careful study of a limited selection of carefully chosen ideas may convey as much of the spirit and essence of a discipline as does a more extended coverage of less carefully chosen ideas.

The crux of the matter lies in teaching for transfer, in developing the capacity to apply whatever is learned in one context to other areas and problems. This suggests that the problem of balance of depth and coverage cannot be solved by consideration of the selection of content alone. It involves also parallel plans for designing learning experiences which cultivate the processes essential to transfer.

PROVISION FOR WIDE RANGE OF OBJECTIVES

Curriculum should provide for the achievement of a wide range of objectives. Mastery of content is only one of the many possible outcomes of learning. As was pointed out in the chapter on objectives, various other types of behaviors are both possible and necessary educational objectives. An effective curriculum provides for acquisition of significant new knowledge *and* for the development of increasingly more effective ways of thinking, desirable attitudes and interests, and appropriate habits and skills.*

Realistic planning for a wide range of objectives is amazingly rare considering the widespread acceptance of the idea itself. Some reasons for this gap between the idea and the practice were pointed out in the chapter on objectives, such as the assumption that learning the content automatically also achieves other types of objectives, a limited analysis of what behavior objectives other than knowledge entail, which has placed them into a category of "intangibles," and the failure to realize that each type of behavioral objectives requires an appropriate opportunity to practice it.

Perhaps the first important consideration in achieving a wider range of objectives is the fact that *the learning experiences, and not the content as such, are the means for achieving all objectives besides those of knowledge and understandings.* The often repeated assertion that it matters not what the students study, but how they go about it, has some truth in it in this sense, but only in this sense. Such aspects of thinking as ability to interpret data or such attitudes as loyalty to democratic values *can* come about through a great variety of content. The achievement of these objectives is relatively independent of any one type of subject matter.

The nature of the content and its organization determines only the outside limits of objectives. For example, an extremely atomistic content makes it difficult, if not impossible, to see relationships between ideas, and hence prevents the possibility of developing generalizations and applying them. Similarly, content which is stripped of all value implications cannot be helpful in extending the sense of values. Conversely, potentially rich subject matter can be implemented with learning experiences which provide opportunities for practicing either a wide or a limited range of behaviors, and hence serve either a wide or a narrow range of objectives. One can, for example, learn geographic

---

* In discussing the nature of knowing, Gilbert Ryle (1960, ch. 2) differentiates two types of knowing: knowing that and knowing how. These two types correspond roughly to the grouping of educational objectives indicated above. Acquisition of knowledge corresponds to "knowing that," while thinking and skills correspond to "knowing how."

facts and principles simply by memorizing them. But it is possible also to learn the same facts by examining the maps of contrasting geographic areas to locate them, to use the facts of latitude, rainfall, and altitude to predict what is grown and produced in these areas in order to develop generalizations about the relationship of geographic conditions to resources, production, or a way of life. These experiences will produce the same knowledge of facts and principles, but in addition encourage the cultivation of many other behaviors at the same time: how to select and evaluate materials, how to infer general ideas from concrete facts, how to relate facts to each other.

The possibility of planning learning experiences to attain a wide range of objectives has never been well understood or practiced, partly because of a traditional separation of planning content from planning learning experiences, and partly because of the assumption that good content will bring about the development of thinking and other mental skills.

The planning for effective attainment of a wide range of objectives requires several things. One of these is an awareness that the *different behaviors involved in different areas of objectives require different types of learning experiences to attain them.* As Kilpatrick phrased it: "To each thing to be learned belongs its own way of being learned. . . . To learn how to form judgments, we must practice forming judgments—under conditions that tell success from failure. To learn to think independently, we must practice thinking independently (*1952, pp. 5-6*).

As Tyler points out, learning experience must provide opportunity to practice appropriate behavior. To develop inductive thinking, students must have opportunities to generalize from a series of specific facts. To develop attitudes, it is necessary (a) to provide an environment which stimulates an assimilation of desired attitudes, (b) to provide experiences which evoke feelings of certain types, or (c) to give opportunities to make the kinds of intellectual analysis which reveal the consequences of events, ideas, or possibilities sufficiently to cultivate either a favorable or unfavorable disposition. Interests can be cultivated primarily by seeing to it that the experiences with areas in which interests are to be developed are satisfying (*Tyler, 1950, pp. 42-53*). To extend sensitivity, students need an opportunity to react with feelings and to identify with feelings of other people, whether in the reality of actual experience or as described in fiction. To learn to apply generalization in solving problems, students must have opportunities to pose problems, to develop generalizations, and to use these to solve the problems. If skill in evaluating sources and facts is among the objectives, then students need to handle sources of various degrees of reliability and not depend solely on the reliable sources which require no judgment.

With a growing sophistication of translating educational objectives into learning experiences, and with an extension of technological aids, it should be possible to extend both the variety and the range of achievable objectives. This possibility is further extended by any increase in thought and time that the curriculum planners devote to designing more varied and productive learning experiences. Yet, the achievement of a broad range of objectives would never become a practical possibility if special learning experiences were needed for each objective. Learning experiences are needed which provide within the same experience opportunities for achieving multiple objectives, or, in other words, for practicing a variety of behaviors. It is possible to go about the learning of the content in such a manner that there are simultaneous opportunities for an active exercise of several mental functions: analyzing problems, inferring and making deductions, discovering and applying ideas and principles, practicing certain skills, and expressing feelings and attitudes. These opportunities are presumably available most consistently in a problem-solving approach but need not be limited to formal exercises in problem solving.

Achieving multiple objectives also involves increasing opportunities for active forms of learning. If one assumes that acquiring knowledge is a passive process, it is easy to postulate that learning and thinking are two different phenomena. Bruner makes such an assumption in speaking of "leaping the barrier from learning to thinking" (*1959*). Learning experiences can be devised, however, in which a variety of active mental processes are imbedded in the very act of acquiring knowledge: experiences which stimulate students to generalize instead of absorbing generalizations; to plan in place of following ready-made plans; to abstract instead of absorbing abstractions.

The principle of active learning has been widely accepted, but equally widely misunderstood. Educational theories have long stressed the importance of active learning. Most of Dewey's writing, for example, centered on propounding the idea of learning as an active transaction between the learner and his environment, including the content of the curriculum (*1938, ch. 3*). Unfortunately, this principle of active learning was in practice often reduced to manipulative activity, such as making clay animals in connection with the farm unit, building a grocery store in connection with the grocery unit, and making adobe bricks and building missions in connection with studying early life in California. Max Wingo has pointed out that "activity programs" have often failed to produce any "doing" except following directions and often have forgotten that one purpose of the "activities" is to provide the conditions for reflective thought, and further, that reflective thought itself is active learning (*1950, pp. 91-97*). Recently the principle of active learning has been restated under the term of learning by discovery (*Bruner, 1961*).

A discussion in an eighth-grade American history course illustrates a classroom technique which is designed both for achieving multiple objectives and for cultivating active learning. This discussion occurred as a part of the study of the "People of America," and followed the committee report on Negroes, one of several ethnic groups that the class had been studying. Previous to this report, the class had read and reacted to stories about Negroes as well as about the problems of other ethnic groups in finding a place in American culture. The committee had studied and reported on such points as the importation of slaves, present-day migration of Negroes from the South to the North, discrimination in housing and employment, why the Thirteenth, Fourteenth, and Fifteenth Amendments were needed, and the reasons for FEPC and for the civil rights legislation. The discussion below is on the last point. The class, as a whole, had only general knowledge about Negroes preceding the report, so they asked many questions of the committee on the points they did not understand.

LEO: You said the Negroes were made citizens and they could vote. Then you said they can't vote.

SAUL: They can, but they haven't got the money for the poll tax.

LEO: Whatzat?

SAUL: It's a tax they have to pay to vote.

ANN: When Negroes voted, the Ku Klux Klan scared them and kept them from voting.

STEPHEN: They could vote by law, but the whites thought of ways to stop them.

VICTOR: What's the good of a law if they can't use it?

GRACE: Some will manage to vote if the law is there.

ELLIE: They were chased away. By law you can vote, but if you are chased away, you can't vote.

SAUL: If they came up North, they could vote, so it does help to have that law written down.

ETHEL: But why did people down South try to stop them?

GRACE: It's about Jim Crow. (Explains again) They don't want them to get ahead of them. (Reads from *One Nation* to verify).

WALTER: I read that practically every state in the United States at one time had a poll tax.

DAN: This book says that the Fifteenth Amendment says that they can't take the right to vote away. How come they do?

STEPHEN: If the poll tax is a law, why can't another law stop it?

WALTER: In the South, the white people make laws for their states, and they're not gonna pass another law like that. And besides, the Federal Government can't make laws for the states.

STEPHEN: But it concerns the whole United States.

SAUL: In the South they didn't want the Civil Rights Bill to go through because the Federal Government will have control of that instead of the states.

STEPHEN: I heard on the radio that they are going to try to destroy the Ku Klux Klan.

CELIA: *Negro Americans: What Now,* tells about Negro cases that were thrown out of court just because they were Negroes. They didn't even get a trial, and they are citizens.

DAN: In this book (*Nation's History*), it told about the poll tax, too. Everybody has to pay—whites and Negroes—not just Negroes. But if a white man is poor and he can't pay, there's a Grandfather Clause and he can vote.

LEO: A what!

DAN: A Grandfather Clause. If your grandfather voted, so can you. But the Negroes' grandfathers were slaves so they couldn't vote [*Taba and Elkins, 1950, pp. 167-68*].

This discussion provided an opportunity to consolidate the facts, ideas, feelings, and skills these students had acquired in activities leading up to it as well as active inquiry into matters suggested by the report. The principle of "learning by doing" finds its rightful place in this type of learning experience. Each objective was implemented by an appropriate "doing" calculated to help the student practice the expected behavior, whether it was critical analysis of data or a sensitive projection into strange people and strange values.

The emphasis on multiple objectives and active learning requires a reconsideration of the way to spend time. If a learning activity is to carry many objectives and provide practice for thinking and inquiry, it may require more time than would be warranted by its content alone, because the students need to learn new behaviors. The time allotted to the discussion above was greater than would have been required simply to learn the facts about the civil rights of Negroes. But this particular learning activity also "covered" learning to deduce ideas from the facts in the report, to relate these generalizations to those developed in the preceding study, to apply them to explain new phenomena, to examine the consistency of and relationship between facts, to use references to support points, and to carry on a logical train of thought.

The teacher's appraisal indicated that learning experiences of this sort, while time consuming, pay off in multiple outcomes:

> These open discussions served many purposes. I could appraise what the children had learned. It was evident that the children had not only acquired a wealth of facts, but also were willing to apply them and could use them precisely in reports and arguments. This reminded me of the time, not so long ago, when I was reluctant to give up the textbook and page-by-page fact-learning because I feared the children would learn less. The introductory stories had given the children a chance to identify with Negroes. Apparently these experiences helped the children to bring *feelings as well as facts into discussions* [*Taba and Elkins, 1950, p. 168. Italics added.*]

LEARNABILITY AND ADAPTABILITY TO EXPERIENCES OF STUDENTS

It seems almost trite to say that curriculum content should be learnable and adaptable to students' experiences. The practical application of this criterion, however, is far from clear. *One factor in learnability is the adjustment of the curriculum content and of the focus of learning experiences to the abilities of the learners.* For effective learning the abilities of students must be taken into account at every point of the selection and organization but especially in planning concrete experiences designed to develop the power to discover general ideas and concepts. A major reason for having a curriculum lies in the fact that many skills, ideas, and insights we want students to learn are beyond their powers to master by themselves. If students are to learn these, they must be introduced in thought forms which are appropriate and under conditions which are especially favorable to learning. In essence, we need to view learning experiences as steppingstones toward an end outcome. Naturally, the number as well as the nature of these steppingstones varies with the ability to learn and with the already existing mental systems and schemata of concepts. Some students require fewer encounters with concrete examples to develop a general idea than do others.

To the extent that powers are assumed which do not exist, curriculum becomes a nonfunctional instrument. Moreover, it is far from simple to apply this criterion, and the errors of overexpectation are as frequent as are those of underexpectation and underachievement. First, as the discussion of intelligence and its testing (in chapter 8) suggested, current methods of assessing ability do not give an adequate picture of the qualitative differences in abilities. Hence the adaptation of curriculum to ability takes chiefly the form of modifying the scope of content covered, or the pace of learning. Since it is possible to distinguish only high and low ability, and fast and slow learners, this seems entirely logical, though quite insufficient from the standpoint of developing and using all variety of talent.

Far more study is needed of the qualitative differences in mental systems in order to plan a curriculum which provides differentiated but equally effective approaches to core learnings for students with differing mental systems and different patterns of social learning and motivation. The current curriculum is too uniform not only in that it covers the same content, but also in that it employs essentially the same learning experiences to penetrate into the structure of the content.

The problem of making the curriculum learnable involves also the task of translating the social heritage into experiences which help each student to make it his own. In some ways the students need to experience whatever they are learning. This means that an approach must be used to learning the essentials of curriculum which connects that which the students have already experienced with that which is yet to be learned. The more heterogeneous or deviate the background or the social learning of the students, the more important it is that there be a variety of bridges between what is now understood, the current concepts and meanings, and that which is to come.

Rightly used, this criterion of appropriateness to life experience is applicable primarily at two points. First, it is applicable in the beginning of a unit or a topic, in selecting the concrete instances through which to discover the general ideas. The nearer these instances are to whatever has meaning to students, the greater the possibility that the general idea will be discovered and understood, and that both the potential of the student and his motivation will be fully engaged. Since ideas of fair scope can presumably be developed through a fairly wide range of content, it is only the better part of wisdom to select these instances of the general ideas in the light of their potential connection with the experience of the students.

Life experience of the student can also supply some of the situations to which application is made of what is learned. The possibility of transfer should be greatly enhanced if the student is not faced with applying what he knows to situations which are totally unfamiliar to him or which have no significance to him.

This method of applying the criterion of relating the curriculum to the life experience of students indicates the use of the life experience of students first as a bridge to new learning and then again as a way of *assuring transfer of learning to new phenomena,* but *not* to determine which ideas or principles it is important to learn. This distinction in the use of life experience as a bridge and as a center of organizing content and learning should eliminate the misunderstandings between the advocates of "experience curriculum" and the critics of it. The former have tended to use the experience approach as a way of organizing the curriculum, without sufficient regard for the quality of the content or the intellectual powers so offered. This, for example, has been the criticism of the life adjustment program, which interpreted the experience approach as an attempt to offer students only what fits their current perceptions, or what is directly applicable to immediate life problems. This same misunderstanding has also been the chief source of the contention that the criterion of relationship to life experience is essentially contradictory to the criterion of fundamental knowledge.

Theoretically, of course, it is not impossible to center the study of everything around life problems. These problems have a way of cutting across areas of knowledge, and their analysis and study would presumably engage any type and level of mental powers and skills. Hence an adroit selection of such problems and a careful development of their dimensions could conceivably bring into play all that needs to be learned. However, the planning of this type of curriculum would require resources which, at least currently, are not available, especially for curricula beyond the primary school. Such a program takes more expert thought and planning than has usually been provided. Consequently, the existing examples are, in all justice, open to the criticism of neglecting disciplined knowledge and thinking.

APPROPRIATENESS TO THE NEEDS AND INTERESTS OF THE STUDENTS

The meaning of the principle that the curriculum should be appropriate to the needs and interests of the learners has been among the most misunderstood issues of education, both by those who have supported it and by those who have opposed it. The so-called "needs" approach to curriculum evolved during a period of sharp criticism that curriculum was ineffective because it was too remote from the needs and concerns of youth. This period coincided with the depression, which caused a large-scale displacement of youth. (Cremin [1961] connects the needs approach with the general progressivist and reformist movement at that time.)

In the early days of this approach vague definitions of the term "need" created many controversies. First, the supporters of the "needs" criterion used it as the main basis for selecting and organizing both the content and learning experiences to the exclusion of all other criteria, at least in theory. The criterion was also considered equally applicable to the selection of content and learning experiences on all levels.

Additional misunderstandings arose from what Featherstone calls the "here and now quality" in the definition of needs which prevailed in some quarters (*1950, p. 68*). This "here and now" quality is clearly expressed by Giles and his associates, who, in discussing the question of scope, state boldly that there are but three choices in determining the scope of curriculum: "They (the teachers) may teach that which always has been taught. They may decide on the knowledges, skills, abilities and attitudes which *adults* find necessary in order to cope with the world, and teach those to their pupils. Or they may ascertain the *present* needs of their adolescent charges and teach the knowledges, skills, abilities, and attitudes necessary to meet these needs" (*1942, p. 77*).

A special storm center was created around the problem of whether the individual or the social needs should have supremacy in determining curriculum content, and whether the studies of children and adolescents were sufficient as a basis for curriculum development. Some educators, among them Boyd H. Bode, argued that, to expect the "felt" needs, the individual wishes and desires, to supply a platform for education smacked too much of Rousseau's "growth from within," and that to expect the "needs" to emerge from the studies of adolescents was like "expecting an architectural design to result from a study of the structural materials that are to be used in building." To his mind, this approach threatened to throw democratic ideals out of the window, because only the purposes of education grounded in democratic philosophy, could supply the proper reference point for the study needs. Individuals cannot be expected to match democratic values to their needs. One must educate individuals to discover their needs in the light of democratic values (*Bode, 1938, pp. 62-70*). (This disagreement actually split the Progressive Education Association in 1942.)

Recent research in psychology, sociology, and social anthropology has added greatly to our understanding of the meaning and the function of needs in educational programs, including a clearer differentiation of the needs which education can and cannot serve. It has also become increasingly clear that the nature of needs is too complex to be served by an orientation which contrasts as antagonistic the demands of adults and the needs of youth. The process of socialization in the culture was not yet widely understood when this juxtaposition was created.

Distinctions have also been made among the requirements to which the term "need" can be applied. One type of needs represents the psychological requirements described in many studies, among the earliest of which was one by Prescott, who distinguished three types of needs: psychological, social, and the ego and integrative. The first have to do with the requirements of the biological nature of human beings, such as the need for food and for activity and rest. Social needs have to do with the relationships which individuals must establish with other human beings, institutions, and organizations; they involve the need for belonging, security, and status. Ego and integrative needs involve certain qualities and conditions of life experience which facilitate the growth of the individual and the finding of the self, such as contact with reality, progressive symbolization of experience, self-direction, balance between success and failure, and harmony and integration of personality (*Prescott, 1938, pp. 114-27*). While other writers have refined the catalog of needs and have used other classifications, in the main the threefold distinction holds. There is a fairly substantial literature on the way the fulfillment of these psychological requirements is related to the mental health of the individual and some clarification of the role of schools in meeting these needs.

Another interpretation of needs is that they represent the requirements of society, such as those discussed in the chapters dealing with socialization and social learning (chapters 10 and 11), and as expressed in the second criterion in this chapter. A classification of personal, social, and civic needs was used by the Curriculum Commission on the Secondary Curriculum of the Progressive Education Association. This Commission set about inquiring into needs in all these areas, in order to derive educational objectives which had more scope than the objectives derived solely from academic considerations (*Thayer, Zachry, and Kotinsky, 1939, chs. 4-9*). In speaking of the "ten imperative needs of youth," such as developing saleable skills, the ability to use leisure time, or learning how to purchase goods and services, the Educational Policies Commission followed a similar definition and grouping of needs and obviously had in mind the things an individual must learn to function in a culture (*1952, p. 216*). Today, the more common practice is to speak of the requirements culture makes on an individual.

Finally, there is the purely educational definition which describes as a need the gap between the present state of an individual and the desirable objectives, such as a need for sensitive awareness of other people and their values, for critical thinking, for competence in social skills, for adequate achievement in arithmetic, for democratic social attitudes, and for skills in group life. The methods of diagnosing many of these needs were described in chapter 16.

In the light of the more sophisticated and scientific understanding of needs, the controversy over the contrasting role of social and individual needs in education seems naïve. Studies of personal problems as students see them are taken for granted, as one way, but only one, of seeking a basis for understanding what the curriculum should accomplish. As chapters 3 and 4 suggest, the concept of social needs has moved closer to a psychological meaning, and the psychological needs are interpreted in the light of their social origin. It seems also that the school's responsibility to serve student needs is neither as comprehensive as was assumed in the first flush of "discovering" the psychological needs nor as limited as was assumed later.

It is clear, for example, that needs representing psychological requirements are less focal to the curriculum of the public school than are the needs representing social demands and the requirements of educational objectives. Many psychological needs lie outside the power of educational approach either within or outside the school. Yet, these psychological needs must be understood and taken into account in curriculum building, because they are a part of the constellation of conditions under which learning takes place. While schools may not be in a position to eliminate deep-seated psychological insecurity, curricula must be adjusted to the demands of security needs, and schools need to provide learning conditions which at least do not create additional insecurities. In this sense, then, all needs are of concern to the educator, but only some of these can be provided for explicitly through the curriculum. Others may be of greater concern to the psychologist and the mental hygienist. (See, for example, *Kotinsky and Coleman, 1955,* for a discussion of the limitations in the school's capacity to meet all needs.)

This means then, that when one speaks of the "curriculum fulfilling the needs of children and youth," one must think in terms of the differentiated types of needs and of the degrees of providing for each. Schools must decide where in the total program certain needs can be met, and to what extent. Perhaps the focal concern of the curriculum lies in one set of needs, with adequate learning conditions provided for another set. It is conceivable that all areas of endeavor in school may add to the establishment of a sense of reality about one's environment, but that it is possible to offer only certain experiences to foster the sense of self-identity and reality about one's self. (For a more extended discussion see *Featherstone, 1950, ch. 4, and R. E. Gross and Zeleny, 1958, pp. 373-75.*)

Similar problems have surrounded the use of the criterion of interests. Often interests have been used as a focus for selecting and organizing units or for organizing the entire program, especially in elementary-school social studies and language arts. Occasionally this practice has led to some interesting excesses, such as developing units from accidental and often whimsical suggestions of children, as from the fact that Johnny had acquired a boat, or Mary had gone to the fair. These experiments with "interest units" were a reaction against the sterile, arbitrary, and often nonsensical "adult-imposed" subject curriculum which prevailed prior to World War I. Those who rebelled against the sterile content tended to rid the curriculum of any shape of adult imposition, including planned curriculum.

But cautious voices were raised even at that time. In a 1926 yearbook on curriculum, Counts tried to classify and limit the function of student interests served in selection and organization of curriculum:

> If learning is to proceed at all, the attention of the learner must be secured and his attention can be secured only through a direct or indirect appeal to his interests. These interests must be utilized to the fullest possible extent, but they cannot be accepted as positive and trustworthy guides in selecting the content of the curriculum. They constitute the raw materials and determine the conditions of education, but they cannot furnish its goals. They reveal the present psychological position of the learner; they do not indicate the direction in which he should move. Until we have found the child's interests we have not found him—he is still lost in the educational woods. Only as his interests set limits to educational possibilities may they be regarded as guides in the choice of objectives of education. In the selection and validation of the content of the curriculum they should serve as negative, rather than as positive factors. *Nothing should be included in the curriculum merely because it is of interest to the children; but whatsoever is included should be brought into closest possible relation with their interests [1926, p. 80].*

Today the dangers of organizing the entire curriculum around the current interests and needs of children, except perhaps for the primary grades, are clearly recognized: these interests are transitory; interest centers tend to sacrifice the subject organization without replacing it with any other; such organization lacks continuity. If individual interests are followed, there is, in addition, a lack of common focus.

While in practice a more reasonable perspective toward the role of interests has been assumed, the theoretical debates about the "interest doctrine" seem to continue. Many interpret the "interest doctrine" to mean letting the whims of the learner control the curriculum. To these persons, considering either the interests or the needs of students at all is so much nonsense and a prostitution of education, even though a reasonably casual acquaintance with research in the psychology of learning, especially the processes of perception, meaning, and motivation, clearly indicates that to begin the study of anything at the point which is in accord with the interests of the learners is but common sense in making learning more effective, no matter whether the content be great books or current news.

The "doctrine of interest" is also accused of soft pedagogy. These accusations grow out of still another misconception about the role of interests in learning: that learning has to be hard to be effective. Recent research indicates the contrary—that learning that is interesting appears to be easier because motivation is stronger and effort less painful.

Dewey, who is largely blamed for the soft pedagogy because of his advocacy of interest as a means for enhancing effort, decries "soft" pedagogy which interprets the doctrine of interest as a method of attaching artificial seductive-ness to otherwise indifferent material. "The remedy is not in finding fault with the doctrine of interest, any more than it is to search for some pleasant bait that may be hitched to the alien material. It is to discover objects and modes of action which are connected with present powers. If the material operates in this way, there is no call either to hunt for devices which will make it interest-ing or appeal to arbitrary, semi-coerced effort" (*1928, p. 149*).

A more reasonable application of the criterion of interests and needs may be exemplified by the following train of reasoning: We know from research that it is foolhardy to overlook the special needs, interests, weaknesses, strengths, and existing concerns of the learners in what is taught and how it is done. To ignore this merely means overlooking potent motivation and courting the possibility of ineffective learning. Furthermore, since one im-portant task of education is to promote personal growth, the interests and needs of the learners themselves should be subject to growth: students can and do become interested in ideas, in the joy of discovery, and in applying their mental powers.

On the other hand, we also know that the range of conscious interest is limited and not an adequate basis for selection of what is to be learned. Some-how, sound education must build a bridge between the existing motivation and concerns of the learners and the essentials of education. The things that for one reason or another constitute the "musts" or "essentials" can be achieved through a range of concrete activities and content, through a mul-titude of details which can be selected according to existing interests and conscious needs, choosing content that either meets already existing interests, or for which interest can be developed. This makes it possible to use existing interests as gateways to learning. If interests in botany can be generated better by growing plants than by first assigning a chapter in the text, it is wiser to grow plants as an introductory activity. If ratios and percentages are "cold potatoes" to lower-class eighth graders, but their own "growing" baffles them, using comparative measurements of their own growth as a way of computing ratios and percentages is wise—provided that these measurements provide the required range of mathematical concepts and processes.

Neither is it necessary to assume that the interests of students are static, or that expressed interests are the true ones. The job of the curriculum mak-ing is to get below the surface and to discover those things that may "engage" the student, to enlarge these, and to connect them with what "has to be learned."

It seems, therefore, that the principle of meeting the demands of essential, significant subject matter and that of adapting education to the needs and interests of the students are not necessarily in conflict. As one differentiates the levels of choice, it is possible to "fix" the essential things to be learned and allow the details through which to learn them to be determined by student interest, thus providing for both.

Organization of Curriculum Content and Learning

Learning in school differs from learning in life in that it is formally organized. It is the special function of the school to so arrange the experiences of children and youth that desirable learning takes place.

If the curriculum is to be a plan for learning, its content and learning experiences need to be organized so that they serve the educational objectives. The type of curriculum organization followed is probably one of the most potent factors in determining how learning proceeds. Often the curriculum is ineffective not because its content is inadequate but because it is put together in a way that makes learning difficult, or because learning experiences are organized in a way that makes learning either less efficient or less productive than it might be. Chaotic content or isolated learning experiences are usually not effective in attaining any important objectives.

THE PROBLEMS OF ORGANIZING

Curriculum organization is both difficult and complex. It poses many questions and requires an application of all we know about the nature of knowledge, about child growth and development, and about learning. To the extent that these theoretical bases are either inadequate or conflicting, the task of curriculum organization also becomes more difficult and a consistent application of the multiple considerations that are needed more hazardous. If one views curriculum planning as a kind of educational engineering, one begins to realize how difficult it is to apply scientific method to this rather crucial task. It is necessary, for example, to sort out, to consolidate, and to apply the principles of learning articulated by a variety of learning theories. At which points is it useful to consider the laws of exercise, effect, and reinforcement as articulated by the associationist theories of learning? Where should one use the more dynamic ideas about learning, such as the development of insight and restructuring of the experience? What do the ideas about social learning suggest for planning sequences of content and approaches to learning that content? How does one plan learning experiences for an economical way of achieving multiple objectives? How does one organize learning for maximum efficiency, using the principles of learning so that any part of the curriculum is justifiable on the basis of its optimum contribution to learning, and nothing is included that does not serve a distinct purpose?

Conflicts and misunderstandings about the nature of knowledge and the ways in which it can be internalized by learners need to be reconciled also. What, for example, is meant by the "logic of subject matter," and how can that logic be reconciled with the fact that there is a psychological order of learning it? How can the way of learning content be so organized that it is possible to develop at the same time a variety of behavioral objectives, such as to acquire a way of thinking and to develop certain relevant attitudes? What has the difficulty of content to do with the level of mental operations that need to be mastered? Can content be so organized that its fundamentals can be acquired by different modes of learning to accommodate differences in mental systems and motivational patterns?

As was true of selection, the problem of organization also is of two dimensions: the organization of content and the organization of learning experiences. Much confusion about curriculum organization is caused by the fact that these two dimensions have not been kept clearly in focus. The validity of some criteria has been questioned because they were applied to one dimension when they were pertinent only to the other, or because they applied more directly and forcefully to one than to the other. This has been true, for example, of the long-standing controversy over the logical vs. the psychological organization of subject matter. Those who defended the primacy of the logical organization used the content as the main reference point and tended to overlook the fact that the student cannot appropriate the "wisdom of the race and the social heritage as he would take an apple from the hand." He must make it his own in some way (*Counts, 1926, p. 81*). Those who stood on the side of psychological organization usually thought of the psychological sequences of learning experiences and tended to underestimate the fact that content of any sort has a certain kind of structure or logic and that this logic should not be violated in organizing content for learning. (This point is discussed more fully on pp. 302-05.)

While the organization of content has received a good deal of attention, relatively little theoretical thinking or empirical experimentation has been devoted to the problem of organizing the learning experiences (see chapter 18). A typical curriculum framework not only lists the subjects and the topics to be covered, but also indicates a sequence for these topics. In contrast, only an unorganized list of learning activities at most is offered for teachers to choose from. The principles of sequence are usually suggested in only very general terms, such as beginning with the simplest and the most concrete and proceeding to the more complex and abstract. Relatively little guidance is given regarding how to combine these proposed learning experiences into an orderly and productive learning pattern. Offering such general criteria is akin to general exhortations to be honest, without a sufficient clarification as to how to make judgments about what constitutes honest behavior under given circumstances. The major curriculum texts treat the organizing of learning experiences in the same manner. Some reduce the problem to that of grade placement (*B. O. Smith, Stanley, and Shores, 1957, ch. 8*). Others treat it incidentally as a subtopic of a certain type of content organization (*Saylor and Alexander, 1954, part 3*).

The decisions affecting the organization of learning experiences are too important and complex to be left to the judgment of individual teachers at the moment of teaching. They deserve as careful theoretical thought as do decisions about organizing content. Therefore in this chapter, as in the preceding one on selection, the problems of organizing content and learning experiences are treated in a parallel fashion, and an effort is made to indicate which criteria or principles have special pertinence to organizing content and which to organizing learning experiences.

Finally, it is important to distinguish the two levels at which organization is needed. Some problems of organization pertain to organizing both content and learning experiences within a unit or a subject. Another level of organization deals with designing the pattern for the entire program, the framework of the content to be taught, the cumulative sequence in the emphasis of the learning experiences, and the relationship of the various subjects to each other. While central problems of organization appear on both these levels, they take a different meaning and form on each. This chapter will stress primarily the first level, leaving the problems connected with the second to another chapter.

ESTABLISHING SEQUENCE

The classical problems of curriculum organization, at least as presented in literature on curricula, are those of establishing a sequence, of cumulative learning or continuity, and of integration. (As we shall see later, the problems of sequence and of cumulative continuity overlap somewhat.) Establishing a sequence in curriculum can be viewed primarily as that of putting the content and materials into some sort of order of succession: this meaning of sequence appears in much of the writing on curricula. Leonard, for example, defines the problem by posing these three questions: what should determine the order of succession of materials of instruction, what follows what and why, and what is the most propitious time to acquire certain learning? (*1950, p. 70*)

When the exposition of content is the primary concern, as in a curriculum organized by subjects, the presumed logic of the subject by and large dictates the order of exposition. Smith, Stanley, and Shores describe four such typical sequences of exposition.

> The first is that which proceeds from the simple to the complex. The simple is defined as that which contains few elements or subordinate parts, as a one-celled animal is simpler than a many-celled animal, or as hydrogen and oxygen are simpler than chemical compounds. Chemistry and biology courses are frequently organized on this principle; and the organization of many other courses, such as grammar and foreign languages, is influenced by it in more or less degree.
>
> The second is an expository order based upon prerequisite learnings. This principle is followed particularly in subjects consisting largely of laws and principles, such as physics, grammar and geometry. Geometry is organized on the supposition that the theorems bear a particular logical relation to one another and are best learned in that relation.
>
> The third form of exposition is that which proceeds from the whole to the part. Geography frequently begins with the globe, with the idea that the earth is a sphere, because this conception serves to interpret many geographic observations, such as differences in time and seasons.
>
> The fourth kind of exposition is chronological. Facts and ideas are arranged in a time sequence so that presentation of later events is preceded by discussion of earlier ones. This is the organization followed in history courses —and frequently in literature courses, literary selections being arranged in time sequence [*1957, p. 233*].

Other sequences have been used, varying somewhat from subject to subject. In history, for example, the reverse order of starting with the present and tracing the development of the present situation backward is frequently used. In skill subjects the sequences from the part to the whole have been used and debated. Some programs use the principle of concentric circles, starting with that which is close at hand and proceeding to the remote. In the development of concepts, the principle of moving from the concrete to the abstract is usually applied.

When the curriculum is viewed as a plan for learning and not merely a plan for exposition of content, additional considerations emerge regarding sequence. One is that of a sequence of learning experiences necessary to master the necessary behavior: to acquire an abstract concept, to develop a method of analyzing problems or an attitude of tolerance toward differences, to master a skill in analyzing data, or to learn a method of inquiry. Learning these behaviors is also a matter of sequence. Further, these behaviors are of different orders of difficulty and involve developmental steps to be internalized. The specific steps in this developmental sequence vary depending on what the object of learning is. The sequence in understanding a concept of tropism is not precisely the same as in understanding the meaning of the concept of "hardships of the pioneers," or the idea that primitive peoples are dependent on their immediate environment while in modern civilization man can use things produced at a distance. Certain general principles apply in planning any of these sequences, such as the principle of moving from the known to the unknown, from the simple to the complex, from an analysis of concrete experiences to developing generalizations, especially if the chief aim is to promote active learning, a "discovery" method of concept formation, or autonomous techniques of inquiry. But each of these concepts also involves a different strategy of learning. To develop the concept of friction, a concrete demonstration can be provided. One can follow this demonstration with verbal exploration of a few contrasting manifestations of friction, compare and contrast the observations, and distill a general principle of a relationship between the nature of the surface and the forces exerted. It is more difficult to develop the idea that primitive people are more dependent on their immediate environment than are modern people, because it is not demonstrable in the same sense as is the idea of friction. The initial experiences might consist of an analysis of examples in our society of how such things as houses, food, clothing, or the materials for them were secured. Next, the students need to acquire information about how similar things are secured in a primitive society. Comparing and contrasting the two ways should enable students to establish an idea of the relative dependence on environment of the modern and the primitive man. In other cases, such as conceptualizing the hardships of pioneers, the developmental sequence might be still more complicated. Because no concrete experience referent is available, the approach has to be considerably more indirect and the evolution of the concept inferential rather than direct. One may need first to establish the feeling of what a hardship is. Since direct experience probably is unavailable, one may need to read fiction or see films as a substitute for experience. Only then can one compare what the pioneers encountered or did with what now happens in similar situations in order to develop a concept of the "hardships of pioneers." Without such experiences verbal descriptions are almost as ineffective as are verbal descriptions of color to a blind person.

Planning learning sequences such as these requires a way of organizing content as well as a sequence of reactions, behaviors, or learning experiences. Both the content and the learning experiences need to be broken into appropriate steps so that an active understanding becomes possible. For this purpose the simple principles, such as proceeding from the simple to the complex and the concrete to the abstract, are insufficient guides. A way has to be found in addition to translate the essence of the particular idea, process, or concept into the thought forms and perception patterns of the students. Since these thought forms and perception patterns vary according to the developmental sequences in the growth of students as well as according to the nature of their social learning and previous experiences, building such developmental sequences requires considerable theoretical understanding as well as practical insight. (A more detailed description of such a sequence of learning experiences is given in chapter 20, on planning a teaching-learning unit.)

The planner also needs to be aware of certain generalized functions that each step must serve. For example, the initial encounter with a concrete "instance" of an idea, a concept, or a feeling needs to connect that which is to come with whatever the student already understands or feels and to open up the possibility of new learning. Following that, the student needs to "take in" new facts, descriptions, or events which extend this first glimmer. This can be done either by subjecting familiar experiences to a new analysis, or by absorbing new facts. A sharp contrasting and comparison of the two sets of ideas and facts furnishes material for a new generalization.*

But planning such sequences also poses several as yet unsolved problems, because little is known about the developmental sequences of concept formation, attitude development, and thought processes. In a recent study of thinking, Bruner suggests several questions regarding concept formation which have pertinence to planning of learning sequences: How does the subject perceive the task—that is, does he approach the task as that of concept formation or simply as that of rote memorization? If we assume that to form general concepts one has to start from a concrete experiential base, then how many and what kind of encounters with the concrete instances of a concept are needed and how does this number vary according to the ability of students or the content of the concept? What relevance does the nature of these concrete examples have to the formation of an idea or a concept—that is, what difficulties are introduced into the process by the fact that the concrete instances are bound to have qualities which are irrelevant to the concept? What is the role of the order in which the concrete instances are introduced? Evidently the pattern of solution that individuals adopt in attempting to attain a concept reflects very sensitively the order in which they encounter the "instances" (*Bruner, Goodnow, and Austin, 1956, pp. 51-64*).

This is an aspect of sequence to which both the formal curriculum theory and practical curriculum planning has paid relatively little attention, either because it has been assumed that the sequence of content automatically provides an appropriate sequence of learning, or because it has been considered simple enough to be left to individual teachers. No doubt the lack of information about such matters as how concepts develop or what is involved in discovering generalizations or developing methods of inquiry has contributed to the meagerness of scientific thinking on this aspect of curriculum planning.

As was pointed out in chapter 11, no one knows what potentialities in growth would be opened up if a sequential development were provided for all types of mental processes, such as abstracting, analyzing, generalizing, differentiating, and categorizing ideas. A few teachers who have experimented with shaping sequences for achieving such objectives as the understanding

---

* A research project on inquiry training is using films which describe certain phenomena of science, such as atmospheric pressure, displacement, and boiling point, as a concrete encounter to demonstrate the need for establishing the necessity and the sufficient conditions for these phenomena and for stimulating questions and hypotheses for experimental inquiry (Suchman, July 1961; Aug. 1961).

of basic concepts, sensitivity to feelings and values, and the ability to generalize have reported unexpected progress, even by students who under
ordinary conditions were classified as retarded. The intellectually more gifted
students responded to this type of program with a progress in maturation that
was a joy to watch.

It is possible that with the scientific planning of sequences for the development of concepts and reflective thinking, formal thinking can develop much
earlier than has been indicated by Piaget. Classroom experimentation suggests
that children can think abstractly and reflectively at the age of seven, provided that what they are asked to think about is simple enough and sufficiently
within the range of their motivation and experience (*Moore, 1929, p. 306*).
Records from classrooms indicate that second graders can generalize, detect
logical fallacies, apply principles to explain new phenomena, and use concepts
usually reserved for much higher maturity level if their learning experiences
have been properly "programmed" to these ends (*Hudson, 1948, pp. 265-67*).

PROVIDING FOR CUMULATIVE LEARNING

Essentially the problem of cumulative learning is
to provide for a progressively more demanding performance: more complex
materials to deal with, more exacting analysis, a greater depth and breadth of
ideas to understand, to relate, and to apply, and a greater sophistication and
subtlety of attitudes and sensitivities. This may involve either short-term or
long-term sequences, depending on the nature of the task.

A first grader, for example, may learn some simple notions concerning
interdependence in connection with studying the way in which the activities
and the needs of the family are dependent on the activities of other people. A
third grader may examine the concept in relation to interdependence among
the community services. A twelfth grader may encounter the same concept,
but with reference to the interdependence of nations, to political decisions, to
the use of resources and commercial exchange. With each return engagement
the difficulty of the "content" of the concept, the level of abstraction, and the
complexity and precision required in using it are increased progressively.

Such a cumulative progression can be applied to all varieties of learning:
thinking, attitudes, and skills. Even young children can begin questioning
simple types of evidence for their sufficiency for drawing certain conclusions.
Step by step they should have experiences leading to the examination of more
complex forms of argumentation, criticism, and analysis of ideas. The development in social sensitivity may begin with the cultivation of identification with
the immediate group and proceed gradually toward sensitivity to abstract
social ideals and to complex social and human relationships (the "generalized
other").

Providing for cumulative progression of learning naturally requires that curriculum experiences be planned so that there is an increasing complexity of material to deal with, accompanied by a requirement for increasingly more mature mental reactions. However, this cumulative progression need not necessarily be tied up with a shift in content. It is conceivable that the same content can be—and often is—studied on two levels, one requiring a more mature understanding, more penetrating analysis, and a deeper insight than the other. The cumulative progression does not depend exclusively on content but also on maturity of thought, levels of abstraction, or sensitivity of feeling. Planning a cumulative progression in learning involves planning learning experiences to create a movement from one level of difficulty or complexity to a higher one, from a more limited use of ideas to a greater breadth and from simpler concepts to increasingly more complex ones. Such a progression involves also planning for a continual use of preceding learning: using what happens at one point to build a foundation for the experiences to follow, such as introducing ideas so that each prepares for the next one, or skills so that at each new step the student perfects and applies what he has mastered before. It involves planning of learning units in which one perception is designed to lift the level of the succeeding one, in which details are examined not for themselves but for their use in building a groundwork for a generalization or a perception of relationships, as, for example, examining the geographic conditions of one country in detail in order to understand a relationship between geographic conditions and resources. This type of development requires organizing a succession of questions and of learning activities to provide for movement of the cognitive and emotional reactions to higher levels, as well as for reinforcing and enlarging the concepts built in the previous activity.

Such a cumulative spiral should provide continual reinforcement by continuing in use that which has been acquired, either through practice or through use in the new context, such as a continuity between learning and applying ideas and skills. There is no guarantee that anything learned at one time is acquired permanently, be it facts, ideas, skills, attitudes, or the power to think. Reinforcement, repetition, and continued use are usually needed.

The current curriculum has evidently paid too little attention to continuity and reinforcement, as the perennial accusation by each level of schooling of the inadequacy of preparation on the preceding level testifies. While it is possible that the initial learning may be inadequate also, a great deal of what is imputed to poor teaching is probably caused by poor organization, or insufficient reinforcement of what has been learned and insufficient attention to a continuous capitalizing and building on ideas and skills already developed. For example, years are spent on accumulating facts to use "later" in thinking. Skills or ideas are acquired at one level and are not used or applied until years later, thus placing a greater burden on memory than is wise. Important elements are forgotten by the time they are needed, and an expensive "maintenance" program is required. If skills taught in arithmetic in the eighth grade are not used again until adult life, they have naturally been partially forgotten.

There is also lack of progression in mental operations. Subjects taught on a lower level of maturity often require a greater capacity to generalize and to abstract than do the subjects taught on upper levels. For example, descriptive civics is often taught in the twelfth grade, while subjects demanding greater abstraction and power to generalize are placed in lower grades.

To develop continuous and cumulative learning requires some clarity about the elements or threads on which to base the sequence. Can they be found in the nature of content itself, as we have tried to find them in composing sequences of subjects in one area, such as in science, mathematics, and social studies? May they be found among the basic ideas and concepts of the kind to which continuous return engagements must be made for mastery, such as the concepts of democracy, interdependence, causality, or social change? Should they be looked for in the powers and mental skills, such as the ability to handle abstractions, the capacity to make increasingly subtle analyses, or to perceive increasingly wide possibilities of application of what is learned? Should these threads be found in skills such as that of reading, interpreting, or performing mathematical computations? It is quite likely that all these elements can be used as threads of continuity if learning is to be both optimally effective and efficient, both because erosion through forgetting is prevented, and because powers are increased by capitalizing on every bit of learning in every new step of learning.

PROVIDING FOR INTEGRATION

The problem of specialization and integration of knowledge has presented a continual dilemma for education, as it has for research. It is recognized that learning is more effective when facts and principles from one field can be related to another, especially when applying this knowledge. Would not the insights gained about American life from reading American literature enrich the perceptions gained from the study of history? Would not the idea of function learned in mathematics reinforce or elucidate the functional relationship expressed in the law of supply and demand? Logical reasoning learned in geometry would be much more realistic when also applied to criticism of a magazine article. This recognized role of integrated knowledge has led to a continued criticism of the fatal disconnectedness of subjects, of the fragmentation and compartmentalization of the curriculum, and of the minds that can bring nothing but a specialist's orientation to bear on problems too complex for such narrow orientation. Unification of subjects has been a theme in education ever since the Herbartians. By far the greatest number of experimental curriculum schemes have revolved around the problem of unifying learning. At the same time we are far from achieving unification, partly because of fear of loss of disciplined learning if the study of specialized subjects is discarded, and partly because as yet no effective basis has been found for unifying school subjects.

Integration as a concept of organization is seen in different ways. Some definitions stress the horizontal relationship of the various areas of curriculum to each other, such as relating what is learned in mathematics to what is learned in science, using the ideas generated in the study of literature to elucidate the perception of a historic period, or relating ideas about historic causality to causality as it functions in the dynamics of community life. This is the definition most frequently used in writing about curricula (*Tyler, 1950, p. 55*). It is also a definition which underlies the experiments in integration of subjects.

But integration is also defined as *something that happens in an individual,* whether or not the curriculum content is organized for that purpose. This conception leads to a concern "with the integrative process in which man engages as he strives to organize in a meaningful fashion knowledge and experiences which at first seem largely unrelated" (*Dressel, 1958, p. 22*). Partly this means achieving an organization of one's own and partly it means seeing relationships between experiences or knowledge that may be separated in one's own experience (*Bloom, 1958, pp. 86-88*).

The problem, then, is that of developing ways of helping individuals in this process of creating a unity of knowledge. This interpretation of integration throws the emphasis from integrating subjects to locating the integrative threads. These threads evidently can be found in certain objectives which are common to several courses, which require relating of facts and broad principles, of theory and life problems, or which combine knowledge, feelings, beliefs, and values (*Pace, 1958, pp. 82-88*). Bloom defines an integrative thread as "any idea, problem, method or device by which two or more separate learning experiences are related" (*1958, p. 91*). He points out, further, that these integrative threads can be used as a basis for organizing curriculum and instruction, or incidentally. Whichever way they are used, certain criteria determine how serviceable they are. If these integrative threads are to help the student organize the subject for inquiry, they must have continuing usefulness in relation to a great variety of problems and questions. By this criterion, the emphasis on the nature of scientific inquiry is a more effective thread than any particular idea or finding in chemistry or physics, and the principles governing the development and use of political controls is a more effective thread than the separate facts about wars and revolutions.

Integrative threads are also effective to the extent that they can be reformulated, altered, and added to as experiences move on. Such an alteration is possible with concepts like freedom and responsibility. They should also provide a basis for comparing and contrasting experiences which would otherwise be unrelated. They should be sufficiently comprehensive to extend over the entire range of subject matter in some area of human experience.

Naturally, none of these threads will be helpful to a student's learning if they hold no meaning for him and are not used by him to integrate *his* learning (*Bloom, 1958, pp. 95-97*).

TYPICAL ATTEMPTS
TO UNIFY THE CURRICULUM

The criteria just discussed have not always been observed in the typical attempts to unify curriculum by establishing relationships between subjects taught simultaneously. One typical method of reducing the unmanageable bulk of specialized subjects to manageable proportions and bringing some unity into atomized specialization is that of combining closely related areas into one broad field, such as replacing grammar, composition, and literature with language arts or combining geography and history into social studies. Correlating two subjects such as English and social studies or mathematics and science is another attempt at integration.

Both these types of curriculum reorganization have tended to be reduced in practice to little more than administrative devices: putting two subjects together into one block of time, on the assumption that the teachers in charge can work out some kind of relationship. Because little thought has been given to the threads around which to integrate, the efforts have not been very successful. Since each subject follows a different scheme of organization, such as a chronological sequence in history and that of literary forms in literature, putting subjects together without developing a new basis for organization which is appropriate for both subjects usually has resulted in one subject becoming a "handmaiden" of the other. When correlated with history, literature is taught in historical sequence, and the language skills are taught according to the requirements of themes drawn from the content of history.

Core programs of the type which center on some broad problems or concepts and draw together from any field whatever knowledge or ideas that seem pertinent represent perhaps the more successful experiments with integration. For example, literature and history have been used as combined sources for understanding American life; mathematical skills are being taught in connection with concepts relevant to consumer education. Often the problems of children and youth have served as focusing centers. The main advantage of this pattern of integration is that it uses, if ever so vaguely, an integrating thread represented by an area of concern as a basis for organizing information and ideas. This organization permits a more natural relationship of ideas, facts, and concepts drawn from different areas of knowledge. If the topics of the core units are chosen adroitly, these relationships can approximate those that prevail in life situations, thus permitting at the same time a maximum of life application. To the extent that there are appropriate integrating threads and the organization of learning experiences is determined by the nature of the problem, integration can be quite successful. Often, however, there has been no such thoughtful determination of the integrative threads or of the organization to follow. The result has been, as one critic points out, the replacement of poorly organized subjects with something that has no organization at all.

As suggested above, combining subjects is not the only way of integrating learning. A good deal can be accomplished toward integrating learning by developing more consistent patterns of thinking in the various subjects, by stressing the broad concepts which the more specialized subjects share in common, and by seeing to it that the students develop a consistent framework for understanding the ways in which these concepts are used in these disciplines.

COMBINING THE LOGICAL AND PSYCHOLOGICAL REQUIREMENTS

From the preceding discussion it should be clear that curriculum organization should preserve and protect both the logic of the subject matter and the psychological sequence of the learning experiences. No matter how the content is put together, it is important that the basic ideas or the patterns of relationships which are important should not be obscured or falsified. Neither can one overlook the task of making the content learnable by organizing the ways of learning according to a psychologically sound sequence, even in curricula in which the learning of content is the sole emphasis.

The merits of the logical unity of the subject matter in contrast to its "psychological organization" has been subject to a long and a heated controversy, which probably arose because the criterion of "logic" and of "psychology" were applied without sufficiently discriminating differentiation either of subject matter and of learning experiences in the first place, and of the levels of content in the second place.

If one views the learning process as a transaction between the learner and whatever content he deals with, one cannot help but decide that the whole controversy is misplaced, because of a dualistic separation of the two ends of the same process. In the first place, there is no such thing as *the* logic of subject matter. Even in the traditional subject organization there are as many "logics" as there are subjects. History, presumably, follows the "logic" of chronology. The various sciences follow either the classifications of phenomena and the laws pertaining to them (as in physics) or a series of morphological divisions, such as those used in teaching about plants. Further, in literature either the authors, the forms of literature, or the historic periods provide the "logic" of organization.

Each subject or discipline can be and has been organized equally logically in several different ways. One can study the historic events either by following the "woof," the events that occur at the same time and that are related to each other, or the "warp," a chain of events through time. Both are equally logical and important. If one is used as a basis of organization, the other has to be introduced as an auxiliary. If the technological developments in our society are studied chronologically, the effects of technology on other aspects of life would need to be studied distributively, and perhaps in a less organized fashion. Similarly, if geography is organized by areas or regions, the study of such aspects as contrasts in climate and resources and the relationship of these factors to products must be distributed. In the end, to achieve full understanding, the two "logics" will have to be brought together.

Perhaps the chief argument has been not over the logic of organization, but conflicting ideas about learning and teaching. The "logical" organization in the traditional sense was adapted to exposition as the chief mode of teaching. This exposition usually followed the sequence of ideas and facts adapted for the purpose of presenting the finished product of thought: it was usually deductive, in that the main ideas were presented first, and then developed. Yet, the way of organizing knowledge for exposition by and for the specialists is not necessarily the type of organization by which knowledge can be most effectively acquired, especially if the generation of active understanding or rational methods of inquiry is to be an important outcome. An inductive approach starting with the study of specific details and evolving from this study the general ideas or principles is much more appropriate for that purpose.

Adopting an organization of content which is most appropriate for effective learning does not mean disregarding the logic of the content, in the sense of arraying facts without any relationship to each other or to the basic principles which they illustrate, or following disconnected topics. The questions pursued about a topic must represent important dimensions that not only make a rational pattern but organize the details in some logically defensible manner.

Actually, what passes for the contrast of logical and psychological organization of content is simply choosing one set of relationships as a basis for organization in place of another set, when both need to be understood. The decision then rests on which set of relationships is harder to learn without the support from organized sequence, namely on a psychological principle.

Perhaps the way to compose an organization for the study of Latin America in the sixth grade can serve as an illustration. Latin America is composed of twenty different countries. Usually certain aspects of life in these countries are considered important to study. The chief elements of content about Latin America can therefore be represented by two sets of items as follows:

Countries to Study	*Things to Study about Each*
Argentina	Economic development
Bolivia	Geographic conditions
Brazil	Patterns of government
Chile	Types of people
Colombia	Social institutions and customs
Mexico	Resources
etc.	Education
	etc.

Either set of items could become the basis for organization. One could use the countries as organizing centers and study in turn the various aspects of life or a sampling of them in each country. Or one could use the aspects of life as centers of organization, and examine the variations in them by countries, by groups of countries, or by a sampling of them. These two ways of organizing this content are shown in figures 1 and 2 below.

FIGURE 1   FIGURE 2

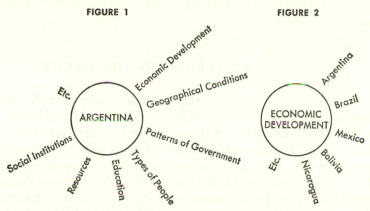

Either way of organizing the content is equally logical. Which pattern one chooses depends on several other considerations. First, which set of relationships is harder to learn when not supported by a pattern of organizations? Second, which relationship represents the more significant learning, and therefore requires support by organization? Is it more important to know every country in detail or to get a clear understanding of certain contrasts in the ways of life, such as the level of industrialization or the use of natural resources, and the environmental conditions which cause these contrasts? Third, which pattern promises the greater depth of understanding about Latin America? Finally, which method of organizing better advances and deepens the understanding of such general concepts as the role of resources in economic life, the relationship of patterns of government to historic background, the relationship of standards of living to educational level and level of technological development, and so on? In other words, the objectives for the study largely determine the choice. If the development of general concepts about Latin America is important, pattern two is indicated. If one is concerned about developing a distinct picture of each separate country, pattern number one is more appropriate.

Considerations of the effectiveness, practicality, and integration of learning enter also. No matter what one thinks about the relative importance of knowing each country as a unit, one must concede that studying each separate country in turn is inefficient: the learning is too atomized, it is difficult to develop important concepts, and the content is bound to be repetitious and burdensome on memory. In contrast, examining contrasting patterns of the ways of life avoids repetition, divides the content into fewer units, and therefore permits the development of basic ideas and the organization of selected details around these ideas.

The chief application of the "psychological" criterion, however, is to organize the learning experiences discussed in the earlier sections of this chapter, so that they are cumulative, to follow the psychological sequences, and to make it possible to internalize whatever is being learned. (See chapter 20, pp. 363-77, for a fuller example of a psychological sequence of learning experiences.)

DETERMINING THE FOCUS

Perhaps the greatest drawback to the usual organization of learning is the lack of focus. Whether the curriculum is organized by subjects, by topics, or by units, one frequent characteristic is its amorphous nature, which makes it difficult to decide which dimensions are important to pursue, which relationships of facts and ideas should be submerged, and which ones should stand out. Descriptive topics such as Japan, the Constitution of the United States, or living plants stake out an area for study, but set no guideposts to what should be emphasized, and what not. Lacking a criterion for focusing, each detail related to the topic seems as important as any other. For all the title "Japan" indicates, anything from the burial customs to the organization of government, traditions governing family life, or economic and technological developments may be equally significant. In one classroom an enormous outline covered the blackboard on three walls. Asked why they were studying Japan, the students said they wondered how Japan, a small country, could develop enough military power to attack the United States. With this focus, and a list of ideas pertinent to it, more than half of what the class had outlined was irrelevant and most of the rest could have been treated in lesser detail. This focus not only reduced the unit to a manageable size but also provided a selective criterion for reading and an orientation for interpreting what was read.

The problem, then, is to decide which element of curriculum can serve as such a focus or a center of organization. Curriculum books describe a variety of centers of organization that have been used: interests, experiences, life problems, content topics. However, none of these centers provides a sufficient criterion for selecting the details to cover, for interpreting what is learned, or for establishing relationships between facts. It seems that only as one formulates the central ideas to pursue can one speak of an *organizing focus* for study. The logic of the basic ideas about the topic, a subject, or a problem usually determines which dimensions of a topic need emphasis, which details are relevant and which not, and in which relationship they are significant. For example, if the study of the economic conditions in Latin America is to develop the idea that the level of industrialization generally determines the level of the standard of living that prevails, then it becomes important to study certain details about comparative progress in industrialization in the various countries and the effect of that progress on standards of living. Thus it is the logic of the ideas that determines which facts are studied and how they are put together. This is true whether the topic deals with economic conditions, the circulation of blood, oxidation, or the Constitution of the United States.

Using core ideas as focusing centers serves several important functions. First, they structure the units or the topics of the subject by giving them a perspective of the dimensions of the content to be treated. If these dimensions are clear, it is possible to make intelligent judgments regarding which details to include, as well as to *sample* content on a rational basis (by its logical dimensions) rather than trying to cover anything and everything, including what is irrelevant and insignificant. The perspective on these dimensions prevents the associative pattern of thinking which characterizes so many teaching units and which leads to a multiplication of more detail in the same dimension. It is, for example, not unusual for the topic of transportation to "cover" one means of transportation after another—boats, trains, airplanes— without ever raising other questions important to understanding transportation, such as what it carries, how it becomes available, and so on.

Focusing the unit on core ideas will assure a fuller scope for the development of the content. For example, in organizing the study of the people of America, the chief content ideas were as follows: People came to America from a variety of places, for a variety of reasons, and at different times. In making adaptations to the American scene, they met many problems, discarded some of the ideas or customs they brought with them (such as language), changed others (such as food habits), and retained still others (such as religion). These people contributed greatly to American life and now play various roles in it.

Converted into questions, these ideas provide a structure of dimensions for a focused study of the various ethnic groups that have come to the United States. These questions are as follows:

1. Who were these people and when did they come to the United States?
2. Where did they come from, and where did they settle?
3. What were the reasons that brought them here (conditions here and in the home country), and what were the historic events that created these conditions?
4. What did they bring with them, and what of this did they change (language, customs, skills, food habits, ideas of government, etc.)?
5. What adjustments did they make, and what were the conditions that forced these adjustments?

6. What contributions did they make to life in the U.S. (e.g., what patterns of government did they set, what skills did they import, etc.)?

7. What position do these people hold now and why?

These questions, structured to follow the core ideas, "structure the subject," make a design for study, and form a basis for comparing information about several ethnic groups and for investigating causes of differences and similarities, such as a comparison of the type of adjustments required of the Pilgrims and of the immigrants in the nineteenth century, or of the nature of contributions made by Germans in contrast to those made by the Spanish. (See chapter 20, p. 361, for a simplified structure of this topic.)

Using ideas as centers of organizing content will also help with the problem of "coverage," the setting of limits to the amount of detail that must be studied. If certain basic ideas are treated as the core of content, it would seem important to cover these ideas, but the detail could be the minimum necessary for understanding, or developing, the core ideas. In other words, basic ideas supply a criterion for sampling content judiciously, as illustrated on page 359. An adequate scope of ideas, combined with a minimum necessary sample of specific content, assures a balanced treatment and balanced understanding without the undue burden of coverage, whereas extensive coverage often results only in learning a little about a lot of things.

"Covering" ideas but sampling detailed content releases time from unproductive mastery of details and makes it available for a more thorough study of that which is offered and for emphasis on such objectives as learning how to handle resources, interpret data, and develop and apply generalization. This type of organization of content also opens up a greater freedom than is otherwise possible to adjust content to the backgrounds and abilities of students without jeopardizing the fundamentals. Since many different samples of detailed content may serve to develop a core idea equally well, these samples can be chosen according to the ability and the maturity of the students, their interests, current experience, or local needs.

For example, the idea that there are contrasting levels of industrial development can be gained by comparing the method of producing any number of different things, from automobiles to pottery. If each is an equally adequate example of the methods of industrial development, there is no reason why the choice of the specific examples should not be dictated by such considerations as what is interesting to students, what materials are available, or what makes the most needed addition to previous studies. In this sampling it should be possible to decide what amount of detail is necessary to enable the particular class, or even different students in the class, to master the idea. (It is interesting to note that in analyzing concept attainment Bruner and his associates point out that in concept attainment one important theoretical point is to determine how many encounters with the relevant specific exemplar of the concept to be attained are necessary to attain the concept with certainty [*1956, p. 54*].)

Finally, ideas as focusing centers can serve as threads for either a vertical continuity or a horizontal integration, as discussed in the preceding pages. They can provide the structure for comparing and contrasting learning experiences which otherwise would bear no similarity to each other. For example, the concept of differences can be extended from simple differences in the roles of members of a family in the first grade to a complex and abstract one among the cultures of the world in the twelfth grade. Or the idea that events have multiple causes can be a thread for relating the study of life in the community to the study of human relations in literature.

The above ideas about organizing the curriculum make it possible to think of the methods of organizing content as one way of translating subject matter into educational process. It is also a way of disposing of the unprofitable arguments which grow out of unnecessary and fruitless contrasting of the content and the learning process. Educational process consists of both, and educational techniques are needed to combine the two into one stream. It seems absurd to have content organization which obstructs rather than facilitates thinking or, at the other extreme, to handle the accommodation to the experience and interest of students so that they cannot be nourished by exciting and significant knowledge.

PROVIDING VARIETY
IN MODES OF LEARNING

We know that not all individuals learn most effectively by the same method, by the same type of activity, or by using the same media. One student may successfully master generalizations about health or about growth of plants from a book, another may get the same thing more effectively from observation or experimentation. While some students are stimulated to thought by books, others need group discussion to accomplish the same purpose. Some people are moved to a clear organization of ideas by having to write about them, while others accomplish the same end by composing a summary chart.

Different individuals also *need* different types of learning activities for their self-development. A shy person *needs* experience in group participation. A person given to overgeneralization *needs* the corrective experience of analyzing precise data and drawing accurate inferences from them. Finally, students *need* to acquire a tool chest of methods of learning which will help them to continue their education beyond school. The wider the range of learning techniques which an individual masters, the better equipped he is for continuing to learn after formal schooling has ceased. Chapter 8 discussed the differences in mental systems and the need for corresponding variations in approaches to learning tasks. For all students to use identical methods of learning, no matter what their abilities and backgrounds, is a highly questionable procedure from the standpoint of efficiency in stimulating and using intelligence.

It is well to remember, further, that interests attach not only to the content of learning but also to the ways of learning. There are preferences and predilections regarding the use of verbal and quantitative materials, the handling of precision data and generalities, and the ways of expressing what has been learned. Additional suggestions for variation in learning activities come from analysis of the effect of groups on individuals. The research on group processes seems to suggest that the patterns of group relations in which an individual finds himself have a great deal to do with his achievement. In heterogeneous groups, some individuals can learn from each other what they cannot gain from books. Others respond to motivational support from peers when they cannot respond to teachers' invitations to learning or to such motivational devices as grades (see chapter 11).

All this seems to suggest that a balanced array in the modes of learning and in the conditions under which learning takes place is required if there is to be equality of opportunity to learn.

What, then, are the kinds of balance that need to be considered? Learning activities need to represent a balance of various *means* of learning: reading, analyzing, doing research, observing, writing, experimenting, manipulating, and constructing. Too often there is a tendency to depend more or less exclusively on one mode of learning and thus to limit the scope of learning. Often either the traditional means, such as reading books, or some new dramatic teaching techniques, such as group discussion, tend to dominate. Such a dependence on one way of learning deprives some students of an adequate access to learning. A physics class in which reading the physics text is the sole means of learning the principles of mechanics offers a less than optimum opportunity to learn physics to those who perceive these principles more readily by operating and manipulating machines, studying blueprints, or experimenting.

A balance is needed also between experiences or activities that represent "intake" and those that represent synthesis, reflection, and expression. Too long a stretch of absorbing new information is bound to result in the erosion of the previous learning by the new. An appropriate rhythm of absorbing and consolidating, internalizing, and reorganizing seems to hold a much greater possibility. It incorporates the idea of intake and of feedback and utilizes what is known about dynamics of creative learning.

A similar rhythm is important for incorporating "feeling insights" into cognitive mastery, especially in areas in which concepts and ideas tend to be colored by feelings and attitudes. This means that the intake of facts and ideas needs to be alternated with learning activities and materials which open up and extend feelings and sensitivities. To use a previous example, in studying the hardships of pioneers it might be important to precede the factual study with films or stories which create new insights into what the "hardships" of pioneers mean.

Providing a rationally balanced variety of learning experiences not only increases the capacity to learn and motivation for learning. It is also one way of dealing with the problem of individual differences and heterogeneity. It is quite possible that making a greater range of means of learning available will also extend the capacity to master the content and to develop the powers of thought and feeling in individuals now deprived of this mastery.

A balanced variety in learning techniques also makes possible a flexibility in the approaches which are so necessary in a heterogeneous group. Usually the problem of heterogeneity is dealt with in two contrasting ways, neither of which is adequate. One is to accommodate to the variation in pace of learning by reducing the material covered: to give fewer and lighter assignments and easier tasks to the less able. In this reducing the fundamentals are likely to be reduced also. The other is to vary the expectations—to cover the same ground but to expect a lower level of understanding or of mastery from the less able. This plan has the danger of leaving some students progressively less able to cope with the curriculum.

Perhaps a more effective way of providing for heterogeneity in ability is to design methods of learning according to differences in needs, levels of comprehension, or ability. This way presents a problem of formulating open-ended tasks which serve a similar purpose for all but which enable students to use alternate procedures and a different level of materials. For example, in one sixth-grade classroom individuals in a group responsible for the study of and reporting on economic conditions of Latin American countries worked on several levels. Some studied fairly abstract materials on the economic status of a given country, from which they derived an analysis of the factors responsible for this status, such as the trade balance. Slow readers in the same group had the task of using the ideas of the bright members in the group, figuring out what the United States exported to Canada and Mexico and imported from these countries, and then making a graphic map of the movement of goods to and from these countries. While the less able readers could not get the idea about the trade balance from books, they could perceive it once it was explained by those who could read well. They could then do an effective job in making the idea concrete. Thus each type of learner got something from the other type of learner, each also contributed to the other, and each mastered the basic idea. Had the assignment been for all to read a chapter in the text, only those with a certain degree of reading ability would have learned. The students of high ability would have worked below their capacity, and the low-ability students would have learned little or nothing.

Evaluation of the Outcomes of Curricula

The use of the term evaluation to cover a great variety of meanings and to describe many processes has caused considerable confusion. In the first place, one can evaluate anything about the schools' curriculum: its objectives, its scope, the quality of personnel in charge of it, the capacities of students, the relative importance of various subjects, the degree to which objectives are implemented, the equipment and materials, and so on.

Secondly, the term evaluation may be used to refer to different processes. It may be simply a rendering of a value judgment based on sheer opinion. This sort of evaluation is illustrated by opinion surveys, such as asking laymen to decide which subjects a public school is neglecting, whether the schools are doing a good job, or what the schools should teach. An illustration of such evaluation is an opinion survey in Denver Public Schools described by Oberholtzer and Madden (*1957, pp. 274-75*). Evaluation by judgment may also represent a fairly systematic description of the various aspects of a program, such as the objectives, the program of studies, the method of curriculum development, and the material used. (See, for example, California Association of Secondary School Administrators, 1955; National School Boards Association, 1960.)

The term evaluation is also used to describe a process which includes a careful gathering of evidence on the attainment of objectives, a forming of judgments on the basis of that evidence, and a weighing of that evidence in the light of the objectives. The judgments may be formed against some criterion or norm, such as the national average, an expectancy formula, or the stated objectives.

Finally, evaluation can be carried on at a variety of levels and by different categories of people. The central administration may be concerned about the general effectiveness of the total curriculum or the extent to which the central goals are being attained—whether the time allowed for arithmetic, for example, is sufficient, and whether the arithmetic curriculum teaches arithmetic as well as it should. Those more immediately concerned with the progress of pupils will want to evaluate curriculum in terms of its efficacy in helping students progress toward the educational objectives. Teachers use evaluation to assess progress toward the specific objectives of a given course or a unit. Students, too, may make judgments about what they have learned and the extent to which they accomplish what is expected of them. And parents evaluate the outcomes of curriculum in terms of what they think their children are or are not achieving.

A NARROW AND A BROAD DEFINITION OF EVALUATION

Since the curriculum is essentially a plan for helping students to learn, ultimately all evaluation goes back to the criterion of effectiveness of learning. But even here many meanings prevail. Some equate evaluation with grading, as is illustrated in the following excerpt from a forthcoming book: "A hotly debated issue in United States education concerns evaluation or 'marking.' Procedures for evaluating the progress of elementary children range all the way from interviews with parents, in which many phases of the child's development are discussed, to the traditional report card on which everything from conduct to reading is graded by letter." The author then proceeds to distinguish three methods for this evaluation: (a) how the student is doing in relation to his ability, (b) how the child stands in his classroom, and (c) how his performance compares with national norms (*McCandless, 1961, pp. 158-60*).

Defining evaluation as marking, reducing everything that is known about the progress of students to one single mark, is the narrowest concept of evaluation. But even within this narrow definition there is confusion, the chief item of dissension being whether grades should represent progress or comparative status. Shaplin points out that novices in teaching have difficulty in assigning grades because "they fail to distinguish adequately between measurement of progress and measurement of degree to which students meet certain standards, relative or absolute." The measurement of progress "requires a pretest–post-test model of evaluation" which allows individual assessment of a student over a given time. The latter requires a scale on which to measure the degree to which students meet certain standards. The former is geared to the status of the individual; the latter is often geared to an absolute notion, an upper limit of learning, or a distribution from which a relative standing can be determined. The uses of the two types of measurement are often very different: the former is a way of rewarding students and deciding upon the next steps for learning; the latter is a means of rating students relative to one another or against an absolute standard for purposes of making recommendations and judgments (*Shaplin, 1961, p. 48*).

At the other extreme, evaluation is described as an intricate and complex process which begins with the formulation of objectives, which involves decisions about means of securing evidence on the achievement of these objectives, processes of interpretation to get at the meaning of this evidence, and judgments about the strengths and weaknesses of the students, and which ends in decisions about the needed changes and improvements in curriculum and teaching.

This definition of evaluation places it in the stream of activities that expedite the educational process; these activities can be reduced to four essential steps: identification of educational objectives, determination of the experiences students must have to attain these objectives, knowing the pupils well enough to design appropriate experiences, and evaluating the degree to which pupils attain these objectives (*Tyler, 1951, p. 48*).

Another point of confusion is that of identifying evaluation with measurement. This error is committed even by many writers of texts on evaluation, which make a bow to evaluation in the first few chapters and then proceed to discuss the varieties of measurement, from intelligence tests to records of height and weight. Measurement is only one part of evaluation. It refers to the process of obtaining a quantified representation of some characteristic, such as certain kinds of achievement or scholastic aptitude. The process of measurement is fundamentally descriptive, inasmuch as it indicates in some quantity the degree to which a trait is possessed. Educational measurement usually tends to concentrate on narrow, specific, and well-defined characteristics. While evaluation depends on measurement, its concern is with a broader profile of characteristics and attainments.

A further confusion surrounds the term "testing." Some limit the use of this term to objective tests. Others use it to describe any controlled way of recording students' behavior so that it can be described with some degree of quantitative precision. In this sense a performance on the typewriter can be a "test" of ability to type, or a reading record an index of reading interests.

The definition of evaluation used in this chapter is based on the following assumptions:

Education is a process which seeks to change the behavior of students. These changes are the objectives of education. While these changes include mastery of content, "knowing that," and while this mastery is achieved in connection with the study of some subject, they also include the reactions of students to this content, such as the ways of thinking, or the skills in "knowing how" (*Ryle, 1960, ch. 2*).

Evaluation is the process of determining what these changes are and of appraising them against the values represented in objectives to find out how far the objectives of education are being achieved. Because human behavior is multidimensional, these objectives are multidimensional.

Methods of evaluation include any way of securing valid evidence on attainment of objectives: paper-and-pencil tests, records of various sorts, observations of behavior and of performance as well as of products of various sorts.*

Defined in this way, evaluation is a broader undertaking than that of giving tests and grading students. It involves: (1) clarification of objectives to the point of describing which behaviors represent achievement in a particular area; (2) the development and use of a variety of ways for getting evidence on changes in students; (3) appropriate ways of summarizing and interpreting that evidence; and (4) the use of information gained on the progress of students or the lack of it to improve curriculum, teaching, and guidance.

The nature of an evaluation program depends, first, on what objectives are pursued and how each objective is defined and, secondly, on the purposes for which the results of evaluation are used. The more comprehensive and complex the objectives, the more complex the task of evaluation. A school concerned only with mastery of information will confine its efforts to assessment of mastery of information. A school that mainly wants to see if its performance is up to par according to the national norms in basic skills, such as reading, will be concerned mainly with comparing the average achievement scores to the national norms. A school whose objectives include development of various intellectual skills and attitudes needs not only a broader range of evidence but also ways of appraising that evidence other than comparing its test scores to national norms. Evaluation conceived in this manner is an integral part of curriculum development, beginning with the concern about objectives and ending with assessment of their attainment.

THE FUNCTION OF EVALUATION

No one doubts that evaluation serves an important role in the curriculum, teaching, and learning. The way of evaluating what is learned dictates the way in which learning takes place. The scope of evaluation determines what types or levels of learning are emphasized, no matter what the curriculum indicates. Furthermore, no matter what the teacher stresses, the student will selectively address himself to that learning on which he is examined (*Brown, 1961, p. 17*). If a thoughtful reorganization of knowledge is stressed in the classroom, but the testing and grading are confined to the mastery of facts, the latter learning is reinforced. If creativity and thinking are stressed in evaluating student progress, factual cramming is less likely to be the order of the day.

In the light of the recognized importance of its role, it is surprising to note several deficiencies in present evaluation programs. First, there is a great dis-

* This rationale was formulated by the evaluation staff of the Eight Year Study, and has been substantially followed ever since in discussions of evaluation. (E. Smith and and Tyler, 1942, pp. 7-15.)

crepancy between the scope of the objectives of curriculum and the scope of evaluation. This is a common criticism of evaluation programs. Dressel points out that the objectives are not furnishing sufficient guidance to curriculum, instruction, or evaluation (*1960, p. 45*). Others point to the fact that measurements or instruments of securing evidence are available only on the simpler variety of objectives and mental processes, such as skills and knowledge of facts, and that the more important and complex the objectives, the less likely it is that there are systematic and dependable devices for measuring their achievement. There are even accusations that the forms adopted in the aptitude and achievement tests are prejudicial to original and creative thinking (*Hoffman, 1961*).

Evaluation serves or can serve many rather central functions in the school and in the development of curriculum. Perhaps the most central and often the least used function of evaluation is to validate the hypotheses upon which the curriculum is based. In a sense all curriculum plans and approaches to instruction are only hypotheses whose efficacy needs to be tested. This is true of established curriculum practices as well as of innovations. A myriad of half-tested assumptions are at the heart of many curriculum practices. These include beliefs, such as that geometry as now taught develops deductive thinking, that it is necessary to organize history chronologically in order to acquire a sense of time, and that the mental powers develop automatically as a by-product of systematic absorption of factual information. Many questions, such as what type of content organization is most effective in developing integrated learning and what the advantages are of using the theory of sets for teaching mathematics, cannot be answered short of fairly thorough evaluation of what happens in or through learning.

Many curriculum innovations are introduced on little more than hunches. Certain materials and content are selected and organized in certain ways in the hope that this will bring certain results. Today, for example, the teaching of science is being reorganized in the hope of producing a greater quantity and quality of scientific talent. Ability grouping is introduced to accelerate learning and to encourage a more vigorous use of the higher mental processes. Different ideas prevail about the ways to strengthen the teaching of critical thinking. Some favor teaching it in separate units, or even in a separate course in logic; others maintain that thinking needs to be taught in connection with every subject and in every curricular activity. And many maintain that nothing short of a complete problem-solving approach will do the job.

These matters cannot be settled on the basis of philosophical arguments alone. One needs to determine what changes these innovations actually produce and what effects they have on the total pattern of educational outcomes. Innovations introduced for a certain limited purpose too often produce other undesirable results. For example, a school which was greatly concerned with the development of scientific objectivity and critical thinking had stressed the use of reliable and dependable materials of unquestionable objectivity.

After administering a battery of tests on thinking, the staff discovered to its amazement that the students were highly gullible. They had a tendency to accept as true almost anything in print because they had had no opportunity to compare poor and good sources. An exclusive diet of excellent and dependable ideas cultivated an unquestioning attitude. Evaluation thus serves not only to check the hypothesis on which curriculum is based but also to uncover the broader effects of a program which may serve its central purpose well, but may, at the same time, produce undesirable by-products.

Careful evaluation has not been made of the innovations of the past, nor is it being made today. This failure to assess the effects of innovations against their total outcomes has been perhaps the cause of the fact that in American education curriculum revision proceeds by replacing one scheme with another and one "approach" with another, not necessarily because objective evidence has demonstrated the merits of one or the failures of the other, but merely because the new scheme or approach somehow has gained attention, is in "fashion" for the time being, or is championed by forceful leaders.

Another important function of the evaluation program is to provide information on the weakness and strengths of the program by assessing the weaknesses and strengths in the achievement of students. A curriculum or a pattern of instruction may systematically underemphasize certain types of outcomes. Studies have shown, for example, that the current mathematics program is weak in developing problem-solving abilities (*Buswell and Hersh, 1956*). Information is usually needed on what prerequisites of particular areas of instructions students do or do not master and what level of concepts and skills they can handle in order to determine how much can be covered, as well as which aspects of learning need special attention. The very continuity of curriculum and learning depends on such information. Many a problem of articulation between the various levels of schooling exists because of insufficient knowledge about what precisely the students have mastered on the previous level.

Information is needed also on variations in achievement of individual students. A student who masters information adequately may be weak in thinking critically about ideas. One who is able to handle generalizations may be inconsistent when it comes to dealing with issues that involve values and controversies. Ability to locate needed information is not necessarily accompanied by strength in getting the most meaning from it, and so on. Since each of these difficulties calls for help of a different sort, curriculum and teaching are effective to the extent that they are addressed to these specific problems of learning and provide help that is appropriate to these difficulties.

Earlier it was pointed out that the nature of evaluation dictates the functioning curriculum because the teachers tend to stress what they can evaluate and students to stress what they know they will be examined on. A broad evaluation therefore is likely to create also a broader motivation for learning.

Finally, evaluation can provide the kind of evidence which can be used for more adequate marking, grading, and reporting. To the extent that grading and marking are based on a wider range of evidence and reflect precise knowledge of achievement rather than a vague appraisal of the relative standing in the group, they are likely to be more objective and reflect less the subjective feeling of teachers. Adequate evaluation data are also likely to encourage a more diagnostic reporting than is possible by reducing all achievement to a single mark or a score. (For further discussion of the functions of evaluation see *Tyler, 1951, pp. 47-67.*)

CRITERIA FOR A
PROGRAM OF EVALUATION

To perform the necessary functions, the evaluation program should have certain characteristics.

Consistency with Objectives

First, evaluation must be consistent with the objectives of the curriculum. It needs to have an integral relationship to the chief intentions of the program and be animated by the same philosophy that underlies the curriculum and teaching. Evaluation should be based on the same perceptions of what is significant achievement as is the curriculum. It should not stress achievement that is not considered the most basic and fail to stress that which is considered important. If the teaching program emphasizes individual development, then evaluation should not submerge individual differences in performance for the sake of group comparisons. It is especially dangerous for an evaluation program to be inconsistent with the chief values in the curriculum and teaching, such as stressing conformity when the curriculum emphasizes creativity, or accurate memory of pedestrian facts when teaching is striving to develop good judgment. This type of inconsistency often occurs when standardized tests are used without a full understanding of their inner workings, or when one depends on instruments which do not reflect the nature of the program. For example, while an integrated social studies is stressed in many schools, the available standardized tests deal almost exclusively with specialized areas, such as history, economics, and geography.

Pace describes such an inconsistency as the difference between the explicit and implicit objectives. He reports that the stated objectives for a college course in Responsible Citizenship were quite clear and the teaching procedures and learning activities of students were related to these objectives. But the examinations conflicted with both the objectives and the teaching emphasis. A major portion of the final examination invariably consisted of true-false and multiple-choice information questions, requiring recall of historical information, definitions of terms, and other factual material. Despite the fact that the classroom activities rewarded critical thinking and the analysis of complex ideas and their relationships, the students in preparing for final examinations concentrated on recall of information, because this was necessary for the objectives implicit in the examination (*Pace, 1958, ch. 4*).

To develop such a consistency, it is of course necessary that the decisions about any specific part of the evaluation program, such as choosing a particular test or employing a particular method of grading, be made in the light of a perspective on the whole program, and that each instrument of evaluation serve a clear function.

Comprehensiveness

Evaluation programs should also be as comprehensive in scope as are the objectives of the school. Perhaps the most flagrant deficiency of the current evaluation programs is their lack of comprehensiveness. While the objectives of education have expanded markedly since the turn of the century, the development of instruments for measuring the attainment of these objectives has not kept pace. This is particularly true of the standardized paper-and-pencil tests. By and large they are still dominantly concerned with mastery of specific information and academic skills, such as reading, arithmetic, and map locations. The supply of evaluation devices tends to be inadequate for most objectives concerned with the higher mental processes, such as thinking, social attitudes, aesthetic development, and moral values (*Ahman and Glock, 1958, pp. 49-51*). This discrepancy is generally recognized, but there is little evidence that it is being corrected. Brown suggests that it is largely due to the inadequacy of the conceptions in educational theory, pointing out that ultimately this "inadequacy comes out in (not out of) the inadequacy of our evaluation of learning. Furthermore, the quality of learning is affected both by what we think to be important as outcomes and by the evaluational incentives that, inevitably, the learners also learn" (*1961, p. 18*). Educators are more likely to suggest that classroom teachers develop devices and tests in areas which are left untouched by standardized tests. Entire books have been devoted to analyzing the needs for and offering models for the needed type of tests and other devices. Among these is the Yearbook of the National Society for the Study of Education devoted to the problem of measuring understanding (*1946*). The need is even recognized by the test-making groups. In discussing the need for measuring achievement in a changing curriculum, Dobbin predicts that future development of tests will put more stress on the general outcomes of the curriculum than on specific information in specific courses (*1958, pp. 103-04*).

The lack of adequate instruments is naturally a great handicap to comprehensive evaluation. The concentration of the formal instruments on information achievement, leaving the development of evaluation devices for the more complex objectives entirely to individual classroom teachers, is hazardous, to say the least. Most teachers know too little about the techniques of developing evaluation instruments. They need the help of experts who could aid them to state clearly what they are trying to teach and devise means to discover what has been learned. The university examiners in some major institutions have played this role with great success. Furthermore, securing evidence on the more complex outcomes is precisely the area in which technical competence is even more important than in information testing. Finally, these are the learning outcomes which matter most in a forward-looking curriculum development. Unless a greater amount of technical resources is harnessed in this area of evaluation, many important curriculum decisions will be made on insufficient evidence, and curriculum innovations are bound to address themselves to less than an adequate range of outcomes. The use of television for mass instruction is one such example. So far these programs are justified largely on the ground that the achievement of information is no worse than in ordinary classrooms. But there is no evidence that reflective thinking, social attitudes, or creativity are not retarded. Would the gain in efficiency and economy be worth that price?

Sufficient Diagnostic Value

Another important criterion of evaluation is that its results be sufficiently diagnostic to distinguish various levels of performance or mastery attained and describe the strengths and weaknesses in the processes as well as in the product of performance.

Broudy illustrates the various levels of mastery by analyzing the meaning of the statement that John has mastered the concept of oxidation under seven different levels of "mastery":

1. In response to the cue, "What is oxidation," John replies with a textbook definition.

2. John makes his response when not warned in advance.

3. John responds with a paraphrase of the textbook definition.

4. John replies with ordinary examples of oxidation: burning, rusting, spontaneous combustion.

5. John replies with an unusual example of oxidation, one not in the text nor discussed in class, such as cellular respiration.

6. When presented with an instance of oxidation, John properly categorizes it.

7. John categorizes properly an unusual or unfamiliar instance of oxidation.

Levels one to three are scarcely illustrations of the mastery of a concept, because all could be a product of rote memory. The last four responses can be regarded as instances of understanding, because they require that John select from his experience the appropriate one. When the student shows understanding of material not studied in class and recognizes the application of the concept or the principle of oxidation in a case which does not permit an easy identification, this demonstrates that he can apply what he knows about oxidation to other kindred chemical principles (*Broudy, 1961, pp. 79-81*).

Besides the necessity of distinguishing the levels of performance, it is also important to distinguish the various processes which lead to acceptable products as well as to errors. Such an analysis is illustrated in several tests produced by the evaluation staff of the Eight Year Study, one of which, dealing with application of the principles of science, is represented below.

PROBLEM:

What happens to the cooking time of an egg when it is cooked in an open kettle of boiling water on a high mountain?

CONCLUSIONS:

    a. It is the same as the cooking time at sea level.

    b. It is less than the cooking time at sea level.

    c. It is greater than the cooking time at sea level.

REASONS: (*Check the reasons which explain the conclusion you choose.*)

1. Everyone who has studied science knows that the boiling point of water decreases as the altitude increases. (*Ridicule*)

2. An egg will not cook as quickly on the mountaintop as at the sea level. (*Assuming a conclusion*)

3. A reduction of the boiling point accompanies the reduction of the pressure above the water. (*Right principle*)

4. Decreased air pressure on mountaintops decreases the efficiency of fire for cooking purposes. (*False principle*)

5. Just as foods cook more slowly at slow temperatures, so will an egg more slowly on a mountaintop where the temperature is low. (*Analogy*)

6. A reduction of air pressure accompanies an increase in altitude. (*Right principle*)

7. A solid in solution raises the boiling point of water. (*Irrelevant*)

8. Experienced mountain climbers report that it takes more time to cook foods at high altitudes than at low altitudes. (*Reference to authority*)

9. The ordinary way of cooking on mountaintops is to use a pressure cooker. (*Irrelevant practicality*)

10. The boiling point of water rises as the pressure above the water becomes less. (*False principle*)

11. Water boils more quickly on mountaintops in order to offset the difference in cooking time. (*Teleology*) [*Progressive Education Association, 1938*]

The scoring of such an exercise can describe the ability to reach valid conclusions by applying known principles to new situations. It is possible also to describe the ability to distinguish the use of right and wrong principles, of acceptable and unacceptable analogies, of relevant and irrelevant facts, controls, or authority. Students may use right principles to support wrong conclusions, in which case they may have memorized the principles but do not know how to use them. (For further exercises of this sort, see *E. R. Smith and Tyler, 1942, chs. 2 and 3.*)

Such distinctions of the level of performance are extremely important in evaluation, both for gearing curriculum to a greater depth and for determining the level of understanding on which the student performs. Such a type of evaluation is especially important in gauging the amount and the distance of transfer which learning has produced, a problem which, as was pointed out earlier (chapter 9), is at the heart of effective curriculum and teaching.

This means that evaluation devices are needed which yield multiple rather than single descriptions. The evidence on which evaluation is based needs to be as descriptive as is practical of both weaknesses and strengths. Because comparisons are easier to make and scoring simpler and less expensive, the tendency is to reduce the analysis of the results and to compound the various facets into some simple score even when instruments sample a variety of behaviors. When grading and reporting is limited to a score or a grade which describes only a student's standing in comparison to a norm or to the scores of other students in the class, specific variations in performance which are useful to know for guidance and correction are obscured. A profile of behavior, which includes both the acceptable and unacceptable reactions and which is expressed in multiple scores or verbal descriptions, is much more useful for this purpose.

To secure this multidimensional information it is necessary that the instruments themselves be shaped and selected according to an analysis of the processes involved in achieving certain objectives. If, besides acquaintance with good sources, ability to use sources of information also involves discrimination between good and bad sources and judging the relevance of sources to certain purposes, then an instrument for evaluating the skill to handle sources must reveal these particular behaviors.

It is, of course, important that the evaluation program yield an objective and a valid picture of the achievement. This means that the data on which evaluation is based should be reasonably free of subjective bias or other deficiencies which mar their objectivity and accuracy. Subjectivity in the sense of personal bias has always been a problem. This difficulty in part explains the popularity of the objective tests over other types of instruments which involve personal judgment. One must not forget, however, that objective tests, too, involve judgment. The important thing is not to eliminate judgment, but to prevent irrelevant factors from influencing the judgment (*Rothney,*

1960, p. 13). Further, no matter how much the variety of objective tests is extended, teachers and curriculum makers will always face the problem of improving the objectivity of the qualitative and informal method of appraisal. The specifications of the behaviors and the development of concrete criteria by which to appraise these behaviors should considerably reduce the subjectivity of judgment in handling nontest evidence.

Validity

Validity, or the capacity of the evidence to describe what it was designed to describe, is even more important in improving curriculum and teaching than dependability and objectivity. If a choice must be made, weakness in the latter may be preferable to weakness in validity. Too often the criterion of validity is overlooked because other considerations, such as economy of time or ease of administering or summarizing, loom large. The validity of evaluation instruments tends to improve in the measure in which they are consistent with objectives, are based on a sufficiently careful analysis of the behaviors to be evaluated, and are addressed to what the students have had an opportunity to learn. For example, the validity of an instrument is jeopardized if the content it uses or the skills it requires are inappropriate to what the group has mastered, such as measuring familiarity with literature by asking students about pieces of literature which are not included in the program or asking students to apply principles with which they are not familiar. The situations used for the purpose of testing or getting evidence should give students a genuine opportunity to reveal the behavior called for and should exclude extraneous factors and unnecessary stumbling blocks. For example, a test or an exercise on interpreting data which involves unusual reading difficulties will measure the ability to read rather than the ability to interpret data. By the same token, the results of a test on interpreting data when used with students with no training in the necessary skills will turn into a reading test and show high correlation with reading ability, because the reading skill is the only differentiating ability.

Difficulties with validity increase when the objectives are diffuse, vague, and abstract and bear no relationship to recognizable behaviors. When objectives are expressed in such terms as "understanding the social order," one is hard put to know whether this means knowing which institutions this social order contains, how these institutions function, how they are related to each other, what forces operate in the society, and so on. Thus it comes about that demonstration of one kind of ability is taken for proof of an ability of a different sort, such as using the knowledge of historic facts as proof of historical judgment. The problem is aggravated by the fact that usually the most important objectives tend to be also the least well understood and the least clearly stated. Thus, least valid evidence usually supports the effects of the curriculum and teaching in areas that represent the most significant growth. There is no doubt that the area of thinking and of values belongs in this category.

Sophistication about the diverse kinds of behavior responses possible in a variety of subject contexts would prevent confusion about what kinds of behavior students are to develop and how to help them develop it, as well as how to test for it. Without this sophistication, teaching as well as evaluation will tend toward the least ambiguous and the least complex level, factual mastery; and other types of mastery, such as understanding the principles and applying them, will be omitted altogether.

It must be pointed out that these characteristics of an evaluation program are not guaranteed by the availability of good instruments. Instruments of high general validity may be invalid in a given school if its program differs from that of the population on which the test was validated.

Unity of Evaluative Judgment

Perhaps the greatest threat to validity lies in the way in which evaluative judgments about individuals or groups are derived from available evidence. By their very nature, evaluation processes are analytic. To "measure" behavior clearly and precisely, and to note the differences among individuals accurately, it is necessary to break down the larger complexes of behavior into smaller units and to measure each of these separately. To permit its evaluation at all, an objective needs to be broken into its component units for an analytical differentiation of the specific behaviors it entails, and specific devices used to secure evidence on these specific behaviors.

However, since human behavior has organic unity, in which each component part is related to another, these component parts need to be put together again at several points. The major objectives, taken together, must represent a reasonably related and unified pattern of the development of the individual. Each single instrument needs to measure closely related aspects of behavior, and a battery of instruments should compose a unified pattern in which instruments are in a sense "mates" to each other, one either checking, extending, or supplementing information secured from the other.

The evidence secured from different instruments and on different aspects of the evaluation program needs then to be brought together into a pattern, so that a meaningful portrait of the individual and of the group is available; otherwise the judgments may be faulty no matter how objective or dependable each piece of evidence is. Thus, test scores on mastery of information need to be related to data on ability, emotional and social backgrounds, and the nature of school experience before a valid judgment is possible. This means, of course, that the principles of interrelatedness of behaviors and of the conditions which affect them must be kept in mind in planning the evaluation program. The battery of devices for securing evidence must also be composed so that they check and countercheck the behaviors which are either closely related or which influence each other. If appreciation of literature is related to the pattern of interests in literature, the two should be appraised in relation to each other. If knowledge of principles affects the ability to apply them, evidence on the one cannot be properly understood without evidence on the other. It is these relationships, rather than the fact that information is needed about knowledge in several areas, that should be the basis for composing a test battery.

A special weakness of current evaluation programs is the fact that data about the progress of students toward educational objectives are evaluated or interpreted without sufficient knowledge of the nature of students as learners and of the nature of the instructional program. This weakness is especially pronounced in the status studies, in which test data on one group are compared with the averages in other groups or with national norms. Too often in such comparisons neither the unique pattern of objectives nor the unique backgrounds of students are taken into account. For example, the level of achievement of information in a group with cultural handicaps is compared with the level of groups without such handicap, or a group which needs special stress on thinking is compared with another in which nothing but information is taught.

Nor do such status studies yield the kind of evidence which permits identification of the causes of the weaknesses observed. For example, a "low" standard average test score in reading might mean any of several things: the time devoted to reading is too short; the teaching method is inappropriate for a given group; the content of reading is inappropriate; there are many individuals with a low cultural background, hence with a weak start in reading; there are many students with emotional problems which prevent them from concentrating on reading. To improve reading one would need to know the specific causes of the poor showing. Otherwise, inappropriate remedial measures may be taken.

Continuity

Finally, it should be pointed out that evaluation should be a continuous process and an integral part of curriculum development and of instruction. Evidence of progress, of strengths and weaknesses, is needed throughout the year. Diagnosis of difficulties and of readiness for the next steps is more useful before than after certain curriculum units or courses. Progress must be observed and recorded when it occurs. This means that the final tests and examinations are only a small part of the total program of evaluation. It should begin with a diagnosis at the start of any new program or unit of a program, continue through its development, and end in whatever checks are appropriate at the conclusion.

A COMPREHENSIVE
EVALUATION PROGRAM

To develop an evaluation program which fits the requirements of a particular type of curriculum and of the criteria discusse in the preceding pages requires answering several questions:

1. What are the objectives which underlie the curriculum program? What behaviors are entailed in achieving (or in demonstrating the achievement of) these objectives? E.g., what do students of a given age who have good working habits do? In relation to what kind of content or experience is this behavior directed? What kinds of information could one expect fourth graders to be able to locate and in what kinds of sources? (*Formulation and clarification of objectives*)

2. Under what conditions or in which situations will students have an opportunity to demonstrate the behavior? E.g., in which situations, either natural or controlled, can students show their ability to formulate and to define problems? (*Selection and construction of the appropriate devices for getting evidence*)

3. By what criteria would one appraise students' achievement of an objective? Thus, in the case of free reading interests, one might want to appraise student growth in terms of (a) quantity—how much he reads, (b) variety—the range of content which he reads, and (c) maturity level—the quality of content represented among his choices. (*Application of evaluative criteria*)

4. What factors determine the attainment of educational objectives and how can one determine these factors? (*Information on the background of students and the nature of instruction in the light of which to interpret the evidence*)

5. What implications do the findings have for curriculum teaching or guidance of students? (*Translation of evaluation findings into improvement of the curriculum and instruction*)

In essence, these questions represent the elements composing the evaluation program. A comprehensive evaluation program, then, is more than a battery of instruments and data on achievement. The order of these questions also suggests the sequence of steps by which to develop an evaluation program. (For a fuller discussion of such steps see *Bradfield and Moredock, 1957, pp. 196-205.*)

Determination of the objectives of the curriculum is the basic and the first step, for it is in terms of these objectives that the evaluation program is to be developed. The problem of formulating an adequate set of objectives was discussed in chapter 13. It is sufficient to say here that one of the most difficult obstacles to adequate curriculum as well as adequate evaluation is the tendency to establish objectives which are vague, diffuse, and general and therefore bear little relationship to what the actual outcomes of curriculum and instruction are and have no resemblance to recognizable student behavior. The evaluation program is only as good as is the platform of objectives which it serves. A narrow and a sterile conception of objectives will lead to a limited program of evalution. Vagueness of objects will naturally be reflected in invalid evidence or evidence which is incapable of being translated into a guide for improvement of curriculum.

When an evaluation program is much narrower than are the objectives of the curriculum, the tail tends to wag the dog, because usually those aspects of curriculum which are evaluated also tend to be emphasized, especially if this evaluation involves comparison with wider norms. Sometimes the curriculum even assumes a direction which is inconsistent with the basic aims because objectives on which tangible evidence is available are apt to be seen out of perspective in comparison to other equally significant objectives which are not supported by similarly convincing evidence.

When the definitions of objectives fail to supply a criterion for distinguishing one level of performance from another, it is difficult to decide what type of evidence is needed or what criteria to apply in appraising it. It would be difficult, for example, to evaluate the outcomes of reading when it is not clear whether one should evaluate the mastery of mechanics or the degree of comprehension, interests, or sensitivity to values. (See chapter 13 for a description of the method of stating and clarifying objectives, and p. 319 for an illustration of the levels of understanding.)

Decisions about the techniques to use in gathering data for evaluation can be made satisfactorily only after the objectives are clarified. Not all behaviors connected with one general objective can be evaluated equally well by the same technique. For example, in assessing problem-solving ability, evidence of the ability to recognize problems and to define them might be best secured through classroom observation. A paper-and-pencil test might be most economical and effective for getting evidence on the ability to apply information and ideas in the solution of problems. Different types of techniques may have unique appropriateness for their purposes. For example, paper and pencil tests may be adequate for measuring the amount of information a student has, or the methods of thinking he employs, but a behavior record may be more appropriate for assessing his ability to cooperate.

A variety of means and methods are available to teachers and curriculum makers, ranging from objective tests to informal procedures, such as checklists, observation, records, and teacher-made exercises. Whatever their nature, they should live up to the criteria described in the preceding section. These devices must be consistent with the purposes for which they are used and give students an opportunity to reveal the behavior that is being evaluated. They must be as free as possible of arbitrary subjective elements—that is, they must be objective. And whatever the instruments or devices, they should represent a sufficient sample of behavior to give valid information. A record of one performance may be sufficient for certain types of behavior, such as the ability to type, while others may require a time sampling or a sampling according to variability of situations. For example, a diary that includes only one weekend would not be an adequate sample of how students spend their time out of school. Nor is one anecdotal record describing an emotional outburst in the history class sufficient to describe the "adjustment" of the student. A more careful sample of behavior in various situations and over a time span is needed. In other words, the criteria employed in the development and use of objective tests need to be applied also to the choice and structuring of all sorts of other evaluation instruments.*

The data secured from the evaluation instruments are usually only descriptions of behavior. To have meaning, they need to be appraised by some criteria. These criteria can be comparative norms, such as are used in standardized tests or distributions in a given class. In an anatomy class a teacher may want the students to know the names of all the bones in the human body. To be able to recite all is the highest value. The performance on a test is then measured by the number of items the student can remember. Or his performance is measured against other performances, and the level is determined by distribution, in which case 80 per cent of correct answers may represent the top performance.

But it is possible also to conceive of another kind of standard based on qualitative difference in the level of performance. The illustration on p. 319 gave an example of an analysis of levels of performance in mastering a concept. Bradfeld and Moredock suggest a generalized scheme for analyzing levels of performance as far as understanding is concerned as follows:

> Level I: Imitating, duplicating, repeating.
> Level II: Recognizing, identifying, remembering, recalling, classifying.
> Level III: Comparing, relating, discriminating, reformulating, illustrating.
> Level IV: Explaining, justifying, predicting, estimating, interpreting, making critical judgments, drawing inferences.
> Level V: Creating, discovering, reorganizing, formulating new hypotheses, new questions and problems [1957, p. 204].

Bloom and others also imply levels of performance in their taxonomy of objectives. The various aspects of cognitive domain are lined up in an ascending order of complexity: knowledge, comprehension, application, analysis, synthesis, and evaluation. The same is true of specific categories within an area, such as analysis of elements, of relationships, and of organizing principles (1954, pp. 47-182).

---

* For a discussion of validity, reliability, and objectivity of evaluation instruments see a section on the characteristics of evaluation instruments in any standard text, such as Ahman and Glock (1958).

Information from various sources and on various dimensions of achievement needs to be interpreted as a unified pattern. If the types of information which bear on each other are interpreted in isolation, the guidance of curriculum development and instruction is bound to be less adequate and imaginative than it could be. Obviously high achievement in science accompanied by high interest is different from similar achievement accompanied by low interest.

Data on achievement need to be interpreted, in addition, in a context of what is known about the background of the students and about the conditions of learning. One cannot judge the ability to interpret data of students who have had little opportunity to learn to do so in the same manner as that of students with a long history of training in processes of interpretation. Nor does failure to appreciate literature mean the same thing for students with ample books around them as it does for students who see books only in school. The batteries of achievement tests need to be supplemented by batteries of other devices, such as were described in the chapters on diagnosis, and the data from all subjected to a patterned interpretation.

It is at this point also that the philosophy and values of education need to be considered. Without applying the standards of significance, the empirical tools cease to be useful servants and become masters. The tools determine what we shall do: it is easy to succumb to stressing the outcomes which are the easiest to understand and to measure. The task of interpretation is to assign significance to behavior according to the philosophy of the school. Furthermore, evaluation data have little meaning until one applies the psychological principles of learning and growth. For example, the meaning of a certain level of competence in the use of language in a fourth grade can be determined only in the light of what we know about the development of language. Interpretation, therefore, is not a mechanical process. It involves judgment in the light of philosophical and psychological principles, and the principles of social values.

The foregoing suggests a definition of a comprehensive program of evaluation which involves a broad scope of data including data on achievement, on factors affecting learning, and on teaching-learning operations. A comprehensive evaluation program should also include the steps and the procedures by which to translate the objectives into evaluation data and these data into hypotheses about the needed changes in curriculum and instruction. Such a definition of a comprehensive evaluation program might be expressed as in the model presented below.*

* This model is the work of the Commission on Evaluation (Hilda Taba, Chairman), Association for Supervision and Curriculum Development created for the purpose of experimenting with a workable pattern of comprehensive evaluation.

Model for a Comprehensive Evaluation Program

1. Deciding what kinds of evaluation data are needed:
   A. *Objectives and Evidence Pertaining to Them*
      Thinking abilities
      Attitudes
      Skills
      Creativity
      Concepts
      Levels of perception
      Etc.
   B. *Factors Affecting Learning*
      Class culture backgrounds
      Peer culture influences
      Social learning
      Initial level of subject matter mastery
      Motivational patterns
      Special abilities
      Feelings
      Etc.
   C. *Teaching-learning Operations*
      Nature of assignments
      Procedures for maintaining control
      Patterns of teacher response to pupil behavior
   D. *Teaching Methods*
      Telling
      Discovery
      Laboratory work
      Recitation
      Discussion
      Use of problems
      Demonstration
      Etc.
2. Selecting or constructing the needed instruments
   and procedures. These may include:
   Objectively scored tests
   Essay tests and other written exercises
   Sentence completion tests
   Tape recorder techniques
   Attitude scales
   Social class scales
   Interest inventories
   Behavior check lists
   Sociograms and participation flow charts
   Questionnaires
   Interviews
   Performance tests
   Rating scales for performance and products
   Anecdotal records
   Etc.
3. Analyzing and interpreting data to develop hypotheses regarding needed
   changes. The broad patterns of relationships to be studied are as follows:

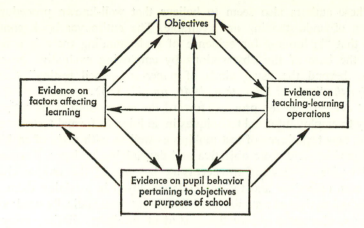

4. Converting hypotheses into action.

TECHNIQUES
FOR SECURING EVIDENCE

Generally the techniques for securing evidence for evaluation are classified into three types: standardized tests, nonstandardized or teacher-made paper and pencil tests, and informal devices.

Usually the evaluation of achievement tends to be confined to the use of paper-and-pencil tests for a variety of reasons: they are supposed to be objective and dependable; they are economical of time and easy to administer; they provide national norms against which to compare a given class; they can be scored in standard scores, which makes possible comparison of levels of achievement between various subject matter areas; and, because several forms of the same test are available, a systematic measurement of progress is possible (*Ahman and Glock, 1958, pp. 351-52*).

However, there are limitations to the use of paper-and-pencil tests, informal or standardized, and as the range of accepted objectives has expanded, these limitations have becomes more severe. There is an insufficient variety of them, and, because many newer objectives are complex and as yet "intangible," the behaviors represented by them cannot be compressed into an objective short-answer test, a form devised largely for measuring the mastery of factual knowledge.

Perhaps the most serious shortcoming is that the paper-and-pencil tests match their virtues of objectivity and economy with inability to measure the more complex and especially the creative forms of mental activity, such as the divergent thinking, described in chapter 8. This deficiency is rather widely recognized. Finley and Scates, for example, point out that the role of the paper-and-pencil tests seems so dominant because it is easier to write about them. These authors also seem to believe that well-known procedures for evaluation of understanding are available. The entire yearbook committee suggests that "in looking for evidence of understanding there is a need to broaden the base of the observations by employing evaluative procedures which go beyond the usual kinds of paper-and-pencil testing" (*National Society for the Study of Education, 1946, pp. 45, 326*).

To get evidence on the progress toward the more complex objectives it is necessary to employ informal techniques in addition to formal tests, to experiment with new techniques of test making as well as with ways of making the informal devices yield more objective and dependable evidence. Furthermore, informal evaluation devices are necessary because of the unique character of classroom objectives and the methods employed in attaining them. Many such informal devices are available, although not systematically used: records of all sorts, classroom observations, student products, diaries, essays, and simple classroom exercises. Many of these are useful at once as instructional devices and as devices for appraising student performance. For example, when students describe what they saw on a trip or react to a story they have read, these reactions not only afford an exercise in writing and contribute to the content of learning, but also can be analyzed for the levels of awareness or social attitudes displayed, as well as for their mastery of forms of writing.

Traditionally there has been a cleavage between these two methods of securing evidence and a distinction between the objectives which each serves. Usually the objective tests concentrate on measurement of information and of academic skills, whereas informal and often carelessly formulated methods are reserved for judging the ability to think, attitudes, and work habits. Somewhat different criteria are applied also to the development and use of these two types of instruments. Objectivity and reliability, for example, are all-important in objective tests, while the range and the significance of the behavior that a test measures sometimes receive only a secondary consideration. On the other hand, far too little attention has been paid to achieving greater objectivity and dependability in teacher ratings, anecdotal records, or assessment of essay tests.

This cleavage is gradually being eliminated. The range of objective tests is being extended, even though not nearly rapidly enough to serve the expanding curricular emphasis. The realm of "intangibles" is gradually being reduced by a more careful analysis of the objectives and by the development of appropriate instruments to measure these behaviors. Many standardized achievement tests are stressing related rather than isolated information and call for an understanding of factors, relationships, and consequences instead of rote memory—for example, the "Sequential Tests of Educational Progress" (*Cooperative Tests, Educational Testing Service, Princeton, New Jersey*). Many test batteries include sections on work-study skills—for example, "The Iowa Every Pupil Tests," or the "SRA Achievement Series" (*Science Research Associates, 57 West Grand Avenue, Chicago*). Models of paper and pencil tests which attempt to evaluate objectives other than mastery of information, such as thinking, are being extended also.* Some of these, such as the ones produced by the evaluation staff of the Eight Year Study, are highly diagnostic and describe mental processes in great detail.†

Much can be and has been done to eliminate subjectivity in informal methods of evidence getting. Some progress has been made in clarifying objectives to the point where teachers know what particular behavior they are looking for, can record without judgment, and can apply stable criteria in appraising it. However, much yet remains to be done to bring the tool chest of evaluation into line with the kind of attainments that are considered central to education, and until this happens, these types of attainment will not play the role in curriculum and in teaching that they should.

There is also a need for a more diagnostic description of the results from all evaluation instruments, such as introducing scoring which describes the processes as well as products and gives the type of errors instead of a single score.

Many of the techniques described in the chapter on diagnosis can also be used for evaluation, provided that the devices are either used continuously or repeated at time intervals. Among these are the discussions of cut-off stories, analysis of records of discussion, records of reading and writing, observation of performance, special assignments and exercises, and sociometric tests. As was pointed out, in all areas in which growth is expected diagnosis is but the first step in evaluation, establishing bench marks for the initial status of students.

INTERPRETATION OF EVALUATION DATA

It is well to remember that the raw test scores or any other descriptions as such carry no message about learning or achievement that is translatable into suggestions about curriculum or instruction. The fact that John marks as liking twenty of the thirty items that have to do with arts does not in itself say whether this is a meager or a high interest, unless one assumes that the thirty items represent absolute perfection. Standards of evaluation of human behavior are established with reference to some kinds of group averages or norms. These norms may represent the average of a given group or the average of the scores made by many students presumably so sampled that their performance reflects the normal range. The national norms may constitute a yardstick against which a given school or a school

* For a list of tests available on thinking skills, see Burton, Kimball, and Wing, 1960, pp. 439-44. For reviews, see Buros, 1959.
† For descriptions of the type they represent see E. R. Smith and Tyler, 1942, and National Society for the Study of Education, 1946, chs. 5 and 6.

district may want to measure itself in order to check against a possible imbalance in its achievement. However, using national norms as standards has its
dangers. They can be misleading in that they may make a successful school
rest on its laurels, or a school or a class with many handicaps to be held to a
standard of performance which is too high for them. Since these norms are
also unidimensional, they can lead to false evaluation. This would be true
when the achievement of specific information in a school which has stressed
the ability to apply general ideas is measured by standards established in
schools in which the achievement of information is the sole and the central
aim.

Probably a better procedure is to make comparisons with groups in other
schools that have a similar program, a similar emphasis, and roughly, a
similar student body. Inasmuch as there are wide differences in the objectives,
emphasis, and population of schools on which norms are compounded, it
would be a poor policy to measure achievement in a school by standards which
are inappropriate for it. Thus a pattern of interests in a slum school in New
York City could not be considered an appropriate standard for a suburban
school in California. And the average of the two would be inappropriate for
both. Nor would one compare the standards in critical thinking from a school
where there is no emphasis on it with the averages in a school whose students
have had a long and careful training in such thinking. The danger is in investing the national norms with a magical significance.

Interpretation also needs to be analytical enough to suggest hypotheses
regarding the causes of strengths and weaknesses in individuals and groups.
This implies the need for an examination of the patterns of behavior shown in
data. An interesting problem in connection with this task is caused by the fact
that evaluation is both an analytic and a synthesizing process. Interpretation
must chiefly serve the synthesizing function. To do this it is necessary to
search for patterns of behavior and to apply the principle of balanced development in assigning meaning to the data. If the idea of an integral and
organic relationship of all aspects of learning, of all outcomes, and of the
preconditions of learning is to be taken seriously by those concerned with
evaluation, it is of utmost importance to so treat the evaluation data that each
bit of it is interpreted in the light of all other available evidence. The student's
successes or failures in his academic work should be seen in the light of his
attitudes, work habits, interests, and social adjustment. What is known about
his interests is helpful in interpreting data about his thinking processes and his
reactions to the school program, and so on. And whatever is known about the
attainment of individuals or groups needs to be appraised in the light of their
known abilities, cultural backgrounds, and the type of learning experiences to
which they are exposed. Therefore, in recent evaluation practices, some provision is usually made for pooling, interpreting, and summarizing all information on students, so that it is possible to see each phase of a student's development in the light of all other relevant facts about him. (For an example of a

case study which brings together a battery of information on one student, see *H. Taba, 1942, pp. 408-29.*)

One important task in interpreting evaluation data is to search for critical imbalance in the profile of attainment, either individual or group. While growth toward the various objectives would naturally be somewhat uneven, it is also clear that no one segment of growth could be developed very far without a simultaneous growth in other important segments. Thus, there may be a danger in cultivating logical thinking to an extreme without sufficient growth in emotional maturity. The possibility of holding rational social attitudes is limited without corresponding growth in social concerns.

To develop such patterned interpretation, questions such as the following need to be answered: What does it mean for teaching and for curriculum if the students achieve high scores on information in American History but make many errors in interpreting historic data? What does a high score in geometry mean when it is accompanied by a low attainment on logical thinking? Does a high frequency of crude errors in interpretation of data mean the same thing for a group that has had training and a class that has had none? Does inability to get accurate meaning from quantitative data combined with evidence of high competency in logical discrimination and skill in quantative techniques mean only a failure to apply oneself and lack of sufficient persistence?

If the plan for evaluation has a unified design, synthesizing the data from various sources in interpretation is a fairly simple task. The interpreter faces not a series of unrelated data into which to bring order, but data that already fit into a pattern. Certain generalized relationships are inherent in the very nature of the data. His task is to detect the variation in individual and group patterns within this generalized framework.

To locate the causes for strengths and weaknesses it is important not only to develop profiles of performance from all available evidence; it is also necessary to see the current status of students in the light of their history and their development up to this point. For example, high uncertainty on beliefs on social issues means one thing when it appears during the process of changing from one set of beliefs to another. It means something else when it seems to be a permanent characteristic, and it has a different meaning for persons with a general tendency toward cautiousness and precision than for people who do not share in this characteristic.

Interpretation also should suggest possible hypotheses regarding remedial action. This step requires a thoughtful judgment. One needs to consider the objectives of the school in relation to each other in order to determine which weaknesses most need to be remedied. A careful analysis of the curriculum and of methods of teaching in the light of the psychological learning principles is needed to determine what might be the best way of remedying any given weakness. The usual automatic answer to most weaknesses is to stress more the performance in which weakness is shown, although the cause of the difficulty may actually lie elsewhere. Therefore, the cause of the difficulty must be clear in order to decide what particular remedial action is likely to be effective. It is important to remember that evaluation data in and of themselves do not solve the problems of what to do in teaching or in guidance. This would be like expecting the thermometer to tell what to do about the weather. Evaluation only calls attention to the problems to be solved; it does not provide the solutions.

Interpretation of evaluation data should also provide the basis for examining the hypotheses that underlie the schools' program. Changes in curriculum are often introduced in the hope of improving student performance. These are assumptions, such as that strengthening the training in phonics will improve reading. These expected changes may not occur, or they may be accompanied by others which are undesirable enough to make the price too high. In one school a core program was introduced for the purpose of clarifying and strengthening social attitudes. These results did occur. But at the same time, students had serious difficulties with techniques of precise thinking. They exhibited little caution in interpreting data. In applying principles and facts they failed to discriminate between the valid and invalid data, and so on. Apparently, in emphasizing social values, the teachers had relied too much on generalizations and stressed the study of precise data too little. In another school the evaluation program revealed that students specializing in mathematics and science showed a more limited appreciation of and interest in literature than all other groups. Upon examining the program it turned out that these students had a special course which concentrated on biographies of scientists and mathematicians, on the assumption that those interested in mathematics and science would not be interested in general literature. Since it was not the intention of the staff to narrow the interests of these students in literature, a broader program of reading was indicated.

Such instances demonstrate that special care is needed to discover whether the intended results in one respect tend to produce other undesirable consequences, or whether the assumptions on which the curriculum emphasis rests may not be faulty. This sort of information is revealed only if all data on students are examined in the light of the total pattern, rather than item by item.

Methods of Interpretation

The particular methods pursued in interpreting evaluation data depend on and are determined by two factors. One is the purpose for which the data are used, and the other is the nature of the data. For example, data are examined differently if they are used to guide individual learning than if they are used to check the effectiveness of the curriculum and teaching in helping students to achieve the designed objectives. Either shortcut summaries or diagnostic descriptions are needed depending on whether evaluation data are used for grading or for diagnosis of weaknesses and strengths of individuals. The analysis of descriptive data, such as diaries, records, and writing, involves different processes from the interpretation of test scores.

All rational processes of interpretation, however, involve one common factor, that of postulating several alternative hypotheses to explain certain patterns of data and checking each against other data to see which one is most likely to be correct. The decisions about which problems are the most serious and which require remedial action can be made safely only after the most likely causes of the patterns shown are discovered.

In interpreting data on individuals, the first task is to understand thoroughly the meaning of all individual data, especially with reference to what the general categories under which the data are summarized represent in fact. The meaning of these data can be established by reference to the pattern of the group or any other available norm. This, however, establishes only a tentative meaning. The next step is to relate each specific score or judgment it suggests, such as a low score on logical thinking, or less than average interest in reading, to the total pattern for the individual. The fewer than average number of books read may in a given instance be accompanied by a thoroughly analytic attitude towards the content of reading, which gives this reading "score" a different meaning than it would have if superficiality were the accompanying behavior. Occasionally this way of examining data reveals the necessity for a radical shift in the original meaning of the score, or judgment. Often in examining a battery of data one needs also to consider the natural relationships between the various sets of data. For example, since interests and social attitudes are known to influence social thinking, data on social thinking need to be scrutinized in the light of data on attitudes and interests. One might discover objective thinking in all areas except those in which bias and feeling prevail, or only in areas of special personal concerns. This would indicate that remedial action needs to be directed to attitudes rather than to thinking.

In interpreting group data it is necessary to determine whether a class or the school is attaining the major objectives. The attention in this case must be focused on averages, distributions of scores, and frequencies. These need to be established first for all categories of data. For example, one needs to determine the average accuracy in interpreting data or in judging the pertinence of information, and what this average means in the light of a particular curriculum pattern. One needs also to discover what type of errors occur most frequently, such as whether students on the whole go beyond the data, or fail to use all that is given in data. From such analysis it is possible to compound the combinations, patterns, or syndromes. For example, one may find a frequency of a combination of high interest in music and art, or of negative responses to anything that has to do with English, writing, and reading. This sort of information does not result from merely looking at means and distributions of individual scores. One must compare also the profiles of high and low performance.

Progress of groups needs to be examined also by comparing the performance of several grade levels with each other. Is there, for example, growth in accuracy in interpreting data from one grade to the next one? Do the errors noted on one level tend to disappear on the next?

The above suggests, then, that interpretation of evaluation data is not merely a technical task to be performed by test experts who are unaware of the curriculum pattern, the methods of teaching, and the schools' objectives. Translating evaluation data into interpretations useful for guiding the curriculum and teaching should be done by persons who are involved in curriculum making and teaching, and the technical processes need to be subordinated to and shaped by the chief purposes of evaluation.

TRANSLATION OF EVALUATION DATA INTO THE CURRICULUM

The translating of evaluation data into curriculum improvement or improvement of teaching is too often done rather mechanically. Low performance is taken as an automatic sign for a need to spend more time on the area of low performance without sufficient analysis of the possible causes for low performance or its meaning in the total pattern of achievement. Nor is the analysis of the performance of the group used as frequently as it might be to project the future curriculum emphasis—that is, for experimentation with developmental curriculum in the light of the analysis of the current performance.

An illustration of how evaluation might serve as a basis for projecting curriculum follows: One senior high school was experimenting with a core program involving social studies and language arts. This program was started in the sophomore year and extended gradually to the junior and senior years. A three-year cumulative plan for developing skills in reflective reading, thinking, and expression was part of the design. In the sophomore year, the skills in locating sources and getting information from them were stressed. During the junior year, personal interpretation of ideas, imaginative insight, and comparison were emphasized. The focus of emphasis during the third year was the development of logical analysis, argumentation, criticism of ideas, and a coherent and consecutive formulation of ideas. These objectives were selected for each grade level partly because they seemed to constitute a good sequence in maturation. They were stressed both in language arts and in social studies, with which the development in language arts was integrated. A plan for diagnosing and evaluation accompanied this curriculum plan, in order to check the hypotheses on which the curriculum was based and to correct the curriculum plan according to whatever weaknesses were discovered.

First, to discover any difficulties in mechanics of reading and written expression, standard tests of reading comprehension and speed, and of the mechanics of English expression were given at the beginning of the tenth grade for diagnosis and repeated again at the end of the twelfth grade. The results were reassuring. These students began with a normal range of skills, and made normal progress in the three years. Evidently the general mechanics of reading were mastered fairly early in the course of high school. Beyond this there remained the tasks of acquiring special reading techniques for special content and of adapting familiar techniques and approaches to reading to new materials and purposes. It seemed possible to accomplish this without formal stress on reading and by using, instead, occasional small group or individual guidance sessions at points where difficulties were noted.

Students kept a continuous record of their free reading, and this record was periodically summarized to diagnose the quantity and quality of free reading. These summaries often suggested corrections in the program emphasis. For example, at the end of the sophomore year it appeared that the reading of brief articles and stories had been overemphasized. Few students had read a whole book through. Fiction was read too infrequently and the reading lists showed practically no poetry or drama. Examination of the writing folders showed that this lack of experience with continuity was reflected in writing also; it seemed fragmentary. To correct this condition the reading of longer books and writing of longer themes was introduced during the junior year. Records also revealed little application of what was learned in free reading to what was discussed or studied in class. Since integration of experience was one of the objectives of the school, the program was revised to stimulate a greater linkage between what was studied in classroom and the personal problems of students, and a wider application of ideas gained from free reading.

During the junior year, the reading of poetry and other imaginative materials was stressed to help students learn to interpret this material both accurately and imaginatively. To diagnose this ability a special test was constructed, consisting of selections from poetry and of prose passages using symbolic and metaphoric language. The analysis of students' interpretation of this material was used as a guide in further reading, and in discussion of that reading.

These efforts showed their effects. As time progressed, the free reading of students became more varied as well as more mature. It seemed to be used for a greater variety of purposes: to enrich study, for pleasure, for self-understanding.

The evaluation and diagnosis of expression followed the same pattern. Book reviews, reports, research papers, and themes were examined continually for maturity of ideas, organization of thought, discrimination in the use of sources, and originality and sensitivity of interpretation. To get a comparative appraisal, the writing for the whole class was filed and examined together at the end of the year.

The analysis of this material at the end of the first year yielded several important insights. For example, students had made remarkable progress in facility in the use of varied resources. But much remained to be learned in making discriminating judgments of the validity and significance of what they used. Every bit of information seemed as important to the students as every other bit. Personal interpretations were rare, and few students could construct an adequate logical argument. These difficulties expressed themselves in poor paragraphing, in inadequately conceived central ideas, and in stereotyped expression.

This diagnosis suggested that more thoughtful assignments were in order. A three-year plan was worked out to simulate the expected qualities for writing and reading. Teachers became vigilant about stimulating more sensitive and imaginative expression. At the end of three years, considerable improvement took place. Students grew in their ability to address themselves to central ideas in reading as well as in writing. Papers and themes became more personal and used fewer dry quotations. Reference lists at the end of research papers became more individual, varied, and mature. The flow of language improved.

In addition to using the evaluation data to improve instruction, they were also applied to check certain hypotheses regarding the curriculum. For example, the curriculum plan was based on the hypothesis that combining the use of reference material and of fiction would produce a greater discrimination in the use of sources, a greater skill in using them, a greater respect for accuracy, and more personalized ideas. The records of writing showed considerable progress in the ability to combine imaginative insight with factual accuracy. Classroom discussions revealed also a marked growth in the ability of students to apply the ideas from books in thinking about their own lives and concerns (*Taba, 1944, pp. 199-204*).

EVALUATION AS A COOPERATIVE ENTERPRISE

Cooperation is needed at all steps of evaluation, though perhaps in a different measure and in a different way at each. A balanced set of objectives is more likely to be developed through the participation of the whole staff. This cooperation is necessary in order to see the specialized lines of growth in a proper perspective, but it is especially important in formulating and clarifying those objectives which can be fully achieved only through a combined emphasis in various subject areas and in various realms of activity in the school. Cooperative formulation is needed especially in the more complex areas of achievement, which are sometimes oversimplified when in charge of only one group of specialists.

Reading is one example. The evaluation of attainments in reading is too often limited to an analysis of difficulties in the mechanics of reading and in vocabulary, while the skills needed to read special materials in special subjects are often overlooked. Reading difficulties may occur because the ideas inherent in the subject matter are not understood. Passages in the history text may elicit meager response because they represent verbal summaries of processes or institutions with which students are unfamiliar. Difficulties with such passages may be caused not so much by vocabulary used, but by hazy notions of such things as what the United Nations means or a lack of any real idea about what a labor union is or does. One can substitute simpler words for the abstract, and shorter sentences for the long, but that would not help comprehension if the difficulty stems from lack of meanings of the things for which the words stand.

Reading is also only one end of a two-way system of communicating ideas: progress in comprehending ideas depends somewhat on the progress in formulating and expressing ideas. For example, as students clarify their ideas about democracy, or about what the Chinese live by and value, their insight into what they read on these topics sharpens also; their ideas about what to look for in a book becomes keener and their ability to discover the organizing principles under the mass of detail increases. Thus neither the diagnosis nor the evaluation of reading is complete apart from the assessment of expressing and using ideas.

Growth in the ability to interpret data, to relate diverse ideas, to apply generalization, and to judge the dependability of information is similarly related to reading. To read effectively about the systems of government in Latin America involves applying some ideas about what a good government is. To understand and to judge the ideas of a certain author about international cooperation requires the application of some facts and ideas about international trade and about social and economic traditions in various countries. Meaningful reactions to mature literature develop only in a measure that students gain in understanding of life, human behavior, values, and motivations.

Thinking is another such objective. It involves processes which take a long time to cultivate, and which need to be practiced in different contexts. Interpreting a play is a different matter from interpreting quantitative data in tables and graphs. The processes for getting meaning from these data differ, as do the criteria for accuracy and validity of judgments made from them. At least in departmentalized programs, these materials and processes are in charge of different teachers. Unless the persons representing these different areas of instruction are involved in identifying and analyzing this objective and in setting up the criteria of evaluation, both curriculum and evaluation are likely to be narrow and one-sided. The clarification of the behaviors involved in such general objectives, therefore, requires a pooling of ideas and insights, because it is difficult to see what is involved in a complex objective except as the possibilities are examined from a variety of angles.

Cooperation is involved also in projecting or selecting the techniques and tools by which to secure evidence. To expand the tool chest of techniques to cover the objectives that are incapable of being evaluated by objective tests or for which appropriate tests are not available, one needs to tap the resources and inventiveness of the entire faculty. Most teachers have a quantity of information on hand which is not available for evaluation because their meaning is not evident. For example, the writing of students can be appraised for evidence other than whether they use grammatically correct language. It does express thinking, often values, and reveals something of the student's interests and social orientation. Teachers have some observations of how students attack problems, or of their work habits. They have some information on students' ability to criticize ideas or to relate facts and ideas. Pooling this evidence adds immeasurably to the total body of evidence on which to evaluate the growth or the achievement of students.

Cooperation is needed also in making plans for the school-wide evaluation program. Such a plan requires distinguishing between the kind of evidence which is needed throughout the school, and the kind that each teacher may secure only for his own class. If the two kinds of evidence are not coordinated, inefficiency is bound to result: there may be overlapping in information secured; important areas of objectives may be overlooked altogether; objectives that are easiest to appraise may be overemphasized; and so on.

Cooperative planning of the evaluation program would help in several ways. Devices now used for limited purposes may be expanded to serve wider purposes without much additional time and effort. For example, if the English teacher keeps a reading record for her purposes, it would not take much more to include in such a record reading that is relevant to other classes. School-wide planning is also needed to make sure that evaluation samples all relevant situations in which achievement or performance can be expressed. Thus, for example, not all outcomes of free reading are necessarily expressed in English classes. They may show themselves in discussion in social sciences. Leadership ability, cultivated in one spot of the program, may express itself in others. Ability to follow a logical argument, developed in mathematics class, may show itself in the critical analysis of an essay or a play. Only by cooperative planning is it possible to determine which areas of school experience to sample for evidence on certain types of achievement. This is especially true of the behaviors which are subject to wide transfer. Unless the evaluation program itself is set to spot such transfer, the important evidence of growth will be missing.

Cooperation is needed also to assure the validity and reliability of the evidence, especially of the informal evidence. Teacher ratings, analysis of writing, anecdotal records, and other such material gain in objectivity and validity when there is agreement on what specific behavior to look for and on the criteria by which to interpret what is observed. For example, if teachers agree that frequent reading of books in free time, frequent expression of personal reaction to them, and an eagerness to talk about books is an index of appreciation of reading, recording of these reactions wherever they occur can take place with a minimum of disagreement regarding the meaning of these behaviors.

Cooperation is especially needed in interpretation of information and the translation of that information into guides for teaching and curriculum making. Even the responsibility for the various steps in interpretation may need to be shared. A person who has been responsible for the securing of the data may be responsible for the first round of interpretation, because only that person could devise appropriate categories for summarizing the information and could distill appropriate meaning from the data. Thus, if an English teacher has collected records of discussion, this teacher is in the best position to summarize the data from these discussions. A record for behavior on the playground may best be first interpreted by a person in charge of the playground.

These data and their interpretations may then be subjected to the scrutiny of others, both for the purpose of enlarging their meaning and for checking unwarranted assumptions in interpretations which are likely to creep in from a person with special concern in an area of behavior. It is easy for a teacher concerned only with academic success to read academic ability into the reasons for sociometric choices, and overlook other reasons to which perhaps a guidance counselor would be more sensitive.

But the chief importance of a collective interpretation is to see to it that each piece of evidence is interpreted in the light of the total picture. Otherwise each teacher knows about only a segment of pupils' behavior, and no one sees the entire picture. This approach to interpretation would avoid the difficulties inherent in establishing corrective measures for one type of weakness without assessing the meaning of this weakness in relation to a strength elsewhere, or without considering the developmental sequence sufficiently in evaluating current performance.

Perhaps the greatest need for cooperative pooling of ideas is at the last and the final step of evaluation, in projecting the needed changes in curriculum and instruction to take care of weaknesses discovered through evaluation. Unless tangible steps are taken to translate into practice whatever is learned about pupil progress, the effort of evaluation will have been largely in vain. Occasional staff meetings dealing with the implications of evaluation data for curriculum and instruction are helpful, as are occasional meetings on problems of individuals. The more significant results are obtained when evaluation data are used systematically at every point of decision making. Whether evaluation data are merely studied generally or used as a basis for making decisions makes an enormous difference in attitudes and insights of a school staff. The evidence acquires a sharper meaning and its interpretations a sharper focus when it is used in connection with making decisions such as what to do about certain pupils' lack of academic success, what kind of program to compose for those who seem unable to master the college preparatory mathematics, whether or not to segregate the gifted students, whether a certain course on a certain grade level is advisable. Decisions involved in routine activities, such as making out schedules or reporting to parents, may create similar occasions for a purposeful use and interpretation of evidence. When these decisions are made cooperatively and in the light of available evidence, not only do teachers acquire a keener insight into the growth of pupils, but there is also a continual clarification of the school's policy and a continual reinforcement of a habit of making decisions of the school's policy scientifically and rationally.

This emphasis on cooperative procedures in planning and interpreting evaluation data is not meant to suggest that the role of experts in evaluation and testing is unnecessary. Their help is needed throughout. Most teachers need help in judging the merits of a given test. Expert help is needed also in devising informal instruments and records of maximum possible validity and objectivity, in developing adequate methods for summarizing data to make them more amenable to interpretation. Teacher-made tests need to be examined to prevent technical flaws, and so on. However, these technical services need to be performed so as not to usurp the functions which teachers should perform in evaluation, if evaluation and curriculum development are to be properly related to each other and if evaluation is to improve instruction. Teachers should determine which objectives the curriculum is to serve and what action should be taken regarding whatever is revealed in evaluation. To do these two things properly, involvement is needed in other steps also.

It would seem, then, that a cooperative approach to evaluation would insure a wider concept of what is involved in promoting growth toward a range of objectives. Cooperative approach also promises an extension of techniques available for securing evidence and a wiser use of the results in curriculum development and planning of instruction (*Taba, Sept. 1942*).

Development
of a Teaching-Learning
CHAPTER TWENTY # Unit

The preceding chapters have discussed the various tasks which go into developing a curriculum and the various processes connected with these tasks: the ways of formulating educational objectives, the methods of diagnosing needs to make it possible to translate objectives into appropriate patterns of learning, the selecting and organizing of both the content of curriculum and the learning experiences, and the ways of evaluating the outcomes of learning. The elements produced by this analytic approach need to be put together into a functioning pattern. This "putting together" occurs at two points: planning units and developing a curriculum design. In essence, developing a unit is translating these elements of curriculum into a dynamic whole, while a design represents an over-all pattern. This chapter will deal with the patterning of a unit, and Chapter 22 will deal with an over-all curriculum design.

THE ROLE OF A MODEL FOR
A TEACHING-LEARNING UNIT

Usually the development of teaching-learning plans is left to classroom teachers. The curriculum guides are at best only skeletal affairs, which merely describe some of the foundations, outline the content, and possibly suggest types of learning activities. Yet the job of organizing the multiple facets into a coherent unit, of applying the multiple criteria to the making of even fairly minute decisions is too complex not to deserve careful theoretical consideration.

Action models and experimentation in classrooms play the same role in the development of a theory of curriculum making as do the laboratory experiments in developing theories in science. In the present writer's views, those responsible for generating theories of curriculum development omit a very important step, that of creating models for the ways of translating theoretical ideas into functioning curriculum and testing these ideas in classroom experiments. Furthermore, this task of creating functioning curriculum units involves practically the whole gamut of theoretical considerations and principles, and cannot be safely left to practitioners without such theoretical training.

This chapter assumes that organizing an instructional plan—whether that plan be for a subject or for a unit is immaterial—is in the category of a major task of curriculum planning. First, in the development of such a plan lie the fundamental seeds of curriculum innovation. Perhaps the deficiencies pointed out by the critics—the lack of coherent curriculum theory, the meager application of what is known about learning, the obsolescent content—go back to the fact that the thinking by curriculum experts has stopped with the delineation of the grand schemes and frameworks, and has not been engaged in putting their knowledge to work creating models for teaching-learning plans. The gap between theory and practice may exist because the preoccupation with reshaping organizational schemes has not been paralleled by experimentation with curriculum as it functions in the teaching-learning situation. The national experimental studies, such as the Eight Year Study and the Intergroup Education Project of the American Council on Education, discovered this necessity: they found it necessary to induce experimentation with creative curriculum patterns on the classroom level along with developing a new conceptual scheme. The current curriculum explorations in science and mathematics are conducted from a similar premise, namely, that a teaching plan is needed along with the reorganization of content. Unfortunately the content specialists working on these plans are also assuming that such a teaching plan can be expressed only in a universal textbook.

The development of a teaching-learning plan is also the point at which the many problems of curriculum making can be worked out realistically. It is at this point that the myriad of decisions are made which incorporate the principles of a good curriculum: how to integrate learning experiences, how to provide for student interests and at the same time preserve the unique contribution of disciplined and systematic knowledge, what it is possible to learn on a given maturity level, how to translate objectives into productive learning activities, how to provide for continuity of learning, and so on.

At this point lies the creative end of curriculum making: experimentation with continuity of learning, with ways of relating learning experiences to life, developing teaching and learning patterns suitable for meeting new needs, exploring ways for achieving multiple objectives. Only as these problems are explored with respect to real variations among the children can one discover new patterns or put old ideas to new uses. These problems need to be faced and solved in a new way before it is possible to develop a new design. Imposing a new curriculum design on top of unrevised teaching-learning units is like putting a new front on an old house whose interior remains the same. In other words, a theoretical development of criteria, of a framework, and of scope and sequence without such concrete experimentation is likely to be one-sided, impractical, and scientifically unfounded. The many curriculum designs which have apparently overlooked many important considerations and consequences seem to testify to this fact. (See chapter 21.)

Secondly, many dilemmas in curriculum development which have remained unresolved on the theoretical level probably could be worked out in a concrete setting. Such questions as what is a reasonable balance between the scope and the depth of learning, which threads are most useful in developing continuity of learning, or how to accommodate student interests without jeopardizing disciplined thinking are much more easily answered in a concrete context and in classroom experimentation than they appear to be on the theoretical level.

Further, the major criteria of a good curriculum and ideas about organizing the curriculum acquire meaning only as they are applied to some tangible content. What integration of learning actually is and which elements of curriculum can be brought into an integrated relationship cannot be determined in the abstract, but only by testing on some concrete subject—or on such sampling of subjects as the variations in their basic structures dictate. One can, for example, find out which particular ideas or facts in science can be usefully related to ideas in social sciences. The possibilities of active discovery methods of learning and their limits can be worked out only by experimenting with a variety of ways of stimulating them.

This means that the development of pilot "units" designed for known groups of students and for tangible circumstances has to be an important part of scientific curriculum development. As these experimental or pilot studies become available, it is then possible to consider on a new basis such problems as an over-all continuity, sequence, and integration of subjects. In this sense, then, curriculum development should be an inductive process, beginning at the grass roots and with natural small units and proceeding into the more general problems of over-all organization.

THE METHODOLOGY
FOR PLANNING A UNIT*

As in any involved undertaking, the total job of planning a unit needs to be broken down into systematic steps to assure orderly thinking, to make possible a systematic study of the elements that compose such a plan, and to provide for a precise and careful study and application of the relevant principles and facts. These steps need to be taken in an orderly sequence. Each step should prepare for the next, which, otherwise, would be too difficult or would be taken uncreatively. In other words, there is a methodology in the development of curriculum units.

* The term *unit* will be used here to refer to an organized segment of a teaching-learning plan. It is used in the generic sense and not as an example of any special variety of "units."

A clear-cut methodology is also needed for handling each step. If the purpose of creating model units is not only to have a unit but also to develop a model for thinking about curriculum planning and about the questions with which a theory of curriculum development needs to deal, no aspect of planning such pilot units can be left to casual treatment. Because planning such units brings into play all considerations and principles important in curriculum development, the decisions made in planning pilot units and the ways of making them should provide important insights into curriculum development in general. Creating such models should at once test the validity of the existing theories, suggest new hypotheses, and point out what gaps exist either in theoretical concepts or in available facts.

To illustrate, planning a teaching-learning unit raises questions about the implications of the demands of culture and society which need to be answered also in planning of the entire program. For example, in the light of the needed orientation into the nature of our technological culture, what are the most significant features to study in the unit on "How People Live in California"? Its history? If so, which particular aspects? Its resources? If so, which? Its population movements? Industrial development? Contrasts between life today and in the past? Current units do not seem to reflect such questioning, with the result that an accidental reason carries the day, such as the teacher's love for missions or Indians, or the fact that the text contains good material on early California but is skimpy on modern.* Current courses on California tend to stress transportation and communication but deal only with its early people, the Indians and the early Spaniards. What does this mean for the social perspective that children acquire? What about their perspective on the manifold cultures that have poured into California since 1849? What about the technology that has turned deserts into orchards?

Surely there is a rational way of deciding whether to spend time on making adobe bricks, carving missions out of soap, comparing the use of land now and in 1849, and so on. And the rationale in making these relatively limited decisions on selecting content in a relatively limited field should be exemplars of making any decision concerning selection of curriculum content and of the way of applying any criteria relevant to selecting content.

A similar array of questions regarding what to include in a unit emerges from considering the students—their backgrounds, their social learning, needs, and motivations. Do all students, from city slums, from wealthy conservative farming centers, or from the families of migrant agricultural workers, need the same emphasis in studying life in California? Will they learn the same things from similar content? How must the details of content, the approach to studying it, and the materials be modified for these different groups? Chapter 10 described a variety of differences in children as learners. These differences have some bearing on what materials and learning experiences can be

---

* For contrasting ways of developing such units, see Los Angeles County Schools (1955) and Sacramento County Schools (undated).

or need to be used, how the essential ideas and concepts are approached, and what background of skills and understandings can be counted on.

The nature of the content needs to be examined also. What are the basic focusing ideas around which the content can be organized? How can one study the geography of California in such a manner that it contributes to the understanding of basic geographic principles and concepts? What is the most "logical" way of organizing this type of content? By basic ideas, and if so, which?

The unit needs to be shaped also according to the educational objectives for it. What can a unit do for the thinking of these particular children with these particular gaps or strengths? What attitudes, habits, and skills must be modified, extended, or strengthened? What understandings are present and, in the light of these, what can be learned next? It is evident, then, that the development of a unit raises all the theoretical issues and brings into play most of the criteria of curriculum development. Therefore, it also calls for the mobilization of all resources—expertness in curriculum planning, scholarship in content, and competence in teaching strategies.

To achieve these purposes in the manner suggested above, one needs to think of planning a unit in terms of a series of steps, each calculated to deal with a specific complex of decisions and each requiring the application of a specific set of criteria. One might call these the steps of inquiry in curriculum thinking and curriculum planning. The sequence given below is a logical one in the sense that some of these steps must be taken ahead of some others, although in practice explorations may begin at different points and the actual steps are not as sequential as they are described here. It would be futile, for example, to plan the learning activities ahead of determining what the objectives are and ahead of having a pretty clear idea of the main ideas to be taught. On the other hand, often the focusing ideas for the unit are redefined after exploring the ways or organizing the learning experiences, because these explorations may suggest certain deficiencies in continuity or scope. Under certain circumstances it is even profitable to start with developing evaluation instruments, because that is one way to sharpen the formulation of objectives (*Ginther, 1961, pp. 241-42*).

Step One: Diagnosing Needs

The diagnosis which precedes the planning of a unit is a fairly general analysis of problems, conditions, and difficulties. Its purpose is to generate a new emphasis and new ideas about the curriculum. It therefore consists of drawing together already existing information or securing easily obtainable new information and scrutinizing these data for whatever they may suggest regarding a new approach or neglected needs. For example, the idea of the study of comparative communities for a third grade emerged from a session with a group of teachers who had noted that the study of the community in the third grade seemed extremely unprofitable. The students did not progress in knowledge much beyond what they had gained in the study of the neighborhood in the second grade. They seemed bored and gained little in maturity. The materials and experiences seemed unchallenging and repetitious. The chief cause seemed to lie in the fact that most of these students lived in suburban communities which, because they depended for most of their services on the adjacent metropolitan areas, had few features of a full-fledged community. These teachers noted further a prevalence of certain parochial and ethnocentric attitudes and smugness about the "rightness of their particular way of life" among both the students and the adults in the community, which suggested that an emphasis on insights into varying ways of life as well as on more realistic attitudes towards cultural differences might be valuable.

A check on mastery of skills and abilities suggested that these students were ready to use a greater variety of reading materials than a dearth of materials pertaining to the local community had permitted. Many teachers had evidence on their students' lack of precision in handling data and interpreting information and on an abundance of misinformation about the world gathered from television. Out of this preliminary diagnosis grew the idea of projecting a year's course in a comparative study of communities across the world (*Contra Costa County Schools, 1961*).

Under certain conditions this type of analysis may lead to an entirely new conception of curriculum. Elkins describes such a shift in orientation: As she watched the "primitive authoritarian attitudes" her students displayed in handling their younger siblings, she began to ponder some other evidence she had collected. The papers on "How I Get Punished" suggested "a startling similarity between the way parents handled these teen-agers and the way teen-agers in turn handled their younger brothers and sisters. Would this abusive pattern continue when these thirteen-year-olds grew up and had families of their own? Would this kind of 'upbringing' and its consequent problems be perpetuated?"

Class discussions in connection with the unit on family and writing on open-ended themes indicated that these students thought that the younger sibling deprived them of parental attention and affection. Many even worried about having to leave school to help support them. Diaries written earlier had shown that these students carried adult responsibilities for their younger brothers and sisters. All this material suggested a need for attention to the problem of relationship with siblings. The teacher decided to give this in the form of a unit on siblings which supplanted what she did in literature and in the group-guidance periods (*Taba and Elkins, 1950, pp. 116-18*).

Once such a decision is made, a host of other questions arise which usually suggest new lines of needed diagnosis and therefore also the need for new information. For example, once Miss Elkins decided to emphasize human relations, and to use group work as one means of teaching, she began to examine her eighth-grade class in a different way.

> Before me sat an eighth-grade class of approximately thirty youngsters, all new to me. Some were noisy; others, quiet. Some smiled; others appeared sad. Some talked all the time; others never said a word. Some were clean and neatly dressed; others, unkempt. That's what appeared on the surface. But what was below the surface?
>
> These children would have to work and play together for a year. What did I know about their pupil society? Could each child find a place in it? Could each child be comfortable in it? Could it facilitate their learning? What had these children learned in their families, on street corners, at work or at play in various groups? What values and ways of behaving had been fixed by their previous experiences? How did these fit into what I was doing? What problems and difficulties were they meeting in growing up and in making their way through the web of human contacts?
>
> These and many other questions troubled me, because I could not start a new program until I had some idea of what needed to be done [*Taba and Elkins, 1950, p. 1*].

In a similar way the group of third-grade teachers who had decided to develop a comparative study of communities found that, in order to make the necessary decisions, they needed a fairly wide range of diagnostic information. It was necessary to know about the levels of ability to decide at what level to pitch the unit or what materials to use. Some information was needed about social relations and home backgrounds to determine which ways of working would be feasible and effective. Information was needed on the concepts students already had about the community, on the special meanings situations might have for them, and on the cultural attitudes which colored their orientation. As the explorations in classrooms progressed, further diagnosis was needed of the specific skills these students had in expressing themselves, in using materials, and in interpreting data.

Naturally the scope of diagnosis and the particular emphasis in it depend on the nature of the contemplated program revision, including the scope of its objectives and the context in which the particular program is to function. The more the contemplated program deviates from the traditional, the greater the need for comprehensive diagnosis, because there are more new decisions to make. Comprehensive diagnosis is especially needed if the unit is to serve as a model for concrete and creative ways of thinking about curriculum planning.

The wider the scope of objectives, the greater the task of diagnosis. If a unit is designed to influence attitudes and feelings, it is important to know what the current attitudes and feelings are, if for no other reason than to know what to change. If the unit is supposed to contribute to critical thinking, the current ways of thinking, including the strengths and weaknesses, need to be described. Thus the diagnostic task corresponds to the concept of learning that is being applied and to the platform of objectives for the unit.

These data for the analysis of needs may come from different sources, through different techniques, and represent different degrees of accuracy and dependability. The school's records may contain some, such as data on achievement and intelligence. The previous teacher may have jotted down in a cumulative record facts about conduct, discipline, and special problems. It may be necessary to interview parents to throw light on the emotional climate at home. Sociometric data may help to describe the climate of interpersonal relations. Themes may be assigned to diagnose prevailing feelings and attitudes. There may be writing or discussion of open-ended questions to probe concepts, meanings, and feelings the students have in the area of a projected unit. (See chapter 16 for a discussion of the available types of techniques.)

Not all this knowledge may be available at the point of planning the unit or at the beginning of the year. Much of it may have to be gathered in the course of experimentation with the unit. One needs, however, to know enough at the start to begin to see the "whites of their eyes." The chief task is to begin to translate the available data into needs with sufficient concreteness and succinctness to develop a rational basis for making preliminary decisions about content, emphasis, and objectives for learning experiences.

Step Two: Formulating Specific Objectives

The diagnosis of needs described above will have provided clues as to which objectives or which aspects of them to emphasize. A unit is likely to generate richer learning if the areas of objectives for it are fairly comprehensive and include some material on each of the following:

1. Concepts or ideas to be learned.
2. Attitudes, sensitivities, and feelings to be developed.
3. Ways of thinking to be reinforced, strengthened, or initiated.
4. Habits and skills to be mastered.

A comprehensive set of objectives is likely to help extend both the content and the learning activities and to point attention to the need for devising learning activities which are capable of carrying multiple objectives. At the same time, some selection and specification are needed in each category, by indicating which particular knowledge or concepts, what particular aspects of thinking, which particular attitudes or skills need to be and can be cultivated in a particular group at a particular level in connection with a particular content.

The task at this point is to translate the general objectives of the school into specific objectives in the light of what the unit encompasses and what the analysis of needs indicates. In doing this, special attention should be given to the cumulative progression in the level of the behaviors indicated in the objectives. If the fourth graders have already developed a general notion of a time line, then the time lines required of the fifth graders should require a greater precision. If the preceding year's work has taught students to make rough comparisons, more analytic or more abstract comparisons might be in order. The skill in writing might be scaled upward from simple descriptions to stories involving sequences, or from description to critical analysis or a sequential argument. If the necessity for gauging a sequential development of the behaviors indicated in the objectives is overlooked, one might plan content and learning activities which require skills, perceptions, and levels of conceptualization beyond the capacity of the students to master. The reverse is also possible, that there is no cumulative progression in the powers or attitudes, and that the program may merely move to new content without also moving to a higher level of performance. Objectives worth their salt are roads to travel, and not fixed terminal end points. Even so specific a thing as "paragraphing" grows in difficulty as the complexity of thought grows. The meaning of cumulative learning is that each new unit of educational experience must take a student an achievable step further.

With the picture of the needs and the above considerations in mind, the objectives for the study of comparative cultures emphasized first the development of an objective attitude toward differences in the ways in which various people serve their needs. Secondly, in the area of knowledge, it was decided to concentrate on basic ideas about the way of life which would apply to communities everywhere, and could be applied comparatively. A list of ideas which constituted the essential knowledge to be achieved was drawn up. (*See pp. 354-55.*)

In the area of thinking, the two main objectives were the ability to interpret such data as they were going to use with some precision and accuracy and an ability to generalize and to apply generalizations about the comparative ways of life. Regarding skills, it was agreed that it was time for these students to begin to handle a variety of sources: stories, maps, films.

In planning the specific objectives for a unit it must be recognized that not all objectives are equally achievable in every unit. Some units may be especially suitable for working on certain attitudes, such as attitudes toward differences, and others for developing a certain specific aspect of critical thinking, such as interpreting quantitative data or analyzing and evaluating biased and controversial material.

It must be noted that at the point of planning a unit, probably neither the analysis of needs nor the formulation of objectives can be complete. Further clarification of objectives is to be expected at other steps of planning the unit. A prolonged time spent on formulating the objectives at the very beginning usually ends only in a stilted formalism and sometimes in discouragement at the complexity. Schools that spend a year or so on formulating objectives may become so engrossed in that process that their implementation never takes place. Since often a clear perception of objectives emerges only at the point of formulating means for evaluating them, the formulation of means of evaluation might be an activity concurrent to formulating objectives.

Step Three: Selecting Content

After a preliminary analysis of needs and a tentative projection of objectives, it is possible to tackle the problem of selecting the content. Both the analysis of needs and the statement of objectives have provided a preliminary guide for suggesting the lines of emphasis. Usually, the development of a unit also takes place within a general framework formulated either by the state or by the school district which determines the general areas of content to be dealt with at any given grade level. While a given school may want to modify the content of these themes or subjects, changes in the areas of content allocated to a grade level are more difficult to make.

It is necessary to be selective about several levels of the content: the central topic and its dimensions, the focusing ideas in the light of which the topic or the unit is to be developed, and the specific facts and details which will serve to develop the focusing ideas.

Selecting topics

Selecting topics is the first task in the development of a unit. This decision is not a matter of whimsical preference but is of some consequence, and should be made rationally and carefully. The nature of the topics or units within a course determines which relationships stand out and which are submerged. Their nature also determines the scope of the study. Unless the topics represent a good sample of the content, the study will be quite limited. The choice of topics also determines what ways of organizing content and learning experiences are possible.

Many a unit lacks significance not because the topic is not worthwhile, but because the dimensions treated are unimportant, or because its development is unidimensional rather than multidimensional. Elementary units on transportation often explore one means of transportation after another, covering cars, boats, trains, and airplanes without ever touching on questions which represent another dimension, such as the changes technology has brought or the ways in which transportation affects life. Such units are narrow in scope and have little value beyond acquiring a bit of descriptive information and providing many opportunities for play.

The selection of the communities to study in the comparative study of communities will illustrate the problems involved in selecting topics. After the decision was made to study communities comparatively, it was necessary to select the kinds of contrasting communities. It seemed clear that the number of communities had to be limited to avoid excessive coverage at the cost of understanding. The idea was to sample the maximum range of contrasts in ways of life through a minimum number of communities. Tentatively it was decided to sample five types of communities: (a) their own, (b) primitives in the African rain forest, (c) a nomadic tribe in the Sahara, (d) Hong Kong boat people, and (e) a Swiss village.*

A rationale supported each choice. A study of the students' own community was needed, both as a point of departure and as a point of comparison. Without comparison to their own community these third graders could hardly be expected to understand much about communities elsewhere. The first obvious contrast was a primitive community. The rain-forest community in Africa was chosen because it served as an obvious contrast and also because materials were available. The nomads in the Sahara provided an opportunity to examine a fairly primitive way of life, but in a geographically contrasting environment.

Next, the group searched for a type of communal life which was both sophisticated and simple, which represented important contrasts in the structure of family life and in the ways of securing food and shelter. A Chinese community seemed ideal, but study of the old China seemed inappropriate, and nothing was available on new China. Hong Kong boat people seemed to fill the bill. A Swiss village was selected to represent life not too unlike our own, yet geographically remote and more self-sufficient than the suburban communities in the Bay Area. It seemed obvious, also, that whatever the choice of topics, they should represent significant knowledge about communities, because even third graders should study significant rather than irrelevant or surface aspects of community life.

The "logic" of the subject matter dictated the dimensions to study. A search of anthropological literature for culturally important categories used in descriptions of a way of life yielded the initial list of the dimensions of these topics. From this list were selected those which were understandable to the third graders, provided appropriate contrasts in the five communities, and, in the light of the backgrounds of these students, promised to make the greatest impact on their attitudes and insights.

By this process the following aspects of life were chosen and became the dimensions of the topic to study: how people get food, shelter, and clothing; their technology (the tools and materials they use for the above); education (the method of rearing children); family life (the structure of the family and the roles of the family members or who does what in the family); government (what rules people live by, their customs, rituals, do's and don't's, festivities and ceremonials).

This selection of dimensions illustrates two theoretical points discussed in previous chapters. In determining the structure of the topics, the criteria of significance and validity of the content were applied and implemented, as were the criteria of learnability and appropriateness to the needs and the

* The selection was by no means ideal, because of the limitation in available material.

developmental levels. Both the so-called logical and the psychological criteria were applied. The formulation of these topics and their dimensions also demonstrates a way of introducing new ideas without having to introduce a new unit or a new subject. In this case, anthropological ideas were introduced as a way of looking at community life. While the third graders probably would not understand anthropology as such, they can understand anthropological ideas if these ideas are translated into terms they can understand and are introduced in a context which they can apprehend.

Selecting basic ideas

Neither the topics nor their dimensions yet represent all the aspects that are important for an adequate unit. It is also necessary to determine what ideas should be taught about a given topic, for, as indicated in chapter 12, it is the basic ideas which represent the *fundamentals* of a subject or a discipline. They are the knowledge.

The functions of the focusing or basic ideas were discussed earlier. It is sufficient to say here that each unit, being a unique piece of content, has its own logic, and the ideas selected for it should be designed to give perspective to this particular area of content. These ideas also should represent the essential knowledge, that is, the knowledge that all students should master. The basic ideas also guide the selection and organization of specific information and its interpretation. Therefore, a list of basic ideas provides a practical check against including the irrelevant and insignificant, whether introduced by the teachers or by the students.

Because of the importance of the basic ideas, care is needed in their selection and formulation. Their selection needs to be tested by experienced teachers, curriculum makers as well as content specialists, because they must be valid, significant, and learnable. Because of their central role, every aspect of the unit—content, learning experiences, and materials—should be organized to support the development of these ideas.

The focusing ideas of the course on comparative communities were as follows:

1. All people have certain basic needs; they work in different ways to meet these needs.

2. People of a primitive culture are extremely dependent upon their immediate environment and their own skills; people of a modern culture use the skills of others and are much less dependent on their environment.

3. In some communities the way of life is greatly influenced by tradition.

4. The family is important in all cultures, but family structures may be different, as are the roles different family members play.

5. All people teach their children the things they think are important for them to learn; they teach them in different ways.

6. Many activities of primitive people are carried on through the family and/or the tribe; a more modern community provides for these activities through organized institutions.

7. Changes are taking place in primitive communities.

8. Modern communities are dependent on each other. Trade helps each community to meet its needs.

9. People develop institutions that support their way of life. Some people live a very simple life even though they are part of a very ancient civilization.

10. Even a very modern community may wish to preserve some of its customs from the past (*Contra Costa County Schools, 1961, pp. 1-90*).*

In this case a slightly different selection of ideas was used in the study of each community, in order to extend the scope of ideas and to provide variations in emphasis. There may be an advantage, however, in following through with the same ideas in all units.

As can be seen from the above illustration, the formulation of the basic ideas involves application of several criteria: that of soundness of content, of learnability, of developmental levels. It is also important to keep the objectives for the unit in mind. For example, ideas 1, 4, 5, and 10 were introduced with an aim to break into the ethnocentricity of this group. A closer attention was needed also to using these basic ideas as integrating threads which run through these several units to organize and tie together the whole year's study. Finally, since the nature of these ideas determined the organization of content, considerations of their sequence entered. No matter how basic each individual idea is, if the ideas cannot be organized into a coherent sequence and if their levels of abstraction are uneven, they fail in their function of providing a basic structure for the unit.

It is useful also to check the extent to which, taken collectively, the ideas express important concepts which should thread throughout the whole program. This unit, for example, deals with the concept of differences in the ways of life of peoples, which has been touched upon in preceding study and to which many return engagements need to be made in subsequent study. It also adds a bit to the concept of social and cultural change, which probably will not be treated directly until much later. It helps to extend the important concept of the dependence of man on his environment and begins to differentiate the degrees of this dependence.

A few comments are needed on what is involved in an attempt to formulate focusing ideas. It is not an easy task, especially when teachers are not trained to think in terms of large ideas and have difficulty in distinguishing interesting facts from basic ideas. This step in the development of a unit, therefore, requires much time and involves considerable study. The higher the grade level, the more difficult the task, because the content becomes more complex and a

---

* For ideas in other types of units, see Taba, Brady, and Robinson, 1952, ch. 3; and Contra Costa County Schools, 1959*b*.

total view of it is more difficult to gain. Because curriculum building is an exercise on an adult level of thinking, the first attempts tend to be in terms of an adult thinker. Constant effort is needed to translate these ideas into the kinds of terms that might represent a child's thinking at the end of the unit. Therefore, knowledge of how children think is extremely relevant.

As is true of the preceding steps, the job of formulating the focusing ideas is not really finished until tested and corrected in the subsequent steps and eventually in the classroom. For example, if the content outlines tend to overlap, it means that the ideas are not distinct enough. If the ideas do not form a natural unit, the content outline tends to be choppy and transitions from one point to another are difficult. The final check comes at the last step, that is, at the point of selecting and organizing learning activities. Many difficulties in devising cumulative learning activities may arise out of poor sequence of content or a poorly stated focusing idea, and revisions of the work done on the preceding steps may be necessary.

Selecting specific content

Once the core ideas are chosen it is possible to begin to select the specific content for their development. This can be done by constructing for each idea an appropriate sample of specific content. The specific content should be a valid example of the general idea, have a definite logical connection with the idea, and not just be vaguely related to the topic. Usually, however, for each idea several samples of detail could be used with equal validity. Therefore, it is not necessary to "cover" the specific content. It is possible to sample it by selecting the contrasts that are necessary to represent the variations contained in the idea. The way of treating the topic of the American Colonies may serve as an illustration of this problem of coverage vs. sampling. The usual temptation is to offer tidbits about each of the thirteen colonies, knowing fully that these details will soon be forgotten. In contrast, let us suppose that one fundamental idea to be understood about the colonies is that each colony set up a pattern of life that represented an adjustment to its physical environment. Should one for that purpose cover all thirteen colonies or could the idea become clear by sampling only two or three contrasting environments and contrasting types of life, such as the Massachusetts and the Virginia colonies?

Sampling content is essential to solving the problem of excessive detail which so burdens students' minds that there is neither time nor room to think, to understand anything in sufficient depth, or to perceive and ponder relationship between facts. This, in turn, tends to induce passivity on the part of the students, their main occupation being to remember facts, with little challenge for understanding or originating ideas.

In developing the units on comparative study of communities, samples of content were constructed for each idea. The content sample for the first main idea that *the primitive people are more dependent on the immediate environment and their own skills and that the people in a modern culture use the skill of others and depend less on the immediate environment,* included the following:

Content Sample

1. Some people make their own homes and secure their food and clothing from their immediate environment; e.g.,
   Zulus build huts
      raise cattle
      plant some food
   Rain-forest primitives build huts
      hunt and gather food
      sometimes raise a little food
2. In some communities many sources are used to secure food, clothing, and shelter; e.g., our own community.

The content sample for the second idea, that *many activities of primitive people are fulfilling needs carried on through the family or tribe, rather than through specialized institutions, as in modern communities,* includes only three types of content:

Content Sample

1. All people provide a means for their children to learn.
   Primitive families/tribes teach their children:
      to secure food, clothing, and shelter
      to learn tribal customs
      to sing and dance
   Modern communities have schools, churches, and libraries to teach the people.
2. All societies expect different things of boys and girls.
3. All people have some laws.
   Primitive people settle problems within their families or tribes.
   Modern communities have courts to settle problems.

Many other activities, such as manufacturing articles or providing for transportation, could have been included. But sampling seemed necessary to avoid overcrowding the unit with detail and consequently not being able to explore anything in sufficient detail to understand the basic idea fully and clearly. The three were thought to provide sufficient contrasts with those aspects of the modern community which children understand. They were considered to be a good enough sample for the purpose of developing the main idea.

Four samples of content were selected to represent the idea that *changes are taking place in primitive communities:*

1. Some primitive people are beginning to use modern inventions and discoveries:
      tools
      transportation
      medicines

2. Some primitive people are using more modern ideas:
    send their children to school
    give up superstitions
    go to hospitals
    wear more and different clothes
3. Many people are bringing new ideas to primitive people:
    missionaries
    United Nations
    traders
4. People are afraid of some changes [*Contra Costa County Schools, 1961,
    pp. 1, 16, 26*].

This sample is also telescoped in several respects. Of all possible types of changes, only three are listed and only a few items are included under each type of change.

Assuming that several different samples of content could be used, the decision on which sample to use depends upon several considerations. One is, of course, validity, which applies to all levels of content. Since ideas with fair scope can be developed through a fairly wide range of detailed content, it is possible to apply several other criteria. For instance, if several kinds of detail develop the same main idea equally well, one can choose those that can accommodate multiple objectives, promise to meet local needs, coincide with student interests, connect with their level of understanding and previous learning, or have life meaning for them. And there is always the practical consideration of whether sufficient material to pursue the study is available or could be devised. No matter how good the selection of content, it is of little use without adequate materials to develop it in the class. There is no point to choosing a content sample which the students either will not or cannot understand or which requires materials that the students cannot handle or which are unavailable.

In actual process, the sampling of the content and the formulation of ideas are mutually corrective: the content sampling suggests possible reclassifications of ideas, if there is overlapping; sharpening, if the focus does not seem clear enough; simplification, if the material needed seems too complex; and so on. Modified ideas, in turn, require new detail sampling.

In the development of the ideas and of the content sample, especially the latter, the aid of a content specialist is required, especially if teachers who work on the unit are not well grounded in the subject. Poor command of the subject matter prevents an overview of the whole field and therefore produces a poor sample of content. And a poor content sample means that students are burdened with irrelevant detail and are denied the optimum development of the central idea. The content specialist's role is to evaluate the validity and significance of the ideas and to check the adequacy of the sample.

The above analysis demonstrates that a systematic and scientifically oriented selection of content is by no means a simple process. It involves balancing of the scope with the necessity of focusing and narrowing. It involves decisions about what is to be universal or common and where a flexibility of choice can be exercised according to special needs of the students or of the situation. It involves also decisions regarding the relative place assigned to mastery of content and to the development of mental powers. These considerations apply to all levels of the structure of content: the topics, their dimensions, the basic ideas, and the specific content details.

Step Four: Organizing Content

Neither the ideas nor the sample of content for each idea as yet represent a teachable content: a sequence and a logical organization is only partly established. The content needs to be arranged so that the dimensions of inquiry are in a sequential order according to a feasible learning sequence. The topics, the ideas, and the concrete content samples need to be arranged so that there is a movement from the known to the unknown, from the immediate to the remote, from the concrete to the abstract, from the easy to the difficult. In other words, an inductive logical arrangement of the content and a psychological sequence for learning experiences need to be established to facilitate learning.* This may require combining in a single cluster several ideas and their samples seen separately in the preceding step. Ideas also need to be arranged in a sequence which proceeds from those which psychologically form the "background" for the perception to other, more complex ideas. They need to be considered also from the standpoint of cumulative development of mental skills: each succeeding idea or question should require an increasingly difficult mental operation, such as an increasingly demanding abstraction, an increasingly differentiating analysis, and an increasingly subtle sensitivity. (See chapter 18 on organizing content.) Since the core ideas represent the structure of thinking about the topic, any flaws in formulating and organizing them are reflected in the quality of thinking of the learners. The very plan for the unit is a method of teaching thinking, a pathway for developing generalizations inductively and for applying them, a way of establishing relationships between ideas and facts, and among ideas. The organization should facilitate these processes rather than obstruct them, as a thoughtless organization often does.

It might be important here to point out that this approach to organization opens a new slant on the perennial argument about what is in the focus or can be taught directly and what indirectly or incidentally. From the standpoint of the content organization as well as to what the students are addressing themselves, the subject matter under study is in focus. But this focus can be planned so that the opportunities to achieve other objectives besides the content details are not left to chance, but are provided for consciously and systematically. This means that at the point of organizing the content, thought

* Shaplin calls this the "psychologizing of the curriculum" (1961, p. 46).

is given to shaping the content so that it facilitates the type of learning activities needed to achieve objectives other than content mastery.

Decisions need to be made also regarding the aspects of content which shall serve as the focusing center, because on this depends which ideas and relationships will stand out and which have to be put together without support from the pattern of organization. For example, in the study of the comparative communities it was necessary to decide whether each of the five communities chosen for the sample were to be studied in turn, or whether each of the main dimensions—ways of securing food, shelter and clothing, technology, education, and institutions—would be studied in turn across the five communities. The former would preserve the unity of the culture pattern of the respective communities but would obscure comparison. The latter would bring sharper comparison, but would make it more difficult to examine precise differences in the various aspects of the ways of life. The first organization would yield more concrete units of study, and the second would call for greater powers of abstraction, possibly too great for third graders to master. Because of this last reason, centering the units in communities was adopted.

The question of the order in which to study the communities then arose. From the standpoint of moving from the known to the less known, the decision should have been to study the students' own community first, the community most similar to it next, and the least familiar last. This would have given a sequence which started with the study of a local Bay Area community, was followed by the study of the Swiss village and ended with the study of primitives of Africa. However, several other considerations made a different order necessary. First, from the standpoint of sharpening the contrasts and comparisons, it seemed best to distribute the study of the local community, using it as a backdrop for the study of each specific aspect of the other communities. Secondly, studying the fairly simple primitive community first would help to establish relationships between the various facets of community life. Therefore, it was decided to start with the African primitives, to move from there to the nomads of the Sahara, then to the Hong Kong boat people, and finally to the Swiss village. The beginning was made with the most contrasting culture, but a simple one, which demonstrates that when several criteria are applied in constellation, the decisions will differ from those derived from consideration of a single criterion, no matter how valid.

The content about each community was then arranged according to questions which followed the dimensions to be studied and which were formulated to develop the meaning of the focusing ideas. (See pp. 368-73 for the pattern of organization.) The focusing ideas, having served as a criterion for selecting the content sample, are now used as criteria for establishing a method of inquiry. The content dimensions are converted into the questions to pursue. These questions represent a more fruitful method of inquiry if they follow the natural flow of inquiry and a learning sequence.

This pattern of organizing content (determining the topic, the basic ideas, the sample of content, and questions representing the dimensions to be studied) has several advantages. First, occasionally a great simplification of the complex elements takes place, especially when one is dealing with older students who can work in committees and study simultaneously several samples. This can be illustrated in the scheme of organization in units on American peoples, which consisted in the study of various groups of people who came to America and were organized around these focusing ideas:

1. The U. S. is a multiculture society; it is composed of many kinds of people, with many different backgrounds and styles of life.

2. These people came from many places, for many different reasons, and over a long period of time.

3. All people who move from one place to another have to make adjustments: they are not accepted at once, nor do they feel at home.

4. The wider the cultural distance of the home background from the new place, the more severe and difficult is the adjustment.

5. All people in the U. S. have contributed something to the shaping of the life, customs, strength, richness and well-being of this country.

Usually the sample of the groups studied included: the families of students (for a comparative backdrop); groups in large numbers in the local city, such as Italians, Polish, Russians, Irish; groups who are important minorities, such as the Spanish-speaking people in California and Negroes.* These were chosen by specific criteria to represent the cultural variations which were important according to the objectives of the study. Each of these groups was studied by following the questions suggested by the focusing ideas. Thus the scheme of organization for the entire sequence of topics was stated very simply, indicating the entire scope of the study as follows:

Topics to Study (Sample of Groups)	Dimensions to Study	Questions for Study
Poles	Place of origin	Who came from which country?
Irish	Time of arrival	
Germans	Place of settlement	When?
etc.	Reasons for migration	When settled?
	Nature of problems and adjustments	Why came?
	Nature of contributions	What problems and adjustments they had to meet
		What contributions they made

Such a scheme of organization is also quite flexible. For example, one can extend or cut down the unit by extending or cutting down the ideas covered, the number of groups studied, or the dimensions for studying each group. Add an idea, and it is necessary to change the sample of people and the ques-

* See Taba and Elkins, 1950, pp. 146-50, for a description of how a particular teacher made selections and decided on questions to study about each.

tions. Delete an idea, and certain portions of the sample and certain questions lose relevance. This flexibility makes it possible to make modifications fairly easily and rationally in the quantity, complexity, or the level of abstraction and sophistication. For example, a gifted class could either "cover" more ideas or answer more penetrating questions about the same ideas, such as comparing the differences in adjustments that different groups had to make by considering such causes as visibility of racial groups or by exploring how the idea of the superiority of certain ethnic groups has come about. One sample of content could be substituted for another. Each question could be explored in greater or lesser detail according to student backgrounds. The relationships between questions could be developed elaborately or kept at the minimum. This flexibility permits each teacher to work out a particular teaching scheme according to the needs of his students. The organization permits adjustments without redoing the whole scheme or substituting some other altogether different content.

The fact that the content is not limited to a statically fixed level of penetration and insight opens up new possibilities for teaching heterogeneous groups in the same classroom. It is quite possible for students of greater intellectual ability or with more adequate academic skills to be working to their limit while others are traveling a more modest distance, without segregating the two groups or giving each group entirely different assignments. All these variations represent differentiations around a common focus which does away with the necessity for developing thirty different curricula in order to provide for individual differences of the thirty different students in the class. All will deal with the same basic curriculum but can explore it in different depths, using different materials, or drawing on different experiences, and sifting them through a different level of perception.

Choices are open also regarding what methods of instruction to pursue. The topics can be studied by committees, each committee studying one group of people but all pursuing the same questions. Or the entire class could study one group of people after another, comparing and contrasting the findings on each group as they proceed. The study could be purely factual or stress the development of sensitivity by using fiction or personal experiences of the students. There is nothing in the structure of the unit organization itself to prevent a teacher from limiting the resources to texts or using a wider range of references. In this sense the scheme of organizations is open-ended and can be adapted to a variety of school conditions. It is not wedded to a particular way of learning and style of teaching.* There are many levels of freedom, even though the outline appears structured.

What is essential, though, is that there be comparing and contrasting of the answers to all questions on each group of people, because this process is necessary for the development of generalizations. It is also essential that

---

* This could be compared to what H. H. Anderson calls an open system of education, which he considers important in producing creative persons (1961).

the students be led step by step toward these generalizations instead of having the generalizations handed to them.

This scheme also makes content revisions over a period of time relatively easy. If in the course of time some new idea seems more significant, it, with its content sample, can be substituted for a less useful one in the outline; if different details become relevant or available, these can replace the ones included at the moment. Revision can be made in parts of the outline without having to redo the whole scheme.

A rational analysis of the horizontal relationships is also facilitated. First, the list of ideas makes visible which cross relationships are important and relevant. Instead of building relationships by entire subjects, integration can be plotted by relevance and need by relating those ideas and insights which can enrich each other; this is the reason for having the idea of integration in the curriculum.

In the outline shown above, one can see clearly the points at which literature is helpful to sensitivity—to differences in values and customs, in identification with the problems and adjustments, and for understanding of what it means to be rejected or to be at a loss in a new place. One does not need to "plot" correlation. It is implicit.

Finally, there is also certain encouragement of creative extensions in the fact that the questions which structure the content are open-ended. Learning outcomes are always conditioned by what a teacher is able to do, what the students can master by way of learning techniques, and what resources are available. But they should not be further limited by the questions asked in the structure of the content. These should be open-ended enough to encourage discovery and the excitement of putting ideas together and discovering something new.

Steps Five and Six: Selecting and Organizing Learning Experiences

With the tentative content outline in hand, it is possible to begin to plan the learning experiences or learning activities. Unless one assumes that mastery of content is the sole objective, a content outline is only a partial plan for learning. As the chapters on objectives and on selection of learning activities pointed out, only a portion of important outcomes can be fulfilled through content. All objectives, except those of knowledge, need to be implemented by appropriate learning activities designed to help students develop and practice the powers and the behaviors they are supposed to learn. Achievement of objectives such as thinking and attitudes are relatively independent of the content but highly dependent on the type of learning experiences or processes which are used.

The first rule to observe in selecting the learning experiences for each idea and its content sample is that each should serve some definite function. There should be no such thing as activity for activity's sake. Learning experiences without a specific function are a waste of students' time. In current practice, too many learning activities are introduced for irrelevant reasons; they are supposed to be modern, or traditional, or the teacher favors them, and so on. In considering the functions of learning experiences, it is naturally important to keep in mind the total range of objectives so that there is assurance for implementing the whole range. The possibilities for inventing learning activities which serve multiple objectives need to be watched for also.

To translate the criteria for effective learning experiences into an actual program, it is important, first, to visualize what students need to do or experience in order to acquire certain behavioral competencies and what the order of these experiences should be. What, for example, must a third grader experience or do to acquire a concept of the primitive? How can data about the modern and the primitive ways of using tools, securing food, or any other activity be handled not only to lead children to see the similarities and contrasts clearly but also to develop skills in interpreting data accurately and in drawing inferences? In other words, in plotting the learning experiences for each focusing idea and the corresponding content sample, the criteria for desirable learning experiences (chapter 18) must be applied by asking questions like the following: Is the activity appropriate for learning the main ideas? Does it serve the objectives of the unit? Is it efficient in the sense of serving more than one objective? Does it promote active learning? Is it appropriate for the maturity level? Can the skills required by it be learned? And it is especially important to be sure that the assumption that certain traditional learning processes automatically achieve many outcomes will not creep in.

Care must be taken also to include a variety of ways of learning—reading, writing, observing, doing research, analyzing, discussing, tabulating, painting, constructing, and dramatizing—and that experiences representing both intake and absorption and those requiring synthesis, reformulation, and expression are properly represented, although not necessarily for each idea or content sample. Knowing what the needs and skills of the students are is useful at this point, as is familiarity with their modes of thinking and learning.

Since it is not easy to invent learning activities with creative possibilities, some experimentation in the classroom with portions of the unit by specially creative teachers is helpful. Otherwise it is difficult to break the traditional round of learning activities.

After a slate of possibilities has been accumulated, it is necessary to plan the organization of the learning experience. Perhaps the most important requirement for adequate learning experiences is that they follow a sequence which makes continuous and accumulative learning possible. A psychologically adequate learning sequence is in effect a programmed learning which includes not only an inductive movement toward generalization and abstraction, at least in units focused on the development of central ideas, but appropriate steps of attaining concepts and attitudes as well.

Introduction, opener, orientation

Generally speaking, a sequence of learning experiences involves at least three main stages. At one stage the learning activities introduced are essentially *introductory, for opening up, for orientation.* These include activities which (a) provide diagnostic evidence for the teacher, (b) help the students make a connection with their own experience, (c) arouse interest, (d) provide concrete descriptive data from which to get a preliminary sense of the problems to be dealt with, and (e) create involvement and motivation. In this sense an opener has a broader meaning than the usual "setting of an environment for learning."

Even though the teacher may have general diagnostic data at her disposal, some diagnosis is still needed in preparation for teaching a specific unit, for detecting the special misconceptions and difficulties, for identifying the sensitivity patterns or probing the attitudes unique to this particular area. Students may be asked to talk or write about the concepts around which the unit is centered to discover special meanings or misunderstandings that need to be corrected. For example, to introduce the sequence about how various people provide opportunities to learn, children can be asked to tell about ways people learn generally what their mothers and fathers have told them about things, about what was a good and bad thing to do, or how they learned certain skills. The study of Latin America may be preceded by a survey of what students know about the United States as a background for comparison, or for what is important to know about any country. If small group work is to be used, sociometric data are needed to provide a psychological basis for composing work groups and committees.

Experiences to orient the students to the unit and to establish a connection with their personal experiences are part of this cluster of learning activities also. For example, if the types of work in the community are studied from the standpoint of the differences in a way of life that occupations entail, the type of work their fathers do can be tabulated and classified, and then discussed in respect to the way such work affects the way each family lives. Similarly, the experiences of the students' families coming to America could be analyzed by using the same questions that will be used to study the people of America. This type of initial activity gives students a preliminary training in the methods of attacking the problem, establishes a connection with something in their experience, and affords the teacher an opportunity to size up what the class can do and what particular skills, ways of viewing facts, and insights they lack and need to learn.

This stage also includes the planning with the students. Even though the main features of the unit are preplanned, it is also useful for students to develop criteria for sampling, to project ways of studying, to allocate the tasks that need to be done, and to discuss methods by which to do them. For example, the eighth grade studying the people of America spent some time in formulating the criteria for selecting the ethnic groups to study and the points to study about each. If the unit requires new ways of learning, some time may need to be spent on initiating students into new skills. In the same class, during the opening period, the students prepared themselves by taking notes from an old text because the new study required the use of many different references, for which note taking was essential (*Taba and Elkins, 1950, pp. 146-49 and 156-71*).

Occasionally the topic requires a preparation of feelings and sensitivities for full comprehension. This may make it necessary to read a story or to see a film as a part of the opening sequence. For example, to prepare students for understanding the multiple family of the primitives, a story about a primitive family that induced identification with a youngster of their own age was read preceding the study of the family structure (*Mirsky, 1952*).

In other words, among the opening activities belong all learning experiences necessary to tone up teacher and students for the proper attack on the task of study. These activities may be fairly brief or quite lengthy, depending on what the class is like, how great a shift in the usual ways of learning the unit involves, or how complex the central task of the unit is. If the transition to the required study skills is abrupt, the preparatory activities may have to be rather elaborate. If the task requires a shift in emotional orientation before factual study, sensitizing experiences may take a long time and require fairly elaborate devices, such as sociodrama or reading of stories and reacting to them.*

Generally this orientation period takes more time, especially in the first unit of a sequence, than teachers anxious to get on with the content are willing to give unless they understand its significance. Since in the beginning the visible productivity is low and the problems many, teachers who are using this method for the first time become anxious about wasting time. However, the more thorough this orientation, the more rapid the progress in subsequent stages.

Development, analysis, study

These consist of learning experiences designed to develop various aspects of the subject and to provide the needed factual material: reading, research, analysis of data, committee work, study of various kinds. Organizing for the study—forming committees, planning ways of presentation—also comes during this period. For example, in studying the people of America, students needed to do research in answering the questions they had planned for the study of each ethnic group. They needed to search for data about the time of arrival, the places of settlement, problems of adjustment, contributions, and so on. This is also the period for acquiring skills needed for the pursuit of various tasks, such as using references, taking notes, and interpreting, com-

* For an opener that took a lot of effort, see Taba and Elkins, 1950, pp. 115-23.

paring, and contrasting data. This period is characterized by an abundance of the "intake" variety of learning activities: reading, digesting information, synthesizing facts, and so on.

For example, in studying activities which the primitive people are carrying on in families but which are accomplished through organized institutions in modern society, the third graders composed precise lists for our own culture and for the primitive society of what children learn, from whom they learn, how they are taught. They examined folk tales as a source of learning in primitive society, studied the roles of family members in our own culture and in the primitive community, the family structure in the two cultures, and so on. The content of some of these activities was derived from the analysis of their own experience; others required a careful study of available materials.

Generalization

Development and analysis need to be followed by the type of assignments and activities which help students to *generalize,* to put their ideas together and reformulate them in their own terms, to compare and contrast, or to formulate conclusions. For example, after studying the times of the coming of various ethnic groups to America, students need to plot these times and then ask themselves why certain people came at certain times and not at another, why there was a greater concentration of immigration to certain places than to others. In the study of comparative communities the generalizing involved a good deal of comparing and contrasting and of exploring the reasons for the similarities and differences discovered. For example, the data on what people learn in a primitive community, how they learn, and what sources they use were compiled into a chart to help the process of generalizing and to make it more precise. This was followed by discussion of differences between learning in school, with teachers, books and experiments, and learning in families by imitation. The data on roles played by the family members was subjected to the same treatment. (See pp. 371-72.) These activities produce generalizations and critical evaluation and set a perspective. While the developmental activities require much individual or small group work, it is more profitable to formulate generalizations in discussion by the entire class.

Application, summary, culmination

Finally there are activities designed to apply what has been learned, to assess and evaluate, or to set what is learned into a larger framework: What do these ideas mean? How do they relate to other ideas? How did we work? What could we do better, or differently, the next time? Another form of summary, testing, or synthesis of what is learned is applying what is known to a new situation, in a new context. Thus, after having studied conditions and feelings during the Civil War, a synthesis might be made by writing a letter such as a Southern belle might write to her boy friend at the front. In the illustration of a sequence that follows, the concluding activities consisted of dramatizing the contrasting aspects of recreation, education, and law in the primitive and modern cultures, and of composing a chart entitled "Big Ideas to Watch For."

An example of an organized sequence
(Contra Costa County Schools, 1961, pp. 16-25.)

Main Idea II. Many activities of primitive people are carried on through the family and/or tribe; a more modern community provides for these activities through organized institutions.

CONTENT

1. All people provide a means for their children to learn.
      Primitive families/tribes teach their children:
         to secure food, clothing and shelter
         to learn tribal customs
         to sing and dance
      Modern communities have schools, churches, and libraries to teach the people.
2. All societies expect different things of boys and girls.
3. All people have some laws.
      Primitive people settle problems within their families or tribes.
      Modern communities have courts to settle problems.

MATERIALS NEEDED

Thirty-One Brothers and Sisters—Mirsky
First Book of Words—Epstein
Living Together Around the World—Cutright
Tales from the Story Hat—Aardena
The Na of the Wa—Aardena
Otwe—Aardena
The Sky God Story—Aardena
Wembi, the Singer of Stories—Cobble
The Illustrated Book about Africa—Sutton
Music Near and Far—Mursell (State Text Bk. IV)
Fun Around the World—Scarry
Equatorial Africa FS 2544 (*Families of the World*)
Wambo and Tawa of the Hot Lands FS 3021

OPTIONAL MATERIALS

Music of Equatorial Africa P402A
or *Pygmies of the Ituri Forest* FE4457B
or *Drums of the Yoruba of Nigeria* P441B

(All are Ethnic Folkways Records)

LEARNING EXPERIENCES

Opener
Ask the children to write on "How Children Learn."

Note: The purpose of this opener is to determine whether the children think of learning only in relation to school.

If the children's responses indicate that they are unaware of how much they learn from parents, experience, etc., discuss with them:

(1) What my Dad and Mother told me about animals, plants, places, *or*
(2) How I learned what was a good or bad thing to do, e.g., don't eat with dirty hands, don't tease younger sister, etc., *or*
(3) How I learned a skill, e.g., setting a table, tying shoes, etc.

Development

1. Have the children list some of the activities of Nomusa and Mdingi (characters in *Thirty-one Brothers and Sisters*). These activities may be listed on the chalkboard.

Now have the children recall from the story who taught the children to do these things, and how they taught them, e.g.,

Jobs for Nomusa	*These people taught her*	*How they taught her*
cooking	Mother	showed
feeding baby	Mother	let her help
entertaining baby	Grandmother	told her stories

Jobs for Mdingi	*These people taught him*	*How they taught him*
hunting	Father	showed
herding cattle	Big Brother	went along
etc.		

2. Let the children look at the column that shows how these children were taught. Let them note that they learned mostly by (1) being shown, (2) story-telling, (3) helping adults, etc. (*Generalizing*)

3. Select an activity with which these children are acquainted, such as cooking. Ask, "How does Mother learn to cook something new?" Question until children bring out that one way of learning to cook is by reading recipes. Ask, "Why could Nomusa not learn from a cookbook?" (*Contrasting two known experiences, learn a new idea*)

4. Ask the children how information from people who lived before us gets learned by children in our community. How does this get done in primitive communities? What is the main difference? (*Generalizing and extending the new idea*)

5. Read *The First Book of Words*, pp. 23-29, and *Living Together Around the World*, pp. 246-47.

Note: It is suggested that information about the Chinese ideographs not be pursued at this time. The children will have an opportunity to learn about them in a later section of the unit.

6. Refer to the list "Primitive People" the children made in experience 11 of Main Idea I. Did they include the lack of a written language as one indication of a primitive society? If not, let them add it to the list. (*Fixing the new learning. Reinforcement*)

7. Let some of the children learn some of the folk tales told in *Thirty-one Brothers and Sisters*, such as those told on pages 43, 107-08, 187. (*New experience to reinforce the new idea of learning*)

8. Select a few African folk tales to read to the children. Discuss what these stories are about and what they teach.

Note: Select stories that teach about a variety of things, such as history, important people, bravery, etc. (Extension of no. 7.) Suggested references:
> *Tales from the Story Hat*
> *The Illustrated Book about Africa*
> *Wembi, the Singer of Stories*

9. Let the children illustrate their favorite African folk tale and make a bulletin-board arrangement of selected illustrations. (One group made shoe-box dioramas of their favorite tales.)

10. Help the children recall stories they know about important people, history, bravery, etc. Where did they learn them—storytellers, books, television, radio? (*Reinforcing*)

11. Discuss with the children why the storyteller is so important in primitive society. How many ways do we have of learning these same things? (*Generalizing the new idea of learning*)

12. Let the boys list the skills boys in primitive society need for hunting, e.g., running, creeping, throwing, etc.

Now let the children practice some of these physical skills on the playground and chart their improvement. (*Extension of the idea of learning via exploring a new experience*)

13. List on the chalkboard as many things primitive children need to learn as the children can recall, e.g.,

> songs and dances of their tribe
> how to play a drum
> folk tales of their people

Discuss where the primitive child learns these things. (*Generalizing—moving to new question*)

14. Let the children create some rhythms on their drums. (*Extension, optional*)

15. Small groups of children might enjoy creating some dances. Others can accompany them on their drums. (*Extension, optional*)

16. Teach the children some folk songs of primitive people. (*Extension, optional*) Suggested references:
> *Music Near and Far*—Mursell
> > Africa: "The Jog Trot," p. 86
> > > "The Magic Tom-Tom," p. 87
> > Tropical Islands: "South Sea Isle," p. 94
> > > "Fish Counting Song," p. 95

Optional experience: If the teacher has access to an album of African music, short selections of a variety of music should be played for the children, such as a hunting song, a riddle game, etc. Suggested references:
> *Music of Equatorial Africa* P402A
> or *Pygmies of the Ituri Forest* FE4457B
> or *Drums of the Yoruba of Nigeria* P441B
> (All are Ethnic Folkways Records)

17. Let the children list many of the skills they learn. Include both physical and academic skills, such as playing ball and spelling.

Discuss where the children learn these skills and why their parents feel they must have schools to teach some of them. (*Comparison. Introducing a new idea*)

18. Ask the children to write on "Should Girls Behave Differently from Boys?" List the ways boys and girls are asked to differ in their behavior.

Note: From these papers the teacher should gain some insight as to how the children feel about such adult expectancies. Their attitudes will guide some of the discussion of this section. (*Opening up attitudes. Diagnosis*)

19. Recall the restrictions placed on Nomusa's behavior? What things was she not supposed to do? Where did she learn these things? (*Preparation for contrast*)

20. Ask the children, "Why are girls and boys taught different things?" Follow through in discussion until children conclude that boys and girls do different things in life. All cultures have boy and girl roles, but these are learned differently. (*Introduction of a way of thinking about similarities and differences. Preparation for contrast*)

21. Summarize on the chalkboard (1) the things people learn, (2) how they learn them, (3) what sources they use, e.g.:

Things people learn	How they learn	Sources
to earn a living	watching	books
to read books	reading	libraries
how to behave	doing	churches
games	experimenting	people
etc.	etc.	etc.

Discuss the differences in learning in school with teachers, books, and experiments, and learning in families with people and imitating what they do. Bring out such differences as:

(1) where one can check information

(2) where one can learn more new things

(3) etc. (*Consolidation. Summary*)

22. Show FS 2544 *Equatorial Africa* (*Families of the World*). Recall with the children that the family is very important to primitive man (MP *Life of a Primitive People*).

Let the children list some of the family activities that take place at the home of a primitive, such as caring for children, eating, playing games, etc. Which of these activities are carried on in the children's own homes? (*New intake to introduce new content*)

23. Ask "Which activities of the family were carried on by men and boys?" "Which by women and girls?" (*Introduction of the idea of roles by reanalyzing already used material*)

24. Recall the number of wives shown in the above filmstrip (experience no. 22). Do all primitive men have the same number of wives? How many did Nomusa's father have? How do Zulus get their wives? (*Thirty-one Brothers and Sisters*, p. 39). (*Same as 24*)

25. Let each child make a diagram of his immediate family structure, e.g.:

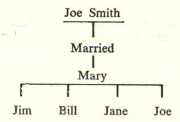

Now with the class plan a diagram of Nomusa's family structure:

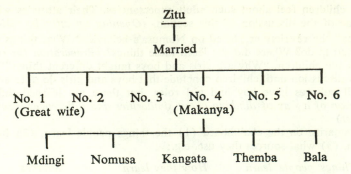

(Consolidation. Comparison. Generalization)

26. Let the children draw pictures of a variety of things a little primitive child might do for recreation.

> *Note:* Observe whether the children's pictures reflect the learning that there are many children to play with in the primitive family. Suggested references:
> *Fun Around the World,* pp. 54, 70-71
> FS *Wambo and Tawa of the Hot Lands*

Alternate experience: Some groups of children planned a tribal party such as the one held by Nomusa's tribe. They planned:

> games: *Thirty-one Brothers and Sisters,* pp. 49, 90-94
> dances: *Thirty-one Brothers and Sisters,* pp. 89, 91
> contests: *Thirty-one Brothers and Sisters,* pp. 79-80
> songs: *Music Near and Far,* pp. 86-87

(Consolidation. Expression in new form)

27. Have the children enter these pictures and their family structure diagram in their notebooks.

28. Let the children write on "How We Settle Disputes."

> *Note:* The purpose of this activity, which is really an opener, is to assess the range of thinking of the children. Is their functional knowledge limited to "fighting," or do they indicate "talking things over" and "recourse to laws or rules"? *(Introduction of a new idea)*

29. Have children list situations which might be taken to court for settlement, e.g., ownership of a bicycle, traffic violations, etc. *(Extension via analysis of experience)*

30. Recall the hunting episode from *Thirty-one Brothers and Sisters.* Who settled the ownership of animals killed on the hunt? Who decided on the punishment of a careless hunter? *(Comparison. Reanalysis of familiar material)*

31. Let the children discuss what might be good and what might be bad about having an all-powerful chief. *(Establishing orientation to contrasting rule)*

32. Who will be the next chief? *(Thirty-one Brothers and Sisters,* p. 72)

> *Note:* Do not let the children overgeneralize on the succession to the role of chief. All tribes do not automatically make the eldest son chief.

33. Let the children write on "How Nomusa's Father Showed He Was a Good Chief."

Examine these writings and help the children identify qualities, e.g., bravery, **fairness, etc.** List on chalkboard. *(Consolidation. Expression)*

34. Ask the children "What other rules regulated the lives of the primitive people studied?"

List these rules on the chalkboard. Ask the children to pick out the ones that

> tell what girls must and must not do
> tell what boys must and must not do
> prevent bad luck
> keep people safe

(*Extension*)

35. Discuss why rules would be necessary in a large family such as Nomusa's family. (*Establishing rationale*)

Conclusion

Have the children dramatize situations that show a sharp contrast between primitive and modern activities, such as

Recreation: A modern family going to a show
A primitive family telling of a hunt with songs, etc.

Education: Modern children learning to read at school
Primitive children listening to a storyteller

Law: A father recovering his stolen car in court
A chief telling his tribe who gets the slain animal

(*Expression. Consolidation*)

Develop a chart of big ideas that might be asked about people anywhere, but using ideas discovered in studying primitive people as a start, e.g.:

BIG IDEAS TO WATCH FOR

1. Is this a primitive culture?
2. What kind of family structure do they have?
3. Is there a reason for the kind of home they have?
4. Do the people have some kind of government?
5. Etc.

Note: Such a chart can be a guide in reading and viewing films through the rest of the unit.

(*Generalization. Establishing a way of thinking*)

A sequence such as shown above represents a way of making learning continuous and accumulative and thereby also more effective. Developing a step-by-step procedure toward the exercise of the higher mental functions is nothing more than a developmental plan to help the mind grasp more and to develop an autonomy in thinking. A marked heightening of the intellectual powers of sensitivity and productive thinking seems to be one result common to all experiences with such cumulative sequences with which the author is acquainted. This occurred even in cases where only a minimum of new teaching techniques was used and the change consisted chiefly of having experiences follow each other in a more dynamic and psychologically coherent order.

Several reasons may account for the phenomenon. This order corrects some of the misplaced uses of deductive thinking imbedded in the current methods, such as starting with definitions and then proceeding to illustrations and application, replacing it with an inductive-deductive sequence. This sequence also introduces learning activities designed for the development of the necessary feelings, sensitivities, and skills as a calculated part of the total learning and at the appropriate points. It is thus a *developmental plan for achieving multiple objectives.*

This type of sequence is also a calculated method for teaching for transfer. First, by approximating the method of discovery, this sequence will help students to internalize this method as a way of learning. Secondly, by explicitly encouraging the formulating of general ideas and perceptions, instead of allowing students to continually absorb predigested material, this sequence teaches students an approach which they can use to develop ideas in other situations. Third, by ending each learning sequence with tasks demanding application, reformulation, and synthesis, students get a direct practice in transfer of learning. (See the discussion of transfer in chapter 9.)

Finally, by permitting variation in approach to learning tasks through making available a variety of ways of learning, there is a greater possibility of offering each individual his optimum opportunity to be stimulated and challenged. Under these conditions heterogeneity ceases to be a handicap as it is under a system of a uniform teaching-learning process. With a wise use of group processes heterogeneity can even become an asset and a stimulant, especially if the focus of teaching is quite clear, and therefore open-ended assignments can be used without causing chaos.

Rhythm of learning activities

A few points about the rhythm of the various learning activities may be useful to know. One is the importance of a rhythm of intake and of organization, synthesis, and expression. The fault of a great many curriculum patterns is that either the one or the other type of mental activity is defectively developed. Too long a period of intake assimilation without integration and reorganization of concepts is apt to burden the memory, induce inhibition of new learning, and fail at internalization. Much expression and personal reaction without sufficient refreshment through new information and without the discipline of knowing accurately tends to develop somewhat careless use of creative tendencies. The extreme emphasis on creative expression, in activity and experience curricula seem to have that effect.

A balanced curriculum is one in which both phases of the total learning act are balanced, which offers opportunities both for mastery of knowledge, and for making it one's own—or "internalizing" it, as the expression now goes— and which requires disciplined knowing, analysis, and reflection.

The rhythm of building feelings and meanings is important also. Extension of feeling is the necessary foundation for understanding many ideas and concepts, particularly the ones that deal with culture, society, and human beings. One cannot understand the primitive culture as long as everything people in that culture do is rejected. A degree of identification is necessary which permits one to raise the persons in that group to a human dignity comparable to one's own.

Alternating individual work with work by the whole class and work in small groups is another type of rhythm. Some matters will require the attention of the entire class, such as experiences which involve development of the main ideas, general conclusions, and explorations of feelings. Some skill training, such as how to outline, is better done with the entire class, if for no other reason than for economy of time. But this training is more effective if offered after small groups of students have tried the skill and if the teacher knows what the common difficulties are. Sharing of small-group plans for research and reporting with the entire class helps also, because students can learn from each other how to improve their designs and to avoid pitfalls.

Class discussion can be used to break the closed tracks of thinking or of feeling that an individual builds for himself. Properly used, group discussion is a means for preventing these tracks from hardening. To use personal expression from the entire group in developing an idea or a pattern of feeling is to open wider possibilities than any individual can build for himself. Again, at the point of drawing the generalizations together, of forming the insights, the group can extend what the individuals have to offer. Hence a rhythm of activities which alternates individual and group work should go a long way to lift the level of learning for everyone.

Some work is done much more effectively individually. One cannot write or do certain kinds of research in groups. Some types of synthesis require individual work. Individuals can also pursue specific projects beyond the group, but care must be taken that these projects have some relationship to what the class is doing. Reports on unrelated topics or projects are a waste of time because the common base of understanding is insufficient for the class to learn from them.

Small groups or teams are perhaps more efficient in doing certain kinds of research, in planning specific reports and summarizing specific aspects of the study. Practice of skills is usually also more effective in small groups than alone. Often they are useful in preliminary canvassing of ideas and approaches to be shared with the entire class. Committee work is especially useful in extending the scope of coverage without extending the repetitive labor required for doing the original work on each sample.

Finally, it must be remembered that any transition in methods of learning requires learning of new skills by students as well as by teachers. It would be disastrous to depend on committees to study and present certain materials not covered by the class when the skills of the committee are so poor that the product is not worth listening to. Students cannot use multiple resources effectively if they only know how to read a chapter and to answer the questions from it. They cannot make a transition to developing generalizations from specific facts if the only thing they have learned is to recollect the facts. Students who are not used to working in a committee cannot undertake a long committee assignment without periodic training in skills that committee work involves. Nor can new skills be learned overnight or all at one time. They are better learned a step at a time. They are also learned more easily when the load of learning is not too heavy, as it is when new material and a new skill for mastering it are taught simultaneously. In climbing stairs one learns to balance on one foot while going upward with the other foot. Something similar should characterize learning new ideas and new skills. When teaching a new skill, it is wise to use known material. When teaching new ideas, use familiar skills.

Questions may be raised about the effect of such precise preplanning on the active involvement of students in planning—so cherished by some educators as an index of absence of teacher dominance. First, there is a difference between preplanning which disregards student interests and involvement and one which focuses on capturing it. If the diagnosis is built into the opening activities of the unit, and if the teachers understand the function of each learning experience, then student planning is necessary only for a clearer perspective or in order to give students experience in planning and possibly for greater motivation. It is likely that curriculum decisions based on good diagnostic evidence meet student interests and needs more adequately than do students' own unenlightened insights.

Also, the detailed preplanning need not prevent planning by the students, should this experience be important in any way. Usually it is a better part of wisdom to plan with students the dimensions of the topic and the questions to ask about each. Preplanning helps clarify the criteria by which to guide the students' planning. If students are guided by the same criteria and are induced to plan with thoughtful care, there is no reason to believe that they will not come out with the same type of selection, or at least one which serves an equivalent function. This type of replanning in class of what the teacher had planned is illustrated by Miss Elkins' choosing of groups of people to study in the unit on the American people and of questions to ask about each group. She describes her procedure as follows:

> I pointed out to the children that we could not possibly study all these groups. I would like them to help choose those we should concentrate on. I told them we would have to consider several things before we made our choice: which people were most numerous in America, which were most numerous in our city, which were most interesting to them, and which we could find material about.
>
> First of all, we discovered that we did not know which groups were largest in our city. One child volunteered to call the Chamber of Commerce for this information. We discovered that the four largest groups in order of size were Italian, Russian, Polish and Irish. The children were amazed that there were so many Russians. I pointed out that many people whom they classified as Jews were probably in this group; a number of them had come from Russia in the early 1900's.

We finally decided to include in our study all four of these groups. I wanted to eliminate the Russian or the Polish group because I felt their problems would be similar, but there were several Polish children in the group who would have none of that. The children who argued for the Russian group said they could do double duty by studying the Jews, too. We wanted to include members of a racial group other than white; we chose Negroes, although there was a bit of grumpiness about leaving out the Chinese and the Japanese. Finally, we wanted a group that was important in another section of the country. For this we chose the Spanish-speaking people of the United States.

This gave us six groups. The number was satisfactory. My class could comfortably be divided into six committees. I finally added Japanese-Americans as one group on which to practice using many references with the whole class before launching committee work [*Taba and Elkins, 1950, pp. 158-59*].

This was a cooperative enterprise in planning. The teacher and the students planned with the same basic understanding about the criteria, time limitations, and other essential considerations. Both understood the goals which the selections were to serve. The rationale for choices would have been defective had not the teacher done some preplanning and articulated the crucial considerations. In planning with students it is important to distinguish what they can do rationally and what they cannot so handle—otherwise a poor curriculum emerges in the name of democracy and freedom. While eighth graders may understand sampling once they have criteria, they could not compose the criteria. While students could plan how to attack a specific problem, they probably could not decide on the educationally appropriate sequence of learning activities for the unit.

Step Seven: Evaluating

As indicated in the preceding chapter, evaluation consists of determining the objectives, the diagnosis, or the establishment of baselines for learning and appraising progress and changes. Naturally all this is much more accurate and objective if the evaluative judgments are based on evidence.

Unavailability of objective tests for particular units or particular objectives is often a reason for not attempting evaluation at all. As the preceding chapter pointed out, there are many ways of securing fairly substantial data on student progress, even in the achievement of goals for which scarcely any objective measuring instruments are available. Much evaluation is actually continuous diagnosis, accompanied by comparison of results. For the evaluation of single units a continuous evaluation built into the very instructional procedures is perhaps wise. For example, if a sociometric test is used to determine the quality of interpersonal relations in the classroom at the beginning, and the data are then used to compose work groups, the assessment of the manner of working itself constitutes evidence of the progress of group relations. Again, the diagnosis of the initial reactions of the students to such stories as *Thirty-one Brothers and Sisters* can be compared with the reactions to the same story when used later in the unit. The initial diagnosis of the apperception of concepts of "primitive" need to be compared with the concepts expressed in the final discussion on the meaning of primitive. If tape recordings are used, an objective comparison of the levels of abstractions and comprehensiveness of ideas can be made. If the concepts developed in one unit are applied to new material in the next, this again is an occasion for noting the adequacy with which students carry on this process.

Some concluding activities should be largely for the purpose of appraisal of progress. Thus an assignment of letters to be written as if one were a Southern girl writing to her sweetheart in the Confederate army after a study of the Civil War would reveal the extent to which the southern feeling was understood.

Several informal devices were used to evaluate the outcomes of the unit on comparative communities. Perception of the relationship between ways of living and environmental conditions was tested by presenting the class with a series of stories describing some facet of environment or a way of life and asking them to write on what else would be true of that situation. "Pogo lives in a tent, herds sheep all day long. How would Pogo be educated?" Or the children were asked to explain certain phenomena, such as the conditions under which a tent would be a good place to live. To test retention of ideas, discussions of the concepts in the unit were conducted six months after the unit was ended and the tapes were analyzed for the adequacy of ideas expressed in comparison to similar discussions at the end of the unit. Creative writing was checked for evidence of transfer of ideas and insights from social studies. Records were kept of the number of books read. It was interesting to discover that the book used frequently in class (*Thirty-one Brothers and Sisters*) was one requested by several children for a Christmas present, a compliment which probably is not shared by any other "text." On a general appraisal of what the students liked about the school, social studies was listed most frequently.

Step Eight: Checking
for Balance and Sequence

After the outline for a unit is completed in writing, it is necessary to check the over-all consistency among its parts. Are the ideas pertinent to the topic? Does the content outline match the logic of the core ideas? Is the sampling of detail as sharp as it could be? Do the learning activities provide a genuine opportunity for the development of the content ideas? Do the activities provide for the achievement of all the objectives as well as they might? Does the sequence of content and of learning experiences flow? Is there proper cumulative progression? Is there a proper balance and alternation in the modes of learning: intake and synthesis and reformulation; reading, writing, oral work; research and analysis? Is there a variety in forms of expression, such as dramatization, creative writing, construction, painting?

By developing each segment of the unit in a separate step, it is quite possible to get off the track, to extend some aspects more than necessary and to have gaps in others. The examination of consistency and balance among the various elements of the unit—the objectives, the main ideas, the content outline, and the learning activities—is important for correcting such flaws. It is also necessary to re-examine the total plan in the light of all criteria for a good curriculum to see that there are no serious oversights or inconsistencies.

An evaluation of the total load for a given amount of available time is also needed. Usually at the planning stage both the content and learning activities tend to be more ambitiously projected than is practical. They need to be screened and combed to reduce the unit to a reasonable scope, for an appropriate developmental level for a given group of students and for proper transitions from one level to another to avoid overloading or too meager a progression. There may be a demand for skills for which there is no preparation, such as locating information in all kinds of sources after merely following pages in a text. Again, there may be too sharp a contrast between the degree of initiative and self-sufficiency expected and that which now exists. Or students who know only how to work individually on standard assignments may be required too abruptly to work in groups, which involves altogether different techniques.

A check is needed also as to whether the organization is sufficiently open-ended to provide alternatives both for content detail to be used and for ways of learning to allow for special needs. Some students may need an abundant opportunity just to open up and talk. Other groups may be beset with interpersonal difficulties. They may require considerable emphasis on and training in the ways and means of group work. This, of course, would have to be achieved at the cost of something else.

Finally, there are practical considerations. While it is important to conceive a unit of work first in the most ideal terms, its final shape should take due account of the limitations of a given school situation, of which there are always many. For example, needed materials may not be available, or teachers may lack the proper background for teaching certain things.

While a variety of materials may be needed, it is not wise to toss out the texts altogether. Texts have the disadvantage of offering too predigested a diet, of giving answers rather than raising questions, organizing thought rather than stimulating it, but they can be used as a resource. It is also important to point out that many ordinary sources, such as the students' own experiences, can be effective, provided they are subjected to rigorous analysis. Not all materials need to be accurate, adequate, and dependable, provided there is opportunity and skill to evaluate them. Undependable materials, when used critically rather than as something to absorb, afford lessons in sifting and evaluating, and in the end yield good ideas.

PART THREE

The
Design
of
the
Curriculum

Current Patterns of Curriculum Organization

Scope, sequence, continuity, and integration are the central problems of curriculum organization. The methods of achieving appropriate scope and of establishing desirable sequence, cumulative continuity, and integration of learning were discussed in the preceding chapter from the standpoint of organizing certain specific aspects of the curriculum, such as a course or a unit. Here they will be discussed as parts of a general framework or pattern in organizing the entire curriculum.

SOME PROBLEMS OF ORGANIZATION

Each pattern of curriculum organization adopts a certain idea of scope because it adopts certain centers of organization. Each also tends to adopt certain special criteria for sequence, continuity, and integration and therefore provides for these characteristics in a different manner. Furthermore, these characteristics of curriculum organization are related. The way one characteristic is provided for influences the method of providing for the next: the decisions on one level of organization determine the pattern on the next. For example, the decision made regarding the center or focus of individual units also determines the way in which the scope of the entire curriculum will be considered. If the basic units are organized in terms of subjects and topics, the coverage of content becomes the main way of determining the scope. If basic ideas and concepts are the important centers for organizing units, then the coverage of ideas and concepts becomes a criterion for scope and their cumulative extension becomes a part of the general design. If the objectives of curriculum experiences are central, then scope can include the range of objectives the curriculum pursues. One cannot apply the criterion of comprehensiveness of scope without considering how various areas of knowledge are related, and vice versa. These considerations represent multiple demands on organization, and while they can be applied either in a different order or simultaneously, it would be difficult to apply them independently of each other.

However, these problems are not always seen as equally important or as equivalent parts of the design, nor are all relationships seen equally well or used with equal consistency. For example, few curriculum designs give equal weight to scope of content covered and scope in intellectual powers, habits of mind, skills, and attitudes to be acquired by students. A broad scope of content may be accompanied by a narrow range of intellectual skills. And, in reverse, it is conceivably possible to develop a wide range of behaviors by studying content of a relatively narrow scope. As Sheffler puts it, the danger of applying only the first definition of scope is superficiality. The danger of applying only the second is ignorance. How to avoid both ignorance and superficiality is a practical problem of great consequence to curriculum organization (*1958, p. 472*).

Some curriculum theorists assume that the selection and organization of curriculum content are the chief theoretical problems and that the sequence is merely a matter of grade placement, subject to considerations of convenience only. Krug, for example, disposes of sequence by saying that the problem of placement is largely a matter of practical school arrangement rather than of intrinsic values, while scope is a matter of intrinsic value into which consideration of administrative feasibility should not enter (*1950, p. 133*). This position overlooks the importance of cumulative learning. In this scheme of thinking, decisions on sequence of learning are reduced to such questions as to whether to teach *Silas Marner* in the eighth or the ninth grade, and then adjusting what is expected of this reading to the level on which it is offered. Whether what is learned from *Silas Marner* represents a higher level of power than what was learned in the preceding piece of literature is presumably of no theoretical concern.

The questions of scope, sequence, and integration of learning experiences have received a good deal of attention in curriculum writing. Debates on and descriptions of the scope and sequence absorb more pages in curriculum texts than any other single topic on curriculum development. Ever since the departure from the traditional classical curriculum, the curriculum theorists have been wrestling with the issues of what should constitute the basis for determining what the curriculum should "cover" and in what order to do it. The problems of cumulative learning have received less attention and are only now coming into prominence.

A balanced treatment of all these problems of organization involves many perplexities, the solutions to which require a careful study and experimentation. Yet of all the major aspects of curriculum theory—determining the bases on which to make curriculum decisions, formulating objectives, developing coherent criteria for selecting learning experiences, and organizing them—the last has received the least systematic attention (*Tyler and Herrick, 1950, p. 59*). Decisions leading to changes in curriculum organization have been made largely by pressure, by hunches, or in terms of expediency instead of being based on clear-cut theoretical considerations or tested knowledge. The scope of the curriculum has been extended vastly without an adequate consideration of the consequences of this extension on sequence or cumulative learning. The order in which subjects are taught has been shifted. All this has been done without fundamental reconsideration of the assumptions underlying the classical curriculum. The result has been to make the curriculum, especially that of the high school, an unmanageable, overcrowded hodge-podge, an atomistic cafeteria table of offerings, and to play havoc with whatever sequence the traditional subjects represented and achieved.

The fact that these perplexities underlying curriculum change have not been studied adequately may account for the proliferation of "approaches" to curriculum making.* In effect, the state of curriculum theory can be compared to the state of biology in the pre-Darwin days, as described by Beck: a careful classificiation of all false starts, because no fundamental theoretical idea is present to pull it all together. The consequence of this difficulty (intricacies which make proof difficult) has been "the proliferation of countless schools of thought—those opinion-holding factions whose outward appearance in many cases suggests nothing quite so much as a frescoed mural depicting a struggle" (*Beek, 1957, p. 15*).

In the light of these difficulties it is interesting to examine some of the current patterns of curriculum organization, especially to determine what is inherent in these structures that either permits or prevents the fulfillment of the criteria for good curriculum, and how well these patterns solve the problems of organization.

THE SUBJECT ORGANIZATION

This is the oldest and still the prevailing form of organizing a curriculum, especially in the high school. It has its origin in the grand simplicity of the Seven Liberal Arts of the classical curriculum, all very broad in character. This classical simplicity of the sweep of knowledge can still be observed in the more modern statements of what the curriculum should cover. In speaking of the ends of education, Sidney Hook describes important powers and areas of knowledge as follows:

> Education should aim to develop students' capacities to write and speak clearly and effectively, to deal competently with number and figure, to think critically and constructively, to judge discriminately and observe carefully, to appreciate and respect personal and cultural differences, to enjoy with trained sensibility the worlds of art and music, and to enrich the imagination and deepen insight into the hearts of men by the study of literature, drama and poetry. . . .

* Smith, Stanley, and Shores describe from three to ten approaches to curriculum organization, depending on how one counts (1957, Part III).

[As to areas of knowledge, they need to acquire] an adequate knowledge . . . of the physical and biological world—of the forces that play upon and govern man's habitat, limit his place in nature, and determine the structure and behavior of his body and mind—[this primarily to make the student's everyday experience intelligible to him]. . . .

The second field of interest and subject matter is history and the social studies . . . [because there is] a universal need for all individuals to understand the society in which they live. . . . Whether or not wars begin in the minds of men, ideological differences may well determine whether these differences result in conflict. Educators disagree only in the relative emphasis to be placed on the distant past, the recent past, and the contemporary civilization. . . .

A third field of study that should be required of all students, particularly in the colleges, is the study of the great maps of life. The value judgments and commitments of the major philosophies and religions that have swayed multitudes, as well as the visions of solitary figures of deeper thought but lesser influence, bear directly upon some of the ideological conflicts of our age. . . . In the end, a decision with respect to the conflicting social philosophies involves a choice among the key moral values [*1959, pp. 7-10*].

Actually, the generalized division of subjects which so simply delineates the scope of education no longer exists. As specialization increases, so does the number of special subjects. The array of high-school subjects of today bears only a faint resemblance to the overarching trivium and quadrivium, even though that is still the pattern in the minds of many contemporary humanists. Further, many subjects now taught—such as problems of democracy and personal adjustment—represent many scientific disciplines.

One assumption of this organization is not only that specific subjects cover the important areas of social heritage, but also that the mastery of them takes care of the full scope of education. For this reason the accommodation to new developments, such as refinements of knowledge and new educational tasks, take the form of adding new subjects. This, naturally, leads to proliferation of subjects, until today in English alone fifty-one different subjects are offered (*Brink, 1955, pp. 372-77*).

Some of the recent recommendations attempt to reduce this conglomeration of subjects to its former cleaner, more classical proportions. For example, Conant (*1959, pp. 47-48, 57*) recommends the following program for the high school:

Program for Academically Talented	Program for All
4 years of English	4 years of English
3 years of social studies	3-4 years of social studies
4 years of mathematics	1 year of mathematics
3 years of science	1 year, at least, of science
4 years of foreign language	

The essence of subject organization is that it follows a logic of the pertinent discipline—that is, both the content and the learning experiences related to acquiring it are divided and organized by the logic of the respective subject areas. This "logic" is determined by the content specialist, and the chief function of the curriculum maker and of the teacher is to find ways for learning the content as organized. Because the mastery of subject matter is the central task, exposition tends to be the chief method of instruction and the textbook the chief source. However, at present the subject curriculum is accompanied by a diversity of methods of presentation developed throughout the first quarter of this century. The standards, including the criteria for evaluation, are set in terms of the amount of subject matter mastered.

Part of the philosophy of subject organization is that there is a hierarchy of priority among the subjects according to their value as mental disciplines. This idea is the basis for the distinction of the "hard" and the "soft" subjects. Not all subjects have the same quality and the same worth in an educational enterprise, even though they may be of some value to some individuals. It is from this vantage point that the "egalitarianism" or the "democracy" of subjects is being questioned.

The Rockefeller Report points out that: "In the great 'democracy of subject matters' which we have allowed to develop, it is only a moderate exaggeration to say that beyond the prescribed subjects (which take only about half the students' time) any subject has been considered as important as any other subject." The report, therefore, suggests a series of priority subjects and a modernization of these courses (*Rockefeller Brothers Fund, 1958, pp. 26-27*). The assumption that certain subjects have a special value as mental discipline by virtue of their content creates a tendency to equate "general education" with "required subjects." This assumption endows the subject organization with a certain compartmentalization and rigidity, especially in subjects which are a part of the presumably immutable college requirements (*Bossing, 1960, pp. 33-44*). This assumption also produces the first point of confusion in the arguments about ways of organizing content. The "subject curriculum" is defended on grounds that no longer exist—the virtues of generalized disciplines and the mental-discipline value of certain types of content. The question is not whether certain subjects have a built-in mental-discipline value, but whether there is "ascertainable content which facilitates other learning" (which was the issue over the classics) and whether this "content is logically central enough to apply to a wide range of problems" (*Sheffler, 1958, p. 470*).

The chief defense of the subject organization is that subjects constitute a logical and effective method of organizing new knowledge and therefore an effective method of learning it. By following organized bodies of subject matter, a student can build his store of knowledge more effectively and economically. Having such a stock of knowledge available makes it possible for individuals to use it when needed. This argument is based on the assumption that storing up organized knowledge is the way of preparing for its later use, an assumption refuted by the more recent data about learning. G. Miller maintains that the principal problem of human memory is not storage but retrieval (*1956*).

The more recent argument for the return to more compartmentalized subjects is that following subjects systematically provides disciplined knowledge and trains in special systems of thought; it is thus most appropriate for the development of intellectual powers. Even the nonspecialist must address his questions in terms of the language of a science whenever he is looking for generalizations from that science to help him with his problems. This capacity to cull from a discipline what is needed cannot be developed without a prolonged and systematic study of a subject *qua* subject (*Cronbach, 1955, pp. 48-51*).

There are also practical advantages. A curriculum organized by subjects is backed by long tradition, and many administrative features, such as accounting of programs and patterns of college entrance requirements, are tied up with it. Teachers are trained in subject areas, hence this organization is more easily planned and taught. Even the techniques of evaluating achievement are centered in subject areas.

Criticisms of the Subject Organization

There is and has been for a long time a host of criticisms of this organization. Some of these pertain to its pattern, but others are really addressed to the methods of teaching and the assumptions about the priority of subjects which have pervaded this method of organization. Perhaps the most long-standing criticism is addressed to the claim that the logical organization of subjects is also the best organization for learning. (See the discussion of the logical and psychological organization of learning in chapter 18, pp. 302-05.)

The questioning of the "logical" order of learning started first as a rebellion against the tight lockstep of sterile knowledge that the subjects represented in the 1920's, but it spread to a rejection of any type of organized content. This rebellion, or organization of dissent, as Cremin calls it (*1961, ch. 7*), was based at first on the semi-intuitive concern for individual development, for independent thinking, creativity, freedom, and the right of childhood to learn actively and to formulate its own thoughts and ideas instead of merely absorbing the social heritage—the platform of the progressive movement of the 1920's and 1930's.

This criticism of sterility of the "logically organized subjects" was not confined to people foreign to intellectual disciplines. Such writers as James Harvey Robinson also spoke out for humanizing knowledge:

> Both the textbooks and manuals used in formal teaching and the various popular presentations of scientific facts written for adults tend, almost without exception, to classify knowledge under generally accepted headings. They have a specious logic and orderliness which appeals to the academic mind.

They, therefore, suit the teachers fairly well, but unhappily do not inspire the learner.

When one has "gone through" a textbook and safely "passed" it, he rarely has any further use for it. This is not because he has really absorbed it and so need not refer to it again. On the contrary, it is associated with a process alien to his deeper and more permanent interests. And it is usually found by those who embark in adult education that textbooks make almost no appeal to grown-ups, who are free to express their distaste for them [*1926, p. 67*].

The criticisms were all the more violent because of insufficient distinction between the consequences of organizing the curriculum by subject and of the way these subjects were taught. Logically, the expository method of teaching and the organization of curriculum by subjects are not requisites of each other. Presumably the organization of learning experiences by subjects does not rule out active intellectual processes on the part of the students. Many good teachers have used subject organization to teach students to think, appreciate, and understand. It is in the teaching of these subjects by the expository or prescriptive methods that the limitations lie. It is evident that some needed modifications cannot be introduced without changing the single-discipline-subject basis of organization, but this does not mean that all difficulties stem from the organization alone. For example, although an extremely atomistic subject pattern limits the development of broad ideas and their life application, subjects with reasonable latitude permit the study of problems and formulation of basic ideas regarding these. However, these processes are harder to establish when: (a) the organization does not support them, (b) there is excessive concern for "covering," and (c) covering means acquiring specific facts. All these features tend to accompany the subject organization, and, chiefly because the criterion of choice is that of coverage and because there is insufficient understanding of the levels of knowledge and of the function of each, the criterion of learning is that of absorption.

As far as ideas about learning and teaching are concerned, research in child development and learning has supplied considerable factual support for these early criticisms. Learning by expository, prescriptive, and deductive methods does foster mental passivity, prevents transfer and fails to encourage active use of what is acquired. There are special psychological sequences to learning, which, if followed, increase its effectiveness. Motivation is found to be one of the chief factors in enhancing learning. And, as recent developments in studies of cognition and of mental functioning show, intelligence and intellectual productivity do involve active processing of information and organization of concepts and mental schemata, not just assimilation of organized knowledge.

Less has been discovered and said about the role of logical organization of content in learning, although there is by now clear evidence that a variety of logical organization is possible and that there is more than one way of acquiring disciplined knowledge and thinking. Moreover, it is quite possible that each school subject can foster a greater range of "habits of mind" than has been suspected. As Sheffler points out, the ability to develop empathy is not restricted to literature (*1958, p. 471*). Other human sciences also provide this opportunity. Nor is the development of logical thinking the monopoly of mathematics, nor scientific method a monopoly of science.

Questions can be raised also about the extent to which a prolonged pursuit of a specialized subject is the necessary condition for acquiring disciplined thinking characteristic of that subject. No doubt the major disciplines exemplify certain unique ways of thinking and unique ways of viewing the world. Science, history, and literature each represent a different key to the world around us. But the question is whether the mastery of these keys is bound up in the consecutive coverage of the entire field or whether "systematic" understanding can come about in some other manner, such as by an intensive study of selected aspects of a discipline or an intensive pursuit of selected basic ideas and principles. At any rate, the question of what it means to be literate in an area is not yet conclusively answered.

However, because of the sterility and inflexibility that has tended to be associated with the subject organization, there has been insufficient experimentation with ways in which to combine the logical organization of content with the psychological patterning of learning without jeopardy either to the psychological criteria of learning or to the logical criteria of disciplined knowledge. Only recently there has been a "breakthrough" in this tradition, but this break has also brought with it a tendency to eliminate the traditional compartmentalized divisions within a larger discipline. The developing mathematics curriculum, in fact, tends to eliminate the distinctions between the "subjects" of arithmetic, geometry, and algebra. (See the discussion of the new mathematics curricula, chapter 12, pp. 177-78, 180-82.)

Atomization of knowledge has been another charge against subject organization. As the specialization of knowledge increased and the demands for additional subjects for various practical and social purposes grew, increasing decimation of knowledge took place. As the special content areas multiplied and the time for each decreased, so also increased the learning of unrelated information, too much of which was forgotten. Because concepts and facts were learned in strict subject-matter compartments, there was little opportunity to relate this knowledge to anything that might have given it perspective and meaning—to consider its utility beyond passing classroom lessons or tests, to enlarge and enrich ideas acquired in one field by principles and facts from another. Each subject thus became a dead-end track. Subjects were "polished off" when courses ended. Closing the book meant closing the matter. Fragmentation of learning decreased the possibility of transfer of learning. These understandable consequences of both the rigidity and the fragmentation of knowledge began to be seriously criticized.

Still another charge had to do with the detachment from life application and from the experiences and interest of students of much of what was learned, which weakened the motivational dynamic. Again, little is known exactly about the extent to which this detachment has been due to the method of teaching or to the method of organizing by subjects. Certainly most life problems are no respecters of subject-matter boundaries, and most practical judgments (in the sense of judgments involving either values or actions) cut across the boundaries of what we would call school subjects. Perhaps the more accurate judgment is that the subject approach to curriculum building and to teaching is less prone to consider students' experience as a starting point, or to cultivate the disposition and the skill to apply what is learned to life problems or even to problems not traditionally within the confines of the subject. Knowledge neither acquired nor put to use in close connection with life experiences can easily end, as the charge goes, as dead baggage. While at the time of these criticisms little was said about what life demanded, the conviction that it did not demand what the academic subjects provided was clear enough. This viewpoint is illustrated by the much quoted, salty passage from Whitehead:

> There is only one subject matter for education, and that is Life in all its manifestations. Instead of this single unity, we offer children—Algebra, from which nothing follows; Geometry, from which nothing follows; Science, from which nothing follows; History, from which nothing follows; a couple of Languages, never mastered; and lastly, most dreary of all, Literature, represented by plays of Shakespeare, with philological notes and short analyses of plot and character to be in substance committed to memory. Can such a list be said to represent Life, as it is known in the midst of the living of it? The best that can be said of it is that it is a rapid table of contents which a deity might run over in his mind while he was thinking of creating a world, and had not yet determined how to put it together [*1929, p. 11*].

It is interesting to note, however, that the very efforts to respond to life demands, such as introducing training in citizenship and in home and family living, and the teaching of such utilitarian skills as homemaking, also eventuated in new and separate subjects. This would suggest that the criticisms were addressed not so much to the idea of subjects, but to the nature of the content of these courses: their academic orientation, their expository and factual emphasis, and the limited conception of the nature of learning.

Perhaps the most serious criticism, and at the same time one which generated the most constructive thought, had to do with the limited scope of objectives of learning and the passive concept of learning. The earlier form of subject curriculum did overstress the learning of details; it paid little attention to the development of active thought processes; it failed to teach for transfer and for active connection between ideas and facts in different fields. Further, by divorcing the content of curriculum from the concerns of the learners at one point and from life application at the other end, a setting was created which was sterile for acquiring values and loyalties. In this setting it was difficult to use the facts to develop attitudes and values, let alone to devote direct attention to their development.

The criticisms that the ideas of what was to be learned through curriculum were limited and that learning was passive sharpened after the movement toward the clarification of behavioral objectives got under way, which in turn was possible after studies of child development had proceeded far enough to make it clear that the individual develops through acquiring a series of specific abilities or behaviors: ability to think, attitudes, sensitivities, and skills. This analysis of objectives threw new light on what active learning as an educative experience might be and how it might change the individual. This development in a sense put a floor under the emphasis on active learning. At least, it put at the disposal of curriculum makers a method of analyzing concretely the behavior and reactions to be cultivated and thereby made it possible for them to see more clearly both the advantages and the disadvantages of subject organization. It became increasingly clear that to learn to think logically, it is not enough to absorb logically organized subject matter. One has to think. To learn to be sensitive to people, values, and feelings, one needs to respond to situations which provoke feelings, and so on. This emphasis has made it clear that presenting content in a predigested form to be mastered by students neither effectively trains the mind nor promotes the achievement of any other educational objectives except of mastering information.

This new emphasis also accentuated the awareness of the limitations of highly compartmentalized subject matter. A strong suspicion was created that fragmented and compartmentalized content is an inadequate vehicle for the fullest development of intellectual powers, no matter what effort teachers make. Furthermore, as long as compartmentalized subject organization also pervades teacher training, it very likely imposes the same limitations on the teacher's mentality: the inability to put ideas together in a context different from that in which he himself learned them, the incapacity to identify important ideas or to classify them, the indisposition to search for wider application of the principles imbedded in a subject. In other words, the suspicion is expressed that both the students and teachers alike were "dwarfed" by this type of curriculum organization (*B. O. Smith, Stanley, and Shores, 1957, p. 245*).

Perhaps the most serious weakness of the traditional concept of subject organization is its assumption that a rigorous training in academic disciplines detached from social reality develops the abilities and skills most needed in meeting the demands of life problems. This weakness was pointed out in the earlier studies of the needs of youth in the 1930's. For example, evidence from the New York Regents' Inquiry into the character and cost of education led to a conclusion that: "A major reason for young people's lack of success in meeting out-of-school problems is that the secondary schools give them insufficient chance to master important abilities which the out-of-school world will require of them. What the schools actually teach they teach with reasonable effectiveness, but they fail entirely to teach many significant things which boys and girls are quite unlikely to learn except as the schools do teach them"

(*Spaulding, 1938, p. 149*). Recent manpower studies similarly suggest that characteristics other than high academic performance—values, motives, and skills in social perception—are important factors which among equally able people differentiate those who succeed in life from those who do not (*McClelland et al., 1953, pp. 248-49*).

Finally, it must be pointed out that the subjects themselves, *qua* subjects, have no built-in criterion of respective importance in providing knowledge essential to survival of the culture, or a strategic perspective, or training in mental capacities.

The foregoing suggests that determining the scope of education by accounting the scope of subjects in the program without knowledge of what these subjects contain or what learnings they entail is an extremely dubious enterprise. Nor can "subjects" per se constitute an adequate sequence. The very number and discontinuity of the special subjects prevents a rational accounting of the scope or the sequence. To say today that the scope of education is represented by the scope of subjects taken, when the subjects may represent any one of the three hundred offered in high school, in any order or combination, is so much nonsense.

In addition to being a poor way of accounting for scope of learning, subject organization tends to limit the scope of knowledge. If new areas of knowledge can be incorporated only by adding new subjects, the scope of new knowledge available at any time is seriously limited. The conventional subject organization simply does not provide enough room for new areas of knowledge, or even for the growing edges of new knowledge, because these do not fit into conventional slots and their number scarcely encourages adding them as new subjects.

In other words, the traditional subject organization has been found wanting on the score of all three basic questions regarding curriculum organization:

1. Subjects alone, *qua* subjects, do not provide a sufficiently adequate basis for developing a scope of well-rounded education, because in themselves they have no inherent criterion for either comprehensiveness or worth, and because subject organization discourages the pursuit of multiple objectives.

2. Subjects alone do not provide a sufficient basis for sequence, especially if they minimize understanding of and concern for analysis of what is learned or of the behavioral objectives.

3. Subject organization, conventionally pursued, practically prevents a pursuit of interrelated learning. It tends toward unnecessary compartmentalization and atomization of learning.

Currently there is again an emphasis on content, disciplined knowledge, and the lifting of the intellectual level by a return to compartmentalized subjects, even in the elementary schools. It is only to be hoped that at least some of the weaknesses noted in the earlier type of subject organization will not be repeated, and that the new emphasis on content will be implemented by a clearer understanding of the ways in which disciplined knowledge can be brought closer to the minds of children and youth.

THE BROAD FIELDS CURRICULUM

Out of the criticisms of the subject organization came a variety of other schemes for reorganizing the scope and sequence of curriculum. Each one of these, evidently, was addressed primarily to some one difficulty or weakness in curriculum design.

The broad fields curriculum is essentially an effort to overcome the compartmentalization and atomization of curriculum by combining several specific areas into larger fields. History, geography, and civics were combined into social studies. Reading, spelling, composition, and handwriting were combined into language arts. Specialized sciences yielded to such general fields as general science, life sciences, and physical sciences. Survey courses in social sciences, physical sciences, and humanities appeared on the college level.

The main advantage of a broad field organization is that it permits a greater integration of subject matter. It was assumed also that this approach to organization would facilitate a more functional organization of knowledge. Studying the conditions of all living things permitted a clearer emphasis on the common principles of environmental influences than was possible while progressing from amoeba to frogs and from there to the higher vertebrae, studying each in turn as an entity, including its specific environmental conditions. This organization also permits a broader coverage and allows the elimination of excessive factual detail which seemed necessary when the units of study were laid out in smaller segments. On the elementary level, especially, a greater flexibility in the choice of content became possible. On this level, also, the broad field approach has practically become a standard. In high schools it has developed only partially, although the influence of this form of organization may be greater than course titles indicate (*Saylor and Alexander, 1954, pp. 267-68*).

While the broad fields curriculum was supposed to disregard the logical fences that specialists have for convenience erected between their subjects, the hoped-for integration and unification of knowledge did not immediately materialize. In many instances the areas were broad in name only, because the reorganization was only formal and the experimentation with reorganizing the content to make it appropriate for integration quite superficial. Separate units on the subtopics of "condensed" courses replaced the separate subjects. The first courses in general science, for example, were composed of special sections of chemistry, physics, zoology, astronomy, and geology.

Only gradually, as thinking about content veered toward lining up essential principles and themes large enough to be a focus for a wider range of content, did the broad fields curriculum assume a coherent and more or less integrated character. This procedure has been especially employed in social sciences, where investigations of the generalizations in various fields provided material for the planning of larger themes, which then served as strands around which to weave the data of social sciences. Many of these themes, such as the Rise of Industrialism, Man's Control of Nature, etc., are now fairly characteristic both of the curriculum outlines and of the textbooks in social sciences. (See, for example, the generalizations brought together by *Billings, 1929; Meltzer, 1925;* and the use of the themes developed from these generalizations in the fourteen-volume social science series by *Rugg [1936 and 1937].* The current California state framework in social studies is also based on generalizations from several social sciences [*California State Department of Education, 1957*].)

An example of a broad field curriculum developed around the "fundamental biological concepts, with stress on ideas and on experimental approach of physiology and biology" is provided by the tentative "blue version" of the biology text of the Biological Science Curriculum Study. It begins with the "basis of life in the properties and organization of matter," moves from there to the "activities of these organizations as seen in the capture and use of energy," and from there to the "organ level" and the level of "the whole organism and populations."

SECTION ONE
1. The Biologist Looks at the World

SECTION TWO: *On Being Alive*
2. The Pattern of Life
3. The Origin of Life

SECTION THREE: *The Composition and Organization of Living Things*
4. Matter and Energy
5. Molecules of Living Organisms
6. Structure in Living Organisms

SECTION FOUR: *The Quest for Energy*
7. Introduction to Photosynthesis
8. Mechanism of Photosynthesis
9. Fermentation and Respiration

SECTION FIVE: *The Uses of Energy*
10. Ways of Using Energy
11. Exchanges of Energy Among Living Organisms

SECTION SIX: *Function and Organization of Man*
12. Introduction to the Study of Man
13. The Body Fluids
14. The Skeleton, Muscles and Skin
15. Nutrition, Excretion and Respiration
16. Integration and Response

SECTION SEVEN: *Genetics*
17. Introduction to Genetics
18. The Cellular and Chemical Bases of Heredity

19. Patterns of Heredity
20. The Chromosome Theory of Heredity
21. Genetic Variety
22. The Ways in which Genes Act
23. Genetics of Population

SECTION EIGHT: *Reproduction and Development*
24. Methods of Animal Reproduction
25. Comparisons of Reproductive Specializations in Animals
26. Events of Development
27. Explanations of Development

SECTION NINE: *Evolution*
28. Introduction: History of the Theory of Evolution
29. Mechanics of Evolution
30. Differences Among Organisms
31. Patterns of Evolutionary Change
32. Physiological Variations

SECTION TEN: *Biology—Known and Unknown*
33. Biology—Known and Unknown *

While the broad fields type of subject organization provides a more functional organization and a more significant content, the very attempt at broad coverage has its dangers. For example, it is possible that this treatment of knowledge fails to produce disciplined knowledge because insignificant details have been replaced by unintelligible generalizations. This is especially true of courses which aim at broad surveys and provide no specific, careful study of any one aspect of the content treated. Such courses are no more helpful in introducing the learner to special methods of thought, ways of using and relating evidence, and the special way of "asking the questions" than were the courses loaded down with unrelated specific facts.

A danger which must also be prevented is that the broad courses will turn into a passive overview of generalizations which offers little opportunity for active inquiry and active learning. It is possible that a condensation of a field, without an opportunity to pursue any part of it in depth, cultivates superficiality. Furthermore, without provision to examine some concepts and principles in sufficient detail to enable students to form their own generalizations, it is as easy to be tempted into "covering" generalizations and principles at the cost of developing active mental responses as it has been to "cover" the detailed facts of the specialized subject organization.

It must be noted that this danger lies not in the organization itself but in the manner of selecting what is put into such courses and in the manner of teaching them. With a clearer understanding of what is involved in teaching the essential ideas of a field, and with a more balanced provision for depth as well as breadth, the broad fields organization should go a long way toward correcting some of the weaknesses of the subject curriculum.

* This outline is from a preliminary edition (Biological Sciences Curriculum Study, 1960), which was revised in the subsequent year.

CURRICULUM BASED ON SOCIAL
PROCESSES AND LIFE FUNCTIONS

The advocates of this approach maintain that organizing the curriculum around the activities of mankind will not only bring about a needed unification of knowledge but will also permit such a curriculum to be of maximum value to students' day-by-day life, as well as to prepare them for participation in a culture. Essentially, this type of curriculum is an attempt to provide a patterned relationship between the content of the curriculum and life.

By making either the social functions, social processes (in some ways these are similar), or social problems the focus around which to organize the curriculum, it was thought possible to remedy several deficiencies, at least in the social studies curriculum.

The basic idea of the social processes or functions of life goes back to Herbert Spencer's five categories of significant types of activities which constitute the common features of life in any culture. The social-process approach to curriculum was originally formulated by Marshall and Goetz, who rather brilliantly defended this scheme. Some of Marshall's arguments still make sense, even though his classification of processes or functions has been superseded by more adequate ones. Marshall and Goetz describe the advantages of this approach as follows:

1. It is an aid to the development of meaning. A classification of social processes, or of areas of living, provides nuclei around which the countless complexities and details of society can be organized in a meaningful fashion. It provides larger units of experience and thus avoids narrow compartmentalization, makes possible better balance and truer perspective—with resultant gains in meaning.

2. It permits the use of experiential background which facilitates learning. Since there can be no pupil who has not had large, personal, and emotionally colored experience in group living, and since in every one of these groups many of the major processes of social living are manifested as truly as they are in adult groups, it follows that most of the great social processes are vividly in the experiential background of every pupil; they need only to be described and thrust into clear relief in order to be recognized and appreciated. The process approach, therefore, provides "a unique opportunity to utilize at every level of the school system an experiential background of a highly intimate and personal character. . . . In some substantial sense, this approach means a laboratory study of social living."

3. It permits a needed overview "of the data of social living of all times, places, and cultures; overview of the analyses of social living supplied by the various specialized study disciplines; overview of the goals and methods of social study curricula."

4. It provides clear-cut standards for curriculum making. "Through all the kaleidoscopic welter of varying techniques, institutions, and activities there run a few constants. . . . [Fundamental social processes] maintain an approximate identity through all forms of group living, and through diverse time periods and areas of the world. Because of this, and because they represent quite large and inclusive unities of experience, they may be thought of as *norms* of social practices and experiences.

"It follows that a social-process approach provides fairly objective standards for use in the organization and presentation of a social study curriculum. . . . It offers a way of clarifying the goals of our understandings which should be attained. . . . It furnishes a continuous check upon the spirit or outlook which should guide the presentation of subject matter. It gives the teacher a touchstone for determining the appropriate relative emphasis upon the maze of facts which make up so much of our current instructional materials."

5. It provides a dependable basis for social engineering (value orientation). The standards of scholarship imbedded in the traditional organization of subjects cause a strain when efforts at evaluation and solution are introduced.

"A social-process approach can make possible social engineering without sacrifice of the standards of scholarship, for it is purely scientific procedure to discover and describe the processes basic to all groups, past or present. . . . A pupil will look with new comprehension upon his familiar social setting when he realizes that the enduring basic processes of cultural living have in the past been performed by scores of institutions and devices which are no longer in existence; by others . . . [which still exist] in greatly changed form; by yet other scores which have not changed greatly. . . . He will be prepared for the appearance of new devices. He will realize that the future will re-sort and re-value all those he now cherishes. . . . Presumably his realization of the inevitability of change will be coupled with a modicum of understanding of the techniques of the control of change. . . .

"So also, a social-process approach fosters objectivity and dispassionate examination of the competence with which current institutions perform their functions, for it makes possible analysis of their contribution to underlying processes or norms of social living without resorting to indoctrination. . . . This means that controversial issues of the day are placed in a setting which permits objective treatment in terms of these norms of human experience without attempting categorically the single, universally 'correct' solution, so impossible to find."

Many topics, such as immigration, would assume richer meaning if placed in the large perspective of population adjustment in which it is related to folk wanderings, colonization, economic penetration, internal migration, and all the rest. Immigration lends itself excellently to analysis of the various motives behind population adjustment. The growth in flexibility of adjustment is clearly seen in the history of immigration. And again, the attempts to encourage, control, reduce, or prohibit immigration provide splendid occasions for the discussion of the role of conscious thought in the planning of population adjustment.

Finally, a social-process approach provides a comprehensive basis for the "comparative study of social living so helpful in the educational process. . . . Comparison of our institutions, for example, with those of primitive people or with those of contemporary groups is obviously more effective when all these institutions are seen in the perspective of underlying purpose and process" (*Marshall and Goetz, 1936, pp. 16-21, 104*).

Perhaps the best-known attempt to organize the curriculum around the processes of life was the Virginia State Curriculum program (*Virginia State Board of Education, 1934*). Eventually the nine areas of life were used as a basis for curriculum organization in several Southern states:

1. Protecting life and health
2. Getting a living
3. Making a home
4. Expressing religious impulses
5. Satisfying the desire for beauty
6. Securing education
7. Cooperating in social and civic action
8. Engaging in recreation
9. Improving material conditions [*Frederick and Farquear, 1937, pp. 672-79*].

There are other variants of search in the patterns of culture or of life for a unifying and perspective-giving focus in curriculum organization. Morrison, for example, used the scheme of the universal social institutions, such as Language, Mathematics, Science, Religion, Art, Health, Government, Commerce, and Industry (1940). These categories are rather abstract, and in their development the "common" is overstressed at the cost of the unique so that the life relationship of these institutions becomes rather tenuous.

The most recent effort to develop a design for scope and sequence based on activities of man is by Stratemeyer, Forkner, and McKim, who used persistent life situations as a scheme around which to group learning experiences and, hence, as the basis on which to decide what constitutes a rounded education and an acceptable sequence. These situations they classify as follows:

A. Situations Calling for Growth in Individual Capacities:
    1. Health
        a. Satisfying physiological needs
        b. Satisfying emotional and social needs
        c. Avoiding and caring for illness and injury
    2. Intellectual Power
        a. Making ideas clear
        b. Understanding the ideas of others
        c. Dealing with quantitative relationships
        d. Using effective methods of work

3. Responsibility for Moral Choices
   a. Determining the nature and extent of individual freedom
   b. Determining the responsibility to self and others
4. Aesthetic Expression and Appreciation
   a. Finding sources of aesthetic satisfaction in oneself
   b. Achieving aesthetic satisfaction through the environment

B. Situations Calling for Growth in Social Participation:
   1. Person-to-Person Relationships
      a. Establishing effective social relations with others
      b. Establishing effective working relations with others
   2. Group Membership
      a. Deciding when to join a group
      b. Participating as a group member
      c. Taking leadership responsibilities
   3. Intergroup Relationships
      a. Working with racial and religious groups
      b. Working with socio-economic groups
      c. Dealing with groups organized for specific action

C. Situations Calling for Growth in Ability to Deal with Environmental Factors and Forces:
   1. Natural Phenomena
      a. Dealing with physical phenomena
      b. Dealing with plant, animal and insect life
      c. Using physical and chemical forces
   2. Technological Phenomena
      a. Using technological resources
      b. Contributing to technological advance
   3. Economic-Social-Political Structures and Forces
      a. Earning a living
      b. Securing goods and services
      c. Providing for social welfare
      d. Molding public opinion
      e. Participating in national and local government [*1957, pp. 155-65*].

This last scheme seems to be an effort to correct one deficiency of the social-process approach, the disregard of the learner. In effect this approach combines the concepts of common activities, needs, and life situations with an awareness of the learner as a factor in curriculum design and uses both to find a unifying scheme. The sequence is usually determined by following either an ever widening circle in a geographic sense (the concentric circle)—such as home, community, the nation, the world—or proceeding from the understanding of the immediate experiences to a wider understanding and to action. For example, Stratemeyer, et al., suggest the following sequence of learning experiences for the life situation of "Making and Enforcing Laws": In early childhood—sharing in agreements necessary to effective living; in later childhood—finding what procedures are used in making laws; in youth—understanding the procedures by which laws are made; in adulthood—taking a responsible part in making and changing laws (*1947, p. 287*).

Several difficulties appeared in using the social-process approach. One was the fact that the concrete implementation of the scheme was not as careful as might have been necessary. Hence, the relationship of the content that was actually taught to the life functions it was supposed to elucidate was somewhat tenuous. Actually, one has an impression from the scope and sequence charts of these curricula that the scheme was superimposed on the existing curriculum with but minor adjustments. Thus, for example, it is hard to discover a relationship between earning a living as a thread, and such array of topics as "Going to School in Japan" (Gr. IV), "Trucking and Gardening in Mississippi" (Gr. V), and "Developing and Using Electricity" (Gr. VI). (*Saylor and Alexander, 1954, pp. 280-81.*)

This difficulty of finding one's way back to adequate content is common to all organizational schemes which depart markedly from the conventional subject organization. It springs from the fact that it was assumed that inventing the scheme was more difficult than selecting and organizing the content with which to implement it. By leaving the implementation to the teachers, there is no assurance either that the functioning curriculum represents the application of the scheme or that the life situations listed actually represent a developmental order of learning. No curriculum scheme which requires as fundamental a reorganization of approach, content, and learning experiences as does the social-process approach can be satisfactorily implemented by teachers who have had little fundamental training for doing so. It is no wonder, then, that one major criticism of these programs was their disregard for valid and significant content.

In some respects, the approach also failed in its central aim, the integration and unification of learning experiences. By using life activities as direct focuses for developing units a new discreteness appeared which was no less sharp than the discreteness observed in the subject curriculum. As Saylor and Alexander point out, this was corrected in the later applications of the scheme by using the various aspects of social living as guiding themes for selection of learning experiences rather than as organizing centers for the units (*1954, p. 285*). However, both these difficulties are probably not inherent in the nature of the scheme but the result of ineffective implementation.

THE ACTIVITY
OR EXPERIENCE CURRICULUM

The activity curriculum is another attempt to meet the criticism of the conventional subject curriculum. Its design is planned specifically to counteract the passivity and sterility of learning and the isolation from the needs and interests of children of the conventional curriculum. It has been especially widely used on the elementary level.

The rationale of the approach is approximately as follows: People learn only what they experience. Only that learning which is related to active purposes and is rooted in experience translates itself into behavior changes. Children learn best those things that are attached to solving actual problems, that help them in meeting real needs or that connect with some active interest. Learning in its true sense is an active transaction. To learn to think logically, one needs to do it—not only to absorb logical arguments or master logically arranged material. To pursue active learning the learner needs to engage in activities which are vital to him, in which he can pursue personal goals and satisfy personal needs. Learning occurs during the process of overcoming obstacles in reaching solutions or goals. Some hold, furthermore, that only by pursuing personal problems is it possible to activate motivation and effort and to experience purposeful activity.

Presumably one essential characteristic of the activity curriculum is the fact that children are encouraged to use problem-solving methods and to set their own tasks. Skills and knowledge are acquired as they are needed, and subject matter from many fields is used according to the requirements of the tasks. Thus, theoretically, the activity curriculum centers in student interests, encompasses in an integrated fashion content from any field, provides for a learning dynamic in a natural setting, and incorporates both the purposes for learning and the application of what is learned. Because reality situations and spontaneous interests play such an important role, preplanning is considered impossible and even undesirable. The ideal instruction is for well-prepared master teachers to help students to fashion study plans as ideas occur and as interests develop. This eliminates rigid scheduling. Overt activity—construction, painting, observing, manipulating—plays an important role. In some orthodox activity schools even discipline was completely self-directive and, presumably, all adult interference was eliminated.

The activity and experience programs have been practiced in a variety of degrees. At one extreme, found more frequently in theoretical statements than in actual practice, is the curriculum in which the centers of activity or of interest constitute both the scope and the sequence: the needs and interests of the children supply the main threads and act as selectors of what to study. The "felt" needs and interests of children, their impulses to investigate, experiment, and construct, fashion the curriculum. Its practical examples are far fewer than one would guess from the furor the approach has raised in the educational literature, and these are confined to the early part of this century.*

* Most noted among these were the Dewey Laboratory School at the University of Chicago (see Mayhew and Edwards, 1936); the University Elementary School and the University of Missouri (Meriam, 1920); the Ellsworth Collings experiment with the project method in the rural schools of MacDonald County, Missouri (Collings, 1923); and the Lincoln School at Teachers College, Columbia University (Tippett et al., 1927). For a description of the role of these schools, see Cremin, 1961, chs. 5 and 8.

More recently the experience curriculum has been represented by a mode of learning in which direct experience and spontaneous interests and activities are an aid rather than an outright organizing center for the development of units of learning, at least beyond kindergarten and first grade. While the experience curriculum follows interests and needs, decisions regarding the nature of needs and interests are based on general knowledge rather than on their immediate spontaneous expression. This knowledge is derived either from empirical experience, from shrewd guesses, or from actual studies. (A great deal of systematic research was done in the 1930's, especially during the Eight Year Study, on student interests in the junior and senior high schools.) These data are then classified into large areas which in turn became the focuses for curriculum. For example, the curriculum scheme developed in 1930 in California was based on the following classification of interest centers, presumably derived from studies of children:

> Home Life
> Natural World
> Local Community and Common Experiences of Children
> Food, its Production and Distribution
> Transportation and Communication
> Community Life in Earlier Times
> Community Life of Other Lands and Peoples
> Social Experiences [*Hockett, 1930, p. 59*].

It is interesting to note that these categories of interest still dominate the scope of sequence of the California State curriculum framework for the elementary school. The recent Los Angeles County course of study, based on this framework, proposed for each grade the following centers which are almost replicas of the earlier centers of interest:

KINDERGARTEN: *How We Live and Work Together*
    How We Live Together at Home
    How We Work Together at School
    What Our Neighborhood Is Like
    Workers Who Help Us at Home, at School, and in the Neighborhood
GRADE 1: *How Home, School, and Neighborhood Help Us Meet Our Needs*
    How the School Helps Meet Needs
    How the Family Helps Meet Needs
    What Our Neighborhood Is Like
    How Workers in Our Neighborhood Help Us Meet Our Needs
GRADE 2: *How People Live and Work in Our Neighborhood*
    How People Live in Our Neighborhood
    How People Provide for Their Needs for Food, Clothing, Shelter
    How People Meet Their Health and Safety Needs
GRADE 3: *How People in Communities Depend upon One Another*
    How People Work Together to Provide Services
    What Our Community Is Like
    How Our Community Is Related to Other Communities
    What Makes for Good Living in Our Community

GRADE 4: *How People Live in California*
How Ways of Living Differ in Various California Communities
How People in California Produce, Process, and Distribute Goods
How Life in California Continues to Change
What Our State Is Like Today

GRADE 5: *How People Live in Our Country*
Why People Are Moving to Our Region
How the Movement of People in Our Country Began
How Our Country Was Discovered and Settled
What Our Country Is Like Today

GRADE 6: *How People Live in the Western Hemisphere*
How Certain Countries in the Western Hemisphere Developed
How All Countries in the Western Hemisphere Are Interrelated
How the Western Hemisphere Is Related to the World

GRADE 7: *How People Live in the Eastern Hemisphere*
What the Eastern Hemisphere Is Like
How Life in Certain Countries of the Eastern Hemisphere Compares with Life
in Our Country
How All Countries of the World Are Interrelated

GRADE 8: *How Our Country Fosters the Democratic Way of Life*
How People Meet Their Needs through Participating in Groups
How Our American Heritage Continues to Grow
How Our Ways of Governing Compare with Other Ways of Governing [*Los
Angeles County Schools, 1955, pp. 86-87*].

This type of curriculum organization has been subject to a good deal of controversy and misunderstanding. As was pointed out, activities, interests, or experiences were used as centers of curriculum organization only in the early stages of the developing emphasis. More recently these aspects of learning have been practiced within the curriculum, whose main centers of organization are in some other terms. Much confusion is centered on the meaning and the role of experience and its relationship to organized knowledge. The various meanings of experience have not been adequately differentiated. It is a word to "swear by" for the proponents of the experience curriculum and for those who oppose it. Dewey's rather moderate statement that learning should be an experience and that "material should be within the experience of the students" has been distorted both by his followers and his critics.

Dewey's emphasis on experience was an argument against a premature pushing of symbolic materials ahead of the primary experience with the things and their relationships which these symbols represent (such as adding $2 + 2$ without understanding "twoness"), and without which symbols and abstractions have little meaning. This means that primary experience is a starting point for all further learning and a prerequisite for learning new ideas.

Raw experience in itself is "merely seen" or "merely had" and has no cognitive value. Only as it is composed into ideas does it acquire meaning. But acquiring meaning in that sense means making selective responses—paying attention to certain features, finding common ones, establishing relationships, applying to the experience a mode of thinking. A grocery store may be regarded as a supply of goods, as an example of a service to the community, or as a nuisance on a nice landscape. These are "frameworks" or systems of thought, each of which raises different questions about the grocery store, and each of which, therefore, requires that different facts be noted. For learning purposes, primary experiences can and should be organized and interpreted by the systems of thought that are appropriate to them. These systems of thought then determine which "details" about the grocery store are important and which are not.

The significance of the experience theory, then, is not only that learning begins with primary experience, but also that the learner must experience the operations by which these facts are compounded into ideas and concepts instead of only absorbing the conclusions of someone else's mental operations. In the heat of arguments about the "progressive" overtones of this theory, the second part of the definition was often lost. Only recently, under the impetus of Piaget, have studies of cognition and intelligence returned to his definition of the operation of intelligence and learning (*Piaget, 1950 and 1953; Hunt, 1961*).

Many of Dewey's followers reduced the definition of experience to overt activity, practical action, direct contact with objects, which in many cases became activity for activity's sake rather than a road to a meaningful symbolic experience.* This definition of experience and activity, combined with revolt against formalism and sterile and rigid content, caused some educators to become allergic to organized content of any sort except in the most immediate sense and in strict relationship to specific activities and problems.

The question of how the transformation of "random" direct experience into organized understanding takes place has never been properly asked or properly studied even by the most ardent advocates of the experience curriculum. Creating a learning sequence which would transform random experience into a mature, organized knowledge was even considered by many to be adult interference. The chief difficulty lay in not distinguishing the organization of subject matter which leads students to organize their own experience and knowledge from organizing it in the sense of predigesting it. Thus, neither Dewey's followers nor his critics, who relish in destroying the "fantasy of experience curriculum," bothered to take seriously the fact that Dewey saw overt experience as only the first step in the learning sequence and that "the next step is the progressive development of what is already experienced into a fuller and richer and also a more organized form, a form that gradually approximates that in which subject-matter is presented to the skilled, mature person" (*1938, pp. 87-89*).

Dewey insists that the orderly development toward organization of subject matter should receive proper attention, as the following quotation shows:

* See Wingo's discussion of activity as a basis for reflective thought (1950, pp. 91-99).

> It is a mistake to suppose that the principle of leading on of experience to something different is adequately satisfied simply by giving pupils some new experiences any more than it is by seeing to it that they have greater skill and ease in dealing with things with which they are already familiar. It is also essential that the new objects and events be related intellectually to those of earlier experiences, and this means that there be some advance made in conscious articulation of facts and ideas. It thus becomes the office of the educator to select those things within the range of existing experience that have the promise and potentiality of presenting new problems which by stimulating new ways of observation and judgment will expand the area of further experience. He must constantly regard what is already won not as a fixed possession but as an agency and instrumentality for opening new fields which make new demands upon existing powers of observation and of intelligent use of memory. Connectedness in growth must be his constant watchword [*1938, pp. 89-90*].

Dewey even points out that a fundamental weakness of progressive education is in its failure to systematically select and organize the intellectual subject matter.

> That up to the present time the weakest point in progressive schools is in the matter of selection and organization of intellectual subject-matter is, I think, inevitable under the circumstances. It is as inevitable as it is right and proper that they should break loose from the cut and dried material which formed the staple of the old education. In addition, the field of experience is very wide and it varies in its contents from place to place and from time to time. A single course of studies for all progressive schools is out of the question; it would mean abandoning the fundamental principle of connection with life-experiences. Moreover, progressive schools are new. They have had hardly more than a generation in which to develop. A certain amount of uncertainty and of laxity in choice and organization of subject-matter is, therefore, what was to be expected. It is no ground for fundamental criticism or complaint.
>
> It is a ground for legitimate criticism, however, when the ongoing movement of progressive education fails to recognize that the problem of selection and organization of subject-matter for study and learning is fundamental. Improvisation that takes advantage of special occasions prevents teaching and learning from being stereotyped and dead. But the basic material of study cannot be picked up in a cursory manner. Occasions which are not and cannot be foreseen are bound to arise wherever there is intellectual freedom. They should be utilized. But there is a decided difference between using them in the development of a continuous line of activity and trusting them to provide the chief material of learning [*1938, pp. 95-96*].

Both aspects of the problem, deciding which first-hand experiences constitute an appropriate introduction to learning and deciding how to transform these experiences into organized knowledge, became more difficult with each advance in the maturity of students, in the complexity of the content, and in the mental reactions to it. As the complexity of learning experience increases, it is increasingly more difficult to channel direct experience into intellectually *organized* knowledge. This difficulty probably explains why the principle of activity and experience has been explored only on a relatively unsophisticated level and why its application has been limited to overt activity. This failure to extend the concept of experience probably also accounts for the dichotomy between the primary curriculum, which is more or less centered in direct experience, and the curriculum in the upper grades and junior and senior high schools, with its almost complete disregard of the role of primary experience in developing abstract ideas.

It is obvious, then, that the principle of "experience" and activity is a criterion for determining a sequence of learning experiences and *not* of organizing content.

Several difficulties appeared in centering the curriculum exclusively on the interests or activities of children, even in primary school. First, interest categories replaced the organized content categories without the introduction of a new organization. Because of this, a curriculum developed on the basis of immediate interests was bound to leave huge gaps in the experience of the children. While this danger was minimized in the early experimental schools with master teachers, it became serious when the plan was taken over by public schools with less well-prepared teachers.

From this difficulty flows another, that it is difficult to build continuity from the centers of interests. In effect, the activity curriculum based on interests could build continuity only on the continuity of growth as a guide, and neither research on the developmental sequences of mental processes nor developmental tasks was sufficiently refined to stake out the principles and sequences for growing maturity (*Ausubel, 1959, pp. 245-47*).

Experimentation with the activity or experience design has made perhaps two lasting contributions to the curriculum. One is the recognition of the role of active learning through manipulation, expression, construction, and dramatization. This emphasis has left a permanent imprint on the nature of instruction in the elementary schools, even in curricula whose design has little resemblance to the interest centers. The second is the impetus it has given to studying child development, the principles and sequences of growth, and an effort to consider these sequences in the planning of the curriculum sequences.

This effect is perceptible in the curriculum outlines of today. Most curriculum guides are introduced by descriptions of the characteristics and sequences in child development, which are chiefly confined to describing the emotional, intellectual, and social characteristics of children by age levels. But the content outlines which follow such introductory statements still leave unanswered the question of how to connect these growth trends and needs with the placements of topics or learning activities. While these introductory statements might guide the teacher in the selection of teaching procedures to be used, they offer little guidance as to which areas of study are appropriate for which types of children, or the order in which to offer them.

There is practically no experimentation with an actual curriculum development in the light of these facts on developmental sequence. Learning experiences are still placed in terms of empirical guesses. Many reasons account for this lack of application. Sequential placement of learning activities by the developmental sequence in interests, in maturity, in thinking, and in capacity to handle problems is more complex than is placement of content by its difficulty. In the first place, since this idea is founded on a more ambitious concept of learning, there are many more factors to take into account than in the subject organization, which disregarded active learning and considered only a limited range of learning. Centuries of empirical experience, which the activity programs lack, also support the subject organization. In order to center on activities and to redistribute and reorganize the knowledge and the concepts to be acquired around these activities, it is necessary to know precisely which aspects of content or of ideas are manageable at which level. Research does not as yet give much help in this respect. The accounts of developmental sequences are concrete regarding only early childhood, but evaporate into vague generalities when describing older children and adolescents.

Further, the studies of developmental sequences in learning have been confined to such skill subjects as reading and arithmetic. Much research has been done to determine the age levels at which it is most appropriate to introduce various processes of arithmetic, but little is available regarding developmental sequences in such important matters as concept development, thinking, and affective reactions. Actually, no one knows what level of conceptualization students of any age would be capable of if the learning of concepts proceeded by properly planned sequences. Such research as is available was conducted under conditions which excluded teaching of concepts and experimentation with active learning in concept formation or in thinking. If we followed current research on the development of reasoning, there would be no place for cultivation of reasoning in primary grades. Yet empirical experience in the classrooms of American schools shows that children generalize, infer, and abstract at a fairly early age, provided they are helped to do so and that they are asked to think about matters in which they have had experience.

THE CORE CURRICULUM

The core curriculum was introduced with rather ambitious aims. This type of curriculum organization was supposed to develop integration, to serve the needs of students, and to promote active learning and significant relationship between life and learning. In this sense it was an epitome of all preceding designs.

The term "core" is used in several different ways. A large portion of curriculum patterns which are designated by this name represent nothing more than a method of distinguishing the portions of curriculum required of all students from those which have specialized functions or are elective. Alberty describes six different program designs as core programs, in the order of their deviation from conventional curriculum organization, as follows:

1. The core consists of a number of logically organized subjects or fields of knowledge each of which is taught independently.

Example: English, world history, and general science are required at the ninth-grade level. They are taught without any systematic attempt to show relationships.

2. The core consists of a number of logically organized subjects or fields of knowledge, some or all of which are correlated.

Example: American history and American literature are required of all twelfth-grade students. When the history teacher is dealing with the Civil War, the English teacher introduces the literature of that period.

3. The core consists of broad problems, units of work, or unifying themes which are chosen because they afford the means of teaching effectively the basic content of certain subjects or fields of knowledge. These subjects or fields retain their identity, but the content is selected and taught with special reference to the unit, theme, or problem.

Example: "Living in the Community" is selected as a unit of work for the tenth grade. The unit is then organized in terms of such subjects as science, art, and social studies and may be taught by specialists or by one teacher.

4. The core consists of a number of subjects or fields of knowledge which are unified or fused. Usually one subject or field (e.g., history) serves as the unifying center.

Example: American history and American literature in the eleventh grade are unified through a series of epochs, such as "The Colonial Period," "The Westward Movement," "The Industrial Revolution." The unification may be extended to include other fields, such as the arts, science, and mathematics.

5. The core consists of broad, preplanned problem areas, from which are selected learning experiences in terms of the psychological and societal needs, problems, and interests of students.

Example: A Unit on "Healthful Living," in the twelfth grade, stresses the health problems of the group and how they are related to the immediate and wider community. The unit is teacher-student planned, but in terms of a basic curriculum structure.

6. The core consists of broad units of work, or activities, planned by the teacher and the students in terms of needs as perceived by the group. No basic curriculum structure is set up.

Example: An eighth-grade group, under guidance of the teacher, decides to landscape the school grounds. The activity meets criteria decided upon by the group [*1953, pp. 119-20*].

Such a broad definition makes the core program practically synonymous with general education, which destroys the usefulness of the concept. Of the types described by Alberty, only types four to six represent a pattern of organization that differs from subject organization. In a great many cases the core program is not actually a curriculum design, but only a way of scheduling classes in larger blocks of time and with more than one teacher being assigned.

Because of this confusion about the meaning of the term there is also some confusion about the extent to which this pattern of organization is used. For example, two surveys conducted in the same year report variously that 57.3 and 31.4 per cent of junior high schools use core programs (*Faunce and Bossing, 1958, p. 69; Wright, 1958a and 1958b, pp. 1-2*). From the description of these programs, it is also evident that the central focus of these designs is largely social studies and that the other disciplines are in a contributing role.

The core programs have several important characteristics. First, they are attempts to promote a greater integration of learning by unifying subject matter. The actual methods of unification vary. Some programs employ systematic correlation of subject matter around themes drawn from the functions of living. This, for example, characterizes the program of the Wells Junior High School in Chicago, as described by Pierce. Materials and topics in social studies, language arts, and science are correlated around such themes as ethical and spiritual character, work, leisure, thought and its communication, health, social relationships, and economic consciousness (*1942, p. 47*). In others, contemporary problems or problems of living provide the main structure of organization. These problems may range from those dealing with orientation to school or personal problems to the problems of contemporary culture and problems of peace.* Still another variety of core programs is organized around the problems and needs of adolescents. One such program was used in the McKinley High School in Honolulu, Hawaii (*Carey, 1947*).

The use of these varieties of centers or focuses of organization means, of course, that the scope is accounted for in a variety of ways also. Usually there seem to be two ways of accounting for scope: what the centers of organization cover and what their balance is, as well as the coverage and the balance in the disciplines which are the part of the core program. Thus, a plan for a core or unified program may include units which are accounted for by topics treated in social studies, such as conservation, community, and responsible citizenship, and may list at the same time the language arts and skills which are being taught, such as use of correct English, principles of oral discussion, or development of writing techniques (*Saylor and Alexander, 1954, pp. 326-27*).

Another important characteristic of the core program, considered one of its main advantages, is its effort to relate the program to life problems and student interests. The most frequent claim of the proponents of this organiza-

---

* See Alberty (1953, pp. 128-29) for a fuller list of the problems used as centers in core programs. Saylor and Alexander (1954, pp. 322-37) have descriptions of patterns of core programs and the focuses for organization.

tion is that it focuses on problems which are real and have meaning for the students. Often this is accompanied by an effort to use problem-solving techniques, which this organization makes more possible than, for example, the subject organization.

In other words, the centers for organizing learning activities in core programs may be, and often are, any of the previously described: broad subject fields, unified or correlated subjects, social functions, life areas, or social or personal problems. The common features are the idea of cutting across subject matter lines and attention to student needs. Many core topics are organized around personal needs of students, and provisions for guidance are usually included in the instructional scheme. Student interests play a role in shaping these units, but they do not furnish the basis for organization. In many instances students are supposed to carry on an active role in selecting and organizing what to study.

Since the time is more flexible and resources of more than one subject are drawn upon, the core programs use broader units, more flexible and freer instructional procedures, and a greater variety of learning experiences than is possible in the subject curriculum. Emphasis is supposed to be on problem-solving methods and critical thinking and on the use of intellectual and academic skills in a meaningful context. The flexibility in arrangements of time and content also facilitates the adaptation of learning experiences to individual needs. The needs for specialization are presumably provided for as they arise, through individual projects or special courses. Skills are taught as needed.

Whatever the focus, whatever materials are used to develop the points of emphasis, at least the start of any learning unit can be made from some experiences familiar to the students. Hence, it is presumably possible to make a connection with the motivating forces, including individual differences and deviate experience. The emphasis on life problems also underscores the social role of the school, to help develop intelligent citizens who can manage the business of life with a modicum of maturity. This type of organization probably also makes it easier for teachers to consider more seriously the developmental sequence of growth and the behavioral objectives.

The core patterns of organizing curriculum also present many dangers and limitations, some connected with the theoretical conception of the design and others representing difficulties of effectively rearranging content around these new focuses. These difficulties may account for the slow spread of these programs despite their seemingly wide acceptance in curriculum literature.

Among the most criticized aspects of the core programs is their failure to offer significant and systematic knowledge. This weakness is caused by the same difficulty which has been typical of several other attempts to deviate radically from the subject organization—that is, insufficient attention to the implementation of the design. The typical implementation consists solely of providing a large block of time and assigning a group of teachers representing the subject areas drawn into the program. While the practice of bringing two or more specialized subjects together represents an improvement over the piecemeal subjects, such a new combination is effective only if a new organization is devised for it. This has not happened as fully and as well as might be expected. Too often the reorganization has been in the hands of persons who themselves are not well enough steeped in the respective disciplines to catch their essence.

Beyond the early grades, the organization of all learning experiences around new centers is more of a task than the proponents of the idea realize. To produce an organized scope of learning experiences, to marshal the kind of content and procedures which give body to such a program, is extremely difficult. The selections made so far by the school systems and by the text writers leave much to be desired in validity and coherence. Materials which are adequate in scope and represent a sound preparation for mature and disciplined understanding are rather scarce. Many outlines and much of the materials used lack intellectual challenge and perspective. They suggest a nondescript flavor of baby food. This is probably the case because the interdisciplinary generalizations are as yet not available, because the interdisciplinary approach to research and materials is as yet in its infancy.

Since the minds of the curriculum makers as well as of the teachers are also conditioned to specialized areas, the integrated thinking about life problems or any other constants which crosscut the current subject divisions is hard to come by. Cooperative thinking by a team of subject specialists is a possibility, but neither the skills nor the time allowances have made it possible to give such planning a real chance. Using content specialists as team members in planning the content presents difficulties also, because applying the knowledge of special fields to these new fields requires a reorientation of focus which the content specialists are not always willing or able to achieve. Nor are the planning procedures so far employed in curriculum making especially designed to overcome this difficulty.

Because of these difficulties, the attempts at integrating learning around broader themes or problems represent at best a patchwork of existing content: combining subjects instead of integrating ideas is the rule rather than the exception. In the process of combining subjects, one field often becomes dominant. Its principles determine the scope and sequence, thus violating the unique qualities and contributions of the "cooperating" fields. New relationships between fields are thus developed at the price of overlooking the essential principles or thought forms inherent in a discipline. This is true whether the particular form is a "unified course" or problem-centered organization.

In the latter, the discovery of problems with sufficient validity and scope for curriculum purposes is an additional difficulty. For example, a consumer unit may deal with the practical aspects of buying and neglect the economic aspects; or mass mediums may be studied apart from the entire problem of communication and opinion forming in our culture.

It is no wonder, then, that a great many core programs can be more accurately described by their time arrangements in scheduling than by the substance of the content or the type of content organization.

Finally, any new design, and among the curriculum patterns this is the newest, suffers in practice from lack of teachers competent to teach with the plan. Core programs or unified programs are especially subject to this difficulty because they require broad competence, while teachers, especially on the secondary level, have fairly specialized training in content areas. This lack, combined with the lack of adequate curriculum guides and materials, has made it difficult to test adequately whether or not this type of organization can serve the purposes it was designed to serve and at the same time provide disciplined thinking and significant and valid content. And the fact that all administrative arrangements, including accounting of credits and the requirements of transcripts for college, have remained in terms of separate subjects has not helped matters. In summary, one could say that the unified or core program design has not yet received a fair test.

A Conceptual Framework for Curriculum Design

Any enterprise as complex as curriculum develop·ment requires some kind of theoretical or conceptual framework of thinking to guide it. To be sure, theoretical considerations are, and have been, applied in making decisions about curriculum, and possibly more theoretical ideas are available than have been applied in practice. What is lacking is a coherent and consistent conceptual framework.

In recent literature there have been signs that this lack has been recognized. Evidently an awareness is growing that an advance in practice cannot continue without some advance in the consolidation of the theory of curriculum development. Bayles points out that today educational theory is "in the state of suspended animation," for until the early 1940's the whole twentieth century had witnessed a flood of energetically fostered proposals for improvement of the educational process, and since then, little of note seemingly has been added. He feels that to improve our theory we must do two things: clarify our thinking about democracy and what it means for keeping school, and reconsider our assumptions regarding the nature of learners and the learning process (*1959, p. 5*).

Caswell points out further that such curriculum theories as exist are beset with confusion, are at odds with each other, and seem to have relatively little effect on practice. There is failure to recognize clearly "the foundations upon which curriculum theory must rest" and a failure to draw from the basic sciences "a consistent body of basic principles, to interpret these principles as they apply to education, and to extend their application so that a clear guide to practice is provided." There is, further, too great a reliance on a particular principle in curriculum designs, as is illustrated by the juxtaposition of the child-centered and subject-centered basis for organizing curricula. Other principles are interpreted too narrowly, such as interpreting experience—the stuff of which curriculum is made—as being its own justification and therefore not subject to adult planning and guidance. Inappropriate theories are applied, as when theories which apply to general education are used in making decisions about vocational education (*1950, pp. 110-13*).

413

He further outlines the issues in curriculum which, though raised decades ago, are no nearer resolution or even clearer now than they were then, such as how to determine the values which should guide curriculum development, how curriculum is to be related to persistent problems of American life, and how one should go about developing curriculum (*Caswell, 1952, pp. 208-09*).

DEFICIENCIES IN THE RATIONALE OF CURRENT CURRICULUM DESIGNS

Some light may be thrown on the nature of needed conceptual framework by an examination of the deficiencies and gaps in the rationale of the current curriculum designs described in the preceding chapter. These designs and the rationale on which they seem to rest involve many difficulties and leave many gaps.

As the preceding chapters have demonstrated, one important characteristic of adequate curriculum development is that the decisions made in the course of planning rest on multiple criteria and consider a multiplicity of factors. In contrast, one common characteristic of the designs described in the preceding chapter is their tendency to center their rationale in some single criterion or principle. The controversy over the child-centered and the subject-centered curriculum is an illustration of such an elevation of a single principle into the sole foundation for the entire "approach" to curriculum. Since obviously a curriculum has to do with teaching something to somebody, it can be neither entirely content centered nor child centered in the sense of neglecting either the nature of the learner or the nature of content. A more or less fundamental choice between the two may be involved in decisions as to whether the interests and activities of children or the content topics shall serve as organizing centers for teaching-learning units. But even here, considerations other than mere juxtaposition of children's needs and interests and the logic of content enter.

A similar tendency is illustrated by the way the principle of integration of knowledge is applied in discussions of the core curriculum. According to theoretical statements, the chief principle of the core curriculum is supposed to be integration of knowledge. Yet trouble brews if this principle overrides the consideration of the unique requirements of the various areas of knowledge and if integration is effected without sufficiently considering what the appropriate threads of integration might be and what aspects of the content of various disciplines can appropriately be brought together.

This tendency to rationalize a curriculum pattern in terms of a single principle, at least in theoretical statements, while overlooking the relevance of other equally important considerations is in effect a gross oversimplification which has many undesirable consequences. One is a kind of myopia in developing and implementing curriculum designs. The patterns for the scope and sequence appropriate for social studies have been discussed as if they were equally appropriate for all subjects. The designs which have been tested only on the elementary level have been extended into high school without testing their appropriateness on that level.

This limitation in rationale has also produced a somewhat doctrinaire position regarding the particular patterns of organizing curricula and rigid concepts of what each pattern entails. These doctrinaire positions resulted not only in a proliferation of "approaches," but each position also tended to rule out, or to allocate an incidental role to, certain types of learning experiences which make perfectly good sense, such as excluding the possibility of studying organized subject matter in some "approaches" and of creative activities or the pursuit of projects animated by individual interests in others. It is intertesting to note that while the practice has moved away from these doctrinaire positions to a more balanced perspective regarding the role of the learner and of the subject matter, the argument persists. Except for the fact that the shoe is on the other foot, the arguments in the 1930's, when the battle was to introduce sufficient consideration of the learners, are duplicated today, when the battle is to reintroduce disciplined content. The problem of balance is unresolved. Only the stakes have changed.

The writer argued for a policy of balance between the requirements of content and of the psychological demands thirty years ago:

> The conflict of policies regarding the central principles of the organization of educational processes and content is a comparatively old one. The discussion of it has taken the form of a conflict between the psychological and the logical organization of the subject matter of instruction.
>
> The general position of those standing for the priority of the logic of the subject matter as a basis for organization of educational materials . . . is that there are binding principles of thought, leading ideas and compelling generalizing concepts . . . which are . . . necessary for a consistent and intelligent way of looking at the phenomena of life. . . . To a certain extent this position is a correct one, especially when viewed in the light of the present prevailing attempts toward the psychological organization. The present practice of using the individual as . . . unit, around which and according to the demands of which, the educational process is to be organized are frequently based on a narrow and one-sided concept of that individual [*Taba, 1932, pp. 224-25*].

Another series of problems and difficulties is introduced by the confusion about which principles or considerations apply at which points of curriculum development. Such principles and criteria as have been articulated are often misapplied: considerations which are relevant to selection are applied to organization, principles relevant to organization of learning experiences are applied to organization of content, and vice versa. While the basic principles and criteria for good curricula apply in some measure across all decisions regarding curricula, certain considerations are logically central to certain aspects of it. Different criteria are logically central to making decisions about objectives, the selection and organization of content, and the selection and organization of learning experiences. In selecting content, for example, its validity and significance are the primary criteria, while the principles of learning are more central to organizing it. The principle of using primary experience is misapplied when primary experience is used as a center for organizing content rather than as a first step in a cumulative learning sequence.

The "doctrine" of interest has been subject to the same type of misapplication. The principle that the curriculum should meet the interests of the students is appropriate in selecting from a larger body of material a specific sample of content detail which is equally potent in elucidating the basic ideas. It is misapplied when used as a criterion for selecting the entire range of content and, worse still, as a center for organizing content on all levels of schooling.

A clearer analysis of the points at which curriculum decisions are being made, and of the principles and considerations that apply to each, should open a way to a more comprehensive approach to curriculum development as well as to identifying more precisely the fundamental differences and agreements among the various theories. It is possible, for example, that there is a genuine difference between educators who insist that intellectual development is the exclusive center to educational effort and those who maintain that it is only one of the many powers to be developed and that cognitive aspects of development in turn depend on other facets of growth. But it is impossible to discover what the difference is as long as one group defines intellectual power as erudition and another as capacity to handle cognitive processes, and as long as both positions mask additional assumptions behind the façade of their chief point of argument, such as assumptions regarding the ways in which intellectual powers develop, whether they are an automatic by-product of the mastery of "disciplines" or require special provisions for ways of learning them. One cannot get far in arguments about the importance of integrated learning as against the virtues of pursuing isolated disciplines as long as there is no clarity about precisely what is being integrated or what the integrating threads are, or can be.

But perhaps the greatest deficiency in the current curriculum theories are the gaps they leave in conceptualizing curriculum development and hence also in implementing it. In most of the designs some important components are missing; the relationships between these elements are not clearly enough stated, or there are no provisions for moving from one point to another. Goodlad illustrates this deficiency by analyzing a document pertaining to curriculum development as follows:

> The document identifies the basic values of democracy and the functions of the school in a democratic society. Apparently, the functions of the school should in some way follow or depend on the values presumed for life in democracy. But the nature of that relationship and the method of deriving

school functions from societal values are not made clear. The document goes on to list the demands imposed by a democratic society and to pose goals for education. Of necessity value-judgments are involved in moving from an analysis of society to an elaboration of desirable educational objectives. Do we educate individuals to adjust to a particular characteristic of society, or do we educate individuals to revise society? Value-theory is involved, but just how and where, the document does not make clear.

Next, the report examines the needs of the individual. The purpose of the examination is to set up methods of teaching. Yet, in the introduction to the section, the authors state that instructional goals are clarified by examining characteristics of the human personality. If the principle is sound, should not the school examine learners to determine what, as well as how to teach? Should not an analysis of learners precede as well as follow the stating of educational objectives? And should not the purpose of examining learners before the formulation of objectives be quite different from the purpose of examining learners after the objectives have been formulated? [*1958, p. 393*].

As was indicated in the chapter on evaluation, the lack of relationship among objectives, the content outline, and the evaluation program has often been noted. Objectives tend to be more ambitious than the provisions for learning experience warrant. Evidently, the conceptual framework of the newer curriculum designs does not provide adequately for moving from objectives to content or the instructional pattern and from both to the methods and the manner of evaluation.

While the newer curriculum patterns extended vastly the concept of desirable objectives, they failed to provide corresponding ways of translating these objectives into appropriate learning experiences. No theoretical distinctions regarding the types of learning experiences required by various types of objectives are made to differentiate the instructional techniques necessary to implement these objectives. The result is that the curriculum guides based on these patterns present somewhat arbitrary and unrealistic expectations. They ask teachers to achieve objectives but provide no foundation for making the necessary practical provisions. No matter how high-sounding the claims for the importance of such objectives as critical thinking and democratic loyalties are, one cannot regard them as anything but pious hopes as long as there is no clear plan for appropriate learning experiences.

A theoretical vacuum seems also to exist between the requirements of a curriculum design and the administrative arrangements necessary to its effective implementation. To be effective, a given curriculum plan, such as a broad field curriculum or a core program, requires a certain type of scheduling, certain instructional materials, and certain ways of using staff talents. One can kill a potentially promising curriculum design by poor scheduling, insufficient materials, inappropriate grouping of students, or an ineffective staff organization. The potentialities of the core curriculum have never been really explored because the conditions under which it was tried seldom lived up to requirements for its success. Neither the staffing nor the accounting for credits accommodated this curriculum pattern. When a transition was made from the rigidly prescribed curriculum sequence to greater freedom for classroom teachers to select and organize the content of the curriculum, there was no corresponding arrangement for communication among teachers to ensure proper sequence and to avoid repetition and overlapping. The current experiments in mass mediums fail to consider such consequences of a shift from small-group to large-group organization as the elimination of the nurturing contacts in small groups. These omissions not only reflect deficiencies of implementation, they also reflect gaps in theoretical thinking and incomplete conceptualization of the relationships among the total outcomes, curriculum, learning, and the conditions under which learning takes place. Therefore, it is possible to propose shifts in grouping and in group sizes without considering any other effects except those on achievement of information.*

The designs described in Chapter 21 also show too meager a consideration of the nature and pacing of the transition from knowledge organized around children's experience to a systematically organized study of a discipline or an area as the maturity of students increases. As understanding matures, a greater emphasis on systematic study is both possible and needed. There is little discussion in curriculum treatises of just how and when this transformation takes place, with the result that, in some designs, the systematic study is rather generally shunned and, in others, specialized subjects may be pushed too far down the age level.

To this array of difficulties one must add the difficulties arising from insufficient analysis of the elements themselves. The treatment of content is one example. The difficulties which flow from treating school subjects and their content without differentiation of the levels of knowledge has already been dealt with (chapter 12). This unanalytic attitude toward content could be summarized by paraphrasing the famous phrase of Gertrude Stein: "A subject is a subject is a subject." This view of school subjects creates an illusory conflict over the functions of content which vanishes when confusion is cleared by examining the different levels of knowledge, and the special function which each serves in the educational process. Such an analysis should also make it possible to differentiate the role that each of these levels plays in organizing content. While subjects conceived and taught as collections of facts might be poor centers of organization, the basic ideas of a discipline, or of a series of disciplines, could be so used without the dangers and difficulties pointed out about the subject of organization. The same difficulty appears in determining the scope and sequence. If the content is seen as consisting of (a) specific facts, (b) basic principles or ideas, and (c) overarching concepts and systems of thinking, the decisions about what to use for determining the scope, sequence, and integration would be less subject to confusion.

All of the above are traps in curriculum thinking and planning which arise out of ineffective or insufficient conceptualization and in turn contribute to

---

* Ward traces the deficiencies in the program for the gifted to the shortcomings in theoretical thinking (1961).

unscientific attitudes toward curriculum development. The doctrinaire positions lead the protagonists of a particular design to defend that design as a credo or a doctrine instead of as a hypothesis and a possibility. Consequently, the problems of curriculum design are argued in an atmosphere of partisanship, and ideas are debated in terms of protagonist and antagonist positions and not in a climate of honest scientific inquiry. Issues which should be subject to scientific research or to the test of experimental evidence are treated as matters of personal beliefs. One "school" believes in correlation of subject matter, and the next one thinks it is a degradation of education. This doctrinaire approach has prevented the systematizing of the perception of the entire complex of factors that need to be considered in curriculum development. Some essential considerations are played down because they do not support the basic beliefs and preferences, and others assume a more dominating role than their contribution warrants.

Under these conditions, it is not surprising that active research and experimentation in the area of comprehensive curriculum development is as meager as it is, and that changes in curricula are introduced on a wide scale without sufficient logical analysis or testing under experimental conditions prior to their adoption. Witness the current avalanche of special programs for the gifted which are being introduced without even settling what the meaning of "gifted" is, or where one draws the line between those who are and those who are not, let alone considering the possible psychological and social consequences of this move.* By settling on the administrative devices of grouping and acceleration as a means for dealing with heterogeneity in ability, the schools are refusing to meet the problems of heterogeneity by making qualitative changes in the curriculum, such as an open-ended curriculum organization which offers more varied opportunities for dealing with the fundamentals of curriculum on several levels of depth.

This doctrinaire and unscientific attitude is also reflected in the manner in which changes are made. When some one aspect of an approach is discredited or found wanting, the entire scheme is discarded in favor of something different, rather than retaining what is useful and correcting what was faulty. This happened when the atomistic and sterile "subject" curriculum provoked an opposition to any planned content in the early progressive movement. It occurred in the reaction to the Herbartian order of five steps in learning, which no doubt were sterile when they were first introduced in this country but which make a good deal of sense when underpinned with a more dynamic interpretation of learning. And today, in the name of excellence, we are supposed to go "back to the fundamentals," to the "hard subjects," in spite of what has been learned in the meanwhile about the role of experience, motiva-

* Getzels and Jackson point out, for example, that the current concept of giftedness tends to be limited not only exclusively to cognitive qualities but even simply to a high IQ (1961, p. 2).

tion, and active inquiry in enhancing learning and in producing intellectual excellence. Whether we want to produce scientists and mathematicians or simply responsible human beings and enlightened citizens for democracy, the curriculum still needs to be child-centered in the sense that a productive learning sequence cannot be constructed apart from starting from where the child is and proceeding developmentally. An effective curriculum still needs to make connection with individual needs and concerns and to build bridges from here to there.

A scientific attitude toward curriculum making should at least cultivate a greater respect for the task and a greater humility in the face of it, to prevent such thoughtless and wild swings of the pendulum as seem to be characteristic of American curriculum development. It would also require a greater investment in careful study and research than is now common in curriculum development or change.

THE FUNCTIONS
OF A CONCEPTUAL FRAMEWORK
FOR CURRICULUM DESIGN

Generally speaking, a conceptual system for the curriculum or a theory of curriculum is a way of organizing thinking about all matters that are important to curriculum development: what the curriculum consists of, what its important elements are, how these are chosen and organized, what the sources of curriculum decisions are, and how the information and criteria from these sources are translated into curriculum decisions.

Only few scattered remarks are available in the curriculum literature about the functions of a curriculum theory or a conceptual framework in designing curriculum. Herrick uses the term "curriculum theory" and suggests three chief functions of such a theory "(1) to identify the critical issues or points in curriculum development, and the generalizations which underlie them; (2) to point up the relationships which exist between these critical points and their supporting structure; and (3) to suggest the approaches that need to be made to resolve these critical issues" (*Tyler and Herrick, 1950, p. 1*). Goodlad uses the term "conceptual system" and indicates that this system must identify the methods of inquiry by which to answer some basic questions about curriculum development (*1958, pp. 391-96*). This volume has identified certain points at which crucial curriculum decisions are made, such as the choice of objectives, the selection and organization of content and of learning experiences, and evaluation. A theory should help to identify what these points of crucial decisions are and the bases on which these decisions are made.

To establish a systematic set of issues with which a theory of curriculum should deal might be as yet premature. However, if one thinks of curriculum theory as a way of asking and answering questions about important issues in curriculum development, and of asking them systematically, the following list of questions might be suggested:

1. What is a curriculum; what does it include and what differences are there between the issues of a curriculum and those of a method of teaching?
2. What are the chief elements of the curriculum and what principles govern the decisions regarding their selection and the roles that they play in the total curriculum?
3. What should the relationships among these elements and their supporting principles be, and what criteria and principles apply in establishing these relationships?
4. What problems and issues are involved in organizing a curriculum and what criteria need to be applied in making decisions about the patterns and methods of organizing it?
5. What is the relationship of a curriculum pattern or a design to the practical and administrative conditions under which it functions?
6. What is the order of making curriculum decisions and how does one move from one to another?

Up to this point this book has dealt with these questions analytically. The introduction attempted a definition of the curriculum. Part I dealt with the sources and the bases for curriculum decisions. Part II analyzed the problems pertaining to the elements of curriculum, or the chief points at which decisions are made—the formulation of objectives, the selection and organization of content and of learning experiences, and the methods of diagnosis and evaluation—discussing also the principles and the criteria which should govern these processes.

But such an analysis does not yet make a design, nor answer all the questions pertaining to making one. These elements need to be organized into a pattern and on two different levels: (1) for a given classroom teaching unit, or for a given subject and (2) for the entire program. A pattern for organizing teaching-learning units was presented in chapter 20. This chapter deals with the problem of a design for the entire curriculum, and the issues and considerations which are pertinent to establishing such a design.

Curriculum design is a statement which identifies the elements of the curriculum, states what their relationships are to each other, and indicates the principles of organization and the requirements of that organization for the administrative conditions under which it is to operate. A design, of course, needs to be supported with and to make explicit a curriculum theory which establishes the sources to consider and the principles to apply. Both are needed in making consistent decisions about the curriculum.

THE ELEMENTS OF THE CURRICULUM

In order to develop a design for a curriculum it is necessary to identify its basic elements. Tyler, for example, points out that "it is important as a part of a comprehensive theory of organization to indicate just what kinds of elements will serve satisfactorily as organizing elements. And in a given curriculum it is important to identify the particular elements that shall be used" (*Herrick and Tyler, 1950, p. 64*).

But even among the meager statements about these elements, there is no consensus as to how to categorize them. Tyler identifies three, which seem to be pertinent mostly to establishing a sequence of learning experiences and are rather similar to the threads of integration discussed in chapter 18. These are the concepts which recur in the sequence of learning experiences, skills which take a long time to master, and values and ideas (*Herrick and Tyler, 1950, pp. 63-64*).

Perhaps one way of identifying these elements is to consider the major points about which decisions need to be made in the process of curriculum development, as described above (pp. 414-16), including such considerations as the principles of learning and ideas about the nature of learners and of knowledge. The points of these decisions—the aims and objectives, the content and learning experiences, and evaluation—then become macroscopic elements of the curriculum.

Most curriculum designs contain these elements, but many have them in defective balance, mostly because these elements are poorly identified or have an inadequate theoretical rationale. For example, the subject design usually pays relatively little attention to objectives, or defines them in too narrow a scope. The core curricula stress learning experiences but are often defective in describing their content, or else the scope of the content is defective. Many curriculum designs eventuate in a program which is inappropriate to the students for whom it is intended, either because it is based on an inadequate concept of the learning process or because a greater uniformity of learning is assumed than is warranted. Few curriculum designs postulate and provide for the upper and lower limits in achieving objectives according to student backgrounds or for different qualities of depth according to differences in ability. Such defects in design usually pose difficulties in implementation.

An analysis of the curriculum designs described either in books on curriculum or in curriculum guides also reveals that, while each involves something of all elements, these elements are inadequately related to the stated central emphasis. For example, an integrated curriculum will usually contain some provisions for specialized knowledge. An experience curriculum usually includes organized subject-matter content, and a subject curriculum will employ first-hand experiences. Either these "extras" are bootlegged, or else what are supposed to be black and white differences in the central emphasis are nothing more than an accentuation of one element over others. The main difference among these designs lies more in how the various elements are balanced than in the complete absence of attention to any one element.

With a greater clarity about the structure of curriculum and about its elements, these black and white differences among the various designs should increasingly disappear. This is noticeable in the curricula for mathematics proposed recently. There is a definite emphasis on content, but its development is related, even though not always consciously, to such objectives as understanding mathematical principles and developing a method of thinking, creativity, and discovery. This is a far cry from the older "content" emphasis which was characterized by sheer mastery of content and manipulative skills with practically no attention to the principles of learning intellectual processes.

An effective design also makes clear what the bases of the selection and the emphases on the various elements are, as well as the sources from which these criteria are derived. It should, furthermore, distinguish which criteria apply to which element. For example, a design should make clear whether its objectives are derived from consideration of the social needs as revealed in the analysis of society, the needs of individual development as revealed by the analysis of the nature of learners and their needs as individuals, or both. In a similar manner, both the choice of content and its organization need to be accounted for by an analysis of the unique characteristics of the knowledge represented by school subjects and of the characteristics of the learning process. When this rationale is not clear, distortions occur in the manner in which content is organized, or else the content is organized in a manner which makes it "unlearnable." Some current designs pay too little attention to the needs of society, or the perspective on these needs is derived from an inadequate analysis of the data on culture and society. This results in objectives of narrowed scope, or objectives which are removed from social realities. Still other designs are based on analysis or the content of the disciplines only, with little or no attention to the characteristics of learners or of the learning process. Many curriculum guides involve all these bases implicitly but fail to state them explicitly. This makes it difficult to establish priorities in applying criteria and principles or their combinations.

Designs with no rationale, or a confusing one, result in a curriculum framework with a high overtone of prescription because the requirements regarding content or the nature of learning experiences are difficult to explain and seem to demand a docile acceptance of directives by those who implement the curriculum in the classroom. As a matter of fact, much of the distance between theory and practice may be caused by just such lack of rationale. Such a curriculum also tends to remain inflexible. An implied rationale is not easily subject to examination and revision according to changes in any of the bases on which it was founded. New data which become available on

learning or on changes in the cultural needs, in the nature of student population, or of the content are not easily translated into the curriculum. Such a
curriculum can be changed only by what could be called an earthquake method
of curriculum revision: a periodic reshuffling of the entire scheme instead of a
continuous readaptation.

RELATIONSHIPS
AMONG THE ELEMENTS

It is especially important for a curriculum design
to make clear how the various elements and the criteria or considerations connected with them are related to each other. A decision made about any one
element out of relationship to others is bound to be faulty, because each element of curriculum acquires meaning and substance in reference to other
elements and by its place in the pattern that encompasses all others. For example, the specific objectives derive their meaning from the larger aims of
the school. If the main aim of the school is to develop intelligent citizenship,
then the development of the ability to think critically becomes important. The
fact that critical thinking is an important objective imposes certain requirements on the selection and organization of learning experiences, and this, in
turn, makes it necessary to include the evaluation of thinking in the program
of evaluation. The type of content organization adopted sets limits on the
learning experiences which are possible. The consideration of the nature of
the students and their backgrounds determines what approaches to the content and to establishing the sequences of learning experiences are effective.
The way in which the content of a subject is organized for curriculum purposes is, in a similar manner, controlled by the structure of the discipline
which the subject represents.

If the essence of learning mathematics is the capacity to handle abstract
symbols and a system of ideas, then the learning experiences in mathematics
need to be designed to develop this capacity. If the essence of literature is to
develop empathy and capacity to identify with human values, problems, and
dilemmas, then the experiences in learning literature must include activities
designed to develop this empathy and not be limited to intellectual analysis
of forms of literature, the quality of expression, or information about characters. Often inadequate decisions are made at points involving such relationships partly because of lack of clarity about the nature of the elements, or a
failure to see the relationship between the criteria which apply to each of
them. We tend to apply first one and then another criterion individually instead of thinking of these criteria as a constellation, in which each has a
bearing on the others.

Herrick illustrates the necessity for examining the relationships among the
elements of the curriculum by analyzing schematic models for curriculum

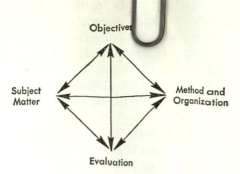

designs (*1950, p. 41*). One of these is a diagram of the elements of a curriculum and their relationships as seen by the curriculum consultants in the Eight Year Study (*Giles, McCutcheon, and Zechiel, 1942, p. i*).

This design describes four elements: objectives, subject matter, method and organization, and evaluation. In essence, it suggests for the curriculum maker four questions: What is to be done? What subject matter is to be used? What methods and what organization are to be employed? How are the results to be appraised? The design also indicates that each of these elements is related to the others and that, therefore, decisions regarding any of them are dependent on decisions made on others.

However, this design fails to indicate the bases on which the decisions regarding these elements are to be made: the sources from which objectives are derived, which criteria, in addition to objectives, govern the selection and organization of content, and what relationships exist among these criteria.

A design also needs to make explicit its relationship to the factors in school organization and the instructional resources which are necessary to implement it. B. O. Smith, Stanley, and Shores include these considerations in their discussion of the various types of curriculum patterns. They point out, for example, that the subject curriculum requires teachers with intensive training in one subject field, that the best training for teachers for the activity curriculum is one which combines broad general training in content fields with "specialized training in child and adolescent development, guidance and project methods of teaching." Flexibility of scheduling and in grouping of students is a special requirement of the core curriculum (*1957, pp. 239, 324*).

While the organization of the school and its institutional facilities should be shaped to implement the curriculum, the reverse is usually the case. The functioning curriculum is fitted into the existing arrangements and shaped by the limitations in these conditions. When the conditions necessary for implementing a curriculum design are not fulfilled, a discrepancy between the intended and the actual curriculum is naturally created. It has already been pointed out that a fully integrated curriculum remains an impossibility as long as evaluation and accounting of the program for college entrance is in terms of separate subject areas, as long as teachers are trained along specific subject-matter lines, and as long as the patterns of team teaching are ineffectively developed. When teaching materials are limited to texts, a curriculum design centered on problem solving and calling for sophistication in handling a variety of resources is somewhat unrealistic. The failure to assess realistically the effect of existing conditions has often led to the discrediting of a given curriculum design when the difficulty may not have been in the design but in the discrepancy between the requirements of the design and the conditions for implementing it.

Further, a good design describes the elements and the relationships among them and their supporting principles in such a fashion as to indicate priorities among the factors and principles to be considered. Not all criteria and principles have equal significance in developing an adequate design, or even as norms for a good curriculum. At present there is little analysis of the priorities of these considerations, with the result that often criteria of least significance have a priority over those of greatest consequence. For example, the criterion of efficiency and economy seems to be the major consideration in such proposals regarding curriculum change as team teaching and the use of television. One wonders also whether the advantage to the development of talent in the few gifted is worth the disadvantage accruing from the ability grouping in the form of social and psychological consequences of such a grouping.

Some curriculum analysts consider the decisions about the centers around which to organize curriculum central to the whole business of curriculum development. Herrick, for example, proposes that a curriculum design becomes more usable in improving educational programs if its major focus is on problems of selecting and organizing the teaching-learning experiences of children and youth (*1950, p. 44*). There are many reasons for allocating a central role to decisions regarding the selection and organization of the curriculum. Certainly, in practice, this is the central task around which decisions regarding selection of objectives revolve. All other decisions, and the criteria and considerations pertaining to them, come into focus in relation to this central decision.

THE PROBLEMS AND PRINCIPLES OF ORGANIZATION

The problems of organization are central to a design of curriculum. A design should, and usually does, convey an idea of how it deals with the major issues of organization: what centers are used for organizing curriculum experiences, what the concept of scope is and how to determine an adequate scope, what provisions are made for sequence of content and of learning experiences, and how to handle integration of knowledge.

The Centers for Organizing
the Curriculum

In curriculum development, decisions about what centers to use for organizing curriculum experiences are rather crucial. As indicated in chapter 20, many other decisions regarding selection and organization come to focus around the problems of centering. The merits and disadvantages of the different centers for organizing curriculum have already been discussed. Here only some general points about the role of centering or focusing need to be made.

First, the decisions connected with focusing, such as those involved in planning a unit, bring all other decisions into perspective and organize the ideas relevant to these decisions. For example, it is around the task of formulating a unit that it is possible to perceive and to examine the relationships among objectives, content, learning experiences, and evaluation. The development of organized teaching units also brings home the extent to which all curriculum decisions need to be made in the light of consciously understood criteria and relationships. It is impossible to make good decisions about the method of learning and teaching apart from considering the objectives that students should attain, or apart from concepts regarding the nature of the learners and the principles of learning. The decisions faced regarding organization of content bring into play the necessity of analyzing the functions of the various levels of content as well as the nature of learners and thus demonstrate a way of applying multiple considerations in making curriculum decisions which curriculum makers cannot learn abstractly.

How the nature of organizing centers influences the selection of the content and learning experiences and vice versa becomes clear also. For example, if the basic ideas are the centers for organizing the unit, these ideas then determine which specific details of information are relevant and which particular learning experiences are useful to develop these concepts and ideas and to achieve other non-content-related objectives.

The organizing focuses are also crucial to the manner of dealing with the problems of scope, sequence, and integration. For example, the kind of centers used in organizing each unit of social studies determines the kind of sequence which can be built into the entire social-science curriculum as well as the relationships which can exist between social sciences and other subjects, such as literature. In reverse, once the scope and sequence are established they determine to a certain extent how the specific areas of curriculum can be organized, such as which centers of organization can be employed or which sequence of learning experiences can be used. It becomes clear that decisions regarding the focusing centers of specific units and those pertaining to scope and sequence as indicated in the framework of the curriculum are interdependent. The decisions about focusing of specific units cannot be made out of context of the total design without the danger of discontinuity and inconsistency.

This means, of course, that the two types of activities, analysis of the various elements of the curriculum and organization, represent two separate but interrelated steps, and this interrelationship needs to be maintained on both the specific and the general level of curriculum organization. The description of ways for dealing with the elements of the curriculum may outline the objectives and set criteria for selection of content and of learning activities in general. These essential aspects of curriculum planning and thinking are faced only at the point of putting these elements together into a functioning unit. A method of curriculum development which devotes a long time to the analysis of objectives and philosophy, and which then omits the organizing of teaching units, usually results in guides on paper which do not function in classrooms.

The general analysis only furnishes the bricks from which to compound a functioning curriculum. But the general analysis is insufficient without the subsequent step of translating general objectives into specific ones and without a methodology of translating into a functioning curriculum the criteria which apply to these decisions severally and collectively. One qualification for the focus or center of curriculum organization, then, is that the organization which it produces lives up to such criteria as adaptability to the ability levels of students, the varied conditions in schools, the resources of the teachers, and the interests of children.*

Scope, Sequence, and Integration

A design should indicate clearly the bases and provisions for the scope and continuity of learning. Scope is a way of describing what is covered, or what is learned. As was pointed out earlier, one needs to determine what is learned in two different dimensions: what content is mastered and what mental processes are acquired (or what non-content objectives are achieved). The failure to see scope as a two-dimensional problem has created the dilemma of breadth and depth. When scope is seen solely as the breadths of content covered, the demands of coverage are in conflict with demands arising out of requirements of depth. The wider the coverage, the less time there is to develop depth of understanding and a high level of conceptualization, to incorporate ideas into a personal system of thinking, and so on. Often these two dimensions are confused and a more extensive coverage of the subject is identified with depth. The continuity of learning has two aspects: that of a vertical progress from one level to another,

---

* Goodlad presents this problem in the form of outlining a three-dimensional planning which takes place on the pre-classroom level and a three-dimensional synthesis which is necessary "if children are to experience a series of dynamic learning-teaching acts" (1956, pp. 11-22).

and that of a relationship between the learnings in various areas of the curriculum which take place at the same time. The first of these is associated with the term *sequence,* the other with the term *integration.* The problem of providing continuity of learning also presents itself on two different levels: the level of organizing specific units of teaching and learning, and the level of the design for the entire curriculum.

Much of the confusion and difficulty in developing cumulative and continuous learning comes from the fact that in setting up sequences in curriculum designs, only the sequence of content is considered, while the sequence of the powers and competencies is largely overlooked. The result is that the curriculum sequence reflects growth in the mental powers only to the extent that the level of content requires it, and not because of a clear plan for the developmental sequence of these powers, competencies, and skills. Out of this confusion grow all sorts of difficulties: poor articulation between the levels of schooling, the perennial complaints by each level of lack of preparation on the preceding level, misplaced expectations, and a lowered amount of growth. The attempts to "cure" these difficulties by changing the content and setting standards of excellence in the light of content achievement alone are bound to be less successful than addressing the standards of excellence to the formulation of developmental sequences in either intellectual or other types of performance.

When the problems of both scope and sequence are seen in two dimensions —one which sketches out the pattern of the content to be covered, and the other which indicates the kinds of powers or capacities to be developed and a sequence of developing them—the dilemma of scope and depth can be put into a more balanced perspective. This perspective would aid in deciding when the extension of the scope of content interferes with the development of the scope of mental powers and how the sequence of content could assure a sequence in levels of mental powers, or vice versa.

This double pattern of scope and sequence makes certain requirements on the centers of organization. Centers of organization need to combine most advantageously the requirements for advancing both the level of content and the level of mental operations. Using the basic ideas as focusing centers has several advantages in this respect. First, if the basic ideas are clearly outlined, it is also easier to see which intellectual powers and operations are necessary to deal with them. If units are organized around ideas, it is, for example, easier to determine what levels of abstraction may be required and what type of relationships between various ideas are possible and necessary than it is when only the topics and their dimensions are available for analysis.

This organization also makes it possible to examine more precisely both the sequence of content that is being employed and the sequence in the powers and capacities that are developed in the successive levels of curriculum. The units on different grade levels can be examined to see what ideas have been added and which are extended, and whether the contexts in which these additions are being made add up to sufficient scope of understanding. It will also be possible to determine whether there is an increment in such powers as the capacity to analyze data, to organize ideas, to respond to feelings and values, to appreciate aesthetic qualities, or to express feelings and ideas.

Below is an attempt to analyze for the elementary social studies the sequence in content and the cumulative maturation of the concept of difference, which is a recurring concept from one grade level to another.

SEQUENCE OF THE CONCEPT OF DIFFERENCE

Grade level	Areas in which the concept is developed	Sequence of the concept of "differences"
I	Home, family, school	Difference in families in: 1. Family composition 2. Occupation 3. Income
II	Work in community: farm, transportation, and supermarket	People do different things to meet life's needs.
III	Comparative communities	People do things in different ways today than long ago, and differently in different cultures.
IV	California—now and before	Differences in reasons for people coming to California, for different kinds of occupations here, etc. Differences in ways of life according to geographic and historical conditions.
V	Life in the United States	Extension of IV. Different feelings about coming to or moving about the U.S. Different patterns of life. Effects of different environments.
VI	The Western Hemisphere— how the various functions of life are carried on, such as economy, education, government	The functions of life are met in different ways as determined by climate, topography, history, type of people.

| VII | World trade | Different ways the various countries process, use, or distribute the natural resources of the earth. |
| VIII | United Nations | Different ways in which the various cultures can be helped to meet life's needs.* |

Content organized around large central ideas is also amenable to analysis of the ideas drawn from various disciplines in order to check validity and significance. For example, the units in the areas described above were analyzed to see what ideas they contained that might be classified as history, sociology, geography, economics, and anthropology. An example of the sociological ideas in social studies from Grades 1-3 is given in the chart that follows.

A Sequence of Mental Operations

A chart of learning activities makes possible a similar analysis of the mental operations represented by the learning experiences. If the learning activities in the various units are clearly stated, they can be examined to determine the scope and range they represent and the cumulative growth they provide in powers other than the understanding of content—thinking, academic and group skills, attitudes, values, and sensitivities. A sequence in developing sensitivity to differences starts in the first grade by reading about a new child in the school and then discussing what it feels like to be one and what the ways are of making a new child feel at home (*Contra Costa County Schools, 1959a, p. 13*). The second-grade unit on the farm inducts the students into feelings about farm life and ends with writing a story, "The Farmer Who Would Not Move Away" (*Contra Costa County Schools, 1959a, pp. 39 and 41*). In the third grade the children have the task of projecting themselves into the life in many cultures, and they begin to explore how the various kinds of people—the primitives in the rain forest, the Hong Kong boat dwellers, the Sahara nomads—feel about their culture. They are asked to write on themes such as, "If I were a primitive child I would like to. . . ." (*Contra Costa County Schools, 1961, p. 13*).

Such an analysis permits a projection upwards. What other aspects of cultural sensitivity can be built on this particular one, and how can an increasing capacity to put oneself in other people's shoes be cumulatively developed? What additional dimensions are necessary to develop the degree of cosmopolitan cultural sensitivity needed and which particular contexts are especially appropriate?

A cumulative sequence is observable also in logical and critical thinking.

* From the minutes of a curriculum planning session, Contra Costa County Schools, Pleasant Hill, California.

A SAMPLE FROM A CONTENT ANALYSIS

Sociological Ideas in Units, Grades 1-3 *

Central Ideas	Grade 1	Grade 2	Grade 3
Groups, Society, and Communication	As students at school we expect to learn certain things and we expect to behave in a particular way. Children feel differently about what schools expect of them. A family group may differ in structure, i.e., one-parent home, foster home, etc. A child has two sets of relatives—his mother's relatives and father's relatives. Families have different rules for their children. The teacher is also a member of a family.	The clerk in the supermarket is also a member of a family and a consumer. The farmer is an employer, a consumer, and a member of a family. A supermarket needs the newspaper for advertising.	A Zulu child and a nomadic Arab child are members of a tribe as well as of a family. A Chinese child has an extended family. A Swiss child has a family structure more nearly like ours. People who have no written language pass along their knowledge and tradition by word of mouth. Our form of writing was first evolved among the Arab people. The Chinese have a pictograph form of writing. Music, dance, and ceremonies can be used to communicate with others. The primitive of Africa, the Arab, the Chinese, and our communities have each developed a certain kind of music. Among the Chinese celebrations are held for the entire family.
Human Ecology	Homes in cities may differ from homes in small towns or on a farm.	People live in different kinds of communities.	Primitive people (Zulu or rain-forest primitives) use the plants

* Contra Costa County Schools, June 1961.

Schools in the country may be different from schools in town or city.

Some "grandparents" receive checks from "the county."

When a community grows larger more services, such as schools, churches, libraries, etc., are needed.

A commuting community needs many roads and filling stations.

A small community may have a volunteer fire service; larger communities have full-time firemen.

A community may not meet all the needs of the people who live there—employment, hospitalization, etc.

Some services (school, fire, etc.) are provided by taxes, some are provided by individuals (TV repairs, barber), and some by companies (banking, electricity).

Irrigation canals are built by the government to bring water to farms.

The farmer needs schools, recreation, etc., just as people in large communities do.

and animals of their environment to provide food, clothing, and shelter.

Modern communities (Swiss people or our community) are less dependent on their environment for food, clothing, and shelter.

Where there is water in the hot, dry lands we find farms. The farmers live in permanent homes.

The nomad of the hot, dry land and the people who live on boats in Hong Kong harbor must trade to meet their basic needs.

The people of Switzerland are concerned with the tourist trade as a result of their natural scenery.

The family and tribe of the primitive community provide religion, recreation, teaching of the young, and enforcement of tribal rules. Our community has schools, churches, and government to do this.

Each community celebrates occasions in a traditional manner.

Modern transportation helps the Swiss people secure chocolate beans from another country and deliver the Swiss chocolate to far-away markets.

Central Ideas	Grade 1	Grade 2	Grade 3
Personality and Socialization Processes	At school where there are many children we have rules for the sake of safety.		Zulu children are taught to accept the ways of their people. Arab, Chinese, and Swiss children are each taught a particular way of behaving.
	Family living demands that we share space, parents' time, etc., with other members.		Each of the four cultures teaches girls to behave in a special way and boys to behave in a special way.
	Families teach their children to behave a certain way. They may punish them for not obeying the rules.		Among the Zulu the oldest son of the chief will inherit the position of chief.
	In some families the role of the "bread-winner" is carried by someone other than or in addition to the father.		Among the Arabs the male has a special position.
	Father's work is very important to the family.		In the Chinese culture age is given great respect.
	Some jobs, such as shopping, fixing things, etc., may be done by different family members.		
Social Processes	Families carry on many work and play activities together.	We have laws related to keeping milk clean and cows free from disease.	
	Parents who commute to work have little time to spend with children in the evening.	We have laws related to keeping food markets clean and free from disease.	
	Fathers who travel have time with their families only on certain days.	All businesses need fire and police protection.	
Social Relations and Culture			Traders and missionaries have brought changes to primitive people.

The United Nations and WHO are bringing many changes among primitives and underdeveloped peoples.

People do not always like the changes that are brought to them. The Zulu have certain rules the members must follow, such as obedience to the chief on a hunt.

Brave behavior is rewarded by the chief.

In our communities there are laws related to trade—a limit on how much a tourist may bring back into this country.

After observing and analyzing what the teacher, principal, custodian, and cafeteria workers do, the first graders develop chart stories on the theme, "We have many helpers at school." They begin to differentiate such things as what must be done for the baby, what is fun to do and what is troublesome, what people might like and dislike about different types of houses, or what responsibilities are carried by different family members. The burden of differentiation and abstraction increases in the second grade, where the children are asked to differentiate the services needed and provided in different types of communities and the ways in which these services are paid for. They now write on topics such as, "This is the day when the electricity failed." In the third grade, the students are asked to analyze a film on the idea of what is primitive by developing a list of qualities and activities which are evidences of a primitive way of life. Subsequently they read a story about life in the rain forest and are then asked to determine which statements in the list are true of the family described in the story and in which way that family shows evidence of being primitive. This requires a degree of abstraction, of logical inference, of contrasting and comparing.

What should be the expectation on the next level of children who have mastered these intellectual processes? In other words, what is the sequence in the processes of thinking? If students in one unit have learned to classify simple ideas, is the next attempt at classification more demanding? If they have learned to derive simple generalizations from fairly simple facts, are they challenged in the next unit to move on to a higher and a more complex level? Do students who have learned to compare and contrast a simple set of conditions have an opportunity next to do the same on a more abstract or complex level? Do those who have learned to state simple sequences of events next learn to state and to discover sequences in argumentation?

As the students return to the same central idea or concept, it is possible to determine whether they only add to its content and meaning or whether these additions also increasingly demand higher levels of mental operations, such as an increasingly higher level of abstraction and an increasingly wider radius of application. In other words, it is necessary to plot a developmental sequence of cumulative growth both in power and in content in order to determine whether the subsequent contexts merely yield new information while requiring the same powers of comprehension and the same level of thinking, or whether there is an increment in both.

Advantages of a Double Sequence

Such a double scheme of composing scope and sequence by ideas and concepts treated and by the behaviors expected has several advantages. Both the behavior reactions and the content are accessible to an objective analysis of their cumulative effect. The scheme of scope and sequence is not jeopardized by a varied type of organization, and, in reverse, no one single type of organization needs to be imposed for the sake of a coherent scope and sequence. It is equally possible to apply such a scheme to a curriculum organized by subjects, by topics which cut across disciplines, or by problems. And it would also be possible to vary the schemes of organization from area to area, such as using problems as the main approach in one and a topical organization in the next. If ideas serve as centers of organization, variety in approaches does not destroy the comparability of the threads.

Such a scheme would also open up the possibility of developing a single consistent pattern of scope and sequence from the elementary through the high school, and across all subjects, which the current curriculum designs do not provide. None of them encompasses all grade levels or everything that the curriculum contains.

The same would be true of establishing and examining the integration or the horizontal relationship among disciplines or subjects. If ideas are used as the basic threads for establishing these relationships, integration can be achieved on several levels and in several ways, and not limited to the combining of particular subjects. For some ideas a crossing of historical, sociological, and anthropological material may be necessary to give proper dimension. Integration of scientific and social facts may be most relevant for others. Still others may require a combination of practical life situations with theoretical principles. In other words, it would not seem necessary to apply a single pattern of integration in all subjects or at every step in their study.

Another advantage of structuring the scope, sequence, and integration by ideas and behaviors rather than by subjects and content topics is that such a scheme has a flexibility which permits adjustments to the nature of student population and to the local conditions in particular schools. As was pointed out, units structured around ideas and developed by dimensions of topics and sampling of content permit a variety of adjustments. Each dimension can be extended or contracted according to the limits in students' perception and their level of understanding. These extensions and contractions can be made at any point: in the depth required, by developing an idea only on a certain level; in the extent of comparisons required, by limiting comparison only to certain aspects of culture or carrying it only to a certain level of exactitude; in the number of the concrete samples used, by using a larger number of concrete examples with the less able. One can require more or less exacting types of analysis, abstracting, and generalizing. Alternatives can be substituted either in specific ideas to be pursued or in specific samples of content, provided these alternatives are equally relevant to the main ideas. Coverage and level of expectation are thus brought into a rational control, and changes in each can be effected without revising the entire scheme.

This makes it possible to have a *common* curriculum pattern without necessitating a uniform curriculum. Teachers can be free to give adequate attention to content without having to submit to the tyranny of uniform, fixed, and static content. While the same threads go through all grade levels and all

A MODEL FOR CURRICULUM DESIGN

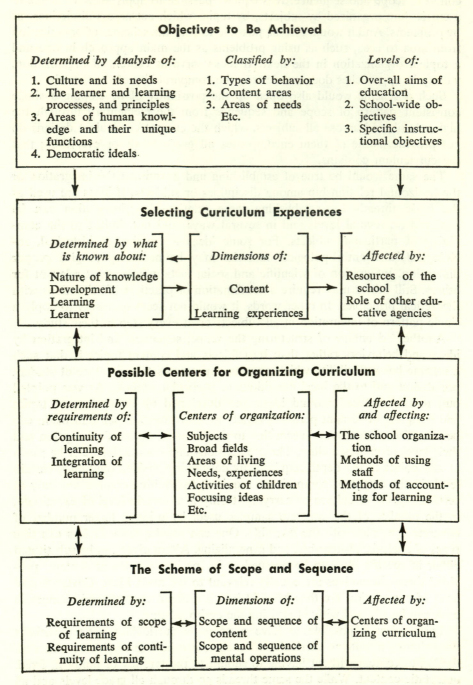

Objectives to Be Achieved

Determined by Analysis of:
1. Culture and its needs
2. The learner and learning processes, and principles
3. Areas of human knowledge and their unique functions
4. Democratic ideals

Classified by:
1. Types of behavior
2. Content areas
3. Areas of needs
   Etc.

Levels of:
1. Over-all aims of education
2. School-wide objectives
3. Specific instructional objectives

Selecting Curriculum Experiences

Determined by what is known about:
Nature of knowledge
Development
Learning
Learner

Dimensions of:
Content
Learning experiences

Affected by:
Resources of the school
Role of other educative agencies

Possible Centers for Organizing Curriculum

Determined by requirements of:
Continuity of learning
Integration of learning

Centers of organization:
Subjects
Broad fields
Areas of living
Needs, experiences
Activities of children
Focusing ideas
Etc.

Affected by and affecting:
The school organization
Methods of using staff
Methods of accounting for learning

The Scheme of Scope and Sequence

Determined by:
Requirements of scope of learning
Requirements of continuity of learning

Dimensions of:
Scope and sequence of content
Scope and sequence of mental operations

Affected by:
Centers of organizing curriculum

areas, these threads may be developed with different student groups in different ways.

This type sequence of scope requires careful experimentation and research. The elements that compose them are not strangers. The idea of teaching for concepts and ideas is older than Mark Hopkins' log, and most people know what is meant by behavioral objectives. What is new and requires new study is the cumulative sequence in achieving them. This would require longitudinal studies of the curriculum and its outcomes, similar to the longitudinal studies of physical growth and development. No such studies have as yet been made.

The schematic model of a curriculum design (*see p. 438*) attempts to organize the considerations presented above: the chief points at which curriculum decisions are made, the considerations that apply to each, the relationships that should exist among these points, and the criteria.*

A METHODOLOGY OF CURRICULUM DEVELOPMENT

Another aspect of the theory of curriculum development is the methodology of the process itself. As one contemplates the variety of tasks involved in curriculum development, one cannot help but discover that there is a rational sequence for attacking them. The current sequence of starting with formulations of the design and of a framework and then developing the learning units to implement the framework tends to reduce the possibilities for creative innovation because it limits the possibilities of experimentation from which new ideas and concepts of curriculum can emerge.

When revision or change starts with changing the framework of scope and sequence, a pattern is fixed before thorough re-examination and testing of what goes into making that pattern. Since, as was shown in chapter 21, the conceptions around which the current curriculum units are organized tend to dictate the new framework, the inadequacies in the current organization of the specific subjects tend to be reflected in the new framework, and the possibility of genuine and radical improvement is reduced. Because it is difficult to develop a new concept of scope and sequence apart from experimenting with the various centers of organization in the specific areas of a curriculum, it seems more efficient to explore first the new possibilities closer to the grass roots. Concrete experimentation with composing specific units is necessary also as a groundwork for other aspects of the curriculum framework. For example, to incorporate in the design the idea of multiple objectives, teaching-

---

* This scheme is an extension of the one presented by Herrick (1950, p. 43).

learning units need to be developed first which are adequate to the task and which demonstrate its possibilities. Experimentation on this level also permits the discovery of new possibilities which otherwise escape attention. Problems such as that of establishing a balance between the scope of coverage and the depth of understanding can be explored in a tangible way. It is possible to examine realistically the relative role of content and of learning experiences in achieving educational objectives. The developmental sequences necessary for learning concepts can be tested. This setting also makes it both possible and necessary to apply multiple criteria and thereby prevent the trap of *either-or* thinking which tends to endanger armchair curriculum designing.

Many problems involved in formulating the framework cannot be realistically explored on the general level at all. The problem of effective integration can be explored with a reasonable functionality and precision only at the point of developing specific units for specific grade levels. One cannot decide flatly that these two or three subjects should be "unified." It is necessary to experiment with relating specific ideas, knowledge, and skills to ascertain what can be integrated, which combinations are of greatest potency and for which type of students. There is no virtue in integration *per se*. The idea of integration has been proposed because some ideas and facts are recognized to be more productive of learning in organized combinations than separately. Arbitrary integration is as great a danger to the development of understanding as is atomization of knowledge.

Creative innovations in types of learning experiences do not come about when decisions such as how to develop consistency between the objectives and what is taught or how to translate ideas about learning into curriculum sequences are deferred until *after* the framework is fixed, especially if these decisions are made by teachers under conditions which do not encourage theoretical thinking. Under these circumstances the designs for scope and sequence are impoverished and the curriculum develops a split personality: the framework of scope and sequence in the curriculum guides points in one direction and the actual teaching in another, or else the relationship between the two is forced, and the design embodies fewer criteria of a good curriculum than would otherwise be possible. By making the development of a framework rather than experimentation with concrete teaching units the main target of efforts at innovation, old wine is poured into new bottles, because the most relevant decisions are made by teachers who are only scantily prepared in theoretical thinking about curriculum, and who, furthermore, are not given sufficient time for careful planning.

This inappropriate methodological sequence together with the dichotomizing of decisions about curriculum content and methods are probably responsible for the fact that so many important and fully accepted criteria and considerations have received only limited application. This, for example, is true of the idea of development. While the criterion of a developmental sequence is elaborated in most up-to-date curriculum guides and is embodied in practically all books on curricula, its application is largely confined to the concept of readiness and to the teaching of reading and arithmetic. The idea of developmental sequence in learning other things has been scarcely explored. The concept of individual differences has been confined to differences in ability, in spite of a spate of data on differences in motivational patterns and social backgrounds. The concept of differences in mental abilities has found application only in varying the pace and quantity of learning the same curriculum and not in varying the quality of understanding and the depth of perception (*Ward, 1961, pp. 534-36; Frazier, 1961*).

A gap between theory and practice thus exists at both ends of curriculum development: theoretical designs of curricula are developed with meager foundation in experimentation with practice, and implementation is carried on with insufficient understanding of theory. This gives theory an unreal quality and fosters black and white thinking. The scope and sequence charts are formalized on paper and lack the dynamics necessary to translate their essence into appropriate practice. This is clearly illustrated by what has happened to the idea of core curricula, which were designed to foster relationships with life needs and integration of content. In practice they have remained largely administrative schemes of blocks of time in which separated subjects are continued and life problems are examined at the cost of sacrificing validity and soundness of content. In other words, because a theory of implementation is lacking, in practice only the form and not the substance is implemented and the essence of the idea is subverted.

It seems, then, that both for the sake of curriculum improvement and for the development of sounder curriculum theory, the sequence in the method of developing curriculum designs needs to be inverted. Instead of starting with general designs, a start needs to be made with reconsidering and replanning learning-teaching units as the first step in curriculum development. The results of experimentation with teaching-learning units should then provide a basis for the general design. For example, the tested centers for such units could provide a new and a more functional basis for determining the scope. Concrete sequences for cumulative learning of concepts, for patterns of thinking, and for acquiring attitudes would provide a basis for sequence in addition to the sequence of subjects. General plans for integration are likely to be more realistic when founded on the more concrete explorations with the most effective threads for integration.

It is possible also that this inversion of the sequence in curriculum building will help bridge the gap between theory and practice. In the first place, since in the development of such units theoretical competence needs to be combined with practical experience in teaching, the first step is taken by infusing theoretical thought into what up till now has been considered strictly the domain of the practitioner. Cooperative planning by curriculum specialists, experts in content, and classroom teachers should enhance at the same time the theoretical insights of teachers and the practical insights of the theoreticians.

Secondly, curriculum guides which are evolved from and implemented by concrete teaching-learning units prepared by teachers should be easier to introduce to the teaching staffs and more readily understood than is possible when only abstract general guides are available. This procedure should also initiate a steadier flow of ideas and facts from the basic behavioral sciences into curriculum development and curriculum practice, because the combined tasks of designing functioning units and a framework requires a greater attention to translating ideas from the basic sciences into educational practice than does the task of developing a general framework. The result should be that curriculum designs will reflect a conceptual framework and experimental knowledge to a greater degree than they do now.

Finally, curriculum guides which consist of both the general framework and tangible models for teaching-learning units are more likely to affect classroom practice than do the current guides which stop short of any guidance for converting the rather sketchy schemes into instructional practices.

This methodology and a sequence in curriculum planning involve a greater extent of preplanning than has been assumed to be necessary or wise. Under the shadow of the concept that preplanning involves rigid outlines of subject content, the idea has grown that a curriculum would be more "developmental" and responsive to the needs of students if a large portion of it were planned in the classroom by students and teachers. Some even defend this procedure on the grounds that it is more democratic. Some of these arguments are rather like shadow-boxing. Featherstone, for example, raises the question as to the extent to which the current schemes of scope and sequence select and control the values selected *by* adults *for* youth. He suggests that the problem of sequence might be solved more easily by shifting the control from the means to the ends. He maintains that the current schemes control only what the student is *exposed* to, and not what they shall *attain* or *become*. In this respect, according to him, "Problems-set-out-to-be-studied are not necessarily better or worse than subject-matter-set-out-to-be-learned. Neither procedure necessarily does anything more than put youth through their paces. Neither makes explicit provisions for controlling or determining the competencies which youth shall acquire as a result of a prearranged exposure." In contrast, developmental planning would allow for the curriculum to develop as the pupils grow and develop. Therefore, it would be important to consider the balance of external and internal control (*Featherstone, 1950, pp. 192, 197*).

Goodlad raises the same question when he suggests that the development of a conceptual system should answer the question of the extent to which synthesis of the components of curriculum can and should be effected for the teacher before he begins his teaching (*1958, p. 396*).

The decision regarding the role of preplanning is related to two matters.

One is the extent to which the curriculum plans are open-ended or rigid. The kind of plan projected in chapter 20, while thoroughly preplanned in great detail, incorporates procedures for introducing alternatives and adaptations and for a diagnosis to determine which of these are appropriate. A teacher who understands the rationale of these preplanned units can reshape the units considerably, provided she avails herself of the diagnostic data on the basis of which to do it.

The second matter is the problem of the degree of freedom which is commensurate with the degree of competency and available time. Curriculum planning, as has been iterated over and over again, is extremely complex. Individual teachers have neither the training nor the time to do a good job if they tackle the whole process, even though only a single teaching-learning unit be involved. Still less insight could be expected from students, including their insights into their own needs. There must, therefore, be different degrees of freedom for planning by teachers and pupils which correspond to the levels of competency and the degrees of complexity involved in making certain decisions adequately. Otherwise the "developmental" freedom adds up to a curriculum which is barren of the very growth this freedom is to protect.

According to the scheme of curriculum development described in this book, the levels of freedom increase as one moves from decisions involving the selection of subjects to teach to the selection of learning experiences. There is little freedom of choice for the classroom and the teacher in the selection of subjects; these decisions are made by the requirements set by agencies beyond the school districts. There is a greater degree of freedom on the next level, the selection of ideas around which to center the sampling of content and to develop learning experiences. These decisions also need to be made after thoughtful study of the requirements of content as well as of the development of students. Because selecting valid ideas around which to organize teaching units is not easy, it is better that this selection be done by groups of teachers under the guidance of the curriculum specialists and with the help of persons competent in the respective subjects.

A much greater degree of freedom is available in the sampling of content necessary to develop the ideas. Since a variety of specific content may be equally useful for the purpose of developing a central idea, there is no reason, as long as there is an understanding of the relationship between a given type of content sample and the idea, to prevent the planning on this level either by teachers or by the students and teachers together. About the same hierarchy of freedoms applies to the selection and organization of learning experiences. Usually teachers are the main source for suggestions of the possible learning experiences, because it is here that their expertness lies. This is also a task in which students can participate effectively. A more difficult task is to balance the learning experiences so that there is a proper opportunity for each of the behaviors implied in the objectives to be practiced. The most difficult task is that of arranging these learning experiences in sequences which promise the greatest cumulative impact. In this, cooperative effort is needed.

However, if models for such sequences are available and teachers are familiar with the way of thinking about them, the best development of these sequences takes place when teachers and students together plan the particular learning experiences for a given unit. This means, then, that the decision regarding the amount of preplanning needs to be made according to the complexity of decisions involved, and the competency and time available for planning. The decision may also depend on whether a transition is being made to a new way of thinking about the curriculum or whether the planning takes place in an accepted framework and serves only to implement the existing pattern of thinking about the curriculum.

One must conclude that the major question about curriculum planning is not whether to plan or not to plan, but how to do it wisely, scientifically, and on the basis of rationally recognized facts and considerations, instead of being guided by an ill-considered mixture of assumptions, beliefs, and personal preferences. The questions pertain also to who plans what, or what to what degree, and in which order. It is more useful to deal with these questions concretely than to argue abstractly about planned and unplanned curriculum or a particular fixed approach to it. If curriculum designs are built so that the roles which different types of personnel and competencies can play in the total process of curriculum development from design down to implementation in the classroom are clearly seen and properly allocated, it should be possible to employ these roles wisely and according to the understood requirements. It is further possible to use the process of curriculum development as a means of in-service training, which will extend the compass of the decisions teachers and students can make as they develop the appropriate competencies and skills.

The Strategy of Curriculum Change

Strategy
for Changing
Curriculum

Since their inception American schools have been subject to recurring reappraisals, criticisms, and modifications. Change has come about in different ways and by different methods but has always been a dominating feature.

CURRICULUM CHANGE
IN HISTORIC PERSPECTIVE

Perhaps the earliest method of curriculum revision consisted of legislation regarding which subjects to teach, and of the writing of textbooks to develop the content to be taught. In the 1890's began what has been called the development of curricula by national committees. The Committee of Ten on the Secondary School Studies (1893) established the four parallel high-school curricula, the principles of "equivalence of subjects" and of election, and opened the way to the introduction of practical subjects. The Committee of Fifteen (1895) established the principle of correlation of elementary-school subjects. The Committee on the Economy of Time in Education (1911) was the first scientific study of the value of subjects, of the placement of materials, and of the social utility of the educational program. The Commission on the Reorganization of Secondary Education (1918) established the Cardinal Principles referred to above in an effort to unify the subject matter of curriculum and to stimulate a life-related, integrated, and continuing process of education.

These committees were initiated to bring order and uniformity into rather diverse and sometimes chaotic programs. Their chief role was to make recommendations regarding the content and the organization of secondary and elementary school curricula. During this period, the responsibility for curriculum development tended to be in the hands of college professors and of content specialists, who developed principles and patterns which the local school systems adopted. Also during this period the curriculum consisted of content outlines in which there were sharp distinctions between subject matter and method.

Following the First World War, the responsibility for curriculum development gradually shifted to local school systems, a trend which has continued to the present day. This shift was accompanied by an extension of the concept of curriculum. Curriculum development began to be viewed as a larger enterprise than simply the outlining of courses of study in the various subjects. The emerging knowledge of the learning process generated efforts to define educational objectives and developed a concept of a more comprehensive curriculum.*

This concept introduced a whole stream of experimental work on curriculum revision, some of which eventuated in the ideas for curriculum design described in chapter 22.

This change in the concept of curriculum and the shift in the responsibility for curriculum development also produced changes in the method of organizing and administering the process of curriculum development. Curriculum experts and teachers began to participate in curriculum production, replacing the content specialists. To organize this participation, committee work became the chief vehicle. The earliest formula for work was "from the top down" or the "administrative approach," in which the committee structure was elaborated in the central office. The superintendent appointed a steering committee, which in turned selected personnel for working groups to define the philosophy and to formulate the objectives. Production committees then worked out course outlines, guides, and new materials. This work was followed by that of installation committees whose task it was to acquaint teachers and principals with the nature of new materials. This procedure was devised for the production of courses of study. It yielded many publications but did not always achieve a corresponding impact on the classrooms, because the changes in curriculum were not accompanied by changes in the skills and attitudes of teaching personnel. Nor were these paper plans sufficient guide to implementation. Since a small group conceived, initiated, and directed the change, the changes did not reach the fundamental arena for curriculum change, the classroom. It was soon found that the courses of study so produced were used ineffectively or not at all.

Gradually both the pattern of participation and the nature of responsibility were extended. The "grass roots" approach replaced the "from the top down" administrative approach and included as much of the schools' personnel as possible on the assumption that the functioning curriculum would be improved only as the professional competence of teachers improved. Under this approach curriculum change usually began with the individual schools or with

---

* Among the first books to describe curriculum making in comprehensive terms are Bobbitt (1922 and 1924). The latter emphasized almost entirely the analysis of objectives. The Twenty-Sixth Yearbook of the National Society for the Study of Education (1927) was another pioneering, comprehensive view of curriculum which delved into the relationship of the curriculum and the American scene.

individual teachers in schools. It also characteristically began with teacher concerns. Increasingly, curriculum work became the responsibility of smaller units. Increasingly, also, the work was done by elected committees of teachers who were responsible for defining objectives, producing the curriculum guides, and suggesting learning activities and materials to be used.

This shift in method was accompanied by a modification of the nature of materials issued and their use. Curriculum outlines became more diversified and were regarded as resources rather than as prescriptions. Classroom teachers acquired a greater autonomy in shaping the instructional patterns and in many instances were encouraged to develop their own programs.

These strands of development established the essential features of the method of curriculum development that prevails today. Today, also, we are witnessing perhaps another beginning of the cycle: again a feeling is being expressed that school programs are too diverse and chaotic, that their content is inadequate, that national effort is needed to establish the main outlines and main patterns, and that therefore a national curriculum commission is needed (*Hanna, 1960; Tyler, 1960*).

CURRENT METHODS
OF CURRICULUM CHANGE

The strategies of organizing and administering the work of curriculum development today are essentially extensions of methods employed when the task of the local school districts was to implement the designs established either by experimental ventures, such as the Eight Year Study, or by the work of national commissions.

Today several types of activity go under the name of curriculum improvement. One of these is the work of supervisors and principals in helping teachers either to implement the existing curriculum guides or to introduce modifications in organizing their content and learning experiences. By and large, though, little of this work is concerned with curriculum change; most of it is on behalf of curriculum maintenance. The work is carried on largely in classrooms with individual teachers and is neither systematic nor developmental. Dealing as they do with specific problems, in a limited amount of time, supervisors conferring with individual teachers find they are supplying "expert" answers to unanalyzed problems and suggesting methods of dealing with problems without being able to see clearly the sources of difficulty. In this process there is little room for theoretical thinking, for designing experiments, or for invention of any consequence. As one supervisor put it, "We always end up in some sort of a dependency relationship, hold their hands, tell them, bring them materials" (*Taba and Noel, 1957, pp. 48-49*).

Another way to improve the curriculum is through in-service training: conducting study groups, workshops, work conferences, and in-service courses.

These devices may or may not be connected with specific plans for curriculum development, even though they are addressed to improvement of curriculum by changing teaching methods, developing curriculum materials, or simply introducing new ideas. Study groups are usually set up to learn about some important aspect of curriculum, such as child development, available resources, or human relations factors in learning.

Workshops and work conferences are usually devoted to a cooperative and continuous study of some problem to the point of making plans for action. Their plans may range from providing for superior students to ways of teaching concepts in social studies. A workshop may also be used to put together the various strands of curriculum analysis into a curriculum guide. Often these in-service devices are used by national or state projects to introduce new emphases and ideas into the existing curriculum; this has occurred in workshops on economic education and human relations.

The chief organizational vehicle for curriculum revision, however, is a committee which either works on a particular subject or produces general guides or "a framework."

Organized effort to provide consultant help and occasions for study and planning on a larger scale is another type of curriculum improvement. Such efforts are illustrated by the Metropolitan Study Council in the New York area, the Illinois Curriculum Project, the Intergroup Education Project of the American Council on Education, and the Horace Mann-Lincoln Institute of School Experimentation. These groups have worked both directly, through planning and study with the local groups, and through publications (*Taba, Brady, and Robinson, 1952, ch. 1; Barnes, 1960;* and *Lawler, 1958*).

In the more ambitious comprehensive programs of curriculum development, a network of committees handles different aspects of curriculum development. Krug, for example, describes a series of committees in local school systems as follows:

1. The central curriculum or instructional council. The function of this group is to identify problems of common concern, to develop an awareness of these problems, to select problems for system-wide study, and to organize the means for their study.

2. System-wide committees set up by the council to carry on revision of curriculum guides or outlines in the particular subjects or areas, such as for social studies or the primary curriculum.

These central curriculum revision committees may be paralleled by committees in the various schools. Krug lists a number of such committees and groups:

1. School-wide faculty group to study philosophy and/or objectives and to establish the general direction.

2. Editorial subcommittee on school philosophy and/or objectives to put in writing the point of view developed.

3. Groups to recommend policy on school problems, to elaborate the policies regarding specific problems in the light of the general philosophy.

4. Committees in instructional fields to develop curriculum guides and to apply the all-school objectives to the problems of selecting and organizing content.

5. Committee on programs for achieving all-school objectives, to deal with aspects of objectives which cut across subject-matter fields.

6. Committees on certain aspects of school programs which cut across the entire program, such as committees to deal with the relationships of curriculum to guidance, student activities, or work experience.

7. Case study discussion and study groups to develop leads to curriculum development from the study of individual children.

8. Resource unit construction groups to develop materials for instruction (*1950, pp. 287-91*).

Often the committee system is elaborated to take care of the problems of developing a curriculum for the sequence of schools, such as for a senior high school and the feeder junior high and elementary schools. In such cases the organization runs into an intricate combination of area committees, under the direction of a steering group or a planning council.*

The general characteristics of the organization and procedures for curriculum improvement are summarized by Passow as follows:

> (a) Widest possible participation in planning, testing, and evaluating by all persons—professional and lay—who are affected by policy and action decisions; (b) assignment of the individual school to a more central role in curriculum activity; (c) use of groups for initiating, planning, executing, and coordinating improvement efforts; (d) fusion of supervision, inservice education, and curriculum activity to concentrate personnel and processes for the improvement of instruction; (e) experimentation with procedures and devices for more effective involvement; (f) extension of kinds and uses of consultative services from many sources—central office, state department, universities and colleges, for example; (g) use of cooperative research in field situations for improving practices; (h) teamwork from many levels in cooperative enterprises; and (i) development of more effective and widespread leadership [*1954, p. 221*].

One key word in describing the current approach is cooperation: of teachers and administrators, of lay groups and school personnel. Four-fifths of the curriculum guides examined by a recent survey were products of cooperative work of teachers and administrators (*Merritt and Harap, 1955, p. 40*). Much is made of cooperation with parents and lay groups. (*See, for example, Ahrens, 1956; Storen, 1946.*)

Wide participation in curriculum work has raised the issue of the best ways

---

* See, for example, the Organization Chart for Curriculum Improvement of Dade County, Florida, in McNally and Passow (1960, p. 147). This volume also includes descriptions of curriculum programs in seven different state, county, and city school systems, chapters 6-11.

of working to assure cohesion and productivity. Consequently, a good deal of attention has been devoted to the elaboration of group processes necessary to develop both democratic participation and productivity, to the definition of the roles of leadership, to the methods of establishing communication and involvement, and of developing consensus out of a multitude of positions and beliefs. Discussions of group processes have been so large a part of most discussions of curriculum change that some writers have wondered whether preoccupation with it may be limiting study in other directions (*McKenzie and Bebell, 1951, p. 231*).

Recently attention has been devoted to the research approach to curriculum development—to ways of developing ideas on curriculum from studies of practical problems. This emphasis has been popularized under the name of cooperative action research, the essence of which is for the practitioners to carry on research with the help of research technicians on problems of immediate concern to them. Action research has been an attempt to bring research data and research methods to bear on the problems of curriculum development and to enlarge the perspective of those who work on curriculum development (*Corey, 1953; Taba and Noel, 1957, pp. 1-2; Association for Supervision and Curriculum Development, 1957*). One of the more extensive series of action research studies has issued from the Horace Mann-Lincoln Institute (*Miel et al., 1952*).

Individually and collectively these procedures and organizational patterns have several deficiencies. There are difficulties inherent in the wide participation. When one considers the current suggestions for developing the total curriculum program, it seems that almost everyone is supposed to participate: the public, the administration, students, curriculum and supervisory staff, teachers, and specialists in curriculum development, learning, child development, and content. This extension in participation has not been accompanied by a corresponding clarity about the roles which each group can legitimately play. As one analyzes the literature on participation of the lay public in curriculum development, one is impressed with the somewhat naïve delight at the necessity and the possibility of cooperation and, at the same time, with the complete absence of a definition of roles for each participant and of a distinction between decisions that involve general wisdom and those that require expertise.

The basic argument that, unless those who are using the curriculum have some part in determining it, they will resist any change, is sound. But this is far from saying that everyone affected by the curriculum must also take part in every decision, such as determining what the scope and sequence should be. It is also far from asserting, as does Ahrens, that "curricula that are planned and developed without participation of all concerned . . . are usually ineffective. . . . Changes in approaches, content, and methods take place only when there are changes in the thinking of those who are concerned" (*1954, p. 338*).

Perhaps "being concerned" is too broad a criterion for participation in curriculum development. Some delineation is needed regarding the nature of this participation. Much grief has come from an indiscriminate participation of everyone in everything. Some analysts have suggested, for example, that laymen have been "invited" to influence decisions which require professional competence, such as what shall be taught in history, when and how to teach reading, and what literature high school students should read.* Teachers are expected to make decisions which require theoretical insights into curriculum even though they do not have such insights. There are expectations that students and teachers in their classrooms will organize the curriculum, that they will outline the topics and decide what to study about each. This, too, seems apt to lead to a thoughtless plan unless there is a clear concept of the limits within which students can contribute. Clearly, there is a distinct function that all these groups can serve in the total job of curriculum development, and the decisions on participation must rest on who can best do what, and not on a sentimental concept of democratic participation.

Secondly, there seems to be an overdependence on administrative arrangements to provide the essence of curriculum change. The committee system, for example, expresses the penchant in American education for solving educational problems by organization alone. However, the committee system of curriculum development can be unproductive, especially if not accompanied by adequate methodology of work, appropriate ways of inducing new theoretical perspective, and ways of generating dynamics of involvement. When these elements are lacking, committee work rarely results in genuine change or new thinking about curriculum.

It is, for example, not unusual for a curriculum guide emanating from committee work to have merely moved pieces of content from one grade level into another one. New curriculum guides rarely offer genuine and systematic modification of curriculum design, even from the standpoint of the brave principles of child development, of learning, or of the nature of society described in the introductions.

The reasons can be found in the nature of the system and in the methods of attacking the task. First, when the members of the committees are chosen primarily as representatives of schools, they are not necessarily the persons most concerned about changing anything, nor necessarily the most competent, nor even representative. Too often they are only persons with the greatest visibility. A group of such persons does not make the best team for curriculum work. Set to the task of producing a design or a framework, such a group tends to be at a loss on how to think together. Often this method of representation produces a group that cannot think together at all because of difficulties with personal status or philosophical incompatibilities.

Second, developing new curriculum patterns through committee work re-

---

* Lieberman (1956) points out that educators have permitted laymen too large a voice in decisions which belong in a professional realm.

quires more adequate strategy of leadership and of work patterns than is usually available. The committee system expresses a new philosophy of participation without a corresponding analysis of responsibilities, roles, and needed competencies to protect sound thinking and creative development of new ideas. When committee membership represents schools rather than ideas, the curriculum planning tends toward the common denominator rather than the new and creative.

Difficulties occur also because of faulty division of labor. Since curriculum development involves many different tasks, each of which requires study and thought, it calls for division of labor. When separate committees are created to take care of each step in curriculum development, as is illustrated by the description of the possible building committees by Krug (page 449-50), the sequential steps in curriculum thinking and planning are separated from each other, which prevents systematic, consistent, and productive thinking. No one group can see the various elements of the curriculum in relation to each other. How, for example, can one group work on resource units without also working on objectives which these units are to help achieve? How can a committee formulate a school philosophy without considering its bearing on instruction, or vice versa? Those who develop curriculum guides need the insights gained from the case studies of children. Philosophy of education is a part of making decisions about objectives, about selecting content, and about the learning activities. These decisions cannot be made wisely by different groups and in different terms.

The whole system of operations in curriculum development is still piecemeal and seems to operate on an oversimplified notion of the task. In the first place, experimentation is fragmentary, and much of planning is cut off from serious classroom experimentation. This tends also to cut off creative ideas about curriculum change and to limit the local planning to building a superstructure over an essentially unchanged understructure: creating on top of a functioning classroom curriculum a framework which may be inconsistent with it. Without solid roots in classroom experimentation, curriculum planning acquires a certain repetitive sterility.

The oversimplified assumptions regarding the nature of the task are also expressed in provisions for curriculum work, such as providing less time than is needed for serious work or expecting committee work to be carried on outside of school time and in addition to other full-time duties (*J. A. Hall, 1952, p. 235*). The time allowed for completing the tasks is often unrealistically short. Because of this twofold time limitation, curriculum revision is often little more than a scissors and paste job.

Questions can be raised also about the ability and training of the people asked to do the task. It was pointed out earlier (chapter 1) that the task of curriculum development is serious enough to require the best minds. Broad participation requires training and organization which call for superior leadership skills. Despite concentrated attention on group processes these are not yet abundant enough.

Perhaps the greatest deterrent to creative curriculum change lies in the fact that there is as yet no methodological sequence in which to tackle curriculum change, nor yet a clear-cut way of appraising the extent or the quality of changes taking place. There is, for example, little evidence that any part of the curriculum is being worked through from beginning to end so as to correlate the various sets of decisions and to carry through the whole cycle of steps necessary to allow generation of new ideas regarding curriculum and to assure the transitions from objectives to content, from content to organization, and from organization into practice. Multiple starts are made and these efforts are scattered in several directions. A rule-of-thumb method still dominates, and often the persons involved do not know why they succeeded or why they failed. The means used today for curriculum improvement may be adequate for generalized improvement, but they do not add up to an adequate strategy of curriculum change.

This conclusion is all the more serious because, concurrently with the shifting of responsibility for curriculum development to the local school districts, various developments in education have made the task vastly more complicated than it was when drafting content outlines by experts was the dominant methods of changing curricula. Not only is the curriculum today supposed to serve a greater variety of objectives than had previously been seriously considered, but the criteria and expectations of a good curriculum have also been extended. For this larger task the local school groups are rather ill prepared: they have neither the theoretical analysis of what the task involves nor the required skills to engineer the efforts of the multiple groups.

THE CONCEPT OF STRATEGY
FOR CURRICULUM CHANGE

Perhaps the first requirement of a strategy for curriculum change is to differentiate between curriculum improvement and change. As currently managed, curriculum improvement means changing certain aspects of the curriculum without changing the fundamental conceptions of it or its organization. Improvement consists mainly of an extension of the existing conception of the curriculum and its organization. A different problem altogether is posed in producing changes in the current curriculum scheme: in the way of organizing it, in ideas about what its content, its scope, and its sequence should be.

To change a curriculum means, in a way, to change an institution. Changing institutions involves changing both goals and means, although, as Merton has pointed out, goals and institutionalized means may not always correspond.

There may be emphasis on goals without an emphasis on means to achieve these goals (*1957*). Educational goals, such as educating the whole child, may be an "aspiration with little attention being paid to the institutional means of achieving it." Such aspirations are "likely to be idealistic or sloganistic." Or institutionalized procedures may be forgetful of goals and become "a virtual ritual, with conformity to procedures elevated to a central value" (*Coffey and Golden, 1957, p. 83*).

Changing the curriculum also involves changing individuals. Coffey and Goldner point out that changing individuals involves two types of changes. One is the change in the way he is oriented to the world around him, what he perceives and apprehends—the cognitive aspects. The other is the change in his emotional orientation—what he feels to be important, what he is motivated to do, and what emotional investment he makes in his goals. The change is effective to the extent that the two become integrated. At times the two are compartmentalized. Teachers may be exhorted and inspired to change without provision of means for change, as is the case with inspirational talks at teacher institutes. Or they may be led to new perceptions and ideas without involving their will to do anything about it (*1957, pp. 72-73*).

An effective strategy of curriculum change, therefore, must proceed on a double agenda, working simultaneously to change ideas about curricula and to change human dynamics. To achieve both the strategy of curriculum change requires a methodology, which may be summarized as follows:

1. Curriculum change requires a systematic sequence of work which deals with all aspects of the curriculum ranging from goals to means. A piecemeal approach, no matter how effective, does not produce sufficient change either in thinking about the curriculum or in the actual practice. A planned strategy, thus, must establish a sequence of steps or tasks in effecting curriculum change. Constructing this strategy involves the following kind of question: In initiating curriculum change, where does one begin? What is the order of steps or tasks that must be followed by a given group working either on a segment of the curriculum, or in developing a total plan?

2. A strategy for curriculum change involves creating conditions for productive work. Under what conditions does productivity flourish or languish? What processes need to be employed to enhance creative productivity? What are the guiding principles for the ways of working? Which human relations factors operate, and how does one deal with these? What role do such devices as committees, study groups, individual experimentation, and work teams play and how do these means operate in the various sequential steps?

3. Effecting curriculum change involves a large amount of training. New skills need to be learned, new cognitive perspective must be acquired, new modes of thinking need to be initiated. Since, as was pointed out above (pp. 291-93), most curriculum decisions, no matter what their scope, require application of theoretical principles, what balance of theoretical insight and

practical know-how is needed? What kind of training does that imply, and how and when should it be provided? What is the role of research and experimentation in this training?

4. Change always involves human and emotional factors. To change thinking about curriculum one also needs to change people's attitudes toward what is significant and perceptions about role, purposes, and motivation. To effect changes means to destroy dependencies on previous habits and techniques of work, with whatever personal meanings these have. To work in groups means to learn new group techniques.

5. Since curriculum development is extremely complex, it requires many kinds of competencies in different combinations at different points of work. These competencies need to be organized into effective working teams so that all resources are made available. Who should be involved at what points? What should be the roles of administrators, curriculum specialists, content specialists, specialists in group dynamics and research, lay people, students? To develop an adequate use of the manifold talents and resources, it is necessary to practice the principle of levels of involvement. Not every type of competency is relevant at every point of curriculum development. Not everyone needs to participate in everything.

6. Managing curriculum change requires skilled leadership. It also requires distributed leadership. What are the chief attributes of such leadership? Who can assume which leadership roles? How do these roles change at various stages of the process? What are the ways of extending leadership roles? What is to be the relationship between the official positions and leadership roles? How self-sufficient is a school system? What resources in leadership roles must the school draw from outside? How should it use these outside consultants? *

These are but a few of the questions involved in planning strategy for curriculum change. The remainder of this chapter is devoted to discussing these questions.

A SEQUENCE OF CURRICULUM DEVELOPMENT

Curriculum revision in a school usually starts with re-examination of the general guide and replanning of the framework. Relatively less attention is paid to renovating the more basic elements of curriculum, the classroom teaching units. As was pointed out in chapters 21 and 22, in this deductive process lie certain difficulties, chief among them the fact

---

* Beyond the aspects of change discussed in this chapter are the factors which are related to changes in institutions. Curriculum change may involve these more profound changes also. Regarding theory of these changes see Coffey and Golden (1957, ch. 4).

that certain aspects of curriculum planning and thinking which are crucial to the development of new ideas are not given their rightful place. Some aspects of a good curriculum, such as implementation of multiple objectives by appropriate learning activities, the relationship of ideas and the specific content, the developmental sequences of learning experiences, can be thoughtfully planned only on the level of specific units.

It is on this level that the problems of how to relate the curriculum to the fundamentals of child development and to the requirements of culture can be worked through. On this level, also, one learns to select and organize content so that there is a needed degree of flexibility and an appropriate integration of ideas across subjects. Work on specific units presents realistic opportunities for identifying the threads for learning sequences with a greater degree of rationality than merely placing subject areas one after another. At this point also one can experiment with applying the principles of learning (such as using different ways of learning to achieve different types of objectives) or with organizing the curriculum under various centers.

A deductive sequence of curriculum development, which starts with the mapping out of a general scope and sequence and then proceeds to the development of specific units to implement the sequence, prevents the development of creative ideas about curriculum because classroom experimentation is confined to the already formulated framework. The use of this sequence in tackling the task of curriculum revision may explain why relatively few new ideas about the basic ways of organizing the curriculum have been created in the last decades. The ideas abroad today are only refinements of the ideas developed in the 1920's and 1930's when classroom experimentation flourished and national studies were opening up new patterns of thought on curriculum development. A systematic strategy aimed at changing the curriculum seems to require an about-face in the general sequence of revising it. Instead of beginning with revising the general guides and developing new designs for scope and sequence as a first step (a plan which assumes that the understructure of that guide is as it should be), one needs to turn back to grass roots and start by creating new models of classroom teaching-learning units which illustrate and incorporate in practice new theoretical ideas and research data.

Translated into strategic steps, this sequence of curriculum change would involve roughly the following steps:

Producing Pilot Units

The first step is an experimental production of pilot units by groups of teachers sampled to represent the necessary grade levels and the arrays of subject areas under consideration. No one school system could afford to tackle the entire program at once, and usually it is necessary to concentrate on some reasonably limited area, such as the elementary curriculum, social studies, or language arts. The decision as to where to start could be made on several different bases: the area of greatest need, of greatest concern to teachers, the most obsolescent, and so on.

These units should be developed as models which illustrate tangibly the characteristics of a good curriculum. This step is also the first link between theory and practice, because many theoretical considerations described in chapters 21 and 22 will need to be worked through in the light both of available research and new local research. These models cannot be created without teacher participation because, in addition to the theoretical principles, developing units involves consideration of actual student needs, experimenting with classroom procedures, and setting objectives that are rooted in classroom reality. (The sequence for this step was described in chapter 20.)

Testing Experimental Units

Since the pilot units are created by individual teachers for individual classrooms, they are not as yet perfect models for other and different classrooms. They need next to be tested in different classrooms and under varied conditions to establish their validity and teachability and to set their upper and lower limits of required abilities. This testing should suggest appropriate modifications and alternate selections of content and of learning experiences and materials to accommodate variations in student population and in available resources. What is adequate coverage for one group may be too much for the next. Learning experiences suitable for one student population may be inappropriate for another. The units need to be examined also for their appropriateness to different teaching styles. A certain amount of induction and training is needed to make sure that the tryouts proceed with appropriate skill and insight. Teachers who have participated in the experimental development of the new materials are helpful in making this training concrete enough to include cues to ways of handling classroom problems by demonstrating specific procedures and materials.

Revising and Consolidating

After tryouts, the modifications need to be assembled and shaped into outlines representing an appropropriate general curriculum for all types of classrooms. To do this it is necessary to examine the outlines for consistency in reflecting the relevant principles and criteria, to check the materials for their validity, and to determine their feasibility in the light of available resources. At this point it is also important to consolidate the rationale for developing the units by stating the principles and theoretical considerations on which the structure of the units and the selection of content and learning activities are based and suggesting the limits within which modifications in the classroom can take place. These considerations and suggestions might be assembled in a handbook explaining the use of the units. If the units so developed are comprehensive enough to cover all grade levels in a given area, such as the social studies for the elementary school, they resemble a course of study. This consolidation is the task for the supervisors, the coordinators of curricula, and the curriculum specialists.

Developing a Framework

Once a sufficient range of units is available, these units need to be examined for sequence and scope by those who are competent in the theoretical aspects of curriculum development. For example, the core ideas need to be studied to see whether they are gradually extended toward the more mature and the complex. The content of the successive units needs to be examined for its adequacy of scope and coverage. Learning activities need to be examined to see if the opportunities for intellectual skills and emotional insights stimulate cumulative growth by students. It is possible that some shifting of content, or of emphasis, will take place at this time. At this point it is also necessary to articulate the rationale for the selection and organization, the reasons for a particular type of learning activities, and the intent and philosophy of the whole pattern. This rationale amounts to a statement of the general framework, which stakes out the scope and sequence; this is also a task for curriculum specialists.

Installing and Disseminating New Units

Finally, there is the task of installation, which involves training large groups of teachers in the use of the units. The more the program deviates from the type to which teachers are accustomed, the greater the task of training. This training may be accomplished through intensive workshops, a series of in-service courses, and other in-service training devices to develop the necessary content background, the requisite teaching skills, and an understanding of the theory underlying the new program. Because of changes in personnel, this is often a perennial task.

Installation and arrangement for the necessary training are essentially administrative tasks. Administrative roles are involved also in making the necessary shifts in practical arrangements, such as provisions for the needed materials or shifts in scheduling.

The length of time for this inductive sequence in changing the curriculum depends, of course, on resources and the degree of change involved. Under the best of circumstances it is a matter of several years, rather than the year or few months usually scheduled for revision of curriculum guides.

INTEGRATION OF PRODUCTION
AND TEACHER TRAINING

Working with teachers who may be concerned about making changes but who lack the competencies for curriculum development makes it necessary to combine curriculum development and training into one integral process. Training in a variety of skills and insights is needed. For example, the development of pilot units involves a series of professional competencies ranging from the techniques for diagnosing the needs of the classroom group to formulating core ideas. If the curriculum is to live up to the criteria described in chapter 17, such as meeting the needs of children and of the culture and following psychologically appropriate learning sequences, teachers need to conduct studies to make these criteria a reality. It is, for example, not enough for teachers to accept the fact that the activities introducing a unit should build a bridge from children's experiences to the content of the unit. They need also to study their classrooms to see what these experiences are and how the content of a unit can be related to them. It is not enough to understand generally that the development of thought patterns requires building upon previously acquired meanings. To develop a learning sequence in a unit, it is necessary to know what these meanings are and how to build upon them. To select and organize content one needs to learn to formulate and to classify ideas, to construct samples of content, and to organize both into a feasible teaching sequence.

Teachers tend to be deficient in all these skills. They are especially inexperienced in the process of identifying, classifying, and organizing the general principles of the content. They tend to depend on shorthand symbols, such as interdependence, without being clear about just what should be taught about interdependence or what interdependence means in various contexts. Creating inductive learning sequences is difficult also because textbooks as well as teacher training tend to employ deductive development, which begins with the statement of the general idea, and then proceeds to illustrate and develop it. To convert this sequence into a discovery method, which starts with concrete experiences and leads to the "discovery" of the generalization by the learners, is more difficult than it might appear on the surface.

New theoretical insights are needed also. While it is not necessary to turn teachers into theoreticians, they must understand and apply many theoretical principles. Connections need to be established between what they know about developmental growth and the placing of particular learning experiences, between the theories about learning and their application in such matters as when and how to use a text, or what to do to induce children to think for themselves. In other words, training is needed to develop a capacity to apply the psychological and social principles on which curriculum making is based. Application of these criteria in determining objectives, in making decisions about the selection of the main ideas around which to organize content, or about the selection of learning activities and their sequences involves many theoretical understandings if these decisions are to be made rationally and scientifically. This is especially true if the expected product is to be not only a better curriculum but also more enlightened teachers who in the future could make these decisions independently.

In addition, a myriad of concepts and insights from behavioral sciences need to be applied, some of which represent recent developments and are therefore not in the perception of many teachers. For example, the staff of the intergroup education project, working by and large in the more forward-looking schools and with teachers who were fairly well trained, reported the following gaps in the concepts and skills:

> Most teachers were unaware of the idea related to social learning. They tended to attribute such matters as attitudes toward school expectations, differences in conformity to school rules, and ability to relate to other people to differences in human nature rather than to specific learning from specific kinds of social environment. While there was a tendency to refer to home background as a source of these differences, the press of such learning was, by and large, rather meagerly understood, and the concept met considerable resistance. This was especially true of the concepts related to socioeconomic and minority status, and the psychological consequences of both behavior and attitudes. . . .
>
> While most teachers had some awareness of techniques pertaining to diagnosis of achievement and ability, far less was known about ways of diagnosing . . . values, socially determined meanings, and skills in interpersonal and group relations. This deficiency, of course, made teachers insensitive to a large area of important needs of children. Even the teachers who accepted and understood the psychological theory of needs were unable to implement their understanding in reasonable and realistic manner. . . . Therefore, the development and use of the appropriate methods of diagnosis in these areas constituted a large part of the work and training. . . .
>
> Training in realistic and rational methods of curriculum planning was an almost universal need. By and large, teachers knew only how to organize materials in already determined areas of subject matter and around topics widely enough used that outlining the scope of subject matter and of learning activities was merely a matter of borrowing from various texts and existing curriculum outlines. The problem was different when it included the complex task of inferring from needs what content should be studied and of selecting both content and learning experiences in the light of their own objectives. . . . Therefore, training in functional methods of curriculum construction seemed even more a necessity in intergroup education than in general education. [*Taba, Brady, and Robinson, 1952, pp. 316-18*].

The need for new skills, especially in research, has been recognized by others also. A recent yearbook which dealt with the research processes in curriculum development pointed out that to do a creditable job teachers need to learn not only the skills in a systematic curriculum development, but also skills needed for conducting research and for translating research data into criteria for selecting and organizing content and learning experiences (*Association for Supervision and Curriculum Development, 1957*).

This training can be separated from curriculum production only at the cost of sterility. The time to help teachers learn the best methods of studying their students is when they face decisions on selecting content. Help with methods of formulating and classifying behavioral objectives is needed at the time when they face the problem of developing learning activities. The problems and issues about the levels of content need to be dealt with in connection with decisions about which topics to study, which core ideas to focus on, and how to sample content in studying these ideas. These are also the points at which the principles pertaining to integration and to variations in abilities, perceptions, and meanings need to be developed.

Actually, only those activities in curriculum development should be encouraged which can be supported by adequate skills. No one should be asked or induced to try to do what he cannot be taught or be helped to learn how to do. If it is necessary to secure certain diagnostic data, provisions are needed for learning the techniques by which to secure these data. If a certain method of conducting discussion is indicated among the learning experiences, help is needed in the ways of conducting such discussions. If a classroom experimentation in using children's experiences is needed, designing this experiment requires some help. Time must then be taken for training in the needed techniques and skills. If this "teaching" is done in a group, while individual teachers try out the techniques in their respective classrooms, production, training in skills, and theory are effectively combined.

A systematic approach to initiating curriculum change encompasses also human engineering—a strategy of modifying attitudes, controlling human factors, and building human relations. Changing personal attitudes and feelings is often a part of the task of producing competency for curriculum development. Feelings are facts to be dealt with for those who build a strategy for curriculum innovation.

Professional skills and personal attitudes go hand in hand, each affecting the other, and changes in one both require changes in the other and produce possibilities for further changes. For example, it is not only important for teachers to understand that it is possible to organize content logically in several different ways, it is also important for them to accept the most appropriate alternatives. This is difficult for persons who "believe" in a particular scheme of organization. It is difficult for a teacher who essentially rejects students whose thinking and motivation differ from what she regards as standard, to adapt learning experiences to meet the needs of the deviating students. This is especially true if this adaptation involves a departure from the usual academic standards in materials or procedure.

A systematic curriculum development requires also a degree of objectivity: one needs to examine unwelcome alternatives, question the merits of cherished teaching procedures as means of achieving objectives, assess the relevance of cherished facts as useful knowledge, and so on. Because changes in personal attitudes have not been adequately stressed in pursuing curriculum change, many curriculum decisions are made on the basis of feelings rather than facts. It is not rare to find espousal of certain centers of organization or of certain learning experiences simply because "one believes in them" and therefore considers them superior to other methods without examining their total effects.

The emotional attachment to a position without a rational basis is well illustrated in the arguments about homogeneous and heterogeneous grouping. The merits and disadvantages of either procedure are argued in a context which involves hidden assumptions, such as convenience to the teacher, or the arguments play up some factors, such as efficiency, and disregard others, such as the effect of segregation on motivation and self-image.

This reasoning from strong unexamined preferences is aided by the fact that the tradition of rigorous scientific thinking about curricula is not as yet well established (*Taba, 1957, pp. 44-46*). Distinctions are lacking on what is essential and universal and what is not. Curriculum designs are espoused on the basis of their concurrence with a set of beliefs and feelings, rather than by their verifiable consequences on learning or their contributions to educational objectives.

At many points ethnocentric and egocentric assumptions and viewpoints rather than scientific data control the thinking. For example, teachers tend not only to be unfamiliar with the concept of acculturation and the processes of socialization but also to reject the whole idea of social-class variation; consequently they cannot relate the content of their students' social learning to the problems of selecting content and learning experiences. The understanding of individual differences in ability and achievement in no way prepares teachers to accept differences in feeling as facts to be worked with, especially differences in attitudes toward school achievement and school values and differences in behavior in emotionally charged and socially difficult situations (*Taba, Brady, and Robinson, 1952, pp. 295-97*).

The idea that a teacher's self-concept is related to the willingness to make changes and to experiment is a fairly recent one. In many school situations the image of a perfect teacher is one who does not have any problems, who knows all the answers, and who, therefore, does not need to explore and experiment. This self-image, fostered by school evaluations as well as by the folklore of the school culture, tends to make it difficult to admit problems and gaps in understanding.

Experimentation involves risks—a risk of making mistakes, of discovering deficiencies, of not succeeding, or of proceeding without sufficient skill. Reorientation in outlook removes the old pegs before the new ones are in place. A new basis for selecting a curriculum while still in the process of formation throws doubt on the old one. Diagnosis of children's needs may turn up points which cast doubt on commonly used classroom methods or on assumptions underlying them. These risks are a sufficient deterrent even for secure teachers. In some situations making mistakes can be both personally and professionally threatening. In a school situation in which little premium is placed on experimentation, errors are looked upon as flaws in professional competence. Those who work with teachers do not always understand that this feeling of threat is a source of resistance. It is usually assumed that teachers are not interested in studying their problems, when actually the teachers may be fearful because of the consequences of experimentation or of their lack of skill.

One baffling aspect in involving teachers in changing a curriculum is their lack of faith in their own ability to tackle curriculum revision. Their whole training and experience has led them to expect answers from "qualified" persons and to depend on "competent" aid in suggesting materials and procedures. Constantly in in-service training situations teachers want immediate answers and even show hostility when the questions are thrown back to them, because that suggests that the "experts" are shirking their responsibility. To be sure, this pressure for immediate answers is generated in part by the urgency of the practical situation. But equally responsible is the tendency of teachers to underestimate their own roles and abilities. This is especially true of anything that smacks of research or study. Teachers are, for example, surprised when it is suggested that in a sense they are the clinical experts in curriculum studies because they have access to data about learning and teaching processes which no one else has. Only they can invent and try out new methods of teaching or new approaches to content organization, and only they are in a position to diagnose how these approaches work.

These images and expectations stand in the way of developing a scientific attitude and a scientific approach to curriculum problems. It is difficult to make a transition from the hope of finding some miraculous solution to a realization that even the simplest problems of teaching and of curriculum have multiple causes, and that, moreover, teachers themselves are almost the only ones who can with proper study, eventually develop the solutions (*Taba, 1957, pp. 47-49*).

Both these problems, the need for training in professional skills and the human factors, need to be taken into account in planning both the manner of working and the sequence and pacing of the work for curriculum change. If the strategy involves the tooling up both of the workers and of productivity, then these gaps in professional skills, personal attitudes, and feelings need to be taken into account in the training offered and in planning the strategy for curriculum development. First, these working methods for change need to give teachers opportunities to learn new skills. Teachers must be helped to discover their own expertness. If work involves transition from one orientation into another, some provisions are needed for protecting self-confidence. Perhaps the greatest need is for protecting experimentation. Teachers need encouragement and help to try out new and unfamiliar ideas. They need help in thinking through the assumptions on which the experiment is based and in evaluating the results. They need to learn what the conditions for experiment have to be and how to set up these conditions. But, above all, they need to feel free to experiment. They need assurance that the mistakes which occur in the course of experimentation will not be held against them.

All of this involves conscious planning of the sequence of work. For example, experiences to change orientation or feelings need to come ahead of tasks that require a changed orientation. If research skills are lacking, these need to be developed in connection with preliminary studies before studies on which serious decisions depend are undertaken. If there is a problem of lack of objective orientation or of personal bias, these need to be worked at before the task of outlining ideas for the unit is tackled. In other words, all aspects of planning and work need to proceed on a double agenda: (1) experiences necessary to produce curriculum patterns, (2) experiences necessary to eliminate clouded vision, fears, and threats, and to create a climate in which change in feelings is both possible and comfortable. It would be fatal to assume that curriculum development can be accomplished by concentrating on either aspect and overlooking the other.

PATTERNS OF WORK

The logical steps and tasks in the development of units were discussed in chapter 20. This section will deal with those aspects of training and strategy which grow out of the psychological and human factors.

One important necessity is to create involvement. One way of creating involvement in curriculum change is to start with the concerns and problems teachers face, even though these concerns may not seem for the time being to be the most central to curriculum development. The first business in the strategy of curriculum change is to create identification with the task and to lay a foundation for a scientific and systematic approach to curriculum development. The data from research and experimentation in group dynamics suggest that in all productive work and activities concerned with innovation, identification with the task is an extremely crucial element. Identification helps the participants to adopt the problem as their own, rather than one for someone else to solve. This adds to the fortitude to face the fairly difficult learning and study that attends the production of curriculum units.

The problems and concerns for the initial study must also be within the competence of teachers and within practical possibility for them to act on. When the problems are beyond teacher competence and their power to act on, creative possibilities are cut off. No one can think profoundly, creatively, or precisely on matters that are out of his reach.

Starting with the identification of problems and concerns serves other important purposes also. First, the identification of problems lays the groundwork for a scientific and research-oriented approach to curriculum making. A careful problem identification and analysis usually leads to a study of the causes of difficulties. The data on these usually encourage an analysis of objectives and of the discrepancies that may exist between them and the curriculum practices.

These exploratory studies also help develop a realistic foundation for applying the criteria of good curricula in developing units because they begin to supply data with which to translate these general criteria into requirements for specific plans. For example, pursuing concrete problems by action-research techniques creates a setting in which theoretical explanations of the criteria of individual needs or social requirements become possible and understandable. As was suggested in the preceding section, gaps in theoretical understanding of the bases for curriculum are many. A research approach to practical curriculum problems permits these gaps to be filled by self-discovery.

Using the analysis of their own data as a way of reaching back into the fundamentals usually introduces teachers to new insights along many lines: a new perspective on learners, on community backgrounds, on the problems involved in translating the necessary content into learning experiences for particular groups of students, on psychological considerations which underlie the selection of effective learning experiences, and so on. These theoretical considerations are not easily communicated to teachers by verbal means in in-service training, at least not in a manner to assure their transfer into practice. When these principles are explored as an integral part of answering questions created by teachers' own studies, their meaning is more readily understood, accepted, and applied.

This integration of theory with the analysis of problems and conditions in classroom also stimulates bolder departures from the usual practices, because these departures can now be seen as clear-cut measures necessary for perceived purposes and on tangible evidence. In this framework, experiments with new content or new methods can be planned consciously as logical consequences of principles that are understood and accepted.

Finally, this method permits a clear and manageable means of translating general ideas into practice, in regard to selection of both the content of the programs and the methods to be pursued. (*Taba, Brady, and Robinson, 1952, pp. 311-12.* See also examples of change in approach in *Taba and Noel, 1957, pp. 35-46.*)

To the leaders and consultants this preliminary exploration provides a diagnosis of the level on which teachers think, feel, and operate. It gives opportunity to diagnose personal needs and feelings, and hence provides a tangible basis for doing something about them. It can reveal the extent to which teachers are capable of experimental procedures, the extent to which their current practices are wrapped up in strong convictions and feelings, the degree of naïvete or sophistication which prevails, and so on.

Insights can be gained into training needs by discovering what teachers understand about learning, what patterns of needs they are aware of, which classroom techniques they handle with security, and what thoughts they have about the curriculum. It is fairly generally recognized that changes in the human factors take time. It is more difficult to accept the slow pace of the actual change this approach requires. For example, it took the author, as a consultant and a county supervisor, a whole year to reorient one teacher whose method of teaching reading readiness to the first graders was to make them reproduce a variety of direct experiences in stories and pictures. While generally this method is quite successful, these particular children did not need it because their observations were extraordinarily perceptive, mature, and exact. At the same time, by the teacher's own admission, the class was quite weak in oral expression and discussion. It was difficult for this teacher to shift to stressing talk and discussion because her professional success was associated with her competency in this particular method. She was also a perfectionist, whose idea of herself, of her status, and professionality were tied up with the idea of making no mistakes. To adopt new procedures in teaching reading readiness involved a risk of making mistakes. She was not willing to get herself into such an eventuality. Many preliminary steps were needed before she was ready to develop a curriculum that was suitable to her students' needs.

Spending time in this initial stage of work on reconditioning attitudes and dispositions pays off in released talent and in the acceleration of subsequent changes at an accumulative pace. Persons who slowly master the basic principles of curriculum making in connection with their first effort at planning a unit can apply these skills to the next one with a relative ease. Once the scientific experimental attitude is established, a matter which at first is slow and difficult, it begins to function in all sorts of other decisions. Once the teachers learn to ask in connection with each classroom experience: What is it for? Can it produce more than one kind of learning?, their effectiveness in classroom teaching increases considerably. In the case described above, once the reorientation was accomplished, the teacher became competent in the new method, enabling her not only to develop a rewarding unit for her class but also to assume a leadership role in training others.

Generally, the efforts to diagnose the initial difficulties and to provide time and help to overcome them pay off in increased productivity and creativity. Teachers who feel extremely insecure about departing from the current guide or the textbook begin to explore new approaches to organizing units, once they are sure that there is an orderly method to it. Persons who feel shaky about using group process for fear of losing control of the class invent many new uses, once they acquire the needed skills and realize that grouping and group processes are not a matter of a wild *laissez-faire* permissiveness but of scientifically planned stimulants and controls.

In contrast, pressure on rapid production without the preliminary reorientation slows down later work, reduces the amount of change in conception, and gives a less creative product. The amount of work and the quality of the product depend on the groundwork laid in this first step.

Because this initial step of problem analysis, pondering, and study serves so many purposes, more care and time are needed than is usually allotted to it in the pressure of getting the work done. Too often this preparatory step is cut down or omitted altogether because the significance of this tooling up is not apparent. This may account for the fact that curriculum revision is often limited to tinkering and produces so little genuine innovation. It probably also accounts for the common complaints about teacher resistance to change.

Similar integration of theory and practice is needed at all other stages in curriculum development discussed in chapter 20. Questions may very well be raised concerning the proper balance between training in the theoretical and the practical, between the general and the specific. For example, how deeply do the teachers, at the point of developing curriculum units, need to go into the various theories about learning? In using (or planning for the use of) diagnostic techniques, what do they need to understand about psychological theories underlying these techniques? To what extent should they probe into the nature of cultural needs?

Those who have worked with teachers in this manner have found two helpful principles. First, it is most efficient to limit the training in theory to those points that elucidate the practical tasks, and second, the best use of theory occurs when theoretical discussions accompany action steps instead of preceding them.

Too elaborate an emphasis on theory ahead of its use usually falls on deaf ears, especially if its relationship to tangible problems is lost. For example, theories of learning, including the psychological sequence of learning, make little sense until someone in the group tries to select learning activities and to put them into a sequence. No amount of explanation of the meaning of sampling content by selecting contrasts is comprehensible until the members of a group face the actual task of selecting content for a given classroom and for a given idea. Philosophical issues can be discussed profitably only when the decisions at hand require value judgments. The concept of scope and sequence does not become clear until the task of determining the basis for a sequence from unit to unit or from one grade level program to another is actually being faced.

But none of these occasions needs to be converted into a protracted seminar on learning theories, values, or sampling theories. Introducing the theoretical principles as an integral part of producing curriculum units, in effect, amounts to applying the principle of discovery to curriculum making and the training involved in it.

LEVELS OF INVOLVEMENT

The way of working described in the preceding section suggests also new criteria for selecting participants for the groups working on curriculum for composing teams.

If both productivity and human factors are to be considered, one needs to plan a developmental strategy of participation. The first pilot development of experimental units needs to start with a fairly small group of volunteers composed of persons who are concerned about something and willing to work out something for their own classrooms. The greater the range of grade levels and types of school situations represented among these volunteers, the better. But for eventual productivity as well as for effective participation it is preferable to make a start with a small group of people willing to change than to harness at this point a large group that has no inherent motivation for changing anything.

This principle of selective participation in curriculum revision on the basis of concern contradicts the current notion that participation in any effort on behalf of curriculum change should be 100 per cent or at least include representation from every school. This insistence on a 100 per cent participation is partly due to equating participation with democracy, to the idea that no one should be left out of important decisions and that burdens should be shared equitably. Partly, however, it stems from the failure to see curriculum making as a developmental sequence in which different groups of school personnel are involved at different stages of work, each playing a different role and at a different point in the sequence. This is the principle of levels of involvement.

Insisting on a 100 per cent participation from the start is a strategical error which creates many problems. One of these is the inclusion of many "reluctant dragons," who by their resistance dampen the atmosphere and impede progress at a time when the participants are the least secure and when resistance and doubt, therefore, have the greatest impact. Many a curriculum committee has become tired before it has won over those who sabotage new ideas. To create new pilot developments with a reluctant group is asking for the impossible, if for no other reason than because the usual public school cannot afford the leadership it takes to guide this job under such circumstances.

This principle of starting with a small group of volunteers needs to be supplemented by a strategy of extending participation at successive levels of work by adding personnel as the nature of work, and therefore also the nature of its appeal, changes. For example, persons not interested in curriculum development as such may be intrigued with some succeeding activities, such as sociometric testing to determine needs, selecting reading materials for experimental units, or trying out experimental units. Once involved, they tend to continue and to enlarge their interest. To continue to involve additional personnel at various steps of curriculum development requires a continual communication and kindling of interest which can happen only if the lines of communication are kept open between the pilot groups and the rest of the staff. This can be done formally and informally. A teacher developing a unit for a third grade on community study may engage the help of few others. A faculty meeting describing what is going on in experimental work may stimulate others to try. A vivid description of what is learned about students by some newer diagnostic devices usually brings request for opportunities to try these techniques.

Some schools have developed a fairly systematic exploitation of levels of involvement after a trial and error with the usual procedures for increasing participation in curriculum work. In one school a core committee of six for elementary social studies had been at work for a year in developing a fifth-grade study unit. As they worked on developing a basis for constructing this unit, they began to realize that the ideas and procedures they were using might be applied to revising the whole social studies program. They therefore set to work on the general objectives and a framework for the social studies. Soon they realized that not only was this task beyond them, but that even if they managed to complete it, they would have trouble in getting it accepted by other teachers. A meeting of all teachers of social studies was called at which the objectives worked out by the core committee were reported and criticisms were asked for. This meeting was a failure because the participants could not enter into the process without at least an opportunity to go through some of the steps in thinking about formulating the objectives. It was clear that more active methods of involvement were needed, so a series of grade-level meetings was held at which teachers of each grade were asked to suggest needs and objectives important to them, ideas to explore, and areas around which to build units. This brought a much more active response, and a few people volunteered to develop units. These people constituted a temporary production committee to criticize and revise each other's units. At a later point, a still larger group tested the tentative units and experimented with the new classroom procedures. Others helped secure needed materials, and so on, making available many levels of involvement and a differentiated participation in the total job over the period of four years. Throughout this period the core committee continued to guide and coordinate the activities. They compared the units, revised them, planned the sequence of development, and did the rewriting. They also were responsible for editing the final units, as well as producing the handbook on how to use them.*

The way of working described above involves not only a methodology of approaching the task but also a way of combining the work of individuals and of groups that is not customary in the usual curriculum committees. It involves, furthermore, varied patterns of leadership. These matters will be discussed in the next chapter.

* For a fuller description of the process, see Taba *et al.* (1950, pp. 223-41). The handbook was issued by the School City of South Bend (1949).

Working with Groups

Working in groups is practically essential in curriculum development, particularly for any work requiring development of new insights and new orientation. A recognition of the importance of the processes of group work has led to a science of groups and group dynamics, which is concerned with the analysis of processes of interaction in small groups and the relationship of these factors to productivity. While by far the greatest number of studies in group dynamics have been confined to groups outside the school context, the application of the principles and theories of group dynamics to educational work has been quite assiduous. (See, for example, *Thelen, 1954; Miles, 1959.*) It is generally recognized also that the "science in the field of human relations and social action has been developed a great deal further than have our technologies for affecting action in valid ways" (*Thelen, 1954, p. 181*). An analysis of the ways in which groups can become more effective and productive and an effort to apply the findings in group dynamics are, therefore, important elements in building the strategy of curriculum change.

Group work serves a variety of functions. One is to release intelligence; another is to provide a potent dynamic to rethinking. In group study and discussion, one person's insight generates another's; one idea suggests another. As new ideas are created by a circular response, by reconciling different ideas, a freeing of intelligence occurs. The greater the range of experience, the greater this learning, provided the members of the group are focused on a similar task. For example, if teachers, community agency personnel, and parents participate in studies of children, a wider range of evidence and broader perspective become available to all.

Groups can also create motivation and courage to proceed. To many individual teachers who struggle with practices they cannot change single-handedly, group work provides moral support and encouragement. Still others, who feel that there is too much to learn, too much to conquer, find in group participation additional energy and courage.

However, these advantages are not automatic by-products of groups as such. Groups can also be wasteful of time, sterile, play the game of passive resistance, and act as hotbeds of "under the table agenda," intrigue and conflict. Many groups do. What role the groups assume depends in part on how they are composed, in part on how skillfully group processes are carried on, and how well human-relations factors are attended to. (See, for example, *Thelen, 1954, ch. 10; Miles, 1959, ch. 6; Benne and Muntyan, 1951, part 3, sec. C and D.*)

COMPOSING WORK TEAMS

This chapter deals with ways of working with groups on curriculum development and with the problems of leadership in such groups. Curriculum work requires integration of many competencies not usually found in one person. Therefore, planned teamwork, in which each individual concentrates on his own task but also in which a range of needed competencies is combined in such a manner that they can support and supplement each other, is one essential requirement for productivity. However, selecting persons who have concerns or problems on which they want to work and who at the same time bring complementary competencies to a team is in itself a difficult task. Normally, neither the school district staffs nor the principals are completely aware of who wants or can do what or of the unique competencies of their various staff members. Nor has selecting and composing work groups been considered important enough to allow time to develop the criteria of choice and the procedure for choosing.

For initial stages of curriculum development, concern about some problem of teaching or of curriculum seems the best chief criterion for selection. On succeeding levels of involvement the criterion of planned heterogeneity is useful. The more extensive the curriculum change, the more important it is to involve representatives from different grade levels and from different areas of specialization, although at the start it may be better not to insist on representation at the expense of the principle of "voluntarism."

On the whole, the kind of thinking involved in curriculum planning, and especially in developing a basis for it, is more easily stimulated in a group that is heterogeneous in experience and background. While it may require greater skill to lead such a group, heterogeneity is more apt to generate new thinking than a group with about the same kind of experience.

For groups whose task it is to produce a curriculum, a combination of several types of experience is necessary. Combining persons with expertness in research techniques, in curriculum development, and in principles of child development with those who are expert about the realities of the classroom and about specific subjects provides the needed ingredients for a dynamic team, making it possible to think about curriculum in a balanced way. Theorists are forced to be in touch with data and experience on the classroom level, and practitioners are compelled to subject their views to theoretical considerations. Communication between these two poles of curriculum thinking is facilitated when the groups representing each orientation—the curriculum directors, consultants, supervisors, and teachers—together focus on tangible tasks and work together on them. This partnership of varied expertness and talent, harnessed to the practical task of producing teaching units, in which the reality situation lends vitality to theory and theory elucidates the reality, is quite fruitful in producing new ideas, experimental designs, and zest to revaluate and to reconsider.

Work teams are more effective when they cross the traditional lines of association and, therefore, the traditional pockets of thinking and orientation. Individuals who have worked together too long develop a climate which favors acceptance of assumptions that should be questioned. In such groups it is difficult to raise new questions and to secure new answers. When teachers of different grade levels or subjects work together, new points of view challenge the crystallized ideas and assumptions because each sees students in a different perspective, each has a different philosophy about content, and a different experience with what children can do. When primary teachers, who usually stress experience, exchange ideas with upper-elementary-grade teachers, who are more apt to stress content, a balanced role of content and of experience can be more readily established. Clearer community assessments come about when knowledge and interpretation of lay persons are combined with those of the social agency and school personnel.

Besides these job-related experiences and competencies, it is useful also to consider the more personal ones, such as ability or inclination to handle quantitative data, conduct interviews, compose questionnaires, or act as an interpreter or pacifier in the group. The more the combined professional or human-relations skills of the group match the demands of the task, the greater the productivity of which such a group is capable.

Various tasks and situations call for different combinations of competencies, of course. If an integrated program of social studies and English for high school is under consideration, then it is most appropriate to include the teachers of these areas. Or teachers of social studies, English, and home economics might work together on a program of orientation to the community. For some purposes it may be profitable to combine individuals with experience on all grade levels in one group. The main point is that combining heterogeneity of job involvement to attack a similar task or a task with similar focus enhances insight and extends understanding. Heterogeneity is a handicap only when the whole group is expected to do the same job and when there is no differentiation of tasks within the group. It is of advantage to combine individualization of specific tasks with commonality of focus, such as when each person works on a different unit or part of a unit and group sessions are held for the purpose of clarifying common theoretical points, or for criticism and suggestions.

Another useful criterion in composing groups for a pilot development in curriculum is what is loosely called "potential leadership"—the ability of the persons chosen to communicate with several different segments of the school and the community. Composing curriculum work groups of persons who can easily communicate with other teachers is itself an insurance for spreading the involvement at the later stages, through involving other teachers in try-outs of the units developed, enlarging the base of the studies made in connection with the pilot development, or merely keeping the wider group of teachers and parents informed about the new developments. Many an experimental venture has become isolated, and even caused a rift in a school system, because no provisions were made for communication during the experimental period or because the communication was confined to official channels, which are always limited and tend to have an alienating air about them.

The size of working groups is a consideration also. Studies in group dynamics have attempted to determine an optimum size of groups. Thelen, for example, recommends nine (1949). Probably this is not a valid recommendation for all groups, for, if productivity and participation are the criteria, and the time the group has together is a dependent variable, then different sizes may be appropriate, depending on the task, the composition of the group, the nature of their interpersonal relations, and the time they have to work together. However, considering the fact that usually curriculum planning meetings last about two hours, generally groups larger than fifteen become difficult to handle. If a combination of individual work and group discussion of the common points and plans is the pattern of work, groups larger than this present difficulties, for individual reports are arranged at too infrequent intervals and participation decreases in proportion to the size of the group.

Whatever the number of persons, work groups should be formed on the basis of job requirements and along the lines promising the most effective teamwork. For example, groups should not be formed ahead of determining what individuals wish to work at, for groups work best when each individual is anchored in a personal commitment and the group tackles the common features of these individual tasks. At least in the beginning, these should be frankly work groups and not committees committed to producing consensus in action decisions.

This is in reverse of the usual procedure of composing committees first and then deciding what they shall do, a practice which has immobilized many a committee because the work pattern that evolves so often turns out to be incompatible with the composition of the group.*

* For ways of developing action groups, see D. M. Hall (1957) and Lippitt, Watson, and Westley (1958, ch. 5).

CLIMATE FOR PRODUCTIVE WORK

Adequate composition of the group does not automatically provide good climate for learning or for productive work. A collection of individuals, even with similar tasks, does not make a functioning group. Good functioning groups are shaped by what happens in them and to them. They need to develop a collective focus and a sense that what is being done has significance beyond the worth of any one individual project—to the group, to the school, to the scheme of things generally. Above all, the method of working must be such as to relate each individual's contribution to that of others. If both productivity and good human relations are desired, certain processes need to be used which help establish aims, standards, and models and, at the same time, create a climate favorable to maximum effort.

The climate of the group determines also the nature of participation and the level of expectations. If objectivity is always sought and maintained in group conferences, whether they deal with interpretation of data or with ideas, objectivity becomes for the individual members an aim toward which to strive and a standard by which to live.

Groups can also give moral support for actions or decisions that may threaten one individual. A person who is afraid to experiment on his own is more likely to do so when a group collectively becomes responsible. A growing edge can be set in a group, one higher than the lowest possible accomplishment but not so high that it can be shared only by the few most advanced. It is possible to develop a climate of mutual responsibility and dependence in which the success of each individual's project depends in part on the creative contribution of others, such as setting an idea suggested by one member into a larger perspective, refining a technique by sharing experience with it, or expanding a plan of action.

A few criteria can be set for developing a good working climate:

1. Groups tend to be more productive when their deliberations are conducted in a permissive atmosphere, when decisions are kept open so that shifts in conclusions are possible with new facts and analysis, when participation is encouraged by incorporating each person's contribution into the thinking of the group, and when critical comments are treated so that their impact is devoid of sharp personal edges. This permissive atmosphere is a cushion against the struggles and the doubts some persons experience, especially in the initial stages of their efforts.

2. Most groups need opportunities to appraise their own thought and work processes in order to become intelligent about them. Individuals can overcome blocks to their thinking when they are aware of them. Realization that appraisal is a functional part of the process makes it easier for individuals to give and accept criticism. Objectivity induced by evaluation helps individuals to accept analysis of ideas and problems that otherwise might seem

threatening. An awareness of the fact that everyone has problems makes it easier to accept help.

3. Protection of individual viewpoints and behavior in groups needs to be assured, even of those who are overaggressive and hostile or who express unsupportable notions. This is especially important in the beginning stages of group work when both morale and task orientation are as yet weak and when the demands on re-orientation are the heaviest.

4. Groups work more effectively when natural leadership is cultivated and distributed. When official leaders are forced into the role of experts, they, instead of the group members, shoulder the responsibility and leadership never emerges. Many unproductive situations are those in which, for one reason or another, the natural leadership never developed, and the consultant or the official chairman remains both the initiator and the change agent.

5. Communication channels must be established. This involves procedures which assure that whatever is said and done has a clear meaning to everyone, such as providing adequate clarification, use of illustrations, developing common definitions, etc. It also involves removal of such road blocks to communication as tenseness, vying for status, and lack of a framework to which to relate the particulars.*

6. Both the composition of the groups and the manner of work need to be flexible. If personnel is fixed and plans change, the composition may become inappropriate to the new task. A group may begin studying one problem which, upon analysis may turn into something else. A group of teachers who were concerned solely with their Mexican students' tardiness and were unaware of the gap between the school's demands and the children's cultural learnings began to see that gap when they investigated the reasons for tardiness. They acquired a new perspective on the kind of curriculum these students needed and turned toward plans for revising some aspects of curriculum instead of pursuing tardiness. This also necessitated reshaping of the group to bring it in line with the new objective. If it is understood that the groups are composed around work tasks, such changes in membership do not constitute the offense that they do in "frozen" committees. In fixed committees change in membership is often embarrassing because members acquire fixed roles and develop a stake in belonging to the committee whether or not their role is effective.

* The literature on group dynamics sets up much more refined criteria for an adequate climate for group productivity. See, for example, Thelen (1951, pp. 84-98) and Thelen (1951 and 1954, ch. 10).

DIFFERENTIATION OF TASKS FOR GROUPS AND INDIVIDUALS

Working in groups becomes burdensome and sterile when everything is done in group sessions. Work can be carried on more effectively when tasks that require participation of the entire group are differentiated from those that can be done more effectively in subgroups, and from those that individuals can do best alone. The following differentiation of individual and group roles seems logical: Individuals are responsible for all the tasks involving active production, such as studying their classrooms, projecting objectives for their units, outlining core ideas, selecting samples of content, projecting and reporting on experiments in classrooms. Group sessions are reserved for planning procedures, analyzing and reflecting upon individual efforts, sharing inventions, and developing the common theoretical principles which underlie all of these specific efforts. Common principles need to be developed in groups partly because group discussion is a better means for clarifying them, and partly because developing them for each individual project would be too time consuming.

Group sessions should, in other words, be devoted to mutual help and to theoretical ideas that are relevant to all individual projects and represent training in insight and orientation for all. Group sessions should also be reserved for matters in which an exchange of a maximum range of ideas and experience is important, such as identifying and analyzing problems, interpreting facts from research and reading, and projecting the general direction of work. For example, each individual on a team for producing model units may attempt to formulate objectives for his own unit. The group discussion would then be addressed to such matters as developing a proper differentiation of categories of behavior and of the criteria by which to appraise objectives. After individuals have attempted to formulate core ideas, a content sample, or a sequence of learning activities, group seminars are also helpful in developing the needed criteria and in examining individual efforts in the light of these criteria.

An astute rotation of group work and individual work does much to keep production alive: it enhances involvement, because each individual is focused on his own task; it makes available for each person new dimensions of thought through comparison with the work of others and through group analysis; the thought of the group is primed continually with new facts and experiences on which it can reflect; and theoretical ideas acquire new pertinence because they can be related to definite individual needs.

LEADERSHIP ROLES

The topic of leadership has received considerable attention recently. There are studies of various patterns of leadership and their effects on the productivity of groups and of the specific functions and roles of leadership in group situations. Numerous analyses of the role of administrative leadership are available. And there are enough "how to do" pamphlets and articles to supply guidelines for practically every level and type of leadership function. There have been numerous leadership training activities both in laboratory settings and in connection with educational conferences and workshops (*Thelen, 1954, ch. 5; Miles, 1957; N. Gross, Mason, and McEachern, 1958; Chase and Cuba, 1955*).

A few central points from this welter of group dynamics literature are relevant here. The scientific approach has helped to explode the common concept of leadership as a trait an individual possesses. Instead, the concept of leadership roles has emerged. These roles serve specific functions in specific group situations. A distinction has also emerged between the official status leadership positions and the functioning leadership roles. In each school system there are many "leadership" positions filled by different members of the professional staff. These positions usually form a hierarchy of authority ranging down from the board to the superintendent, the school principals, and the supervisors or curriculum consultants. While the responsibilities of these positions may be fairly clearly defined, the functional leadership roles they perform are not. There is considerable confusion, for example, between the roles of the supervisor or consultant and of the principal. It is not always clear exactly what the "leadership" role of an administrator is in curriculum development. Is it limited only to giving the green light? Is it something more functional? If so, what degree of participation is required in the process of curriculum development and at which points?

Some difficulties are experienced also in the role expectations of the outside consultant. Outside consultants are often put in a position of initiating change, instead of supplying expert knowledge and skill at points where the local curriculum development needs it and can use it. Smith suggests that the use of outside consultants "as agents of change" is a perversion of the consultant role, and that the importation of the dynamics of change from outside assures a short tenure for the change (*B. O. Smith, Stanley, and Shores, 1957, p. 458*). The dynamics of change must be located in the local situation. While an outside expert may be helpful in the analysis of the situation requiring change, in the methods of initiating change, or in the required techniques and knowledge, the focal point of initiating and carrying on curriculum change must remain the responsibility of local leadership.

It appears, then, that the functional roles important to curriculum development, including the functions of official personnel, need to be more sharply defined to avoid role confusion and to permit allocation of particular roles according to specific competencies as well as according to professional status and responsibilities.

As far as work in groups is concerned, the more widely the leadership roles are distributed, the more energetic and responsible is the participation. In discussions and meetings, for example, the chief function of the official leader is to induce a functioning leadership in the members of the group. The chief function of the official leaders in school systems is often also found in their ability to induce growth and the distribution of the functional leadership roles.

In the complex task of curriculum development, as in any task-centered activity, multiple leadership roles are required. These multiple roles can be classified into two types: those of group maintenance and those involving professional expertness in knowledge and skill. One difficulty in using groups in curriculum development, as in other professional undertakings, is that there is insufficient analysis of the requirements of these two types of leadership roles.

Often leadership is identified exclusively with expertness and knowledge. Persons who know the most are supposed to be the leaders and are often appointed as official leaders. Yet, supplying information and ideas is but one of the many functions of leadership. It is necessary also to recognize leadership roles which enable the group to be productive, to work harmoniously and more or less contentedly. The fact that most productive groups carry double agenda, that of producing something and that of shaping the human conditions, makes it necessary also to look at leadership from this double viewpoint: leadership in the sense of ability to contribute expert knowledge or skill to the task, and leadership in a sense of keeping the wheels moving smoothly.*

Curriculum development requires expertness of many varieties, not the least of which is the expertness which teachers have by virtue of the fact that they are the only ones who actually face groups of children and have experience in guiding them. Someone needs to know how to mobilize groups, to initiate them into curriculum work, to diagnose their concerns, and to develop problems and plans from these. Someone needs to have sufficient grasp of the method of formulating objectives to help with the processes of clarification and classification. Sufficient familiarity is needed with the content of specific fields to guide the processes of selecting valid core ideas and samples of content. Someone must be capable of projecting hypotheses from research, whether local or general, and of translating these hypotheses into curriculum possibilities. Someone must know enough about learners and processes of learning to help guide the selection of learning activities and the formulation of their sequences. Technical understanding is needed regarding

* On the group-maintenance roles of leadership, see Benne and Sheats (1948); Miles (1959, pp. 15-26); Lippitt, Watson, and Westley (1958).

the choice of diagnostic and evaluation devices, of research methods and of the methods of interpreting research data.

In addition to these professional competencies there are requirements for "human engineering." A diagnosis is needed of the human factors affecting the participants and their interpersonal relations to determine the degree of change each can take, the blocks to be overcome, the levels of perception, and the attitudes, so as to shape the working methods and to pace the work according to actual rather than hypothetical possibilities. And, of course, someone needs to be familiar enough with group processes to guide the groups through their initial bafflements and confusions and to help establish group goals and a psychological continuity as well as a climate conducive to productive and satisfying work.

This is a wide array of competencies. When a clear-cut analysis of these functions is lacking, leadership in curriculum work tends to be confined to a narrower range of roles than is necessary, or the emphasis falls exclusively either on production or on group processes. Neither alone generates creative productivity. The combination of these two types of leadership roles demands that the persons who assume them be thoroughly disciplined both in the knowledge of curriculum development and in the "knowledge of, and skill in, human relations and social diagnosis and communication" (*B. O. Smith, Stanley, and Shores, 1957, p. 461*). Rarely is one person or one type of personnel equipped with all this, nor can these functions be automatically designated according to the official positions.

As one considers the state of curriculum leadership in the school systems, one would tend to agree that no current professional staff in a school district is completely competent in all roles that are needed in curriculum development: the technical skills in curriculum making, the mastery of intellectual discipline, the knowledge of social and educational values which underlie educational decisions, and the understanding of the processes of educational engineering and human relations. The skills in managing curriculum development are not highly developed. Most persons in charge of curricula are familiar with the various schematic approaches; they know what a good curriculum should be. But because curriculum theories are vague at this point, there is relatively little understanding of the elements which go into making that kind of curriculum, and particularly of the action steps that are necessary to combine these elements into a functioning curriculum. Therefore, many tactical errors are made, such as tackling curriculum development from the least movable points, undertaking tasks without analyzing the steps by which they can be accomplished, and generally in expecting too much in too little time.

While teachers, on the whole, are fairly competent in their respective subject areas, this competency tends to be limited to the factual details and does not represent disciplined knowledge, nor always an up-to-date grasp of their subjects. They need help in weeding out the chaff and in determining the important ideas. While there is a fair understanding of the democratic values, less is understood about the relationship of these values to the curriculum and about the method of translating "democracy" into school practices. Nor is the profession on the whole well enough trained in the research processes needed to form a good foundation for curriculum development. The curriculum staffs have not mastered sufficiently the techniques of mobilizing human resources to make the best of whatever talents and energies are available.

To initiate and carry on curriculum changes of consequence in the sense discussed in the preceding chapters requires that the profession either possess these competencies or acquire them in the process of curriculum development. This is the burden of leadership imposed by the transition to a grass-roots approach to curriculum development. Because the grass-roots approach emphasizes wide participation, it also faces the task of developing the procedures, strategies, and competencies for a sophisticated level of leadership.

From these considerations emerge several criteria for developing and using leadership in curriculum development in practical situations:

1. A clear analysis is needed of the functional roles necessary in the various aspects of work, so that the competencies required by these roles can be considered in making up the work teams and supplied at needed points.

2. Since change in those who participate in curriculum development is a necessary condition for producing a curriculum that is in any essential way different from the existing one, leadership is needed to deal with the human factors. The range of required leadership functions goes beyond the usual professional competencies and extends into psychological insights and into the techniques for managing the human dynamics.

3. The strategy of systematic curriculum work involves a projection of a sequence of the essential steps and of the essential leadership roles for each step. It is clear that the type of help needed is not the same at all these points.

4. A new look is needed at the way of using outside consultants, and the type of consultants needed. It is not unreasonable to assume that instead of a consultant on content or an expert in techniques of curriculum development, a group at certain points of its work may need a consultant on human relations and group processes to shape the strategy for work and to provide training in the procedures of conducting groups to produce optimum cooperative effort and to avoid or minimize cleavages and conflicts. Lawler identifies a host of consultant functions which include help in defining problems, in planning steps for the study of the problems, in examining ways of working, in developing a favorable climate of working, and in getting in touch with ideas and resources (1958, chs. 3-5).

5. In most school situations experimentation and training is needed to develop these leadership skills, to organize the leadership functions into an adequate team pattern, and to use them according to the developmental sequences in the work of the groups.

A CASE STUDY OF DEVELOPING
LEADERSHIP ROLES

This case study (a composite of work on curriculum in two county school systems) is a description of the stages in the leadership functions played by a county staff and outside consultants in the course of initiating curriculum change and of producing a curriculum pattern which differed considerably from the existing one. Several stages can be identified in this work, each of which required different leadership roles in different combinations and allocations. The allocation of the roles was in part affected by the fact that the county staffs were being trained for leadership in a varied context of working on the curriculum with teachers.

Initiating

The analysis of the problems requiring change in the curriculum and in the approach to making this change was made by the county curriculum staff in cooperation with the school principals. This analysis suggested that the usual efforts—institutes, lectures, required attendance of college classes—had not over a period of years produced much curriculum improvement and did not seem promising for making changes in the structure of the curriculum. Furthermore, since the county staff had been responsible for developing curriculum guides and units, the teachers in various districts tended to regard the county as authoritarian and it was difficult to kindle their initiative for curriculum improvement. For these reasons, the county staff was searching for some kind of grass-roots approach that would promise greater participation and involvement in the whole process of curriculum improvement, and at the same time improve the human relations between the schools and the county office.

This decision to look at the problem was made by the county administration. It initiated the search for a consultant who could help with the human-relations aspect and was oriented to a grass-roots approach to curriculum building.

Next, it was necessary to decide on an approach and a pattern of work. In this the entire staff and the outside consultant participated. The strategy grew from questions like these: (1) Is the initial effort to be directed toward a "guide" or a series of models of curriculum units? (2) What would be a chief method of working: should the work be centered in the county office, or in districts and individual schools? Where should one start? (3) What is the total sequence and about how much time will it take? (4) What will be the roles of the county staff, of the outside consultants, of teachers, and of the local school principals? How should leadership teams be composed?

From the discussion of these questions the following principles evolved:

1. The program should be aimed at re-education of the whole staff, and at producing pilot models of curriculum and teaching. The program should seek especially to enhance the democratic quality in supervisory leadership.

2. The program should pursue an action-research approach. It should start with concerns and problems identified by teachers and study these problems scientifically, diagnosing their causes and factors. The formulations of the curriculum should be undertaken following these preliminary studies. By and large the new program should adhere to the state framework.

3. The project should extend over at least a three-year span, allowing roughly the first year for exploratory studies, the second for development and experimentation, and the third for consolidation. In other words, there should be no pressure for immediate results, and as much time for training as seemed necessary. (Actually a longer time was needed for a variety of reasons, among them the mortality in the initial groups.)

4. The county staff should be involved in all aspects of the program: planning with teachers, recording, evaluating. In addition, there should be special training sessions with the county staff, so that at the end of the project their leadership skills would be mature enough to continue without outside help.

The specific roles for the staff and the consultant were also spelled out. The county staff members agreed to attach themselves to the work groups in line with their usual work assignments and to perform any roles that seemed necessary. from locating and supplying needed materials and giving emotional support to keeping adequate process records of the training and consultation sessions. The outside consultant agreed to help with the methods of analyzing these problems, with the planning of the research procedures and techniques, and with designing the experiments and studies on the basis of the findings (*Taba and Noel, 1957, pp. 6-7*).

Mobilizing

Planning the method of initiating and mobilizing and the general strategy was the responsibility of the whole staff. Such questions as the following were raised: What is the sample for the experimental curriculum development to be? Should the project sample geographic areas, areas of curriculum, grade levels? How large a sample is feasible in the light of available competencies and resources? For how large a group can the county staff actually provide leadership? What dangers are there in overstretching leadership? What cautions need to be exercised and what criteria need to be applied in selecting participants?

At this point the role of the outside consultant was to raise questions about the practical implications of the general plan, but the staff as experts on the local situation analyzed it to see what conditions prevailed and which measures were needed.

The final decision was to start with a fairly small group of volunteers in order to make the pilot experience as effective as possible and to take care of a spread at a later step. It was also decided that the next step was to approach the principals to get their reactions to the idea and to secure their help in locating interested teachers. Selecting participants for curriculum work was their official role, and they would also know which teachers could be approached and had the power to encourage them to join the pilot group. The county staff would have overstepped their role had they issued the invitations to teachers directly and would have thereby added to the already brewing animosity between the county staff and the principals. This action also represented a step in the involvement of the administrations on the level congruent with their job role.

Since both the idea of selecting volunteers and the particular approach to curriculum development were new, the county staff with the consultant planned the proceedings of the meeting with principals quite carefully to make sure that the idea was discussed open-endedly enough to permit a reshaping of it in the light of their perceptions.

This meeting dealt with several concerns, such as that if each person concentrates on problems of concern to him, how can one make sure that the sum total of work adds up to something of school-wide significance? How does one assure that the explorations and ideas developed by a few can be compounded into the total program?

The criteria for selection were articulated as follows:

1. Select persons:
   (a) Who have something to work on and who want to work.
   (b) Who believe that they can stay with the project more than one year.
   (c) Whose problems or projects seem significant to the school concerned.
   (d) Who are likely to exercise some leadership with other teachers, so that the limited pilot program will eventually affect the total program in the school.

2. The distribution of grade levels and subject areas should be as wide as possible, although this criterion should not dominate the initial selection.

3. Representation by schools should not be attempted. Small teams from fewer schools would be preferable to a single representative from every school (*Taba and Noel, 1957, p. 9*).

Conducting Preliminary Studies

In the work of the first year, which was largely concerned with identifying and analyzing the problems of teachers, team roles were distributed as follows: The planning of the general steps and procedures was the responsibility of the consultants and the entire county staff.

The county staff members also assumed responsibility for keeping records of all group and individual conferences in order to study the dynamics in the development of ideas, in methods of problem analysis, and in handling the human-relations problems. These records were used as a material for the staff training sessions. The county staff also helped teachers with locating materials and with any practical problems that arose between group sessions. They held conferences with principals to keep them informed of what their teachers were doing.

The outside consultant was chiefly responsible for helping individuals and groups identify their problems and analyze them. She was in charge of the process and acted as a translator of the research ideas and techniques. She diagnosed the levels of perception, feelings, and attitudes, developed, adapted, and invented the techniques of gathering the necessary data, conducted the problem analysis conferences, and developed assignments for individual work.

Teachers were the researchers and analysts. They secured the necessary data and made the needed observations. In group sessions they applied new perspective and insights to the problems they had stated, reflected on each other's problems and findings, and formulated the action hypotheses which these reflections suggested.

Two leadership functions are crucial at this stage. One is to enhance and preserve initiative and to aid self-discovery through encouraging studies by participants, helping them attain a rational perspective toward curriculum problems through their own efforts rather than by being told or taught. This involves a patient questioning. The chief activity of the leader or the consultant is to induce analysis, to help make needed distinctions, to evoke questioning of assumptions. While the leader must be aware of the possible factors involved in the problems proposed by the participants, his role at this stage requires that he refrain from articulating this analysis himself and, instead, guide the group to making studies designed to reveal these factors. For the same reason, the analysis of problems must be so conducted as to focus on problems as the participants see them, so that the diagnosis of problems does not substitute a new problem. While it is important that individuals arrive at a fuller and a more rational perspective toward their problems, this should not be done at the cost of short-cutting self-discovery or of cultivating dependency on the leader and of depriving the group of initiative.*

The other important function is that of human engineering. Since a change in orientation is apt to be threatening, the leader's role at the initial stage is to protect feelings, to foster security with novel tasks, to develop teamwork. Both the consultant and the county staff need to be highly supportive, to pace the work according to individual capacities to change, and to employ indirect rather than direct methods in inducing change and reorientation. The same attitude was needed in the respective schools. To protect self-discovery, it

---

* For a further illustration of this process, see Washington School District (1956a and 1956b).

was important that principals allow the members of work groups to secure the necessary data. Their support was needed for teachers to feel free to experiment in their classrooms and to communicate their ideas to other teachers. Frequent conferences with principals were held to make sure that they understood what the work groups were about and that the new developments in their school were not canceled out by contradictory arrangements made by other divisions of the school system. Experimental programs are in jeopardy when they are carried on under the auspices of one segment of the school system while another segment uses procedures that nullify them.

When problem analysis reaches a point at which research techniques are needed, the consultant role changes into that of a trainer, describing methods and techniques, explaining ways of using them, suggesting procedures by which to obtain valid data and criteria by which to interpret them objectively. Technically trained outside consultants may be used at this point. As competence grows, the active trainer role recedes. In all this, the consultant is more effective if he identifies with the problems of the group, is a learner himself, and does not approach his task with set ideas about how the problems are to be studied, what questions need to be asked, and what kinds of answers must be found.

Since it was important for the county staff to develop the necessary theoretical insights and skills, training sessions were held with them at regular intervals, usually following each series of conferences with work groups in preparation for eventually transferring to the county staff the roles which the consultant assumed at the start. These sessions dealt with such matters as the method of conducting the problem census, the rationale and the method of problem identification, formulating and checking hypotheses and relating them to study assignments, the essential features of the diagnostic techniques used, the methods of asking open-ended questions, and so on. Training was needed even in the methods of recording to reproduce with perception the dynamics of meetings and to strengthen the habit of recording the processes by which conclusions and decisions were reached, rather than only the conclusions and decisions themselves. In this, the outside consultant acted as a trainer while the staff group decided what lines of training they needed.

Planning Pilot Units

At this stage the roles of participants as well as of leadership shifted. The activity of the work groups intensified. Individuals formulated objectives they wanted to attain, outlined content ideas, projected learning experiences, and conducted experiments in their classrooms. As the work progressed, group sessions took on a more theoretical tone and serious reading increased. It was possible, for example, to consider directly some principles which at the earlier stage were handled indirectly and rather incidentally. Some of this work, such as outlining the main ideas and sampling content, required a good deal of training and guidance. In others, such as projecting appropriate learning activities, teachers were the only appropriate experts. The formulation of core ideas and the sampling of content was done under close supervision of the outside consultant because this process involves abstraction and differentiation of dimensions, a process at which few teachers are adept. Teachers, on the other hand, were more expert at designing learning experiences. Many invented entirely new procedures for teaching, for organizing content, and for diagnosis. As their understanding of the objectives for which they worked grew, their skills and security increased, as well as their inventiveness.

At this point, the outside consultant assumed the role of the trainer and the gatekeeper of the principles of curriculum development, and functioned as a reorganizer and systematizer of ideas and proposals rather than as an originator. She became the specialist in the method of thinking, but did not dictate either the objectives or the specific content. The chief task of the consultant as a curriculum specialist was to suggest methods for clarifying and grouping objectives, to aid the formulation of the main ideas, the establishing of their validity, and the checking of their consistency with the principal aims, to help sharpen the content samples proposed, and to check the sequences of learning experiences for their consistency with the principles of learning.

Since the work pattern had stabilized and the needs of the groups were known, it was now possible to extend the number of outside consultants and to use them in "one-shot" sessions for training. Content specialists were brought in to help whenever there was a deficiency in content background in the existing team. Their special task was to check the validity of the main ideas and to help the group select fruitful content samples and materials. Other types of consultants were employed for special skill sessions, such as ways of conducting open-ended classroom discussions or of using literature in social studies.

The county staff searched for materials, determined the practical limits of what could be done in the classroom, assisted in classroom experimentation, and suggested specific teaching techniques. They observed and evaluated the classroom experiments and selected records of learning activities to be used in the eventual collective units to be developed from these experiments. They took responsibility for interpreting the experiments to principals and sometimes to other teachers. They began to diagnose special difficulties encountered and assembled these for discussion at seminars of the staff with the curriculum consultants. In other words, they began to take a more active role than they had taken during the preliminary stage.

More intensive work was also needed in schools with principals and other teachers to protect the atmosphere for experimentation. Principals needed to understand their role in making teachers feel that they were engaged in an important job, that their contribution was relevant and useful, that mistakes were normal in experimentation, and, above all, that they were front-line experts in the classroom. To do this the principals needed to understand what experimentation means logically and psychologically. They needed to learn how to sustain effort, when results seemed hard to come by. This represented a shift in their usual role of responsibility for action, a role which tended to focus attention on attaining results rapidly. The central task of the trainer is different; it is to discover spots in which changes can be initiated and to work with individuals to help him to produce these changes. It is difficult for some administrators to shift from the administrative role to that of trainer and then back again, probably because their administrative responsibility weighs on them more heavily than that of a trainer (*Taba and Noel, 1957, pp. 48-53*).

Toward the end of this step, the county staff was ready for theoretical training in curriculum development. They therefore asked for a series of seminars to develop a systematic rationale for dealing with the various problems of curriculum development: what are the steps in curriculum development and why; what are the functions of the learning activities; how can one check a completed teaching unit for the balance of these and for an adequate sequence; how can one evaluate the teaching-learning units for their contribution to the general plan. In general, the need for training roles increased, while the demands for the management of human-relations roles decreased. As the county staff gained in experience and in understanding the theory of curriculum development, they also assumed a more active part in directing the project; they began to use the curriculum consultant only as an adviser and as a clinician to criticize and evaluate the steps they had taken and to help project the next steps.

Consolidating and Editing

As the teachers completed their plans and experiments, it was necessary to put these materials together into coherent drafts. Since teachers are not necessarily skilled in writing and editing, the county staff assumed the editorial task. Teachers were asked to record what they did and what happened in their classrooms. In some instances the information was secured from teachers by a tape-recorded interview because the flavor of some exciting experiences was lost when the teachers tried to write them out. These descriptions of classroom experiences were analyzed at staff conferences and compounded into sequential units, combining the experiments of several teachers. In the editorial role, each county staff member took charge of the material on one grade level. This edited material, arranged in the form of a teaching-learning unit, became the sample units to be tried out.

The work of the outside consultants was now limited to working almost exclusively with the county staff in helping them with such points as the consistency of the main ideas around which the units were organized, adequacy of the content sample, and the balance and sequence of learning activities. The rationale developed in the preceding step was now systematically consolidated around the problems arising in connection with editing the units.

Trying Out Units

Trying out the units in a larger sample of classrooms involved a new cycle of training sessions. First, sessions with the principals were needed again to plan procedures for giving information about the new program to the rest of their staffs. Their help was also needed for locating persons to try out the units. Second, training sessions were needed with the corps of teachers who either were selected or volunteered for the task.

Preparation for the tryouts also involved a new series of problems. First, it was necessary to compose a pattern of sampling for the tryouts in order to include all varieties of student backgrounds and school conditions. Problems arose also regarding the method of inducting the new groups of teachers into the rationale of the units—their structure, the basis for learning experiences indicated, and particularly the sequence. Since one aim of the tryouts was to modify the units according to the needs of varied groups of students, the participating teachers needed to understand the structure of these units and the points at which modifications were useful and helpful, such as replacing one learning experience with another one having a similar function without destroying the learning sequences, or contracting and expanding the sample of content according to the abilities of their classes.

Since it was not clear how much explanation and demonstration was needed to convey the necessary understanding, the county staff, with the aid of the consultant and a few teachers from the experimental group, constructed a model session. This session was conducted by the consultants and aided by explanations and demonstrations by the experimental teachers. The analysis of this session provided a model for the subsequent ones which were led by the county staff. The teachers who had developed successful units and had employed or invented new learning activities were used as consultants for other teachers, demonstrating their work and describing certain teaching techniques.

The results of the tryouts were again edited and consolidated by the county staff. Alternatives for learning experiences were inserted to take care of the differences in the ability levels and the experiential backgrounds of the children. Notes were inserted about the difficulties inherent at various points. At this point, also, a further check was made of the quality of the material. References were checked and extended. The sequences of learning activities were examined minutely. In other words, the finishing touches were made to produce the final drafts of units.

During this period, the county staff also began to examine seriously the entire plan of curriculum development, including its psychological and social foundation. They began to plot the scope of the main ideas in the various units and to examine the continuity of the basic concepts on which these ideas rested. (See chapter 22 for samples of these.)

Questions such as the following guided this inspection: What are the recurring concepts imbedded in the grade-level units, and how can their vertical development be assured? What are the recurring universals, and how are these extended and augmented at each subsequent level? How can one check learning activities through several grade levels to make sure that there are appropriate increments in the complexity and in the mental powers they require?

A careful analysis was made of the units to check on the scope and sequence of the concepts and of the intellectual skills. Content was re-examined to discover any inadvertent overlapping in what was covered on different grade levels. A study was made of the new teaching techniques that the new curriculum might require so as to determine how to help the teachers with these procedures: how to conduct open-ended discussions, how to help students focus on ideas, how to use a wide range of sources, etc. Plans were made for the kind of handbook which would explain the rationale of the design of the curriculum and the basic principles on which its specific aspects, such as the order of learning experiences, rested. In other words, the county staff now entered into the role with which curriculum work customarily begins: the formulation of a curriculum guide dealing with the problems of scope and sequence and with the articulation of the work on all grade levels. By ending rather than beginning with this task, however, the staff now operated with a different rationale and a greater competence in the theoretical principles involved. Therefore, the scheme of framework which they now projected differed markedly from the one they would have composed had they done it at the start.

Installing the Units

Because of the gradual involvement of an increasingly large group of teachers in the curriculum development, the installation was less difficult than had been anticipated. Furthermore, no attempt was made to enforce the acceptance of the new program in every district. Rather, it was expected that the program would stand and be accepted on its own merits. Every effort was made, however, to "spread the gospel." School districts which were interested were helped with organizing training sessions. The county staff prepared a special demonstration kit showing examples of student work and slides of classroom activities, to be used with school staffs, boards, and parent groups. At this point, also, the usual device of the university or college extension courses came into good use for training the extended groups in the needed skills, for extending the content background, and for developing an understanding of the rationale of the program. While the work on curriculum development was done almost exclusively in small groups, it was possible to conduct this training in larger classes.

CONCLUSION

A word may be needed about the dynamics of teamwork. Teamwork is more than simply cooperating in groups. It involves planning and streamlining many kinds of competencies so that they can complement each other. Teachers have an expertness which needs to be given full play and which should not be submerged for that of a researcher, or planner. A research technician has skills, which if exercised with judicious recognition of the cooperative nature of the enterprise, can be used to lift the level of insight on both sides. A planner can foresee consequences of an immediate decision to which the group may be blind. Cooperation is not merely working together—it needs to be a true meshing of ideas, approaches, insights, and skills. Creativity depends on this meshing—and inventiveness is a much needed quality in this process.

How this partnership in thinking and inventing works might be illustrated by what took place in developing the idea for the third-grade unit described in chapter 20. Teachers had complained that the units on community life were a bore and were getting nowhere because the schools were located in bedroom communities which had too few of the characteristics of full-fledged communities. In effect, the units in studying these communities only repeated the work of the second grade. The curriculum consultant, a person fairly well grounded in the theory of curriculum development and with a fairly long experience in working with teachers, responded to this criticism by suggesting that it might be possible to study communities comparatively. Such a study could extend the concept of what communities are like. While including the study of the immediate community, such a program would make it possible to lift the understanding of community life to a new level by introducing the idea of cultural differences in patterns of community life. The curriculum consultant could not have had this idea without stimulation from the criticism. The teachers would not have accepted the possibility of comparative study of communities had they not been dissatisfied with what they had been doing, for this idea cut them loose from the existing texts, from their common moorings of teaching experience, and required a great deal of additional work.

Next came the question: What type of communities? Perhaps the class could first study their own community. Perhaps next they could study a nearby city or a small town, and then perhaps one "monolithic" community centered in one industry, following that with a rural area. These suggestions were offhand, but they illustrated how a sampling of contrasts could be made.

This idea of sampling simmered in the heads of the teachers and supervisors, who began to produce another sampling. Why not use a cultural and a geographic sampling, one that would simultaneously reach into a variety of geographic settings and help decrease the ethnocentricity of these suburban children? Thus was born the notion of sampling a rain-forest village in Africa, a nomadic tribe in a desert, possibly some locale in Europe, and a Chinese or a Japanese community. The exact nature of the sampling was left open for a while. It was first necessary to try to work out one sample in order to see what should be taught about each, what materials were available, whether jumping such distances, both geographically and culturally, was not too much for the third graders, and so on.

It should be noted that different combinations of competencies are required at different points of curriculum development. For example, competency in content disciplines is seldom constructive if called into play ahead of decisions regarding desirable aims and the general nature of content needed to implement these aims. Psychological competencies are needed at the point of diagnosis and again at the point of selecting and organizing learning experiences.

One must realize, also, that, in order for research to function productively in curriculum development, it is necessary not only to draw on existing research, but for those who are involved in curriculum development to become researchers also—at least in a sense of acquiring a research orientation in making curriculum decisions and evaluating their results, and, if possible, in conducting local research to sharpen the basis for these decisions. Such an approach has consequences beyond improving curriculum making. The experience described in the case study demonstrated that the action research approach helps the participating teachers to become increasingly self-propelling and less dependent on ready-made answers, be these from books, supervisors, or principals. Because the processes employed are essentially those of scientific inquiry used to solve professional problems, their use also tends to create permanent changes in the ways of thinking about and tackling educational problems, as well as in skills that make possible an experimental approach to curriculum and teaching. The tendency to lean on "gimmicks" is reduced while the disposition to sift discriminately the ideas and methods that apply to a given situation is increased.

The foregoing analysis of the ways of working and the case study has tried to demonstrate the fallacy of the concept of a "strong personal leadership" as the nub of curriculum development on theoretical as well as practical grounds. The shadow of such a concept tends to color the discussions of the conditions under which dynamic curriculum development is possible. It is hoped that these chapters have demonstrated the fact that leadership in curriculum development is not a mystical entity but a process that can be analyzed rather specifically, and that its various roles in curriculum development can be identified fairly clearly. To the extent that this is possible, it will also be possible to locate the specific competencies required and to allocate them appropriately. What is needed is a scientifically designed part-nership of competencies rather than leadership of any one person.

The method of working described here seemed to effect growth in local leadership. Local teacher groups became increasingly self-dependent. An increasing number of persons began to be able to conduct meetings. In the third year the local advisory group in one of the workshops planned its own procedures, conducted evaluation, and made decisions about the nature of reports needed. The individuals who were more experienced set the pace in supporting more effective and independent ways of working. The tendency to be disturbed at plunging into a new enterprise whose end products were not clear decreased, because many persons had learned to derive their as-surance from clear-cut process steps. The final evaluations usually pointed up improvement in skills in cooperative work and made clear the fact that this method of working allows educators to "free" their intelligence for work on problems of primary concern to them (*Taba, Brady, and Robinson, 1952, ch. 7; Taba and Noel, 1957, pp. 54-58*).

Another by-product of this method of working appears to be a general improvement in human relations and in communication. The evaluation of the projects described in the case study indicated that lines of communica-tion became clearer and easier. Fewer individuals asked about authority roles. The concern was with "who can do what," irrespective of their posi-tions in the hierarchy of job and authority. One county reported that divi-sions between the county staff, the district administrators, and the teachers began to disappear. Ideas and suggestions began to flow easily back and forth with less threat to individuals.

A natural outcome of these methods of working is an enhanced produc-tivity and participation; growth in these tends to accumulate. Experience in many groups showed quite clearly that a modest start can develop into something respectable both qualitatively and quantitatively speaking. Usually the number of participants in the enterprise grows steadily under the im-petus of applying the principle of levels of involvement. For example, in one school system thirteen teachers were involved during the first year. In the third year, one hundred teachers and twenty-six administrators were taking part in one role or another. Procedures that in the beginning re-quired laborious planning and discussion gradually became a part of indi-viduals' equipment, which increased their productivity. And this productivity gained momentum with time.

All these procedures and their by-products are important aspects in pro-fessionalization of curriculum making as a local enterprise. They help to take curriculum development on this level out of the realm of the rule-of-thumb procedure and to move it into the realm of rational and scientific planning to which both theoretical thinking and practical experience can contribute productively.

Bibliographical Index

References are listed alphabetically by date of publication.
Boldface numbers following each entry indicate the pages
of the text on which each reference is cited.

Adler, M. J., and M. Mayer. *The Revolution in Education.* Univ. of Chicago Press (1958). **19**

Adorno, T. W., *et al. Authoritarian Personality.* Harper (1950). **218**

Adventures in American Education Series. Harper (1942-43). **3-4, 28**

> Aiken, W. M. *The Story of the Eight Year Study.*
>
> Chamberlin, D., *et al. Did They Succeed in College?*
>
> Giles, H. H., S. P. MacCutcheon, and A. N. Zechiel. *Exploring the Curriculum.*
>
> Progressive Education Association. *Thirty Schools Tell Their Story.*
>
> Smith, E. R., and R. W. Tyler. *Appraising and Recording Student Progress.*

Ahman, J. S., and M. D. Glock. *Evaluating Pupil Growth.* Allyn and Bacon (1958). **317, 326, 329**

Ahrens, M. "Parents and Staff Cooperate in System-Wide Improvement." *Educational Leadership, 11* (Mar. 1956), 337-42. **450, 451**

Aiken, W. M. (*see* Adventures in American Education Series)

Albany Public Schools. *Explorations in Character Education.* Albany Unified School District, Albany, Calif. (Nov. 1953). Mimeo. **247**

Alberty, H. "Designing Programs to Meet the Common Needs of Youth." In National Society for the Study of Education, *Adapting the Secondary School Program to the Needs of Youth.* Fifty-second Yearbook, Pt. I. Univ. of Chicago Press (1953). **407-09**

Alexander, W. M. (*see* Saylor, J. G., and Alexander)

Allinsmith, W., and G. W. Goethals, "Cultural Factors in Mental Health: An Anthropological Perspective." *Rev. of Educational Research, 26* (Dec. 1956). **6, 49, 56, 145**

Anastasi, A. *Differential Psychology.* Macmillan (1958). **93**

Anderson, G. L. "Theories of Behavior and Some Curriculum Issues." *Jour. Educ. Psychol., 39* (Mar. 1948), 133-40. **84**

————. (*see also* Swenson, E. J., Anderson, and Stacey)

————, and A. I. Gates. "The General Nature of Learning." In National Society for the Study of Education, *Learning and Instruction.* Forty-ninth Yearbook, Pt. I. Univ. of Chicago Press (1950), 16-35. **152**

Anderson, H. H. (ed.). *Creativity and Its Cultivation.* Harper (1959). **151**

————. "Creativity and Education." *College and Univ. Bulletin, 13* (May 1961). **362**

Anthropological Society of Washington. *Some Uses of Anthropology: Theoretical and Applied.* Washington, D.C. (1956). **33**

Asch, S. E. *Social Psychology.* Prentice-Hall (1952). **80, 171**

————. "Effects of Group Pressure upon the Modification and Distortion of Judgments." In E. E. Maccoby, T. Newcomb, and E. E. Hartley (eds.), *Readings in Social Psychology.* Rev. ed. Holt (1958), 174-83. **153**

Association for Supervision and Curriculum Development. *Research for Curriculum Improvement.* Fifty-seventh Yearbook. Washington, D.C. (1957). **239, 451, 462**

Atkinson, G. "The Sociogram as an Instrument in Social Studies Teaching and Evaluation." *Elementary School Jour.* (Oct. 1949). **253**

Austin, G. A. (*see* Bruner, J. S., Goodnow, and Austin)

Ausubel, D. P. "Viewpoints from Related Disciplines: Human Growth and Development." *Teachers College Record, 60* (Feb. 1959). **90, 93, 96, 128, 272, 406**

————. "In Defense of Verbal Learning." *Educational Theory, 11* (Jan. 1961). **116, 215**

Bales, R. F. (*see* Hare, A. P., Borgatta, and Bales)

Barnes, F. P. "The Illinois Curriculum Program." In H. J. McNally and H. Passow, *Improving the Quality of Public School Programs: Approaches to Curriculum Development.* Teachers College, Columbia Univ. (1960), 113-65. **449**

Bartlett, F. E. *Thinking: An Experimental and Social Study.* Basic Books (1958). **151, 153**

Bayles, E. "Present Status of Educational Theory in the U.S." *School and Soc., 87* (Jan. 1959). **413**

Beam, J. C. "Serial Learning and Conditioning Under Real Life Stress." *Jour. Abnorm. Social Psychol., 51* (Nov. 1955). **165**

Bebell, C. (*see* McKenzie, G. N., and Bebell)

Beberman, M. "Improving High School Mathematics." *Educational Leadership, 17* (Dec. 1959), 162-88. **154, 177**

Beck, W. S. *Modern Science and the Nature of Life.* Harcourt, Brace & World (1957). **384**

Becker, C. *The Heavenly City of the Eighteenth-Century Philosophers.* Yale Univ. Press (1932). **5**

Benedict, R. *Patterns of Culture.* Penguin Books (1946). **149**

Benne, K. D., and B. Muntyan. *Human Relations in Curriculum Change.* Dryden Press (1951), 142-292. **472**

————, and P. Sheats. "Leaders Are Made, Not Born." *Childhood Education, 25* (Jan. 1948), 203-08. **227, 479**

————. "Functional Roles of Group Members." In K. D. Benne and B. Muntyan, *Human Relations in Curriculum Change.* Dryden Press (1951), 98-104.

Berkowitz, L., and B. Levy. "Pride in Group Performance and Group-Task Motivation." *Jour. Abnorm. Social Psychol., 53* (Nov. 1956), 300-06. **165**

Bestor, A. *The Restoration of Learning.* Knopf (1955). **21**

————. "Education and Its Proper Relationship to the Forces of American Society." *Daedalus* (Winter 1959). **21**

Bettelheim, B. "Segregation, New Style." *School Rev., 66* (Autumn 1958), 251-72. **99, 168**

Billings, N. *A Determination of Generalizations Basic to the Social Studies Curriculum.* Baltimore. Warwick and York (1929). **176, 394**

Biological Sciences Curriculum Study. "Annual Report." *Newsletter,* No. 6 (Dec. 1960). **395**

Birch, H. C., and H. S. Rabinowitz. "The Negative Effect of Previous Experience on Productive Thinking." *Jour. Exp. Psychol., 41* (Feb. 1951), 121-25. **125**

Bloom, B. S. "Methods of Increasing Competence in Purposeful Reading in Mathematics." In W. S. Gray (ed.), *Improving Reading in Content Fields. Supplementary Educational Monograph,* No. 62. Univ. of Chicago Press (Jan. 1947), 156-60. **232**

————. (ed.). *The Taxonomy of Objectives.* Longmans, Green (1954). **201, 205, 206, 216, 217, 326**

————. "Ideas, Problems and Methods of Inquiry." In National Society for the Study of Education, *Integration of Educational Experiences.* Fifty-seventh Yearbook, Univ. of Chicago Press (1958). **299, 300**

Bobbitt, J. F. *Curriculum Making in Los Angeles.* Univ. of Chicago Press (1922). **447**

————. *How to Make a Curriculum.* Houghton Mifflin (1924). **447**

Bode, B. H. *Progressive Education at the Crossroads.* New York. Newson (1938). **285**

————. *How We Learn.* Heath (1942). **84**

Boole, M. E. *The Preparation of the Child for Science.* Oxford. The Clarendon Press (1904). **126**

Borgatta, E. F. (*see* Hare, A. P., Borgatta, and Bales)

Bossing, N. R. "Comments on Conant's Recommendations: Curriculum (I)." In *Perspectives on the Conant Report,* Social Science Research Center, Univ. of Minnesota (1960). **386**

————. (*see also* Faunce, R. C., and Bossing)

Bowman, P. H. "Personality and Scholastic Under-achievement." In Association for Supervisors and Curriculum Directors, *Freeing Capacity to Learn.* Washington, D.C. (1960), 40-55. **236**

Bradfield, J. M., and H. S. Moredock. *Measurement and Evaluation in Education.* Macmillan (1957). **324, 326**

Brady, E. (*see* Taba, H., Brady, and Robinson)

Brameld, T. *Cultural Foundations of Education.* Harper (1957). **43, 45**

Brim, O. G., Jr. *Sociology and the Field of Education.* Russell Sage Foundation (1958). **6, 27, 33, 48**

Brink, W. G. "Patterns of Curriculum Organization in Large Secondary Schools." *School Rev., 63* (Oct. 1955), 372-77. **385**

Brookover, W. B. "A Social Psychological Conception of Classroom Learning." *School and Soc., 87* (Feb. 28, 1959). **131, 158**

Broudy, H. S. "Mastery." In B. O. Smith and R. H. Ennis (eds.), *Language and Concepts in Education.* Rand McNally (1961). **318-19**

Brown, M. "Knowing and Learning." *Harvard Educational Rev., 31* (Winter 1961). **313, 317**

Brownell, W. A., and G. Hendrickson. "How Children Learn Information, Concepts and Generalizations." In National Society for the Study of Education, *Learning and Instruction.* Forty-ninth Yearbook, Pt. I. Univ. of Chicago Press (1950), Ch. 4. **154, 155, 214**

Brubacher, J. S. *Modern Philosophies of Education.* McGraw-Hill (1950). **18, 20, 24**

Bruner, J. S. "Learning and Thinking." *Harvard Educational Rev., 29* (Summer 1959), 184-92. **274, 280**

————. *The Process of Education.* Harvard Univ. Press (1960). **78, 81, 86, 109, 119, 121, 127, 128, 155, 175, 176, 270**

————. "The Act of Discovery." *Harvard Educational Rev., 31* (Winter 1961), 21-32. **155, 215, 280**

—————, J. J. Goodnow, and G. A. Austin. *A Study of Thinking*. Wiley (1956). 122, 295, 306-07

Brunswick, E. "Scope and Aspects of the Cognitive Problem." In *Contemporary Approaches to Cognition,* a symposium held at the University of Colorado. Harvard Univ. Press (1957). 78

Burke, K. *Permanence and Change: An Anatomy of Purpose*. New York, New Republic, Inc. (1935). 44, 45

Buros, O. K. *Fifth Mental Measurements Yearbook,* Highland Park, N.J. Gryphon Press (1959). 331

Burton, W. N. *The Guidance of Learning Activities*. Appleton-Century (1952). 154

—————, R. B. Kimball, and R. L. Wing. *Education for Effective Thinking*. Appleton-Century-Crofts (1960). 331

Buswell, G. T., and B. Y. Hersh. *Patterns of Thinking in Solving Problems*. Univ. of California Press (1956). 115, 232, 315

Calandra, A. "Some Observations of the Work of the PSSC." *Harvard Educational Rev., 29* (Winter 1959). 268

California Association of Secondary School Administrators. "Procedures for Appraising California Secondary Schools." 2220 Bancroft Way, Berkeley, Calif. (1955). 310

California State Department of Education. *Building Curriculum in Social Studies for the Public Schools of California*. Bulletin, *26,* No. 4, Sacramento, Calif. (May 1957). 177, 394

Carey, M. E. "Learning Comes Through Living." *Educational Leadership* (May 1947), 491-95. 409

Cartwright, D., and A. Zander. *Group Dynamics: Research and Theory*. 2nd ed. Row, Peterson (1960). 162

Casserley, J. V. L. "Technology and the Foundations of Morality." In "Science and Human Responsibility: A Round Table," Emory University Law School, *Journal of Public Law, 4* (1956). 44

Caswell, H. L. "Sources of Confusion in Curriculum Theory." In V. E. Herrick and R. W. Tyler, *Toward Improved Curriculum Theory,* Supplementary Educational Monograph No. 71, Univ. of Chicago Press (1950). 413

—————. "Significant Curriculum Issues." *Educational Leadership, 9* (Jan. 1952). 414

Chamberlin, C. D., *et al. Did They Succeed in College?* Harper (1942). (*see also* Adventures in American Education Series) 123

Charters, W. W. *Job Analysis*. Macmillan (1938). 83

Chase, F. S. *Education Faces New Demands*. Univ. of Pittsburgh Press (1956). 36, 37, 41

—————, and E. G. Cuba. "Administrative Roles and Behavior." *Rev. of Educational Research, 25* (Oct. 1955), 281-98. 478

Childs, J. L. "Should the School Seek Actively to Reconstruct Society?" *Annals of American Acad. of Political and Social Science, 182* (Nov. 1935), 1-9. 25, 26

—————. "Education and the American Scene." *Daedalus* (Winter 1959). 26

Clark, R., and C. McGuire. "Sociographic Analysis of Sociometric Valuations." *Child Development, 23* (June 1952), 129-40. 253

————— (*see also* McGuire, C., and Clark)

Coffey, H. S., and W. P. Golden, Jr. "Psychology of Change Within Institutions." In National Society for the Study of Education, *In-Service Education for Teachers, Supervisors and Administrators*. Fifty-sixth Yearbook, Pt. I, Univ. of Chicago Press (1957), Ch. 4. 455, 456

Coleman, J. V. (*see* Kotinsky, R., and Coleman)

Collings, E. *An Experiment with the Project Curriculum.* Macmillan (1923). **401**

Combs, A. W. "Intelligence from a Perceptual Point of View." *Jour. Abnorm. Social Psychol., 47* (1952), 662-73. **134**

————, and D. Snygg. *Individual Behavior: A Perceptual Approach to Behavior.* Harper (1959). **81, 153**

Commission for the Reorganization of Secondary Education. *The Cardinal Principles of Secondary Education.* U.S. Bureau of Education, Washington, D.C., G.P.O. (1918). **207**

Commission on Secondary School Curriculum, Progressive Education Association. Appleton-Century (1938-40). **4**

Thayer, T. V., C. Zachry, and R. Kotinsky. *Reorganizing Secondary Education.*

Zachry, C., and M. Lighty. *Emotion and Conduct in Adolescence.*

————. *Language, Science, Mathematics, Social Studies and Visual Arts in General Education.* **4**

Committee for the White House Conference. *Report to the President.* Washington, D.C., G.P.O. (Apr. 1956). **29**

Conant, J. B. *Education in a Divided World.* Harvard Univ. Press (1948). **18**

————. *The American High School Today.* McGraw-Hill (1959). **385**

Contra Costa County Schools. *Social Studies, Grades 1-6.* Pleasant Hill, Calif. (1959a). **213, 431**

————. "United States History with a World History Background." Grades 10-11. Pleasant Hill, Calif. (1959b). **355**

————. "A Content Analysis of the Contra Costa County Social Studies Curriculum." Pleasant Hill, Calif. (June 1961). Dittoed. **431**

————. "A Study in Comparative Communities." Social Studies, Grade 3. Pleasant Hill, Calif. (1961). **347, 355, 358, 368, 431**

————. Unpublished Curriculum Study. **245, 431**

Corey, S. M. *Action Research to Improve School Practices.* Teachers College, Columbia Univ. (1953). **239, 451**

Corle, C. "Thought Processes of Sixth Grade Students While Solving Verbal Problems in Arithmetic." Pennsylvania State Univ. (1958). **185**

Cottrell, L. S. "Some Neglected Problems in Social Psychology." *Am. Sociol. Rev., 15* (Dec. 1950). **223**

Counts, G. S. "Some Notes on the Foundations of Curriculum Making." In National Society for the Study of Education, *The Foundations of Curriculum Making.* Twenty-sixth Yearbook, Pt. II. Bloomington, Ind. Public School Publishing Co. (1926). **288, 291**

————. "Dare Schools Build a New Social Order?" No. 11, John Day Pamphlets, John Day (1932). **26**

————. *Education and American Civilization.* Teachers College, Columbia Univ. (1952). **36, 40**

Craig, R. C. *The Transfer Value of Guided Learning.* Teachers College, Columbia Univ. (1953). **125**

Cremin, L. A. (ed.). *The Republic and the School. Horace Mann on the Education of Free Men.* Teachers College, Columbia Univ. (1957). **23**

————. *The Transformation of the School.* Knopf (1961). **1, 2, 4, 5, 24, 26, 285, 401**

Cronbach, L. (ed.). *Text Materials in Modern Education.* Univ. of Illinois Press (1955). **119, 190-91, 387**

Crouch, E. Unpublished report. Director of Curriculum, Carmel Public Schools, Carmel, California. **170, 253**

Cuba, E. G. (*see* Chase, F. S., and Cuba)

Cunningham, R., *et al. Understanding Group Behavior of Boys and Girls.* The Horace Mann–Lincoln Institute of School Experimentation, Teachers College, Columbia Univ. (1951). **227**

Dahlke, H. O. *Values in Culture and Classroom.* Harper (1958). **163**

Danziger, K. "Independence Training and Social Class in Java, Indonesia," and "Parental Demands and Social Class in Java, Indonesia." *Jour. Social Psychol., 51* (Feb. 1960), 65-74, 75-86. **141**

Davie, J. S. "Social-Class Factors in School Attendance." *Harvard Educational Rev., 23* (Summer 1953), 175-85. **104, 139**

Davis, A. "Socialization of the Personality." In National Society for the Study of Education, *Adolescence.* Forty-third Yearbook, Pt. I. Univ. of Chicago Press (1944), Ch. 11. **145**

———. *Social Class Influences on Learning.* Harvard Univ. Press (1952). **49, 107, 135, 137**

——— (*see also* Havighurst, R. J., and Davis)

Deutsche, J. M. *The Development of Children's Concepts of Causal Relations.* Univ. of Minnesota Press (1937). **111**

Dewey, J. *Democracy and Education.* Macmillan (1928). **24, 288-89**

———. *My Pedagogic Creed.* Reprinted by Progressive Education Association (1929). **23**

———. *How We Think.* Rev. ed. Heath (1933). **86, 214**

———. *Art as Experience.* New York. Minton, Balch (1934). **151**

———. *Experience and Education.* Macmillan (1938). **280, 404, 405**

———. "Education and Social Change." *Social Frontier, 3* (May 1937), 235-38. **25**

"Dewey and Creative Education." A manifesto by a group of educators. *Saturday Review of Literature* (Nov. 21, 1959). **151, 152**

Dobbin, J. E. "Measuring Achievement in a Changing Curriculum." *Proceedings of the 1958 Conference on Testing and Measurement.* Princeton, N.J. Educational Testing Service (1958). **317**

Dollard, J., and N. E. Miller. *Personality and Psychotherapy.* McGraw-Hill (1950). **132**

Downey, L. W. "Secondary Education: A Model for Improvement." *School Rev., 68* (Autumn 1960). **167, 173**

Dressel, P. "The Meaning and Significance of Integration." In National Society for the Study of Education, *The Integration of Educational Experiences.* Fifty-seventh Yearbook, Pt. III. Univ. of Chicago Press (1958), Ch. 1. **314**

———. "Measurement and Evaluation." In *Recent Research and Developments and Their Implications for Teacher Education.* Thirteenth Yearbook. Washington, D.C., American Association of Colleges for Teacher Education (1960). **299**

Duncker, K. "On Problem Solving." *Psychological Monographs, 58* (1945), No. 270. **125**

Durkheim, E. *Education and Sociology.* Free Press (1956). **33**

Dyer, H. S., Robert Kalin, and Frederic M. Lord. *Problems in Mathematical Education.* Princeton, N.J. Educational Testing Service (1956). **115, 268**

Easley, J. A., Jr. "The Physical Science Committee and Educational Theory." *Harvard Educational Rev., 29* (Winter 1959). **269, 271**

Educational Policies Commission. *The Purposes of Education in American Democracy.* Washington, D.C. National Education Association (1938). **207-08**
————. *The Education for All American Youth: A Further Look.* Washington, D.C. National Education Association (1952). **208, 286**
Edwards, A. K. (*see* Mayhew, K. C., and Edwards)
Eells, K. "Some Implications for School Practice of the Chicago Studies of Cultural Bias in Intelligence Tests." *Harvard Educational Rev.,* Pt. II, *23* (Fall 1953), 284-97. **107**
———— (*see also* Warner, W. L., Meeker, and Eells)
Elam, S. L. "Acculturation and Learning Problems of Puerto Rican Children." *Teachers College Rec.,* 61 (Feb. 1960), 258-64. **57, 145, 146**
Elkins, D. (*see* Taba, H., and Elkins)
Ennis, R. H. (*see* Smith, B. O., and Ennis)
Erikson, E. H. *Childhood and Society.* Norton (1950). **90**
————. "Growth and Crises of the Healthy Personality." In C. Kluckhohn, H. A. Murray, and D. M. Schneider (eds.), *Personality in Nature, Society, and Culture.* Rev. ed. Knopf (1955), Ch. 12. **96, 134**

Fadiman, C. "The Case for Basic Education." In J. D. Koerner (ed.), *The Case for Basic Education.* Little, Brown (1959), 6-10. **21**
Farquear, L. (*see* Frederick, O. I., and Farquear)
Faunce, R. C., and N. R. Bossing. *Developing the Core Curriculum.* 2nd ed. Prentice-Hall (1958). **409**
Featherstone, W. B. *A Functional Curriculum for Youth.* American Book (1950). **285, 287, 442**
Ferguson, G. "On Transfer and the Abilities of Man." *Canadian Jour. of Psychol., 10* (Sept. 1956), 121-31. **101**
Fisher, M. S. "Children in the World Today." In Linton, Fisher and Ryan, *Culture and Personality.* American Council on Education. Washington, D.C. (1953). **58**
Floud, J. E., and A. H. Halsey. "Education and Social Structure: Theories and Methods." *Harvard Eductional Rev., 29* (Fall 1959). **28, 31, 33, 48**
Floyd, O. R. "General Science as Preparation for the Study of Biology, Chemistry and Physics." *Jour. Educational Research, 31* (Dec. 1937), 272-77. **122**
Frazier, A. "Needed: A New Vocabulary for Individual Differences." *Elementary School Jour., 61* (Feb. 1961), 260-68. **441**
Frederick, O. I., and L. Farquear. "Areas of Human Activity." *Jour. Educational Research, 30* (May 1937), 672-79. **398**
French, E. G., and F. H. Thomas. "The Relation of Achievement Motivation to Problem-Solving Effectiveness." *Jour. Abnorm. Social Psychol., 56* (Jan. 1948), 45-48. **165**
French, W., *et al. Behavioral Goals of General Education in High School.* Russell Sage Foundation (1957). **210**
Friedenberg, E. Z. *The Vanishing Adolescent.* Beacon Press (1959). **167**
Fromm, E. "Individual and Social Origin of Neurosis." *Am. Sociol. Rev., 9* (Aug. 1944). **57**
————. *Man for Himself.* Rinehart (1947). **60**
————. *The Sane Society.* Rinehart (1955). **38, 39, 58, 60, 62**
Fruchter, B. (*see* Guilford, J. P., Fruchter, and Kelly)

Gardner, J. W. "National Goals for Education." In *The Goals for Americans.* Prentice-Hall (1960). **265**

Gates, A. I. (*see* Anderson, G. L., and Gates)

Gerard, M. W. "The Psychogenic Tic in Ego Development." *Psychoanal. Stud. Child, 2.* International Univ. Press (1946), 133-63. **90**

Gesell, A., and F. L. Ilg. *Infant and Child in the Culture of Today.* Harper (1943). **88**

————, *et al. The First Five Years.* Harper (1940). **88**

Getzels, J. W. "The Acquisition of Values in School and Society." In F. S. Chase and H. A. Anderson (eds.), *The High School in the New Era.* Univ. of Chicago Press (1958). **221**

————, and P. Jackson. *Creativity and Intelligence: Explorations with Gifted Children.* Wiley (1962). **102, 105, 106, 419**

————, and H. A. Thelen. "The Classroom Group as a Unique Social System." In National Society for the Study of Education, *The Dynamics of Instructional Groups.* Fifty-ninth Yearbook. Univ. of Chicago Press (1960), pp. 68-82. **163, 164**

Giles, H. H., S. P. MacCutcheon, and A. N. Zechiel. *Exploring the Curriculum.* Harper (1942). (*See also* Adventures in American Education Series.) **285, 425**

Gillin, J. (ed.). *For a Science of Man.* Macmillan (1954).

————. "The School in the Context of Community." In G. D. Spindler, *Education and Anthropology.* Stanford Univ. Press (1957). **47**

Ginther, J. "News and Comment." *Elementary School Jour., 61* (Spring 1961). **347**

Gladwyn, T. "The Need: Better Ways of Teaching Children." In Association for Supervision and Curriculum Development, *Freeing the Capacity to Learn.* Washington, D.C. (1960). **104**

Glock, M. D. (*see* Ahman, J. S., and Glock)

Goethals, G. W. (*see* W. Allinsmith and G. W. Goethals)

Goetz, R. M. (*see* Marshall, L. C., and Goetz)

Golden, W. P., Jr. (*see* Coffey, H. S., and Golden)

Goodlad, J. L. "Three Dimensions for Organizing the Curriculum for Learning and Teaching." In Vincent Glennon (ed.), *Frontiers of Elementary Education III.* Proceedings of a Conference on Elementary Education, Syracuse Univ. Press (1956). **428**

————. "Toward a Conceptual System for Curriculum Problems." *School Rev., 66* (Winter 1958), 391-96. **416-17, 420, 442**

Goodnow, J. J. (*see* Bruner, J. S., Goodnow, and Austin)

Goodson, M. In *The Dynamics of Instructional Groups.* National Society for the Study of Education. Fifty-ninth Yearbook. Univ. of Chicago Press (1960). **17**

Gordon, C. W. *The Social Life in the High School: A Study in the Sociology of Adolescence.* Free Press (1955). **74**

Gorer, G. *The American People.* Norton (1948). **51**

————. "Themes in Japanese Culture." In D. I. Haring (ed.), *Personal Character and Cultural Milieu.* Syracuse Univ. Press (1949). **131**

————. "The Concept of National Character." In C. Kluckhohn, H. Murray, and D. Schneider (eds.), *Personality in Nature, Society and Culture.* Rev. ed. Knopf (1955), 246-59. **55**

Griswold, A. W. "What We Don't Know Will Hurt Us." *Harper's* (July 1954), 76-82. **122**

————. *Liberal Education and Democratic Ideal.* Yale Univ. Press (1959). **20**

Gronlund, N. E. *Sociometry in the Classroom.* Harper (1959). **161, 253**

Gross, N. "Some Contributions of Sociology to the Field of Education." *Harvard Educational Rev.,* 29 (Fall 1959), 275-87. **33, 166**

————, W. S. Mason, and A. W. McEachern. *Explorations in Role Analysis.* Wiley (1958). **478**

Gross, R. E., and L. D. Zeleny. *Educating Citizens for Democracy.* Oxford Univ. Press (1958). **287**

Grubb, B. S. *Proposal for Emphasizing Modern Mathematics in Elementary Algebra.* Iowa State Teacher's College, Cedar Falls (1958). M.A. Thesis. **185**

Guilford, J. P. "The Structure of Intellect." *Psychological Bulletin,* 53 (July 1956), 267-93. **103, 114**

————. "Traits of Creativity." In H. H. Anderson (ed.), *Creativity and Its Cultivation.* Harper (1959), Ch. 10. **151**

————. "Basic Conceptual Problems in the Psychology of Thinking." in *Fundamentals of Psychology: The Psychology of Thinking.* Annals of the New York Academy of Sciences, *91* (1961), Art. 1. **103**

————, B. Fruchter, and P. Kelly. "Development and Application of Tests of Intellectual and Special Aptitudes." *Rev. Educational Research,* 29 (Feb. 1959), 26-41. **101**

Gustafson, C. V. "The Portland High School Curriculum Study." *School and Soc.,* 88 (Dec. 3, 1960). **268-69**

Haggard, E. "Learning: A Process of Change." *Educational Leadership, 13* (Dec. 1955). **78**

————. "Socialization, Personality and Academic Achievement in Gifted Children." *School Rev., 15* (Winter 1957). **168**

Haigh, G. V., and W. Schmidt. "The Learning of Subject Matter in Teacher-Centered and Group-Centered Classes." *Jour. Educational Psychol., 47* (May 1956), 295-301. **165**

Hall, D. M. *Dynamics of Group Action.* Danville, Ill. Interstate Printers and Publishers (1957). **227, 474**

Hall, J. A. "Organization for Curriculum Improvement." *Educational Leadership, 9* (Jan. 1952). **453**

Halsey, A. H. (*see* Floud, Jean, and Halsey)

Handlin, O. "Textbooks That Don't Teach." *Atlantic Monthly, 200* (Dec. 1957). **153**

Hanna, P. R. "National Curriculum Commission?" *Jour. Nat. Ed. Assoc., 49* (Jan. 1960), 25-27. **448**

Hanson, J. "Learning by Experience." In B. O. Smith and R. E. Ennis, *Language and Concepts in Education.* Rand McNally (1961), Ch. 1. **152**

Harap, H. (*see* Merritt, E., and Harap)

Hare, A. P., E. F. Borgatta, and R. F. Bales. *Small Groups.* Knopf (1955). **162**

Harlow, H. F. "The Formation of Learning Sets." *Psychol. Rev., 56* (1949).

————. "Analysis of Discrimination Learning by Monkeys." *Jour. Exp. Psychol., 40* (1950), 26-36. **103, 125**

————. "Learning Theories." In W. Dennis (ed.), *Current Trends in Psychological Theory.* Univ. of Pittsburgh Press (1951), 57-84. **103**

Harvard Educational Review. Sociology and Education, Special Issue, *29* (Fall 1959). **34**

Havighurst, R. J. *Human Development and Education.* Longmans, Green (1953). **96, 97**

————, and A. Davis. "Social Class and Color Differences in Child-Rearing." In C. Kluckhohn, H. A. Murray, and D. M. Schneider (eds.), *Personality in Nature, Society and Culture.* Rev. ed. Knopf (1955), 308-20. **145**

————, and H. Taba. *Adolescent Character and Personality*. Wiley (1949), **132**

———— (*see also* Janke, L. L., and Havighurst; Warner, W. L., Havighurst, and Loeb)

Heaton, M. *Feelings Are Facts*. National Conference of Christians and Jews (1952). **160, 225, 247**

————, and H. Lewis. *Reading Ladders for Human Relations*. Rev. and enl. ed. Washington, D.C. American Council on Education (1955). **160, 225**

Heilbroner, R. L. "The Future of America. II. The Dilemmas of Abundance." *The Reporter* (Jan. 21, 1960). **35**

————. *The Future as History*. Harper (1960). **35, 36, 37, 38, 39, 43, 45**

Hendrickson, G., and W. H. Schroeder. "Transfer of Training in Learning to Hit a Submerged Target." *Jour. Educational Psychol., 32* (1941), 205-13. **124**

———— (*see also* Brownell, W. A., and Hendrickson)

Hendrix, G. "Learning by Discovery." *Mathematics Teacher, 54* (1961), 290-99. **116, 128, 215**

Henry, J. "Docility or Giving the Teacher What She Wants." *Journal of Social Issues, 11* (1955), 33-41. **71, 154**

Herrick, V. E., and R. W. Tyler. *Toward Improved Curriculum Theory*. Supplementary Educational Monograph No. 71. Univ. of Chicago Press (1950). **420, 422, 424-25, 426, 439**

Hersh, B. Y. (*see* Buswell, G. T., and Hersh)

Hildebrand, E. H. C. "Mathematical Modes of Thought." *The Growth of Mathematical Ideas,* Grades K-12. National Council of Teachers of Mathematics. Twenty-fourth Yearbook. Washington, D.C. (1959). **181**

Hilgard, E. R. *Theories of Learning*. 2nd ed. Appleton-Century-Crofts (1956). **78, 80, 81, 84, 87**

————. *Introduction to Psychology*. 2nd ed. Harcourt, Brace & World (1957). **89, 92**

————. "Creativity and Problem Solving." In H. H. Anderson (ed.), *Creativity and Its Cultivation*. Harper (1959), Ch. 11. **151**

————, R. P. Irvine, and J. E. Whipple. "Rote Memorization, Understanding and Transfer: An Extension of Katona's Card-Trick Experiments." *Jour. Exp. Psychol., 46* (1953), 288-92. **124**

Hockett, R. M. (ed.) *Teacher's Guide to Child Development: A Manual for Kindergarten and Primary Teachers*. California State Curriculum Commission, California State Dept. of Education, Sacramento, Calif. (1930). **402**

Hoffman, B. "The Tyranny of Multiple-Choice Tests." *Harper's, 2220* (March 1961). **314**

Holland, J., and B. F. Skinner. *The Analysis of Behavior: A Program for Self-instruction*. McGraw-Hill (1961). **80, 83**

Hollingshead, A. B. *Elmtown's Youth: The Impact of Social Classes on Adolescents*. Wiley (1949). **49**

Honigman, J. J. *Culture and Personality*. Harper (1954). **51, 53, 62, 131**

Hook, S. "Education in the Age of Science." *Daedalus* (Winter 1959). **384-85**

Horney, K. *The Neurotic Personality of Our Time*. W. W. Norton (1953). **58**

Hudson, F. "How Much Grass?" *Social Education, 12* (Oct. 1948). **296**

Hughes, B. O. (*see* Olson, W. C., and Hughes)

Hughes, M., *et al. Development of the Means for the Assessment of the Quality of Teaching in the Elementary Schools*. Univ. of Utah (1959). Mimeo. **71, 154, 180**

Hull, C. L. *An Introduction to Behavior Theory*. Appleton-Century (1943). **80**

Hunt, J. McV. *Intelligence and Experience.* Ronald Press (1961). **92, 107, 109, 110, 111, 404**
Hutchins, R. M. *The Higher Learning in America.* Yale Univ. Press (1936). **19, 20**
————. *Education for Freedom.* Louisiana State Univ. Press (1943). **264**

Ilg, F. L. (*see* Gesell, A., and Ilg)
Inhelder, B. (*see* Piaget, J., and Inhelder)
Irvine, R. P. (*see* Hilgard, E. R., Irvine, and Whipple)
Irving, A. "Socio-psychological Aspects of Acculturation." In R. Linton, *The Science of Man in the World Crisis.* Columbia Univ. Press (1945). **133**
Isaacs, S. *Intellectual Growth in Young Children.* London. Routledge & Kegan Paul (1930). **111**

Jackson, P. W. (*see* Getzels, J. W., and Jackson)
Jahoda, M. *Current Concepts of Positive Mental Health.* Joint Commission on Mental Illness and Health, Monograph Series No. 1. Basic Books (1958). **150**
Janke, L. L., and R. J. Havighurst. "Relations Between Ability and Social Status in a Midwestern Community, II, Sixteen-year-old Boys and Girls." *Jour. Educational Psychol., 36* (Nov. 1945), 499-509. **104**
Jennings, H. H. *Leadership and Isolation.* 2nd ed. Longmans, Green (1950a). **162**
————. "Sociodrama as an Educative Process." In *Fostering Mental Health in Our Schools,* Yearbook of the Association for Supervision and Curriculum Development. Washington, D.C. (1950b), Ch. 16. **160, 247**
————. *Sociometry in Group Relations.* 2nd ed. Washington, D.C. American Council on Education (1959). **161**
Jensen, G. "The Socio-Psychological Structure of the Instructional Group." In National Society for the Study of Education, *The Dynamics of Instructional Groups.* Fifty-ninth Yearbook. Univ. of Chicago Press (1960). **163, 164**
Joyce, B. R. "Science, the Curriculum, and the Young Conscience." *Elementary School Jour., 61* (Jan. 1961). **276**
Judd, C. H. "The Relation of Special Training to General Intelligence." *Educational Rev., 36* (1908), 28-42. **124**

Kahl, J. A. "Educational and Occupational Aspirations of 'Common Man' Boys." *Harvard Educational Rev., 23* (Summer 1953), 186-203. **104, 139**
Kalin, R. (*see* Dyer, H. S., Kalin, and Lord)
Kardiner, A. *The Psychological Frontiers of Society.* Columbia Univ. Press (1945). **52-53**
Kazamian, A. M. " 'What Knowledge Is of Most Worth?' An Historical Conception and a Modern Sequel." *Harvard Educational Rev., 30* (Fall 1960). **172**
Kearney, N. C. *Elementary School Objectives.* Russell Sage Foundation (1953). **210**
Keedy, M. L. "Mathematics in Junior High School." *Educational Leadership, 17* (Dec. 1959), 176-81. **177**
Kelly, P. (*see* Guilford, J. P., Fruchter, and Kelly)
Kilpatrick, W. H. *Foundations of Method. Informal Talks on Teaching.* Macmillan (1925). **279**
———— (ed.) *The Educational Frontier.* Century (1933). **26**
————. "Public Education as a Force for Public Improvement." *School and Soc., 41* (April 1935), 521-27. **25**
————. *Education for a Changing Civilization.* Macmillan (1935). **25**
Kimball, R. B. (*see* Burton, W. N., Kimball, and Wing)

Kluckhohn, C. *Mirror for Man*. Whittlesey House (1949). 51
————. "Student Teacher." In M. Hughes (ed.), *People in Your Life*. Knopf (1951). 65, 72, 137
————. "Foreword." In T. Brameld, *Cultural Foundations of Education*. Harper (1957). 47, 70
————, and H. A. Murray. "Personality Formation: The Determinants." In C. Kluckhohn, H. A. Murray, and D. M. Schneider (eds.), *Personality in Nature, Society and Culture*. Rev. ed. Knopf (1955), 53-67. 134-35
————, Murray, H. A., and D. M. Schneider (eds.). *Personality in Nature, Society and Culture*. Rev. ed. Knopf (1955). 50
Köhler, W. *The Mentality of Apes*. Harcourt, Brace & World (1927). 81
Koerner, J. D. (ed). *The Case for Basic Education: A Program of Aims for Public School*. Little, Brown (1959). 20
Koffka, K. *Principles of Gestalt Psychology*. Harcourt, Brace & World (1935). 81
Kotinsky, R. (*see also* Thayer, V. T., Zachry, and Kotinsky)
————, and J. V. Coleman. "Mental Health as an Educational Goal." *Teachers College Rec.*, 56 (Feb. 1955). 148, 287
Krug, E. *Curriculum Planning*. Harper (1950). 383, 449-50
Kubie, L. S. "The Psychiatrist Considers Curriculum Development." *Teachers College Rec.*, 50 (Jan. 1949), 241-46. 151

Langer, S. K. *Philosophy in a New Key*. Mentor (1951). 38
Lawler, M. *Curriculum Consultants at Work*. Teachers College, Columbia Univ. (1958). 449, 481
Leonard, J. P. "Some Reflections on the Meaning of Sequence." In V. E. Herrick and R. W. Tyler, *Toward Improved Curriculum Theory*. Supplementary Educational Monograph No. 71. Univ. of Chicago Press (1950), Ch. 7. 292
Levy, B. (*see* Berkowitz, L., and Levy)
Lewin, K. *Resolving Social Conflict*. Harper (1945). 162
————. "Behavior and Development as a Function of the Total Situation." In L. Carmichael (ed.), *Manual of Child Development*. 2nd ed. Wiley (1954), Ch. 15. 81
————, and R. Lippitt. "Patterns of Aggressive Behavior." In E. E. Maccoby, T. M. Newcomb, and E. E. Hartley (eds.), *Readings in Social Psychology*. Holt (1958), 496-511. 162
Lewis, H. (*see* Heaton, M., and Lewis)
Lieberman, M. *Education as a Profession*. Prentice-Hall (1956). 452
Life (April 14, 1949), 105. 89
Lilienthal, J., III. (*see* Tryon, C., and Lilienthal)
Lindgren, H. C. *Educational Psychology in the Classroom*. Wiley (1956). 94
Linton, R. In A. Kardiner, *The Psychological Frontiers of Society*. Columbia Univ. Press (1945a). 53
————. (ed.) *The Science of Man in the World Crisis*. Columbia Univ. Press (1945b). 32
————. In Linton, Fisher, and Ryan, *Culture and Personality: Three Lectures to Educators*. Washington, D.C. American Council on Education (1941). 68, 69, 158
Lippitt, R. (*see also* Lewin, K., and Lippitt)
————, J. Watson, and B. Westley. *The Dynamics of Planned Change*. Harcourt, Brace & World (1958). 474, 479
————, *et al.* "The Dynamics of Power: A Field Study of Social Influence in Groups of Children." In E. Maccoby, T. Newcomb, and E. Hartley (eds.), *Readings in Social Psychology*. Holt (1958), 251-64. 153

Little, E. P. "The Physical Science Study Committee." *Harvard Educational Rev., 29* (Winter 1959). **268**

Loban, W. "A Study of Social Sensitivity (Sympathy) Among Adolescents." *Jour. Educational Psychol., 44* (Feb. 1953), 102-12. **160**

————, M. Ryan, and J. R. Squire. *Teaching Language and Literature.* Harcourt, Brace & World (1961). **160**

Loeb, M. "Implications of Status Differentiation for Personal and Social Development." *Harvard Educational Rev., 23* (Summer 1953). **146**

———— (*see also* Warner, W. L., Havighurst, and Loeb)

Lord, F. M. (*see* Dyer, H. S., Kalin, and Lord)

Los Angeles County Schools. *Educating the Children of Los Angeles County.* A Course of Study in the Elementary School. Office of the County Superintendent of Schools, Los Angeles, Calif. (1955). **346, 403**

Lovell, K. "A Follow-up Study of Some Aspects of the Work of Piaget and Inhelder on the Child's Conception of Space." *British Jour. Educational Psychol., 29* (June 1958), 104-17. **111**

————, and E. Ogilvie. "A Study of the Conservation of Substance in the Junior School Child." *British Jour. Educational Psychol., 30* (June 1960), 109-18. **111**

McCandless, B. R. "Evaluating Curriculum Mastery." *School and Soc., 89* (Mar. 25, 1961). From the forthcoming book: *Children and Adolescents: Behavior and Development.* Holt, Rinehart and Winston. **311**

McClelland, D. C., *et al. The Achievement Motive.* Appleton-Century-Crofts (1953). **141, 392**

————, *et al. Talent and Society.* Van Nostrand (1958). **102**

McEachern, A. (*see* Gross, N. W., Mason, and McEachern)

McFee, J. K. *Preparation for Art.* San Francisco. Wadsworth (1961). **151**

McGuire, C. "The Behavioral Sciences and Research in Curriculum." (An unpublished paper read before AERA, Feb. 1957.) **101**

————. "The Textown Study of Adolescence." *Texas Jour. of Science* (Sept. 1956). **165**

————, and R. Clark. "Age-Mate Acceptance and Indices of Peer Status." *Child Development, 23* (1952), 141-54. **253**

————, I. Phillips, and R. F. Peck. "Mediation of Moral Values in Early Adolescence." University of Texas (n.d.). Mimeo. **135**

———— (*see also* Clark, R., and C. McGuire)

McKeachie, W. J. "Students, Groups and Teaching Methods." *American Psychologist, 13* (Oct. 1958), 580-84. **165**

McKenzie, G. N., and C. Bebell. "Curriculum Development." *Rev. Educational Research, 21* (June 1951). **451**

McNally, H. J., and A. H. Passow. *Improving the Quality of Public School Programs: Approaches to Curriculum Development.* Teachers College, Columbia Univ. (1960). **450**

MacCutcheon, S. P. (*see* Giles, H. H., MacCutcheon, and Zechiel)

Madden, R. (*see* Oberholtzer, K. E., and Madden)

Malinovsky, B. *Freedom and Civilization.* New York. Ray (1944). **63-64**

Mannheim, K. *Diagnosis of Our Time.* Oxford Univ. Press (1944). **33, 38**

————. *Essays on the Sociology of Knowledge.* Oxford Univ. Press (1952). **33**

————. *Essays on the Sociology of Culture.* Oxford Univ. Press (1956). **33**

Marshall, L. C., and R. M. Goetz. *Curriculum-Making in the Social Studies: A Social Process Approach.* Scribner (1936). **176, 398**

Martin, W. E., and C. B. Stendler. *Child Behavior and Development.* Rev. ed. Harcourt, Brace & World (1959). **84, 90, 91, 132, 133**

Mason, W. S. (*see* Gross, N. W., Mason, and McEachern)

Mayer, M. (*see* Adler, Mortimer J., and Mayer)

Mayhew, K. C., and A. K. Edwards. *The Dewey School.* Appleton-Century (1936). **401**

Mead, M. *And Keep Your Powder Dry.* Morrow (1942). **51**

————. "The Impact of Culture on Personality Development in the United States Today." *Understanding the Child, 20* (Jan. 1951). **55**

————. "Social Change and Cultural Surrogates." In C. Kluckhohn, H. Murray, and D. Schneider (eds.), *Personality in Nature, Culture and Society.* Rev. ed. Knopf (1955). **55, 56**

Meeker, M. (*see* Warner, W. L., Meeker, and Eells)

Melton, A. W. "The Science of Learning and the Technology of Educational Methods." *Harvard Educational Rev., 29* (Spring 1959). **76, 79, 86**

Meltzer, H. *Children's Social Concepts: A Study in Their Nature and Development.* No. 192. Teachers College, Columbia Univ. (1925). **176, 394**

Meriam, J. L. *Child Life and the Curriculum.* World Book (1920). **401**

Merritt, E., and H. Harap. *Trends in the Production of Curriculum Guides.* George Peabody College for Teachers. Nashville, Tenn. (1955). **450**

Merton, R. K. *Social Theory and Social Structure.* Free Press (1957). **63, 454-55**

Meyer, A. E. *Education for New Morality.* Macmillan (1957). **44, 45**

Miel, A., et al. *Cooperative Procedures in Learning.* Teachers College, Columbia Univ. (1952). **451**

Miles, M. B., *Learning to Work in Groups.* Teachers College, Columbia Univ. (1959). **471, 472, 478, 479**

Miller, G. A. "The Magical Number Seven, Plus or Minus Two." *Psychological Rev., 63* (1956), 81-87. **387**

Miner, J. B. *Intelligence in the United States.* New York, Springer (1957). **100, 103, 104, 105, 114, 117**

Mirsky, R. *Thirty-one Brothers and Sisters.* Chicago. Wilcox and Follett (1952). **366**

Mogar, M. "Children's Causal Reasoning About Natural Phenomena." *Child Development, 31* (March 1960), 59-65. **112**

Moholy-Nagy, L. *Vision in Motion.* Chicago. Paul Theobald (1947). **150**

Moore, T. V. *The Reasoning Ability of Children in the First Years of School Life.* Williams and Wilkins (1929). **296**

Moredock, H. S. (*see* Bradfield, J. M., and Moredock)

Morris, V. C. "The Other-Directed Man." *Teachers College Rec., 57* (Jan. 1956). **61**

Morrison, H. C. *The Practice of Teaching in Secondary Schools.* Rev. ed. Univ. of Chicago Press (1931). **127**

————. *The Curriculum of the Common School.* Univ. of Chicago Press (1940). **398**

Mowrer, O. H. *Learning Theory and Behavior.* Wiley (1960). **80**

Murdock, G. P. "Sociology and Anthropology." In J. Gillin (ed.), *For a Science of Social Man.* Macmillan (1954). **33**

Murphy, G. "Human Potentiality." *Supplement to the Journal of Social Issues,* No. 7 (1953). **149**

————. *Human Potentialities.* Basic Books (1958). **149**

Murray, H. A. (*see* Kluckhohn, C., Murray, and Schneider)

National Council of the Teachers of Mathematics. "The Secondary Mathematics Curriculum." Report of the Secondary Curriculum Committee. *The Mathematics Teacher* (May 1959). **178, 268**

National Education Association. *Report of the Committee of Ten on Secondary School Studies*. Washington, D.C. G.P.O. (1893). **122**

National School Boards Association and American Association of School Administration. *Quest for Quality*. Booklets 1-14 (1960). **310**

National Society for the Study of Education. *Curriculum-Making: Past and Present*. Twenty-sixth Yearbook, Pt. I. Bloomington, Ind. Public School Publishing Co. (1926). **8, 447**

————. *The Foundations of Curriculum Making*. Twenty-sixth Yearbook, Pt. II. Bloomington, Ind. Public School Publishing Co. (1927). **447**

————. *The Psychology of Learning*. Forty-first Yearbook. Bloomington, Ind. Public School Publishing Co. (1942). **80**

————. *The Measurement of Understanding*. Forty-fifth Yearbook, Pt. I. Univ. of Chicago Press (1946). **244**

————. *Science Education in American Schools*. Forty-sixth Yearbook, Pt. I. Univ. of Chicago Press (1947), Chs. 2 and 3. **177, 215**

————. *The Dynamics of Instructional Groups, Sociopsychological Aspects of Teaching and Learning*. Fifty-ninth Yearbook, Pt. II. Univ. of Chicago Press (1960). **162**

Niblett, W. R. *Education—The Lost Dimension*. Wm. Sloane Associates (1955). **150, 224**

Noel, E. (*see* Taba, H., and Noel)

Northway, M. L., and L. Weld. *Sociometric Testing*. Univ. of Toronto Press (1957). **253**

Oberholtzer, K. E., and R. Madden. "Evaluating the Social Studies Program." In National Society for the Study of Education, *Social Studies in the Elementary School*. Fifty-sixth Yearbook, Pt. II. Univ. of Chicago Press (1957). **310**

Oeser, O. A. "Achievement Levels in High-School Mathematics: The Role of Peer Groups in Task-Centered Teaching." *School Rev., 68* (Autumn 1960). **165**

Ogilvie, E. (*see* Lovell, K., and Ogilvie)

Ojeman, R. H. "An Integrated Plan for Education in Human Relations and Mental Health." *Jour. School Health, 20* (1950), 99-106. **157**

————, *et al.* "The Effects of a 'Causal' Teacher Training Program and Certain Curricular Changes in Grade School Children." *Jour. Exper. Education, 24* (Dec. 1955), 95-114. **112, 157**

Olson, W. C., and B. O. Hughes. "Growth of the Child as a Whole." In R. G. Barker, J. S. Kounin, and H. F. Wright (eds.), *Child Behavior and Development*. McGraw-Hill (1943), 199-208. **90**

Oppenheimer, R. "An Inward Look." *Foreign Affairs, 36* (Jan. 1958), 209-20. **184, 190**

Pace, C. R. "Educational Objectives." In National Society for the Study of Education, *The Integration of Educational Experiences*. Fifty-seventh Yearbook, Pt. III. Univ. of Chicago Press (1958), Ch. 4. **197, 299, 316-17**

Packard, V. *The Status Seekers*. McKay (1959). **61**

Parker, E. P. "Basic Geographic Ideas." In National Society for the Study of Education, *The Teaching of Geography*. Thirty-second Yearbook. Bloomington, Ind. Public School Publishing Co. (1933), Ch. 8. **177**

Parsons, T. "The School Class as a Social System: Some of Its Functions in American Society." *Harvard Educational Rev., 29* (Fall 1959). **53**

Passow, A. H. "Organization and Procedures for Curriculum Improvement." *Rev. Educational Research, 24* (June 1954). **450**

————. (*see also* McNally, H. J., and Passow)

Peck, R. F. (*see* McGuire, C., Phillips, and Peck)

Phillips, I. (*see* McGuire, C., Phillips, and Peck)

Piaget, J. *The Psychology of Intelligence.* Harcourt, Brace & World (1950). **107, 109, 404**

————. *Logic and Psychology.* Basic Books (1953). **107, 404**

————. *The Construction of Reality in the Child.* Basic Books (1954). **107**

————. "Principal Factors Determining Intellectual Evolution from Childhood to Adult Life." In L. E. Hartley and R. E. Hartley (eds.), *Outside Readings in Psychology.* 2nd ed. Crowell (1957), 43-55. **107**

————, and B. Inhelder. "Diagnosis of Mental Operations and Theory of Intelligence." *American Jour. Mental Deficiency, 51* (1947), 401-06. **107**

————, B. Inhelder, and A. Szeminska. *The Child's Conception of Geometry.* London. Routledge & Kegan Paul (1960). **107**

Pierce, P. R. *Developing a High School Curriculum.* American Book (1942). **409**

Post, R. "A Study of Certain Factors Affecting the Understanding of Verbal Problems in Arithmetic." Teachers College, Columbia Univ. (1958). Unpublished dissertation. **185**

Powers, S. R. "The Achievement of High School and Freshman College Students in Chemistry." *School Science and Mathematics, 21* (1921), 366-77. **122**

Prescott, D. A. *Emotion and the Educative Process.* Washington, D.C. American Council on Education (1938). **97, 286**

Pressey, S. L. *Psychology and the New Education.* Harper (1944). **124**

Progressive Education Association. "Application of Principles in Physics." *Evaluation of the Eight Year Study.* Test 1.32. Columbus, Ohio (1938). Mimeo. **319**

Quillen, J., and L. Hanna. *Education for Social Competence.* Scott, Foresman (1961). **177**

Rabinowitz, H. S. (*see* Birch, H. C., and Rabinowitz)

Read, H. *Education Through Art.* Faber (1943). **151**

Redfield, R. *The Little Community.* Univ. of Chicago Press (1955). **51**

Report of the Harvard Committee. *General Education in a Free Society.* Harvard Univ. Press (1945). **19, 271**

Review of Educational Research. "Human Relations in Education." *29* (Oct. 1959). **162**

Riesman, D. *The Lonely Crowd: A Study of a Changing American Character.* Yale Univ. Press (1950). **59, 60, 61, 63**

Robinson, J. (*see* Taba, H., Brady, and Robinson)

Robinson, J. H. *The Humanizing of Knowledge.* Doran (1926), 387-88

Rockefeller Brothers Fund, Inc. *The Pursuit of Excellence.* A Panel Report V of the Special Studies Project, America at Midcentury Series. Doubleday (1958). **3, 386**

Rogers, C. R. "Toward a Theory of Creativity." In H. H. Anderson (ed.), *Creativity and Its Cultivation.* Harper (1959), Ch. 6. **151**

Rosen, B. C. "Race, Ethnicity and the Achievement Syndrome." *Am. Sociol. Rev., 24* (1959). **141**

Rothney, J. W. "Evaluating and Reporting Pupil Progress." Department of Classroom Teachers, American Educational Research Association, *What Research Says to Teachers,* No. 7, (1960). **320**

Rotter, J. B. (*see* Schroeder, H. M., and Rotter)

Rourke, R. E. K. "Some Implications of Twentieth Century Mathematics for High Schools." *Mathematics Teacher, 51* (Feb. 1958). **178, 179**

Rugg, H. *Man and His Changing Society.* Rugg Social Science Series, Elementary School Course. 14 vols. Ginn (1936-37). **394**

————, and Ann Shumaker. *The Child-Centered School.* World Book (1928). **28**

Ryan, C. (*see* Linton, R., Fisher, and Ryan)

Ryan, M. (*see* Loban, W., Ryan, and Squire)

Ryle, G. *The Concept of Mind.* Barnes & Noble (1960). **274, 278, 312**

Sacramento County Schools. *Social Studies Science: Source Material for Unit Development.* Expanded Grade Outline, Grades 1-8. Course of Study Supplement No. 1. Sacramento, Calif. (n.d.). **346**

Salinger, J. D. "Seymour: An Introduction." *The New Yorker* (June 6, 1959), 42. **220**

Sargent, S. S. *Social Psychology: An Integrative Interpretation.* Ronald (1950). **50**

Saylor, J. G., and W. M. Alexander. *Curriculum Planning for Better Teaching and Learning.* Rinehart (1954). **9, 292, 393, 400, 409**

Schmidt, W. (*see* Haigh, G. V., and Schmidt)

Schneider, D. M. (*see* Kluckhohn, C., Murray, and Schneider)

School City of South Bend, The Elementary Social Studies Core Committee. *For Our Time: A Handbook for Elementary Social Studies Teachers.* South Bend, Ind. (May 1949). **229, 230, 470**

Schroeder, H. M., and J. B. Rotter. "Rigidity as Learned Behavior." *Jour. Exp. Psychol., 44* (Sept. 1952), 141-50. **125**

Sears, R. R. "A Theoretical Framework for Personality and Social Behavior." *Am. Psychologist, 6* (Sept. 1951), 476-83. **78**

Shaftel, F. R. (*see* Shaftel, G., and Shaftel)

Shaftel, G., and F. R. Shaftel. *Role Playing the Problem Story.* New York. National Conference of Christians and Jews (1952). **160, 247**

Shaplin, J. T. "Practice in Teaching." *Harvard Educational Rev., 31* (Winter 1961). **311, 359**

Sheats, P. (*see* Benne, K., and Sheats)

Sheffler, I. "Justifying Curriculum Decisions." *School Rev., 66* (Winter 1958). **383, 386, 389**

Shoben, E. J., Jr. "Viewpoints from Related Disciplines: Learning Theory." *Teachers College Rec., 60* (Feb. 1959). **277**

Shores, H. J. (*see* Smith, B. O., Stanley, and Shores)

Shumaker, A. (*see* Rugg, H., and Shumaker)

Skinner, B. F. *Science and Human Behavior.* Macmillan (1953). **80**

————. "The Science of Learning and the Art of Teaching." *Harvard Educational Rev., 24* (Spring 1954), 86-97. **83**

———— (*see also* Holland, J., and Skinner)

Smith, B. O. "Concept of Teaching." *Teachers College Rec., 61* (Feb. 1950), 229-41. **180**

————. "Social Perspective as the Basic Orientation of the Curriculum." In R. W. Tyler and V. Herrick, *Toward Improved Curriculum Theory.* Supplementary Educational Monograph No. 71. Univ. of Chicago Press (March 1950). **26, 27, 38, 45**

————. "Logic, Thinking and Teaching." *Educational Theory, 7* (Oct. 1957).

————. Project No. 258, College of Education, Bureau of Educational Research, University of Illinois, Urbana, Ill. *A Study of the Logic of Teaching.* Unpublished report (n.d.). **183**

Smith, B. O., and R. H. Ennis (eds.). *Language and Concepts in Education.* Rand McNally (1961).

————, W. O. Stanley, and H. J. Shores. *Fundamentals of Curriculum Development.* World Book (1957). 9, 27, 292, 384, 391, 425, 478, 480

Smith, E. R., and R. W. Tyler. *Appraising and Recording Student Progress.* Harper (1942). (*see also* Adventures in American Education Series). 209, 216, 217, 219, 313, 320, 331

Smith, H. "The Scientist and His Duty." *Saturday Review of Literature* (April 2, 1955). 35, 44

Smith, M. B. "Anthropology and Psychology." In John Gillin (ed.), *For a Science of Man.* Macmillan (1954), 40-62. 44, 49, 50, 52

Spaulding, F. T. *High School and Life.* McGraw-Hill (1938). 392

Spence, K. W. "The Relation of Learning Theory to the Technology of Education." *Harvard Educational Rev., 29* (Spring 1959), 84-95. 6, 78, 85

Spindler, G. D. *Education and Anthropology.* Stanford Univ. Press (1955). 6, 48

————. "New Trends and Applications in Anthropology." In National Council for the Social Studies, *New Viewpoints in the Social Sciences.* Twenty-eighth Yearbook, Washington, D.C. (1958), Ch. 7. 48, 269

————. *The Transmission of American Culture.* Harvard Univ. Press (1959). 58

Spitz, R. A. "The Role of Ecological Factors in Emotional Development in Infancy." *Child Development, 20* (Sept. 1949), 145-55. 90

Squire, J. R. (*see* Loban, W., Ryan, and Squire)

Stacey, C. L. (*see* Swenson, E. J., Anderson, and Stacey)

Stanley, W. D. (*see* Smith, B. O., Stanley, and Shores)

Stendler, C. B. (*see* Martin, W. E., and Stendler)

Stiles, F. S. "Developing an Understanding of Human Behavior at the Elementary School Level." *Jour. Educational Research, 43* (March 1950), 516-24. 157

Stoltz, H. R., and L. M. Stoltz. *Somatic Development of Adolescent Boys.* Macmillan (1951). 91

Stoltz, L. M. (*see* Stoltz, H. R., and Stoltz)

Stone, M. "School Mathematics for Tomorrow." In F. S. Chase, and H. A. Anderson (eds.), *The High School in the New Era.* Univ. of Chicago Press (1958). 182, 268

Storen, H. *Laymen Help Plan the Curriculum.* Washington, D.C. Association for Supervision and Curriculum Development (1946). 450

Stratemeyer, F. B., *et al. Developing a Curriculum for Modern Living.* Teachers College, Columbia Univ. (1947). 398-99

Strauss, A. (*see* Schuessler, K., and Strauss)

Strodtbeck, F. L. "Family Interaction, Values and Achievement." In D. McClelland, *et al., Talent and Society.* Van Nostrand (1958). 138, 141-42

Suchman, J. R. "Inquiry Training in the Elementary School." *Science Teacher, 27* (Nov. 1960). 128

————. "Inquiry Training: Building Skills for Autonomous Discovery." *Merrill-Palmer Quarterly* (July 1961). 112, 215, 295

————. "Relational Constructs in Inquiry Training Films." California State Department of Education, Sacramento, Calif. (Aug. 1961). Mimeo. 155

Swenson, E. J., G. L. Anderson, and C. L. Stacey. *Learning Theory in School Situations.* University of Minnesota Studies in Education. Univ. of Minnesota Press (1949). 81

Symonds, P. M. "What Education Can Learn from Psychology, VII: Transfer and Formal Discipline." *Teachers College Rec.* (Oct. 1959). 123, 127

Szeminska, A. (*see* Piaget, J., Inhelder, and Szeminska)

Taba, H. *Dynamics of Education.* Harcourt, Brace & World (1932). **415**
————. *Social Sensitivity.* Progressive Education Association (1936). Mimeo. **224**
————. "Significant Aspects of Growth in Learning Situations." In W. S. Gray (ed.), *Reading and Pupil Development.* Supplementary Educational Monograph No. 51. Univ. of Chicago Press (Oct. 1940), 11-19. **216**
————. "Basic Issues and Cooperative Techniques in Evaluation with Special Reference to Reading." In W. S. Gray (ed.), *Cooperative Effort in Schools to Improve Reading.* Supplementary Educational Monograph No. 56. Univ. of Chicago Press (Sept. 1942), Ch. 23. **342**
————. "Evaluation of Social Sensitivity." In E. R. Smith and R. W. Tyler, *Appraising and Recording Student Progress.* Harper (1942). **224, 333**
————. "What Is Proof?" *Educational Leadership, 1* (April 1944). **218**
————. "Evaluation in High Schools and Junior Colleges." In W. S. Gray (ed.), *Reading in Relation to Experience and Language.* Supplementary Educational Monograph No. 58. Univ. of Chicago Press (Dec. 1944), 199-204. **338**
————. "General Techniques of Curriculum Planning." In National Society for the Study of Education, *American Education in the Post War Period: Curriculum Reconstruction.* Forty-fourth Yearbook, Pt. I (1945), Ch. 5. **12, 267**
————. "The Problems in Developing Critical Thinking." *Progressive Education, 28* (Nov. 1950). **219**
————. *Cultural Attitudes and International Understanding.* Occasional Paper No. 5, Institute of International Education (1953). **52**
————. *School Culture.* Washington, D.C. American Council on Education (1955a). **141, 228, 258, 259**
————. *With Perspective on Human Relations: A Study of Peer Group Dynamics in an Eighth Grade.* Washington, D.C. American Council on Education (1955b). **74, 157, 160, 161, 165, 167, 169, 249, 253, 260**
————. "Problem Identification." In Association for Supervisors and Curriculum Directors, *Research for Curriculum Improvement.* 1957 Yearbook (1957). Washington, D.C. Ch. 3. **251, 463, 464**
————. "Learning by Discovery." Talk at the Symposium of the American Educational Research Association Convention, Atlantic City (Feb. 20, 1962). **155, 215**
————, E. Brady, and J. Robinson. *Intergroup Education in Public Schools.* Washington, D.C. American Council on Education (1952). **74, 224, 227, 355, 493**
————, and D. Elkins. *With Focus on Human Relations.* Washington, D.C. American Council on Education (1950). **160, 167, 225, 246, 247, 248, 249, 253, 260, 281, 282, 348, 349, 361, 366, 377**
————, and E. Noel. *Action Research: A Case Study.* Association for Supervisors and Curriculum Directors. Washington, D.C. (1957). **239, 242, 448, 457, 483, 484, 488, 493**
————, et al. *Curriculum in Intergroup Relation: Secondary School.* Washington, D.C. American Council on Education (1949). **227**
————, et al. *Elementary Curriculum in Intergroup Relations.* Washington, D.C. American Council on Education (1950). **118, 138, 142, 167, 169, 227, 470**
————, et al. *Diagnosing Human Relations Needs.* Washington, D.C. American Council on Education (1955). **161, 167, 246, 247, 253, 259**
———— (*see also* Havighurst, R. J., and Taba)
Thayer, V. T., C. B. Zachry, and R. Kotinsky. *Reorganizing Secondary Education.* Appleton-Century (1939). (*see also* Commission on Secondary School Curriculum.) **286**

Thelen, H. A. "Principle of Least Group Size." *School Rev., 57* (March 1949), 141-47. **474**

————. "Theory of Group Dynamics." In K. D. Benne, and B. Muntyan, *Human Relations in Curriculum Change.* Dryden (1951), 84-98. **476**

————. *Dynamics of Groups at Work.* Univ. of Chicago Press (1954). **471, 472, 476, 478**

————. "Classroom Grouping of Students." *School Rev., 67* (Spring 1959), 60-78. **167, 253**

————. (*see also* Getzels, J. W., and Thelen)

Thomas, F. H. (*see* French, E. G., and Thomas)

Thompson, M. A. "The Levels of Educational Objectives." *Harvard Educational Rev., 13* (May 1943), 196-211. **196, 206**

Thorndike, E. L. *The Principles of Teaching.* New York. A. G. Seiler (1906). **122**

————, and R. S. Woodworth. "The Influence of Improvement in One Mental Function Upon the Efficiency of Other Functions." *Psychological Rev., 8* (1901). **122**

Time. "Wasted Talent" *76,* Pt. II (Nov. 21, 1960), 53-56. **113**

Tippett, J. S., *et al. Curriculum Making in the Elementary School.* Ginn (1927). **401**

Tomkins, S. S. "Personality and Intelligence: Integration of Projective and Psychometric Technics." In P. H. Hoch, and J. Zubin, *Relation of Psychological Tests to Pure Psychiatry.* Grune & Stratton (1951), 87-95. **103**

Torrance, F. P. *Educational Achievement of the Highly Creative: Eight Partial Replications of the Getzels-Jackson Study.* Bureau of Educational Research. Univ. of Minnesota (1960). **106**

————. "Measurement and Development of Creative Thinking Abilities." In *1961 Yearbook of Education.* London. Evans Brothers, Ltd. (1961). **106**

Tryon, C., and J. Lilenthal, III. "Developmental Tasks: The Concept and Its Importance." In Association for Supervisors and Curriculum Directors, *Fostering Mental Health in Our Schools.* Washington, D.C. (1950). **97**

Tyler, R. W. *Basic Principles of Curriculum Development.* Univ. of Chicago Press (1950). **12, 200, 266, 279, 299**

————. "Do We Need a National Curriculum?" *National Association of Secondary Principals Bulletin, 44* (Feb. 1960), 76-85. **448**

————. "The Function of Measurement in Improving Instruction." In E. F. Lindquist (ed.), *Educational Measurement.* Washington, D.C. American Council on Education (1951), 47-67. **312, 316**

————, in V. Herrick and R. W. Tyler, *Toward Improved Curriculum Theory,* Supplementary Educational Monograph No. 71. Univ. of Chicago Press (Mar. 1950). **422**

———— (*see also* Herrick, V. E., and Tyler; Smith, E. R., and Tyler)

Virginia State Board of Education. *Tentative Course for Virginia Elementary Schools.* Richmond, Va. (1934). **398**

Wall, W. D. *Education and Mental Health.* A report based upon the work of a European conference called by UNESCO. Paris. UNESCO (1955). **150**

Ward, V. S. "The Function of Theory in Programs for the Gifted." *Teachers College Rec., 62* (April 1961), 532-36. **441**

Warner, W. L., R. J. Havighurst, and M. B. Loeb. *Who Shall Be Educated?* Harper (1944). **49, 137**

————, M. Meeker, and K. Eells. *Social Class in America.* Harper (1960). **255, 257**

Warren, C. E. *Growing Up: An Experimental Unit in Seventh Grade Arithmetic.* San Francisco State College (1955). M.A. thesis. 98

Washington School District. "Helping Retarded Readers." Curriculum Bulletin No. 1, West Sacramento, Calif. (Feb. 1956a). 485

————. "Identifying and Helping the Slow Learner." Curriculum Bulletin No. 2, West Sacramento, Calif. (Feb. 1956b). 242, 485

Weld, L. (*see* Northway, M., and Weld)

Wertham, F. *Seduction of the Innocent.* Rinehart (1953). 56

Wertheimer, M. *Productive Thinking.* Rev. ed. Harper (1959). 81, 115-16, 117, 127, 128

Wesman, A. G. "A Study of Transfer from High School Subjects to Intelligence." *Jour. Educational Research, 39* (1945), 254-64. 122

Whipple, J. E. (*see* Hilgard, E. R., Irvine, and Whipple)

White, G. "The Changing Dimensions of the World Community." In F. S. Chase and H. A. Anderson (eds.), *The High School in the New Era.* Univ. of Chicago Press (1958). 175, 187, 191, 263

Whitehead, A. N. *Aims of Education.* Macmillan (1929). 198, 390

Whyte, W. H. *The Organization Man.* Simon & Schuster (1956). 61

Wing, R. L. (*see* Burton, W. N., Kimball, and Wing)

Wingo, M. "Theoretical Basis for Activities Program." In V. E. Herrick and R. W. Tyler, *Toward Improved Curriculum Theory.* Supplementary Educational Monograph No. 71. Univ. of Chicago Press (1950), 91-99. 280, 404

Witkin, H. A., *et al. Personality Through Perception.* Harper (1954).

Woodring, P. "National Goals in Education." *Saturday Review of Literature* (Dec. 17, 1960), 49-50. 148

Woodworth, R. S. (*see* Thorndike, E. L., and Woodworth)

Wright, G. S. *Core Curriculum Development: Problems and Practices.* Bulletin No. 5, U.S. Office of Education. G.P.O. (1958a). 409

————. *Block Time Classes and the Core Program in the Junior High School.* Bulletin No. 6, U.S. Office of Education. Washington, D.C. G.P.O. (1958b). 409

Yolo County Schools. "Explorations in Reading." Woodland, Calif. (1956). Mimeo. 95

Zachry, C. B. (*see* Thayer, V. T., Zachry, and Kotinsky)

Zander, A. (*see* Cartwright, D., and Zander)

Zechiel, A. N. (*see* Giles, H. H., MacCutcheon, and Zechiel)

Zeleny, L. D. (*see* Gross, R. E., and Zeleny)

Index

Accommodation, 110
Acculturation, 49, 56-57, 91
  effect of on learning, 145-47
Achievement
  diagnosis of, 232-34
  effect of classroom climate on, 164, 165-66
  effect of social class on, 141
  evaluation of, 325-31
Achievement orientation, 141-42
Age-level development. *See* Development, age-level norms of
Ahrens, M., 451
Alberty, H., 407-09
Alexander, W. M., 400, 409
Alienation, 61, 70
  in complex society, 38-39
American character
  conflicts in, 58
  conformity in, 59-62
  cultural origin of, 57
  inner-direction in, 59-60
  other-direction in, 60-62
Anderson, H. H., 362
Animism, 93, 109, 111
Anthropology
  absence of in social studies curricula, 269
  concept of acculturation in, 145
  concept of conformity in, 62-64
  concept of cultural learning in, 131-34
  concept of culture in, 48-52
  definition of learning in, 130-31
  and education, 47, 48
  influence of on education, 48-50
Anxiety, 145
  in the classroom, 164-65
Application, 216-18
Arithmetic Project, The, 128
Assimilation, 110

Associationism. *See* Behaviorist-associationist theory
Attitudes. *See* Values
Ausubel, D. P., 93, 116, 128, 272
Authority, 138, 139. *See also* Discipline
Autonomy, 70-73

Bartlett, Sir Frederic, 151, 152, 153
Basic ideas. *See* Core ideas
Bayles, E., 413
Beck, W. S., 384
Becker, Carl, 5
Behavior
  of adolescents, 135
  classification of types of, 209
  group, 143-44
  sequence in achieving objectives of, 439
  standards of evaluation of, 331-32
  study of development of, 88
Behavioral environment, 104-05
Behavioral objectives, 3-4
  concept of critical thinking in, 215-20
  consistency in, 228-29
  from general to specific, 228-30
  levels of knowledge in, 211-15
  as part of model for curriculum design, 439
  sensitivity as consideration in, 223-25
  sequence in achieving, 439
  skills to be considered in, 225-28
  values and attitudes in, 220-23
Behavioral sciences
  developments in, 5
  and education, 5-6, 33-34, 47-48
  educational implications of, 74-75

Behaviorist-associationist theory, 78, 80
  and curriculum organization, 83
Benedict, Ruth, 149
Bestor, A., 20, 21
Bettelheim, B., 168
Biological Science Curriculum Study. 394
Bloom, B. S., 206, 232, 299, 326
Bobbitt, J. F., 83
Bode, B. H., 285
Bond, H. M., 113
Boole, M. E., 126
Bradfeld, J. M., 326
Brameld, T., 43
Brookover, W. B., 158
Broudy, H. S., 318
Brown, M., 317
Brownell, W. A., 214
Bruner, J. S., 86, 112, 118, 127, 128, 155, 176, 274, 280, 295, 306
Brunswick, E., 78
Burton, W. N., 154
Buswell, G. T., 115, 232

Cardinal Principles, The, 207, 446
Caswell, H. L., 413
Character
  American. See American character
  definition of, 57
  mode of change of, 67
  as molded by society, 59
  socially adaptive, 132
Chase, F. S., 36, 40-41
Childs, J. L., 25
Clark, R., 253
Classicists. See Rational humanists
Classroom
  open-ended interview in the, 244-46
  social climate of the, 164-67
  social structure of the, 163
Classroom learning, 81. See also Learning
Classroom technique
  for active learning, 280-82
  prescriptive, 154
Coffey, H. S., 455
Cognition, 102. See also Thinking
  and creativity, 151
  development of, 107-09
  effect of subject matter on, 174
  function of, 109-10

Cognition (Cont.)
  studies on development of, 111-12
  training in, 119-20
Commager, H. S., 1
Commission on Evaluation, 327
Commission on the Reorganization of Secondary Education, The, 446
Committee of Fifteen, The, 446
Committee of Ten, The, 122, 446
Committee on School Mathematics, 128
Committee on the Economy of Time in Education, The, 446
Complementation, 169
Conant, J. B., 18, 385
Concepts
  hierarchical order of, 110
  levels of mastery of, 318-19
  sequence of development, example of, 430-31
Conceptual framework
  for curriculum development, 13
  functions of for curriculum, 420-21
Concrete operations, 108-09
Concomitant learning. See Indirect learning
Conformity
  in American character, 59-62
  anthropological concept of, 62-64
  in the classroom, 70-73
  dangers of, 62-63
  designs for, 153-54
  in generalizing, 152-53
  reactions to, 63
  reduction of, 63-64
Content. See also Curriculum content
  analysis of, example, 432-35
  as basis for curriculum development, 11
  concepts as, 178
  contribution of to learning, 181-84
  criticism of organization by, 387-93
  integration of, 189-92
  levels of, 175-81
  logic of, 354
  obsolescence of, 184-85, 268
  organization by, 384-87
  sample of selection of, 357
  sampling, 356-58
  scope of, 186-88
  scope and sequence of developed by life activities, 398-99
  selection of, 352, 356

Content (Cont.)
sequence in, 430-31
sequence of, 356
sequence of, example, 368
structure of, 176-78
thought systems in, 178-81
topics as, 352-54
unanalytic attitude toward, 418
views on, 173
Content organization, 179, 359-63
analysis of, 301-04
atomization of, 389
broad fields, example, 394-95
chart of contrasting methods of, 302-03
double model for, 303
example, 361
by life processes, 398
logical, 387
relationship of to teaching, 388
and selection, 12
Convergent thinking, 102
limitations of, 114-17
Core ideas, 305-07
selection of, 354-56
illustrations of, 357-58
Core program, 300-01
characteristics of, 409-10
criticism of, 410-11
definition of, 408-09
lack of teachers for, 412
organization of, 410
Correlation, 300-01
Counts, G. S., 26, 40, 288
Craig, R. C., 125
Creativity, 151
cognitive aspects of, 114-17
of groups, 491
and rejection, 164
Cremin, L. A., 2, 5, 387
Cronbach, L. J., 190
Cues, 133, 142-44
Cultural agents, 132
Cultural learning, 10, 131-34. See also Social learning
Culture. See also Social class; society
anthropological concept of, 48-52
changed by education, 67
common norms imposed in, 63
concept of change in, 53-57
dangers of ethnocentricity in, 73-74
effect of on learning, 152-53

Culture (Cont.)
influence of on human nature, 50-52
influence of on readiness, 93-94
influence of technology on, 54
and learning requirements, 10-11
preserved by education, 18-22
and the schools, 17
transformed by education, 22-28
Curriculum
age-patterned, 94
balanced, 374
based on cyclical advance, 94-95
centers for organization of, 427
decisions, 231
definition of, 9, 10
definition of as prescription, 268
determining scope of, 285
developing individuality in, 70-73
diagnosis of problems in, 237-43, 244-62
effect of concept of sequential development on, 91
effect of sequential learning on, 188-89
emphasis on factual information in, 213
emphasis on subject matter in, 152
evaluation of, 13. See also Evaluation
gap between theory and practice in development of, 439-41
and heterogeneity of backgrounds, 113-14
importance of ideas about learning to, 76-79
improvement, 450
influence of behaviorist theories on, 81-82
integrated, 189-92, 270
learnability of, 282-84
major elements of, 265
need for diagnosis in, 95
"needs" approach to, 284-89
as plan for learning, 293-94
postwar development of, 5
problems of formulating framework of, 440
provision for variation in, 96
reason for, 282-83
relation of to life experiences, 284
role of science and mathematics in, 172

Curriculum (Cont.)
 stereotyped processes in, 153
 structure of, 422-26
Curriculum change
 case study of functions of leadership
  in, 482-91
 creating involvement in, 465-68
 current methods of, 448-54
 experiments in, 156
 history of, 446-48
 involving teachers in, 460-65
 leadership roles required for, 478-
  81
 levels of involvement in, 469-70
 method of, 9
 sequence of, 457-59
 strategy for, 454-56
Curriculum content. See also Curriculum organization
 adaptation of to ability, 282-84
 atomistic, 278
 criteria for selection of, 265-67
 determined by needs, 285-89
 "doctrine of interest" selection of,
  287-89
 need for balance in, 276-78
 orientation of to past, 275
 selection of, 263-65
 social significance of, 272-76
 validity and significance of, 267-72
Curriculum design
 common patterns of, 437
 conceptual framework for, 420-21
 deficiencies in theories of, 414-20
 definition of, 421
 doctrinaire approach to, 416-19
 elements of, 422-24
 implementation of, 425
 misapplication of principles in, 415-
  16
 a model for, 425, 438
 relationships among elements of,
  424-26
 scope, sequence, and integration by
  behaviors in, 437
 theories of, 413-14
Curriculum development
 committee approach to, 449-50
 conceptual framework for, 13
 and content, 11
 criteria for, 10-11, 174
 decisions to be made in, 6-7, 10, 12-
  13

Curriculum development (Cont.)
 diagnosis as essential part of, 231-
  43
 group work in, 471-72
 influence of technology on, 41-46
 methodology of, 439-44
 methods of change in, 13-14. See
  also Curriculum change
 participation in, 450-53
 productive function of research in,
  492
 progressive education and, 30
 questions to be asked in, 421
 research approach to, 451
 role of models in, 343-45
 scientific, 10
 sequence of, 456-59
 theory of, 3-5, 10
 trends in, 17
 work teams for, 472-74
Curriculum organization
 and associationist theory, 83
 broad fields, 393-95
 centers for, 427-28
 core approach to, 407-12
 criteria of logic and psychology in,
  301-04
 criticisms of, 387-93
 for cumulative learning, 296-98
 double sequence in, 436-39
 by experience, 400-07
 by experience, example, 402-03
 and field theory, 83-84
 focus of, 304-07
 integration as concept of, 298-300
 by life processes, example, 398-99
 planning sequence in, 292-96
 problems in, 290-92, 382-84
 scope, sequence, and integration in,
  428-30
 sequence of concept of difference
  for, 430-39
 and sequence of mental operations,
  431-36
 by social processes, 396-400
 by subject, 384-93
 unification in, 300-01
 use of evaluation data in, 336-38
 for variety of learning modes, 307-
  09
Curriculum planning
 and acculturation problems, 145
 to aid critical thinking, 220

Curriculum planning (Cont.)
concept of developmental tasks and, 97-99
conflicts in, 7-8
for developmental continuity, 204
for direct experience, 156
for disciplined thinking, 179-81
essential problem of, 274-75
for intuitive thinking, 156
levels of freedom for, 443-44
for multiple learning, 158-60
for multiple objectives, 278-82
for productive learning, 118-20
role of diagnosis of needs in, 347-50
for social differences, 144
steps in planning units in, 347-79
for transfer of learning, 125-29
use of teaching-learning unit in, 344-45
Cyclical development. See Development, cyclical

Danziger, K., 141
Davie, J. S., 104
Davis, A., 49, 107, 137, 145
Development
age-level norms of, 94
areas of, 88
classification of types of, 210
and concept of readiness and pacing, 91-96
cyclical, 94-95
emotional, 90
interrelationship among areas of, 89-91
physical, 89
sequential, 91, 94
Developmental tasks, 96-97
and curriculum planning, 97-99
Dewey, J., 23-24, 28, 126, 151, 175, 183-84, 214, 271, 280, 288-89, 403, 404-05
Diagnosis. See also Evaluation
of achievement, 232-34
by classroom interview, 244-46
in curriculum development, 231-32
of curriculum problems, 237-43, 244-62
function of, 95
of needs, 12, 347-50

Diagnosis (Cont.)
of out-of-school environment, 254-60
a program for, 261-62
by questions and themes, 246-47
records used for, 248-50
as a role of opener, 365
sociometric test used for, 252-54
special assignments used for, 250, 252
of students as learners, 234-37
by unfinished stories, 247
use of diaries for, 259-60
Direct learning, 157-60, 161
Discipline. See also Mental discipline
effect of classroom climate on, 165
social class attitudes toward, 138, 144
Divergent thinking, 102
Dobbin, J. E., 317
Downey, L. W., 172
Dressel, P., 314
Drives, 132, 134
secondary, 133, 158

Easley, J. A., Jr., 271
Education
autonomous thinking developed by, 71-73
basic, 20-21
behavioral objectives of, 3-4
and the behavioral sciences, 47-48
classical tradition of, 19-20
cultural change and, 53-57
and cultural heritage, 18-22
current concepts of, 16-18
effects of technology on, 40-46
of emotions, 160
function of, 194
individual development as function of, 28-30
influence of on society, 40
intellectual development as function of, 20-21
mobility as goal of, 29-30
objectives of, 312. See also Educational objectives
philosophy of, 195
preserving function of, 18-22
problems in, 1-3
program for in high school, 385
progressive, 22-30

Education (Cont.)
    recent criticisms of, 173
    role of, 148
    role of in controlling values, 68-70
    role of in society, 31
    the social function of, 23-28
    social responsibilities of, 65-68
    and social sciences, 5-6, 33-34
    tasks of, 40-46, 158
    transforming function of, 22-28
    in values, 273-74
Educational objectives. *See also* Behavioral objectives
    classification of, 206-10
    formulation of, 199-205
    functions of, 196-99
    in the social studies, 229-30
    statement of, 211
    types of, 196
Educational Policies Commission, The, 207-08, 286
Eight Year Study, The, 28, 122, 208, 319, 331, 344, 402, 425, 448
Elam, S. L., 146
Elkins, D., 348, 349, 376-77
Emotions
    class variation in control of, 136-37
    and learning, 150
Environmental stimulus, 104-05
Erikson, E. H., 90, 96, 134
Ethnocentricity, 45-46, 52, 73-74
    of assumptions, 463
    perpetuated by curriculum, 273
Evaluation, 102. *See also* Diagnosis
    based on multidimensional information, 320
    comprehensive program of, 317-18, 324-29
    as continuous process, 323
    cooperative approach to, 338-42
    and curriculum objectives, 316-17
    and curriculum organization, 13
    data used for, 325-31
    deficiencies in programs of, 313-14
    definitions of, 311-13
    diagnostic value of, 318-21
    function of, 313-16
    informal devices of, 378
    interpretation of data used for, 331-36
    judgments derived from, 322-23
    model for comprehensive program of, 328-29

Evaluation (Cont.)
    nature of program of, 313
    obstacles to, 324-25
    as step in sequence of curriculum development, 377-78
    techniques to be used in, 325-26
    use of for curriculum improvement, 336-38
    validity of instruments of, 321-22
    weakness of programs of, 323

Faculty psychology. *See* Mental discipline, theory of
Fadiman, C., 21
Featherstone, W. B., 285, 442
Field theory, 78, 80-82
    and curriculum organization, 83-84
Finley, 329
Fisher, M. S., 58
Forkner, 398, 399
Formal operations, 109
Framework
    conceptual, 13, 420-21
    developing a, 459
    problems of formulating, 440
Friedenberg, E. Z., 167
Fromm, E., 38, 57, 62
Fundamentals, 184-86
    basic ideas as, 354

Gardner, J. W., 265
Generalizing, 114-17, 120, 127, 216, 367
    curriculum planning for, 126
    determined by culture, 152-53
    development of process of, 362-63
    levels of, 119
    need for practice in, 279
    need for reality experiences in, 128-29
    in science, 181
    in second grade, 118, 296
    and transfer of learning, 124-25
Gesell, A., 88, 89, 92, 94
Gestalt theory, 80-81
Gestalten, 81, 108
Getzels, J. W., 102, 105, 106, 163, 164, 221, 419
Gifted child, 106
Giles, H. H., 285
Gladwyn, T., 104

Goals, 166. *See also* Motivation
Goetz, R. M., 396-97
Golden, W. P., Jr., 455
Goodlad, J. L., 416-17, 420, 428, 442
Goodson, M., 17
Gorer, G., 55, 134
Gross, N., 33
Group activity, 227. *See also* Group work
Group behavior, 143-44
Group discussion, 375
Group relations. *See also* Interpersonal relations
    concept of, 162-63
    role of in learning, 160-62
Group work. *See also* Teamwork
    as part of a rhythm of learning activities, 375
    climate of, 475-76
    composing teams for, 472-74
    differentiation of tasks for, 477
    function of, 471-72
    skills for, 375-76
Grouping
    by ability, 167-68
    for complementation, 169
    dangers of, 95
    for direct learning, 161
    to facilitate learning, 168-71
Growth. *See* Maturation
Guilford, J. P., 101, 102, 105, 114
Gustafson, C. V., 268

Haggard, E., 168
Handlin, O., 153
Harlow, H. F., 125, 127
Harvard Report on General Education, The, 19
Havighurst, R. J., 104
Heilbroner, R. L., 35, 36, 38, 39, 42-43, 45
Hendrickson, G., 124, 214
Herrick, V. E., 420, 424-25, 426, 439
Hersh, B. Y., 232
Heterogeneity
    of cultural backgrounds, 113-14
    providing for, 309
Higher Horizons, 114
Hildebrand, E. H. C., 180
Hilgard, E. R., 86-87, 92, 124, 151
Hook, S., 384
Horace Mann-Lincoln Institute, 451

Human nature, 50-52. *See also* Character; Personality
Hunt, J. McV., 92, 109
Hutchins, R. M., 264

Identification, 132, 158
Ilg, F. L., 89
Imitation, 132, 158
Indirect learning, 157-60
Individual development, 28-30
Individual differences
    in learning needs, 307-09
    in reacting to stimuli, 111-12
Individualism, 222
Inhelder, B., 107
Inner-directedness, 59-60
In-service training, 448-49
Insight, 80-81, 212
    in apes, 124
    in learning, 155
Intellect. *See also* Mental systems
    factors of, 101
    model for structure of, 101
    operations of, 102
Intelligence
    concrete operations stage of, 108
    conditioning agents of, 105
    and creativity, 151
    effect of study of Latin on, 123
    evolutionary sequences of, 107-12
    formal operations stage of, 109
    nature of, 100-01
    sensory-motor, 108, 110
    studies on development of, 111-12
    variables affecting, 103-05
Intelligence test scores
    effects of cultural origins on, 106-07
    factors affecting, 107
Intelligence tests, 100, 101
    criticisms of, 105-07
Interests doctrine, 287-89
Intergroup Education Project, 226, 227, 344
Internalization, 132
Interpersonal relations, 160-63, 164-67
    diagnosis of pattern of, 252-54
    problems revealed by themes, 246
    skills needed for, 226
Interpretation, 216. *See also* Evaluation

Intuition. *See* Thinking, intuitive

Isaacs, S., 111

Jackson, P. W., 105, 164, 419
James, W., 122, 123
Janke, L. L., 104
Jensen, G., 163
Judd, C. H., 124

Kahl, J. A., 104
Kardiner, A., 52, 53
Kazamian, A. M., 172
Kilpatrick, W. H., 160, 279
Kluckhohn, C., 47, 65, 69-70, 72, 137
Knowledge
    atomization of, 389
    characteristics of areas of, 172-73
    integration of, 298-300
    intuitive, 155
    levels of, 191, 212-15
    levels of mastery of, 318-19
    specialized, 189-90
    static, 175
Köhler, W., 81, 124
Koffka, K., 104
Kotinsky, R., 148
Krug, E., 383, 449, 453
Kubie, L. S., 150

Latin
    effect of study of on intelligence,
        123
    effect of study of on vocabulary,
        124
Lawler, M., 481
Leadership
    case study of functions of, 482-91
    growth of, 493
    roles, 478-81
Learning. *See also* Direct learning; In-
    direct learning; Social learning
    active forms of, 280
    activities for application of, 367-68
    climate for, 475-76
    contribution of subject matter to,
        181-84
    cultural. *See* Cultural learning
    cumulative progression in, 188-89,
        296-98
    and curriculum decisions, 76-79

Learning (Cont.)
    diagnosis of, 234-37
    difficulties of planning, 55
    by discovery, 215, 280
    effect of group relations on, 160-62
    effect of pacing on, 92
    effect of social climate on, 164-67
    effect of social setting on, 160-62
    emotional aspects of, 84, 150
    factors affecting, 103-05
    grouping for, 167-71
    integration of, 77
    kinds of, 78, 85
    limited by culture, 152-53
    method of assuring continuity of,
        373-74
    modes of, 307-09
    multiple, 158-60
    nature of, 130-31
    passive and active, 390
    potentiality for, 148-51
    principles of, 87
    processes of, 11, 86, 132-33
    as a product, 154
    productive, 118-20, 155
    through responses, 81
    role of experience in, 151-57, 401,
        403
    by rote, 158-59
    science of, 85-87
    sequence of, 188-89, 293-95
    situation, 81
    as social process, 82
    transfer of. *See* Transfer of learning
    transition in methods of, 375-76
Learning experiences
    adaptation of to ability, 282-84
    balance of, 308-09, 378-79
    cumulative, 356
    mental operations represented by,
        431-36
    multiple objectives in planning, 279,
        282
    organization of by subject, 384-93
    planning of, 363-64
    psychological sequence for, 359
    rhythm of, 374-77
    selection and organization of, 12-13
    sequence of, 293, 365-68
    sequence of, example, 368-73
Learning theories, 78, 79-82
    capacity for survival of, 77
    influence of on curriculum, 83-84

Leonard, J. P., 292
Lewin, K., 81, 162
Linton, R., 31-32, 53, 54, 68, 158
Lippmann, W., 16
Locke, J., 122
Logic, 218-20

McClelland, D. C., 141
McGuire, C., 135, 165, 253
McKim, 398, 399
Madden, R., 310
Malinovsky, B., 63-64
Mann, H., 23
Mannheim, K., 37
Marshall, L. C., 176, 396-97
Maslow, 102
Mathematics
    approach to, 177, 180-81
    consolidation in, 179
    curriculum, 268, 270
Maturation
    intellectual, 90
    physical, 89, 90
    and readiness, 93
Mead, M., 55, 134
Melton, A. W., 76, 86
Memory. *See* Retention
Mental ability. *See* Intelligence
Mental discipline, 173-74, 179-81, 183
    theory of, 79-80
Mental systems
    qualitative differences in, 283
Merton, R. K., 454
Meyer, A. E., 44
Miller, G., 386-87
Miner, J. B., 100, 103, 105, 107, 117
Modal character, 66-67
Modal personality, 51-52
Mogar, M., 112
Moholy-Nagy, L., 150
Moredock, H. S., 326
Morris, V. C., 61
Morrison, H. C., 127, 398
Motivation, 103-04, 388
    and acculturation, 146
    effect of classroom climate on, 164,
        165
    and intelligence, 110
    and learning, 82
    social class variations in, 138-40
    and underachievement, 117-18
Motives, 131. *See also* Motivation

Mowrer, O. H., 80
Murphy, G., 149

Needs, 133
    approach to through concept of de-
        velopmental tasks, 98-99
    curriculum geared to, 284-89
    definitions of, 286
    diagnosis of, 347-50
    gratification of, 136
    psychological vs. educational con-
        cept of, 97
New York Regents' Inquiry, 391
Nonlearning, 146, 147
Norms, 331-32

Oberholtzer, K. E., 310
Objectives. *See also* Educational ob-
        jectives; Behavioral objectives
    achieving multiple, 280-81
    behaviors involved in, 279
    effect of multiple on planning learn-
        ing experiences, 282
    formulation of, 12, 350-52
    need for wide range, 278-79
Oeser, O. A., 165
Ojeman, R. H., 112, 156
Oppenheimer, R., 184, 190
Organismic age, 90-91
Organismic theory. *See* Field theory
Orientation, 365-66
Other-directedness, 60-62
Overachievers, 106

Pace, C. R., 316-17
Pacing, 92. *See also* Readiness
Parker, E. P., 176
Parsons, T., 53
Passow, A. H., 450
Peer groups, 134-35, 161, 163, 164,
        165
Performance
    levels of, 318-19
    processes leading to adequacy of,
        319
    qualitative difference in levels of,
        326
Personality
    effect of rejection on, 140
    influences on, 134-35

Personality (Cont.)
  nature and timing of, 52-53
  shaped by culture, 50-52
Physical Science Study Committee, 271
Piaget, J., 93, 107, 111, 115, 118, 296
Pierce, P. R., 409
Potential, 103, 148-51
Powers, S. R., 122
Preconceptual   symbolism.   See
  Thought, preconceptual symbolic
Prescott, D. A., 286
Prescriptive teaching, 115-17
Pressey, S. L., 124
Preverbal intelligence. See Sensory-
  motor intelligence
Problem solving, 216-18
  for curriculum planners, 237-43
Productive learning, 155
  curriculum strategies for, 118-20
Progressive education, 22-30
Progressive Education Association, 3-
  4, 271
  Curriculum   Commission   on   the
    Secondary Curriculum of the,
    286
Punishment. See Discipline

Rational humanists, 19-20
Read, H., 151
Readiness
  criticisms of, 92-93
  influence of culture on, 93-94
  and maturation, 93
  principles of, 92
Reasoning. See Logic; see also Think-
  ing
Redfield, R., 51
Reductionism, 43
Reflective thinking, 181, 183-84, 215
Reinforcement, 85
Response, 133
Retention, 102, 122
Reversibility, 108, 109
Riesman, D., 4, 59, 61, 63
Robinson, J. H., 387-88
Rockefeller Report, The, 386
Rogers, C. R., 102, 151
Roles, 162-63. See also Leadership
Rosen, B. C., 141
Rote drill, 77
Rote learning, 158-59

Rugg, H., 8, 30
Ryle, G., 274, 278

Saylor, J. G., 400, 409
Scates, 329
Schools. See also Education
  criticisms of, 1-2, 22
  as a culture, 47, 65-66, 145-47, 163
  function of, 148
  socializing functions of, 65-68
  society and the, 16-18
  teaching values in the, 65-70
  value conflicts in, 58
Schroeder, H. M., 124
Science
  approach to, 177
  instruction in, 271
Scientific curriculum development, 10
Scientific inquiry, 128
Self-concepts
  revealed by themes, 246
  of teachers, 463
Self-expectation, 140-41, 159
Self-image, 133, 140-41
Sensitivity
  analysis of, 223-24
  definition of, 223
  education for, 224-25
  method of extending, 279
Sensory-motor intelligence, 108, 110
Sequence
  checking for, 378-79
  of the concept of differences, 430-
    31
  of curriculum development, 456-59
  of curriculum organization, 292-96,
    428-30
  double, 436-39
  of learning, 188-89, 293-95
  of learning experiences, 366-73
  of mental operations, 431-36
  of method in curriculum planning,
    441
  structured by behaviors, 437
Sequential development. See Development, sequential
Shaplin, J. T., 311, 359
Sheffler, I., 383, 389
Shoben, E. J., Jr., 277
Shores, H. J., 293, 384, 425
Signals. See Cues

Skills
    in group activity, 227
    in leadership, 228
    in managing authority, 226-27
    in problem solving, 225
    social, 225-26
Skinner, B. F., 80, 83
Smith, B. O., 26, 37, 180, 293, 384, 425, 478
Smith, M. B., 52
Social class
    and achievement, 141-42
    and cleanliness, 137
    diagnosis of, 255-57
    and educational aspiration, 139-41
    effect of on group behavior, 143-44
    effect of on meaning, 142-44
    and emotional control, 136-37
    and family authority, 137-38
    and gratification of needs, 136
    and motivation, 138-40
    and punctuality, 137
    and verbal expression, 144
Social learning, 50. See also Social class
    and acculturation, 145-47
    and class differences, 135-44
    concepts of, 130-31
    effect of change on, 274-75
    effect of peer attitudes on, 162-67
    effect of setting on, 160-62
    influence of curriculum content on, 272-76
    influences in, 134-35
    perceptual limitations in, 142-44
Social psychology, 48, 50-52
Social realities, 272-76
Social Studies, California State Commission on, 177
Social studies
    criticisms of programs in, 268-69
    objectives in, 229-30
    sequence in, example, 430-31
Socialization. See Social learning
Society
    analyses of, 31-34
    character structure of, 51-52
    conflict of values in, 55-56
    curriculum organized by processes of, 396-400
    effect of on character, 59
    effects of technology on, 34-36

Society (Cont.)
    inner-direction in, 59-60
    other-direction in, 60-62
    psychological pressures of, 38-39
    responsibility of schools to, 65-68
    tradition-directed, 59
Sociometric test, 252-54
Spence, K. W., 85
Spencer, H., 396
Spindler, G. D., 48
Stanley, W. D., 293, 384, 425
Stereotyping. See Conformity
Stoltz, H. R., 91
Stoltz, L. M., 91
Stratemeyer, F. B., 398, 399
Subject matter. See Content
Suchman, J. R., 112, 128
Symonds, P. M., 127

Task-centeredness, 165
Teacher training, 460-65, 467
Teachers
    and classroom conformity, 71
Teaching
    limiting productive thought in, 153-54
    mathematics, 177, 179, 180-81
    open-ended technique of, 157, 160
    prescriptive, 115-17
    for productive thinking, 117
    science, 177
    strategies of, 119, 120
    for transfer, 277, 374
Teaching-learning unit
    diagnosing needs for a, 347-50
    experimental, 457-59, 486-90
    methodology for a, 345-47
    model for a, 343-45
    objectives for a, 350-52
    organizing content for a, 359-63
    preplanning of, 376, 442-44, 486-91
    selecting basic ideas for a, 354-56
    selecting learning experiences for a, 363-77
    selecting specific content for a, 356-59
    selecting topics for a, 352-54
    use of evaluation in planning a, 377-78
Teaching machines, 83, 85

Teamwork, 491. *See also* Group work
Technology
    effects of on education, 40-46
    effects of on man, 38-39
    effects of on society, 34-36
    influence of on culture, 54
    need for control of, 36-37, 39
Tests. *See also* Intelligence tests
    interpretation of performance on,
        331-36
    measuring performance on, 326
    objective, 325-26, 330
    paper-and-pencil, 325, 329-30
    standardized, 330
Textbooks
    criticisms of, 153
    descriptive approach in, 156-57
Thelen, H. A., 163, 167
Thinking. *See also* Convergent think-
        ing; Divergent thinking; Reflec-
        tive thinking
    in abstractions, 109
    critical, 215-20
    disciplined, 179-81, 183
    intuitive, 108, 155
    limited by culture, 152-53
    modes of in subject areas, 181-84
    productive, 127-29
    processes of, 216-20
    sequence of development of, 219-20
Thorndike, E. L., 122
Thought. *See also* Cognition; Intelli-
        gence
    preconceptual symbolic, 108
Time and motion observation, 251
Tomkins, S. S., 103
Transactional experience, 214
Transfer of learning
    aptitude for, 127
    automatic, 121-22
    curriculum planning for, 125-29
    early studies of, 122-23
    inconsistencies in, 123-24
    recent studies of, 124-25
    role of self-discovery in, 126
    teaching for, 374

Translation
    of behavioral sciences to education,
        74-75
    of evaluation data into curriculum
        improvement, 336-38
    from general to specific objectives,
        228-30
Tyler, R. W., 279, 422

Underachievement, 117-18
Unit plan. *See* Teaching-learning unit

Value education, 68-70, 273-74
Value orientation, 43-44
Values
    American, 55-56, 57-64
    Christian, 222
    conflicts of, 55-56
    cultural, 49
    cultural stereotypes in, 153
    effects of technology on, 37-38, 43-
        45
    interpretations based on, 217-18
    leading to high achievement, 141-42
    problem of, 220-23
    schools' responsibility for, 65-70
    teaching of, 222-23
Verbalization, 155-56

Ward, V. S., 418
Warner, W. L., 49, 255
Wertham, F., 56
Wertheimer, M., 81, 115, 127, 128
Wesman, A. G., 122
White, G., 175, 187, 191
White House Conference, The,
        (1950), 29
Whitehead, A. N., 198, 390
Wingo, M., 280
Woodworth, R. S., 122

Yearbook of the National Society for
    the Study of Education, 317

M 5
N 6
O 7
P 8